MARRIAGE AND FAMILY 96/97

Twenty-Second Edition

Editor

Kathleen R. Gilbert
Indiana University

Kathleen Gilbert is an associate professor in the Department of Applied Health Science at Indiana University. She received her B.A. in Sociology and her M.S. in Marriage and Family Relations from Northern Illinois University. Her Ph.D. in Family Studies is from Purdue University. Dr. Gilbert's primary areas of interest are loss and grief in a family context, trauma and the family, family process, and minority families. She has published several books and articles in these areas.

Annual Editions

A Library of Information from the Public Press

Cover illustration by Mike Eagle

**Dushkin Publishing Group/
Brown & Benchmark Publishers
Sluice Dock, Guilford, Connecticut 06437**

The Annual Editions Series

Annual Editions is a series of over 65 volumes designed to provide the reader with convenient, low-cost access to a wide range of current, carefully selected articles from some of the most important magazines, newspapers, and journals published today. Annual Editions are updated on an annual basis through a continuous monitoring of over 300 periodical sources. All Annual Editions have a number of features designed to make them particularly useful, including topic guides, annotated tables of contents, unit overviews, and indexes. For the teacher using Annual Editions in the classroom, an Instructor's Resource Guide with test questions is available for each volume.

VOLUMES AVAILABLE

Abnormal Psychology
Africa
Aging
American Foreign Policy
American Government
American History, Pre-Civil War
American History, Post-Civil War
American Public Policy
Anthropology
Archaeology
Biopsychology
Business Ethics
Child Growth and Development
China
Comparative Politics
Computers in Education
Computers in Society
Criminal Justice
Developing World
Deviant Behavior
Drugs, Society, and Behavior
Dying, Death, and Bereavement
Early Childhood Education
Economics
Educating Exceptional Children
Education
Educational Psychology
Environment
Geography
Global Issues
Health
Human Development
Human Resources
Human Sexuality

India and South Asia
International Business
Japan and the Pacific Rim
Latin America
Life Management
Macroeconomics
Management
Marketing
Marriage and Family
Mass Media
Microeconomics
Middle East and the Islamic World
Multicultural Education
Nutrition
Personal Growth and Behavior
Physical Anthropology
Psychology
Public Administration
Race and Ethnic Relations
Russia, the Eurasian Republics, and Central/Eastern Europe
Social Problems
Sociology
State and Local Government
Urban Society
Western Civilization, Pre-Reformation
Western Civilization, Post-Reformation
Western Europe
World History, Pre-Modern
World History, Modern
World Politics

Cataloging in Publication Data
Main entry under title: Annual Editions: Marriage and Family. 1996/97.
    1. Family—United States—Periodicals. 2. Marriage—United States—Periodicals. I. Gilbert, Kathleen, *comp.* II. Title: Marriage and Family.
ISBN 0-697-31711-0   301.42'05   74-84596

© 1996 by Dushkin Publishing Group/Brown & Benchmark Publishers, Guilford, CT 06437

Twenty-Second Edition

Printed in the United States of America

To the Reader

In publishing ANNUAL EDITIONS we recognize the enormous role played by the magazines, newspapers, and journals of the *public press* in providing current, first-rate educational information in a broad spectrum of interest areas. Within the articles, the best scientists, practitioners, researchers, and commentators draw issues into new perspective as accepted theories and viewpoints are called into account by new events, recent discoveries change old facts, and fresh debate breaks out over important controversies.

Many of the articles resulting from this enormous editorial effort are appropriate for students, researchers, and professionals seeking accurate, current material to help bridge the gap between principles and theories and the real world. These articles, however, become more useful for study when those of lasting value are carefully *collected, organized, indexed,* and *reproduced* in a *low-cost format,* which provides easy and permanent access when the material is needed. That is the role played by ANNUAL EDITIONS. Under the direction of each volume's *Editor,* who is an expert in the subject area, and with the guidance of an *Advisory Board,* we seek each year to provide in each ANNUAL EDITION a current, well-balanced, carefully selected collection of the best of the public press for your study and enjoyment. We think you'll find this volume useful, and we hope you'll take a moment to let us know what you think.

The purpose of *Annual Editions: Marriage and Family 96/97* is to bring to the reader the latest thoughts and trends in our understanding of the family, to identify current concerns as well as problems and possible solutions, and to present alternative views of family process. The intent of this anthology is to explore intimate relationships as they are played out in marriage and family and, in doing this, to reflect the family's changing face.

The articles in this volume are taken from professional publications, semiprofessional journals, and popular lay publications aimed at both special populations and a general readership. The selections are carefully reviewed for their currency and accuracy. In some cases, contrasting viewpoints are presented. In others, articles are paired in such a way as to personalize the more impersonal scholarly information. In the current edition, approximately 50 percent of the articles have changed from the previous edition upon updating and responding to reviewers' comments. As the reader, you will note the tremendous range of tone and focus of these articles, from first-person accounts to reports of scientific discoveries as well as philosophical and theoretical writings. Some are more practical and applications-oriented, while others are more conceptual and research-oriented.

This anthology is organized to cover many of the important aspects of marriage and family. The first unit looks at varied perspectives on the family. The second unit examines the beginning steps of relationship building as individuals go through the process of exploring and establishing connections. In the third unit, means of finding and maintaining a relationship balance are examined. Unit four is concerned with issues of crises and ways in which these can act as challenges and opportunities for families and their members. Finally, unit five takes an affirming view as it looks at families, now and into the future.

Instructors can use *Annual Editions: Marriage and Family 96/97* as a primary text for introductory marriage and family classes, particularly when they tie the content of the articles to basic information on marriage and family. It can also be used as a supplement to update or emphasize certain aspects of standard marriage and family textbooks. Because of the provocative nature of many of the articles in this anthology, it works quite well as a basis for class discussion about various aspects of marriage and family relationships.

I would like to thank everyone involved in the development of this volume. My thanks go to those who sent in *article rating forms* and comments on the previous edition as well as those who suggested articles to consider for inclusion in this edition. Finally, to all of the students in my Marriage and Family Interactions class who have contributed critiques of articles, I would like to say thanks.

Anyone interested in providing input for future editions of *Annual Editions: Marriage and Family* should complete and return the postage-paid *article rating form* at the end of this book. Your suggestions are much appreciated and contribute to the continuing high quality of this anthology.

Kathleen R. Gilbert
Editor

Contents

Unit 1

Varied Perspectives on the Family

Six articles explore different views on where our images of family come from and how they are influenced by our life experiences as well as societal and cultural constraints.

The concepts in bold italics are developed in the article. For further expansion please refer to the Topic Guide and the Index.

Unit
2

Exploring and Establishing Relationships

Thirteen articles address factors that influence the formation of close relationships, both romantic and generative.

The concepts in bold italics are developed in the article. For further expansion please refer to the Topic Guide and the Index.

The concepts in bold italics are developed in the article. For further expansion please refer to the Topic Guide and the Index.

Unit 3

Finding a Balance: Maintaining Relationships

Twelve articles consider the complex issues related to keeping a relationship going. From marriage to parent/child relationships and in our sibling relationships and the "grand" alliance, relationship maintenance requires thought and commitment from members.

The concepts in bold italics are developed in the article. For further expansion please refer to the Topic Guide and the Index.

Unit
4

Crises—Challenges and Opportunities

A wide variety of crises, normative and catastrophic, are
detailed in thirteen articles. Ranging from broad cultural
factors impacting on families to the intimate crises of
infidelity and divorce, these articles provide accounts of
devastation and hope.

The concepts in bold italics are developed in the article. For further expansion please refer to the Topic Guide and the Index.

Unit 5

Families, Now and into the Future

Four articles look at means of establishing and/or maintaining health and healthy relationships in families.

Topic Guide

This topic guide suggests how the selections in this book relate to topics of traditional concern to students and professionals involved with the study of marriage and family. It is useful for locating articles that relate to each other for reading and research. The guide is arranged alphabetically according to topic. Articles may, of course, treat topics that do not appear in the topic guide. In turn, entries in the topic guide do not necessarily constitute a comprehensive listing of all the contents of each selection.

TOPIC AREA	TREATED IN	TOPIC AREA	TREATED IN
Abuse	32. Helping Children Cope with Violence 33. After He Hits Her 34. Where Do We Go from Here? 35. Passion Kills	**Culture**	1. Is the Family Obsolete? 5. Ache for Home 6. Growing Up in Black and White 15. Men, Sex, and Parenthood 18. Adolescent Childbearing 23. Staying Power 28. Family Heart 32. Helping Children Cope with Violence 39. Family, Work, and Gender Equality 46. Happy Families 48. Rituals for Our Times
Adolescence	11. Choosing Mates—The American Way 13. Psychotrends 18. Adolescent Childbearing		
Adoption	19. Lifelong Impact of Adoption		
Aging	13. Psychotrends 22. Receipts from a Marriage 40. Caregiving 41. Long Road Back 45. Trace your Family Tree	**Dating/Mate Selection**	7. Love: Immutable Longing for Contact 8. What Makes Love Last? 11. Choosing Mates—The American Way 12. Mating Game 35. Passion Kills
Biological Issues	7. Love: Immutable Longing for Contact 9. Why Don't We Act Like the Opposite Sex? 13. Psychotrends 16. Baby Love	**Divorce**	2. New Crusade for the Old Family 20. What's Happening to American Marriage? 36. Beyond Betrayal 42. Should This Marriage Be Saved? 43. Lessons from Stepfamilies
Children and Childcare	1. Is the Family Obsolete? 3. New Family: Investing in Human Capital 6. Growing Up in Black and White 7. Love: Immutable Longing for Contact 17. What a Baby Really Costs 18. Adolescent Childbearing 19. Lifelong Impact of Adoption 21. Peer Marriage 26. Vanishing Dreams of America's Young Families 27. Effective Fathers 29. I Don't Sweat the Small Stuff Anymore 32. Helping Children Cope with Violence 44. Myths and Misconceptions of the Stepmother Identity 46. Happy Families	**Family Systems**	4. Bringing Democracy Home 5. Ache for Home 21. Peer Marriage 28. Family Heart 30. Siblings and Development 31. Secret World of Siblings 41. Long Road Back 43. Lessons from Stepfamilies 46. Happy Families 47. Rewriting Life Stories 48. Rituals for Our Times
		"Family Values" Conflict	1. Is the Family Obsolete? 2. New Crusade for the Old Family 3. New Family: Investing in Human Capital 4. Bringing Democracy Home
Communication	7. Love: Immutable Longing for Contact 10. Back Off! 12. Mating Game 23. Staying Power 24. But What Do You Mean? 25. Saving Relationships 27. Effective Fathers 43. Lessons from Stepfamilies 46. Happy Families	**Gender Roles**	4. Bringing Democracy Home 9. Why Don't We Act Like the Opposite Sex? 11. Choosing Mates—The American Way 12. Mating Game 13. Psychotrends 15. Men, Sex, and Parenthood 16. Baby Love 21. Peer Marriage 23. Staying Power 24. But What Do You Mean? 25. Saving Relationships 27. Effective Fathers 33. After He Hits Her 34. Where Do We Go from Here? 38. Myth of the Miserable Working Woman 44. Myths and Misconceptions of the Stepmother Identity

TOPIC AREA	TREATED IN	TOPIC AREA	TREATED IN
Health Concerns	13. Psychotrends 14. Choosing a Contraceptive 15. Men, Sex, and Parenthood 16. Baby Love 28. Family Heart 29. I Don't Sweat the Small Stuff Anymore 34. Where Do We Go from Here? 40. Caregiving 41. Long Road Back 45. Trace Your Family Tree	**Poverty**	1. Is the Family Obsolete? 2. New Crusade for the Old Family 18. Adolescent Childbearing 26. Vanishing Dreams of America's Young Families
Infidelity	12. Mating Game 36. Beyond Betrayal 37. Sex in America	**Pregnancy/ Childbirth**	15. Men, Sex, and Parenthood 16. Baby Love 17. What a Baby Really Costs 18. Adolescent Childbearing
Intimacy/Romantic Love	5. Ache for Home 7. Love: Immutable Longing for Contact 8. What Makes Love Last? 10. Back Off! 11. Choosing Mates—The American Way 12. Mating Game 20. What's Happening to American Marriage? 21. Peer Marriage 25. Saving Relationships 35. Passion Kills 36. Beyond Betrayal 37. Sex in America 46. Happy Families	**Race/Ethnicity**	5. Ache for Home 6. Growing Up in Black and White 18. Adolescent Childbearing 26. Vanishing Dreams of America's Young Families
		Remarriage	43. Lessons from Stepfamilies 44. Myths and Misconceptions of the Stepmother Identity
		Sex/Sexuality	12. Mating Game 13. Psychotrends 14. Choosing a Contraceptive 15. Men, Sex, and Parenthood 18. Adolescent Childbearing 21. Peer Marriage 25. Saving Relationships 36. Beyond Betrayal 37. Sex in America
Laws/ Governmental Roles/Policy	1. Is the Family Obsolete? 2. New Crusade for the Old Family 3. New Family: Investing in Human Capital 16. Baby Love 18. Adolescent Childbearing 26. Vanishing Dreams of America's Young Families 34. Where Do We Go from Here? 39. Family, Work, and Gender Equality	**Siblings**	30. Siblings and Development 31. Secret World of Siblings
		Single-Parent Homes	1. Is the Family Obsolete? 3. New Family: Investing in Human Capital
Marriage	8. What Makes Love Last? 11. Choosing Mates—The American Way 20. What's Happening to American Marriage? 21. Peer Marriage 22. Receipts from a Marriage 27. Effective Fathers 36. Beyond Betrayal 38. Myth of the Miserable Working Woman 42. Should This Marriage Be Saved? 43. Lessons from Stepfamilies 46. Happy Families	**Values**	1. Is the Family Obsolete? 5. Ache for Home 6. Growing Up in Black and White 11. Choosing Mates—The American Way 15. Men, Sex, and Parenthood 20. What's Happening to American Marriage? 21. Peer Marriage 28. Family Heart 39. Family, Work, and Gender Equality 42. Should This Marriage Be Saved? 46. Happy Families 48. Rituals for Our Times
Parents/Parenting	6. Growing Up in Black and White 7. Love: Immutable Longing for Contact 17. What a Baby Really Costs 18. Adolescent Childbearing 21. Peer Marriage 22. Receipts from a Marriage 26. Vanishing Dreams of America's Young Families 27. Effective Fathers 28. Family Heart 42. Should This Marriage Be Saved? 43. Lessons from Stepfamilies 44. Myths and Misconceptions of the Stepmother Identity 46. Happy Families	**Work and Family**	3. New Family: Investing in Human Capital 21. Peer Marriage 26. Vanishing Dreams of America's Young Families 38. Myth of the Miserable Working Woman 39. Family, Work, and Gender Equality

Varied Perspectives on the Family

Our image of what family is and what it should be is a powerful combination of personal experience, family forms we see, and attitudes we hold. Once formed, this image informs decision making and interpersonal interaction throughout our lives. It has far-reaching impacts: On an intimate level, it influences individual and family development as well as relationships both within the family and without. On a broader level, it affects social policy and programming.

In many ways, this image can be positive. It can act to clarify our thinking and facilitate interaction with like-minded individuals. It can also be negative, as it can narrow our thinking and limit our ability to see other ways of carrying out the functions of family as having value. Their very differentness makes them "bad." In this case, interaction with others can be impeded because of contrasting views.

This unit is intended to meet several goals with regard to perspectives on the family: (1) to sensitize the reader to sources of beliefs about the "shoulds" of the family: what the family should be and the ways in which family roles should be carried out, (2) to show how different views of the family can influence attitudes toward community responsibility and family policy, (3) to show how views that dominate one's childhood can influence awareness of alternative ways of structuring family life.

The first article, "Is the Family Obsolete?" explores the problems faced by families of today and advocates a social policy that promotes child health and supports families. The next three articles provide dramatic examples of the changing face of the family. The first two address broad societal responsibilities for these "new" families and their members. In the third, "Bringing Democracy Home: Shere Hite Reports on the Family," an alternative view is provided—an optimistic picture of the family moving from patriarchal control to democratic family functioning. The next two articles look at the ways in which images of family can be restrictive and possibly harmful. In "The Ache for Home," family therapist Monica McGoldrick describes her personal journey toward awareness of culture, gender, class, and race, all of which had been "invisible" to her as she grew up. "Growing Up in Black and White" looks at the societal factors that influence images of self-identity, particularly in young black children. Unless they are countered by images that encourage these children to value themselves, these factors can do serious damage to the self-images of these children.

Looking Ahead: Challenge Questions

If you had the power to propose a government program to support today's families, what would it be? What image do you have of families that would take advantage of that program?

What type of intervention would you propose to help children growing up in troubled families?

Discuss why you are—or are not—hopeful for the future of children and families.

How would you go about expanding your ideas of what is acceptable in terms of family relationships and family roles? How far do you think you should go in this?

Is the Family Obsolete?

Leon Eisenberg

Leon Eisenberg, M.D., is Presley Professor of Social Medicine and professor of psychiatry at the Harvard Medical School. This article is adapted from a lecture he gave as a Phi Beta Kappa Visiting Scholar in 1994–95.

When politicians become nostalgic about the "old fashioned" American family and talk about "family values," the family they idealize has husband-father as breadwinner, wife-mother as housekeeper, and children who are seen but not heard. These sentiments memorialize a past when patriarchal values were dominant and when legal restrictions and women's economic dependence combined to make divorce a seldom-used alternative. Even then, of course, there was no *one* American family, traditional or otherwise. Wives in black families, in immigrant families, and in working-class families have always had to share the breadwinning role with their husbands.

Because families of the past were more economically interdependent they were more stable; but we don't know how many couples stayed together for lack of acceptable alternatives and how many for love. Even the image of once-upon-a-time families as centers of concerned child care is uncertain. When families were production units, children did work alongside their parents; they had to, and they worked hard. Would we wish to return to family solidarity based on the inexorable demands of the farm and the cottage industry, with no opportunity for education or social mobility?

Even if we agree that we can't go back to the days of the McGuffey readers and even if you share my doubts that McGuffey had it quite right, it does not follow that today's families are thriving. The size, the composition, the structure, and the living arrangements of families in the United States and Western Europe have undergone changes so profound as to raise the question, Is the family as we have known it becoming outmoded and obsolete? Out-of-wedlock births are an ever-higher proportion of all births. Nonmarital cohabitation, separation, and divorce have become more common, as has remarriage. Children living with only one parent (24 percent) or living with one biological and one stepparent are increasing in number. Each year an increasing proportion of mothers with young children enter the labor force.

The magnitude and significance of these changes have yet to register fully in public or professional awareness. Are these "new" family forms constructive adaptations to modernity? Or are they more like the environmental degradation that accompanies industrialization? That is, are revolving-door family arrangements incompatible with child health? And if they are, what can be done about this problem?

The Need for the Family

The universality of the family in every society testifies that it meets essential human needs: to love and be wanted, to give rise to children, to rear them until they become independent, and to preserve property rights. Are modern families adequate to these tasks?

Put simply, children need two parents, as recent U.S. studies show. Analysis of six nationally representative data sets by McLanahan and Sandefur[1] has demonstrated that children growing up in single-parent households, whether the parents were never married, are separated, or are divorced, have twice the risk of dropping out of high school, of being out of work, and of becoming teenage parents themselves.

Separation and divorce are obvious stressors for children. The split family loses about 40 percent of its income; children have much less time with their fathers (one-third see them once a week, another third not at all); they are twice as likely to have to change residence and school, losing friends in the process. Because remarriage is common, many children must adapt to stepparents and stepsiblings; further stress may be in the offing because one-third of second marriages end in divorce. The long-term outcome depends on the circumstances of the custodial parent after the separation and on the quality of the relationship with each parent.

The 1988 U.S. National Health Interview Survey reveals similar epidemiologic findings: Children living with single mothers *or* with mothers and stepfathers are more likely than those living with both biological parents to have to repeat a grade at school, to be expelled from school, to be treated for emotional or behavioral problems, and to have elevated scores for behavioral problems and

[1] S. S. McLanahan and G. Sandefur, *Growing Up with a Single Parent* (Cambridge, Mass.: Harvard University Press, 1994).

 From *The Key Reporter,* Spring 1995, pp. 1-5. © 1995 by Phi Beta Kappa Society. Reprinted by permission.

health risks. Adjusting for social class and ethnic factors reduces those differences; nonetheless, even when income and ethnicity are taken into account, children from single-parent families fare worse.[2]

Sweden vs. the United States

The evidence is clear: Children are at risk when families are incomplete. Why are such families becoming more common in Europe and the United States? In trying to answer this question, I will contrast the United States with Sweden, which exemplifies an effective welfare state.

First, families in the lowest income quintile in Sweden receive 70 percent more of national income than do those in the corresponding quintile in the United States (8 percent versus 4.7 percent). A second telling difference is relative ranking on the Human Development Index (HDI). The United Nations Development Program each year ranks nations on an HDI, the principal components of which are longevity, knowledge (that is, schooling and literacy), and per capita real income, appropriately weighted in the final index. Overall, the United States and Sweden are ranked fifth and sixth on the world HDI, but when HDI is recalculated to take into account equity in the treatment of women, Sweden rises to the top of the list and the United States falls to ninth.

In 18th-century America, women had had an average of eight children by the time they reached the end of childbearing age; about half to two-thirds of those children reached maturity. The total fertility rate per woman in the United States fell from 7 in 1800 to just under 4 in 1900, to less than 2.5 in 1970, and to 2.1 in 1990. Women in Sweden and the United States today have fewer children and cease childbearing at an earlier age. The total fertility rate in both countries is 2.1.

At the turn of the century, when a woman's life expectancy was about 48 years, she spent almost all her adult life bearing and rearing children. Today, with an expectancy of 80 years, women have a long post-reproductive life; for most women, that longer life includes years of separation, divorce, or widowhood. Acquiring marketable skills is ever more a necessity for women in the modern world.

Most women today work because they have to and because the economy needs them in the work force. Family economics is the major determinant. Paid employment for both members of a couple is a compelling need in an era when real wages are declining. Married women who have children under 18 are more likely to be employed than are childless women in the United States.

In Sweden more than 80 percent of mothers with children under age two and more than 90 percent of mothers whose children are age three or older are employed. The corresponding figure for married women in the United States is 60 percent. When women work full time and year round in the United States, they earn about 74 percent of what men earn for the same jobs. In Sweden, the ratio is 89 percent.

Swedish women have come to regard paid employment as a far more socially desirable role than that of housewife.[3] With paid employment, wives have become less dependent on their husbands. Divorce, once a luxury restricted to the wealthy who could afford to buy it, is now a recourse more common among the working class. Divorce rates in Sweden and the United States have increased markedly.

Today most Swedes who marry have lived in a consensual union for some years before; many have had at least one child. In 1992 the number of newly established consensual unions in Sweden was *double* the number of marriages. Unfortunately, consensual unions do not assure the stability of the subsequent marriage. Parents who have cohabited before marriage separate more often after they marry than those who have not.[4]

As the result of changes in types and venues of work, in vocational characteristics, in the economics of family life, and in custom and law, the stability of the family has declined sharply in Western Europe and America. Europe and the United States differ greatly in the percentage of births that take place out of wedlock. In 1992 the percentage for Greece was 2.6, well below that for any other country in the European Union (compare: Italy 5.8, Ireland 11.7, and France 26.3 percent). The figure for the United States is now 27 percent, 2.5 times greater than it was two

---

Infants born out of wedlock in Sweden enter a family of two parents living in a consensual union; such infants in the United States most often have only a mother to care for them—a mother living in poverty, to boot.

---

decades ago. The rate for Sweden is twice again as high; *half the births* take place out of wedlock. Yet there is little public alarm in Sweden but widespread consternation in the United States about an "epidemic of teenage pregnancy." Why the difference?

Out-of-wedlock births occur under entirely different social circumstances in the two countries. Births to unwed teenagers have been increasing in the United States at the same time that they have been decreasing in Sweden. Infants born out of wedlock in Sweden enter a family of two parents living in a consensual union; such infants in the United States most often have only a mother to care for them—a mother living in poverty, to boot.

Among industrialized nations, the United States has the highest teenage pregnancy rate *and* the highest teenage childbirth rate *despite* the highest teenage abortion rate. This is *not*

---

[2]D. A. Dawson, "Family Structure and Children's Health and Well-being: Data from the 1988 National Health Interview Survey on Child Health," *Journal of Marriage and the Family* 53 (1991):573-84.

[3]B. Hoem and J. M. Hoem, "The Swedish Family: Aspects of Contemporary Developments," *Journal of Family Issues* 9 (1988): 397-424.

[4]Ibid.

because we have the highest rates of nonmarital adolescent cohabitation; the rate for Sweden is actually higher. Public school education about human sexuality and access to contraception have been systematically provided to Swedish adolescents for many years; in contrast, both education and access have been restricted in the United States for fear of "encouraging promiscuity." Americans seem to believe that if you don't tell kids about sex, they won't find out.

U.S. statistics averaged across our heterogeneous population conceal as much as they reveal. When the data are disaggregated by ethnic group, profound differences become apparent. Overall, 29.5 percent of all 1991 births were to unmarried women; the rate for blacks was 67.9 percent, for whites 21.8 percent, and for Hispanics 38 percent. The disparity in life circumstances among whites, blacks, and Hispanics becomes evident when their statuses on the HDI are calculated separately. U.S. whites rank first on the international list, blacks 31st (at the level of Trinidad and Tobago), and Hispanics 35th (just below Estonia). The reasons for this stratification have little to do with biology and everything to do with timing and mode of immigration, past and present discrimination, and extent of ghettoization.[5]

Lower rates of marriage and higher rates of divorce and separation leave more children under age 18 living with a single parent: 25 percent in the United States and 15 percent in Sweden. The U.S. figure has doubled since 1970; the figure for Sweden has increased one-third since 1975. Even when they work full time, most single mothers in America remain near or below the poverty line because their wages are so low. They are vulnerable to frequent layoffs; high expenses for child care deplete their meager earnings; they lose Medicaid if they work. Single parents in Sweden benefit from an extensive social support system— housing subsidies, child support, day care, and medical care—that cushions the mother and her children against adversity.

Why These Social Changes?

What accounts for the increase in consensual unions, the decline in marriage, and the increase in divorce during successive decades in this century? There is no simple or completely satisfactory explanation. The striking differences among countries demonstrate the importance of local variations in custom, in history, in the influence of religion, and in economics. Increasing divorce rates regularly accompany industrialization in the West; yet Japan, at the leading edge of pace and power, continues to enjoy very low divorce and out-of-wedlock childbirth rates.

In earlier centuries, husbands and wives were tightly bound to each other. Traditional family economy enforced mutual dependence; there were simply no viable alternatives for a place to live, for subsistence, or for security. When divorce was difficult or impossible to obtain, abandonment was common; even when husbands and wives continued to live with each other, many marriages were hollow shells. As women earned wages, they gained independence; it became possible to choose to leave.

Decisions about whether to marry, to stay married, and to have children are influenced by job availability, tax structure, housing markets, the rules governing social welfare benefits, and other economic considerations. This situation is readily apparent in changing marriage patterns among young Americans. The route to economic self-sufficiency has become longer and requires more educational preparation with each succeeding decade. Class cleavage is becoming sharper. Advantaged youth adapt to the new situation by later median ages of marriage and parenthood far more often than do low-income and minority youth.

The disappearance of blue-collar jobs has shut adolescents with only a high school education or less out of the workforce. Whereas once manual and semiskilled jobs in the industrial economy supported large numbers at relatively good pay, the replacement of industry by a service economy has resulted in a sharp decline in the wage scale. In 1990, 40 percent of 19- to 24-year-old Americans working full time earned less than the poverty level for a family of four (and just above it for a family of three); this is more than twice the rate for 1980!

These factors have had an especially severe effect on black Americans. In 1974, 46 percent of young black males were in relatively high-paying blue-collar positions; by 1986 that figure had been halved. During that interval, the percentage of two-parent family groups among blacks fell from 64 percent to 40 percent.

The evidence is clear: Children are at risk when families are incomplete.

Wilson[6] has focused on the relationship between employment and marriage by computing a "male marriageable pool index": the number of employed men per 100 women of the same age and race. In the mid-1960s in the United States, the black marriageable pool index was about the same as the white. In the years since, the index for blacks has plummeted so far that there are only 18 employed males for every 100 females age 16 or older on Chicago's South Side. It can hardly be coincidental that the proportion of births to black unmarried mothers under age 20 has increased from 64 percent to 90 percent, and the proportion among those 20 to 24 years old, from 31 percent to 66 percent. For a young woman to marry a man with no prospects for employment is to take responsibility for him as well as the infant and to lose eligibility for certain benefits.

Does the expansion of welfare benefits account for single motherhood? Both welfare benefits and single parenthood *did* increase in parallel in the 1960s and '70s. During the past 20 years, however, benefits have *de-*

---

[5]D. S. Massey and N. A. Denton, "Hypersegregation in U.S. Metropolitan Areas: Black and Hispanic Segregation along Five Dimensions," *Demography* 26 (1989): 373-91.

[6]W. J. Wilson, *The Truly Disadvantaged: The Inner City, the Underclass, and Public Policy* (Chicago: University of Chicago Press, 1987).

clined in real dollar value by 26 percent, whereas single parenthood has continued to increase. Rates of out-of-wedlock births are about the same for Britain, Canada, and France as the rate for the United States; the rate for Denmark—like that for Sweden—is more than 50 percent higher! The structure of the family is changing rapidly throughout the Western world.

Some Solutions

What social policies can support the family and promote child health in a world in which family life has been changing so rapidly? Moral exhortation for premarital chastity and an end to divorce is unlikely to succeed in reconstituting family stability. After all, the increases in premarital sex, desertion, and divorce have all occurred despite jeremiads from the pulpit in virtually every church. Reconstruction of the family must begin with economic and legal policies to promote family formation and stability, and education in public schools for responsible parenting.

National values are decisive in the way debates on policy are framed. Discussion in the United States focuses on protecting children against harm rather than on promoting their well-being, and on protecting the right of the family to privacy; the home is a fortress that can be breached only when serious danger threatens. In Scandinavia, in contrast, state policies are formulated with the goal of strengthening parental rights, roles, and responsibility. That is the framework I urge: active intervention to promote the welfare of the family, teaching adolescents to nurture younger children.

Employment policy must factor family needs into the social cost-benefit equation. Work patterns must be designed to enhance family life; they should include flexible schedules, alternative work locations, and part-time work. It is essential to guarantee that fringe benefits are not lost in the process. Employment patterns must be redesigned to take into account the needs and preferences of employees. Work schedules should

encourage the participation of both men and women in family-oriented programs.

The federal government must implement a full-employment policy to give young adults who enter the labor market incomes sufficient to support families. Increasing the minimum wage is merely the first step. At present, poor two-parent families receive *less* help than do well-off intact families or single-parent families. Nearly all middle-income households receive tax-subsidized medical insurance through work; single mothers in poverty are eligible for Medicaid. There is no safety net for poor two-parent families. A comprehensive family assistance policy should provide a decent basic living standard, cover unemployed two-parent as well as single-parent families, subsidize low-income housing, assure access to health care, and provide work training to enhance adult skills.[7]

Six months of paid leave after childbirth or adoption, already the case in Sweden, should be available here for either parent with guaranteed job protection. Paid parental leave permits infant care in the home and provides an opportunity for care givers to learn to become competent parents; skillful parenting is not instinctive. Payments to single mothers should guarantee a decent standard of living in conjunction with subsidized housing. Family benefits will not solve the problem of too little time, or end loneliness. They will halt the superimposition of poverty on other life stresses.

Access to good-quality infant and child day care should be assured for all families. Although there is a nominally "free market" in day care, that market is seriously flawed because parents do not know the criteria that distinguish good from poor-quality centers and therefore cannot purchase services for their children intelligently. Moreover, in many states licensing standards are weak or missing. The wages of women working in

child care are low. As a result, staff satisfaction is low and turnover is high. State standards must be raised *and enforced*; there is a pressing need for consumer education to enable parents to discriminate quality.

Both parents should take responsibility for children. Nonresident fathers who are employed should be expected to share their income with their children; child support awards should be vigorously enforced. Security for mothers and children could be assured by a guaranteed minimum child support benefit paid directly by the government and recouped from the father so far as possible. Unlike welfare, a guaranteed child support benefit would not depend on the mother's income, and therefore would not be reduced if the mother worked.

Public schooling should include education for family life and child care. Children need help in understanding that happy marriages are not made in Hollywood; success in marriage requires shared values, reasonable expectations, willingness to compromise, and moral commitment. The goals of family life education include educating preteens and teens about sexuality and reproduction in a context of responsible sexuality, and assuring that children are planned by making contraception information and services accessible. Researchers have found that young men educated about reproductive health are more effective contraceptors than those who are not, and that sex education can delay the onset as well as promote the safety of teenage sex.[8]

Will these policies bring about a Golden Age of the Family? Clearly not. They will cushion children against neglect and misfortune. Providing the best care we know how to give is no guarantee of a trouble-free future. Nothing is. But it will increase the likelihood that our children will be more competent than we have been at managing the affairs of the world.

[7]J. T. Gibbs, "The Social Context of Teenage Pregnancy and Parenting in the Black Community," in M. K. Rosenheim and M. F. Testa, eds., *Early Parenthood and Coming of Age in the 1990s* (New Brunswick, N.J.: Rutgers University Press, 1992), 71-88.

[8]A. Grunseit and S. Kippax, *Effects of Sex Education on Young People's Sexual Behavior* (Geneva: World Health Organization, 1993).

The New Crusade for the Old Family

Arlene Skolnick and Stacey Rosencrantz

Arlene Skolnick, a research psychologist at the Institute of Human Development at the University of California (Berkeley), is the author of Embattled Paradise: The American Family in an Age of Uncertainty. *Stacey Rosencrantz is a graduate student in Stanford University's psychology department.*

What is the root cause in America of poverty, crime, drug abuse, gang warfare, urban decay, and failing schools? According to op-ed pundits, Sunday talking heads, radio call-in shows, and politicians in both parties, the answer is the growing number of children being raised by single parents, especially by mothers who never married in the first place. Restore family values and the two-parent family, and America's social problems will be substantially solved.

By the close of the 1992 presidential campaign, the war over family values seemed to fade. Dan Quayle's attack on Murphy Brown's single motherhood stirred more ridicule on late night talk shows than moral panic. The public clearly preferred Bill Clinton's focus on the economy and his more inclusive version of the family theme: "family values" means "valuing families," no matter what their form—traditional, extended, two-parent, one-parent.

Yet Clinton's victory was quickly followed by a new bipartisan crusade to restore the two-parent family by discouraging divorce as well as out-of-wedlock childbearing. The conservative right has for years equated family values with the traditional image of the nuclear family. The new crusade drew people from across the spectrum—Democrats as well as Republicans, conservatives, liberals, and communitarians. Eventually, even President Clinton joined in, remarking that he had reread Quayle's speech and "found a lot of good things in it."

While the new family restorationists do not agree on a program for reducing the number of single-parent families, they generally use a language of moral failure and cultural decline to account for family change. Many want to revive the stigma that used to surround divorce and single motherhood. To change the cultural climate, they call for government and media campaigns like those that have discouraged smoking and drinking. They propose to make divorce harder or slower or even, as the late Christopher Lasch proposed, to outlaw divorce by parents with minor children. And some have also advocated restricting welfare benefits for unmarried mothers or eliminating benefits entirely for mothers who have an additional out-of-wedlock child.

Focusing attention on the needs and problems of families raising children could be enormously positive. But the current crusade draws on the family values scripts of the 1980s, posing the issue in a divisive way (are you against the two-parent family?) and painting critics into an anti-family corner. Restricting legal channels for divorce, cutting off welfare to unmarried mothers, and restoring the old censorious

Reprinted with permission from *The American Prospect*, Summer 1994, pp. 59-65. © 1994 by New Prospect, Inc.

Despite these strong claims of scientific backing, the research literature is far more complicated than the family restorationists have let on.

attitudes toward single parenthood may harm many children and deepen the very social ills we are trying to remedy.

There's nothing new in blaming social problems on "the breakdown of the family" or in making the "fallen woman" and her bastard child into objects of scorn and pity. Throughout our history, public policies made divorce difficult to obtain and penalized unwed parents and often their children. In the 1960s and 1970s, however, public opinion turned more tolerant and legal systems throughout the West became unwilling to brand some children as "illegitimate" and deprive them of rights due others. Now we are being told that this new tolerance was a mistake.

Most Americans, even those most committed to greater equality between women and men, are deeply uneasy about recent family changes and worried about crime and violence. The new case for the old family owes much of its persuasive power to the authority of social science. "The evidence is in," declares Barbara Dafoe Whitehead, author of a much-discussed article, "Dan Quayle Was Right," which appeared in the April 1993 *Atlantic Monthly*. Divorce and single-parent families, Whitehead argues, are damaging both children and the social fabric. Another family restorationist, Karl Zinsmeister, a fellow at the American Enterprise Institute, refers to "a mountain of evidence" showing that children of divorce end up intellectually, physically, and emotionally scarred for life.

Despite these strong claims of scientific backing, the research literature is far more complicated than the family restorationists have let on. Whitehead says, "The debate about family structure is not simply about the social-scientific evidence. It is also a debate over deeply held and often conflicting values." Unfortunately, the family restorationists' values have colored their reading of the evidence.

Few would deny that the divorce of one's parents is a painful experience and that children blessed with two "good enough" parents generally have an easier time growing up than others. Raising a child from infancy to successful adulthood can be a daunting task even for two people. But to decide what policies would improve children's lives, we need to answer a number of prior questions:

■ Are children who grow up in a one-parent home markedly worse off than those who live with both parents?

■ If such children are so disadvantaged, is the source of their problems family structure or some other factor that may have existed earlier or be associated with it?

■ How effectively can public policies promote a particular form of family and discourage others? Will policies intended to stigmatize and reduce or prevent divorce or single parenthood cause unintended harm to children's well-being? Would positive measures to help single-parent families or reduce the stress that accompanies marital disruption be of more benefit to children?

Finally, is there a direct link, as so many believe, between family structure and what a *Newsweek* writer calls a "nauseating buffet" of social pathologies, especially crime, violence, and drugs? In his Murphy Brown speech, given in the wake of the Los Angeles riots, Quayle argued that it wasn't poverty but a "poverty of values" that had led to family breakdown, which in turn caused the violence. The one sentence about Murphy Brown in the speech—borrowed incidentally from an op-ed by Whitehead—overshadowed the rest of the message. Charles Murray was more successful at linking family values with the fear of crime. In a *Wall Street Journal* article, he warned that because of rising white illegitimacy rates, a "coming white underclass" was going to engulf the rest of society in the kind of anarchy found in the inner cities. But what is the evidence for this incendiary claim? And why do countries with similar trends in family structure not suffer from the social deterioration that plagues us?

The family restorationists do not provide clear answers to these questions. And the answers found in the research literature do not support their extreme statements about the consequences of family structure or some of the drastic policies they propose to change it.

Of course, it's always possible to raise methodological questions about a line of research or to interpret findings in more ways than one. The perfect study, like the perfect crime, is an elusive goal. But some of the family restorationists seem to misunderstand the social science enterprise in ways that seriously undermine their conclusions. For example, they trumpet findings about correlations between family structure and poverty, or lower academic achievement, or behavior problems, as proof of their arguments. Doing so, however, ignores the principle taught in elementary statistics that correlation does not prove causation.

For example, suppose we find that increased ice cream consumption is correlated with increases in drownings. The cause, of course, has nothing to do with ice cream but everything to do with the weather: people swim more and eat more ice cream in the summer. Similarly, single parenthood may be correlated with many problems affecting children, but the causes may lie elsewhere—for example, in economic and emotional problems affecting parents that lead to difficulties raising children and greater chances of divorce. Making it hard for such parents to divorce may no more improve the children's lives than banning ice cream would reduce drowning. Also, causation can and often does go in two directions. Poor women are more likely to have out-of-wedlock babies—this is one of the oldest correlates of poverty—but raising the child may impede them from escaping poverty. In short, finding a correlation between two variables is only a starting point for further analysis.

The social science research itself is also plagued by methodological problems. Most available studies of divorce, for example, are based on well-educated white families; some are based on families who have sought clinical help or become embroiled in legal conflict. Such families may hardly be representative. Comparing one study with one another is notoriously difficult because they use different measures to assess children of different ages after differing periods have elapsed since the divorce. Some studies, such as Judith Wallerstein's widely cited work on the harm of divorce reported in the 1989 book *Second Chances* by Wallerstein and Sandra Blakeslee, use no comparison groups at all.

Others compare divorced families with intact families—both happy and unhappy—when a more appropriate comparison would be with couples that are unhappily married.

In addition, the family restorationists and some researchers lump together children of divorce and children whose parents never married. Yet never-married mothers are generally younger, poorer, and less educated than divorced mothers. And by some measures children living with never-married mothers are worse off than those living in divorced families.

The restorationists paint a far darker and more simplistic picture of the impact of divorce on children than does the research literature. Researchers agree that around the time their parents separate almost all children go through a period of distress. Within two or three years, most have recovered. The great majority of children of divorce do not appear to be impaired in their development. While some children do suffer lasting harm, the family restorationists exaggerate the extent and prevalence of long-term effects. For example, they may state that children of divorce face twice or three times the psychological risk of children in intact families. But the doubling of a risk may mean an increase from 2 to 4 percent, 10 to 20 percent, or from 30 to 60 percent. The effects of divorce tend to be in the smaller range.

In fact, a meta-analysis of divorce findings published in 1991 in the *Psychological Bulletin* reported very small differences between children from divorced and intact families in such measures of well-being as school achievement, psychological adjustment, self concept, and relations with parents and peers. (A "meta-analysis" combines data from separate studies into larger samples to make the findings more reliable.) Further, the more methodologically sophisticated studies—that is, those that controlled for other variables such as as income and parental conflict—reported the smallest differences.

In general, researchers who interview or observe children of divorce report more findings of distress than those who use data from large sample surveys. Yet even in the clinical studies the majority of children develop normally. One point that researchers agree on is that children vary greatly in response to divorce, depending on their circumstances, age, and psychological traits and temperament.

Where differences between children of divorce and those in stable two-parent families show up, they may be due, not to the divorce itself, but to circumstances before, during, and after the legal undoing of the marital bond. Most researchers now view divorce not as a single event but as an unfolding process. The child will usually endure parental conflict, estrangement, and emotional upset, separation from one parent, and economic deprivation. Often divorce means moving away from home, neighborhood, and school. Particular children may go through more or fewer such jolts than others.

Researchers have known for some time that children from intact homes with high conflict between the parents often have similar or even worse problems than children of divorced parents. Recent studies in this country as well as in Australia and Sweden confirm that marital discord between the parents is a major influence on chidren's well-being, whether or not a divorce occurs.

Some of the family restorationists recognize that children in high-conflict families might be better off if their parents divorced than if they stayed together. They want to discourage or limit divorce by parents who are simply bored or unfulfilled. But how should we draw the line between unfulfilling and conflict-ridden marriages? And who should do the drawing?

High-conflict marriages are not necessarily violent or even dramatically quarrelsome like the couple in Edward Albee's *Who's Afraid of Virginia Woolf?*. One major recent study operationally defined a high-conflict family as one in which a spouse said the marriage was "not too happy" or the couple had arguments about five out of nine topics, including money, sex, chores, and in-laws. A number of recent studies do show that even moderate levels of marital dissatisfaction can have a detrimental effect on the quality of parenting.

The most critical factor in a child's well-being in any form of family is a close, nurturant relationship with at least one parent. For most children of divorce, this means the mother. Her ability to function as parent is in turn influenced by her physical and psychological well-being. Depression, anger, or stress can make a mother irritable, inconsistent, and in general less able to cope with her children and their problems, whether or not marital difficulties lead to divorce.

Until recently, the typical study of children of divorce began after the separation took place. However, two important studies—one directed by Jack Block and another by Andrew Cherlin—examined data on children long before their parents divorced. These studies found that child problems usually attributed to the divorce could be seen months and even years earlier. Usually, these results are assumed to reflect the impact of family conflict on children. But in a recent book analyzing divorce trends around world, William J. Goode offers another possibility:

> ... the research not only shows that many of the so-called effects of divorce were present befofe the marriage, but suggests an even more radical hypothesis: in at least a sizeable number of families the problems that children generate may create parental conflict and thereby increase the likelihood of divorce.

The problems of never-married single mothers and their children set off some of today's hottest buttons—sex, gender, race, and welfare. Dan Quayle's attack on Murphy Brown confused the issue. It is true that more single, educated, middle-class women are having children. The rate nearly tripled in the last decade among women in professional or managerial occupations. But despite this increase, only 8 percent of professional-status women are never-married, Murphy Brown mothers. Out-of-wedlock births continue to be far more prevalent among the less educated, the poor, and racial minorities.

Most people take the correlation between single parenthood and poverty as proof of a causal relation between the two. But the story is more complex. In his book *America's Children*, Donald Hernandez of the Census Bureau shows that if we take into account the income of fathers in divorced and unwed families, the increase in single mothers since 1959 probably accounts for only 2 to 4 percentage points of today's childhood poverty rates. As Kristen Luker has pointed out in these pages ("Dubious Conceptions: The Controversy Over Teen Pregnancy," *TAP*, No. 5, Spring 1991), the assumption that early childbearing causes poverty and school dropouts is backward; these conditions are as much cause as effect.

Elijah Anderson, Linda Burton, William Julius Wilson, and other urban sociologists have shown the causal connections linking economic conditions and racial stigma with out-of-wedlock births and the prevalence of single-mother families in the inner cities. Cut off from the rest of society, with little or no hope of stable, family-supporting jobs, young men prove their manhood through an "oppositional culture" based on machismo and sexual prowess. Young women, with little hope of either a husband or economic independence, drift into early sexual relationships, pregnancy, and childbirth.

Middle-class families have also been shaken by economic change. The family restorationists, however, have little to say about the impact of economic forces on families. In her *Atlantic* article, Whitehead mentions—almost as an afterthought—that the loss of good jobs has deprived high school graduates across the country as well as inner-city young people of the ability to support families. "Improving job opportunities for young men," she writes, "would enhance their ability and presumably their willingness to form lasting marriages." Yet these considerations do not affect the main thrust of her arguments supporting Quayle's contention that the poor suffer from a "poverty of values."

There is no shortage of evidence on the impact of economic hardship on families. The studies of ghetto problems have their counterparts in a spate of recent books about other groups.* Much quantitative research reinforces these analyses. As Glen Elder and others have found, using data

from the Great Depression to the 1980s, economic conditions such as unemployment are linked to children's problems through their parent's emotional states. Economic stress often leads to depression and demoralization, which in turn lead to marital conflict and such problems in child-raising as harsh discipline, angry outbursts, and rejection. Child abuse and neglect as well as alcoholism and drug use increase with economic stress.

New research has confirmed earlier findings that poverty and inadequate income are major threats to children's well-being and development. Poverty has a deep impact because it affects not only the parent's psychological functioning but is linked to poor health and nutrition in parents and children, impaired readiness for education, bad housing, the stress of dangerous neighborhoods, and poor schools as well as the stigma of being poor. One recent study comparing black and white children across income levels found that family income and poverty were powerful determinants of children's cognitive development and behavior, controlling for other differences such as family structure and maternal schooling.

Child poverty in the United States, as the family restorationists point out, is higher than it was two decades ago among whites as well as blacks. It is also much higher in the United States than in other Western countries. But it is not an unalterable fact of nature that children born to single mothers have to grow up in poverty. Whereas our policies express disapproval of the parents, the policies of other Western countries support the well-being of the children.

The family structure debate raises larger questions about the changes in family, gender, and sexuality in the past three decades—what to think about them, what language to use in talking about them. The language of moral decay will not suffice. Many of the nation's churches and synagogues are rethinking ancient habits and codes to accommodate new conceptions of women's equality and new versions of morality and responsibility in an age of sexual relationships outside of marriage and between partners of the same gender.

The nation as a whole is long overdue for a serious discussion of the upheaval in

---

* John E. Schwarz and Thomas J. Volgy's *The Forgotten Americans* portrays the fast growing population of working poor, people who "play by the rules" but remain below the poverty line. Lillian Rubin's *Families on the Fault Line* documents the impact on working-class families of the decline of well-paying manufacturing jobs. Katherine Newman's ethnographic studies, *Falling from Grace* and *Declining Fortunes*, document the effects of downward mobility in middle-class families.

American family life since the 1960s and how to mitigate its social and personal costs, especially to children. The point of reference should not be the lost family of a mythical past conjured up by our nostalgic yearnings but the more realistic vision offered by the rich body of historical scholarship since the 1970s. From the beginning, American families have been diverse, on-the-go, buffeted by social and economic change. The gap between family values and actual behavior has always been wide.

Such a discussion should also reflect an awareness that the family trends we have experienced over the past three decades are not unique. Every other Western country has experienced similar changes in women's roles and family structure. The trends are rooted in the development of the advanced industrial societies. As Andrew Cherlin puts it, "We can no more keep wives at home or slash the divorce rate than we can shut down our cities and send everyone back to the farm."

However, our response to family change has been unique. No other country has experienced anything like the cultural warfare that has made the family one of the most explosive issues in American society. Most other countries, including our cultural sibling Canada, have adapted pragmatically to change and developed policies in support of working parents, single-parent families, and all families raising children. Teenagers in these countries have fewer abortions and out-of-wedlock births, not becase they have less sex, but because sex education and contraceptives are widely available.

Sooner or later, we are going to have to let go of the fantasy that we can restore the family of the 1950s. Given the cultural shocks of the past three decades and the quiet depression we have endured since the mid-1970s, it's little wonder that we have been enveloped by a haze of nostalgia. Yet the family patterns of the 1950s Americans now take as the standard for judging family normality were actually a deviation from long-term trends. Since the nineteenth century, the age at marriage, divorce rate, and women's labor force participation had been rising. In the 1950s however, the age of marriage declined, the divorce rate leveled off, the proportion of the population married reached a new high, and the American birth rate approached that of India. After the 1950s, the long-term historical trends resumed.

Most of us would not want to reverse all the trends that have helped to transform family life—declining mortality rates, rising educational levels for both men and women, reliable contraception, and greater opportunities for women. Barring a major cataclysm, the changes in family life are now too deeply woven into American lives to be reversed by "just say no" campaigns or even by the kinds of changes in divorce and welfare laws that the restorationists propose.

The task is to buffer children and families from the effects of these trends. Arguing for systematic economic reform in *Mother Jones*, John Judis writes that between the new economic realities and the kinds of broad measures needed to address them, there is "a yawning gulf of politics and ideology into which even the most well-meaning and intelligently conceived policy can tumble." A similar gulf lies between the new realities of American family life and the policies needed to address them.

Yet the potential for ameliorative reform may be greater than it now appears. As E.J. Dionne has pointed out, the debate is more polarized than the public. The 1992 Democratic convention showed how an inclusive pro-family message could be articulated and combined with proposals for economic and social reform. Such a message, recognizing both the diversity of family life and the continuing importance of family, appealed to a broad cross-section of Americans. It continues to make more sense and offer more hope than the punitive and coercive prescriptions of the family restorationists.

THE NEW FAMILY
INVESTING IN HUMAN CAPITAL

DAVID A. HAMBURG

Mr. Hamburg is president of the Carnegie Corporation of New York.

The dramatic changes in the American family can be highlighted by comparing its structure and function as it was in 1960 with what it had become in 1990. Until 1960 most Americans shared a common set of beliefs about family life. Family should consist of a husband and wife living together with their children. The father should be the head of the family, earn the family's income, and give his name to his wife and children. The mother's main tasks were to support and facilitate her husband's, guide her children's development, look after the home, and set a moral tone for the family. Marriage was an enduring obligation for better or worse. The husband and wife jointly coped with stresses. Sexual activity was to be kept within the marriage, especially for women. As parents, they had an overriding responsibility for the well-being of their children during the early years—until their children entered school, they were almost solely responsible. Even later, it was the parents who had the primary duty of guiding their children's education and discipline. Of course, even in 1960, families recognized the difficulty of converting these ideals into reality. Still, they devoted immense effort to approximating them in practice.

Over the past three decades these ideals, although they are still recognizable, have been drastically modified across all social classes. Women have joined the paid labor force in great numbers stimulated both by economic need and a new belief in their capabilities and right to pursue opportunities. Americans in 1992 are far more likely than in earlier times to postpone marriage. Single-parent families—typically consisting of a mother with no adult male and very often no other adult person present—have become common. Today at least half of all marriages end in divorce. Most adults no longer believe that couples should stay married because divorce might harm their children.

Survey research shows a great decrease in the proportion of women favoring large families, an upsurge in their assertiveness about meeting personal needs, and an attempt by women to balance their needs with those of their children and the men in their lives. A clear and increasing majority of women believe that both husband and wife should be able to work, should have roughly similar opportunities, and should share household responsibilities and the tasks of child rearing. A majority of mothers of preschool children now work outside the home. A growing minority of young married women, often highly educated and career oriented, are choosing not to have any children and have little interest in children's issues—yet one more indication of the dramatic transformation of American families that has been taking place in recent decades.

While the rate of pregnancy among adult women has declined since 1970, that among American adolescents, especially girls under age fifteen, is one of the highest among technically advanced nations. Teenagers account for two-thirds of all out-of-wedlock births. There are 1.3 million children now living with teenage mothers only about half of whom are married. Six million children under the age of five are living with mothers who were adolescents when they gave birth.

Childbearing in adolescence has been a common feature of human history. But traditional societies provided relatively stable employment and had reliable networks of social support and cultural guidance for young parents. For such adolescents to set up a household apart from either family was rare in pre-industrial societies. Even rarer was the single-parent family. Rarest of all was a socially isolated, very young mother largely lacking an effective network of social support.

It is startling to realize that today, whether through their parents' divorce or never having been married, most American children spend part of their childhood in a single-parent family. The increase in the proportion of children living with just one parent (usually the mother) has strongly affected large numbers of white, black, and Hispanic children. Female-headed families with children are much more likely to be poor than are married-couple families with children, regardless of race. By conservative estimates, one-fifth of young American children are raised in poverty, many by their mothers alone. Black families with children are more likely to be poor than white families with children, regardless of family type.

By the time they reach age sixteen, close to half the children of married parents will have seen their parents divorce. For nearly half of these, it will be five years or more before their mothers remarry. Close to half of all white children whose parents remarry will see the second marriage dissolve during their adolescence. Black women not only marry less often and experience more marital disruption but they also remarry more slowly and less often than do white women. Generally, as compared with other countries, the United States exhibits a pattern of attachments and disruptions in marriage that is certainly stressful for developing children and adolescents.

Divorce and remarriage create a complex set of new relationships, resulting in many different family configurations. About two-thirds of the children in step-families will have full siblings plus either half- or step-siblings. Many children will have multiple sets of grandparents. On the other hand, children of single mothers or mothers who do not remarry will have a more restricted set of active family relationships than children with two parents.

CHILD CARE In the United States especially, but in many other nations too, mothers of children under three are the fastest-growing segment of the labor market, so child care arrangements at the preschool level are of enormous practical significance. Even though remarriage after a divorce is common, there are still complicated problems of handling child care responsibilities in blended families. For parents who have never been married, the strain is probably greatest. They have all the responsibility as head of household and the least help available. About two-thirds of single mothers with preschool children are employed, most of them full time. No matter how poor they may be, they must find some kind of arrangement for care of their very young children. More often than not, this means a child care center or other home that can take them in.

Child care is thus increasingly moving outside the home, with children's development often placed in the hands of strangers and near-strangers. As late as 1985 only 14 percent of preschool children were cared for in an organized child care facility. This figure has doubled in the last five years. By 1990 half of all children of working parents were either being cared for in a center or in another home. In 1985, 25 percent of working mothers with children under five used a child care facility as the primary form of care, compared with 13 percent in 1977. This transformation was unforeseen, unplanned, and is still poorly understood. With rapid, far-reaching social changes, it is not surprising that public opinion surveys find that many American parents are deeply troubled about raising their children, and two-thirds say they are less willing to make sacrifices for their young than their parents were. Neither they nor the nation's social institutions have had much time to adjust to the new conditions.

HOW PARENTS ARE COPING

Young people moving toward parenthood today face more rapidly changing circumstances and a wider spectrum of life choices than ever before. But choices and decisions as well as transitions can be burdens, even as they offer attractive opportunities and privileges. Young couples today often agonize over decisions taken for granted as recently as a generation ago. Should they get married? If yes, should they wait until one or both have a steady job? What about the fateful decision to have children?

Once married, it is very likely that both husband and wife will be in the paid labor force, and with the advent of the baby, they will have to renegotiate their relationship. How will they divide up the baby-care chores? What sort of parental leaves, if any, will either take? How will they handle the housework? How can they balance work and family life? If the mother takes off from work for a while, when is it sensible to go back, and how can she make the transition in the best interests of the child? Can they afford quality child care? If not, what alternatives are there?

Some studies have been done on the efforts of parents to balance their various interests and responsibilities in new ways. The results show that this is a complicated process that is in its earliest stages. Sociologist Arlie Hochschild of the University of California, the coauthor of *The Second Shift: Working Parents and the Revolution at Home*, has conducted systematic research that illuminates the tension between work and family. She describes the tremendous penalty women pay whether they choose to work at home or to have a paid job. The housewife pays the cost of remaining outside what is today the mainstream of society; the working woman pays the cost in time and energy for family commitments. The evidence clearly indicates that men are sharing very little of the burden of raising children and care of the home. Hence, as Hochschild points out, women are coming home from a paid job to work "a second shift." Most men devote long hours to their jobs. Even if they want to be helpful at home, their institutional settings usually do not make it easy for them to do so.

There is no reason to believe that this phenomenon of the two-parent working family is a transient one. Indeed, a variety of economic and psychological factors reinforce the persistence of the pattern as a financial necessity. The actual and proportionate costs of child raising today are much higher than they were in the 1950s and 1960s. In many families, both husband and wife must have an earned income if the family is to attain or maintain a middle-class standard of living. This is now much harder than it used to be. In the past few decades the shift from a manufacturing to a service-based economy has brought a decline in wages for many people. The industries that have declined in the United States in relation to foreign competition are precisely the ones that historically provided relatively high-earning positions for men, especially those who did not go on to higher education. On the other hand, the new growth in the American economy has been mainly in the sectors that are major employers of women, where the pay is less. One effect of this is that parents have a great deal less leisure time than they used to have and not enough time perhaps for their children.

NEW REALITIES

For all the attractive features of technological progress and economic success, the recent changes have served to attenuate human relationships in the family. Concerns have grown about the effects of the changing family patterns—single-parent families as well as working mothers, and remote fathers—on their availability for intimate, sensitive parenting of young children. The change in the frequency and quality of contact between children and their adult relatives is remarkable.

Not only are mothers home much less, fathers do not seem to spend more time at home to compensate. Only about 5 percent of all American children see a grandparent regularly, a much lower level than in the past. Children spend a huge chunk of time during their years of most rapid growth and development in out-of-home settings or looking after themselves, which often means gazing at the mixture of reality and fantasy presented by television. Adolescents increasingly drift into a separate "teen culture" that is often lacking in adult leadership, mentorship, and support, and is sometimes manifested in violence-prone gangs.

Such attenuation in family relationships is most vividly reflected in rising indicators of adverse outcomes for infants, children, and adolescents. Over the past several decades, the largely unrecognized tragedy of moderately severe child neglect has been accompanied by more visible, flagrant child neglect. This is most obvious in the growing number of adolescents—even pre-teens—who have babies and then walk away from them. Adolescent mothers are often less responsive to the needs of the infant than are older mothers. They also tend to have more babies in rapid succession than older mothers, placing their infants at greater biological and behavioral risk. Children of adolescent mothers tend to have more cognitive, emotional, behavioral, and health problems at all stages of development than do children of fully adult mothers.

But insidious problems have arisen in a much wider portion of the society. Not only are more children growing up in poverty than was the case a decade or two ago, but they are increasingly mired in persistent, intractable poverty with no hope of escape. They lack constructive social support networks that would promote their education and health. They have very few models of competence. They are bereft of visible economic opportunity. *POVERTY*

The fate of these young people is not merely a tragedy for them, it affects the entire nation. A growing fraction of our potential work force consists of seriously disadvantaged people who will have little if any prospect of acquiring the skills necessary to revitalize the economy. If we cannot bring ourselves to feel compassion for these young people on a personal level, we must at least recognize that our economy and our society will suffer along with them.

As society puts greater emphasis on options, freedom, and new horizons—an accentuation of the longstanding American emphasis on individuality—one side effect clearly is a sharp increase in the divorce rate. Conventional wisdom on this issue had it that if the parents handled the situation with enough sensitivity, the effect of divorce on the children would be minimal. And this certainly can be the case. But practically speaking, divorcing couples find it exceedingly difficult to handle such situations over a long enough period of time and to protect their children from the psychological and economic fallout of divorce.

Studies of divorcing families reveal several recurrent themes. Marital separation commonly involves major emotional distress for children and disruption in the parent-child relationship. Single parents, try as they will, tend to diminish parenting for several years after the break-up. Improvement occurs gradually and is enhanced by the formation of a close, dependable new relationship. Over the years, the non-custodial parent's involvement with the child tends to fade. The effects of marital disruption vary with the age of the children involved. Children aged six to eight react with grief, fear, and intense longing for reconciliation. Those aged nine to twelve tend to be openly angry. They are inclined to reject a stepparent. At both ages, the children's behavior at home and at school often deteriorates. The tranquil passage through middle childhood is altogether disrupted by drastic family changes.

The economic impact of divorce on children is often profound. Most children of divorce end up living with their mother. Since women do not earn as much as men on average, and absent parents frequently fail to provide child support, children growing up in single-parent households headed by women are likely to fall into poverty. In one study of divorce during the 1970s, poverty rates for children rose from 12 percent before divorce to 27 percent after divorce. The 1987 poverty rate among female-headed families with children was 46 percent, compared with 8 percent among married-couple families.

In addition to having fewer financial resources, single parents may be less able to supervise their adolescent children. There is evidence that an adolescent living in a single-parent family and having little parental supervision will be susceptible to delinquent behavior and substance abuse. Of course, some single parents do in fact maintain adequate supervision and overcome many difficulties, but on the average the situation is not conducive to successful child rearing.

FAMILY SUPPORT

While all these remarkable changes of the last three decades were increasingly jeopardizing healthy child development, the nation took little notice. Until a few years ago, political, business, and professional leaders had very little to say about the problems of children and youths. Presidents tended to pass the responsibility to the states and the private sector. State leaders often passed responsibility to the federal government or to the cities. One arcane, but important, manifestation of this neglect has been the low priority given to research and science policy for this field. As a result, the nature of this new generation of problems has been poorly understood, emerging trends have been insufficiently recognized. Authority was substituted for evidence, and ideology for analysis.

All this is now changing. While the government has thus far provided little encouragement or incentive for employers to help parents balance their work and family responsibilities, the debate is growing among decision makers over what measures would strengthen today's families—family leave for new mothers and fathers, job sharing, part-time work, flexible schedules, and the like. Within the scientific and professional communities, a remarkable degree of consensus is emerging concerning conditions that influence child and adolescent development and how parents can cope with the changes within themselves and in the world around them. Much has become known about ways to prevent the damage being done to children.

SUPPORT PROGRAMS   There has been an upsurge in programs. Community organizations, churches, schools, and youth service organizations provide child care, support, and guidance for parents and their young. Successful interventions have taken many forms in programs in many cities. They include home visits, parent-child centers, child and family resource programs, school-based and school-linked services, life-skills training, mentoring, self-help programs, and other supports. These programs have found ways of compensating for a damaging social environment by creating conditions that can build on the strengths and resiliency of those caught in difficult circumstances.

Sadly enough, the emerging consensus and the positive results of some interventions are not widely understood by the general public or, for that matter, by many policymakers in public and private sectors. It is crucial now to have a well-informed, wide-ranging public discussion and to link experts with open-minded policymakers in an ongoing process of formulating constructive policy options. No single approach to families and children can be a panacea; many different approaches are needed to span the years of early childhood, when main growth and development occur, and continuing through middle childhood and adolescence. Social neglect is no answer to the crisis families face.

During their years of growth and development, children need dependable attachment, protection, guidance, stimulation, nurturance, and ways of coping with adversity. Infants, in particular, need caregivers who can promote attachment and thereby form the fundamental basis for decent human relationships throughout the child's life. Similarly, early adolescents need to connect with people who can facilitate the momentous transition to adulthood gradually, with sensitivity and understanding. Despite the radical transformations of recent times, such people are usually within the child's immediate family. If not, they exist in the extended family. But if these caregivers cannot give a child what it needs to thrive, we must make an explicit effort to connect the child with people outside the family who have the attributes and skills, and also the durability, to promote healthy child development.

PRENATAL CARE

Early prenatal care for both parents is fundamental in helping families with children in the crucial formative years. The essential components of prenatal care are medical care, health education, and social support services. Good prenatal care dramatically improves the chances that a woman will bear a healthy baby. Those who do not have access to such services suffer higher rates of infant mortality or may give birth to premature or low-birthweight babies. Yet, one-quarter of all pregnant women in the United States now receive insufficient or no prenatal care.

We can prevent nutritional deficiencies by educating expectant mothers and by providing supplementary nutrition and primary health care. This integrated approach has been demonstrated to work well in the federal Women, Infants, and Children Food Supplementation Program. Through prenatal care, pregnant women can also be informed and provided necessary support and skills to help them stop smoking, minimize alcohol consumption, and avoid drugs if they are to have a healthy baby. The educational component of prenatal care can be expanded beyond pregnancy to include a constructive examination of options for the life course. Such a thrust can lead to job training, formal schooling, or other education likely to improve prospects for the future of the mother and her new family.

A major facilitating factor is the ready availability of a dependable person who can provide social support for health and education through the months of pregnancy and beyond. In one intriguing set of innovations, pregnant girls are connected with "resource mothers." These are women living in the same neighborhood as the adolescent mother. They have assimilated life's experiences in a constructive way, have successfully raised their own children, and have learned a lot that can be useful regarding life skills most relevant for the young mother. They convey what they have learned about the problems facing the young mother and in general provide sympathetic, sustained attention as well as gateways to community resources.

"RESOURCE MOTHERS"

Such examples highlight the value of social support for health and education throughout childhood and adolescence. It is vital that national, state, and local policymakers recognize the importance of prenatal care for all women. They need to understand that it will be much less expensive to society in the long run than is medical care for low birthweight and otherwise unhealthy babies, particularly those born to poor women. Intervention helps two generations at once and can have lifelong significance not only for the children but for their young parents as well.

PREVENTIVE CARE

Well-baby care oriented toward prevention of lifelong damage is vital not only for child health but for building parental competence. Immediately after delivery, the pediatrician assesses the newborn's health and informs the parents. In addition to providing immunizations during infancy, pediatricians also monitor children's growth carefully to detect nutritional problems and treat infectious diseases. Pediatricians nowadays provide well-informed guidance and emotional support to help families attain healthy lifestyles. They foster attachment between mother and baby and help prepare her for coping with unpredictable difficulties with her infant. They answer parents' questions and anticipate questions about growth and development. They provide other vital services, for example, early treatment of ear infections and correction of vision deficits so that hearing and visual impairments do not interfere with learning.

As the infant becomes a toddler, the pediatrician or other primary care provider, in addition to assessing the child's health and growth, can check the child for injuries or signs of neglect and abuse. They can help guide parents in providing safe play areas, dealing with difficult behavior, and easing the child's transition to out-of-home care and preschool. Since pediatricians are often in short supply, particularly in poor city neighborhoods and remote rural areas, it is essential to enlist the aid of pediatric nurse practitioners, home visitors, parent support groups, and primary prevention program directors. Neighborhood health centers have proved to be effective in reaching low-income children with preventive services, but they are not widespread.

More policymakers are seeing the wisdom of such preventive care for children, but greater progress has to be made on the most critical fronts: immunization, low birthweight, child abuse, and health education. Still not widely understood is the fact that the major health hazards for American children no longer stem from disease but from injuries—both accidental or unintentional and intentional. Injuries account for half of all deaths of children and are an increasing source of long-term disability and serious health problems for children and adolescents. Intentional injury and neglect—child abuse—is a very unpleasant subject, but it is slowly being faced as a national problem. Abused children are likely to suffer severe psychological and sexual problems later in life, and all too commonly perpetuate violent behavior in the way they treat their own children. The risk of child mistreatment is increased when parents endure a high level of stress, such as unemployment and social isolation.

Despite the limited amount of research that has been done in this area, preventive efforts have been launched that aim mainly at preventing repeated abuse in families rather than preventing the first incident. These interventions include parent education about child development and parenting behavior, counseling, parent self-help support groups, crisis centers, and protective day care, home visitor programs, and programs to promote stronger early attachment between mother and infant. Such preven-

HEAD
START

tive efforts are a good deal less costly than paying for problems of seriously neglected and abused children later on. They deserve vigorous exploration and research.

As child rearing moves beyond the home, the quality of custodial care becomes crucial. The vast majority of responsible parents are eager to ensure that the care their children get will facilitate their healthy development. Just as they want a competent doctor to foster their children's health, so too, they want a capable caregiver. Yet, the more I have probed this issue, the more I have become impressed with how difficult it is to meet this need. There is little precedent for outside-the-home care on such a vast scale as is now emerging in the United States. The crucial factor in quality of care is the nature and behavior of the caregiver. As the demand for child caregivers has surged, those trying to provide it have frantically sought to recruit more child care workers. Even with the best of intentions, this field has been characterized by low pay, low respect, minimal training, minimal supervision, and extremely variable quality. Although most child-care workers try very hard to do a decent job, the plain fact is that many of them do not stay with any one group of children very long. This in itself puts a child's development in jeopardy; it is especially damaging for young children, for whom long-term caretaking relationships are crucial.

At present most professionals recommend that parents defer day care beyond infancy if possible. But in the absence of policies for paid maternity leave, the trend seems to lean increasingly toward day care for infants. Many clinicians and researchers are working to develop effective models and standards of dependable day care that will promote normal, vigorous child development. At present the issue of what constitutes high-quality care and how it can be accomplished in practice is still unresolved. We can learn some lessons from other nations that have addressed this problem seriously. We need a better sense of how powerful institutions might help to fulfill the potential of this extraordinary movement. While there is an emerging consensus on what can be achieved, we do not yet know how to respond to this great challenge.

One of the most important research findings shows that the children who benefit most from child care are those who come from relatively poor families. Perhaps the rich experiences at the center provide such children with opportunities they might be missing at home. Can we extract the essential ingredients and heighten the efficiency of these good effects, so that they may become standard practice?

High-quality child care and preschool education in the mode of Head Start has proven valuable for children age four and now is being offered to those age three. Overall, individuals who have been in good early education programs have better achievement scores in elementary school, are less likely to be classified as needing special education, have higher rates of high school completion and college attendance, and lower pregnancy and crime rates than comparable students who were not in preschool programs.

The lessons of Head Start have wide applicability. Such valuable early stimulation, encouragement, instruction, and health care provided in quality preschool programs (all with substantial family involvement) can be incorporated into a variety of child care settings. Early education should not be seen as a one-time event akin to immunization but as an important component of a constructive series of developmental experiences throughout childhood and adolescence.

PARENTAL COMPETENCE

One of the most important and recurring themes in the research on early intervention is the potential value of teaching young parents to deal effectively with their children. Ideally, such education should begin before the baby is born. Thus, as indicated, a good prenatal care regimen would involve not only obstetrical, nutritional, and other measures that would protect mother and infant throughout pregnancy, labor, and delivery but also some basic preparation for both parents regarding their tasks as parents and their own life course; in the case of poor parents at least, this would include connection with opportunities to develop occupational skills.

Because the first few years of a child's life are a critical period of development, physical, emotional, and psychological, the family's capacity to nurture—or its failure to do so—has the most profound effect on a child's growth. Research findings strongly support the centrality of a loving, dependable relationship for a good start in life. This does not mean that only one person matters to that child or that the biological mother must be that person. Certainly, a baby can form secure attachments with other caregivers and with siblings. But research evidence indicates the great importance of one central caregiver who creates a sustaining, loving relationship with the infant. Expectant or new mothers or other adults in the consistent caregiving role can be taught effective parenting techniques including those that foster attachment.

As their children grow, parents can be helped by programs that promote verbal interaction among family members and the verbal responsiveness of adults to children. Numerous studies confirm that the mother's responsiveness strengthens her child's learning and sense of self-sufficiency and thereby opens doors to development that would otherwise be closed. Parents can also be helped to understand that there is an optimal range for the intensity and variety of stimulation for a child's healthy development. The great challenge is to devise on a broader scale family-centered interventions that will enhance children's cognitive development and emotional resiliency despite the problems of chronic poverty and relative social isolation.

SOCIAL SUPPORTS

As parent education programs spread, it is essential to avoid the extremes of dogmatism on the one hand and vague, wishful, uninformative approaches on the other. We have to look to the scientific and scholarly community as well as experienced practitioners in relevant fields to devise a standard of reference for prospective and actual parents to use.

Studies in a variety of contexts show that social supports for families (that are eroded, disintegrated, or otherwise weakened under circumstances of persistent poverty and social depreciation) can buffer the effects of stressful life transitions for both parents and children. We can no longer take for granted the supportive systems that were built into human experience over millions of years. Even the most successful, capable parents cannot teach their children the wide array of skills needed for today's complex, rapidly changing society. Increasingly, we must consider crucial skills for education and health that have a strong bearing on survival and the quality of life in contemporary American society.

Institutions and organizations beyond the family can provide the social support necessary for strengthening the family and/or offering surrogates for parents, older siblings, or an extended family. Examples of such interventions are in communities across the country, in churches, schools, agencies, and minority-run organizations. They build constructive networks for families that serve parents and attract youngsters in ways that foster their health, their education, and their capacity to be accepted rather than rejected by the mainstream society.

Whereas parent education efforts have historically focused on the child, family support efforts view the entire family as one unit. Their goals are to augment parents' knowledge of a skill in child rearing, to enhance their skills in coping with the child and other family matters, to help families gain access to services and community resources, to facilitate the development of informal support networks among parents, and to organize to counteract dangerous trends in the community. Most of these programs are served by para-professionals who are members of the community, although professionals are also involved.

Social supports for adolescent mothers are particularly vital, especially for those who are poor and socially isolated. Such programs not only teach parenting skills and ensure the provision of health and educational services, they help mothers stay in school and acquire skills for gainful employment. Evaluations of some interventions show that young mothers improve their diets, smoke less, and generally take better care of themselves and their babies than those who do not have such services; they also have fewer children.

FAMILIES WITH ADOLESCENTS

Compared to families with young children, families with adolescents have been neglected. Even for the affluent sector, little work has been done on strengthening support networks for families during the stresses of the great transition from childhood to adulthood. Still less attention has gone into strengthening networks for families who live in poverty or culturally different situations. Although adolescents are moving toward independence, they are still intimately bound up with the family, which is much more important to them than is evident. This is especially true in early adolescence. For that reason, we need to pay attention to the ways in which family relationships can be utilized to help adolescents weather the conditions of contemporary life. This is a difficult time for parents, too. Their own marital relationships, their own coping skills, are often in transition. They may need help in renegotiating family relationships at this time.

Stephen Small has identified for the Carnegie Council on Adolescent Development forty-one programs to help families strengthen their capacity to tackle problems associated with adolescent development. Most of these programs center on curricula developed for this purpose and made available for use by local organizations. Some of the more promising ones are initiated and maintained by voluntary youth-serving organizations such as the Boys Clubs of America, the 4-H Clubs, and the Parent-Teacher Association. One of Small's strongest recommendations is for a network through which parents can obtain social support from other parents—sharing experience, pooling information and coping strategies. A mutual-aid ethic among parents who have a common concern for the well-being of their developing adolescents and yet bring diverse experiences to the encounter can be helpful.

LIFE SKILLS TRAINING

Adolescents have to navigate through a mine field of risks to their healthy education and development. They need attention from adults who can be positive role models, mentors, and sources of accurate information on important topics. They need to understand the biological changes of puberty and the immediate and long-term health consequences of lifestyle choices. They need to learn interpersonal and communication skills, self regulation, decision making, and problem solving. Today there are few guidelines for behavior available to children or even to adults. Many of the messages they receive are conflicting or ambiguous. Clearly, our adolescents need life skills training—the formal teaching of requisite skills for surviving, living with others, and succeeding in a complex society.

Formal education can provide or at least supplement the life skills training that historically was built into the informal processes of family and kin relationships. Successful school programs are typically administered by agencies outside of the schools. Many use some variant of social skills training and use peers in their interventions. Across the nation, most communities have programs outside the schools that offer youngsters recreation or teach them skills. Youth agencies, such as Girls, Inc., serve about 25 million young people annually and thus are in regular contact with almost as many children as are the schools. Their aim is to help teens acquire social skills, develop a constructive personal identity, and build a dependable basis for earned respect. Their strengths are that they are free to experiment, they reach children early, and they typically work in small groups with ten to fifteen young people at a time. Effective programs tend to respond to more than one serious problem or risk factor and try to create incentives for dealing with them that adolescents perceive as relevant to their own lives.

Based on the lessons of experience with all such approaches that work for families and children, it should be possible in the foreseeable future to design interventions that go beyond what has been possible up to now. First, we can use our experience from the programs so far undertaken, ascertain which are the most effective and which need the most attention, and construct informed models for future interventions. With so much at stake, terrible suffering, grievous loss of talent and life, we can surely find ways to make these programs available on a much wider scale.

STRENGTHENING DISADVANTAGED FAMILIES

Democratic societies are being challenged as never before to give all children, regardless of social background, the opportunity to participate in the modern technical world. This means preparing them to qualify for modern employment opportunities; to achieve at least a decent minimum of literacy in science and technology as part of everyone's educational heritage; to make lifelong learning a reality so that people can adjust their knowledge and skills to technical change; and to foster a scientific attitude useful both in general problem solving throughout society and in understanding scientific aspects of the major issues on which an informed citizenry must decide.

Traditionally, America's technologically educated work force, which has by and large been very efficient by world standards, has come from a small fraction of the white, male, college-educated population. We have skimmed the cream of a very preferred, fortunate group, while blacks, Hispanics, American Indians, and even women have historically been under-represented in the fields that require technical competence. Even if we were not interested in rectifying historical injustices, we must consider that the traditional white male source of scientists and engineers has become inadequate at the very time when more technically trained people are needed. This brings the country to a point where equity intersects with economic vitality, democratic civility, and military security. Because of this intersection, there are now broader and more urgent reasons than ever before to support an unprecedented effort in the education of disadvantaged minority children. What must motivate us is not only decency but also national interest.

In the immediate years ahead, the number of young people in the United States will be smaller than in recent decades. Fewer young people will enter the work force. By the year 2000, about one-third of these young people will be black or Hispanic, the groups now at the bottom of the educational and economic ladder. Already, in the 1990s, racial and ethnic minorities constitute the majority of primary and secondary school students in twenty-three of the twenty-five largest American cities. In another eight years, they will be the majority in fifty-three cities.

While the lives of individual members of minority groups have greatly improved since the 1960s, many of the millions remaining in the inner cities have been relegated to marginal status in our society. They are the poorest and least-educated Americans and are served by the least-adequate health care in the nation. As in past generations, those who can escape severely damaged environments do so, leaving behind those who have come of age on the streets, without stable adult models and constructive support systems and often without parents.

For the majority of American schoolchildren to be excluded from the mainstream of education and worthwhile jobs in the next century would be a personal loss and a tragic waste of human resources that will weaken the country's economic and social foundations. Increasingly, this injustice threatens our democratic foundations as well as the economic vitality of the United States. Plain national interest demands that minority students be educated equally with majority students, particularly in the science-based fields. The country can no longer endure the drain of talent that has been the norm up to now. The entire sequence of developmentally useful interventions must be applied in a concerted effort to poor and disadvantaged communities. There is much that can be achieved if we think of our entire population as a large extended family, tied by history to a shared destiny, and requiring a strong ethic of mutual aid.

WEIGHING COST

The biology of our species makes necessary a huge parental investment in order to achieve the fulfillment of each child's potential. This means far more than an economic investment. It is a continuing, relentless, recurrent demand for investment of time, energy, thought, consideration, and sensitivity. It is an investment in patience, understanding, and coping. It requires persistence, determination, commitment, and resiliency. The awareness of such a large investment, however vaguely formulated, is inhibiting many young people from undertaking childrearing now that the choice is more readily available to them. Others have gone ahead and started families, only to find they are unprepared for the challenge.

If they cannot or will not give their children what they need, then others must do so. But who? In general, parents have responded that they are willing to do a good deal of what is necessary but cannot do all of it. Therefore, we have seen the rise of institutions that provide parent-equivalent functions. We are in mid-passage in this process; no one can say with justifiable confidence what the consequences will be for the generation of children in crisis.

In almost all cases, the expenditures for optimal child and adolescent development are not simply add-ons but can be at least partly achieved by wiser use of existing funds. Huge amounts are already spent for these purposes. Much of this current spending could be greatly improved and redirected by some of the measures suggested here. To replace inadequate interventions would in some cases cost less and in other cases cost more than we are now spending. This sort of analysis must largely be done on a case-by-case, place-by-place basis. What is likely is that the total economic and social costs of present child-relevant activities could be greatly reduced.

We are all paying heavily for the neglect of our children—however inadvertently and regretfully. These costs have many facets: economic inefficiency, loss of productivity, lack of skill, high health care costs, growing prison costs, and a badly ripped social fabric. In one way or another, we pay. The vital investments outlined have to be viewed as the responsibility, not only of the family, but of the entire society—not just the federal government but other levels of government; not just business but labor; not just light-skinned people but dark-skinned ones as well; not just the rich but the middle class and the poor. We are all in this huge leaking boat together. We will all have to pay and reason and care and work together. Our habitual short-term view will not suffice. There are many useful, constructive steps to be taken but no quick fix, no magic bullet, no easy way will do. We will not get rich quick on the backs of our children.

We have to move beyond the easy and pervasive recourse of passing the buck. It is the responsibility of every individual, every institution and organization, of every business, and all levels of government. We cannot lose sight of the fact that wise investment in human capital is the most fundamental and productive investment any society can make. Constructive development of our children is more important than oil or minerals, office buildings or factories, roads or weapons. The central fact is that all of these and much more depend in the long run on the quality of human resources and the decency of human relations. If these deteriorate, all else declines.

BRINGING DEMOCRACY HOME

SHERE HITE REPORTS ON THE FAMILY

Shere Hite is the author of, among other books, "The Hite Report on Female Sexuality" (Pandora) and "The Hite Report on Men and Male Sexuality (Ballantine).

In this prepublication excerpt from Shere Hite's new book, The Hite Report on the Family: Growing Up Under Patriarchy, *Hite presents a new analysis of the family. Based on responses from more than 3,000 people primarily from Western nations, this* Hite Report *asserts that families are undergoing a process of modernization, finally adopting the democratic principles that were established in the political realm more*

than two centuries ago. Where others see chaos in the rise of alternative families— such as those with single or same-sex parents—Shere Hite sees progress. These and other changes in personal life, such as women's increased independence and men's more active role as nurturers, are much needed, she says, both to enhance individual satisfaction—and to prevent democracy from sliding toward fascism. Hite's ideas are provocative, as always. She offers great hope for the survival of the many kinds of families we see evolving today, but only if we—as a society—are willing to nurture and support difference.

Love and anger, love and obedience, love and power, love and hate. These are all present in family relationships. It's easy to say that they are inevitable, that stresses and strains are unavoidable, given "human nature." To some extent this is true, but these stresses and strains are exaggerated by a tense and difficult family system that is imposed upon our emotions and our lives, structuring them to fit its own specified goals.

Is the family as we have known it for so long the only way to create safe, loving, and caring environments for people? The best way? To understand the family in Western tradition, we must remember that much of what we see, say, and think about it is based on the archetypal family that is so pervasive in our society—Jesus, Mary, and Joseph. There is no daughter icon. This is the "holy family" model that we are expected, in one way or another, to live up to. But is this model really the right one for people who believe in equality and justice? Does it teach a good understanding of love and the way to make relationships work when we become adults?

One constantly hears that the family is in trouble, that it doesn't work anymore, that we must find ways to help it. If the family doesn't work, maybe there is something wrong with its structure. People must have reasons for fleeing the nuclear family: human rights abuses and the battering of women are well documented in many governments' statistics.

The family is changing because only in recent decades has the process of democratization, which began in Western political life more than two centuries ago, reached private life. Although John Stuart Mill wrote in favor of women's rights in the egalitarian democratic theory he helped develop, the family and women's role in the world were left out of most discussions of democracy, left in the "sacred" religious domain. Women and nonproperty owners, as well as "minorities," did not have the vote when democracy first began. Men made a fatal mistake. The democracy they thought they could make work in the public sphere would not really work without democracy in private life.

Some people, of course, are alarmed by changes in the family. Reactionary fundamentalist groups have gone on the offensive to try to stop this process. Yet most people are happier with their personal lives today than people were 50 years ago. Women especially have more choices and freedom than they did in the past. There is a positive new diversity springing up in families and relationships today in Western society. This pluralism should be valued and

In the words of Hite's respondents:

Parents on Changing Family

"I am home for more of the time than my wife. In fact, she's the main breadwinner. I had no difficulty in reversing roles with my wife when our younger son was three months old. She got thoroughly fed up with being in the house and with my long working and traveling hours. The walls seemed to stifle her enthusiasm for living, while I felt that my participation in family life was too little. So my wife found a teaching position not far from home, I changed to a part-time sales job, and we immediately gained more time together as a family."

●

"I loved touching and holding my children, and walking with them in my arms, up and down the floor on a cold winter night. I changed them, fed them after they left their mother's breast, cared for them when they were sick, spent hours with them, neglecting other work."

●

"It is important to let your child know that you love her but not necessarily that you like her one hundred percent of the time. It is good for kids to know that they don't always have to like you either, and that

encouraged: far from signaling a breakdown of society, it is a sign of a new, more open and tolerant society springing up, a new world being born out of the clutter of the old.

Democracy could work even better if we changed the aggressive personality that is being created by the patriarchal family system. Children brought up with choice about whether to accept their parents' power are more likely to be confident about believing in themselves and their own ideas, less docile or habituated to bending to power. Such a population would create and participate in public debate very differently. And there are many more advances we are on the threshold of achieving: naming and eliminating emotional violence, redefining love and friendship, progressing in the areas of children's rights and in men's questioning of their own lives.

My work salutes the gentler and more diverse families that seem to be arising. They are part of a system that does not keep its members in terror: fathers in terror lest they not be "manly" and able to support it all: mothers in terror lest they be beaten in their own bedrooms and ridiculed by their children: children in terror of being forced to do things against their will and having absolutely no recourse, no door open to them for exit.

What I am offering is a new interpretation of relationships between parents and children, a new theory of the family. My interpretation of the data from my questionnaires takes into account not only the individual's unique experiences, as is done in psychology, but also the cultural backdrop—the canvas of social "approval" or "disapproval" against which children's lives are lived. This interdisciplinary theory also takes into account the historical ideology of the family; those who took part in my research are living in a world where perception of "family" is filtered through the Christian model of the "holy family" with its reproductive icons of Jesus, Mary, and Joseph. But no matter how beautiful it appears (especially in its promise of "true love"), this family model is an essentially repressive one, teaching authoritarian psychological patterns, meekness in women, and a belief in the unchanging rightness of male power. In this hierarchical family, love and power are inextricably linked, a pattern that has damaging effects not only on all family members but on the politics of the wider society. How can there be successful democracy in public life if there is an authoritarian model in private life?

So used have we become to these symbols that we continue to believe—no matter what statistics we see in the newspapers about divorce, violence in the home, mental breakdown—that the icons and the system they represent are right, fair, and just. We assume without thinking that this model is the only "natural" form of the family, and that if there are problems it must be the individual who is at fault, not the institution.

We need a new interpretation of what is going on. We may be at one of the most important turning points of the Western world, the creation of a new social base that will engender an advanced and improved democratic political structure.

What Is the Family All About?

Creating new, more democratic families means taking a clear and rational look at our institutions. We tend to forget that the family was created in its current form in early patriarchy for political, not religious, reasons. The new political order had to solve a specific problem: How could lineage or inheritance flow through men (and not women as it had previously) if men do not bear children?

The modern patriarchal family was created so that each man would "own" a woman who would reproduce for him. He then had to control the sexuality of "his" woman, for how else could he be sure that "his" child was really his? Restrictions were placed on women's lives and bodies by men; women's imprisonment in marriage was made a virtue, for example, through the later archetype of the self-sacrificing Mary,

there are times when a parent will be wrong and that all you can hope to do is your best. Making a mistake is natural and everyone is allowed to do it!"

Girls on Their Families

"When I was 18, I became pregnant and decided to have an abortion. Mom, who had guessed already, spent a day helping me come to terms with my fears and my decision. Mom told Dad—he had a right to know—just before I got home. He didn't have time to adjust, everything came boiling up. He hated the boy—said it was his fault—and on and on.

"Next day, Dad took me out for a drink and apologized and talked about the way he felt and why. He then took me through the whole abortion procedure, which required signing some papers and talking with the doctor, as well as taking me to the actual operation. I got through to the real man for the first time then, the vulnerable and human side, the side that makes mistakes and gets confused. It was a bonding that continues.

"I love both my parents. They work hard at their relationship, and love and respect each other. If I ever marry I think I have a good example. I can see what the ingredients are for a successful partnership."

who was happy to be of service, never standing up for herself or her own rights. Mary, it is important to note, is a later version of a much earlier Creation Mother goddess. In her earlier form, she had many more aspects, more like the Indian goddess Kali than the "mother" whom the Christian patriarchal system devised.

Fortunately, the family is a human institution: humans made it and humans can change it. My research indicates that the extreme aggression we see in society is not a characteristic of biological "human nature" (as Freud concluded), nor a result of hormones. "Human nature" is a psychological structure that is carefully implanted in our minds—for life—as we learn the love and power equations of the family. Power and love are combined in the family structure: in order to receive love, most children have to humiliate themselves, over and over again, before power.

In our society, parents have the complete legal, economic, and social "right" to control children's lives. Parents' exclusive power over children creates obedience. Children are likely to take on authoritarian emotional, psychological, and sexual patterns, and to see power as one of the central categories of existence.

Love is at the heart—so to speak—of our belief in the importance of the family. The desire for love is what keeps us returning to the icons. Even when they don't seem to work in our lives, we try and try again. We are told that we will never find love if we don't participate in the family. We hear repeatedly that the only place we will ever be able to get security, true acceptance, and understanding is in the family; that we should distrust other forms of family; that we are only "half a family" or a "pretend family" if we create any other human group; that without being a member of the family we will be forever "left out," lonely, or useless. No one would want to deny the importance of love, or of lasting relationships with other people. But the violent, distorted definitions of love created by the patriarchal family make it difficult for love to last, and to be as profound as it could be.

How confusing it is for children, the idea of being loved! They are so often told by their parents, "Of course we love you, why do you even ask?" It is easy for children to believe that the emotion they feel when faced with a powerful person is "love"—or that the inscrutable ways of a person who is sometimes caring and friendly, and other times punitive and angry, are loving. The problem then is that, since the parents are still the providers and "trainers" of the children, legally and economically the "owners" of the children, they exercise incredible power over the children—the very power of survival itself.

Children must feel gratitude, and so, in their minds, this gratitude is mixed with love. How much of the love they feel is really supplication before the power of the parents? How will they define love later in life? Won't they be highly confused by passion (either emotional or physical) and what it means, unable to connect it with other feelings of liking and concern? Of course, long-term caring for others is something positive that can also be learned in families, but it can be learned in other kinds of families, not just the nuclear model.

Does "Love" Include Sex? The Body?

And what definition of love do children learn from the way their parents relate physically? Isn't it strange to think of your parents having sex? Finding parents in any kind of physical embrace comes as a fascinating shock to most children: 83 percent of children in my research say their parents seem completely asexual.

It would be logical if children drew the conclusion that "real love" is never sexual, or even physically affectionate. But isn't affection a great part of what love is? If parents don't hug and kiss each other, is the definition of adult "love" different? And if so, what is it? Why do parents feel that they shouldn't touch each other in front of the children? Because the children would be jealous? Because it would give the children sexual feelings and ideas? Or, do many parents really not

"I often received compliments from my parents on how pretty I looked, when what I wanted to hear was how smart or strong or perceptive I was. I remember when I won an academic award, the night of the public awards announcements my father told me how pretty I looked. Never once did I hear how great it was that I was such a scholar."

●

"Without a father around was a great way to grow up. There were no male or female roles in our house. Mom taught both my brother and me how to do housework, then he and I would trade. I liked to iron so I did all the ironing; he liked to vacuum, so he did that."

●

"My father talks freely with me now, and there have been some important talks in the past that gave me permission to be sexual, to adopt a child if I wanted to, to live with a woman. Only once did we tangle seriously, when I wished to return to a relationship with a man that was, indeed, destructive for me. My father is always very fond, strong, and steady in his affections, very willing to listen."

●

"Dad will eulogize Mom for her determination,

want to touch each other? Children wonder, if the parents don't want to be affectionate, why exactly are they together? If they are only together "for the sake of the children," this puts an awfully big burden on the children to be "worth it" or to "make their parents happy," thus confusing the definitions of love even further.

Another way children learn that power and domination are part of love is through observing the relationship of their parents. Gender tension and especially second-class treatment of the mother by the father is reported by the majority of people from two-parent families in this study. Girls in particular find this gender inequality mixed with "love" confusing, even psychologically violent and terrifying. Why? Because for girls it means coming to terms with what this power relationship will mean for them: Will they inherit this gender inequality? Can they avoid being considered lesser beings when they become women? How can they love a father who represents this system? Or a mother who lets herself participate in it?

Are Single-Parent Families Bad for Children?

There are very few carefully controlled studies of the effects of single-parent families on children. Today, much popular journalism assumes that the two-parent family is better for children. My data show that there are beneficial effects for the majority of children living in single-parent families. It is more positive for children not to grow up in an atmosphere poisoned by gender inequality.

Do girls who grow up with "only" their mother have a better relationship with her? According to my study, 49 percent of such girls felt that it was a positive experience; 20 percent did not like it; and the rest had mixed feelings. Mothers in one-parent families are more likely to feel freer to confide in daughters because no "disloyalty to the spouse" is implied. Daughters in such families are less likely to see the moth-

The Psyche of Patriarchy: A New Way of Seeing How We Grow Up

1. Oedipus revisited

The major crisis in boys' lives is created during puberty, when boys are flooded with sexual feelings, first attain full orgasm, and often play sex games with other boys. Boys are heavily pressured by the culture to demonstrate "toughness" in sport, to stay away from girls, not to hang around at home with mother: "Don't be a sissy or a wimp," i.e., "Don't act female or feminine." If boys learn that they should demonstrate contempt for the female world and the mother they love, they can grow up to be men who feel extreme ambivalence toward women. This is Oedipus in torment. Men often desire power and control in a sexual relationship with a woman in order to avoid these feelings of confusion and "danger."

2. Why do girls fight with their mothers?

The relationship most essential to disrupt, in order for patriarchy to work, is the relationship between mother and daughter. Mothers and daughters are not "natural enemies" competing for the father, as Freud imagined, but "natural friends," as they have many things in common. If this relationship is not broken, however, patriarchy could not continue, since all power would no longer be in the hands of men. Distrust of women, and the double standard, are hallmarks of patriarchal psychology.

3. Torn loyalties of children in two-parent families

A crisis of loyalty is the unseen psychosexual drama for children. Most parents' relationships, according to children in my study and many government statistics, still reflect gender stereotypes: most men don't do housework and they condescend to women at home, while many women are psychologically and emotionally dominated by men. Children in my research over and over again document feeling pressure to "choose," "take sides," or help the weaker one—or else feel cowardly. Children are sometimes better off with a single parent than with two who are unequal and thus present the child with an insoluble loyalty conflict.

4. Girls' double identity

Girls learn very early to connect their sexual identities with shame, not pride. Menstruation is not celebrated, and they cannot discuss sexual matters such as masturbation. Thus girls develop a double identity, one a "good girl," and the other a private sexual identity. Friendship between girls is important and represents the underground "self" of the girl.

5. Children do not need the archetypal family model

Children need warm and mature people around them. We should construct positive new families that meet children's needs, not close our eyes because the world does not fit our icons. We should begin to reach out to one another in new ways, to groups wider than our own nuclear families, and to think of the whole society as part of our family too.

dedication to the family, her tireless work, but in daily life he often belittles her or lectures her for things he feels she hasn't done, or has done inadequately. I grew up thinking that a woman's love meant submission."

Boys on Their Families

"In second grade I won a reading contest and was allowed to pick a book as a prize. I chose one about a nurse. It was decided that the teacher could not give me that one—not masculine enough! My parents stood up for me and I got the book."

•

"My mother and I are quite close. I like and admire her a lot. She's generous with her affection, honest about her feelings, willing to stand up for herself, and has a good sense of humor. We share a similar passion for music and metaphysical ideas. Lately, we've been helping each other with our various struggles. "

•

"My sister was my best friend. We did things together as equals with no role barriers. But it was never the same after I left her to play hockey with the boys. After that, we took off into our masculine and feminine roles, which were enforced more and more until we became adults. Now it is almost impossible er as a "wimp"—she is an independent person.

Boys who grow up with "only" their mother experience less pressure to demonstrate contempt for things "feminine" and for nonaggressive parts of themselves. In *The Hite Report on Men and Male Sexuality*, I was surprised to find that boys who grew up with their mother alone were much more likely to have good relationships with women in their adult lives: 80 percent of men from such families had formed strong, lasting ties with women (in marriage or long-term relationships), as opposed to only 40 percent from two-parent families. This does not mean that the two-parent family cannot be reformed so that it provides a peaceful environment for children—indeed this is part of the ongoing revolution in the family in which so many people today are engaged.

Single-parent families are mostly headed by mothers, yet there is an increasing number of single-father families. Many single fathers don't take much part in child care but instead hire female nannies or ask their mothers, sisters, or girlfriends to take care of the children. Men could change the style of families by taking more part domestically, and by opening up emotionally and having closer contact with children. My research highlights men's traumatizing and enforced split from women at puberty [see "The Psyche of Patriarchy"]. Healing this is the single most important thing we as a society could do to bridge the distance men feel from "family."

Democracy of the Heart: A New Politics

If you listen to people talk about their families, it becomes clear that we must

to be 'friends' with a woman. The roles we are assigned don't allow it."

●

"I was well informed about sex by my parents. I was told the names of all the parts and how babies were conceived. Mother talked about love in relation to sex, but never tried to push opinions on me."

give up on the outdated notion that the only acceptable families are nuclear families. We should not see the new society that has evolved over the last 40 years as a disaster simply because it is not like the past.

The new diversity of families is part of a positive pluralism, part of a fundamental transition in the organization of society that calls for open-minded brainstorming by all of us: What do we believe "love" and "family" are? Can we accept that the many people fleeing the nuclear family are doing so for valid reasons? If reproduction is no longer the urgent priority that it was when societies were smaller, before industrialization took hold, then the revolt against the family is not surprising. Perhaps it was even historically inevitable. It is not that people don't want

to build loving, family-style relationships, it is that they do not want to be forced to build them within one rigid, hierarchical, heterosexist, reproductive framework. Diversity in family forms can bring joy and enrichment to a society: new kinds of families can be the basis for a renaissance of spiritual dignity and creativity in political as well as personal life.

Continuing this process of bringing private life into an ethical and egalitarian frame of reference will give us the energy and moral will to maintain democracy in the larger political sphere. We can create a society with a new spirit and will—but politics will have to be transformed. We can use the interactive frame of reference most often found today in friendships between women. Diversity in families can form the basic infrastructure for a new and advanced type of political democracy to be created, imagined, developed—a system that suits the massive societies that communications technology today has made into one "global village."

One cannot exaggerate the importance of the current debate: there has been fascism in societies before; it could certainly emerge again, alongside fascism in the family. If we believe in the democratic, humanist ideals of the last 200 years, we have the right, almost the duty, to make our family system a more just one; to follow our democratic ideals and make a new, more inclusive network of private life that will reflect not a preordained patriarchal structure, but our belief in justice and equality for all—women, men, and children. Let's continue the transformation, believe in ourselves, and go forward with love instead of fear. In our private lives and in our public world, let's hail the future and make history.

THE ACHE FOR HOME

Monica McGoldrick

Monica McGoldrick, M.S.W., is the director of the Family Institute of New Jersey. Address: 312 Amboy Ave., Metuchen, NJ 08840.

"The ache for home lives in all of us, the safe place where we can go as we are and not be questioned. It impels mighty ambitions and dangerous capers. We hope that by doing these things, home will find us acceptable, or, failing that, that we will forget our awful yearning for it."

Maya Angelou

"Going Home." What is the meaning of that familiar and evocative phrase? Until recently, I understood it primarily in terms of the ideas of Murray Bowen, family therapy's pioneering theorist, which have so long influenced my thinking and my own family ties. As a therapist, I had always thought that "going home" meant developing a more adult, personal relationship with your parents and your siblings so you could be more fully your grown-up self even when you were with them. In recent years, however, my notions of home have changed.

I turned 50 last July. I now have a 9-year-old son, and, last year, my 80-year-old mother died. Along with my husband, sisters and friends, I am now somewhat startled to find myself a member of the oldest generation.

For me these days, "going home" means not just evoking in memory the house of my childhood, but trying to imagine how to create a safe haven for all of us on this planet. But, I am discovering, it is impossible to think about this larger vision of home, this deeper sense of human connection, without recognizing how the constraints of culture, gender, class and race have kept so many of us from feeling at home in our society in

the first place. In fact, so many people are systematically abused, despised, devalued and kept invisible—women, children, people of color, the poor, gays— that for millions of us, "going home" means going to a place where we have never been in the first place. "Home" for too many of us is no safe haven, no home at all.

How can we break through these iron bars of hatred, bigotry, arrogance and invisibility that shut out so many? How can we come to understand the links between our individual stories, secrets and silences, and the ways that the lives of all of us are part of one inextricable pattern, that we all do share a common home? How can we come to realize that, as Susan Griffin says, "our personal stories and the history of the world are all one story"?

UNTIL A VERY FEW YEARS AGO, FOR me, culture, gender, class and race were, to borrow Betty Friedan's famous phrase, issues with "no name." It had never occurred to me that any of them affected the relationships in *my* family, *my* schooling or the communities in which *I* lived. None of these crucial determinants of our life experience was ever mentioned during my childhood, my adolescence, my college or graduate education, or, for that matter, during my family therapy training.

So, even though I spent much of my childhood in what was really an interracial family—my primary caretaker was African American—race was never mentioned. Even though I grew up in a family run by two women who raised three daughters, a family with preferential rules regarding males (a family in which my father was treated like a visiting dignitary), gender was never mentioned. The influence of my Irish background would have been obvious to anyone who could recognize Irish behavior, yet I never

thought of myself as Irish. And I grew up in a family in which class was never mentioned, even though we learned implicitly who was above us and below us on the socioeconomic ladder, and we learned rules for behavior that were utterly defined by class hierarchies. In short, we learned to organize our relationships completely according to prescribed, biased and utterly unspoken rules of culture, race, class and gender.

A few years before my mother died, she talked with me about how she had been defined throughout her life—first as a daughter, then as a wife, and finally as a mother:

"I was accustomed to people saying, 'Oh, you're Inspector Cahalane's daughter,'" she told me, "'and then I was accustomed to everybody saying, 'Oh, you're Joseph McGoldrick's wife,' so that I was always somebody's something, just as today I'm Monica's mother. Just once I want to be known as, 'This is Helen McGoldrick. She stands on her own two feet.' But that's never to happen, Monica. So I was always somebody else's something."

My mother's history, her fears and inadequacies, her struggles, continue through me. The pain of always being "somebody's something" is a problem I have to take responsibility for, because during the era in which she lived, she was not able to be all that she could have been. Along with her two sisters and their Barnard classmates in the 1930s, she was part of a privileged and dynamic group of women who, in spite of their education and talents, were raised to submerge their identities in the men and children in their lives. My mother was our nurse, manager, chauffeur, host, and the encourager of our projects. She was a brilliant, courageous and remarkable woman. Yet, for much of her life, I hated her—for her inability to be a "traditional mother," for her foibles and, most of all, for her class pretensions.

In college, when I switched fields from Russian studies to social work, she was embarrassed, because it indicated such a nose dive in class status. She used to introduce me by saying, "This is my daughter Monica, who is doing Psychiatric at Yale." For years, I resented her time of my birth until her death while I was in college. It was to her that I confided my problems—about boyfriends, about teachers, about my mother. After our family moved to the country, How incredible that she learned to read from racist books about fair-haired, blue-eyed little *Dick and Jane*, books that invalidated her own experience by leaving it invisible.

I didn't recognize Margaret's white uniform as a symbol of her status in our family or know that she didn't learn to read until after I did.

for what I viewed as bragging and for hiding who we really were by embellishing her stories to impress others. Only now do I feel shame about my anger, because I realize she did it because she was so unsure of her *own* status, and had been made to feel invisible and inadequate all her life. I have come to see it as my business that my mother was not free to be all she could have been. Her invisibility made our lives visible.

I have come to realize that it is not so much our mothers who have let us down, as the yardsticks by which we have measured them. When I speak, you hear, along with the voice of my beloved father, whose love, wisdom and humor I grew up knowing to cherish, the voice of my mother, whose great strengths it took me many years to recognize. And there were many other unsung voices in my family. For one, my Great-Aunt Mamie, only sister of seven brothers and a widowed father, whose family discouraged all suitors, for fear of losing their caretaker. Aunt Mamie took care of her father and brothers until they died or left home. And then she became the Santa Claus for five generations of our family, as well as for her whole court at 90 Saint Marks Place on Staten Island. Yet she lived in poverty for the last years of her life—"on relief," as it was called then—because, not having the education for work that our society sanctions with remuneration, she could not make ends meet. She taught me a great deal about what you can give others beyond your pocketbook—about humor and generosity of soul, about sacredness that has nothing to do with physical beauty or great accomplishments of the sort that get rewarded in our individualistic, competitive, materialistic society. Her invisibility also made my life visible.

There were other unsung "sheroes" in my family. One of them was my primary caretaker, Margaret Bush, who was descended from slaves in Asheville, North Carolina. She was the person I was closest to, emotionally and physically, from the like so many African-American domestic workers, she had to live away from her own family much of the time to stay with us. She was always there for me and she loved me unconditionally. I am what she made me. I miss her every day, and she, like my parents, lives in my soul. When I speak, you hear her voice too.

But there is another side to this relationship. Last year, a friend of mine became tearful when I spoke of Margaret. Her own African-American mother, like so many others, had worked in the homes of white families, giving those families love and care that took away from what she had left for her own children. This is the story of racism: black women serving white families at the expense of themselves and their own families. And this is one of the unacknowledged benefits I have received from racism.

I grew up thinking I was innocent—that I had nothing to do with racism and certainly not with slavery. My mother, only a few years ago, told me that I was raised to be so "color blind" that I once tried to describe a black girl in my brownie troop by telling another friend everything about her *except* the color of her skin. My mother had no awareness that this was because I had learned the lessons of racism all too well—I knew you did not refer to skin color. Nor did I recognize the fact of Margaret's white uniform as a symbol of her status within our family. Or the fact that she did not learn how to read until after I did, when she was 50 years old. This, too, reflects the history of slavery, when slaves could be killed for learning to read, as could anyone who taught them. During my childhood, when Margaret learned to read with a local teacher, it was a big secret. I remember I used to go up and spy on her, anxious to discover what she was doing, up there in her room with her teacher, Audrey. How appalling it is now to realize the barriers she had to overcome to get where she did with her life.

I now realize how much I benefited from racism, including the fact that most books were written for me as a white person. I am also coming, slowly and painfully, to realize what it means to carry around, in Peggy MacIntosh's terms, a kind of "invisible knapsack of privilege" that contains special provisions, maps, passports, visas, blank checks and emergency gear. We cannot see this knapsack, but those who don't have one see it all too clearly.

I GREW UP NOT KNOWING I WAS Irish, because my family was trying to "pass" for WASP. Of course, "passing" is what everyone in this country is pressed to do—we are urged to accommodate, to fit the preferred images, to keep invisible the parts of ourselves that do not conform to the dominant culture's values. So growing up, I did not even know that I myself had a cultural background.

It wasn't until the mid-1970s, when my interest in Bowen theory had finally led me to explore my own roots, that I took a trip with my entire family to Ireland. From the moment we landed in Dublin, I had an overwhelming sense of having come home. I seemed to see my relatives everywhere, people using humor, teasing or ridicule to keep others in line or to maintain distance in male-female relationships, failing to talk about vital emotional issues staring them in the face, and expressing anger by giving others the silent treatment. Suddenly, patterns I had taken for granted all my life fit into a larger picture. It wasn't that my family was "crazy"—I was just Irish! It was a transforming experience that has never left me. In some deep way, I still think of Ireland as home.

It was only some years after realizing I was Irish that I first became aware of gender as an issue in my own life, an awareness that created enormous turmoil in my personal, as well as my professional, life. With regard to my Irishness, I could maintain a certain distance. I could get away from it. But with gender, there was no escape. Wherever I went, the rules for gender inequality still applied. I had a sexist husband who thought he was helping me if he did any chores around the house. But I came to realize that I, too, was sexist, for I felt grateful to him for "helping" me. When I went on a business trip, my husband described me as "abandoning" him and going on vacation. I prepared days ahead for my absence and I would make up for it for days afterward. This was so unlike the treatment of my father when I was a child; he traveled frequently and we did everything we could to make him as welcome as possible on his return.

As I became aware of the unequal nature of my relationship with my husband, I struggled with how to address it—how could I bring up a touchy issue without overloading the circuits? Certainly not when he'd had a hard day or was in a bad mood. But when I would finally decide the time was right, my husband would accuse me of "ruining our relationship." And a part of me would believe this, that it was somehow my fault: If I were only more generous or better at expressing myself, I would have been able to work things out by myself.

In the family therapy field as well, there was no getting away from the pervasive influence of gender and the emotional heat triggered by discussing it. I remember well the first panel on gender at a meeting of the American Family Therapy Academy in 1985. Virginia Goldner, one of the earliest and most articulate voices of feminism in family therapy, pointed out how family therapists had been trained to emphasize generation, but to ignore gender. I marveled at her clarity, the precision and utter truth of what she was saying—how could I not have seen it myself? But afterward, many men disparaged her talk, including one of the leaders in the field, who described her as "Darth Vader." Later, at a national family therapy conference, when the program included—for the first and only time—predominantly female presenters, many men within the organization expressed their outrage and their belief that this shift represented the desire of the women to "kill off" the men.

Over the years, I have been mystified by the reactivity of men to these issues. No matter how carefully we tried to explain that feminism was about equality, partnership and a new construction of gender relationships and not about women taking over, reasoned conversations were all but impossible. There were threats that men would withdraw from

the field if women didn't get off "this kick." Longtime male colleagues came up to me and said, "Monica, you used to be so *nice*. What's happened to you? Why are you so angry at men? Did you hate your father? Are you having trouble with your husband? *I'm* not sexist. I've never mistreated a woman. So why are you blaming me for all this? Why are you saying we have the power? I feel quite powerless. We men have problems too, you know. After all, we're not allowed to feel."

Of course, it is in the nature of patriarchy for men not to experience their power, because in a society that measures everyone hierarchically, there is always someone ahead of you or nipping at your heels to take your place. But it often almost seemed impossible for men to envision a way of being with other people that wasn't about winning or losing.

Within the past few years, I began to be confronted with race and racism and now it was *I* who was on the other side of the power imbalance. Immediately, I heard the issues quite differently. Suddenly, I wanted to say to others the same things men had been saying to me: "Why are you so angry? You used to be so nice. Now you're being divisive. I have nothing to do with racism, slavery or segregation. I've never mistreated a person of color. I'm a nice person, not a racist. I would love to change things, but I don't have the power, either. White people have experienced oppression, too—let me tell you about it." I wanted to justify myself, as I had heard men do so often by referring to their good intentions, their own experience of class or ethnic oppression, or their kindness to individual women. And as I heard my own reactivity, I realized that I must be part of the problem. Otherwise, I wouldn't need to be so defensive.

We "right-thinking" liberals react almost viscerally to being called racist. The accusation of racism sounds so damning, conjuring up images of lynchings or the Ku Klux Klan. But when people of color use the term, they often are referring to something much more subtle, the everyday micro-aggressions and insults that we who are white unthinkingly inflict through our ignorance of their history and experience.

Inevitably, when an African American expresses frustration or anger at a family therapy meeting, the white people want to get him or her "feeling okay" in the course of a single conversation. It reminds me of how much I always hated it when men indicated that they hoped each conversation about gender inequality would be the last—women would then

feel alright and not be angry anymore. I realize I have taken this attitude myself in conversations about racism, but I now recognize the arrogance of my refusal to see that the pain of racism can't be taken care of so easily. How can we demand that black people's anger and sense of injustice disappear, when the problems that evoke them remain?

To the men who told me they weren't sexist, I used to say, "If you're not actively working on the solution, you're part of the problem." I realize now that unless my own life is about overcoming racism and my invisible knapsack of privilege disappears, I am also a part of the problem—and therefore I am a racist. I must work so that everyone is entitled to those privileges. Then we will all have a home.

Going home—or being unable to do so—is also about class. Until very recently, in my heart, I thought class was a boring, sociological topic, irrelevant to therapy. "I don't know what there is to say about class," I once told a group of students, "except that it's better off not to be poor." Then, one day a few years ago, I got involved in a discussion with some faculty members from the Family Institute of Westchester about the class rules in our families. During the discussion, I remember thinking, then on the way home it hit me—my *whole life* has been organized by class values. The clothes I wear are a class statement, the car I drive, my house, my furniture, the pictures on my walls, the music I listen to, even the language I use to write this article.

The topic of social class was never mentioned in my training—nor is it ever mentioned among family therapists. Everyone knows the class code for the degrees in our field—M.D., Ph.D., Ed.D., D.S.W., M.S.W., M.A. and so forth—yet we don't talk about it. We know, too, the complex hierarchical code for colleges and universities—the Ivy League, the Seven Sisters, Berkeley, Georgetown, Howard, Spellman, Trenton State. This concept of class is exquisitely comprehensive; it governs all social interactions; the rules of class insidiously influence our feelings of otherness, of not being okay.

In one situation or another, the myth of our having a classless society leads to our lying about who we are, whether to hide our WASP roots or the money that would distance us socially in the mental health field, or whether to hide our poverty and working-class origins. Class is about whether you grow up believing the American Dream applies to you, whether you can grow up believing you will ever be able to support yourself

My mother was our nurse, manager, chauffeur, host, and the encourager of our projects. Yet, for much of her life, I hated her.

through work, whether you can feel protected by society's laws, entitled to society's goods and so forth. Class is also about who is in and who is out, who gets bullied, picked on, excluded, made fun of. While patterns of social exclusion develop most intensely during children's school years, rejection and the concomitant pressure to conform—to "pass"— continue to define us all our lives.

Whatever we cannot acknowledge— the secrets we keep about our own class background, our unspoken feelings about race, or sexual orientation, or gender— carries a cost. Guarding secrets consumes our energy and compromises our relationships. It continues to go unsaid that where you come from *does* matter, that you cannot shed your past and become whatever you want merely through hard work and desire. It goes unsaid that anybody *cannot* become president—not a woman, not an African American, not even a white man if he happens to be gay or Jewish. It goes unsaid that the concept of "liberty and justice for all" was never meant to apply to everyone in this country. We must begin to acknowledge our own beliefs and feelings about class, race and gender, to dare to put our assumptions and prejudices on the table so we can examine them and see what they cost us and what they cost others.

AN EARLY 19TH-CENTURY AMERI-can physician, Samuel Cartwright, described "drapetomania," a mental disorder prevalent among slaves, which was characterized by a single symptom— the uncontrollable urge to escape slavery. This diagnosis turned the desire for liberty into a sickness that was the problem of the slave, not the slave owner or the institution of slavery. Naming is an enormously powerful act. The use of labels to control others continues almost unabated in many sectors of our society, including family therapy. We are much more ready to diagnose the victims of abuse than the abusers. We have numerous acronyms—MPD (multiple personality disorder), PTSD (post-traumatic stress disorder), SCS (survivors of child sexual abuse)—that define the entire life course of those who have experienced trauma. But we omit from our descriptions those who traumatize others, just as we did more

than a century ago with slavery. Why, as Ken Hardy and others have asked repeatedly, isn't racism defined as a mental disorder and labeled as psychopathology? Or sexism? Or battering?

Families of color, families of the poor, and immigrant families, whose norms and values are different from those within our naming scheme, remain pathologized as deficient or dysfunctional, or, worse, invisible within our society. They are labeled "dependent," while the dependence of the dominant groups on society is left invisible and they are left to imagine they are autonomous rather than benefiting from schools, health care and legal institutions that silently serve their needs. Many family therapists still are trained without reference to the insidious role that hierarchies related to culture, class, race and gender play in the United States. They are taught concepts of human development, psychopathology, family functioning from the skewed, patriarchal, classist framework of the dominant white groups in our society. They believe that you can learn about "men's issues" and not include issues of African-American men, that you can learn about "couples therapy" or "child sexual abuse" or "the family life cycle" or "dual career families" or "genograms" without including people of color in the discussion.

The problem with naming is not only with the labels we apply to others, but also with the ones we apply to ourselves. A name both includes and excludes. By defining myself as "Irish American," I may be reassured by a sense of belonging to a group, but at a certain point I am also distancing myself from those who are not Irish in ways that may undermine our mutual sense of "home." Focusing on any fixed group identity, whether based on ethnicity or class or race or gender, clarifies some things, but necessarily obscures others. As we try to create a truly multicultural society, enormous challenges face us. We must find ways to appreciate the many levels of our identities, while finding a balance between validating the uniqueness of each of us *and* acknowledging the common humanity we all share.

"All of us are more a hodgepodge of identities, cultural and otherwise, than anything else. So any restrictive characterization inevitably misses much of who

we are. This complexity has been captured brilliantly in Louise Erdich and Michael Dorris's novel, *The Crown of Columbus*. With different details, this might be the story of any one of us:

I belong to the lost tribe of mixed bloods, that hodgepodge amalgam of hue and cry that defies easy placement. When the DNA of my various ancestors—Irish and Coeur d'Alene and Spanish and Navajo and God knows what else— combined to form me, the result was not some genteel indecipherable puree that comes from a Cuisinart. You know what they say on the side of the Bisquick box under instructions for pancakes? "Mix with fork. Leave lumps." That was me. There are advantages to not being this or that. You have a million stories, one for every occasion, and in a way they're all lies and in another way they're all true. When Indians say to me, "What are you? I know exactly what they're asking and answer Coeur d'Alene. I don't add, "Between a quarter and a half," because that's information they don't require, first off—though it may come later if I screw up and they're looking for reasons why. If one of my Dartmouth colleagues wonders, "Where did you study?" I pick the best place, the hardest one to get into, in order to establish that I belong. If a stranger of the street questions where [my daughter] gets her light-brown hair and dark skin, I say the Olde Sodde and let them figure it out. There are times when I control who I'll be, and times when I let other people decide. I'm not all anything, but I'm a little bit of a lot. My roots spread in every direction, and if I water one set of them more often than others, it's because they need it more. . . . I've read anthropological papers written about people like me. We're called marginal, as if we exist anywhere but on the center of the page. We're parked on the bleachers looking into the arena, never the main players, but there are bonuses to peripheral vision. Out beyond the normal bounds, you at least know where you're not. You escape the claustrophobia of belonging, and what you lack in security you gain by realizing—as those insiders never do—that security is an illusion. . . . Caught between two worlds is the way we're often characterized, but I'd put it differently. We are the catch."

I grew up in a family with preferential rules regarding males— a family in which my father was treated like a visiting dignitary.

THERE ARE TWO COMMON PITFALLS in discussions of diversity. The first is to be so inclusive that the pervasive injustice of racism is trivialized in the rush to embrace the multiplicity of other "isms." The second pitfall is for discussion to get polarized, with the "black/white" issues becoming so predominant that other groups feel their issues have no place or that the discussion turns into an endless argument over which oppression is the worst or most important.

Last year, at a workshop on diversity, several panelists were giving impassioned presentations about the impact of white racism on African Americans. During the break, a gay, white colleague expressed distress that his perceptions about homosexuality were difficult to voice in the context of the presentation. Later, a Latina presenter spoke movingly of how discussions of black/white racism made her feel invisible. A third colleague became upset at some joking about his behavior as a white male. The panel also triggered for him some resentments from his working-class upbringing, but, in the context of this particular discussion, these feelings seemed to him somehow trivial and small-minded. Each of these panelists felt a strong urge to withdraw.

Anyone who has been through a heated public discussion about diversity issues knows how easily it can turn into a divisive contest triggered by the many legacies of oppression found in our society. It is hard for most of us to stay together when our particular "otherness" is not the focus. If we are to keep the conversation going, we have to learn to tolerate ambiguities and hold several different ideas in our minds at the same time. We must realize it is much easier to present ourselves in the position of the oppressed than to take responsibility for our role as the oppressor.

One thing is clear to me: in order for people to embrace a multicultural outlook, they first need to feel safe. We must acknowledge the horror of racism to make it safe for people of color to discuss sexism or homophobia in their communities. Similarly, our acknowledgment of homophobia will make it easier for those who are gay or lesbian to acknowledge the racism and classism of their communities.

Making cultural diversity into something more than a catch phrase requires sensitivity, flexibility and the ability to maintain a wider perspective. That means we must take into account the special invisibility of African-American men and the particular way that racism has been directed against them, without ignoring the invisibility of African-American women and the role African-American men play in the oppression of African-American women. While doing this, we must not humiliate or dehumanize white men, even as we must continue to hold them accountable for their privilege, entitlement and lack of awareness of their role in perpetuating the current system.

We must also struggle against the backlash that accompanies profound shifts in deeply held social attitudes. For several years, the family therapy field has been reeling from the reaction to the feminist critique. Many men have withdrawn from professional meetings. Now, as issues of culture and race are beginning to assert themselves, we are witnessing similar efforts to keep these subjects invisible. There is the frequent warning that "We'd better go slow, or the whites will retreat in droves from our organizations." Or those with the power to employ staff say, "We would love to hire a senior minority family therapist, but we can't find any," without questioning their standards for a senior family therapist. (Most clinicians of color have not defined themselves as family therapists, so we are looking in the wrong places for them.) Or those with the power to plan conferences say, "We did cultural diversity last year. We need something new for this year." Or minorities are pitted against one another, with articles written blaming women for the oppression of poorly paid, minority child-care workers or about how the stereotypes minorities have about one another are stronger than the stereotypes whites have about any of them. Of course, this framework makes invisible the social structure created and held in place by the dominant groups that pits minorities against one another.

We must work actively to overcome the forces that divide us. The forces for segregation are so powerful that, unless we make strong and deliberate efforts to nurture diversity, the status quo will prevail. We cannot assume that racism will disappear just by our being "good people," or by leaving people of color to deal with it. This means that we who are white must confront racism rather than ignore it. We must learn to become uncomfortable in segregated situations and with reading books that pertain only to white people. We must become so uncomfortable that we are moved to do something about it.

But to do what we must do, we need each other. We must consciously divest ourselves of our myths of separateness, our false beliefs that the injustice that traps the other does not also trap us, that the suffering we experience in our own group or culture or gender, class or race is inherently more serious than the suffering of others. We can no longer tolerate the barriers that have kept us separate for so long. To take pleasure and strength in the particular heritage to which we were born is fine; to buttress our own identities by humiliating or demonizing or rendering invisible those of other heritages is a sure recipe for our own disaster. Isolated in our self-declared tribes, we will surely be defeated by the forces that have traditionally had so much to gain by keeping us divided and encouraging us to blame each other for the social ills of the whole.

Alone, we will be mystified, silenced, invalidated; we will burn out in the struggle. But, together, we can help each other pull down the walls that separate us, demolish the invisible barriers that keep us from the connection that is our human birthright. It will never be easy. We are none of us yet fully formed human beings; in my view, we are all still just half-baked. So we will continue to blurt out racist or sexist or classist or homophobic comments, often without realizing what we are saying. If we are lucky, someone will draw our prejudices to our attention, and, if we have the patience and good grace to listen, to quell our own instinctive self-righteousness and defensiveness, we may learn a little more about our world, about each other and about ourselves. We may then be able to transcend, little by little, the false haven of our prejudice and blindness, to hold ourselves accountable for the fate of each other, and to gradually widen our vision of what we call home until it becomes a safe place for us all.

GROWING UP IN BLACK AND WHITE

For African-American children, learning to love themselves is a tough challenge

Jack E. White

"Mommy, I want to be white."

Imagine my wife's anguish and alarm when our beautiful brown-skinned three-year-old daughter made that declaration. We thought we were doing everything right to develop her self-esteem and positive racial identity. We overloaded her toy box with black dolls. We carefully monitored the racial content of our TV shows and videos, ruling out *Song of the South* and *Dumbo,* two classic Disney movies marred by demeaning black stereotypes. But we saw no harm in *Pinocchio,* which seemed as racially benign as *Sesame Street* or *Barney,* and a good deal more engaging. Yet now our daughter was saying she wanted to be white, to be like the puppet who becomes a real boy in the movie. How had she got that potentially soul-destroying idea and, even more important, what should we do about it?

That episode was an unsettling reminder of the unique burden that haunts black parents in America: helping their children come to terms with being black in a country where the message too often seems to be that being white is better. Developing a healthy self-image would be difficult enough for black children with all the real-life reminders that blacks and whites are still treated differently. But it is made even harder by the seductive racial bias in TV, movies and children's books, which seem to link everything beautiful and alluring with whiteness while often treating blacks as afterthoughts. Growing up in this all pervading world of whiteness can be psychologically exhausting for black children just as they begin to figure out who they are. As a four-year-old boy told his father after another day in the overwhelmingly white environment of his Connecticut day-care facility, "Dad, I'm tired of being black."

In theory it should now be easier for children to develop a healthy sense of black pride than it was during segregation. In 1947 psychologists Kenneth and Mamie Clark conducted a famous experiment that demonstrated just how much black children had internalized the hatred that society directed at their race. They asked 253 black children to choose between four dolls, two black and two white. The result: two-thirds of the children preferred white dolls.

The conventional wisdom had been that black self-hatred was a by-product of discrimination that would wither away as society became more tolerant. Despite the civil rights movement of the 1960s, the black-is-beautiful movement of the '70s, the proliferation of black characters on television shows during the '80s and the renascent black nationalist movement of the '90s, the prowhite message has not lost its power. In 1985 psychologist Darlene Powell-Hopson updated the Clarks' experiment using black and white Cabbage Patch dolls and got a virtually identical result: 65% of the black children preferred white dolls. "Black is dirty," one youngster explained. Powell-Hopson thinks the result would be the same if the test were repeated today.

Black mental-health workers say the trouble is that virtually all the progress the U.S. has made toward racial fairness has been in one direction. To be accepted by whites, blacks have to become more like them, while many whites have not changed their attitudes at all. Study after study has shown that the majority of whites, for all the commitment to equality they espouse, still consider blacks to be inferior, undesirable and dangerous. "Even though race relations have changed for the better, people maintain those old stereotypes," says Powell-Hopson. "The same racial dynamics occur in an integrated environment as occurred in segregation; it's just more covert."

Psychiatrists say children as young as two can pick up these damaging messages, often from subtle signals of black inferiority unwittingly embedded in children's books, toys and TV programs designed for the white mainstream. "There are many more positive images about black people in the media than there used to be, but there's still a lot that says that white is more beautiful and powerful than black, that white is good and black is bad," says James P. Comer, a Yale University psychiatrist who collaborated with fellow black psychiatrist Alvin F. Poussaint on *Raising Black Children* (Plume).

The bigotry is not as usually as blatant as it was in Roald Dahl's *Charlie and the Chocolate Factory.* When the book was published in 1964, the New York *Times* called it "a richly inventive and humorous tale." Blacks didn't see anything funny about having the factory staffed by "Oompa-Loompas," pygmy workers imported in shipping cartons from the jungle where they had been living in the trees.

Today white-controlled companies are doing a better job of erasing racially loaded subtexts from children's books and movies. Yet those messages still get through, in part because they are at times so subtle even a specialist like Powell-Hopson misses them. She recently bought a book about a cat for her six-year-old daughter, who has a love of felines. Only when Powell-Hopson got home did she discover that the beautiful white cat in the story turns black when it starts behaving badly. Moreover, when the products are not objectionable, they are sometimes promoted in ways that unintentionally drive home the theme of black inferiority. Powell-Hopson cites a TV ad for dolls that displayed a black version in the background behind the white model "as though it were a second-class citizen."

Sadly, black self-hatred can also begin at home. Even today, says Powell-Hopson, "many of us perpetuate negative messages, showing preference for lighter complexions, saying nappy hair is bad and straight hair is good, calling other black people 'niggers,' that sort of thing." This danger can be greater than the one posed by TV and the other media because children learn so much by simple imitation of the adults they are closest to. Once implanted in a toddler's mind, teachers and psychologists say, such misconceptions can blossom into a full-blown racial identity crisis during adolescence, affecting everything from performance in the classroom to a youngster's susceptibility to crime and drug abuse. But they can be neutralized if parents react properly.

In their book, Comer and Poussaint emphasize a calm and straightforward approach. They point out that even black children from affluent homes in integrated neighborhoods need reassurance about racial issues because from their earliest days they sense that their lives are "viewed cheaply by white society." If, for example, a black little girl says she wishes she had straight blond hair, they advise parents to point out "in a relaxed and unemotional manner . . . that she is black and that most black people have nice curly black hair, and that most white people have straight hair, brown, blond, black. At this age what you convey in your voice and manner will either make it O.K. or make it a problem."

Powell-Hopson, who along with her psychologist husband Derek has written *Different and Wonderful: Raising Black Children in a Race-Conscious Society* (Fireside), takes a more aggressive approach, urging black parents in effect to inoculate their children against negative messages at an early age. For example, the authors suggest that African-American parents whose children display a preference for white dolls or action figures should encourage them to play with a black one by "dressing it in the best clothes, or having it sit next to you, or doing anything you can think of to make your child sense that you prefer that doll." After that, the Hopsons say, the child can be offered a chance to play with the toy, on the condition that "you promise to take the very best care of it. You know it is my favorite." By doing so, the Hopsons claim, "most children will jump at a chance to hold the toy even for a second."

White children are no less vulnerable to racial messages. Their reactions can range from a false sense of superiority over blacks to an identification with sports superstars like Michael Jordan so complete that they want to become black. But if white parents look for guidance from popular child-care manuals, they won't find any. "I haven't included it because I don't feel like an expert in that area," says T. Berry Brazelton, author of *Infants and Mothers* and other child-care books. "I think it's a very, very serious issue that this country hasn't faced up to." Unless it does, the U.S. runs the risk of rearing another generation of white children crippled by the belief that they are better than blacks and black children who agree.

As for my daughter, we're concerned but confident. As Comer says, "In the long run what children learn from their parents is more powerful than anything they get from any other source." When my little girl expressed the wish to be white, my wife put aside her anguish and smilingly replied that she is bright and black and beautiful, a very special child. We'll keep telling her that until we're sure she loves herself as much as we love her.

Exploring and Establishing Relationships

- **Emotions and Relating (Articles 7–10)**
- **Finding a Partner (Articles 11 and 12)**
- **Sexuality in Relationships (Articles 13–15)**
- **The Next Generation (Articles 16–19)**

By and large, humans are social animals and, as such, we seek out meaningful connections with other humans. John Bowlby, Mary Ainsworth, and others have proposed that this drive toward connection is biologically based and at the core of what it means to be human. However it plays out in childhood and adulthood, the need for connection, to love and be loved, is a powerful force moving us to establish and maintain close relationships.

As people explore various possibilities, they engage in the complex business of relationship building. In this business, many processes simultaneously occur: messages are sent and received; differences are negotiated; assumptions and expectations are or are not met. The ultimate goals are closeness and continuity.

How we feel about others and what we see as essential to these relationships play an important role in our establishing and maintaining relationships. In this section, we look at factors that underlie the establishment of relationships as well as the beginning stages of relationships.

The first subsection takes a broad look at factors that influence the building of meaningful relationships. The first two articles explore the nature of love itself. "Love: The Immutable Longing for Contact" uses attachment theory as the basis for a depiction of the need for a strong connection as a force pushing people toward meaningful relationships. "What Makes Love Last?" considers different ways in which love is played out in long-term relationships. The approach taken in "Why Don't We Act Like the Opposite Sex?" is sociobiological and is used to explain the difficulties faced by couples as they struggle to understand gender differences. The final article in this subsection, "Back Off!" takes what may seem to be a contrary position in suggesting that, just as time together is important for a relationship, so too do individuals need time alone for themselves.

The second subsection looks at one way in which we establish adult-to-adult relationships in the mate selection process. The first subsection article, "Choosing Mates—The American Way," traces the history of mate selection, contrasting the qualities considered desirable in the past with those considered to be so today. The next essay focuses on the physical and sexual components of "The Mating Game," factors that, incidentally, have not changed much over the centuries.

In the third subsection, an important aspect of adult relationships is explored as we look at sexuality in relationships. Particular attention is given in this section to the idea of responsibility to oneself and others in acting out our sexuality. "Psychotrends: Taking Stock of Tomorrow's Family and Sexuality" is a broad look at current sexual attitudes and behaviors and their implications for the family. The following article, "Choosing a Contraceptive," looks at the strengths and weaknesses of contraceptives available in the United States. Contraception often is seen as a woman's responsibility, in interpersonal relationships and in social policy. The final subsection article takes an international perspective as it examines the role of men in family planning.

In the final subsection, building family relationships is explored. The author of "Baby Love" takes a hard look at high-technology approaches to having a baby, questioning the legitimacy of these approaches, but ultimately reasoning that those seeking these treatments must be the final decision makers. Readers of "What a Baby *Really* Costs" may find themselves amazed at the high cost of having an uncomplicated birth.

The next subsection article, "Adolescent Childbearing: Whose Problem? What Can We Do?" asks the reader to step back and look at the bigger picture of childbearing. What *are* the implications for society of teens having and raising children?

The final article in this section addresses issues of another way of creating parent-child bonds, adoption. "The Lifelong Impact of Adoption" is a cautionary look at the long-term impacts, particularly those related to a sense of loss, that are found among those who have been touched by adoption.

Looking Ahead: Challenge Questions

How easy is it to understand and communicate with members of the opposite sex? What still confuses or frustrates you? Do you find the idea of giving your partner "space" to be contrary to a healthy committed relationship?

What is your definition of love? How do you know you are in love? How do you know you love someone? What does it take for you to believe someone loves you? What can you do when love fades?

What do you look for in a mate? Would you be willing to settle for less? Why or why not?

What are your beliefs about appropriate sexual behavior in intimate relationships? Whose responsibility is contraception? Would you feel comfortable discussing this with your partner? Why or why not?

Do you see children as a part of your life? Why or why not? Discuss whether or not you would consider adopting. How do children enrich a relationship? What are the drawbacks of having children? If you do have children, how will it affect you and your relationship with your partner?

LOVE

The Immutable Longing for Contact

*As the child is connected to the parent, to be connected with another person is
the only security we ever have in life. In that sense, we never grow up.*

**Susan Johnson, Ed.D.,
with Hara Estroff Marano**

An illusion. An anesthetic. An irrational compulsion. A neurosis. An emotional storm. An immature ideal. These are the descriptions of love that have long populated the psychological literature. Let us not even consider the obvious fact that they are highly judgmental and dismissive. The question I want to pose is, does any one of them, or even all of them together, come close to capturing the extraordinary experience that for most people is an enormous part of the meaning of life—an experience that fosters well-being and growth?

As a marital therapist, my job is to help people experience love, to move from distance and alienation to contact and caring. But in order to help distressed couples change, I realized early on that I needed a model of what a good relationship is. For too long, the choices have been confined to two. There is the psychodynamic, or psychoanalytic, view, which holds that adult relationships are more or less reflections of childhood relationships—replays of old conflicts. And there is the behaviorist view: Love is a rational exchange in which couples make deals based on their needs, and they succeed to the degree that they master the negotiation process. Love is then either a crazy compulsion or, after couples calm down, a kind of rational friendship where partners make good deals.

I can assure you that if I tried to persuade the couples I see in therapy to leave with an understanding of their childhood or a rational friendship, they would not be satisfied. The truth is that these conventional descriptions do not adequately reflect the process of marital distress or the rekindling of love that I observe as a marital therapist. Possessing insights as to why you have certain sore spots or honing negotiation skills seems to somehow miss the mark. Neither addresses the intense emotional responses that consume distressed couples. As I watch couples, I see that raw emotion, hurt, longing, and fear are the most powerful things in the room. Couples seem to have a desperate need to connect emotionally—and a desperate fear of connecting.

'Couples seem to have a desperate need to connect and a desperate fear of connection.'

There are, of course, many elements to a relationship. It is true that echoes of the past are present in relationships, but this focus does not capture enough of what goes on and ignores the power of present interactions. Couples do also make bargains. But the essence of their connection is not a bargain. It is, rather, a bond.

The bond between two people hinges on two things-their accessibility and responsiveness to each other. The notion that the tie between two people is created through accessibility and responsiveness is an outgrowth of attachment theory. First put forth by the late British psychiatrist John Bowlby 30 years ago and later elaborated both by him and psychologist Mary Ainsworth in America, attachment theory is only now gathering significant momentum. It promises to be one of the most significant psychological ideas put forth in the 20th century. As many researchers are now demonstrating, it is certainly the most viable way of making sense of the mother-infant (and father-infant) bond.

VIEWING LOVE THROUGH A LENS

Over the past decade, a number of psychologists, including myself, have begun to see in attachment theory an understanding of adult relationships. In my experience attachment is the best lens for viewing adult love. When viewed through this lens, love relationships do not seem irrational at all; we do not have to pronounce them mysterious or outside our usual way of being. Nor do we have to shrink them to fit the laws of economic exchange. They make perfect—many would say intuitive—sense. And attachment theory goes a long way toward explaining what goes wrong in relationships and what to do about it.

John Bowlby observed that the need for physical closeness between a mother and child serves evolutionary goals; in a dangerous world, a responsive caregiver ensures survival of the infant. Attachment theory states that our primary motivation in life is to be connected with other people—because it is the only security we ever have. Maintaining closeness is a bona fide survival need.

Through the consistent and reliable responsiveness of a close adult, infants, particularly in the second six months of life, begin to trust that the world is a good place and come to believe they have some value in it. The deep sense of security that develops fosters in the infant enough confidence to begin exploring the surrounding world, making excursions into it, and developing relationships with others—though racing back to mom, being held by her, and perhaps even clinging to her whenever feeling threatened. In secure attachment lie the seeds for self-esteem, initiative, and eventual independence. We explore the world from a secure base.

Thanks to Mary Ainsworth, a large and growing body of research supports attachment theory. She devised a procedure to test human attachment. Called the "strange situation," it allows researchers to observe mothers and children during a carefully calibrated process of separation and reunion. Ainsworth found that whenever children feel threatened or can no longer easily reach their attachment figure, they engage in behavior designed to regain proximity—they call, they protest, they seek, they cry, they reach out. Closeness achieved, they do all they can to maintain it: They hug, they coo, they make eye contact, they cling—and, that all-time pleaser, they smile.

Ainsworth noticed that children differ in their attachment security and their patterns of behavior sort into three basic "attachment styles." Most children are securely attached: They show signs of distress when left with a stranger, seek their mother when she returns, hold her for a short time, then go back to exploring and playing. These infants develop attachment security because they have mothers who are sensitive and responsive to their signals.

On the other hand, she found, 40 percent of kids are insecurely attached. Some are anxious/ambivalent. They show lots of distress separating, and on reunion, they approach and reject their mother. Their mothers usually respond inconsistently to them, sometimes unavailable, other times affectionate. So preoccupied are these infants with their caregiver's availability that they never get to explore their world.

The third group of children have an avoidant attachment style. They do not seem distressed during separation, and they don't even acknowledge their mother during reunion. These infants keep their distress well-hidden; though they appear to dismiss relationships entirely, internally they are in a state of physiological arousal. These children are usually reared by caregivers who rebuff their attempts at close bodily contact.

These responses are not arbitrary but universal. Evolution has seen to that because they serve survival needs. Some researchers are busy identifying the neurobiological systems that underlie attachment behavior and mediate the response to attachment threats. They are finding specific patterns of changes in biochemistry and physiology during experimental separation experiences.

Attachment bonds are particularly durable, and once an infant is attached, separation—or the threat of it—is extremely stressful and anxiety-producing. In the absence of attachment danger, children explore the world around them. But if the accessibility of a caregiver is questionable or threatened, the attachment behavior system shifts into high gear. Facing the loss or unreliability of an attachment figure, infants typically are thrust into panic and they mount an angry protest. Eventually, however, the protest dies down and they succumb to a despair that looks like classic depression.

The implications of attachment theory are extraordinary and extend to the deepest corners of our psyche. Attachment impacts the way we process information, how we see the world, and the nature of our social experience. Our attachment experience influences whether we see ourselves as lovable. Research now shows that we carry attachment styles with us into life, where they serve as predispositions to later behavior in love relationships.

We seek close physical proximity to a partner, and rely on their continuing affections and availability, because it is a survival need. What satisfies the need for attachment in adults is what satisfies the need in the young: Eye contact, touching, stroking, and holding a partner deliver the same security and comfort. When threatened, or fearful, or experiencing loss, we turn to our partner for psychological comfort. Or try to.

The core elements of love are the same for children and adults—the need to feel that somebody is emotionally there for you, that you can make contact with another person who will respond to you, particularly if you are in need. The essence of love is a partner responding to a need, not because it's a good deal—but even when it's not. That allows you to sense the world as home rather than as a dangerous place. In this sense, we never grow up.

It is growing clear that the dynamics of attachment are similar across the life span. Implicit in the anger of a couple who are fighting over everything is the protest of the child who is trying to restore the closeness and responsiveness of a parent. In the grief of adults who have lost a partner is the despair of a child who has lost a parent and experiences helplessness and withdrawal.

THE MUSICALITY OF EMOTION

Attachment theory makes sense of a matter that psychology has just begun to puzzle over—how we come to regulate our emotions. We regulate feelings, specifically negative ones—fear, sadness, anger—through the development of affectional bonds with others, and continuing contact with them. Through

After the Fight

Anger and hostility in marital relationships are usually interpreted by a partner as rejection. They are felt as distancing behaviors, and set off attachment alarms; you respond as if your life is threatened. But hostility itself is often an outgrowth of feelings of fear; your partner is perhaps feeling threatened. It is important to recognize that it may be an attempt to bring you back into contact rather than to control you. In one sense, the appropriate response to hostility may be a hug rather than a return of verbal barrage. But we fight for our life when threatened; we defend ourselves with anything that comes to mind.

It's after the fight that you have a real chance to reprocess the events more accurately, to enlarge the experience to include elements that were left out of the argument while you were trying to win. An attachment lens on relationships encourages us to look at aggression in intimate relationships as a common way of dealing with fear. It also implies there's nothing wrong with dependency needs; it gives us permission to have feelings of wanting to be cared for without feeling weak or judging ourselves as "dependent." After the fight, you need to recapitulate the events with the inclusion of these feelings.

After a fight, in non-distressed relationships, the immediate emotionally reactivity dies down. (The problem in distressed relationships is that it never quite dies down.) When it does die down, if you have a secure base in a relationship, then is the time to talk about fears and attachment concerns.

This creates the opportunity for real closeness. As in: "When I heard you saying that you wanted to go away with your friends for a golfing vacation, I just got scared all to hell. You're saying that you don't need to be with me as much as I need to be with you. I get totally terrified if I think I'm hearing that."

If I have a secure base, I'm much more likely to allow myself to access the feeling that I'm afraid. I'm much more likely to tell my partner I'm afraid. Hopefully, my partner will actually help me with that fear. My fear level will be reduced. My partner's response will help me see myself as lovable, and that exchange also then becomes a positive intimacy experience in the history of the relationship.

This kind of sharing is what adult intimacy is all about. You and your partner find each other as human beings who need comfort, contact, and caring.

---

the lens of attachment we also come to understand that the expression of emotion is the primary communication system in relationships; it's how we adjust closeness and distance. Emotion is the music of the interpersonal dance. And when attachment is threatened—when we feel alienated from a partner or worry about our partner's availability—the music either gets turned way up, into the heavy metal of angry protest, or way down, shut off altogether.

'The expression of emotion is the primary communication system in relationships; it's how we adjust to closeness and distance.'

The lens of attachment sharply illuminates the dangerous distortion personified in a popular icon of Western culture: the John Wayne image of the self-contained man, the man who is never dependent and never needs anyone else. Our need for attachment ensures that we become who we are as individuals because of our connection with other people. Our personality evolves in a context of contact with other people; it doesn't simply arise from within. Our attachment needs make dependence on another person an integral part of being human. Self-sufficiency is a lie.

A PLACE FOR VULNERABILITY

The most basic message of attachment theory is that to be valid adults, we do not need to deny that we are also always, until the end of our life, vulnerable children. A good intimate adult relationship is a safe place where two people can experience feelings of vulnerability—being scared, feeling overwhelmed by life, being unsure of who they are. It is the place where we can deal with those things, not deny them, control them, or regulate them, the old John Wayne way. Relatedness is a core aspect of our selves.

Yet Western psychology and psychiatry have often labeled feelings of dependency as pathologic and banished them to childhood. Our mistaken beliefs about dependency and self-sufficiency lead us to define strength as the ability to process inner experience and regulate our emotions all by ourselves. Attachment theory suggests that, not only is that not functional, it is impossible. We are social beings not constituted for such physiological and emotional isolation. For those who attempt it, there are enormous costs. A great deal of literature in health and psychology shows that the cost of social isolation is physical and psychological breakdown. Under such conditions, we simply deteriorate.

There is nothing inherently demeaning or diminishing in allowing someone else to comfort you. We need other people to help us process our emotions and deal with the slings and arrows of being alive—especially the slings and arrows. In fact, the essence of making intimate contact is sharing hurts and vulnerability with someone else. You allow someone into a place where you are not defended. You put contact before self-protection. In marital distress the opposite happens, self-protection comes before contact. If you cannot share, then a part of your being is excluded from the relationship.

The couples I see have taught me that it is almost impossible to be accessible, responsive, emotionally engaged with someone if you are not able to experience and express your own vulnerabilities. If you cannot allow yourself to experience and show your vulnerability, you cannot tell others what you need and explicitly ask others to respond to you. But troubled couples naturally want to hide and protect their vulnerability although that usually precludes any satisfying kind of emotional contact.

Like psychoanalytic theory, attachment theory sees early relationships as formative of personality and relationships later on. But unlike Freudian theory, it sees our view of ourselves and relationship styles as subject to revision as we integrate new experiences. This capacity makes growth possible. The past influences the present, but we are not condemned to repeat it.

The attachment system involves attachment behaviors, emotional responses, and internal representations, or models. In our psyches, we create working models of attachment figures, of ourselves, and of relationships. Built from our experience in the world, these internal working models are at the same time cognitive and affective, and they in turn guide how we organize our experience and how we respond to intimate others.

The reason our behavior in relationships is relatively stable is that, although they are susceptible to revision, we carry these internal working models into new social situations. They write the script by which we navigate the social world. Our internal working models of ourselves, our relationship, and our close ones create expectations of support and nurturance—and become the architects of the disappointments we feel. They are the creators of self-fulfilling prophecies.

But the existence of internal models also explains why you can have very different experiences in two different relationships. Essentially, you meet a new potential partner who brings a different behavioral repertoire. This allows you to engage in a different dance of proximity and distance—she is home to receive your phone calls, he doesn't react with veiled hostility when you call him at the office. Being accessible and responsive, your new partner doesn't ignite your anxiety and launch you into attachment panic. What's more, with a different set of internal working models, your new partner appraises your behavior differently and then offers a different response. From such new experience, a tarnished inner vision of relationships or of your sense of self can then begin to change.

A NEW WAY OF CONTACT

That may be what passionate love really is—we find someone who connects with us and alleviates our attachment fears, which opens up a whole new possibility of acceptance and responsiveness. Love is transforming—not just of the world but of the self. We find a whole new way of contacting another human being, and this emotional engagement opens up new possibilities of becoming ourselves. That is the intoxicating thing about the relationship. It modifies how people experience themselves and how they see other people.

From my point of view, attachment theory also redefines the place of sexual behavior. For the past 40 years, we seem to have come to believe that sex is the essence of love relationships. That is not my experience in working with couples. Sex per sex is often but a small part of adult intimacy. Attachment theory tells us that the basic security in life is contact with other people.

We need to be held, to be emotionally connected. I think that the most basic human experience of relatedness is two people—mother and child, father and child, two adults—seeing and holding each other, providing the safety, security, and feeling of human connectedness that for most, in the end, makes life meaningful. Many people use sex as a way to create or substitute for the sense of connection they are needing. I would guess that many a man or woman has engaged in sex just to meet a need for being held.

So perhaps now the mystery of love is becoming clear. We fall in love when an attachment bond is formed. We stay in love by maintaining the bond. We use our repertoire of emotions to signal the need for comfort through contact, the need for a little distance. We help each other process our inner and outer worlds and experience each other's pain, fear, joy.

What, then, goes wrong in couples? As I see it, healthy, normal attachment needs go unmet and attachment fears begin to take over the relationship.

We know that distressed couples settle into rigid interaction patterns. Perhaps the most distressed pattern is that of the disappointed, angry, blaming wife demanding contact from a man who withdraws. Couples can stay stuck in this for years. We know from the research of John Gottman that this is a sure killer of marriages.

But it is only through the lens of attachment that we come to understand what makes such patterns of behavior so devastating. The answer is, they block emotional engagement; they stand in the way of contact and exacerbate attachment fears. As partners hurl anger and contempt at each other or withdraw, emotional engagement becomes more and more difficult. Patterns of attack-defend or attack-withdraw are highly corrosive to a relationship because they preclude a safe way for a couple to emotionally engage each other and create a secure bond.

What couples are really fighting about is rarely the issue they seem to be fighting about—the chores, the kids. It is always about separateness and connectedness, safety and trust, the risk of letting someone in to see the exposed, vulnerable self.

Marital distress, then, is not a product of personality flaws. Nor is anger in relationships irrational. It is often a natural part of a protest that follows the loss of accessibility and responsiveness to a partner. It is an adaptive reaction—anger motivates people to overcome barriers to reunion. Self-defeating as it may be, anger is an attempt to discourage a partner from further distancing.

A COMPELLING EMOTION

But fear is the most compelling emotion in a distressed relationship. Hostility in a partner is usually a sign that the fear level has gone way up—the partner feels threatened. Attachment fears—of being unlovable, abandoned, rejected—are so tied to survival that they elicit strong fight or flee responses. In protecting ourselves, we often undermine ourselves as a secure base for our partner, who becomes alarmed. Our partner then confirms our fears and becomes the enemy, the betrayer.

Such fear sets off an alarm system. It heightens both the anger of those experiencing anxiety in attachment and the dismissal of emotional needs by those given to avoidance.

A NEW FRAME FOR BEHAVIOR

The lens of attachment puts a whole new frame on our behavior in relationships. The angry, blaming wife who continues to pursue with blame, even though she understands this behavior may drive her husband away, is not acting irrationally. Nor do her actions necessarily reflect a lack of communication skill. She is engaged in a desperate intensification of attachment behaviors—hers is an entreaty for contact. She perceives her husband as inaccessible and emotionally unresponsive: a threat that engages the attachment behavioral system. Of course, the defensiveness and conflict make safe contact increasingly less likely, and the cycle of distress escalates. It keeps going because the person never gets the contact and the reassurance that will bring closure and allow the attachment fears to be dealt with.

In working with couples, my colleague Les Greenberg and I have elaborated a therapy, "Emotionally Focused Couples Therapy," that views marital distress in terms of attachment insecurities. It recognizes that relationship problems are created by how individuals react to, cope with, and disown their own attachment needs and those of their spouse. A major goal of therapy is owning and validating needs for contact and security, helping people to expand their emotional range, rather than shut their feelings down or constantly control them. It is not about ventilating feelings, but about allowing people to immerse themselves more deeply in their experience and process elements of it they usually protect against—the desperation and loneliness behind anger, the fear and helplessness behind silent withdrawal.

The most powerful change agent in a distressed relationship seems to be the expression of the tender, more disarming emotions, such as longing, fear, and sadness. It is the most powerful tool to evoke contact and responsiveness from a significant other. If I help couples create contact, couples can then solve their own problems.

Most couples begin by declaring how incredibly angry they are. They have good reason to be angry. As they come to feel more of their anger, not justify or contain it, they usually begin to explore and experience more of what it is about. The experience starts to include elements they don't usually focus on, which they may even [see] as inappropriate. In fact one reason for feeling so angry is that they feel totally helpless and unlovable, which scares them.

Soon one partner begins talking to the other about what happened one second before lashing out—an incredible sense of helplessness, a voice that comes into the head and said, "I'm not going to feel this way. I refuse to feel so helpless and needy. This is unacceptable." And now the experience has been expanded beyond anger and partners start to contact hidden parts of themselves—in the presence of the other.

This is a new and compelling experience for them that enables one partner to turn to the spouse and confide, "Somehow, some part of me has given up the hope of ever feeling cherished, and instead I've become enraged because I am so sure that you could never really hold me and love me." This kind of dialogue redefines the relationship as one where a person can be vulnerable and confide what is most terrifying about him or herself or the world. And the partner, with the therapist's help, is there both for comfort and as a validating mirror of those experiences of the self.

BUILDING A SECURE BASE

The relationship is then starting to be a secure base where people can be vulnerable, bring out the neediness or other elements of themselves that frighten them, and ask for their attachment needs to be met. In this safe context, the husband or wife doesn't see the partner as weak but as available—not dangerous. I may hear one say: "That's the part I fell in love with." In a sense, the language of love is the language of vulnerability. While Western psychology focuses on the value of self-sufficiency, in our personal lives we struggle to integrate our needs for contact and care into our adult experience.

Attachment theory is an idea whose time has finally come because it allows us to be whole people. It views behavior gone awry as a well-meaning adaptation to past or present experience. And it views the desire for contact as healthy. Secure attachments promote emotional health and buffer us against life's many stresses. Love then becomes the most powerful arena for healing and for growth, and from this secure base, both men and women can go out and explore, even create, the world.

PSYCHOLOGISTS
AT THE "LOVE LAB"
ARE USING SCIENCE
TO UNCOVER THE
REAL REASON
WHY MARRIAGES
SUCCEED OR FAIL.

What Makes Love Last?

Alan AtKisson

Alan AtKisson is a writer, songwriter, and consultant living in Seattle, Washington. He and partner, Denise Benitez, recently celebrated their ninth wedding anniversary by hiking in the North Cascades.

My old friends Karen and Bill, married since 1955, recently celebrated another anniversary. "I wore the same nightgown I wore on our wedding night," confessed Karen to me over the phone. "Just as I have every anniversary for thirty-nine years."

"I wore pajamas on our wedding night," offered Bill. "But last night I didn't wear nothin'." They laughed, and even over three thousand miles of telephone wire I felt the strength of their love for one another.

Long-lasting marriages like Bill's and Karen's are becoming increasingly rare. Not only do more than 50 percent of all first marriages in the United States end in divorce (make that 60 percent for repeat attempts), but fewer people are even bothering to tie the slippery knot in the first place. One fourth of Americans eighteen or older—about 41 million people—have never married at all. In 1970, that figure was only one sixth.

But even while millions of couples march down the aisle only to pass through the therapist's office and into divorce court, a quiet revolution is taking place when it comes to understanding how long-term love really works. Inside the laboratories of the Family Formation Project at the University of Washington in Seattle—affectionately dubbed the Love Lab—research psychologists are putting our most cherished relationship theories under the scientific microscope. What they're discovering is that much of what we regard as conventional wisdom is simply wrong.

"Almost none of our theory and practice [in marital therapy] is founded on empirical scientific research," contends the Love Lab's head, John Gottman, an award-winning research psychologist trained both as a therapist and a mathematician. Indeed, it is this lack of solid research, Gottman believes, that contributes to a discouraging statistic: for 50 percent of married couples who enter therapy, divorce is still the end result.

Gottman believes that, although relationship counseling has helped many people, much of it just doesn't work. Not satisfied with warm and fuzzy ideas about how to "get the love you want," Gottman is scouting for numbers, data, *proof*—and he's finding it.

From *New Age Journal,* September/October 1994, pp. 74-79, 146-148. © 1994 by New Age Publishing, Inc. Reprinted by permission.

For the past twenty years, in a laboratory equipped with video cameras, EKGs, and an array of custom-designed instruments, Gottman and his colleagues have been intensely observing what happens when couples interact. He watches them talk. He watches them fight. He watches them hash out problems and reaffirm their love. He records facial expressions and self-reported emotions, heart rhythms and blood chemistry. He tests urine, memories, and couples' ability to interpret each other's emotional cues. Then he pours his data, like so many puzzle pieces, into a computer. The resulting picture, he says, is so clear and detailed it's like "a CAT scan of a living relationship." [See "Putting Love to the Test," at right.]

What Gottman and his colleagues have discovered—and summarized for popular audiences in a new book, *Why Marriages Succeed or Fail* (Simon & Schuster) —is mind-boggling in its very simplicity. His conclusion: Couples who stay together are . . . well . . . *nice* to each other more often than not. "[S]atisfied couples," claims Gottman, "maintained a five-to-one ratio of positive to negative moments" in their relationship. Couples heading for divorce, on the other hand, allow that ratio to slip below one-to-one.

If it ended there, Gottman's research

Fighting, whether rare or frequent, is sometimes the healthiest thing a couple can do for their relationship.

might remain just an interesting footnote. But for him and his colleagues, this discovery is just the beginning. In fact, Gottman's novel and methodical approach to marriage research is threatening to turn much of current relationship therapy on its head. He contends that many aspects of wedded life often considered critical to long-term success— how intensely people fight; whether they face conflict or avoid it; how well they solve problems; how compatible they are socially, financially, even sexually

—are less important than people (including therapists) tend to think. In fact, Gottman believes, none of these things matter to a marriage's longevity as much as maintaining that crucial ratio of five to one.

If it's hard to believe that the longevity of your relationship depends primarily on your being five times as nice as you are nasty to each other, some of Gottman's other conclusions may be even more surprising. For example:

❤ Wildly explosive relationships that vacillate between heated arguments and passionate reconciliations can be as happy—and long-lasting—as those that seem

more emotionally stable. They may even be more exciting and intimate.

❤ Emotionally inexpressive marriages, which may seem like repressed volcanoes destined to explode, are actually very successful—so long as the couple maintains that five-to-one ratio in what they do express to each other. In fact, too much emotional catharsis among such couples can "scare the hell out of them," says Gottman.

❤ Couples who start out complaining about each other have some of the most stable marriages over time, while those who don't fight early on are more likely to hit the rocky shoals of divorce.

Putting Love to the Test

How the "Love Lab" researchers decode blood, sweat, and tears.

THE STUDIO APARTMENT IS TINY, BUT IT affords a great view of Seattle's Portage Bay. The ambiance is that of a dorm room tastefully furnished in late-'80s Sears, Roebuck. A cute kitchen table invites you to the window. A Monet print graces one wall. Oh, and three video cameras—suspended from the ceiling like single-eyed bats—follow your every move.

Welcome to the "Love Lab," wherein Professor John Gottman and a revolving crew of students and researchers monitor the emotions, behaviors, and hormones of married couples. Today, lab coordinator Jim Coan—a calm, clear-eyed, pony-tailed young man in Birkenstocks who started out as a student volunteer three years ago—is giving me the tour.

The Love Lab is actually two labs. I have entered through the "Apartment Lab," whose weekly routine Coan describes: A volunteer couple arrives on a Sunday morning, prepared to spend the day being intensely observed (for which they are modestly compensated). Special microphones record every sound they make; videotape captures every subtle gesture. The only true privacy is found in the bathroom, but even there science has a presence: A cooler by the toilet has two

little urine collection bottles, today marked "Bill" and "Jeannie."

At the end of a relaxed day doing whatever they like (and being watched doing it), the couple welcomes a house guest—a psychologist who listens to the story of how they met, fell in love, and began building a life together. This "oral history," which most people greatly enjoy telling, will later be closely scrutinized: Gottman and company have learned that how fondly a couple remembers this story can predict whether they will stay together or divorce.

Then, after a sleep-over on the Lab's hide-a-bed (cameras and microphones off) and a blood sample, a technician takes the pair out for breakfast, gives them their check, and sends them on their way. The videotapes will later be analyzed in voluminous detail. Every affectionate gesture, sarcastic jab, or angry dispute will be recorded and categorized using Gottman's "specific affect" emotional coding system (the lab folks call it SPAFF for short). At the same time, the couple's blood and urine will be sent to another lab and tested for stress hormone levels. Finally, in four years or so (depending on the study), the lab will follow up with the

❤ Fighting, whether rare or frequent, is sometimes the healthiest thing a couple can do for their relationship. In fact, blunt anger, appropriately expressed, "seems to immunize marriages against deterioration."

❤ In happy marriages, there are no discernible gender differences in terms of the quantity and quality of emotional expression. In fact, men in happy marriages are more likely to reveal intimate personal information about themselves than women. (When conflict erupts, however, profound gender differences emerge.)

❤ Men who do housework are likely to have happier marriages, greater physical health, even better sex lives than men who don't. (This piece of news alone could cause a run on aprons.)

❤ Women are made physically sick by a relentlessly unresponsive or emotionally contemptuous husband. Gottman's researchers can even tell just how sick: They can predict the number of infectious diseases women in such marriages will suffer over a four-year period.

❤ How warmly you remember the story of your relationship foretells your chances for staying together. In one study that involved taking oral histories

from couples about the unfolding of their relationship, psychologists were able to predict—with an astonishing 94 percent accuracy—which couples would be divorced within three years.

THE THREE VARIETIES OF MARRIAGE

In person, Gottman is a fast-talking, restless intellect, clearly in love with his work. Now in his late forties and seven years into a second marriage (to clinical psychologist Julie Schwartz), he seems very satisfied. Yet, in his book, he sheds

---

couple to see if they're still together—and take another look at the data they gathered to see if a predictable pattern can be discerned.

OTHER COUPLES WHO VISIT THE FAMILY Formation Project, as the "Love Lab" is more formally known, merely pass the pleasant apartment on their way to a less cozy destination: the "Fixed Lab." Here they are seated ("fixed") in plain wooden chairs and hooked up with a dizzying array of instruments—EKG electrodes, finger-pulse detectors, and skin galvanometers ("a fancy word for sweat detectors," says Coan). A thick black spring stretched across their chests registers breathing. Their chair itself is a "jiggleometer," recording every fidget and tremor.

A "facilitator" first interviews the pair about what issues cause conflict in their marriage, then gets them talking about the most contentious ones. Video cameras focus on the couple's faces and chests. Computers track the complex streams of data coming in through the sensors and displays them on a color monitor in a rainbow of blips and graphs.

After fifteen minutes of surprisingly "normal" and often emotional conversa-

tion, the couple are stopped by the facilitator, who plays back the videotape for them. While watching, each partner rates his or her own emotional state at every moment during the conversation, using a big black dial with a scale running from "extremely negative" through "neutral" to "extremely positive." Then the pair watch the tape again, this time in an attempt to similarly judge their partner's emotional state (with widely varying levels of success).

Later, students trained by Coan will review the tape using a specially designed dial and the SPAFF coding system, to chart the feelings being displayed. It's eerie to see the range of human emotional expression represented on a high-tech instrument panel: disgust, contempt, belligerence, domination, criticism, anger, tension, tense humor ("very popular, that one," Coan tells me), defensiveness, whining, sadness, stonewalling, interest, validation, affection, humor, joy, and positive or negative surprise (students made Gottman aware of the two different kinds). In the middle is a neutral setting for when couples are merely exchanging information without noticeable emotion.

BACK IN THE APARTMENT LAB, COAN SHOWS me videos of couples who have agreed to be involved with the media. Two young parents from Houston discuss the stress around caring for their new baby, and Coan gives me the play-by-play: "He's being very defensive here" or "See that deep sigh? She's feeling sad now" or "Now that was a nice validation."

Coan says that most people seem to enjoy the lab experience—and even get some benefit from it (though it's not meant to be therapeutic). Amazingly, even with sensors attached to their ears and fingers and chests, the couples seem to forget that they're being watched. They giggle and cry and manage to create a genuine closeness while fixed under a physiological microscope.

"It's a real privilege to work here," Coan says thoughtfully. Even in a short visit, I feel it too. The observation of intimacy, both its joy and its pain, is more than just scientific video voyeurism. It's as though the love these couples are trying so devotedly to share with each other seeps out of the box, a gift to the watchers.

— A. A.

the mantle of guru in the first sentence: "My personal life has not been a trail of great wisdom in understanding relationships," he says. "My expertise is in the scientific observation of couples."

Gottman began developing this expertise some twenty years ago, when a troubled couple who came to him for help didn't respond well to conventional therapy. In frustration, Gottman suggested that they try videotaping the sessions. "Both the couple and I were astonished by the vividness and clarity on the tape of the pattern of criticism, contempt, and defensiveness they repeatedly fell into," he recalls. "It shocked them into working harder . . . [and] it gave me my life's work."

Struck by the power of impartial observation, Gottman became fascinated with research. His goal: to systematically describe the differences between happy and unhappy couples, and from those observations develop a scientific theory capable of predicting marital success. This seemed a daunting task, both because "marriage is so subjective" and because "personality theory, in psychology, has been a failure at predicting anything."

The result of Gottman's passion is a veritable mountain of data: tens of thousands of observations involving thousands of couples, gathered by the Love Lab's researchers and stored in its computer data-bases. The geography of that mountain reveals a surprising pattern: Successful marriages come in not one but three different varieties, largely determined by how a couple handles their inevitable disagreements. Gottman calls these three types of stable marriages *validating*, *volatile*, and *conflict-avoiding*.

Validating couples are what most people (including most therapists) have in mind when they think of a "good marriage." Even when these couples don't agree, they "still let their partner know that they consider his or her opinions and emotions valid." They "compromise often and calmly work out their problems to mutual satisfaction as they arise." And when they fight, they know how to listen, acknowledge their differences, and negotiate agreement without screaming at each other. "These couples," Gottman notes, "look and sound a lot like two psychotherapists engaging in a dialogue."

But where modern therapy often goes wrong, says Gottman, is in assuming that this is the only way a marriage can work—and trying to force all couples

Couples who start out complaining about each other have some of the most stable marriages over time.

into the validating mold. While "viewing this style of marriage as the ideal has simplified the careers of marital therapists," it hasn't necessarily helped their clients, he says, who may fall into the other two types of stable pattern.

Volatile couples, in contrast to validating ones, thrive on unfiltered emotional intensity. Their relationships are full of angry growls and passionate sighs, sudden ruptures and romantic reconcilia-

Men who do housework are likely to have happier marriages, greater physical health, even better sex lives than men who don't.

tions. They may fight bitterly (and even unfairly), and they may seem destined for divorce to anyone watching them squabble. But Gottman's data indicate that this pessimism is often misplaced: These couples will stay together if "for every nasty swipe, there are five caresses." In fact, "the passion and relish with which they fight seems to fuel their positive interactions even more." Such couples are more romantic and affectionate than most—but they are also more vulnerable to a decay in that all-important five-to-one ratio (and at their worst, to violence). Trying to change the style of their relationship not only isn't necessary, Gottman says, it probably won't work.

Nor will conflict-avoiding couples, the third type of stable marriage, necessarily benefit from an increase in their emotional expression, he says. Gottman likens such unions to "the placid waters of a summer lake," where neither partner wants to make waves. They keep the peace and minimize argument by constantly agreeing to disagree. "In these relationships, solving a problem usually means ignoring the difference, one partner agreeing to act more like the other . . . or most often just letting time take its course." The universal five-to-one ratio must still be present for the couple to stay together, but it gets translated into a

Four Keys to a Happy Relationship

DESPITE ALL HIS SOPHISTICATED ANALYSIS of how relationships work (and don't work), researcher John Gottman's advice to the lovelorn and fight-torn is really quite simple.

LEARN TO CALM DOWN.
This will cut down on the flooding response that makes further communication so difficult. "The most brilliant and philosophically subtle therapy in the world will have no impact on a couple not grounded in their own bodies to hear it," he says. Once couples are calm enough, suggests Gottman, they can work on three other basic "keys" to improving their relationship.

LEARN TO SPEAK AND LISTEN NONDEFENSIVELY.
This is tough, Gottman admits, but defensiveness is a very dangerous response, and it needs to be interrupted. One of the most powerful things you can do—in addition to working toward the ideal of listening with empathy and speaking without blame—is to "reintro-

much smaller number of swipes and caresses (which are also less intensely expressed). This restrained style may seem stifling to some, but the couple themselves can experience it as a peaceful contentment.

Things get more complicated when the marriage is "mixed"—when, say, a volatile person marries someone who prefers to minimize conflict. But Gottman suggests that, even in these cases, "it may be possible to borrow from each marital style and create a viable mixed style." The most difficult hurdle faced by couples with incompatible fighting styles lies in confronting that core difference

---

duce praise and admiration into your relationship." A little appreciation goes a long way toward changing the chemistry between people.

VALIDATE YOUR PARTNER.
Validation involves "putting yourself in your partner's shoes and imagining his or her emotional state." Let your partner know that you understand how he or she feels, and why, even if you don't agree. You can also show validation by acknowledging your partner's point of view, accepting appropriate responsibility, and apologizing when you're clearly wrong. If this still seems too much of a stretch, at least let your partner know that you're *trying* to understand, even if you're finding it hard.

PRACTICE, PRACTICE, PRACTICE.
Gottman calls this "overlearning," doing something so many times that it becomes second nature. The goal is to be able to calm yourself down, communicate nondefensively, and validate your partner automatically—even in the heat of an argument.

---

and negotiating which style (or combination of styles) they will use. If they can't resolve that primary conflict, it may be impossible to tip the overall balance of their relational life in the direction of five-to-one.

The important thing here is to find a compatible fighting style—not to stop fighting altogether. Gottman is convinced that the "one" in that ratio is just as important as the "five": "What may lead to temporary misery in a marriage —disagreement and anger—may be healthy for it in the long run." Negativity acts as the predator in the ecosystem of marriage, says Gottman. It's the lion that feeds on the weakest antelopes and makes the herd stronger. Couples who never disagree at all may start out happier than others, but without some conflict to resolve their differences, their marriages may soon veer toward divorce because their "ecosystem" is out of balance.

THE FOUR HORSEMEN OF THE APOCALYPSE

Even the most stable marriages of any style can fall apart, and Gottman and company have observed an all-too-predictable pattern in their decline and fall. He likens the process to a cascade—a tumble down the rapids—that starts with the arrival of a dangerous quartet of behaviors. So destructive is their effect on marital happiness, in fact, that he calls these behaviors "The Four Horsemen of the Apocalypse."

The first horseman is criticism: "attacking someone's personality or character" rather than making some specific complaint about his or her behavior. The difference between saying, say, "I wish you had taken care of that bill" (a healthy and specific complaint) and "You never get the bills paid on time!" (a generalizing and blaming attack) is very significant to the listener. Criticism often engenders criticism in return and sets the stage for the second horseman: contempt.

"What separates contempt from criticism," explains Gottman, "is the intention to insult and psychologically abuse your partner." Negative thoughts about the other come out in subtle put-downs, hostile jokes, mocking facial expressions, and name-calling ("You are such an idiot

---

around money"). By now the positive qualities that attracted you to this person seem long ago and far away, and instead of trying to build intimacy, you're ushering in the third horseman.

Defensiveness comes on the heels of contempt as a seemingly reasonable response to attack—but it only makes things worse. By denying responsibility, making excuses, whining, tossing back counter-attacks, and other strategies ("How come I'm the one who always pays the bills?!"), you just accelerate your speed down river. Gottman also warns that it's possible to skip straight to the third horseman by being oversensitive about legitimate complaints.

Once stonewalling (the fourth horseman) shows up, things are looking bleak. Stonewallers simply stop communicating, refusing to respond even in self-defense. Of course, all these "horsemen" drop in on couples once in a while. But when a partner habitually shuts down and withdraws, the final rapids of negativity (what Gottman calls the "Distance and Isolation Cascade") can quickly propel the marriage through whirlpools of hopelessness, isolation, and loneliness over the waterfall of divorce. With the arrival of the fourth horseman, one or both partners is thinking negative thoughts about his or her counterpart most of the time, and the couple's minds—as well as their bodies—are in a perpetual state of defensive red alert.

The stress of conflict eventually sends blood pressure, heart rate, and adrenaline into the red zone—a phenomenon Gottman calls *flooding*. "The body of someone who feels flooded," he writes, "is a confused jumble of signals. It may be hard to breathe. . . . Muscles tense up and stay tensed. The heart beats fast, and it may seem to beat harder." Emotionally, the flooded person may feel a range of emotions, from fear to anger to confusion.

The bottom line is that flooding is physically uncomfortable, and stonewalling becomes an attempt to escape that discomfort. When flooding becomes chronic, stonewalling can become chronic, too. Eighty-five percent of the time the stonewaller (among heterosexual couples) is the man. The reason for this gender discrepancy is one of many physiological phenomena that Gottman sees as critical to understanding why mar-

Women are made physically sick by a relentlessly unresponsive or emotionally contemptuous husband. Gottman's researchers can even tell just how sick.

riages go sour, and what people can do to fix them.

Though flooding happens to both men and women, it affects men more quickly, more intensely, and for a longer period of time. "Men tend to have shorter fuses and longer-lasting explosions than women," says Gottman. Numerous observations in the laboratory have shown that it often takes mere criticism to set men off, whereas women require something at least on the level of contempt. The reasons for this are left to speculation. "Probably this difference in wiring had evolutionary survival benefits," Gottman conjectures. An added sensitivity to threats may have kept males alert and ready to repel attacks on their families, he suggests, while women calmed down more quickly so they could soothe the children.

Whatever its origin, this ancient biological difference creates havoc in contemporary male-female relationships, because men are also "more tuned in to the internal physiological environment than women," Gottman reports. (For example, men are better at tapping along with their heartbeat.) Men's bodily sensitivity translates into greater physical discomfort during conflict. In short, arguing hurts. The result: "Men are more likely to withdraw emotionally when their bodies are telling them they're upset." Meanwhile, "when men withdraw, women get upset, and they pursue [the issue]"—which gets men more upset.

Here is where physiology meets sociology. Men, says Gottman, need to rely on physiological cues to know how they're feeling. Women, in contrast, rely on social cues, such as what's happening in the conversation.

In addition, men are trained since early

childhood not to build intimacy with others, while women "are given intense schooling on the subject" from an equally early age. Socially, the genders are almost totally segregated (in terms of their own choices of friendships and playmates) from age seven until early adulthood. Indeed, it would seem that cross-gender relationships are set up to fail. "In fact," Gottman writes, "our upbringing couldn't be a worse training ground for a successful marriage."

Yet the challenge is far from insurmountable, as millions of marriages prove. In fact, Gottman's research reveals that "by and large, in happy marriages there are *no* gender differences in emotional expression!" In these marriages, men are just as likely to share intimate emotions as their partners (indeed they may be more likely to reveal personal information about themselves). However, in unhappy marriages, "all the gender differences we've been talking about

Men's bodily sensitivity translates into greater physical discomfort during conflict. The result: Men are more likely to withdraw emotionally.

emerge"—feeding a vicious cycle that, once established, is hard to break.

Married couples who routinely let the Four Horsemen ransack their living rooms face enormous physical and psychological consequences. Gottman's studies show that chronic flooding and negativity not only make such couples more likely to get sick, they also make it very difficult for couples to change how they relate. When your heart is beating rapidly and your veins are constricting in your arms and legs (another evolutionary stress response), it's hard to think fresh, clear thoughts about how you're communicating. Nor can the brain process new information very well. Instead, a flooded person

relies on "overlearned responses"—old relationship habits that probably just fan the flames.

All this physiological data has enormous implications for relationship therapists as well as their clients. Gottman believes that "most of what you see currently in marital therapy—not all of it, but most of it—is completely misguided."

For example, he thinks it's an exercise in futility when "the therapist says 'Calm down, Bertha. Calm down, Max. Let's take a look at this and analyze it. Let's remember the way we were with our mothers.' Bertha and Max can do it in the office because he's doing it for them. But once they get home, and their heart rates get above 100 beats per minute, whew, forget about it."

Teaching psychological skills such as interpreting nonverbal behavior also misses the mark. "We have evidence that husbands in unhappy marriages are terrible at reading their wives' nonverbal behavior. But they're great at reading other people's nonverbal behavior. In other words, they have the social skills, but they aren't using them." The problem isn't a lack of skill; it's the overwhelming feelings experienced in the cycle of negativity. Chronic flooding short-circuits a couple's basic listening and empathy skills, and it undermines the one thing that can turn back the Four Horsemen: the repair attempt.

HEADING OFF DISASTER

Repair attempts are a kind of "meta-communication"—a way of talking about how you're communicating with each other. "Can we please stay on the subject?" "That was a rude thing to say." "We're not talking about your father!" "I don't think you're listening to me." Such statements, even when delivered in a grouchy or complaining tone, are efforts to interrupt the cycle of criticism, contempt, defensiveness, and stonewalling and to bring the conversation back on track.

"In stable relationships," explains Gottman, "the other person will respond favorably: 'Alright, alright. Finish.' The agreement isn't made very nicely. But it does stop the person. They listen, they accept the repair attempt, and they actually change" the way they're relating.

Repair attempts are "really critical," says Gottman, because "everybody screws up. Everybody gets irritated, defensive, contemptuous. People insult one another," especially their spouses. Repair attempts are a way of saying "we've got to fix this before it slides any deeper into the morass." Even people in bad marriages make repair attempts; the problem is, they get ignored.

Training people to receive repair attempts favorably—even in the middle of a heated argument—is one of the new frontiers in relationship therapy. According to Gottman, "Even when things are going badly, you've got to focus not on the negativity but on the repair attempt. That's what couples do in happy mar-

> *Even people in bad marriages make repair attempts; the problem is, they get ignored.*

riages." He's convinced that such skills can be taught: One colleague has even devised a set of flash cards with a variety of repair attempts on them, ranging from "I know I've been a terrible jerk, but can we take this from the top?" to "I'm really too upset to listen right now." [See Upfront, July/August 1993.] Even in mid-tempest, couples can use the cards to practice giving, and receiving, messages about how they're communicating.

Breaking the Four Horsemen cycle is critical, says Gottman, because "the more time [couples] spend in that negative

perceptual state, the more likely they are to start making long-lasting attributions about this marriage as being negative." Such couples begin rewriting the story of how they met, fell in love, made commitments. Warm memories about how "we were so crazy about each other" get replaced with "I was *crazy* to marry him/ her." And once the story of the marriage has been infected with negativity, the motivation to work on its repair declines. Divorce becomes much more likely (and predictable—consider that 94 percent accuracy rate in the oral history study).

Of course, not all relationships can, or should, be saved. Some couples are trapped in violent relationships, which "are in a class by themselves." Others may suffer a fundamental difference in their preferred style—validating, volatile, or conflict-avoidant—that leaves them stuck in chronic flooding. With hard work, some of these marriages can be saved; trying to save others, however, may do more harm than good.

In the end, the hope for repairing even a broken marriage is to be found, as usual, in the courage and effort people are willing to invest in their own growth and change. "The hardest thing to do," says Gottman, "is to get back to the fundamentals that really make you happy." Couples who fail to do this allow the Four Horsemen to carry them far from the fundamentals of affection, humor, appreciation, and respect. Couples who succeed cultivate these qualities like gardeners. They also cultivate an affirming story of their lives together, understanding that that is the soil from which everything else grows.

The work may be a continuous challenge, but the harvest, as my long-mar-

ried friends Bill and Karen would say, is an enormous blessing: the joy in being truly known and loved, and in knowing how to love.

The Lovers' Library

A slew of new books appearing in 1994 address some of the most entrenched problems facing long-term lovers:

■ *Hot Monogamy: Essential Steps to More Passionate, Intimate Lovemaking*, by Patricia Love and Jo Robinson (Dutton, 1994). This is a wonderful guide to enriching your sex life in a host of imaginative ways, and to reducing the shame and anxiety caused by differences in sexual appetite. (Also available as an excellent workshop on cassette from The Sounds True Catalog, 800-333-9185.)

■ *When Opposites Attract: Right Brain/ Left Brain Relationships and How to Make Them Work*, by Rebecca Cutter (Dutton, 1994). A very helpful and thorough guide to dealing with the wide range of problems that can stem from fundamental differences in brain wiring.

■ *The Couple's Comfort Book: A Creative Guide for Renewing Passion, Pleasure, and Commitment*, by Jennifer Louden (HarperSanFrancisco, 1994). A highly usable compendium of nurturing and imaginative things to do together, cross-referenced so you can hop around the book and design your own program of relationship rebirth.

Why Don't We Act Like The Opposite Sex?

*The new field of sociobiology prompts arguments as to whether
different behavior by men and women is inherited or learned.*

Anthony Layng

Dr. Layng is professor of anthropology, Elmira (N.Y.) College

Social scientists long have been aware of the distinctive sex roles characteristic of tribal societies around the world, but many are reluctant to conclude that this is anything other than learned behavior. Most American cultural anthropologists have assumed that sex roles are largely arbitrary. This is illustrated by citing examples characteristic of males in one population and females in another—as in the American Southwest, where Navajo weavers are women and Hopi weavers are men.

To suggest that female roles are determined to any significant degree by biological factors invites an implication that the lower social status of women found in most societies also might be attributed to innate differences between the sexes, that "anatomy is destiny." American anthropologists have been influenced by social liberalism to such an extent that any scholarly proponent of biological determinism (racism, sexism, etc.) is likely to be challenged immediately. Their argu-

ments against racism have pointed out that there is no reliable correlation between race and social behavior; people of the same race may have sharply contrasting cultures; and a given population can alter its culture dramatically without, presumably, altering its genes. For instance, the Aztecs and Apache were of the same race, but the former evolved a complex state civilization while the latter remained primitive nomads. The post–World War II Japanese have shown us how much a homogeneous racial population can change its culture in a very short time.

When it comes to sexism—the belief that the distinctive behavior of females and males is influenced significantly by their differing physiology—ethnographic challenges are less convincing. One major difficulty is the fact that there are no societies where men and women act alike. Even where conscious attempts have been made to eliminate behavioral differences between the sexes, distinctions remain. A study of American communes in the 1970s found that none have "come anywhere near succeeding in abolishing sex-role

distinctions, although a number . . . have made this their highest ideological priority."

It is far more usual for women to be in favor of the binding relationship of marriage, while men are reluctant to commit themselves.

Another reason why cross-cultural comparisons have been relatively ineffectual in undermining sexist thinking is that, regardless of the great variability of sex roles from one society to another, there are certain behavior patterns and attitudes that appear to be the same in both traditional and modern societies. For example:
• Women generally prefer older men

as mates, while most males prefer younger females.

- In courtship and mating behavior, most men are more sexually aggressive and most women are more coy.
- Males are more inclined to delay marriage.
- Men are more likely to seek a variety of mates.
- Women tend to be more tolerant of adulterous mates.
- Females are more likely to be domestic and nurturing.

In some societies, women prefer men who are considerably older than themselves; in others, the age discrepancy is slight. What is constant is that, on average, the male in each couple is older. Unlike bands of apes, where females are the usual initiators of copulation, "presenting" themselves to males, it is far more common for men to initiate sex, while women are more likely to take a relatively passive role beyond flirtation. Nearly everywhere, shyness or coquettishness is associated strongly with female sexual behavior.

Although some males may have to sell the idea of marriage to their mates, it is far more usual for women to be in the position of favoring such a binding relationship and men to be reluctant to commit themselves. However, males are less reticent about participating in purely sexual relationships, often doing so with more than one partner concurrently. Females seem far more inclined to restrict themselves to one mate, or at least to one at a time. These behavioral differences often are reflected in the "double standard"—the attitude that female infidelity is a far more serious moral breech than male unfaithfulness. Typically, both men and women are more inclined to condemn the adultress. This is not to say that wives do not disapprove strongly of spouses who cheat on them. The point is that a woman far more often will put up with such a husband. Men, on the other hand, are more likely to leave, severely beat, or even kill an unfaithful mate.

Finally, men are far less inclined toward "nesting" and nurturing. It is the women in all societies who are the most domestic and more adept at nurs-

ing the sick and comforting those who are troubled. Both sexes generally agree that it is a woman's nature that makes her so well suited to these activities.

If women and men naturally are inclined to view each other in programmed ways regardless of their class or culture and naturally are predisposed to act toward each other in similarly uniform ways, it might seem reasonable to conclude that female human nature is clearly distinct from that of males and that an Equal Rights Amendment goes against nature. As an active proponent of the ERA and an opponent to all sexism, I am troubled by such a conclusion, but unable simply to dismiss it.

In light of such global uniformity in behavior and attitudes, it is difficult to account for these patterns solely in terms of socialization. Cultures differ dramatically from one to another, and religious beliefs, kinship systems, social structures, political traditions, and subsistence systems vary. So why do men in such contrasting societies all behave so aggressively in the pursuit of sex? Why do male hunters, farmers, and warriors tend to show such interest in seducing new sex partners? Why do Latin American and Asian women put up with adulterous husbands? Why do females in primitive tribes and industrial societies usually prefer older men? Why do peasant women and debutantes tend to want marriage before their male counterparts do? Why are both American and African men relatively disinterested in domestic chores? If it is all a matter of learning, of cultural conditioning, why are there not some societies where most men and women do not conform to these patterns?

Are these traits determined to some extent by the biological peculiarities of the different sexes? If so, it is distressing to consider the social and political implications of such a finding. If human nature (and not only nurture) leads females to behave in a distinctive way, is it therefore not suitable that they be treated in a discriminating fashion? If chasing women only is doing what comes naturally to men, then promiscuous females should have less

excuse for their infidelities. Should husbands, even of working wives, be excused from house cleaning and child care? Clearly, one need not be a militant feminist to be made very uncomfortable by such questions.

It is further disturbing to liberals to learn about the findings of sociobiology, a new discipline which suggests some rather startling explanations for behavior traits such as those cited above. According to many sociobiologists, mating practices are the result of an evolutionary process favoring genes that most successfully replicate themselves. This theory states that those most successful in this regard give rise to behavior and attitudes maximizing reproductive success.

The reproductive strategy of a female stresses quality of offspring, therefore they are inclined to seek established and mature males as providers and protectors of their children.

Supposedly, genetically inherited behavior that causes people to have the most offspring eventually results, through natural selection, in such action becoming more and more common. Genes which induce people to behave otherwise, by the same selective process, are weeded out since people who behave this way have fewer children—that is, they do not produce as many carriers of their genes. Over time, as the result of this process, genes which most successfully cause men and women to produce carriers of these genes become more and more prevalent.

The most convincing illustrations of sociobiological explanations have been provided by studies of animal populations. For example, when a male langur monkey takes over a harem from an older male, he proceeds to kill all the infants of nursing mothers in the troop. From the perspective of Darwin's Theory of Evolution (survival of the fittest), this makes no sense at all, for it destroys healthy and fit infants as well as any others. From a sociobiological perspective, however, this wholesale infanticide is a sound reproductive strategy because it ensures that the genes of this newly dominant male soon will be replicated and in maximum numbers. Were he to wait until each female weaned her infant and ceased to lactate—a prerequisite to coming back into heat—it would be that much longer before he could impregnate them. By killing all the infants carrying some other male's genes, he speeds up the process whereby his genes begin to predominate. Also, he does not waste any energy protecting infants not carrying his genes.

The females of any species, goes this theory, are likely to develop very different kinds of reproductive strategies given the fact that they produce fewer offspring than do males. The genes of males, in competition with those of other males, induce behavior that results in the greatest number of offspring. Females, who are not able to produce nearly as many offspring as are males, compete for quality, rather than quantity, behaving so as to ensure that each child produced will be likely to survive and reproduce. In these ways, males and females alike are directed by their genes to see to it that they reproduce them as successfully as possible.

REPRODUCTIVE STRATEGIES

Among human beings, the fact that men prefer younger wives is fully consistent with their desire to have children since young women are highly fertile and the most likely to bear full-term healthy offspring. A young wife may devote her entire reproductive potential to producing children fathered by her husband. Since the reproductive strategy of women stresses *quality* of offspring, they are inclined to seek established and mature men as providers and protectors of their children. Male sexual aggressiveness serves to

spread male genes. Female coyness helps to assure a potential mate that pregnancy has not occurred already. Her fidelity helps to convince him to stay around to protect what he therefore can assume to be his own offspring. (The sexual aggressiveness of female apes would be inappropriate in a human population, but not for them since male apes are not providers. Given the human sexual division of labor, men and women are economically dependent on each other; apes are not.)

By delaying marriage, a man is free to impregnate more women who will bear his children (his genes) without obligating him to care for them. A woman seeks marriage to monopolize not a man's sexuality, but, rather, his political and economic resources, to ensure that her children (her genes) will be well provided for. She may worry about her husband's infidelities, but only because this can siphon off resources she wants for her children. He, on the other hand, is far more concerned about sexually monopolizing her. He wants assurance that he is the father of any child she gives birth to; otherwise, he will be providing for those who do not carry his genes. Moreover, if she becomes pregnant by another man, it will be many months before she can produce a fetus carrying her husband's genes. With or without her husband's faithfulness, she can get pregnant and produce the maximum number of children carrying her genes. Thus, a wife's affair is less tolerable to her husband for, according to the sociobiological perspective, it threatens to diminish the number of offspring he can produce by her.

The domesticity of women and the wanderings of men also are consistent with the differential reproductive strategies each sex has evolved. In stressing the quality of her offspring, since she can have relatively few, a woman provides a comfortable domicile for her children and stays home to nurture them, to better ensure their survivability so they are most likely to mature and further reproduce her genes. Meanwhile, the man is off chasing women, producing as many children as possible and being far less concerned

with sticking around to guarantee their welfare. If he were to limit himself sexually to one woman, he greatly would diminish the number of children he potentially could propagate. In short, from a sociobiological perspective, she "succeeds" by being faithful to her husband since this helps to ensure that he will provide for her children; he does so not only by monopolizing her as a producer of his offspring, but by having children with other women as well.

By this point, you probably are thinking of people who exemplify sociobiologically sound traits of lecherous males and the women who put up with them. Certainly, we all are familiar with this behavior. Even though it often runs counter to accepted moral standards, we frequently hear people say, "That's the way men (or women) are." Sociobiologists seem to be offering theoretical confirmation of this folk wisdom.

Is human social behavior influenced by our genes? Whether further research will confirm or refute sociobiological theory as it applies to human behavior, we shall have to wait until far more information is available. No matter what the effect on our behavior, we should keep in mind that learning plays an important role. Consequently, social policy should not be based on any assumption that biological determinants of human behavior and attitudes are more instrumental than learning, for cultural factors can counteract human genetic predispositions. Our early ancestors were subject to natural selection. Since the time of the Neanderthals, though, human populations have adapted to environmental change almost entirely by altering their learned behavior and attitudes—their culture, not their genes. There are individuals whose behavior conforms to sociobiological generalizations, but, especially among the educated, one finds many contrasting examples—men who do not chase young women, females who are sexually aggressive and/or disinterested in marriage, and couples who choose to have no children at all.

If traditional social inequality between men and women somewhat is perpetuated by genetically determined and sexually specific reproductive strategies, why are contraceptives and abortions so popular in modern society? Even most modern women may seem to conform to sociobiologically correct behavior (being attracted to older men, tolerating unfaithful spouses, accepting primary responsibility for domestic duties, etc.). Since most males still earn more than females do and since

society continues to socialize boys and girls quite differently (encouraging girls to play with infant dolls, rewarding boys for being physically aggressive, etc.), the continuation of such behavior may be more a matter of cultural inertia than genetic compulsion.

So, even if inborn factors influence male and female human sexual behavior, the extent to which they do so clearly is limited and subordinate to

learning and conditioning. Consequently, we neither need fear intellectually the findings of sociobiologists nor allow them significantly to influence interpersonal behavior and social attitudes regarding gender-specific behavior. If men and women continue to behave differently (and it seems there is no clear trend away from this pattern), we may yet learn just why we do not act like the opposite sex.

BACK OFF!

We're putting way too many expectations on our closest relationships. It's time to retreat a bit. Consider developing same-sex friendships. Or cultivating a garden. Whatever you do, take a break from the relentless pursuit of intimacy.

Geraldine K. Piorkowski, Ph.D.

You can't miss it. It's the favorite topic of Oprah and all the other talk shows. It's the suds of every soap opera. And I probably don't have to remind you that it's the subject of an extraordinary number of self-help books. Intimate relationships. No matter where we tune or turn, we are bombarded with messages that there is a way to do it right, certainly some way of doing it better—if only we could find it. There are countless books simply on the subject of how to communicate better. Or, if it's not working out, to exit swiftly.

We are overfocused on intimate relationships, and I question whether our current preoccupation with intimacy isn't unnatural, not entirely in keeping with the essential physical and psychological nature of people. The evidence suggests that there is a limit to the amount of closeness people can tolerate and that we need time alone for productivity and creativity. Time alone is necessary to replenish psychological resources and to solidify the boundaries of the self.

All our cultural focus on relationships ultimately has, I believe, a negative impact on us. It causes us to look upon intimate relationships as a solution to all our ills. And that only sets us up for disappointment, contributing to the remarkable 50 percent divorce rate.

Our overfocus on relationships leads us to demand too much of intimacy. We put all our emotional eggs in the one basket of intimate romantic relationships. A romantic partner must be all things to us—lover, friend, companion, playmate, and parent.

We approach intimate relationships with the expectation that this new love will make up for past letdowns in life and love. The expectation that this time around will be better is bound to disappoint, because present-day lovers feel burdened by demands with roots in old relationships.

We expect unconditional love, unfailing nurturance, and protection. There is also the expectation that the new partner will make up for the characteristics we lack in our own personality—for example, that he or she will be an outgoing soul to compensate for our shyness or a goal-oriented person to provide direction in our messy life.

If the personal ads were rewritten to emphasize the emotional expectations we bring to intimacy, they would sound like this. "WANTED: Lively humorous man who could bring joy to my gloomy days and save me from a lifetime of depression." Or, "WANTED: Woman with self-esteem lower than mine. With her, I could feel superior and gain temporary boosts of self-confidence from the comparison."

From my many years as a clinical psychologist, I have come to recognize that intimacy is not an unmitigated good. It is not only difficult to achieve, it is treacherous in some fundamental ways. And it can actually harm people.

The potential for emotional pain and upset is so great in intimate relationships because we are not cloaked in the protective garb of maturity. We are unprotected, exposed, vulnerable to hurt; our defenses are down. We are wide open to pain.

Intuitively recognizing the dangers involved, people normally erect elaborate barriers to shield themselves from closeness. We may act superior, comical, mysterious, or super independent because we fear that intimacy will bring criticism, humiliation, or betrayal—whatever an earlier relationship sensitized us to. We develop expectations based on what has happened in our lives with parents, with friends, with a first love. And we often act in anticipation of these expectations, bringing about the result we most want to avoid.

The closer we get to another person, the greater the risks of intimacy. It's not just that we are more vulnerable and defenseless. We are also more emotionally unstable, childish, and less intelligent than in any other situation. You may be able to run a large company with skill and judgment, but be immature, ultrasensitive, and needy at home. Civilized rules of conduct often get suspended. Intimacy is both unnerving and baffling.

HEALTHY RETREATS

Once our fears are aroused in the context of intimacy, we tend to go about calming them in unproductive ways. We make excessive demands of our partner, for affection, for unconditional regard. The trouble is, when people feel demands are being made of them, they tend to retreat and hide in ways that hurt their partner. They certainly do not listen.

Fears of intimacy typically limit our vulnerability by calling defensive strategies into play. Without a doubt, the defense of choice against the dangers of intimacy is withdrawal. Partners tune out. One may retreat into work. One walks out of the house, slamming the door. Another doesn't call for days. Whatever the way, we spend a great deal of time avoiding intimacy.

After many years of working with all kinds of couples, I have come to believe that human nature dictates that intimate relationships have to be cyclical.

When one partner unilaterally backs off, it tends to be done in a hurtful manner. The other partner feels rejected, uncared about, and unloved. Typically, absolutely nothing gets worked out.

However, avoidance is not necessarily unhealthy. Partners can pursue a time out, where one or both work through their conflict in a solitary way that is ultimately renewing. What usually happens, however, is that when partners avoid each other, they are avoiding open warfare but doing nothing to resolve the underlying conflicts.

Fears of intimacy can actually be pretty healthy, when they're realistic and protective of the self. And they appear even in good relationships. Take the fears of commitment that are apt to surface in couples just before the wedding. If they can get together and talk through their fears, then they will not scare one another or themselves into backing off permanently.

After many years of working with all kinds of couples, I have come to believe that human nature dictates that intimate relationships have to be cyclical. There are limitations to intimacy and I think it is wise to respect the dangers. Periods of closeness have to be balanced with periods of distance. For every two steps forward, we often need to take one step back.

An occasional retreat from intimacy gives individuals time to recharge. It offers time to strengthen your sense of who you are. Think of it as constructive avoidance. We need to take some emphasis off what partners can do for us and put it on what we can do for ourselves and what we can do with other relationships. Developing and strengthening same-sex friendships, even opposite-sex friendships, has its own rewards and aids the couple by reducing the demands and emotional expectations we place on partners.

In our culture, our obsession with romantic love relationships has led us to confuse all emotional bonds with sexual bonds, just as we confuse infatuation with emotional intimacy. As a result, we seem to avoid strong but deeply rewarding emotional attachments with others of our own sex. But having recently lost a dear friend of several decades, I am personally sensitive to the need for emotionally deep, same-sex relationships. They can be shared as a way of strengthening gender identity and enjoying rewarding companionship. We need to put more energy into nonromantic relationships as well as other activities.

One of the best ways of recharging oneself is to take pleasure in learning and spiritual development. And there's a great deal to be said for spending time solving political, educational, or social ills of the world.

Distance and closeness boundaries need to be calibrated and constantly readjusted in every intimate relationship. Such boundaries not only vary with each couple, they change as the relationship progresses. One couple may maintain their emotional connection by spending one evening together a week, while another couple needs daily coming together of some sort. Problems arise in relationships when partners cannot agree on the boundaries. These boundaries must be jointly negotiated or the ongoing conflict will rob the relationship of its vitality.

S.O.S. SIGNALS

When you're feeling agitated or upset that your partner is not spending enough time with you, consider it a signal to step back and sort out internally what is going on. Whether you feel anxiety or anger, the emotional arousal should serve as a cue to back off and think through where the upset is coming from, and to consider whether it is realistic.

That requires at least a modest retreat from a partner. It could be a half hour, or two hours. Or two days—whenever internal clarity comes. In the grip of emotion, it is often difficult to discriminate exactly which emotion it is and what its source is. "What is it I am concerned about? Is this fear realistic considering Patrick's behavior in the present? He's never done this to me before, and he's been demonstrating his trustworthiness all over the place, so what am I afraid of? Is it coming from my early years of neglect with two distant parents who never had time for me? Or from my experiences with Steve, who dumped me two years ago?"

Introspective and self-aware people already spend their time thinking about how they work, their motives, what their feelings mean. Impulsive people will have a harder time with the sorting-out process. The best way to sort things out is to pay attention to the nature of the upset. Exactly what you are upset about suggests what your unmet need is, whether it's for love, understanding, nurturance, protection, or special status. And once you identify the need, you can figure out its antecedents.

The kinds of things we get upset about in intimacy tend to follow certain themes. Basically, we become hurt or resentful because we're getting "too much" or "too little" of something. Too many demands, too much criticism, too much domination. Or the converse, too little affectional, conversational, or sexual attention (which translates into "you don't feel I'm important" or "you don't love me"). Insufficient empathy is usually voiced as "you don't understand me," and too little responsibility translates into failure to take on one's share of household and/or financial tasks. All these complaints require some attention, action, or retreat.

SHIFTING GEARS

It's not enough to identify the source of personal concern. You have to present your concerns in a way your partner can hear. If I say directly to my partner, "I'm afraid you're going to leave me," he has the opportunity to respond, "Darling, that's not true. What gave you that idea?" I get the reassurance I need. But if I toss it out in an argument, in the form of "you don't care about me," then my partner's emotional arousal keeps him from hearing me. And he is likely to back away—just when I need reassurance most.

If people were aware that intimate relationships are by nature characterized by ambivalence, they would understand the need to negotiate occasional retreats. They wouldn't feel so threatened by the times when one partner says, "I have to be by myself because I need to think about my life and where I'm going." Or "I need to be with my friends and spend time playing." If people did more backing off into constructive activities, including time to meditate or to play, intimate relationships would be in much better shape today.

If couples could be direct about what they need, then the need for retreat would not be subject to the misrepresentation that now is rampant. The trouble is, we don't talk to each other that openly and honestly. What happens is, one partner backs off and doesn't call and the partner left behind doesn't know what the withdrawal means. But he or she draws on a personal history that provides room for all sorts of negative interpretations, the most common being "he doesn't care about me."

No matter how hard a partner tries to be all things to us, gratifying all of another's needs is a herculean task—beyond the human calling. Criticism, disappointment, and momentary rejection are intrinsic parts of intimate life; developing a thicker skin can be healthy. And maintaining a life apart from the relationship is necessary. Energy invested in other people and activities provides a welcome balance.

GOOD-ENOUGH INTIMACY

Since our intimate partner will never be perfect, what is reasonable to expect? The late British psychiatrist D. W. Winnicott put forth the idea of "good-enough mothering." He was convinced that mothering could never be perfect because of the mother's own emotional needs. "Good-enough mothering" refers to imperfect, though adequate provision of emotional care that is not damaging to the children.

In a similar vein, I believe there is a level of imperfect intimacy that is good enough to live and grow on. In good-enough intimacy, painful encounters occasionally occur, but they are balanced by the strength and pleasures of the relationship. There are enough positives to balance the negatives. People who do very well in intimate relationships don't have a perfect relationship, but it is good enough.

The standard of good-enough intimacy is essentially subjective, but there are some objective criteria. A relationship must have enough companionship, affection, autonomy, connectedness, and separateness, along with some activities that partners engage in together and that they both enjoy. The relationship meets the needs of both partners reasonably well enough, both feel reasonably good about the relationship. If one person is unhappy in the relationship, then by definition it is not good enough for them.

People looking for good-enough intimacy are bound to be happier than those seeking perfect intimacy. Their expectations are lower and more realistic. Time and time again, those who examine the intricacies of happiness have found the same thing—realistic expectations are among the prime contributors to happiness.

Choosing Mates—The American Way

Martin King Whyte

Martin King Whyte is professor of sociology and faculty associate in the Center for Chinese Studies at the University of Michigan. He has published numerous works on family sociology and contemporary Chinese social organization. His is currently involved in a comparative study of mate choice and marital relations in China and the United States. His latest book is Dating, Mating, and Marriage.

As America's divorce rate has been soaring, popular anxieties about marriage have multiplied. Is it still possible to "live happily ever after," and if so, how can this be accomplished? How can you tell whether a partner who leaves you breathless with yearning will, as your spouse, drive you to distraction? Does "living together" prior to marriage provide a realistic assessment of how compatible you and your partner might be as husband and wife? Questions such as these suggest a need to examine our American way of mate choice. How do we go about selecting the person we marry, and is there something wrong with the entire process?

For most twentieth-century Americans choosing a mate is the culmination of a process of dating. Examination of how we go about selecting mates thus requires us to consider the American dating culture. Dating is a curious institution. By definition it is an activity that is supposed to be separate from selecting a spouse. Yet, dating is expected to provide valuable experience that will help in making a "wise" choice of a marital partner. Does this combination work?

How well dating "works" may be considered in a number of senses of this term. Is it easy or difficult to find somebody to go out with? Do dates mostly lead to enjoyable or painful evenings? However, these are not the aspects of dating I wish to consider. The issue here is whether dating works in the sense of providing useful experience that helps pave the way for a successful marriage.

Dating is a relatively new institution. The term, and the various practices associated with it, first emerged around the turn of the century. By the 1920s dating had more or less completely displaced earlier patterns of relations among unmarried Americans. Contrary to popular assumptions, even in colonial times marriages were not arranged in America. Parents were expected to give their approval to their children's nuptial plans, a practice captured in our image of a suitor asking his beloved's father for her hand in marriage. Parental approval, especially among merchants and other prosperous classes, put some constraint on the marriages of the young. For example, through the eighteenth century, children in such families tended to marry in birth order and marriage to cousins was not uncommon. (Both practices had declined sharply by the nineteenth century.) However, parents rarely directly arranged the marriages of their children. America has always exhibited "youth-driven" patterns of courtship. Eligible males and females took the initiative to get to know each other, and the decision to marry was made by them, even if that decision was to some degree contingent on parental approval. (Of course, substantial proportions of later immigrant groups from Southern and Eastern Europe, Asia, and elsewhere brought with them arranged marriage traditions, and contention for control over marriage decisions was often a great source of tension in such families.)

How did young people get to know one another well enough to decide to marry in the era before dating? A set of customs, dominant for the two centuries, preceded the rise of the dating culture. These activities came to be referred to as "calling" and "keeping company." Young people might meet in a variety of ways—through community and church socials, informally in shops or on the street, on boat and train trips, or through introductions from friends or relatives. (America never developed a system of chaperoning young women in public, and foreign observers often commented on the freedom unmarried women had to travel and mix socially on their own.) Usually young people would go to church fairs, local dances, and other such activities with family, siblings, or friends, rather than paired off with a partner. Most activities would involve a substantial degree of adult and community supervision. Nonetheless, these gatherings did encourage some pairing off and led to hand holding, moonlit walks home, and other romantic exploration.

By late nineteenth century, a formal pattern of "calling" developed among the upper and middle classes.

As relationships developed beyond the platonic level, the suitor would pay visits to the home of the young woman. By the latter part of the nineteenth century, particularly among the middle and upper classes, this activity assumed a formal pattern referred to as "calling." Males would be invited to call on the female at her home, and they were expected to do so only if invited. (A bold male could, however, request an invitation to call.) Invitations might be extended by the mother of a very young woman, but eventually they would come from the young woman herself. Often a woman would designate certain days on which she would receive callers. She might have several suitors at one time, and thus a number of men might be paying such calls. A man might be told that the woman was not at home to receive him, and he would then be expected to leave his calling card. If this happened repeatedly, he was expected to get the message that his visits were no longer welcome.

Initiative and control in regard to calling were in the hands of women (the eligible female and her mother). Although some variety in suitors was possible, even in initial stages the role of calling in examining potential marriage partners was very clear to all involved. The relatively constrained and supervised nature of calling make it certain that enjoyment cannot have been a primary goal of this activity. (During the initial visits the mother was expected to remain present; in later visits she often hovered in an adjacent room.) If dating is defined as recreational and romantic pairing off between a man and a woman, away from parental supervision and without immediate consideration of marriage, then calling was definitely not dating.

The supervised and controlled nature of calling should not, however, lead us to suppose that propriety and chastity were always maintained until marriage. If the relationship had deepened sufficiently, the couple might progress from calling to "keeping company," a

precursor of the twentieth-century custom of "going steady." At this stage, the primary activity would still consist of visits by the suitor to the woman's home. However, now she would only welcome calls from one man, and he would visit her home on a regular basis. Visits late into the evening would increasingly replace afternoon calls. As the relationship became more serious, parents would often leave the couple alone. Nineteenth-century accounts mention parents going off to bed and leaving the young couple on the couch or by the fireplace, there to wrestle with, and not infrequently give in to, sexual temptation.

Even though some women who headed to the altar toward the end of the nineteenth century had lost their virginity prior to marriage, premarital intimacy was less common than during the dating era. (The double standard of the Victorian era made it possible for many more grooms to be non-virgins at marriage than brides. Perhaps 50 percent or more of men had lost their virginity prior to marriage, as opposed to 15 to 20 percent of women, with prostitutes and "fallen women" helping to explain the differential.) What is less often realized is that the formalization of the calling pattern toward the end of the nineteenth century contributed to a decline in premarital sexual intimacy compared to earlier times. America experienced not one but two sexual revolutions—one toward the end of the eighteenth century, at the time of the American Revolution, and the other in the latter part of the twentieth century.

The causes of the first sexual revolution are subject to some debate. An influx of settlers to America who did not share the evangelical puritanism of many early colonists, the expansion of the population into the unsettled (and "unchurched") frontier, the growth of towns, and the individualistic and freedom-loving spirit of the American revolution may have contributed to a retreat from the fairly strict emphasis on premarital chastity of the early colonial period. Historians debate the extent to which the archetypal custom of this first sexual revolution, bundling, (which allowed an unmarried couple to sleep together, although theoretically fully clothed and separated by a "bundling board") was widespread or largely mythical. Whatever the case, other evidence is found in studies of communities, such as those by Daniel Scott Smith and Michael Hindus, which found that the percentage of married couples whose first births were conceived premaritally increased from about 11 percent before 1700 to over 33 percent in the last decades of the eighteenth century.

This first sexual revolution was reversed in the nineteenth century. The reasons for its demise are also not clear. The closing of the frontier, the rise of the middle class, the defensive reactions of that new middle class to new waves of immigrants, the growth of Christian revivalism and reform movements, and the spread of models of propriety from Victorian England (which were in turn influenced by fear of the chaos of the French Revolution)—all these have been suggested as having contributed to a new sexual puritanism in the nineteenth century. According to Smith and Hindus, premarital conceptions decreased once again to about 15 percent of first births between 1841 and 1880.

It was in the latter time period that the customs of calling and keeping company reached their most formal elaboration—calling, in less ritualized forms, can be traced back to the earliest colonial period. Not long after reaching the formal patterns described, calling largely disappeared. In little more than a generation, dating replaced calling as the dominant custom.

Dating involved pairing off of couples in activities not supervised by parents, with pleasure rather than marriage as the primary goal. The rules governing dating were defined by peers rather than by adults. The initiative, and much of the control, shifted from the female to the male. The man asked the woman out, rather than waiting for her invitation to call. The finances and transportation for the date were also his responsibility. The woman was expected to provide, in turn, the pleasure of her company and perhaps some degree of romantic and physical intimacy. By giving or withholding her affection and access to her body, she exercised considerable control over the man and the date as an event. Nonetheless, the absence of parental oversight and the pressure to respond to a man's initiatives placed a woman in a weaker position than she was in the era of calling.

The man might pick up the woman at her home, but parents who tried to dictate whom their daughters dated and what they did on dates generally found such efforts rejected and evaded. Parents of a son might not even know where junior was going or whom he was dating. Dates were conducted mostly in the public arena, and in some cases—such as at sporting events or school dances—adults might be present. But dates often involved activities and venues where no adults were present or where young people predominated— as at private parties or at local dance halls. Or in other cases the presence of adults would have little inhibiting effect, as in the darkened balconies of movie theaters. American youths also developed substantial ingenuity in finding secluded "lovers' lanes" where they could escape the supervision of even peers. (Localities varied in the places used for this purpose and how they were referred to. In locales near bodies of water young people spoke of "watching submarine races;" in the

rural area of upstate New York where I grew up the phrase was "exploring tractor roads.") Community dances and gatherings for all generations and ages practically disappeared in the dating era.

Greater privacy and autonomy of youths promoted romantic and physical experimentation. Not only kissing but petting was increasingly accepted and widespread. Going beyond petting to sexual intercourse, however, involved substantial risks, especially for the female. This was not simply the risk of pregnancy in the pre-pill era. Dating perpetuated the sexual double standard. Men were expected to be the sexual aggressors and to try to achieve as much intimacy as their dates would allow. But women who "went too far" risked harming their reputations and their ability to keep desirable men interested in them for long. Women were expected to set the limits, and they had to walk a careful line between being too unfriendly (and not having males wanting to date them at all) and being too friendly (and being dated for the "wrong reasons").

Rules governing dating were defined by peers rather than adults.

During the initial decades of the dating era, premarital intimacy increased in comparison with the age of calling, but still a majority of women entered marriage as virgins. In a survey in the greater Detroit metropolitan area, I found that of the oldest women interviewed (those who dated and married prior to 1945), about one in four had lost her virginity prior to marriage. (By the 1980s, according to my survey, the figure was closer to 90 percent.) Escape from parental supervision provided by dating weakened, but did not immediately destroy, the restraints on premarital intimacy.

When Americans began dating, they were primarily concerned with enjoyment, rather than with choosing a spouse. Indeed, "playing the field" was the ideal pursued by many. Dates were not suitors or prospects. Seeing different people on successive nights in a hectic round of dating activity earned one popularity among peers. One of the early students and critics of the dating culture, Willard Waller, coined the term "rating and dating complex" to refer to this pattern. After observing dating among students at Pennsylvania State University in the 1930s, Waller charged that concern for impressing friends and gaining status on campus led to superficial thrill-seeking and competition for popularity, and eliminated genuine romance or sincere communication. However, Waller has been accused of both stereotyping and exaggerating the influence of this pattern. Dating was not always so exploitative and superficial as he charged.

Dating was never viewed as an endless stage or an alternative to courtship. Even if dates were initially seen as quite separate from mate selection, they were always viewed as only the first step in a progression that would lead to marriage. By the 1930s, the stage of "going steady" was clearly recognized, entailing a commitment by both partners to date each other exclusively, if only for the moment. A variety of ritual markers emerged to symbolize the increased commitment of this stage and of further steps toward engagement and marriage, such as wearing the partner's high school ring, being lavaliered, and getting pinned.

Growing affluence fueled new industries designed to entertain and fill leisure time.

Going steady was a way-station between casual dating and engagement. Steadies pledged not to date others, and they were likely to become more deeply involved romantically and physically than casual daters. They were not expected explicitly to contemplate marriage, and the majority of women in our Detroit survey had several steady boyfriends before the relationships that led to their marriages. If a couple was of a "suitable age," though, and if the steady relationship lasted more than a few months, the likelihood increased of explicit talk about marriage. Couples would then symbolize their escalated commitment by getting engaged. Dating arose first among middle and upper middle class students in urban areas, and roughly simultaneously at the college and high school levels. The practice then spread to other groups—rural young people, working class youths, to the upper class, and to employed young people. But what triggered the rapid demise of calling and the rise of dating?

One important trend was prolonged school attendance, particularly in public, co-educational high schools and colleges. Schools provided an arena in which females and males could get to know one another informally over many years. Schools also organized athletic, social, and other activities in which adult supervision was minimal. College campuses generally allowed a more total escape from parental supervision than high schools.

Another important influence was growing affluence in America. More and more young people were freed from a need to contribute to the family economy and had more leisure time in which to date. Fewer young people worked under parental supervision, and more

and more fathers worked far from home, leaving mothers as the primary monitors of their children's daily activities. These trends also coincided with a rise in part-time and after-school employment for students, employment that provided pocket money that did not have to be turned over to parents and could be spent on clothing, makeup, movie tickets, and other requirements of the dating culture. Rising affluence also fueled the growth of entire new industries designed to entertain and fill leisure time—movies, popular music recording, ice cream parlors, amusement parks, and so on. Increasingly, young people who wanted to escape from supervision of their parents found a range of venues, many of them catering primarily to youth and to dating activities.

Technology also played a role, and some analysts suggest that one particular invention, the automobile, deserves a lion's share of the credit. Automobiles were not only a means to escape the home and reach a wider range of recreation spots. They also provided a semi-private space with abundant romantic and sexual possibilities. New institutions, such as the drive-in movie theater, arose to take advantage of those possibilities. As decades passed and affluence increased, the borrowed family car was more and more replaced by cars owned by young people, advancing youth autonomy still further.

All this was part of a larger trend: the transformation of America into a mass consumption society. As this happened, people shifted their attention partially from thinking about how to work and earn to pondering how to spend and consume. Marketplace thinking became more and more influential. The image of the individual as *homo economicus* and of modern life typified by the rational application of scientific knowledge to all decisions became pervasive. The new ideological framework undermined previous customs and moral standards and extended to the dating culture.

Dating had several goals. Most obviously and explicitly, dates were expected to lead to pleasure and possibly to romance. It was also important, as Waller and others have observed, in competition for popularity. But a central purpose of dating was to gain valuable learning experience that would be useful later in selecting a spouse. Through dating young people would learn how to relate to the opposite sex. Dating would increase awareness of one's own feelings and understanding of which type of partner was appealing and which not. Through crushes and disappointments, one would learn to judge the character of people. And by dating a variety of partners and by increasingly intimate involvement with some of them, one would learn what sort of person one would be happy with as a marital partner. When it came time to marry one would be in a good position to select "Mr. Right" or "Miss Right." Calling, which limited the possibilities of romantic experimentation, often to only one partner, did not provide an adequate basis for such an informed choice.

What emerged was a "marketplace learning viewpoint." Selecting a spouse is not quite the same as buying a car or breakfast cereal, but the process was seen as analogous. The assumptions involved in shopping around and test driving various cars or buying and tasting Wheaties, Cheerios, and Fruit Loops were transferred to popular thinking about how to select a spouse.

According to this marketplace learning viewpoint, getting married very young and without having acquired much dating experience was risky, in terms of marital happiness. Similarly, marrying your first and only sweetheart was not a good idea. Neither was meeting someone, falling head over heels in love, and marrying, all within the course of a month. While Americans recognized that in some cases such beginnings could lead to good marriages, the rationale of our dating culture was that having had a variety of dating partners and then getting to know one or more serious prospects over a longer period time and on fairly intimate terms were experiences more likely to lead to marital success.

Eventually, this marketplace psychology helped to undermine America's premarital puritanism, and with it the sexual double standard. The way was paved for acceptance of new customs, and particularly for premarital cohabitation. Parents and other moral guardians found it increasingly difficult to argue against the premise that, if sexual enjoyment and compatibility were central to marital happiness, it was important to test that compatibility before marrying. Similarly, if marriage involved not just hearts and flowers, but also dirty laundry and keeping a budget, did it not make sense for a couple to live together prior to marriage to see how they got along on a day-to-day basis? Such arguments on behalf of premarital sex and cohabitation have swept into popular consciousness in the United States, and it is obvious that they are logical corollaries of the marketplace learning viewpoint.

Our dating culture thus is based upon the premise that dating provides valuable experience that will help individuals select mates and achieve happy marriages. But is this premise correct? Does dating really work? What evidence shows that individuals with longer dating experience, dates with more partners, or longer and more intimate acquaintances with the individuals they intend to marry end up with happier marriages?

Surprisingly, social scientists have never systematially addressed this question. Perhaps this is one of those cherished beliefs people would prefer not to examine too closely. When I could find little evidence on the connection between dating and other premarital experiences and marital success in previous studies, I decided to conduct my own inquiry.

Dating was to give valuable experience to help in future mate selection.

My desire to know whether dating experiences affected marriages was the basis for my 1984 survey in the Detroit area. A representative sample of 459 women was interviewed in three counties in the Detroit metropolitan area (a diverse, multi-racial and multi-ethnic area of city and suburbs containing about 4 million people in 1980). The women ranged in ages from 18 to 75, and all had been married at least once. (I was unable to interview their husbands, so unfortunately marriages in this study are viewed only through the eyes of women.) The interviewees had first married over a sixty year span of time, between 1925 and 1984. They were asked to recall a variety of things about their dating and premarital experiences. They were also asked a range of questions about their marital histories and (if currently married) about the positive and negative features of their relations with their husbands. The questionnaire enabled us to test whether premarital experiences of various types were related to marital success, a concept which in turn was measured in several different ways. (Measures of divorce and of both positive and negative qualities in intact marriages were used.)

The conclusions were a surprise. It appears that dating does not work and that the "marketplace learning viewpoint" is misguided. Marrying very young tended to produce unsuccessful marriages. Premarital pregnancy was associated with problems in marriage. However, once the age of marriage is taken into account, none of the other measures—dating variety, length of dating, length of courtship or engagement, or degree of premarital intimacy with the future husband or others—was clearly related to measures of marital success. A few weak tendencies in the results were contrary to predictions drawn from the marketplace learning viewpoint. Women who had dated more partners or who had engaged in premarital sex or cohabited were slightly less likely to have successful marriages. This might be seen as evidence of quite a different logic.

Perhaps there is a "grass is greener" effect. Women who have been led less sheltered and conventional lives prior to marriage may not be as easily satisfied afterward. Several other researchers have found a similar pattern with regard to premarital cohabitation. Individuals who had been living together prior to marriage were significantly less likely to have successful marriages than those who did not.

Individuals who had been living together were less likely to have successful marriages.

In the Detroit survey, these "grass is greener" patterns were not consistent or statistically significant. It was not that women with more dating experience and greater premarital intimacy had less successful marriages; rather, the amount and type of dating experience did not make a clear difference one way or the other.

Women who had married their first sweethearts were just as likely to have enduring and satisfying marriages as women who had married only after considering many alternatives. Similarly, women who had married after only a brief acquaintance were no more (nor less) likely to have a successful marriage than those who knew their husbands-to-be for years. And there was no clear difference between the marriages of women who were virgins at marriage and those who had had a variety of sexual partners and who had lived together with their husbands before the wedding.

Dating obviously does not provide useful learning that promotes marital success. Although our dating culture is based upon an analogy with consumer purchases in the marketplace, it is clear that in real life selecting a spouse is quite different from buying a car or a breakfast cereal. You cannot actively consider several prospects at the same time without getting your neck broken and being deserted by all of them. Even if you find Ms. Right or Mr. Right, you may be told to drop dead. By the time you are ready to marry, this special someone you were involved with earlier may no longer be available, and you may not see anyone on the horizon who comes close to being as desirable. In addition, someone who is well suited at marriage may grow apart from you or find someone else to be with later. Dating experience might facilitate marital success if deciding whom to marry was like deciding what to eat for breakfast (although even in the latter regard tastes change, and toast and black coffee may replace bacon and eggs). But these realms are quite different,

and mate selection looks more like a crap-shoot than a rational choice.

Is there a better way? Traditionalists in some societies would argue that arranged marriages are preferable. However, in addition to the improbability that America's young people will leave this decision to their parents, there is the problem of evidence. The few studies of this topic, including one I have been collaborating on in China, indicate that women who had arranged marriages were less satisfied than women who made the choice themselves. So having Mom and Dad take charge is not the answer. Turning the matter over to computerized matchmaking also does not seem advisable. Despite the growing sophistication of computers, real intelligence seems preferable to artificial intelligence. As the Tin Woodman in *The Wizard of Oz* discovered, to have a brain but no heart is to be missing something important.

Perhaps dating is evolving into new patterns in which premarital experience will contribute to marital success. Critics from Waller onward have claimed that dating promotes artificiality, rather than realistic assessment of compatibility. Some observers suggest that the sort of superficial dating Waller and others wrote about has become less common of late. Dating certainly has changed significantly since the pre-Second World War era. Many of the rigid rules of dating have broken down. The male no longer always takes the initiative; neither does he always pay. The sexual double standard has also weakened substantially, so that increasingly Americans feel that whatever a man can do a woman should be able to do. Some writers even suggest that dating is going out of style, replaced by informal pairing off in larger groups, often without the prearrangement of "asking someone out." Certainly the terminology is changing, with "seeing" and "being with" increasingly preferred to "dating" and "going steady." To many young people the latter terms have the old fashioned ring that "courting" and "suitor" had when I was young.

My daughter and other young adults argue that current styles are more natural and healthier than the dating experienced by my generation and the generation of my parents. Implicit in this argument is the view that, with formal rules and the "rating and dating" complex in decline, it should be possible to use dating (or whatever you call it) to realistically assess compatibility and romantic chemistry. These arguments may seem plausible, but I see no evidence that bears them out. The youngest women we interviewed in the Detroit survey should have experienced these more informal styles of romantic exploration. However, for them dating and premarital intimacy were, if anything, less closely related to marital success than was the case for the older women. The changes in premarital relations do not seem to make experience a better teacher.

While these conclusions are for the most part quite negative, my study leads to two more positive observations. First, marital success is not totally unpredictable. A wide range of features of how couples structure their day-to-day marital relations promote success—sharing in power and decision-making, pooling incomes, enjoying similar leisure time activities, having similar values, having mutual friends and an active social life, and other related qualities. Couples are not "doomed" by their past histories, including their dating histories, and they can increase their mutual happiness through the way they structure their marriages.

Second, there is something else about premarital experience besides dating history that may promote marital success. We have in America not one, but two widely shared, but quite contradictory, theories about how individuals should select a spouse: one based on the marketplace learning viewpoint and another based on love. One viewpoint sees selecting a spouse as a rational process, perhaps even with lists of criteria by which various prospects can be judged. The other, as song writers tell us, is based on the view that love conquers all and that "all you need is love." Love is a matter of the heart (perhaps with some help from the hormonal system) and not the head, and love may blossom unpredictably, on short notice or more gradually. Might it not be the case, then, that those couples who are most deeply in love at the time of their weddings will have the most successful marriages? We have centuries of poetry and novels, as well as love songs, that tell us that this is the case.

In the Detroit study, we did, in fact, ask women how much they had been in love when they first married. And we did find that those who recalled being "head over heels in love" then, had more successful mar-

riages. However, there is a major problem with this finding. Since we were asking our interviewees to recall their feelings prior to their weddings—in many cases weddings that took place years or even decades earlier—it is quite possible and even likely that their answers are biased. Perhaps whether or not their marriage worked out influenced these "love reports" from earlier times, rather than having the level of romantic love then explain marital success later. Without either a time machine or funds to interview couples prior to marriage and then follow them up years later, it is impossible to be sure that more intense feelings of love lead to more successful marriages. Still, the evidence available does not question the wisdom of poets and songwriters when it comes to love. Mate selection may not be a total crap-shoot after all, and even if dating does not work, love perhaps does.

READINGS SUGGESTED BY THE AUTHOR:

Bailey, Beth. *From Front Porch to Back Seat.* Baltimore: Johns Hopkins University Press, 1988.

Burgess, Ernest W. and Paul Wallin. *Engagement and Marriage.* Chicago: Lippincott, 1953.

Modell, John. "Dating Becomes the Way of American Youth," in *Essays on the Family and Historical Change,* Leslie P. Moch and Gary Stark (eds.). College Station, Tex.: Texas A&M University Press, 1983.

Rothman, Ellen K. *Hands and Hearts: A History of Courtship.* New York: Basic Books, 1984.

Smith, Daniel S. and Michael Hindus. "Premarital Pregnancy in America, 1640-1971: An Overview and Interpretation," *Journal of Interdisciplinary History,* 4 (1975), 537-570.

Waller, Willard, "Rating and Dating Complex," *American Sociological Review,* (1937), 2:737-739.

Whyte, Martin King. *Dating, Mating, and Marriage.* New York: Aldine de Gruyter, 1990.

THE
Mating
GAME

The sophisticated sexual strategies of modern men and women are shaped by a powerful Stone Age psychology.

It's a dance as old as the human race. At cocktail lounges and church socials, during office coffee breaks and dinner parties—and most blatantly, perhaps, in the personal ads in newspapers and magazines—men and women perform the elaborate ritual of advertisement and assessment that precedes an essential part of nearly every life: mating. More than 90 percent of the world's people marry at some point in their lives, and it is estimated that a similarly large number of people engage in affairs, liaisons, flings or one-night stands. The who, what, when and where of love, sex and romance are a cultural obsession that is reflected in everything from Shakespeare to soap operas and from Tristram and Isolde to 2 Live Crew, fueling archetypes like the coy ingénue, the rakish cad, the trophy bride, Mrs. Robinson, Casanova and lovers both star-crossed and blessed.

It all may seem very modern, but a new group of researchers argues that love, American style, is in fact part of a universal human behavior with roots stretching back to the dawn of humankind. These scientists contend that, in stark contrast to the old image of brute cavemen dragging their mates by the hair to their dens, our ancient ancestors—men and women alike—engaged in a sophisticated mating dance of sexual intrigue, shrewd strategizing and savvy negotiating that has left its stamp on human psychology. People may live in a thoroughly modern world, these researchers say, but within the human skull is a Stone Age mind that was shaped by the mating concerns of our ancient ancestors and continues to have a profound influence on behavior today. Indeed, this ancient psychological legacy

HOW WE CHOOSE

Women are more concerned about whether mates will invest time and resources in a relationship; men care more about a woman's physical attractiveness, which in ancient times reflected her fertility and health.

influences everything from sexual attraction to infidelity and jealousy—and, as remarkable new research reveals, even extends its reach all the way down to the microscopic level of egg and sperm.

These new researchers call themselves evolutionary psychologists. In a host of recent scientific papers and at a major conference last month at the London School of Economics, they are arguing that the key to understanding modern sexual behavior lies not solely in culture, as some anthropologists contend, nor purely in the genes, as some sociobiologists believe. Rather, they argue, understanding human nature is possible only if scientists begin to understand the evolution of the human mind. Just as humans have evolved

specialized biological organs to deal with the intricacies of sex, they say, the mind, too, has evolved customized mental mechanisms for coping with this most fundamental aspect of human existence.

Gender and mind. When it comes to sexuality and mating, evolutionary psychologists say, men and women often are as different psychologically as they are physically. Scientists have long known that people typically choose mates who closely resemble themselves in terms of weight, height, intelligence and even earlobe length. But a survey of more than 10,000 people in 37 cultures on six continents, conducted by University of Michigan psychologist David Buss, reveals that men consistently value physical attractiveness and youth in a mate more than women do; women, equally as consistently, are more concerned than men with a prospective mate's ambition, status and resources. If such preferences were merely arbitrary products of culture, says Buss, one might expect to find at least one society somewhere where men's and women's mating preferences were reversed; the fact that attitudes are uniform across cultures suggests they are a fundamental part of human psychology.

Evolutionary psychologists think many of these mating preferences evolved in response to the different biological challenges faced by men and women in producing children—the definition of success in evolutionary terms. In a seminal paper, evolutionary biologist Robert Trivers of the University of California at Santa Cruz points out that in most mammals, females invest far

 From *U.S. News & World Report*, July 19, 1993, pp. 57-63.

more time and energy in reproduction and child rearing than do males. Not only must females go through a long gestation and weaning of their offspring, but childbirth itself is relatively dangerous. Males, on the other hand, potentially can get away with a very small biological investment in a child.

Human infants require the greatest amount of care and nurturing of any animal on Earth, and so over the eons women have evolved a psychology that is particularly concerned with a father's ability to help out with this enormous task—with his clout, protection and access to resources. So powerful is this psychological legacy that nowadays women size up a man's finances even when, as a practical matter, they may not have to. A recent study of the mating preferences of a group of medical students, for instance, found that these women, though anticipating financial success, were nevertheless most interested in men whose earning capacity was equal to or greater than their own.

Healthy genes. For men, on the other hand, reproductive success is ultimately dependent on the fertility of their mates. Thus males have evolved a mind-set that homes in on signs of a woman's health and youth, signs that, in the absence of medical records and birth certificates long ago, were primarily visual. Modern man's sense of feminine beauty—clear skin, bright eyes and youthful appearance—is, in effect, the legacy of eons spent diagnosing the health and fertility of potential mates.

This concern with women's reproductive health also helps explain why men value curvaceous figures. An upcoming paper by Devendra Singh of the University of Texas at Austin reveals that people consistently judge a woman's figure not by whether she is slim or fat but by the ratio of waist to hips. The ideal proportion—the hips roughly a third larger than the waist—reflects a hormonal balance that results in women's preferentially storing fat on their hips as opposed to their waists, a condition that correlates with higher fertility and resistance to disease. Western society's modern-day obsession with being slim has not changed this equation. Singh found, for instance, that while the winning Miss America has become 30 percent thinner over the past several decades, her waist-to-hip ratio has remained close to this ancient ideal.

Women also appreciate a fair face and figure, of course. And what they look for in a male's physique can also be explained as an evolved mentality that links good looks with good genes. A number of studies have shown that both men and women rate as most attractive

— WHOM WE MARRY —

more than 90 percent of all people marry and, they typically choose mates who closely resemble themselves, from weight and height, to intelligence and values, to nose breadth and even earlobe length.

faces that are near the average; this is true in societies as diverse as those of Brazil, Russia and several hunting and gathering tribes. The average face tends to be more symmetrical, and, according to psychologist Steven Gangestad and biologist Randy Thornhill, both of the University of New Mexico, this symmetry may reflect a person's genetic resistance to disease.

People have two versions of each of their genes—one from each parent—within every cell. Sometimes the copies are slightly different, though typically each version works just as effectively. The advantage to having two slightly different copies of the same gene, the researchers argue, is that it is harder for a disease to knock out the function of both copies, and this biological redundancy is reflected in the symmetry in people's bodies, including their faces. Further evidence for a psychological mechanism that links attractiveness with health comes from Buss's worldwide study of mating preferences: In those parts of the world where the incidence of parasites and infectious diseases is highest, both men and women place a greater value on attractive mates.

Some feminists reject the notion that women should alter physical appearance to gain advantage in the mating game. But archaeological finds suggest that the "beauty myth" has been very much a part of the human mating psychology since the times of our ancient ancestors—and that it applies equally to men. Some of the very first signs of human artistry are carved body ornaments that date back more than 30,000 years, and findings of worn nubs of ochre suggest that ancient humans may have used the red and black chalklike

substance as makeup. These artifacts probably served as social signs that, like lipstick or a Rolex watch today, advertised a person's physical appearance and status. In one grave dating back some 20,000 years, a male skeleton was found bedecked with a tunic made from thousands of tiny ivory beads—the Stone Age equivalent of an Armani suit.

Far from being immutable, biological mandates, these evolved mating mechanisms in the mind are flexible, culturally influenced aspects of human psychology that are similar to people's tastes for certain kinds of food. The human sweet tooth is a legacy from a time when the only sweet things in the environment were nutritious ripe fruit and honey, says Buss, whose book "The Evolution of Desire" is due out next year. Today, this ancient taste for sweets is susceptible to modern-day temptation by candy bars and such, though people have the free will to refrain from indulging it. Likewise, the mind's mating mechanisms can be strongly swayed by cultural influences such as religious and moral beliefs.

Playing the field. Both men and women display different mating psychologies when they are just playing around as opposed to searching for a lifelong partner, and these mental mechanisms are also a legacy from ancient times. A new survey by Buss and his colleague David Schmitt found that when women are looking for "short term" mates, their preference for attractive men increases substantially. In a study released last month, Doug Kenrick and Gary Groth of Arizona State University found that while men, too, desire attractive mates when they're playing the field, they will actually settle for a lot less.

Men's diminished concern about beauty in short-term mates reflects the fact that throughout human evolution, men have often pursued a dual mating strategy. The most successful strategy for most men was to find a healthy, fertile, long-term mate. But it also didn't hurt to take advantage of any low-risk opportunity to sire as many kin as possible outside the relationship, just to hedge the evolutionary bet. The result is an evolved psychology that allows a man to be sexually excited by a wide variety of women even while committed to a partner. This predilection shows up in studies of men's and women's sexual fantasies today. A study by Don Symons of the University of California at Santa Barbara and Bruce Ellis of the University of Michigan found that while both men and women actively engage in sexual fantasy, men typically have more fantasies about anonymous partners.

Surveys in the United States show

that at least 30 percent of married women have extramarital affairs, suggesting that, like men, women also harbor a drive for short-term mating. But they have different evolutionary reasons for doing so. Throughout human existence, short-term flings have offered women an opportunity to exchange sex for resources. In Buss and Schmitt's study, women value an "extravagant lifestyle" three times more highly when they are searching for a brief affair than when they are seeking a long-term mate. Women who are secure in a relationship with a committed male might still seek out attractive men to secure healthier genes for their offspring. Outside affairs also allow women to shop for better partners.

Sperm warfare. A woman may engage the sexual interest of several men simultaneously in order to foster a microscopic battle known as sperm competition. Sperm can survive in a woman's reproductive tract for nearly a week, note biologists Robin Baker and Mark Bellis of the University of Manchester, and by mating with more than one man within a short period of time, a woman sets the stage for their sperm to com-

---

JEALOUS PSYCHE

Men are most disturbed by sexual infidelity in their mates, a result of uncertainty about paternity. Women are more disturbed by emotional infidelity, because they risk losing their mate's time and resources.

---

pete to sire a child—passing this winning trait on to her male offspring as well. In a confidential survey tracking the sexual behavior and menstrual cycles of more than 2,000 women who

said they had steady mates, Baker and Bellis found that while there was no pattern to when women had sex with their steady partners, having sex on the side peaked at the height of the women's monthly fertility cycles.

Since in ancient times a man paid a dear evolutionary price for being cuckolded, the male psychology produces a physiological counterstrategy for dealing with a woman's infidelity. Studying the sexual behavior of a group of couples, Baker and Bellis found that the more time a couple spend apart, the more sperm the man ejaculates upon their sexual reunion—as much as three times higher than average.

This increase in sperm count is unrelated to when the man last ejaculated through nocturnal emission or masturbation, and Baker and Bellis argue that it is a result of a man's evolved psychological mechanism that bolsters his chances in sperm competition in the event that his mate has been unfaithful during their separation. As was no doubt the case in the times of our ancient ancestors, these concerns are not unfounded: Studies of blood typings show that as many as 1 of every 10 babies born to couples in North America is not the offspring of the mother's husband.

Despite men's efforts at sexual subterfuge, women still have the last word on the fate of a man's sperm in her reproductive tract—thanks to the physiological effects of the female orgasm. In a new study, Baker and Bellis reveal that if a woman experiences an orgasm soon after her mate's, the amount of sperm retained in her reproductive tract is far higher than if she has an earlier orgasm or none at all. Apparently a woman's arousal, fueled by her feelings as well as her mate's solicitous attentions, results in an evolutionary payoff for both.

Cads and dads. Whether people pursue committed relationships or one-night stands depends on their perceptions of what kind of mates are in the surrounding sexual environment. Anthropologist Elizabeth Cashdan of the University of Utah surveyed hundreds of men and women on whether they thought the members of their "pool" of potential mates were in general trustworthy, honest and capable of commitment. She also asked them what kinds of tactics they used to attract mates. Cashdan found that the less committed people thought their potential mates would be, the more they themselves pursued short-term mating tactics. For example, if women considered their world to be full of "cads," they tended to dress more provocatively and to be more promiscuous; if they thought that the world was populated

---

BEAUTY QUEST

---

the most attractive men and women are in fact those whose faces are most average, a signal that they are near the genetic average of the population and are perhaps more resistant to disease.

---

by potential "dads"—that is, committed and nurturing men—they tended to emphasize their chastity and fidelity. Similarly, "cads" tended to emphasize their sexuality and "dads" said they relied more on advertising their resources and desire for long-term commitment.

These perceptions of what to expect from the opposite sex may be influenced by the kind of home life an individual knew as a child. Social scientists have long known that children from homes where the father is chronically absent or abusive tend to mature faster physically and to have sexual relations earlier in life. Psychologist Jay Belsky of Pennsylvania State University argues that this behavior is an evolved psychological mechanism, triggered by early childhood experiences, that enables a child to come of age earlier and leave the distressing situation. This psychological mechanism may also lead to a mating strategy that focuses on short-term affairs.

The green monster. Whether in modern or ancient times, infidelities can breed anger and hurt, and new research suggests subtle differences in male and female jealousy with roots in the ancient past. In one study, for example, Buss asked males and females to imagine that their mates were having sex with someone else or that their mates were engaged in a deep emotional commitment with another person. Monitoring his subjects' heart rates, frowning and stress responses, he found that the stereotypical double standard cuts both ways. Men reacted far more strongly than

EVOLVED FANTASIES
Eroticism and gender

For insights into the subtle differences between men's and women's mating psychologies, one need look no further than the local bookstore. On one rack may be magazines featuring scantily clad women in poses of sexual invitation — a testimony to the ancient legacy of a male psychology that is acutely attuned to visual stimulus and easily aroused by the prospect of anonymous sex. Around the corner is likely to be a staple of women's erotic fantasy: romance novels.

Harlequin Enterprises Ltd., the leading publisher in the field, sells more than 200 million books annually and produces about 70 titles a month. Dedicated romance fans may read several books a week. "Our books give women everything," says Harlequin's Kathleen Abels, "a loving relationship, commitment and having sex with someone they care about." Some romance novels contain scenes steamy enough to make a sailor blush, and studies show that women who read romances typically have more sexual fantasies and engage in sexual intercourse more frequently than nonreaders do.

Sexual caricature. Since sexual fantasy frees people of the complications of love and mating in the real world, argue psychologists Bruce Ellis and Don Symons, it is perhaps not surprising that in erotic materials for both men and women, sexual partners are typically caricatures of the consumer's own evolved mating psychology. In male-oriented erotica, for instance, women are depicted as being lust driven, ever willing and unencumbered by the need for emotional attachment. In romance novels, the male lead in the book is typically tender, emotional and consumed by passion for the heroine, thus ensuring his lifelong fidelity and dependence. In other words, say Ellis and Symons, the romance novel is "an erotic, utopian, female counterfantasy" to male erotica.

Of course, most men also enjoy stories of passion and romance, and women can be as easily aroused as men by sexually explicit films. Indeed, several new entertainment ventures, including the magazine *Future Sex* and a video company, Femme Productions, are creating erotic materials using realistic models in more sensual settings in an attempt to appeal to both sexes. Still, the new research into evolutionary psychology suggests that men and women derive subtly different pleasures from sexual fantasy — something that even writing under a ghost name can't hide. According to Abels, a Harlequin romance is occasionally penned by a man using a female pseudonym, but "our avid readers can always tell."

---

women to the idea that their mates were having sex with other men. But women reacted far more strongly to the thought that their mates were developing strong emotional attachments to someone else.

As with our evolved mating preferences, these triggers for jealousy ultimately stem from men's and women's biology, says Buss. A woman, of course, has no doubt that she is the mother of her children. For a man, however, paternity is never more than conjecture, and so men have evolved psychologies with a heightened concern about a mate's sexual infidelity. Since women make the greater biological investment in offspring, their psychologies are more concerned about a mate's reneging on his commitment, and, therefore, they are more attentive to signs that their mates might be attaching themselves emotionally to other women.

Sexual monopoly. The male preoccupation with monopolizing a woman's sexual reproduction has led to the oppression and abuse of women worldwide, including, at its extremes, confinement, domestic violence and ritual mutilation such as clitoridectomy. Yet the new research into the mating game also reveals that throughout human evolution, women have not passively acquiesced to men's sexual wishes. Rath-

DUELING SPERM

If a couple has been apart for some time, the man's sperm count goes up during sex at their reunion — an ancient, evolved strategy against a female's possible infidelities while away.

---

er, they have long employed a host of behavioral and biological tactics to follow their own sexual agenda — behaviors that have a huge impact on men's behavior as well. As Buss points out, if all women suddenly began preferring to have sex with men who walked on their hands, in a very short time half the human race would be upside down.

With its emphasis on how both men and women are active players in the mating game, evolutionary psychology holds out the promise of helping negotiate a truce of sorts in the battle of the sexes — not by declaring a winner but by pointing out that the essence of the mating game is compromise, not victory. The exhortations of radical feminists, dyed-in-the-wool chauvinists and everyone in between are all spices for a sexual stew that has been on a slow boil for millions of years. It is no accident that consistently, the top two mating preferences in Buss's survey — expressed equally by males and females worldwide — were not great looks, fame, youth, wealth or status, but *kindness* and *intelligence*. In the rough-and-tumble of the human mating game, they are love's greatest allies.

WILLIAM F. ALLMAN

PSYCHOTRENDS

Taking Stock of Tomorrow's Family and Sexuality

Where are we going and what kind of people are we becoming? Herewith, a road map to the defining trends in sexuality, family, and relationships for the coming millenium as charted by the former chair of Harvard's psychiatry department. From the still-rollicking sexual revolution to the painful battle for sexual equality to the reorganization of the family, America is in for some rather interesting times ahead.

Shervert H. Frazier, M.D.

Has the sexual revolution been sidetracked by AIDS, and the return to traditional values we keep hearing about? In a word, no. The forces that originally fueled the revolution are all still in place and, if anything, are intensifying: mobility, democratization, urbanization, women in the workplace, birth control, abortion and other reproductive interventions, and media proliferation of sexual images, ideas, and variation.

Sexuality has moved for many citizens from church- and state-regulated behavior to a medical and self-regulated behavior. Population pressures and other economic factors continue to diminish the size of the American family. Marriage is in sharp decline, cohabitation is growing, traditional families are on the endangered list, and the single-person household is a wave of the future.

AIDS has generated a great deal of heat in the media but appears to have done little, so far, to turn down the heat in the bedroom. It is true that in some surveys people *claimed* to have made drastic changes in behavior— but most telling are the statistics relating to marriage, divorce, cohabitation, teen sex, out-of-wedlock births, sexually transmitted diseases (STDs), contraception,

and adultery. These are far more revealing of what we *do* than what we *say* we do. And those tell a tale of what has been called a "postmarital society" in continued pursuit of sexual individuality and freedom.

Studies reveal women are more sexual now than at any time in the century.

Arguably there are, due to AIDS, fewer visible sexual "excesses" today than there were in the late 1960s and into the 1970s, but those excesses (such as sex clubs, bathhouses, backrooms, swinging singles, group sex, public sex acts, etc.) were never truly reflective of norms and were, in any case, greatly inflated in the media. Meanwhile, quietly and without fanfare, the public, even in the face of the AIDS threat, has continued to expand its interest in sex and in *increased,* rather than decreased, sexual expression.

Numerous studies reveal that women are more sexual now than at any time in the century. Whereas sex counselors used to deal with men's complaints about their wives' lack of "receptivity," it is now more often the women complaining about the men. And women, in this "postfeminist"

era, are doing things they never used to believe were "proper." Fellatio, for example, was seldom practiced (or admitted to) when Kinsey conducted his famous sex research several decades ago. Since that time, according to studies at UCLA and elsewhere, this activity has gained acceptance among women, with some researchers reporting that nearly all young women now practice fellatio.

Women's images of themselves have also changed dramatically in the past two decades, due, in large part, to their movement into the workplace and roles previously filled exclusively by men. As Lilian Rubin, psychologist at the University of California Institute for the Study of Social Change and author of *Intimate Strangers,* puts it, "Women feel empowered sexually in a way they never did in the past."

Meanwhile, the singles scene, far from fading away (the media just lost its fixation on this subject), continues to grow. James Bennett, writing in *The New Republic,* characterizes this growing population of no-reproducers thusly: "Single adults in America display a remarkable tendency to multiply without being fruitful."

Their libidos are the target of million-dollar advertising budgets and entrepreneurial pursuits that seek to put those sex drives on line in the information age. From video dating to computer coupling to erotic faxing, it's now "love at first

From *Psychology Today,* January/February 1994, pp. 32-37, 64, 66. Excerpted from *Psychotrends: What Kind of People Are We Becoming?* by Shervert H. Frazier, M.D. © 1994 by Shervert H. Frazier, M.D. Reprinted by permission of Simon & Schuster, Inc.

byte," as one commentator put it. One thing is certain: the computer is doing as much today to promote the sexual revolution as the automobile did at the dawn of that revolution.

Political ideologies, buttressed by economic adversities, *can* temporarily retard the sexual revolution, as can sexually transmitted diseases. But ultimately the forces propelling this revolution are unstoppable. And ironically, AIDS itself is probably doing more to promote than impede this movement. It has forced the nation to confront a number of sexual issues with greater frankness than ever before. While some conservatives and many religious groups have argued for abstinence as the only moral response to AIDS, others have lobbied for wider dissemination of sexual information, beginning in grade schools. A number of school districts are now making condoms available to students—a development that would have been unthinkable before the outbreak of AIDS.

Despite all these gains (or losses, depending upon your outlook) the revolution is far from over. The openness that it has fostered is healthy, but Americans are still ignorant about many aspects of human sexuality. Sexual research is needed to help us deal with teen sexuality and pregnancies, AIDS, and a number of emotional issues related to sexuality. Suffice it to say for now that there is still plenty of room for the sexual revolution to proceed—and its greatest benefits have yet to be realized.

THE REVOLUTION AND RELATIONSHIPS

The idea that the Sexual Revolution is at odds with romance (not to mention tradition) is one that is widely held, even by some of those who endorse many of the revolution's apparent objectives. But there is nothing in our findings to indicate that romance and the sexual revolution are inimical—unless one's defense of romance disguises an agenda of traditional male dominance and the courtly illusion of intimacy and communication between the sexes.

The trend now, as we shall see, is away from illusion and toward—in transition, at least—a sometimes painful reality in which the sexes are finally making an honest effort to *understand* one another.

But to some, it may seem that the sexes are farther apart today than they

ever have been. The real gender gap, they say, is a communications gap so cavernous that only the most intrepid or foolhardy dare try to bridge it. Many look back at the Anita Hill affair and say that was the open declaration of war between the sexes.

The mistake many make, however, is saying that there has been a *recent* breakdown in those communications, hence all this new discontent. This conclusion usually goes unchallenged, but there is nothing in the data we have seen from past decades to indicate that sexual- and gender-related communication were ever better than they are today. On the contrary, a more thoughtful analysis makes it very clear they have always been *worse.*

What has changed is our *consciousness* about this issue. Problems in communication between the sexes have been masked for decades by a rigid social code that strictly prescribes other behavior. Communication between the sexes has long been preprogrammed by this code to produce an exchange that has been as superficial as it is oppressive. As this process begins to be exposed by its own inadequacies in a rapidly changing world, we suddenly discover that we have a problem. But, of course, that problem was there for a long time, and the discovery does not mean a decline in communication between the sexes but, rather, provides us with the potential for better relationships in the long run.

Thus what we call a "breakdown" in communications might more aptly be called a *breakthrough.*

Seymour Parker, of the University of Utah, demonstrated that men who are the most mannerly with women, those who adhere most strictly to the "code" discussed above, are those who most firmly believe, consciously or unconsciously, that women are "both physically and psychologically weaker (i.e., less capable) than men." What has long passed for male "respect" toward women in our society is, arguably, *disrespect.*

Yet what has been learned can be unlearned—especially if women force the issue, which is precisely what is happening now. Women's views of themselves are changing and that, more than anything, is working to eliminate many of the stereotypes that supported the image of women as weak and inferior. Women, far from letting men continue to dictate to them, are making it clear they want more *real* respect from men and will accept

nothing less. They want a genuine dialogue; they want men to recognize that they speak with a distinct and equal voice, not one that is merely ancillary to the male voice.

The sexual revolution made possible a serious inquiry into the ways that men and women are alike and the ways that each is unique. This revolutionary development promises to narrow the gender gap as nothing else can, for only by understanding the differences that make communication so complex do we stand any chance of mastering those complexities.

SUBTRENDS

Greater Equality Between the Sexes

Despite talk in the late 1980s and early 1990s of the decline of feminism and declarations that women, as a social and political force, are waning, equality between the sexes is closer to becoming a reality than ever before. Women command a greater workforce and wield greater political power than they have ever done. They are assuming positions in both public and private sectors that their mothers and grandmothers believed were unattainable (and their fathers and grandfathers thought were inappropriate) for women. Nonetheless, much remains to be achieved before women attain complete equality—but movement in that direction will continue at a pace that will surprise many over the next two decades.

Women voters, for example, who have long outnumbered male voters, are collectively a sleeping giant whose slumber many say was abruptly interrupted during the Clarence Thomas–Anita Hill hearings in 1991. The spectacle of a political "boy's club" raking the dignified Hill over the coals of sexual harassment galvanized the entire nation for days.

On another front, even though women have a long way to go to match men in terms of equal pay for equal work, as well as in equal opportunity, there is a definite *research* trend that shows women can match men in the skills needed to succeed in business. This growing body of data will make it more difficult for businesses to check the rise of women into the upper echelons of management and gradually help to change the corporate consciousness that still heavily favors male employees.

As for feminism, many a conservative wrote its obituary in the 1980s, only to find it risen from the dead in the 1990s. Actually, its demise was always imaginary. Movements make headway only in a context of dissatisfaction. And, clearly, there is still plenty for women to be dissatisfied about, particularly in the wake of a decade that tried to stifle meaningful change.

The "new feminism," as some call it, is less doctrinaire than the old, less extreme in the sense that it no longer has to be outrageous in order to call attention to itself. The movement today is less introspective, more goal oriented and pragmatic. Demands for liberation are superseded—and subsumed—by a well-organized quest for power. Women no longer want to burn bras, they want to manufacture and market them.

The New Masculinity

To say that the men's movement today is confused is to understate mercifully. Many men say they want to be more "sensitive" but also "less emasculated," "more open," yet "less vulnerable." While the early flux of this movement is often so extreme that it cannot but evoke guffaws, there is, nonetheless, something in it that commands some respect—for, in contrast with earlier generations of males, this one is making a real effort to examine and redefine itself. The movement, in a word, is *real*.

Innumerable studies and surveys find men dissatisfied with themselves and their roles in society. Part of this, undoubtedly, is the result of the displacement men are experiencing in a culture where *women* are so successfully transforming themselves. There is evidence, too, that men are dissatisfied because their own fathers were so unsuccessful in their emotional lives and were thus unable to impart to their sons a sense of love, belonging, and security that an increasing number of men say they sorely miss.

The trend has nothing to do with beating drums or becoming a "warrior." It relates to the human desire for connection, and this, in the long run, can only bode well for communications between humans in general and between the sexes in particular. Many psychologists believe men, in the next two decades, will be less emotionally closed than at any time in American history.

More (and Better) Senior Sex

People used to talk about sex after 40 as if it were some kind of novelty. Now it's sex after 60 and it's considered not only commonplace but healthy.

Some fear that expectations among the aged may outrun physiological ability and that exaggerated hopes, in some cases, will lead to new frustrations—or that improved health into old age will put pressure on seniors to remain sexually active beyond any "decent" desire to do so.

But most seem to welcome the trend toward extended sexuality. In fact, the desire for sex in later decades of life is *heightened,* studies suggest, by society's growing awareness and acceptance of sexual activity in later life.

Diversity of Sexual Expression

As sex shifts from its traditional reproductive role to one that is psychological, it increasingly serves the needs of the individual. In this context, forms of sexual expression that were previously proscribed are now tolerated and are, in some cases increasingly viewed as no more nor less healthy than long-accepted forms of sexual behavior. Homosexuality, for example, has attained a level of acceptance unprecedented in our national history.

More Contraception, Less Abortion

Though abortion will remain legal under varying conditions in most, if not all, states, its use will continue to decline over the next two decades as more—and better-contraceptives become available. After a period of more than two decades in which drug companies shied away from contraceptive research, interest in this field is again growing. AIDS, a changed political climate, and renewed fears about the population explosion are all contributing to this change.

Additionally, scientific advances now point the way to safer, more effective, more convenient contraceptives. A male contraceptive that will be relatively side-effect free is finally within reach and should be achieved within the next decade, certainly the next two decades. Even more revolutionary in concept and probable impact is a vaccine, already tested in animals, that some predict will be available within 10 years—a vaccine that safely stops ovum maturation and thus makes conception impossible.

Religion and Sex: A More Forgiving Attitude

Just a couple of decades ago mainstream religion was monolithic in its condemnation of sex outside of marriage. Today the situation is quite different as major denominations across the land struggle with issues they previously wouldn't have touched, issues related to

adultery, premarital sex, homosexuality, and so on.

A Special Committee on Human Sexuality, convened by the General Assembly of the Presbyterian Church (USA), for example, surprised many when it issued a report highly critical of the traditional "patriarchal structure of sexual relations," a structure the committee believes contributes, because of its repressiveness, to the proliferation of pornography and sexual violence.

All this will surely pale alongside the brave new world of virtual reality.

The same sort of thing has been happening in most other major denominations. It is safe to say that major changes are coming. Mainstream religion is beginning to perceive that the sexual revolution must be acknowledged and, to a significant degree, accommodated with new policies if these denominations are to remain in touch with present-day realities.

Expanding Sexual Entertainment

The use of sex to sell products, as well as to entertain, is increasing and can be expected to do so. The concept that "sex sells" is so well established that we need not belabor the point here. The explicitness of sexual advertising, however, may be curbed by recent research finding that highly explicit sexual content is so diverting that the viewer or reader tends to overlook the product entirely.

Sexual stereotyping will also be less prevalent in advertising in years to come. All this means, however, is that women will not be singled out as sex objects; they'll have plenty of male company, as is already the case. The female "bimbo" is now joined by the male "himbo" in ever-increasing numbers. Sexist advertising is still prevalent (e.g., male-oriented beer commercials) but should diminish as women gain in social and political power.

There's no doubt that films and TV have become more sexually permissive in the last two decades and are likely to continue in that direction for some time to come. But all this will surely pale alongside the brave (or brazen) new world of "cybersex" and virtual reality, the first erotic emanations of which may well be experienced by Americans in the coming two decades. Virtual reality aims to be just that—artificial, electronically induced experiences that are virtually indistinguishable from the real thing.

The sexual revolution, far from over, is in for some new, high-tech curves.

FROM BIOLOGY TO PSYCHOLOGY: THE NEW FAMILY OF THE MIND

Despite recent pronouncements that the traditional family is making a comeback, the evidence suggests that over the next two decades the nuclear family will share the same future as nuclear arms: there will be fewer of them, but those that remain will be better cared for.

Our longing for sources of nurturance has led us to redefine the family.

Demographers now believe that the number of families consisting of married couples with children will dwindle by yet another 12 percent by the year 2000. Meanwhile, single-parent households will continue to increase (up 41 percent over the past decade.) And household size will continue to decline (2.63 people in 1990 versus 3.14 in 1970). The number of households maintained by women, with no males present, has increased 300 percent since 1950 and will continue to rise into the 21st century.

Particularly alarming to some is the fact that an increasing number of people are choosing *never* to marry. And, throughout the developed world, the one-person household is now the fastest growing household category. To the traditionalists, this trend seems insidious—more than 25 percent of all households in the United States now consist of just one person.

There can be no doubt: the nuclear family has been vastly diminished, and it will continue to decline for some years, but at a more gradual pace. Indeed, there is a good chance that it will enjoy more stability in the next two decades than it did in the last two. Many of the very forces that were said to be weakening the traditional family may now make it stronger, though not more prevalent. Developing social changes have made traditional marriage more elective today, so that those who choose it may, increasingly, some psychologists believe, represent a subpopulation better suited to the situation and thus more likely to make a go of it.

As we try to understand new forms of family, we need to realize that the "traditional" family is not particularly traditional. Neither is it necessarily the healthiest form of family. The nuclear family has existed for only a brief moment in human history. Moreover, most people don't realize that no sooner had the nuclear family form peaked around the turn of the last century than erosion set in, which has continued ever since. For the past hundred years, reality has chipped away at this social icon, with increasing divorce and the movement of more women into the labor force. Yet our need for nurturance, security, and connectedness continues and, if anything, grows more acute as our illusions about the traditional family dissipate.

Our longing for more satisfying sources of nurturance has led us to virtually redefine the family, in terms of behavior, language, and law. These dramatic changes will intensify over the next two decades. The politics of family will be entirely transformed in that period. The process will not be without interruptions or setbacks. Some lower-court rulings may be overturned by a conservative U.S. Supreme Court, the traditional family will be revived in the headline from time to time, but the economic and psychological forces that for decades have been shaping these changes toward a more diverse family will continue to do so.

SUBTRENDS

Deceptively Declining Divorce Rate

The "good news" is largely illusory. Our prodigious national divorce rate, which more than doubled in one recent 10-year period, now shows signs of stabilization or even decline. Still, 50 percent of all marriages will break up in the next several years. And the leveling of the divorce rate is not due to stronger marriage but to *less* marriage. More people are skipping marriage altogether and are cohabiting instead.

The slight dip in the divorce rate in recent years has caused some prognosticators to predict that younger people, particularly those who've experienced the pain of growing up in broken homes, are increasingly committed to making marriage stick. Others, more persuasively, predict the opposite, that the present lull precedes a storm in which the divorce rate will soar to 60 percent or higher.

Increasing Cohabitation

The rate of cohabitation—living together without legal marriage—has been growing since 1970 and will accelerate in the next two decades. There were under half a million cohabiting couples in 1970; today there are more than 2.5. The trend for the postindustrial world is very clear: less marriage, more cohabitation, easier and—if Sweden is any indication—less stressful separation. Those who divorce will be less likely to remarry, more likely to cohabit. And in the United States, cohabitation will increasingly gather about it both the cultural acceptance and the legal protection now afforded marriage.

We need to realize the "traditional family" is not particularly traditional.

More Single-Parent Families and Planned Single Parenthood

The United States has one of the highest proportions of children growing up in single-parent families. More than one in five births in the United States is outside of marriage—and three quarters of those births are to women who are not in consensual unions.

What is significant about the single-parent trend is the finding that many single women with children now *prefer* to remain single. The rush to the altar of unwed mothers, so much a part of American life in earlier decades, is now, if anything, a slow and grudging shuffle. The stigma of single parenthood is largely a thing of the past—and the economic realities, unsatisfactory though they are, sometimes favor single parenthood. In any case, women have more choices today than they had even 10 years ago; they are choosing the psychological freedom of single parenthood over the financial security (increasingly illusory, in any event) of marriage.

More Couples Childless by Choice

In the topsy-turvy 1990s, with more single people wanting children, it shouldn't surprise us that more married couples *don't* want children. What the trend really comes down to is increased freedom of choice. One reason for increasing childlessness among couples has to do with the aging of the population, but many of the reasons are more purely psychological.

With a strong trend toward later marriage, many couples feel they are "too old" to have children. Others admit they like the economic advantages and relative freedom of being childless. Often both have careers they do not want to jeopardize by having children. In addition, a growing number of couples cite the need for lower population density, crime rates, and environmental concerns as reasons for not wanting children. The old idea that "there must be something wrong with them" if a couple does not reproduce is fast waning.

The One-Person Household

This is the fastest growing household category in the Western world. It has grown in the United States from about 10 percent in the 1950s to more than 25 percent of all households today. This is a trend that still has a long way to go. In Sweden, nearly *40 percent* of all households are now single person.

"Mr. Mom" a Reality at Last?

When women began pouring into the work force in the late 1970s, expectations were high that a real equality of the sexes was at hand and that men, at last, would begin to shoulder more of the household duties, including spending more time at home taking care of the kids. Many women now regard the concept of "Mr. Mom" as a cruel hoax; but, in fact, Mr. Mom *is* slowly emerging.

Men *are* showing more interest in the home and in parenting. Surveys make clear there is a continuing trend in that direction. Granted, part of the impetus for this is not so much a love of domestic work as it is a distaste for work outside the home. But there is also, among many men, a genuine desire to play a larger role in the lives of their children. These men say they feel "cheated" by having to work outside the home so much, cheated of the experience of seeing their children grow up.

As the trend toward more equal pay for women creeps along, gender roles in the home can be expected to undergo further change. Men will feel less pressure to take on more work and will feel more freedom to spend increased time with their families.

More Interracial Families

There are now about 600,000 interracial marriages annually in the United States, a third of these are black-white, nearly triple the number in 1970, when 40 percent of the white population was of the opinion that such marriages should be illegal. Today 20 percent hold that belief. There is every reason to expect that both the acceptance of and the number of interracial unions will continue to increase into the foreseeable future.

Recognition of Same-Sex Families

Family formation by gay and lesbian couples, with or without children, is often referenced by the media as a leading-edge signifier of just how far society has moved in the direction of diversity and individual choice in the family realm. The number of same-sex couples has steadily increased and now stands at 1.6 million such couples. There are an estimated 2 million gay parents in the United States.

And while most of these children were had in heterosexual relationships or marriages prior to "coming out," a significant number of gay and lesbian couples are having children through adoption, cooperative parenting arrangements, and artificial insemination. Within the next two decades, gays and lesbians will not only win the right to marry but will, like newly arrived immigrants, be some of the strongest proponents of traditional family values.

The Rise of Fictive Kinships

Multiadult households, typically consisting of unrelated singles, have been increasing in number for some years and are expected to continue to do so in coming years. For many, "roommates" are increasingly permanent fixtures in daily life.

In fact housemates are becoming what some sociologists and psychologists call "fictive kin." Whole "fictive families" are being generated in many of these situations, with some housemates even assigning roles ("brother," "sister," "cousin," "aunt," "mom," "dad," and so on) to one another. Fictive families are springing up among young people, old people, disabled people, homeless people, and may well define one of the ultimate evolutions of the family concept, maximizing, as they do, the opportunities for fulfillment of specific social and economic needs outside the constraints of biological relatedness.

THE BREAKUP OF THE NUCLEAR FAMILY

It's hard to tell how many times we've heard even well-informed health professionals blithely opine that "the breakup of the family is at the root of most of our problems." The *facts* disagree with this conclusion. Most of the social problems attributed to the dissolution of the "traditional" family (which, in reality, is *not* so traditional) are the product of other forces. Indeed, as we have seen, the nuclear family has itself created a number of economic, social, and psychological problems. To try to perpetuate a manifestly transient social institution beyond its usefulness is folly.

What *can* we do to save the nuclear family? Very little.

What *should* we do? Very little. Our concern should not be the maintenance of the nuclear family as a *moral* unit (which seems to be one of the priorities of the more ardent conservative "family values" forces), encompassing the special interests and values of a minority, but, rather, the strengthening of those social contracts that ensure the health, well-being, and freedom of individuals.

CHOOSING A CONTRACEPTIVE

What's Best for You?

Joseph Anthony

Joseph Anthony is a Contributing Editor at AMERICAN HEALTH.

If you've been frustrated by a lack of contraceptive choices, there's good news: In the last couple of years, several new forms of contraception specifically, the long-lasting, hormone-based products Depo-Provera and Norplant and the female condom have been approved for use in the U.S., which means that we're finally catching up with the rest of the world. Depo-Provera and Norplant have been in use in other countries for years. But much ballyhooed new methods, such as contraceptive "vaccines" and a male birth control pill, are still probably a decade or more away.

Why? Manufacturers worry about boycotts and other protests from the religious right and antiabortion activists. And, says Dr. Michael Policar, vice president for medical affairs at the Planned Parenthood Federation of America, "the threat of litigation has had an incredibly chilling effect on contraceptive development in the last 10 years."

What are in the pipeline are mostly variations on existing themes—a two-capsule Norplant (instead of today's six); redesigned, baggier male condoms that promise greater comfort; intrauterine devices (IUD's) that release hormones; barrier methods that release spermicides, creams or gels with anti-HIV as well as antisperm properties; and perhaps some new injectables. There has also been some movement toward making the Pill available over the counter (without a prescription), although the Food and Drug Administration (FDA) is not currently considering any formal proposals to do so.

Here's a rundown on newly available methods of birth control, followed by more-established and better-known alternatives.

THE FEMALE CONDOM: This device looks like a large, floppy tube closed at one end. Marketed by Wisconsin Pharmacal under the name Reality, the polyurethane barrier (thinner, stronger and a better conductor of heat than latex) was approved by the FDA last May. Like other barrier methods this one can take some time and patience to use correctly. The device has two rings, one around the outer rim and one inside. The inner ring is designed to fit over the cervix, anchored in place behind the pubic bone, like a diaphragm. The outer ring covers the labia and the base of the penis during intercourse. Some women have complained that the condom can rise into the vagina if not sufficiently lubricated; it can'also twist around if not inserted properly.

The one-year failure rate with "typical use" is high, estimated at 21% to 26%, which means that about one in four women using it may become pregnant over the course of a year. (The pregnancy rate for "perfect use" would be much lower—about 5%.)

DEPO-PROVERA: This injectable prescription contraceptive, first available in New Zealand in 1969 and subsequently used by 30 million women in 90 countries, was finally approved in the U.S. in late 1992. One injection of this synthetic version of the female hormone progesterone every three months blocks ovulation.

The drug, which provides no protection against sexually transmitted diseases (STD's), may cause irregular periods, and women may not regain fertility until six to 12 months after they stop taking it.

Side effects of Depo-Provera are similar to those of other hormonal contraceptives and may include weight gain, headaches and fatigue. Women usually experience some irregular bleeding or spotting during the first months of use. On the plus side, studies by the World Health Organization have found a link between Depo-Provera use and a reduced risk of cancer of the endometrium (the lining of the uterus).

NORPLANT: This implant of six thin capsules, placed under the skin of a woman's arm, releases the hormone levonorgestrel, which keeps the body from producing the hormones necessary for ovulation. Norplant is effective for up to five years.

The implant was approved after two decades of testing on more than 50,000 women. More than 900,000 American women have received Norplant since it was introduced in February of 1991 by U.S. distributor Wyeth-Ayerst Laboratories. It's not appropriate for women who have liver disease, blood clots, inflammation of the veins or a history of breast cancer, or for those who are breast-feeding in the first six weeks after delivery. Fertility returns soon after the implant is removed.

The most common side effect of Norplant is irregular menstrual bleeding during the first six months after implantation. Norplant provides no STD protection.

Wyeth-Ayerst Laboratories has been charging $365 for Norplant in the U.S. (With doctor's fees, Norplant generally costs between $500 and $800.) After congressional hearings last year revealed that the drug sells for as little as $23 in other countries, the company announced that the price to public clinics would be lowered in 1995. But company officials won't comment on what the new price will be.

STERILIZATION: Every year more than 600,000 women in the U.S. have their fallopian tubes surgically blocked or severed, thus preventing eggs from reaching the uterus. About 25% of all women at risk of pregnancy (sexually active, heterosexual and fertile) aged 15 to 50 have had this procedure, called a tubal ligation; among such women 35 to 44 the number soars to more than 60%, according to the Alan Guttmacher Institute, a nonprofit group studying contraceptive issues. In addition, each year about half a million American men have vasectomies, in which the tube that carries sperm from the testes is cut and sealed. Vasectomy, which is performed under local anesthesia, carries less surgical risk than tubal ligation, which requires general anesthesia.

Both forms of sterilization are more than 99% effective and virtually permanent. (Though surgical sterilizations can sometimes be reversed—the success rate for such procedures is better for vasectomies than for tubal ligations—but anyone contemplating surgical sterilization is generally advised to consider the operation irreversible.)

ORAL CONTRACEPTIVES: Commonly known as the Pill,

oral contraceptives, which suppress ovulation, are the most popular form of birth control for women in the U.S. About 28% of American women at risk of pregnancy between 15 and 44 use oral contraceptives. Fewer than 1% of women using oral contraceptives properly will become pregnant in the course of a year.

Literally hundreds of studies over the past four decades have attempted to analyze the effect of the Pill on women's health. No solid connections between taking the Pill and getting breast cancer have been made. The Pill does appear to increase the risk of blood clots, heart attack and stroke for women over 35 who smoke. The authors of *Contraceptive Technology,* a leading reference manual in the field, characterize the risk for non-smokers and smokers under 35 as relatively minor.

While the Pill has been linked to circulatory problems in women who have high cholesterol, hypertension or any heart or vascular disease, as well as those who have a family history of heart disease, oral contraceptives also have been associated with several health *benefits.* Some studies indicate that birth control pills can actually reduce a woman's chances of developing ovarian or endometrial cancer, as well as lower her risk of pelvic inflammatory disease. Women taking the Pill also have fewer ovarian cysts and benign breast tumors than other women.

There are more than a dozen side effects attributed to the Pill, including breast tenderness, fluid retention, weight gain and headaches.

BARRIER METHODS: Condoms, diaphragms, cervical caps, sponges and spermicides all operate on the same basic principle: preventing sperm from reaching an egg. Latex condoms have the added benefit of providing the most protection against STD's, although all barrier methods, even spermicides, are thought to provide some protection when used properly.

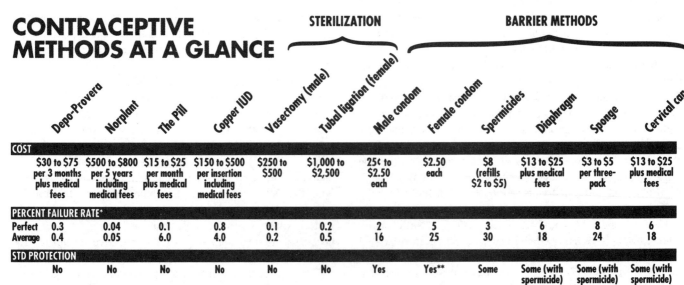

CONTRACEPTIVE METHODS AT A GLANCE

	Depo-Provera	Norplant	The Pill	Copper IUD	STERILIZATION Vasectomy (male)	STERILIZATION Tubal ligation (female)	BARRIER METHODS Male condom	BARRIER METHODS Female condom	BARRIER METHODS Spermicides	BARRIER METHODS Diaphragm	BARRIER METHODS Sponge	BARRIER METHODS Cervical cap
COST	$30 to $75 per 3 months plus medical fees	$500 to $800 per 5 years including medical fees	$15 to $25 per month plus medical fees	$150 to $500 per insertion including medical fees	$250 to $500	$1,000 to $2,500	25¢ to $2.50 each	$2.50 each	$8 (refills $2 to $5)	$13 to $25 plus medical fees	$3 to $5 per three-pack	$13 to $25 plus medical fees
PERCENT FAILURE RATE*												
Perfect	0.3	0.04	0.1	0.8	0.1	0.2	2	5	3	6	8	6
Average	0.4	0.05	6.0	4.0	0.2	0.5	16	25	30	18	24	18
STD PROTECTION	No	No	No	No	No	No	Yes	Yes**	Some	Some (with spermicide)	Some (with spermicide)	Some (with spermicide)

*Estimated percentage of women who get pregnant unintentionally in the first year of use. "Perfect use" is calculated from pregnancies occurring among couples who use the method correctly each time they have intercourse; "average use" combines perfect use figures with pregnancies occurring among couples who use the method sporadically or incorrectly.

**Although the female condom does provide protection against sexually transmitted diseases (STD's), its manufacturer is required by the Food and Drug Administration to note that for "highly effective protection" against STD's, including AIDS, it is important to use latex condoms for men.

FAILURE RATE DATA: ALAN GUTTMACHER INSTITUTE.

RU-486 and MORNING-AFTER TREATMENTS

Women who fear they may have become pregnant because they experienced condom rupture or otherwise engaged in unprotected intercourse have a little-publicized "morning-after," or postcoital, contraceptive option. Take what Dr. Felicia Stewart, director of research for the Sutter Medical Foundation in Sacramento, Calif., calls emergency contraceptive pills as soon as possible after the unprotected intercourse but no later than 72 hours afterward.

The "emergency pills" are regular birth control pills, but taken in two larger-than-usual doses (the second 12 hours after the first). The number of pills per dose depends on the brand: two Ovral, or four Lo/Ovral, Nordette, Levlen or yellow-colored Triphasil or Tri-Levlen (the yellow versions of both are the strongest formulas). By taking a larger-than-normal dose of birth control pills, you'll disrupt your body's natural hormone patterns, thereby reducing your chances of becoming pregnant by about 75%.

Obviously, the morning-after option shouldn't be looked at as a regular birth control method—it's a one-time emergency measure. And the procedure may not be suitable for women suffering from severe liver disease, blood clots or other circulation problems. Up to half of all women using this approach report short-term nausea or vomiting.

The drug RU-486, which prevents a fertilized egg from implanting itself in the uterine wall, might also find a secondary use as a morning-after contraceptive if it's approved for sale in the U.S. A University of Edinburgh study published in *The New England Journal of Medicine* found that if taken within 72 hours of unprotected sexual intercourse, RU-486 also prevents pregnancy. The women surveyed in the study reported much milder side effects than those taking birth control pills as morning-after measures.

Last year RU-486 manufacturer Roussel-Uclaf announced it would grant U.S. rights to the drug to the nonprofit research organization the Population Council, which would market and test the drug. As of the beginning of this year, however, the final details of the agreement had not been ironed out.

The main side effects of barrier methods are allergies or sensitivity to latex or spermicides. (The sponge is off-limits to women who have had toxic shock syndrome.)

INTRAUTERINE DEVICES (IUD's): IUD's are placed in a woman's uterus, where they prevent pregnancy by interfering with sperm transport and egg fertilization. The Dalkon Shield gave IUD's a terrible name in this country during the 1980s. After more than 10,000 lawsuits over pelvic inflammatory disease linked to the shield, IUD's have fallen out of favor. Fewer than 2% of women in the U.S. currently use them, a fact some experts regard as unfortunate.

"Compare that to around 30% of the women in Finland who choose an IUD," says Dr. Daniel Mishell, chairman of obstetrics and gynecology at the University of Southern California School of Medicine. "The IUD is effective and is one of the least expensive forms of long-term contraception, but it is also one of the least used in the U.S. because of the perception that it is dangerous." Recent studies have shown modern copper IUD's present little, if any risk of pelvic inflammatory disease.

The only IUD's currently sold in the U.S. are the Copper T-380A, which can be used for up to eight years, and the Progestasert, which releases progesterone and can be used for up to one year.

What form of contraception is right for you? People who have new or multiple partners have to be concerned about STD's as well as pregnancy. That means they should use condoms for maximum STD protection. A survey of 678 women receiving Norplant in Texas indicated that about half who had previously used condoms intended to keep doing so at least some of the time. "Until the last few years, nobody even *asked* questions about whether women using a hormonal contraceptive like Norplant would also continue to use barrier methods like condoms," says Margaret Frank, a contraceptive researcher at the University of New Haven in Connecticut and coauthor of the Texas study. People in monogamous, long-term relationships shouldn't have to worry about diseases and may focus instead on effective contraception.

But there's no way of saying that any one choice is "best." "Some women are going to get along really well with a particular method, and that's great," says *Contraceptive Technology* coauthor Dr. Felicia Stewart, director of research for the Sutter Medical Foundation, a managed-care organization in Sacramento, Calif. "If you have a method that is a comfortable fit with your hormonal makeup or your anatomy and your habits, then that method is fine for you. Trying, to say there's one best method is just ridiculous."

Men, Sex, *and* Parenthood *in an* Overpopulating World

Because women bear the primary responsibility for childrearing and family life in every country, they are also presumed to bear the primary responsibility for excess population growth. But family planning is unlikely to succeed—and population is unlikely to stabilize—until men share fully in those responsibilities.

Aaron Sachs

Aaron Sachs is a staff researcher at the Worldwatch Institute.

In almost all mammalian species, the male lives the life of a philanderer. From pandas to pumas, mammalian fathers tend to abandon their mate right after conception, leaving to the mother the entire burden of childrearing. The very classification "mammal" refers to a mother's independent capacity to nurse her babies: it's always the female bear that people see feeding, training, and protecting the cubs.

But human males are different. From the beginning, they have tended to stay with their mates and their children, and today many anthropologists and biologists believe that men's participation in the family played a critical role in the evolution of *homo sapiens*' most distinctive features, especially our capacity for psychosocial development. The children of very few other species, over the millennia, have been lucky enough to receive the attention of two caring adults.

Unfortunately, as human culture continues to evolve, more and more men are breaking with tradition and shirking their childrearing responsibilities. And the world's women and children are bearing the costs of this neglect. According to Judith Bruce, a senior associate at the Population Council in New York, the amount of time contributed by mothers to childcare is commonly seven times greater than that contributed by fathers, and the mothers' share only seems to be increasing. While important social revolutions in the industrialized world have begun to free women from an imposed dependence on men, some husbands and fathers are using this broadening of women's opportunities as an excuse to contribute less time and money to their families. By 1980, for instance, American men aged 20 to 49 were spending almost 50 percent less time living with their young children than they were in 1960. In less developed countries, even when there is a long tradition of male financial contributions to the family, men often abandon their wives and children because of increasing economic pressures: fewer and fewer are able to succeed as breadwinners. A recent Chilean study of low-income adolescent couples and their first-born children found that, by the children's sixth birthday, 42 percent of the fathers were providing no child support whatsoever.

Male sexual behavior, too, puts a strain on society: besides the indirect stresses caused by men's failure to avoid fathering children they might not be able to support later, their higher fertility levels contribute disproportionately to population growth. Because men stay fertile much longer than women do, and because they tend to be more promiscuous, the average man, by the end of his lifetime, is responsible for more children than the average woman. In the 18th century, a Moroccan emperor had reportedly fathered more than 1,000 children by the time he turned 50. Though childrearing is becoming more expensive and parents are finding themselves with fewer resources to pass on to their children (whether in the form of cash or land), many men have continued to have large families. In some sub-Saharan African countries, the average man wants to have more than 10

Of 333 fathers with eight-year-old children, only 22 percent were still living with their child.

children, in part because large families serve as cultural symbols of a man's virility and wealth. Consequently, under male-dominated social systems that tend not to hold fathers accountable for the well-being of their children, the women of the Third World are increasingly finding themselves doing hard labor for food as well as walking several miles every day for water and fuelwood—all with babies on their backs or at their breasts.

Society has long expected women to take ultimate responsibility for the duties of raising a family. Currently in the United States, fathers head only one of every 40 single-parent households: men just aren't expected to juggle childcare and a job. Single women often end up simply raising their children by themselves, whether or not they have access to resources. In all parts of the world, both women and children would no doubt be better off if women faced fewer barriers to economic independence—and if men fulfilled their familial obligations. According to a recent study in Barbados, of 333 fathers with eight-year-old children, only 22 percent were still living with their child, and the children of the fathers who stayed were doing significantly better in school than all the others. And in the Chilean study, children's diets and nutrition levels tended to be much healthier when their fathers were living at home.

Men's failure to embrace their familial responsibilities begins with a failure to acknowledge that families get started through sex. A growing body of sociological research suggests that a family's eventual size and welfare depend largely on how the father and mother interact in bed—that men who are attentive to their partner's concerns tend later to be attentive to their family's concerns. Unfortunately, many men continue to see sex not as a shared experience but as their prerogative, as simply an opportunity to fulfill their desires. When interviewed by the demographer Alex Chika Ezeh, men in Ghana explained bluntly that their large families reflected, most of all, their desire to assert their culturally sanctioned sexual dominance over their wives. "The woman has no right to choose the number [of children] she prefers," said one man, "since it is you, the man, who decides when to have sex with her."

Over the past decade, then, many advocates for women's and children's welfare have turned to fam-

ily planning as a way of addressing men's irresponsibility. And many family planning organizations, in turn, have recognized a need to supplement their efforts to provide women with safe, appropriate contraception with efforts to educate men. In the mid-1980s, for instance, the poster campaigns of many national-level affiliates of the International Planned Parenthood Association (IPPF) targeted men's sexual attitudes quite explicitly. They attempted to make men empathize with women, to help them understand that, though they themselves do not get pregnant, they do have a role in reproduction.

Family planners reason that if men take full responsibility for their potential to procreate by participating in family planning, then each of the children they do father will be both expected and wanted—and presumably they will father only the number of children for whom they are able to provide. No culture directly encourages men not to care about their families, after all. Emphasizing male responsibility in family planning, therefore, is a key to getting men both to fulfill their broader responsibilities as husbands and fathers and to contribute their fair share to population stabilization.

THE HIGHER FERTILITY OF MEN

Of course, family planning is still, at heart, a women's issue. The development of the birth control pill, the IUD, and safe methods of female sterilization have remained the most important and revolutionary innovations in the history of family planning, because they finally gave a significant number of women control over their own fertility. After all, as Margaret Sanger, America's family planning pioneer of the early 20th century, frequently noted, it is the woman who risks her life in childbirth. Even at the end of the 20th century, maternal mortality rates remain high in the developing world. In Afghanistan and Sierra Leone, for instance, according to the World Health Organization (WHO), one mother dies for every 100 live births—a rate 250 times higher than that of some European countries. And many maternal deaths in developing countries are attributed by WHO to excessive childbearing.

The focus of family planning policies and programs, then, should not be shifted away from women, but rather broadened to include men as well. Though the importance of female methods of birth control seems to lie in their very independence from male influence, and though many women would not be using contraception were it not for private, female-only clinics, the exclusion of men from family planning has also had some negative consequences for women that were not foreseen by many activists. "Putting all the responsibility onto women," says Gill Gordon of IPPF's AIDS prevention unit, "has the effect of marginalizing men and making them *less* likely to behave responsibly." In many places where female birth control methods predominate, the connection between sexuality and reproduction has disappeared in the minds of many men, and they simply haven't had to confront or even consider the very serious reasons women might have for wanting to limit their childbearing. Though giving all women control over their fertility would be a significant accomplishment, it would not insure their well-being, or the well-being of any children they might eventually want to have.

The reality in many developing countries is that if a man's wife resists childbearing, he will often simply withdraw his financial support and marry another woman. Even worse, many men have resorted to violence in order to keep their wives from using contraception. One recent study showed that more than 50 percent of Mexican women using state-sponsored birth control services do so secretly, for fear of being physically abused by their husbands. A woman's ability to regulate her own fertility is often contingent upon her partner's recognition of her right to do so—which means that family planners need to work that much harder to make men empathize with women and understand their own responsibilities.

Changing men's sexual attitudes in a patriarchal world is delicate, time-consuming, expensive work, and the cost-effectiveness of education campaigns aimed at men is always difficult to measure, since progress is inevitably so slow. It would be a mistake, then, to let male-focused policies and programs take away any of the already limited resources currently devoted to women and family planning. But changing men's attitudes about familial decision-making is still crucial, especially since men currently tend to be responsible for more children than do women. All around the developing world, the population pressures caused by high fertility are contributing at least indirectly to problems as varied as wood and water shortages, joblessness, inadequate sanitation, the spread of infectious diseases, and the accumulation of waste—all of which have a direct impact on families. And, if current demographic trends continue, the globe's current population of almost 5.6 billion will probably have risen to about 8.4 billion by 2025. Ninety-five percent of those new babies will be born in the Third World.

Traditionally, population programs and policies have held women responsible for high fertility, at least implicitly. For years, national censuses and surveys did not even consider men's fertility. A country's fertility rate—the target of most programs and policies—is always measured as the average *female* fertility rate, because women are the ones who actu-

MEN HAVE MORE CHILDREN

Average Number of Living Children of Men and Women over 50, Selected Countries in Sub-Saharan Africa.

COUNTRY	MEN	WOMEN	PERCENTAGE BY WHICH MALE RATE IS HIGHER
CAMEROON	8.1	4.8	69
NIGER	6.7	4.9	37
KENYA	9.6	7.9	22
GHANA	8.5	7.4	15

Source: Demographic and Health Surveys

ally have children. Over the last decade, however, as demographers have begun to provide more relevant data, population policies guided solely by analyses of women's fertility have begun to seem less appropriate. Especially in societies where polygyny is common, family planning programs would do better to focus on men, since most of the excess childbearing in such societies can be traced to sexual pairings of older men—who might be able to provide child support for only a few more years—with much younger women. In Kenya, Ghana, and Cameroon, for instance, married men over the age of 50, who might continue to father children until their death, tend to have between eight and 10 living children. Married women at the end of their reproductive years report having five to eight.

THE POLITICS OF CONTRACEPTION

Since so many men in the developing world are so strongly predisposed to reject family planning, and since progress in changing their attitudes is so hard to measure in the short term, Third World development experts have tended to focus their family-planning efforts on couples who are already interested in limiting childbearing. Most development funders like to support programs that aspire to deliver a certain number of contraceptives to a certain number of people and achieve a measurable decline in fertility. And, without question, expanding access to birth control devices is crucial in the struggle both to improve women's and children's health and welfare and to help stabilize the world's burgeoning population. A 1992 study by Population Action International (then called the Population Crisis Committee) found 22 countries in which men and women still have no access, in effect, to birth control information or services. The contraceptive prevalence rate—or percentage of married women of reproductive age (15 to 49) using birth control—has surpassed 50 percent in a few countries in Latin America and Asia, but in sub-Saharan Africa, for example, it averages only 14 percent.

Simply flooding developing nations with contraceptives will go only so far, however. To make a significant contribution to population stabilization on a global scale, family planning programs will have to change people's attitudes, and especially men's attitudes, about the number of children they want to have. Unfortunately, in addition to the broad social and cultural factors that discourage men from participating in family planning, there are several more intimate factors about which men tend to express concern. Some men worry, for instance, that their wives would become promiscuous if provided with the means of preventing pregnancy. More generally, many men fear—probably with good reason—that, whether or not their wives ended up using birth control for extramarital affairs, the simple fact that it would allow them to assert a new form of control over sex and their bodies would probably change the power dynamics of the marriage. And men often have genuine concerns about the threats to their partner's health that many contraceptive devices are reputed to pose. Some of their fears—about pelvic inflammatory disease from IUDs, and nausea and headaches from the pill—are valid, while others—that the pill causes arthritis and sterility—are myths perpetuated by failings in information and education systems.

Men usually have even stronger negative feelings about the three birth control methods commonly thought of as male-initiated—withdrawal, the condom, and vasectomy. Withdrawal and the condom represent an unreasonable sacrifice of sexual pleasure to many men. Family planning field workers commonly report that suggestions of condom use are most often greeted with smiles and quickly composed maxims, such as "You can't wash your feet with your socks on," or "That would be like eating a sweet with the wrapper still on it." Vasectomies are even less acceptable in many parts of the developing world, because it seems highly unnatural to many men to have surgery on their sexual organ, or because they don't understand exactly what the operation entails. In the Sudan, 34 percent of male participants in a recent study thought that getting a vasectomy was equivalent to being castrated.

Many of these concerns could be easily overcome, though, since they stem from simple gaps in information or services. Family planning programs that cater to the specific concerns of men, and that offer a wider selection of contraceptive options, with

complete explanations of their risks and how they are to be used, could make converts of millions. Already, more men than ever before are at least considering the use of family planning, if only, in many cases, for spacing their children further apart.

In the early 1970s, surveys of men in sub-Saharan Africa showed consistently that more than half fervently disapproved of birth control. In the 1990s, though, outright rejection of contraception is rare even in this region. Approval ratings are still low in some countries, such as Mali, where only 17 percent of men aged 20 to 55 support family planning; but in Burundi, for instance, male approval has soared to 94 percent. In 10 other recent Third World surveys cited in a paper written by Cynthia Green for WHO, countries reported contraceptive approval rates among men of between 56 percent and 96 percent. Of course, a positive survey response hardly guarantees that a man will practice contraception, but it is a first step. Some men have even begun to express a more philosophical attitude about so sensitive an issue as female promiscuity. If a woman "wants to go out," noted a member of a 1989 focus group in Burkina Faso, "whether she takes the pill or not, she can go out." And a young telephone operator in Quito, Ecuador, went so far as to connect family planning with shared parental responsibility: "Even if you have enough money to ensure the children have a good education, they probably suffer from lack of attention if there are too many. And men here never help the women at home—she has to do everything. These kinds of decisions must be taken together by the man and the wife."

JUST FOR MEN

One way for a man to begin sharing the burden of planning and caring for a family is to offer to use a male method of birth control. Unfortunately, though, because contraceptive research has always been guided by the assumption that contraception is woman's work, men's options remain limited. While women theoretically have access to several modern, semi-permanent but fully reversible methods, ranging from the pill and the IUD to Norplant and injectables such as Depo-Provera, research on modern methods for men seems to have stopped at vasectomy. The IPPF's *Medical Bulletin* estimates that "only approximately 8 percent of the world contraceptive budget is spent on the development of male methods." It is true that certain chemical methods just aren't well suited to male physiology: developing a "male pill," for instance, would mean finding a way of blocking the ongoing production of millions of sperm without blocking the production of male hormones, a task much more daunting than chemically blocking the production of one egg every month. "Physically," however, as Elaine Lissner, the director of the Male Contraception Information Project in Santa Cruz, points out, "it's easier to stop millions of sperm than one egg. The sperm all travel through the vas deferens, a small, easily accessed tube, where they can be incapacitated or blocked." In any case, family planning researchers have hardly even begun to develop the potential range of useful contraceptive services for men.

Meanwhile, about one quarter of the world's couples who are currently using contraception rely on male methods. Withdrawal is perhaps the most dubious birth control method, with a failure rate of about 18 percent. But it has a long and notable history. Withdrawal was especially important in the 19th century during Europe's massive demographic transition to replacement-level fertility (when each man and woman have, on average, just two surviving children). The men of the Victorian era, perhaps aided by a pervasive cultural prudery, present the ultimate example of male responsibility, remembering their duty to their family even at the height of passion. Today, withdrawal still provides a free, safe method of birth control for about 15 million couples in the developing world who perhaps have no other options.

Vasectomy remains an important birth control method for men who don't want any more children. Because so many births are accidental, and because sterilization is almost 100 percent successful as a birth control method, the average vasectomy in the developing world is thought to prevent about two births. More reproductive health clinics are expanding their services and offering comprehensive vasectomy programs. PRO-PATER, in Sao

Of 204 published references on the Latin American family, only two discussed the role of fathers.

Paulo, Brazil, has been particularly successful in attracting men, thanks to a carefully planned, high-profile outreach program. Its staffers go to workplaces to talk about family planning with men in settings where they feel at ease. The clinic also runs a series of television advertisements that describe vasectomy as "an act of love" and reassure men that it does not affect sexual functioning—a key strategy with male sterilization. Nick Danforth, men's programs advisor for the Association of Voluntary Surgical Contraception in New York, likes to point out that although vasectomy—increasingly performed without a scalpel—is technically simpler, safer, and quicker than female sterilization, it is still used only a third as often.

Overall, condom use is probably the most significant male method, because it is not only cheap, easy, highly effective, and free of side effects, but it is also the one contraceptive additionally capable of preventing the spread of sexually transmitted diseases (STDs), including AIDS. Unfortunately, the condom's association with disease makes it that much more controversial as a birth control device. Many men and women, especially in regions where STDs have become widespread, take suggestions of condom use as insults: the person making the suggestion is either admitting that he or she might have a disease or expressing the fear that his or her partner might have a disease. In both cases, the implication is that someone has been unfaithful. For this reason, many couples feel uncomfortable about even acquiring condoms. "The condom is not seen as a contraceptive like, for example, the pill," explains a 50-year-old man in Burkina Faso. "It has come with AIDS. . . . If you want a condom, then that means you want to have an affair. So you have to get it via a third person. You cannot go yourself." Obtaining condoms may be even more problematic for women, because of the double standard operating in so many cultures. Men are expected to be discreet if they want to be promiscuous, but women are simply not expected to be promiscuous. Many women, intimidated by such strong stigmatization and by their male-dominated societies, end up risking pregnancy and disease rather than risking their partner's wrath by asking him to use a condom.

As with all male methods, condoms leave the woman in a particularly vulnerable situation: she

MEN WANT MORE CHILDREN

Average Number of Desired Children of Men and Women, Selected Countries in Sub-Saharan Africa.

COUNTRY	MEN	WOMEN	PERCENTAGE BY WHICH MALE RATE IS HIGHER
CAMEROON	11.2	7.3	53
NIGER	12.6	8.5	48
GHANA	7.6	5.3	43
BURUNDI	5.5	5.5	0
KENYA	4.8	4.8	0

Source: Demographic and Health Surveys

must depend on her partner to use them, and use them correctly. But AIDS is making condoms increasingly important to women's health in the developing world. HIV is passed much more easily from a man to a woman than from a woman to a man, and it has already infected a significant portion of the adult, heterosexual population in Africa and Asia, where prostitution and male promiscuity are common. For now, women have to rely on male condoms for their safety, and while the female condom might give women slightly more control, using it will still probably entail complicated sexual negotiations. It is essential, then, that men acknowledge the sensitivity of the situation and take the lead in encouraging condom use. Perhaps family planners and AIDS activists can join forces to produce education campaigns that will help to inform couples about the specifics of sexually transmitted diseases and their consequences, and help to dissipate sexual tensions by allowing partners to anticipate and understand each other's anxieties.

In the end, a willingness to participate in sexual and familial decisions as a concerned, forthcoming, equal partner is the real key to male responsibility. More than being willing to use a male method of birth control, men have to be willing to listen—to learn how to be sensitive to their partners' health, welfare, and desires. As Mary Daly, a leader of the modern feminist movement, has remarked, true responsibility is defined by an ability to be responsive.

NOT-SO-GREAT EXPECTATIONS

In almost all matters of policy, the family is defined as the mother-child unit: policymakers and program directors forget about gender dynamics, or simply don't expect men to take part. All too often, well-intentioned representatives of industrialized countries simply press packages of pills into the outstretched palms of Third World women, "as if women alone," in the words of the Population Council's Judith Bruce, "could bring about fertility decline, and as if their sexual and parental roles were determined autonomously." The United Nations Educational, Scientific, and Cultural Organization (UNESCO) recently asked a sociologist to do a review of the current literature on the Latin American family. Of the 204 documents she examined, only two mention fatherhood or the situation of men.

In the 1990s, men's family planning and parenting responsibilities need to be explicitly defined. A logical starting point would be prioritizing the goal of establishing paternity and enforcing child support payments—as leaders have in Nigeria, where, according to the new national population policy,

children have a legal claim on their father's time and money. Even in so "advanced" a country as the United States, where most of the so-called "deadbeat dads"—fathers who have abandoned their partner and child to the welfare system—could actually afford to pay child support, only about 18 percent do.

Changes in men's roles will not emerge quickly or with anything resembling ease. In some places, as economies modernize, the direct costs of child-rearing—from medicines and nutritious foods to schooling fees—are increasing, and familial resources are getting tight. Instead of having smaller families, though, many fathers simply shift the financial burden to the mother or the older children. And even when men genuinely want to act more responsibly, they sometimes believe they are unable to because of certain social and economic factors that continue to be neglected by policymakers. Both fathers and mothers, for instance, feel in many cases that children provide them with their only means of achieving economic and social security. And many fathers insist that they would have fewer children if they could be sure that more of them would survive: a study by the World Bank revealed that, on average, the prevention of 10 infant deaths results in one to five fewer births. But fathers in sub-Saharan Africa, where the infant mortality rate has remained as deplorably high as 10 percent—compared to one percent in the industrialized world—feel that they cannot afford to take chances with their fertility. And some fathers are contributing no financial resources to their children simply because they have none to give. Often they are desperately searching for work, perhaps in a far-off city.

YOU REAP WHAT YOU SOW

Still, educational efforts—ideally in tandem with pointed policy initiatives that force men to take up some of the economic burden of raising children—have considerable potential. If more field workers sought out men and provided them with better information, they would surely have more influence over men's family planning decisions. Good strategies for increasing male responsibility range from integrating family planning into community development programs to integrating sex and gender education into primary school systems. A recent IPPF report stated that, in general, field workers have had the most success changing men's attitudes and behavior through peer counseling: when men felt they were being advised by people who really identified with their concerns, whether sexual or financial, they were much more likely to respond favorably to suggestions of taking on more familial responsibility.

In Colombia, men started turning out in droves at vasectomy clinics modeled after Sao Paulo's PRO-PATER when male clinicians began offering more reproductive health services, including urological exams, infertility treatment, and sexuality counseling. Between 1985 and 1987 the number of vasectomies being performed quadrupled in Bogota and increased tenfold in Medellin.

The National Family Planning Council of Zimbabwe ran an intensive media campaign in 1989 designed specifically to increase men's responsibility in family planning and encourage joint decision making among couples. Male educators gave a series of 80 informational and motivational talks, and an entertaining serial drama about the consequences of irresponsible sexual and familial behavior was broadcast over the radio twice a week for six months, reaching about 40 percent of the country's men. By the end of the campaign, 61 percent of the men who had tuned in to "Akarumwa Nechekuchera"—variously translated as "Man is his own worst enemy" or "You reap what you sow"—reported a change in their attitudes about their families, and 17 percent of the men who had attended at least one talk reported that they actually started using a family planning method. Most importantly, the number of men saying that family planning decisions ought to be made jointly by husband and wife had risen by 40 percent: the council's educational programs were getting men and women to talk.

Some fatalists argue that because of undeniable evolutionary and physiological differences between men and women, men aren't likely ever to take much responsibility as parents: they are no better than all the other mammalian males. But such arguments overlook thousands of years of male contributions to family welfare—from big-game hunting to protection, wage earning, counseling, mentoring, and even nurturing. Men have the potential to participate fully in planning and raising a family. It is only because they have society's implicit permission that some men still limit their participation to the act of sex.

Baby love

Fertility treatments are expensive, risky and often ineffective. Yet banning them would be a setback for women.

Rickie Solinger

Rickie Solinger is a visiting scholar at the University of Colorado. She is the author of *Wake Up Little Susie: Single Pregnancy and Race Before Roe v. Wade* (Routledge) and *The Abortionist: A Woman Against the Law* (The Free Press).

Reports of technological breakthroughs in reproductive technologies have tended to focus on the sensational and the singular: on the putative grotesqueries of post-menopausal pregnancies; and on surrogacy cases, which are invariably transformed into melodrama, described as if gender, class and sometimes race exploitation were not at their heart. The media trendsetter, of course, was the "Baby M" case, reported as if it were about one lowdown, unstable and insufficiently maternal female welching on the good-faith deal she made with a proper middle-class couple—lacking only a baby in their quest for perfection.

The media dishes out these tales of perversity with relish; but the big impact of the new technologies is on the lives of ordinary women, hundreds of thousands of them, who have participated in fertility-enhancing programs in recent years. These women, who for one reason or another are apparently unable to conceive in the usual way, undergo treatments ranging from IUI (intra-uterine insemination) to egg harvesting, embryo implantation, embryo and egg freezing, the micro-injection of sperm and the micro-manipulation of ova.

Lately there has been a great deal of controversy among feminists, most often expressed in heated political terms, about the broader implications of such treatments. Such discussion generally proceeds as if it is possible to embrace or reject any given modality of procreation for straightforwardly political reasons.

But, in this arena as in so many others, the personal is always threatening to trump the political—in ways that might be familiar, say, to progressives who feel compelled to go to extraordinary expense and other inconveniences in order to raise their children in a safe neighborhood with good schools, despite their commitment to improving the lot of all children in society. In a capitalist society, it is the rare individual who foregoes on principle the chance to buy what one values—in this instance motherhood—if one has the resources, even when it takes a special effort to fit an essentially personal choice into a deeply held politics of justice.

And so, to begin with, I'd better identify my own reproductive history: I have two biological children conceived through intercourse. It may also be relevant that I have a close relative deeply enmeshed in the full array of new reproductive technology treatments. I say this because I have the feeling that readers of this kind of article are, like me, always sleuthing the subtext. Is the writer herself a mother? And if so, what kind? A biological mother? An adoptive mother? A technologically assisted mother? Or is she a voluntarily child-free person?

The differences between those supporting and those opposing the new technologies is stark. Those who oppose them insist that the new technologies constitute a new form of violence against women, alienating them from their reproductive processes, reducing them to what critic Janice Raymond, author of *Women as Wombs*, calls "experimental raw material" or "womb environments." Supporters, such as Carol Sternhell, director of women's studies at New York University, argue that the technologies can be potentially liberating for women. "All the new alternative forms of family building are ... challenges to our culture's dominant ideas about family," Sternhell suggests.

Raymond and the other critics can draw upon a great deal of history to back up their opposition to the new technologies. One need only recall the horrifying examples of thalidomide and the Dalkon Shield to prove that real danger can lurk in the heart of technology's promise to women desperate to manage their fertility. And it is clear that technologically assisted conception has been overhyped. The statistics are terrible, yet desperate women keep coming, a fact suggesting that the customers are actually being duped and even coerced into undergoing treatments that are not only physically risky but often futile.

Equally troublingly, the new technologies use up vast social and financial resources that could potentially be better spent solving existing problems such as high infant mortality rates in some parts of the United States and around the globe. (In the United States alone, fertility clinics do $2 billion of business a year.) And the technologies pose tougher issues for the ethicists. They mandate a "normalcy" standard for fetuses: all participants in the programs have the right to demand perfect babies, so fetuses that fail the test will be selectively eliminated.

In addition, the mere existence of the new technologies creates new worldwide inequities. The procedures are terribly expensive: in vitro fertilization, for example, costs $10,000 or more. And so there are multiple new opportunities for exploitation, both of women desperate to be pregnant and of poor women who, out of an extreme lack of resources, can be pressed into service as egg donors or so-called surrogate mothers.

The new technologies, Raymond suggests, are dangerous to women and to feminism because they take power and control over fertility away from desperate women and hand it over to doctors and technicians who manage and profit from the infertility empire. "Women as a class have a stake in reclaiming the female body," Raymond argues, "by refusing to yield control of it to men, to the fetus, to the state, and most recently to those liberals who advocate that women control our bodies by giving up control."

Given this house of horrors (and the sci-fi scenarios anyone can conjure up, based on what seems to be possible and acceptable in the realm of reproduction today), the theorists believe that the only effective check on the evils inherent in the new technologies is a curiously "liberal" one—that the state must outlaw the whole business on the grounds that these technologies are necessarily used in ways that are unethical, dangerous for women, costly and out of sync with the common good.

While the feminists who categorically oppose the new technologies are a relatively homogeneous group, those who support them share no common analysis or creed. No single ideology fits the diverse perspectives of researchers, doctors, business types and participants in fertility programs. And, of course, the doctors and technicians who develop and deliver the new technologies and the average women who buys them may or may not identify with feminism in any form.

While Raymond and her colleagues concentrate on the big picture, the supporters of the new technologies focus on the rights of individual women. They may sometimes have the less powerful argument, medically and politically. But I am struck by their references to the sheer number of women moving through infertility programs—women ready to make sacrifices and take risks simply to be able to give birth. In some ways, their desire for control over their own reproductive capacities is not all that different than that of the countless women who sought abortions even when a large measure of social opprobrium was attached to women trying to determine their fate that way.

The woman entering a fertility program simply wants to be a mother, probably in pretty much the same way that most other women, feminist or not, want to be mothers. She wants to be a mother so badly (maybe partly because of the cultural mandate that presses women into motherhood,

partly because motherhood seems so genuinely, emotionally grand) that even though she knows something about the lousy stats, the painful procedures, the possible risks, she enrolls in an fertility program anyway, glad to have the *choice* to do so, and glad to have the resources to pay for it. The odds tell her there is a good chance that at the end of the process she will be frustrated, disgusted, depressed and much poorer—though not necessarily sorry she tried everything she could.

This woman may also see herself as a feminist, someone who cares about ethics and justice and issues of equity. She simply wants her life to meet her expectations, and having a baby is a key expectation. And so she justifies her participation in the program on roughly the same principles as her like-minded friends when they explain why they choose to live in safe neighborhoods or send their children to private schools or colleges or why they use so much of their disposable income to pay for summer vacations instead of, let's say, sending all their excess dollars to organizations devoted to ending world hunger

What's more—and this is the most painful part—she doesn't believe it is her personal responsibility to engage in orphan-saving just because she or her partner is infertile, or lesbian, any more than it is the responsibility of the lawyer couple next door with one conventionally conceived 6-year-old and tons of money. She is concerned about the high infant mortality rate in the United States and abroad, but she doesn't see how her forbearance from participating in a fertility-enhancing program will reduce the rate of infant deaths. She doesn't believe that her infertility or her sexual orientation requires her to redress this particular human problem. She herself would find paying another woman to be a "surrogate mother" repugnant and unacceptable. Like the theorists, she assumes that the state should have a role in this arena, but for her, the much more limited role of regulator is sufficient.

Given the competition between the logic of the opponents of reproductive technology and the strength of the desire of unwillingly childless women to become pregnant, how does one formulate a position regarding the new technologies? Surely we have to find a position that allows us to reject the medico-cultural mandates that rigidly define infertility as a disease requiring a medical "cure" and that leaves it to the infertility establishment alone to define what is and is not a legitimate mode of procreation. And certainly we must insist that the possibility of male infertility be equally scrutinized in each case where appropriate, and treated accordingly.

Just as important, we need to evaluate the controversy between the supporters and the opponents of the new technologies in light of what we know about the politics of parental worthiness in the United States at the end of the 20th century and the enduring race and class biases that continue to shape these politics. Specifically, it would not do to consider the politics of fertility without attention to the fact that the new technologies can contribute, on the one hand, to the enduring anxiety about poor and non-white women who have "too many" children and must have their fertility controlled, while, on the other hand, it drums up sympathetic concern for "deserving" white middle-class women beset by infertility problems who must be given the chance to enhance their child-bearing possibilities.

These issues cut to the heart of gender and class politics in this era. Together with the politics of abortion and welfare of which they are a part, they define the huge, problematic terrain in which many women now live, a terrain substantially unreconstructed after 20 years in which feminist politics has had an impact on many facets of our national life.

And yet, to construct a meaningful position with regard to the new technologies, one must listen carefully to the voices of women who use them. We must ask why women keep on seeking out and undergoing fertility treatments, despite the poor statistics and the political implications.

And it would be best if we could imagine that these legions of women filing into burgeoning infertility programs around the country are just like those of us who conceived in the old-fashioned way. They've sized up the options, and they've sized up their hearts, realizing that the costs (emotional, financial, medical and political) of the new technologies—like the costs of living through one's child's adolescence or paying for a child's college education—are very high. But no one can tell them—or me—that it's not worth it. Nor, in the end, does it seem fair to me to impose a demographic politics of justice on the backs of women who simply want the same thing that I got without even trying.

What a baby *really* costs

Grab that calculator and see what you can expect to spend during your child's first year.

Jessica Rosenthal Benson
and Maija Johnson

The average first baby costs his parents approximately $8,000 by the time he celebrates his first birthday, according to the Family Economics Research Group of the U.S. Department of Agriculture (USDA). But your cost may be much more or less than that: Where you live, how many gifts you receive, and how much you can afford, or want, to spend are just a few of the factors involved in the accounting. Plus, what you dub a lifesaver may be considered an unnecessary expenditure by another parent.

One cost that the USDA omits is that of prenatal care and delivery—an average $4,720 for a normal pregnancy and birth, and $7,826 if a cesarean is needed. These numbers, however, don't shed much light on actual regional costs. An uncomplicated pregnancy and birth in New York City might cost $10,000, while in Oregon the cost could be half that amount.

In addition to taking into account regional costs, you should check your health-insurance policy. Traditional fee-for-service plans often do not reimburse obstetrical costs until after the delivery. And under some insurance plans, well-baby care is not covered.

Once they are home with their baby, many new parents are surprised how the cost of indispensable items, such as diapers, adds up, not to mention the cost of incidentals, such as film. And then there are the totally unexpected expenses, such as take-out food. "My husband I were too overwhelmed to go grocery shopping and prepare meals, so we ordered in a lot," says Nancy Brower, of Madison, Wisconsin.

New parents may also face a jump in housing costs. Depending on whether you are decorating a nursery, remodeling, or moving to a bigger home, the cost of making room for a baby can range from under $100 to thousands of dollars.

In compiling these lists, we discovered that calculating costs for the first year is tricky at best. Besides some of the variables already mentioned, manufacturer and store prices vary widely, as does product quality. Nevertheless, you an use the lists, or individual items within them, to get an idea of how much you can expect to spend during your baby's first year of life. And no parent has ever been known to complain that having a child wasn't worth the expense!

Feeding
Breast-feeding:
4 nursing bras,$52–$116
360 disposable bra pads for early months, $40
Breast pump, $26–$165
Lactation consultant, $0–$225
6 waterproof lap pads, $8
6 bibs, $6–$46
total: $132–$600

Bottle-feeding:
8 eight-ounce bottles, $9–$28
4 four-ounce bottles, $4–$14
18 nipples, $21–56
Formula, $616–$956
Bottle and nipple brush, $1–$2
6 waterproof lap pads, $8
6 bibs, $6–$46
total: $665–$1,110

Solids:
24 boxes of infant cereal, $24–$30
432 jars of baby food, $127–$217
156 jars of infant juice, $42–$73
Food grinder, $8
Feeding dish, $2–$9
3 baby spoons, $4–$8
3 training cups, $5–$13
6 large bibs, $15–$51
High chair, $25–$100
Hook-on chair, $28–$35
total: $280–$544

Dressing
Chest of drawers, $200–$350
20 undershirts, $36–$125
6 "onesies" or bodysuits, $19–$36
4 drawstring nightgowns, $20–$28
6 pairs of pajamas, $20–$69
10 stretchies, coveralls, or creepers, $90–$200
2 pairs of overalls, $32–$80
7 jumpsuits, $133–$280
6 tops, $54–$78
4 pairs of pants, $28–$36
2 dresses, $34–$56
4 pairs of booties, $16–$18
8 pairs of socks, $8–$10
1 pair of walking shoes, $25–$32
3 sweaters, $30–$60
3 sunsuits, $30–$63
2 cool-weather hats, $4–$10
1 sunbonnet, $4–$5
1 snowsuit, $48–$60
2 jackets, $64–$120
total: $895–$1,716

Bathing and skin care
Baby bathtub, $10–$20
Baby bath seat, $13–$15

6 washcloths, $4–$9
6 hooded bath towels, $48–$60
2 containers of liquid baby soap, $5
Baby shampoo, $3–$4
Baby lotion, $2
Baby powder or cornstarch, $2–$3
Baby oil, $2–$3
Baby nail clippers, $2
Isopropyl rubbing alcohol, $1
520 cotton balls, $10–$11
Baby brush and comb, $2–$14
total: $104–$149

Diapering

Home-laundered:
4-dozen cloth diapers, $36–$432
Water, utilities, laundry products, $243
Diaper pail, $8–$20
12 diaper pins, $2–$6
18 pairs of waterproof pants, $24–$90
4,160 diaper wipes, $156
Diaper-rash ointment, $3–$4
Changing pad, $9–$30
Changing table, $70–$100
total: $551–$1,081

Diaper service:
Weekly supply of cloth diapers for one year, $552–$803
Diaper pail, $8–$20
12 diaper pins, $2–$6
18 pairs of waterproof pants, $24–$90
4,160 diaper wipes, $156
Diaper-Rash ointment, $3–$4
Changing pad, $9–$30
Changing table, $70–$100
total: $824–$1,209

Disposable diapers:
2,600 diapers for one year, $676–$884
Diaper pail, $8–$20
360 diaper-pail liners, $29
4,160 diaper wipes, $156
Diaper-rash ointment, $3–$4
Changing pad, $9–$30
Changing table, $70–$100
total: $951–$1,223

Outings

Infant car seat, $30–$83
Convertible car seat, $40–$118
Stroller, $20–$200
Soft front carrier, $15–$40
Metal-framed back carrier, $30–$89
Diaper bag, $7–$20
Stroller bag, $8–$9
Travel bassinet, $45
Portable crib, $70–$142
total: $265–$746

Sleeping

Crib, $100–$600
Mattress, $20–$200
2 waterproof mattress covers, $6–$12
2 quilted mattress pads, $4–$16
6 fitted sheets, $54–$80
6 receiving blankets, $24–$48
3 crib blankets, $27–$57
Quilt or comforter, $17–$21
Bumper pads, $23–$30
Dust ruffle, $16–$20
Night-light, $4–$5
Musical mobile, $25–$30
total: $320–$1,119

Playing

Infant seat, $25–$50
Play yard, $47–$120
Baby swing, $24–$110
Toys, $143
total: $239–$423

Child care

One parent cares for child: $0 (does not account for loss of income if this parent has left a full-time job)
Day-care center: $3,326
Family day care: $2,650
At-home sitter: $3,703
Relative: $2,151
Occasional baby-sitter: $448
If these numbers seem particularly low or high to you, keep in mind that they are national averages. Fees vary according to region. For example, fees in the Northeast and West are relatively higher than in the South and Midwest. Centers in the Northeast average $4,534 per year, while centers in the South cost about $2,683.

Health care and safety

Well-baby care, $617
Vitamin and mineral supplements, $80
Thermometer, $2–$10
Liquid acetaminophen, $4–$6
Nasal aspirator, $2
Cool-mist humidifier, $15–$150
Syrup of ipecac, $2–$3
8 pacifiers, $8–$22
Nursery monitor, $29–$49
2 safety gates, $30–$80
Smoke detector (includes battery), $12–$25
Safety gadgets (such as outlet covers and latches), $20–$130
total: $821–$1,174

Nice-to-haves

Cradle, $69–$100
Household help, $3,265–$11,821
35-mm camera, $50–$1,250
14 rolls of film, $52–$62
Film processing, $61–$122
Camcorder, $700–$2,300
22 camcorder tapes, $77–$242
Washing machine, $280–$900
Clothes dryer, $249–$799
Cordless phone, $59–$280
total: $4,862–$17,876

Grand total

From the low end to the high end, here is what your bottom-line expenses—excluding childbirth and child-care costs—could amount to:
total: $3,607–$26,080

Cost Cutters

Gifts and hand-me-downs.
Clothing can be a big expense, but there is good news: You'll probably receive some clothing as gifts—and more as hand-me-downs—which will help cut costs.

Secondhand equipment.
If you are given—or if you buy—a used piece of baby equipment, you must be absolutely sure that it is in good condition and safe for your child to use. For a free safety checklist called *Safe and Sound for Baby*, send a self-addressed, business-size envelope to the Juvenile Products Manufacturers Association, Public Information, 2 Greentree Centre, Box 955, Marlton, NJ 08053.

Free or at cost.
There are programs that offer car seats, either free or at cost. Your health-insurance carrier or the hospital where you plan to deliver may provide such a service.

Renting.
Breast pumps can be rented. To locate a rental station near you, call Ameda/Egnell, Inc., at 1-800-323-8750; or call Medela at 1-800-TELL-YOU (call collect from Illinois, Alaska, or Hawaii at 815-363-1166).

—J.R.B. and M.J.

Adolescent Childbearing

Whose Problem?
What Can We Do?

Diane Scott-Jones

DIANE SCOTT-JONES is an associate professor in the Department of Psychology, Temple University, Philadelphia.

ATTENTION to the phenomenon of adolescent childbearing typically focuses on its most sensational and titillating aspects. The image of an impoverished 13- or 14-year-old African American or Latino female with more than one baby becomes imprinted in the public mind as the symbol of the problem. Yet the issues surrounding adolescent childbearing are more complex than this stereotypical image suggests. Even the statistics are often presented in a dramatic and misleading fashion.

A careful examination of the data on adolescent childbearing yields the following statistical composite of the typical adolescent mother in the U.S.: she is white and in her late teen years. Childbearing among her peers is not an "epidemic." Indeed, the rate is lower than in the 1950s. However, she is more likely to bear children than are her counterparts in any other industrialized democracy in the world.

Our understanding of adolescent childbearing and our efforts to ameliorate its attendant problems are diminished by unexamined, emotionally charged beliefs regarding race/ethnicity, poverty, gender, and even the transitional nature of adolescence in the course of life. As is often true of issues about which we care deeply, the problem of adolescent childbearing is surrounded by myths that are perpetuated in the mass media and in everyday discussions of concerned and caring individuals. In order

> **Young people in our society become biologically mature at very early ages, putting biological forces at odds with social ones.**

to understand complex problems, we sometimes oversimplify our explanations and proposed solutions. We come to see such problems as limited only to certain groups, and we ignore the broader social contexts — thus allowing normal aspects of human behavior to be defined as problematic. Pregnancy and parenthood are, after all, highly valued in American society. Unlike other problems of adolescence, such as drug abuse or delinquency, pregnancy and parenthood are problematic only because of their early timing in the lifecourse.

As we explore adolescent childbearing and consider what we can do to prevent it, we must keep in mind the enormous changes adolescents experience. The dramatic physical changes of adolescence occur very rapidly; this rate of growth is unsurpassed at any point in life, with the exception of the prenatal period and infancy. To this great change within individuals, we must add the changes in social expectations for adolescents, changes in the structure and

content of formal education for middle and high school students, and the effect of difficult conditions in our society. Then one can imagine how tough the transition into adulthood can be for many adolescents. As a society, we must ask how we can establish more supportive contexts for adolescents' transition to adulthood. It is in that spirit that I ask "whose problem" adolescent childbearing is and what we can do about it.

WHOSE PROBLEM?

As is the case with any social phenomenon, we need to begin our analysis with an accurate and thorough description. Adolescent childbearing is embedded in pervasive societal problems and cannot be understood completely as a problem *within* individual adolescents. Adolescent childbearing affects many segments of society and is not limited to ethnic minority groups. Moreover, the behavior of males is an important factor. Finally, the problems are different for younger and older adolescents.

For the most part, *adolescence* is defined as ages 13 through 19, although some studies have used slightly different age ranges. For example, adolescent fertility is often reported as live births to females 15 to 19 years of age. The reason for this range is that relatively few births occur to females younger than 15. Age differences within the adolescent years are very important for any research or intervention program.

NOT JUST INDIVIDUAL ADOLESCENTS

Sometimes we mistakenly assume that adolescents' problems are *within* the adolescents themselves. Yet adolescents must make the transition from childhood to adulthood in a society that places many obstacles in their paths. For some adolescents, the prospects for adult life look bleak. For many families and communities the recession of the early 1990s might well be called a depression. And in these tough economic times, some individuals have created lucrative businesses from the manufacture and distribution of drugs in the communities that are least able to fight them. Our social climate is infected with racism, sexism, and class bias that we have not overcome despite valiant efforts.

Current social conditions make it generally difficult to become a responsible adult, and developing sexual responsibility is particularly difficult for those making the transition to adulthood. We are plagued with the mysterious and uncontrolled sexually transmitted disease AIDS. In spite of the life-threatening nature of AIDS, the mass media continue to bombard adolescents with sexual stimuli and sexual themes in all genres, from rock videos to product advertisements.[1] At the same time, sexual harassment too frequently invades the workplace. As a result, adolescents have few positive role models for adult sexual behavior and lack clear standards for accepting themselves as sexually mature and sexually responsible individuals.

In addition, two important changes have occurred in the *timing* of adolescence in the life span. First, girls today reach biological maturity at very early ages. The average age of menarche is 12.5 years, and for some girls the first menstrual period occurs as early as age 9. We can contrast this early age with the average for European populations in the 19th century: the average age for the first menstrual period in the mid-19th century was 16.5 to 17 years.[2]

Why does menarche occur so early today? Menarche is triggered by a girl's proportion of body fat. High-calorie diets and a relatively sedentary lifestyle have combined to lower the average age of menarche. The current average age of menarche may be the earliest possible for the human species. Boys are, on average, two years behind girls in attaining reproductive maturity.

But as young people in our society become biologically mature at very early ages, we have not responded by accepting them as adults at earlier ages. Instead, we have done just the opposite. We have delayed the time that adolescents can begin to function as adults.

We now expect girls and boys to complete many more years of education than was true in the past. Advanced education is now needed for adequate employment outside the home. Marriage is often delayed, and many women delay childbearing until they are close to the end of their reproductive years.[3] Thus, at the same time that young girls become biologically ready to have children at very early ages, we as a society expect them to wait until they are much older before they behave as adults. Biological forces and social forces are at odds.

The current trend toward later marriage and childbearing in our society, especially among affluent women, causes us to consider adolescent childbearing quite inappropriate. Yet, in the not too distant past, early childbearing was the norm in our society, just as adolescent childbearing remains the norm throughout most of the world. Biologically, optimal time for childbearing begins in the late adolescent years. In fact, in *Walden Two* B. F. Skinner advocated childbearing in late adolescence. In the United States in the 1950s, many young women in their late teens became pregnant, and the adolescent birthrate was higher than in recent years. For every 1,000 females between 15 and 19 years of age, there were 90 births in 1955, 68 births in 1970, and 51 births in 1986.[4] These facts are surprising to those who think that adolescent childbearing is a recent phenomenon and that it has become an epidemic.

Adolescent childbearing was not widely acknowledged as a problem in the 1950s because pregnant adolescents tended to get married, to remain in stable families, and to live relatively prosperous lives. Even men with little formal education could find good jobs in factories, steel mills, and so on. But those manufacturing jobs are no longer widely available, and young people with the same level of education today are faced with low-paying service jobs, such as those in the fast-food industry. Thus today's economy makes it very difficult for young people to form families as they did in the 1950s. Marriage is made still more unlikely by the current economic recession. Many young fathers are not able to find employment that would allow them to support a family. The situation today is vastly different from that of the 1950s.

The fact that adolescent childbearers tend to be unmarried must be placed in the context of the increase in nonmarital childbearing for older women in our society. A re-

> **For every 1,000 females between the ages of 15 and 19, there were 90 births in 1955, 68 births in 1970, and 51 births in 1986. These facts are surprising to those who think that adolescent childbearing is a recent phenomenon and that it has become an epidemic.**

cent Census Bureau report of data from June 1992 indicates that approximately 24% of single adult women had given birth.[5] The greatest increases in the rate of childbearing among single adult women occurred among women who were college-educated, employed, and white. Nonmarital childbearing actually declined slightly for African American women at the same time as it rose sharply, almost doubling, for white women. Although higher percentages of nonmarital childbearing still occur among African American women and women who have not completed high school, these figures indicate that nonmarital childbearing among adult women does not fit stereotypes and cuts across ethnic and socioeconomic lines.

It is in the current social and economic environment that we must try to understand the challenges facing adolescents and the opportunities we can provide them as they move into their adult lives. The current focus on adolescent childbearing as a social problem of enormous magnitude results at least partly from changed societal conditions. Thus we can conclude that adolescent childbearing is a socially constructed problem and not simply the result of individual pathology. In addition to interventions with individuals, social change is necessary to eliminate the problems associated with adolescent childbearing.

NOT JUST AFRICAN AMERICANS AND LATINOS

There is a bias among researchers and the mass media that shifts the focus of adolescent sexual behavior, pregnancy, and childbearing almost exclusively to African Ameri-

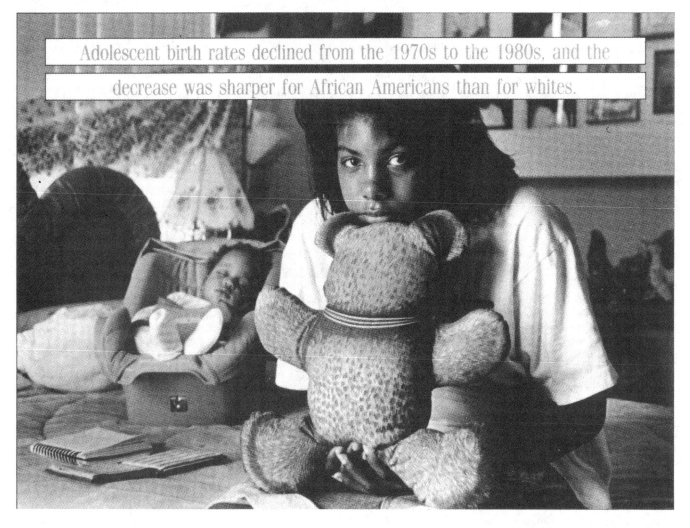

Adolescent birth rates declined from the 1970s to the 1980s, and the decrease was sharper for African Americans than for whites.

cans and Latinos and ignores the same problems in white adolescents. Rates of sexual activity, pregnancy, and childbearing are higher for African American adolescents than for white adolescents. Yet many problems exist for white adolescents as well. In addition, statistical comparisons of racial and ethnic groups can be misleading, because a disproportionate number of members of ethnic minority groups are poor. Differences attributed to race or ethnicity often stem at least partly from socioeconomic differences. With that caveat, I will briefly review the data on sexual activity, pregnancy, and childbearing. (The comparisons are reported most frequently for African Americans and whites, and data are not as readily available for other American racial and ethnic groups.)

The largest increase in adolescent sexual activity over the past two decades has occurred for white adolescents. Consequently, the difference between African Americans and whites in rates of sexual activity has declined dramatically in the past two decades, almost to a point of convergence. In 1970, 27% of white adolescent females

and 46% of black adolescent females had become sexually active. In 1988, the figures were 51% for white and 59% for black adolescent females.[6] Furthermore, older (18- to 19-year-old) black adolescent females' rate of sexual activity actually declined, from 83% in 1985 to 77% in 1988. The rate of sexual activity for white 18- to 19-year-old females, in contrast, increased from 61% in 1985 to 73% in 1988.

Adolescent females of all racial and ethnic groups are becoming sexually active at earlier ages. In 1988, 25.6% of 15-year-old female adolescents reported having had sexual intercourse, compared to 4.6% in 1970.[7] Once they become sexually active, white adolescent females have sex more frequently and with more partners than do black adolescent females.[8]

The pregnancy rate for 15- to 19-year-old adolescents has been approximately 11% since 1982, which is an increase over the rate of 9.9% in 1974.[9] The overall increase in the pregnancy rate is the result of increases for white adolescents. The pregnancy rates for African American and white adolescents are not close to convergence,

however. In 1985 the adolescent pregnancy rate of 18.6% for African Americans was twice that of the 9.3% rate for white adolescents.[10]

However, white adolescents who become pregnant are more likely than pregnant African American adolescents to be married, and both groups are less likely to be married than were pregnant adolescents in the past. In the 1950s one-third of first births to adolescents were conceived out of wedlock; in the 1980s two-thirds of first births to white adolescents were conceived out of wedlock, and 97% of first births to African American adolescents were conceived out of wedlock. White adolescents who become pregnant are somewhat more likely to have abortions than are their African American counterparts. In 1985, 41% of 17- to 19-year-old pregnant African American adolescents had abortions, compared to 46% of white adolescents in this age group.[11]

Adolescent birthrates declined from the 1970s to the 1980s, and the decrease was sharper for African Americans than for whites. The birthrate for African American adolescents between the ages of 15 and 19 was 12.3% in 1973 and 9.5% in 1983. Corresponding rates for white adolescents were 4.9% in 1973 and 4.4% in 1983.[12] From 1986 to 1988, birthrates for both African American and white adolescents increased but remained below the 1973 rates. The birthrate for African American adolescents remains double that of white adolescents. Although adolescent birthrates are higher for African Americans, two-thirds of adolescent childbearers are white.[13]

The U.S. has the highest adolescent birthrate of all industrialized, democratic nations. Even if only white adolescents are considered, the U.S. rate remains higher than that in all other similar countries.[14] Included in this cross-national comparison were 37 countries selected on the basis of two criteria: a relatively low fertility rate for women overall and a relatively high per-capita income. Canada, England (including Wales), France, the Netherlands, and Sweden were chosen for more extensive analyses because of their similarity to the U.S. in cultural heritage and economic growth.

In addition to the higher birthrate, the adolescent pregnancy rate is higher in the U.S. than in any other Western country.[15] In addition, the adolescent abortion rate in the United States in 1983 was the highest of any country for which data were available.[16]

These comparisons with other developed countries strongly suggest that the common stereotypes regarding adolescent sexuality in this country cannot explain our higher adolescent childbearing rate. The U.S. rate is not higher because of African Americans, for the rate remains higher when only white adolescents in the U.S. are considered. In addition, other countries in the cross-national comparisons also include nonwhite minority groups. Moreover, U.S. adolescents do not have a higher rate of sexual activity than adolescents in the comparison countries. Nor does U.S. welfare assistance explain higher rates of pregnancies and births; the comparison countries have more generous welfare provisions.

One important difference, however, is that the comparison countries have a more equitable distribution of income and more extensive benefits in such areas as health and unemployment. A second pronounced difference is that sex education, contraceptives, and abortion services are more widely available in the comparison countries.[17] I should point out that the availability of abortion typically coincided with the availability of contraception in the comparison countries, so that the need for abortion

among adolescents in those countries was minimized. Another important difference is that the comparison countries have a more open and accepting attitude toward sexual activity among young people. The rate of sexual activity among adolescents is not greater in the comparison countries than in the U.S., but apparently adolescents in the comparison countries are more responsible when they become sexually active.

In addition to the notion that adolescent childbearing is almost exclusively a problem of ethnic minorities, another common stereotype is that children born to African American adolescent mothers will themselves become adolescent parents. It is assumed that a cycle of early parenting is repeated generation after generation. How-

---

Apparently adolescents in the comparison countries are more responsible when they become sexually active.

---

ever, the majority of daughters of adolescent mothers delay their first birth beyond the adolescent years. In a 20-year follow-up of urban African American adolescent mothers, Frank Furstenberg, Judith Levine, and Jeanne Brooks-Gunn found that nearly two-thirds of the daughters had delayed their first birth until they were 19 years of age or older. The three researchers found the same result when they examined data for African Americans in the National Longitudinal Survey of Youth; two-thirds of the daughters of adolescent mothers delayed their first birth until age 19 or older.[18] This research clearly demonstrates that the cycle of adolescent childbearing is not repeated generation after generation in African American families.

NOT JUST FEMALES

The role of males in adolescent childbearing has received too little attention. Adolescent males who become fathers typically are not included in intervention programs for adolescent parents. However, the majority of fathers of babies born to adolescent females are not adolescents; they are men older than 20. This creates a serious problem in understanding early unplanned pregnancies as an *adolescent* issue. The interactions of an adolescent female and a young adult male may involve a compelling power

differential that is not acknowledged in research or in prevention and intervention programs. Thus the sexual encounters of adolescent females may involve some elements of coercion, whether psychological or physical.

Curbing the physical and psychological intimidation of females in schools is also important. The Educational Foundation of the American Association of University Women sponsored a national survey of eighth-through 11th-graders in 1993. The survey found that sexual harassment is widespread in our middle schools and high schools. Although males were also victims of sexual harassment, far more females than males had experienced and were disturbed by sexual harassment. Some females reported being afraid in school because of the sexual harassment they experienced.[19]

Males' attitudes toward females and sexuality are especially important, given that adolescents, when they do use contraception, rely heavily on a male contraceptive method — the condom.[20] Adolescent males, however, tend not to use contraceptives regularly. Estimates of contraceptive nonuse range from approximately one-half to two-thirds of adolescent males in research samples, including a study of black male inner-city junior and senior high school students and the 1988 National Survey of Adolescent Males.[21]

Although adolescent males do not use contraceptives regularly, most indicate that they are willing to share the responsibility for contraceptive use.[22] Joseph Pleck and his colleagues used a perceived costs-benefits model to test the importance of different motivations for condom use and found that adolescent males' belief in male responsibility for pregnancy prevention was related to condom use. However, the personal benefit that would result from preventing pregnancy was not a factor in their decision to use condoms. Other important factors were the perception that their female partners expected them to use condoms, and the perception of personal risk of acquiring AIDS. Perceptions of reduced sexual pleasure and of embarrassment were negatively related to condom use.[23]

Ethnic differences may exist in adolescent males' use of contraceptives, but current research is not consistent on this point. African American adolescents in the 1979 and 1988 national surveys conducted by Pleck and his colleagues reported the highest consistency of condom use, compared to white and Hispanic adolescents. However, in a small sample of 13- to 14-year-olds, of those who used contraception of any kind, African Americans tended to use withdrawal, which is not effective as a contraceptive, and whites tended to use condoms.[24] Age and the lower rates of sexual activity among younger adolescents may account for the inconsistencies between these studies.

Media warnings delivered by a highly regarded celebrity may have some limited impact on risky sexual behaviors, but adolescents may be influenced even less than young adults. The November 1991 announcement that basketball star Earvin "Magic" Johnson was infected with the human immunodeficiency virus (HIV) appears to have affected some but not all risky sexual behaviors of young patients in a suburban Maryland clinic.[25] The study was ongoing at the time of Johnson's announcement; comparisons were made of those interviewed prior to and after the announcement. The participants were 60% male and 73% African American; 85% had at least a high school diploma. Their average age was 25. No difference was found in reported condom use before and after Johnson's announcement. However, the number of sexual partners reported by participants was significantly lower for those interviewed after the announcement than for those interviewed prior to the announcement. Unfortunately, this reduction took effect for patients aged 25 and older but not for the younger patients (16 to 24 years of age).

YOUNGER AND OLDER ADOLESCENTS

The majority of births to adolescents are to older adolescents. Only 1% to 2% of all births to adolescents are to those younger than 15.[26] Childbearing and related issues are very different for older adolescents than for younger ones. With adolescent mothers who are at least 15 years of age, the medical risks of pregnancy could be normalized with adequate nutrition and adequate prenatal care.[27] Older adolescent childbearers face issues related to the transition to adulthood: completing school, finding employment, and forming stable adult relationships.

Although childbearing occurs less frequently in young adolescents, the potential negative outcomes are great. Adolescents younger than 15 face serious biomedical risks when they become pregnant. In addition, the younger the adolescent female is when she becomes sexually active, the more likely she is to experience little intimacy and some degree of coercion in her relationships. The transition from late childhood to early adolescence is often difficult, and early sexual relations, pregnancy, and childbearing greatly exacerbate the normal developmental challenges.

Although childbearing occurs less frequently in young adolescents, the potential negative outcomes are great.

WHAT CAN WE DO?

What can we do to help adolescents make good choices about sexual activity, pregnancy, and childbearing? Adolescents need guidance at many decision points. They need comprehensive sex education programs to prevent early sexual activity and unplanned pregnancies.

We also need to reframe the question of adolescents' motivation. Too frequently, researchers and practitioners assume that adolescent sexual activity is a problem behavior whose origins are the same as those for drug use and delinquency. The association of adolescent sexual activity with pathology needs to be replaced by an acknowledgment that becoming sexually active is a normal aspect of human development as adolescents make the transition into adulthood. In our present society, however, early sexual activity and early pregnancy greatly diminish the possibility of positive developmental outcomes for adolescents. We need to learn more about how to motivate adolescents to delay sexual activity and to avoid unplanned pregnancy.

In addition to sex education programs, adolescents need programs that indirectly help to reduce the risk of unplanned pregnancy by focusing on educational expectations, educational achievement, and career preparation. Although controversial, abortion and adoption are possible resolutions of unplanned pregnancy, and they need careful consideration, along with acknowledgment of and respect for differing values on these issues. When adolescents have children, they need to continue in school, and child-care programs are important ways of helping them do so. Prevention and intervention programs should target males as well as females. Finally, separate strategies are needed for younger and for older adolescents.

Claire Brindis offers some excellent practical information on preventing unplanned pregnancy among adolescents — drawing on and evaluating the efforts of a number of communities.[28] Although some general guidelines apply broadly, local communities will need to develop prevention plans that are suited to the particular issues and problems they face.

COMPREHENSIVE SEX EDUCATION

The sex education that adolescents receive may be too little, too late. In a study of African American adolescent females, Sherry Turner and I found that the majority had had sex education programs in school.[29] The majority also said that they had discussed sexual topics with their parents. But our analyses indicated that one-half to two-thirds of the adolescents became sexually active *before* they had had a sex education program. And many young adolescents in our study who were not sexually active had not yet had a sex education program. In addition, one-half of the adolescents found the information typically provided them to be inadequate. So, although most adolescents receive some form of sex education, the *quality* and *timing* of their programs and discussions of sexuality are crucial.

However, objections to sex education programs in the schools continue. Only 17 states and the District of Columbia include sex education as a mandated part of the school curriculum.[30] Moreover, many sex education programs promote abstinence without also providing information about contraception. U.S. policy regarding sex education stands in sharp contrast to that of other Western democracies, where sex education is far more extensive. Indeed, the only federal program for adolescent pregnancy prevention, the Adolescent Family Life Act, will not support programs that focus on contraception unless they are targeted toward the prevention of second pregnancies among adolescents who have experienced first pregnancies. The thinking represented in this federal legislation is that it is acceptable to talk about contraception with teens who have already had one baby but not acceptable to talk about contraception with teens who have yet to become pregnant!

Despite current sex education policies, some adolescents do use contraceptives. This is evidenced by the fact that adolescent pregnancies have not increased at the same rate as adolescent sexual activity has increased.[31]

In some communities, sex education is seen as the cause of adolescent pregnancy.

Many people believe that giving teens accurate information about sex and contraception will increase the numbers who are sexually active and become pregnant. There is no research to support this idea. In one small town in a rural area of California where only 25 girls were in the graduating class, more than half were pregnant or had

Adolescents who have high expectations for their own attainment are less likely to become sexually active.

already had a baby at the time of graduation. The response of the community and school was to ban sex education programs in the school.

In many instances, sex education is a small part of a health course and is not given sufficient attention. But comprehensive sex education programs that give adolescents accurate information about reproduction and contraception are needed, and they are needed before adolescents become sexually active.

Technical information about sexuality should be augmented with discussions of the close personal relationships in which the responsible expression of sexuality occurs. The current trend in our society is toward delayed marriage. And we don't have clear age norms for the appropriate time for the initiation of sexual activity. Moreover, some early sexual encounters may occur in the context of sexual harassment. Thus attention to the *relationship* in which sexual expression occurs is critical in sex education programs.

Most adolescents who attend sex education programs do so in schools. In our research, Turner and I found that very few adolescents had sex education programs in community centers or churches. The resources of these organizations could be used in a comprehensive sex education program and might be very important to adolescents' understanding of community values related to sexuality, pregnancy, and the relationships in which pregnancy occurs.

EDUCATION AND CAREER PROGRAMS

Comprehensive sex education programs are necessary but not sufficient to prevent unplanned pregnancies. In addition to programs that focus directly on sexuality and

pregnancy prevention, we need programs that focus on educational expectations and educational achievement. These programs reduce the risk of unplanned pregnancy indirectly by giving adolescents a positive focus for their lives. Anne White and I found that adolescents who have high expectations for their own educational attainment are less likely than others to become sexually active and more likely to use contra-

ceptives when they do become sexually active. Adolescents who see formal education as a viable route to adult success have a *reason* to delay sexual activity and childbearing.[32] As the Children's Defense Fund puts it, "The best contraceptive is a real future." Programs for adolescents need to emphasize the good things they can do with their lives and not just the negative possibilities that we want to prevent. If pregnancy pre-

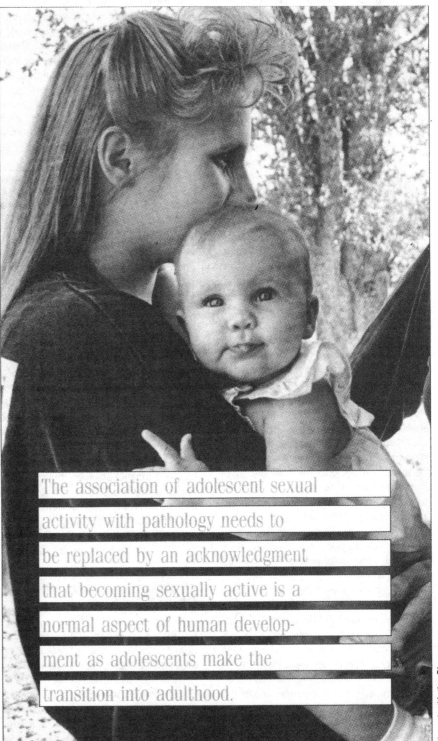

The association of adolescent sexual activity with pathology needs to be replaced by an acknowledgment that becoming sexually active is a normal aspect of human development as adolescents make the transition into adulthood.

Photo by Kathy Sloane

vention programs focusing on abstinence can be characterized by the slogan "Just say no," then the programs I am advocating here could be characterized by the slogan "Just say yes." Adolescents need to be shown positive options that they can embrace.

Many adolescent childbearers were not performing well in school prior to their pregnancy.[33] The developmental trajectory that leads to poor outcomes for adolescent childbearers appears to be set in motion before the pregnancy and includes low achievement, low engagement in school, and even dropping out of school. Thus having a child usually does not deflect an adolescent from a positive developmental trajectory; many adolescents who bear children were already moving in a negative direction.

Therefore, we must consider the meaning and value of schools for adolescents. Schools today may not be educating and socializing adolescents appropriately for the transition to adulthood. At a time in their lives when they need more guidance from caring adults, adolescents may get less attention from them. For many adolescents, school becomes less and less meaningful. Few high school students, especially those who are not college-bound, believe that they will use the material they are expected to learn in school. Some are already working part-time jobs similar to the kinds of jobs that await them upon graduation. From their own experience, they may know that what they are expected to learn in school is not related to the employment available to them.

An apprenticeship system for adolescents, similar to that in Germany, has been proposed for the U.S.[34] In programs of this type, adolescents would be socialized to perform well not only on academic tasks but also in a real job setting.

Some current efforts to make high schools more meaningful for adolescents include a Public Service Academy, located in a high school in a very poor area of Washington, D.C. This program orients students toward careers in government — the largest employer in their community — and provides them appropriate internships and part-time government jobs. Public schools, private companies and foundations, and universities collaborated to create the Pubic Service Academy. A second example is Houston's High School for Health Professions, which has been operated as a partnership of the public school district and a Houston medical school since 1972. The majority of students in these high school programs will go

on to college. However, similar programs could provide an avenue toward employment for those who do not attend college.

Overall, the educational attainment of adolescent childbearers has increased from the 1950s, and the educational attainment of African American adolescent childbearers has increased more than that of whites. Dawn Upchurch and James McCarthy investigated educational attainment among three cohorts of women who were 21 to 29 years of age in 1958, in 1975, and in 1986. Although women who delayed childbearing were more likely to have graduated from high school than adolescent childbearers, adolescent mothers in 1986 were more likely to have graduated than their 1975 or 1958 counterparts. For black adolescents who were 17 years of age or younger when their first child was born, only 16.6% had graduated in 1958, compared to 60.6% in 1986. The corresponding rates for their

---

Child rearing places enormous demands on adolescents, who must also complete their schooling and enter the workplace.

---

white counterparts were 19.6% in 1958 and 53.7% in 1986.[35]

African American adolescent mothers appear to fare better educationally than both their white and their Hispanic counterparts. The National Longitudinal Survey of Youth revealed that, among adolescent mothers whose children were in elementary school, African American mothers had achieved higher educational levels than whites or Hispanics.[36] In addition, in a study of the birth records of one midwestern state, African American childbearers deviated less from expected educational attainment than did Hispanic or white childbearers.[37]

ABORTION: A CONTROVERSIAL OPTION

Perhaps no issue involved in adolescent childbearing is more controversial than abortion. Adolescents' minor status means that their right to obtain abortions is more restricted than that of adult females.

More than 30 states have laws that require the involvement of a parent or a third party in a minor's decision regarding abortion. The "third party" requirement exists so that

adolescents have the option of attempting to convince a third party — typically a judge — that they are competent to make the decision independently or that the abortion is in the adolescent's best interest. This "third party" mechanism is a way of bypassing the parental consent requirement for adolescent abortion. Data from actual court hearings indicate that adolescent minors' requests to bypass parental consent are almost always granted. Judges may find the determination of maturity or best interest difficult and may therefore grant all requests. Anita Pliner and Suzanne Yates question whether the consent legislation meets the goals of encouraging communication between parents and adolescents and protecting the rights of minor adolescents.[38] They found that health professionals working with adolescents before and after passage of the legislation indicated that psychological and medical counseling were needed more than pro forma legal procedures. Time spent on the legal proceedings might have been better spent on psychological and medical counseling.

Pliner and Yates recommend that states follow the example of Maryland, where a physician or mental health provider, instead of a judge, makes the determination of maturity and best interest. A second option they suggest is to include mandatory counseling in the legislation, as is done in Maine and Connecticut. Finally, Pliner and Yates recommend that the parental notification and consent laws be limited to adolescents 15 years of age and younger.

Although legal constraints may prevent some adolescents from seeking an abortion, many adolescents do not choose abortion in any case. We might wonder why more adolescents do not seek abortion. Laurie Zabin and Sarah Hayward found that attitudes toward abortion were not different between adolescents who chose abortion and those who carried their babies to term. The difference was that those who chose abortion were very unhappy — unequivocally so — about the pregnancy. Although other adolescents did not indicate that they had wanted or planned to become pregnant, many were ambivalent rather than completely negative about having a child. Zabin and Hayward concluded that, unless there is an "overriding reason to avoid childbearing" — a bright future that will be damaged by early childbearing — the adolescent will have the child rather than choose abortion.[39]

Despite strong feelings on all sides of the abortion controversy, little research exists to help determine the effect on an adoles-

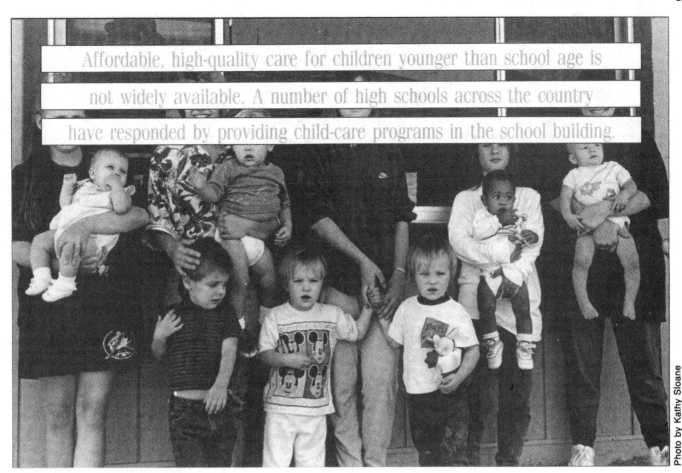

Affordable, high-quality care for children younger than school age is not widely available. A number of high schools across the country have responded by providing child-care programs in the school building.

Photo by Kathy Sloane

cent of having an abortion compared to completing a pregnancy. More research and monitoring of outcomes of legislation should lead to appropriate policy in this area. More research is also needed on adolescents' capabilities to make various decisions about health care.[40] It may not be possible to reach consensus on the issue of abortion, but those who work to create pregnancy prevention programs must find ways to acknowledge differing values and beliefs in this area.

ADOPTION: AN INFREQUENTLY USED OPTION

When adolescents have babies, they very rarely place them for adoption.[41] The overwhelming majority — approximately 97% — of all adolescent childbearers keep their babies. Because of private adoptions and confidential records, however, statistics on adoption may not be entirely accurate. White adolescents are more likely to give their babies up for adoption than are ethnic minority adolescents. But over the past two decades the adoption rate for white adolescent parents has declined sharply, from 19% to 3%, whereas the adoption rate for African American adolescents has re-

mained relatively constant at 1%. It has been suggested that, for African American adolescent parents, an informal type of adoption may occur, with members of the extended family helping to care for the baby.

Research on factors that contribute to adolescents' decision not to place their babies for adoption suggests that adolescents feel emotionally attached to their babies and are thus unable to give them to someone outside their families. In addition, the mothers, peers, and partners of pregnant adolescents may not encourage adoption. Finally, the current organization of adoption procedures may mean that a pregnant adolescent is not given accurate information about adoption as an alternative, may feel pressured into adoption, or may be frightened by the requirement of a complete severing of ties with the baby. Together, these factors may lead adolescent parents to equate adoption with abandonment of the child.

Research on adoption outcomes is sparse. The small number of studies on mothers' responses following adoption often use clinical samples and inadequate research design. However, these studies suggest that mothers experience a long-term sense of loss following adoption and have no accept-

able outlets for expressing their emotions. Michael Sobol and Kerry Daly recommend increasing the involvement of birth parents in the adoption plan as a means of alleviating adolescent parents' belief that placing a baby for adoption is irresponsible.[42] Programs encouraging pregnant adolescents to choose adoption are funded by the federal Adolescent Family Life Act.

CHILD-CARE PROGRAMS

Although child rearing places enormous demands on adolescents, who must also complete their schooling and find a place in the work world, some adolescents are able to manage these developmental tasks. Continued education becomes a key factor in the resilience of adolescent parents. Sherry Turner and I studied three groups of African American women aged 20-24, 25-34, and 35-44 who were part of the National Survey of Family Growth. We found that women who had their first birth during adolescence generally completed fewer years of school and earned lower incomes than women who delayed childbearing.[43] Some of those who had been adolescent mothers, however, had stayed in school longer, and, when we controlled for educational attainment, we found that adolescent childbearing was not a significant predictor of adult income. The number of years of education completed was a stronger predictor of women's income than was the experience of adolescent childbearing.

Social and material support from the family, the community, and the school are essential if the adolescent mother is to remain in school. Adequate child care is especially important for adolescent parents who are enrolled in school. Affordable, high-quality care for children younger than school age is not widely available. But the provision of child care may allow adolescent mothers to resume their schooling more quickly and more easily than would otherwise be possible.

A number of high schools across the country have responded to this situation by providing child-care programs in the school building. We are in the process of studying child-care programs for the children of adolescent mothers as part of our research at the National Center on Families, Communities, Schools, and Children's Learning.

One of our study sites is Orr Community Academy, a public high school in Chicago that maintains an impressive child-care facility. Before the child-care facility was opened, the high school had already established a rich array of programs linking the school to the community and to families. The child-care center was planned in the context of an active umbrella program that connected the high school with surrounding elementary schools and with the community. In June 1989 this urban high school, 13 elementary feeder schools in the area, and a local bank initiated the Orr School Network. This network connects the schools to one another and to the city's educational, cultural, and social service resources. Network principals meet each month to plan and implement programs revolving around three major initiatives: intervening in early childhood, enriching the school years and removing academic deficits, and increasing family and community support for children. One component of the early childhood initiative is the child-care center in the high school.

The high school also contains a comprehensive health clinic for students and a prekindergarten program. The health clinic provides a broad range of health services, including contraception, to adolescents whose parents give written consent. The prekindergarten program operates four days a week in two half-day shifts; 20 children are enrolled in each shift. The high school is also a site for the Women, Infants,

Sexual restraint and pregnancy prevention should be presented as necessary prerequisites for a bright future.

and Children program, a federally funded supplemental program that provides food packages and nutritional counseling to eligible mothers. Another special program that operates out of the high school building is Enrichment for Latinas Leading to Advancement, a comprehensive career program for Latina students that emphasizes nontraditional areas of work for females, such as real estate, banking, medicine, and engineering.

The Orr Infant and Family Development Center, which is operated by Jane Addams Hull House, a Chicago social service agency, is licensed to serve 24 adolescent parents and their children from 6 weeks to 3 years of age. The center has an exemplary physical layout for the care and education of young children. It has its own separate entrance and an outdoor playground separated by a wall from the rest of the school grounds. A bus provides transportation exclusively for the adolescent parents and their children.

To use the center, the adolescent parent must be enrolled in school, must work in the child-care facility for one hour a day, and must take a parenting class. Adolescent parents and *their* parents must sign a contract agreeing that the adolescent will attend and pass all classes. Adolescent parents also complete a plan detailing goals that they wish to accomplish with their children. The Orr Infant and Family Development Center provides much-needed assistance to adolescent parents, but it also encourages responsibility and achievement on the part of the young parents.

PROGRAMS FOR YOUNG FATHERS

Most programs focus on adolescent females. Because the majority of fathers of babies born to adolescent mothers are young adult males, programs that seek to reach young fathers may be more effective if they are based in the community rather than in the school. One example of such a community-based program is the Responsible Fathers Program, run by the Philadelphia Children's Network. This program, which in 1992 served 57 young unwed fathers between the ages of 16 and 25, focuses on

parenting skills and encourages the men to be actively involved in their children's lives. The young men are also linked to educational resources, employment opportunities, and social services. The program promotes communication and cooperation between fathers and mothers as they raise their children. Claire Brindis provides some examples of other programs for males.[44]

SEPARATE STRATEGIES FOR DIFFERENT AGE GROUPS

The developmental needs of early adolescence, which involves the transition from late childhood, are very different from the developmental needs of late adolescence, which involves the transition to adulthood. Thus programs for older adolescents need to address such matters as completing formal schooling, entering the labor force, and maintaining responsible relationships.

Young adolescents, on the other hand, need sex education programs that begin before they become sexually active. Open discussions with parents, teachers, and counselors are also important. In these discussions, the adults should listen to adolescents, in addition to conveying adult beliefs and values. Young adolescents need accurate information about sexuality and contraception, and they need the opportunity to discuss with adults the close personal relationships in which responsible sexual expression occurs. Sexual restraint and pregnancy prevention should not be presented in negative terms but as necessary prerequisites for a bright future that would be tarnished by an unplanned pregnancy.

When young adolescents do become pregnant, they are more likely than older adolescents to face medical risks that need attention. In addition, the number of years of school remaining for young adolescent parents affects program strategies. For example, in school-based child-care programs for adolescent parents, the children served are usually under age 3. This age range is appropriate for the needs of older adolescents and would allow them to have child care until they completed high school. Children born to younger adolescents, however, would be older than 3 before the adolescent parent completed high school and would need care through a different program.

N SPITE of the difficulties adolescents face as they grow into adulthood, we must remain optimistic. Adolescents encounter many problems as they become adults in the imperfect world we have created. Gary Melton has written about the importance of recognizing adolescents as *persons*.[45] We must respect them as such in the programs we plan for them. They are not children, even though we do not yet recognize them as adults. Adolescents' views need to be incorporated into the design and evaluation of pregnancy prevention programs. Through the dreams and aspirations of our adolescents and through the opportunities we provide them to grow into productive adults, we might truly change our society.

1. Issues of the newsletter of the National Coalition on Television Violence, June-August 1991.

2. Phyllis B. Eveleth, ''Timing of Menarche: Secular Trends and Population Differences,'' in Jane B. Lancaster and Beatrix A. Hamburg, eds., *School-Age Pregnancy and Parenthood* (New York: Aldine, 1986), pp. 39-52.

3. Linda H. Holt, ''Medical Perspectives on Pregnancy and Birth: Biological Risks and Technological Advances,'' in Gerald Y. Michaels and Wendy A. Goldberg, eds., *The Transition to Parenthood: Current Theory and Research* (New York: Cambridge University Press, 1988), pp. 157-75.

4. Wendy H. Baldwin, *Adolescent Pregnancy and Childbearing — Rates, Trends, and Research Findings from the Center for Population Research* (Washington, D.C.: National Institute of Child Health and Human Development, 1984); and Tom Luster and Mary Mittelstaedt, ''Adolescent Mothers,'' in Tom Luster and Lynn Okagaki, eds., *Parenting: An Ecological Perspective* (Hillsdale, N.J.: Erlbaum, 1993), pp. 69-100.

5. *Fertility of American Women: June 1992* (Washington, D.C.: U.S. Bureau of the Census, Current Population Reports, Series P-20, No. 470, 1993).

6. ''Sexual Risk Behaviors of STD Clinic Patients Before and After Earvin 'Magic' Johnson's HIV-Infection Announcement — Maryland, 1991-1992,'' *Morbidity and Mortality Weekly Report*, Centers for Disease Control, 29 January 1993, pp. 45-48.

7. Ibid.

8. Laurie S. Zabin and Sarah C. Hayward, *Adolescent Sexual Behavior and Childbearing* (Newbury Park, Calif.: Sage, 1993).

9. Stanley Henshaw et al., *Teenage Pregnancy in the United States: The Scope of the Problem and State Responses* (New York: Alan Guttmacher Institute, 1989); and Select Committee on Children, Youth, and Families, U.S. House of Representatives, *Teen Pregnancy: What Is Being Done?* (Washington, D.C.: U.S. Government Printing Office, 1986).

10. Henshaw et al., op. cit.

11. Ibid.

12. Luster and Mittelstaedt, p. 69.

13. Claire D. Brindis et al., *Adolescent Pregnancy Prevention: A Guidebook for Communities* (Palo Alto, Calif.: Stanford Center for Research in Disease Prevention, 1991).

14. Elise Jones et al., *Teenage Pregnancy in Industrialized Countries* (New Haven, Conn.: Yale University Press, 1986).

15. Charles F. Westoff, ''Unintended Pregnancy in America and Abroad,'' *Family Planning Perspectives*, vol. 20, 1988, pp. 254-61.

16. Henshaw et al., op. cit.

17. Jones et al., op. cit.

18. Frank Furstenberg, Judith Levine, and Jeanne Brooks-Gunn, ''The Daughters of Teenage Mothers: Patterns of Early Childbearing in Two Generations,'' *Family Planning Perspectives*, vol. 22, 1990, pp. 54-61.

19. *Hostile Hallways: Survey on Sexual Harassment in American Schools* (Washington, D.C.: American Association of University Women, 1993).

20. Leo Hendricks, *Unmarried Adolescent Fathers: Problems They Face and the Ways They Cope with Them* (Washington, D.C.: Institute for Urban Affairs and Research, 1979); Diane Scott-Jones and Anne B. White, ''Correlates of Sexual Activity in Early Adolescence,'' *Journal of Early Adolescence*, vol. 10, 1990, pp. 221-38; and Freya Sonenstein, ''Risking Paternity: Sex and Contraception Among Adolescent Males,'' in Arthur B. Elster and Michael E. Lamb, eds., *Adolescent Fatherhood* (Hillsdale, N.J.: Erlbaum, 1986), pp. 31-54.

21. Loretta S. Jemmott and John B. Jemmott, ''Sexual Knowledge, Attitudes, and Risky Sexual Behavior Among Inner-City Black Male Adolescents,'' *Journal of Adolescent Research*, vol. 5, 1990, pp. 346-69; and Joseph H. Pleck, Freya L. Sonenstein, and Leighton C. Ku, ''Adolescent Males' Condom Use: Relationships Between Perceived Cost-Benefits and Consistency,'' *Journal of Marriage and the Family*, vol. 53, 1991, pp. 733-45.

22. Hendricks, op. cit.

23. Joseph H. Pleck, Freya L. Sonenstein, and Scott O. Swain, ''Adolescent Males' Sexual Behavior and Contraceptive Use: Implications for Male Responsibility,'' *Journal of Adolescent Research*, vol. 3, 1988, pp. 275-84; and Pleck, Sonenstein, and Ku, op. cit.

24. Scott-Jones and White, op. cit.

25. ''Sexual Risk Behaviors.''

26. Zabin and Hayward, op. cit.

27. Joy D. Osofsky, Howard J. Osofsky, and Martha O. Diamond, ''The Transition to Parenthood: Special Tasks and Risk Factors for Adolescent Parents,'' in Gerald Y. Michaels and Wendy A. Goldberg, eds., *The Transition to Parenthood: Current Theory and Research* (New York: Cambridge University Press, 1988), pp. 209-34.

28. Brindis, op. cit.

29. Diane Scott-Jones and Sherry L. Turner, ''Sex Education, Contraceptive and Reproductive Knowledge, and Contraceptive Use Among Black Adolescent Females,'' *Journal of Adolescent Research*, vol. 3, 1988, p. 171-87.

30. Brindis, op. cit.

31. Janet Gans et al., *America's Adolescents: How Healthy Are They?* (Chicago: American Medical Association, 1990); and Luster and Mittelstaedt, op. cit.

32. Scott-Jones and White, op. cit.

33. Dawn M. Upchurch and James McCarthy, ''The Timing of a First Birth and High School Completion,'' *American Sociological Review*, vol. 25, 1990, pp. 224-34.

34. Stephen F. Hamilton, *Apprenticeship for Adulthood: Preparing Youth for the Future* (New York: Free Press, 1990).

35. Upchurch and McCarthy, op. cit.

36. Tom Luster and Eric Dubow, ''Predictors for the Quality of the Home Environment That Adolescent Mothers Provide for Their School-Aged Children,'' *Journal of Youth and Adolescence*, vol. 19, 1990, pp. 475-94.

37. Diane Scott-Jones, ''Adolescent Childbearing: Risks and Resilience,'' *American Journal of Education*, vol. 24, 1991, pp. 53-64.

38. Anita J. Pliner and Suzanne Yates, ''Psychological and Legal Issues in Minors' Rights to Abortion,'' *Journal of Social Issues*, vol. 48, 1992, pp. 203-16.

39. Zabin and Hayward, p. 80.

40. *Adolescent Health — Vol. I: Summary and Policy Options* (Washington, D.C.: U.S. Congress Office of Technology Assessment, OTA-H-468, April 1991).

41. Michael P. Sobol and Kerry J. Daly, ''The Adoption Alternative for Pregnant Adolescents: Decision Making, Consequences, and Policy Implications,'' *Journal of Social Issues*, vol. 48, 1992, pp. 143-61.

42. Ibid.

43. Diane Scott-Jones and Sherry L. Turner, ''The Impact of Adolescent Childbearing on Educational Attainment and Income of Black Females,'' *Youth and Society*, vol. 22, 1990, pp. 35-53.

44. Brindis, op. cit.

45. Gary B. Melton, ''Are Adolescents People? Problems of Liberty, Entitlement, and Responsibility,'' in Judith Worell and Fred Danner, eds., *The Adolescent as Decision-Maker: Applications to Development and Education* (San Diego: Academic Press, 1989), pp. 281-306.

Selected Resources

REPORTS

☑ *Adolescent Health — Vol. I: Summary and Policy Options*. Washington, D.C.: U.S. Congress Office of Technology Assessment, OTA-H-468, April 1991.

☑ Hayes, Cheryl D., ed. *Risking the Future: Adolescent Sexuality, Pregnancy, and Childbearing, Vol. I*. Washington, D.C.: National Academy Press, 1987.

☑ Hofferth, Sandra L., and Cheryl D. Hayes, eds. *Risking the Future: Adolescent Sexuality, Pregnancy, and Childbearing, Vol. II: Working Papers and Statistical Appendices*. Washington, D.C.: National Academy Press, 1987.

☑ Ooms, Theodora, and Lisa Henrendeen. *Teenage Pregnancy Prevention Programs: What Have We Learned?* Washington, D.C.: Family Impact Seminar, 1990.

☑ *Teenage Drug Use: Uncertain Linkages with Either Pregnancy or School Drop-Out*. Gaithersburg, Md.: U.S. General Accounting Office, GAO/PEMD-91-3, January 1991.

INFORMATION RESOURCES

☑ Brindis, Claire D., et al. *Adolescent Pregnancy Prevention: A Guidebook for Communities*. Palo Alto, Calif.: Stanford Center for Research in Disease Prevention, 1991.

☑ Creighton-Zollar, Ann. *Adolescent Pregnancy and Parenthood: An Annotated Guide*. New York: Garland, 1990.

☑ Data Archives on Adolescent Pregnancy and Pregnancy Prevention, Sociometrics, Los Altos, Calif.

☑ *Family Planning Perspectives* (journal published by the Alan Guttmacher Institute).

☑ ''Special Issue: Adolescence in the 1990s: Risk and Opportunity.'' *Teachers College Record*, Spring 1993.

ORGANIZATIONS AND CLEARINGHOUSES

Alan Guttmacher Institute
2010 Massachusetts Ave. N.W.
Washington, DC 20036

Center for Population Options
1025 Vermont Ave. N.W.
Washington, DC 20005

Children's Defense Fund
122 C St. N.W.
Washington, DC 20001

Girls Clubs of America
205 Lexington Ave.
New York, NY 10016

National Urban League
500 E. 62nd St.
New York, NY 10021

Share Resource Center on Teen Pregnancy Prevention
P.O. Box 2309
Rockville, MD 20852

The Lifelong Impact of ADOPTION

In many cases, birthparents have trouble dealing with giving up their offspring; adoptees want to know more about their biological roots and genetic history; and adoptive parents are being confronted with issues concerning the raising of their adopted children that no one had warned them about.

Marlou Russell

Dr. Russell is a clinical psychologist in private practice in Santa Monica, Calif., specializing in adoption. She is an adoptee who has been reunited with her birthmother and two brothers.

IMAGINE BEING an adoptive parent who has gone through years of infertility treatment. You recently have adopted an infant and are at a party with it. Someone exclaims, "What a cute baby. Why, I didn't even know you were pregnant!" You wonder if you need to explain.

Now, try to imagine being a birthmother who relinquished a child 25 years ago. You since have married and had two more offspring. You strike up a conversation with someone you've just met. She asks, "How many children do you have?" You hesitate for a moment, then answer, "Two."

Finally, imagine that you were adopted as an infant. You have an appointment to see a new physician for the first time. When you arrive at the office, you are given a two-page form asking for your medical history. When you meet the doctor, he asks, "Does cancer run in your family?" You respond, "I don't know."

The adoption triad has three elements: the adoptive parent or parents, the birthparents, and the adoptee. All members are necessary and all depend on each other, as in any triangle.

There have been many changes in adoption over the years. The basic premise of adoption in the past was that it was a viable solution to certain problem situations. The infertile parents wanted a child; a birthparent was pregnant and unable to raise her offspring; and the infant needed available parents. It was thought that all the triad members would get their needs met by adoption. The records were amended, sealed, and closed through legal proceedings, and the triad members were expected never to see each other again.

It was discovered, however, that there were problems with closed adoption. Some birthparents began having trouble "forgetting" that they had had a child and were finding it hard "getting on with their lives," as suggested by those around them. There were adoptees who wanted to know more about their biological roots and had questions about their genetic history. Some adoptive parents were having difficulties raising their adopted children and were being confronted with parenting issues that no one had told them about.

Clinicians and psychotherapists became involved because more and more adopted children were being brought in for psychotherapy and being seen in juvenile detention facilities, inpatient treatment centers, and special schools. Questions began to be raised about the impact and process of closed adoption.

From these questions, it became clear that there are new basic tenets in adoption. One is that adoption usually is a second choice for all the triad members. For example, most people don't imagine that they will grow up, get married, and adopt children. They expect that they will grow up, get married, and have kids of their own. Girls and/or women also don't expect to get pregnant and give their child to strangers to raise.

Coping with loss

A second basic tenet of adoption is that it involves loss for all involved. A birthparent loses a child; the adoptee loses biological connections; and infertile adoptive parents lose the hope for biological children. Those indirectly involved in adoption also experience loss. The birthparents' parents lose a grandchild, while the siblings of the birthparent lose a niece or nephew.

Since loss is such a major part of adoption, grieving is a necessary and important process. The five stages of normal grief and mourning, as set forth by psychologist

Elisabeth Kübler-Ross, are denial—feeling shocked, numbed, and detached; anger—maintaining that the situation is unfair; bargaining—wanting to make a deal or trade-off; depression—feeling helpless and hopeless; and acceptance—integrating and resolving the loss enough to function.

For triad members, grief holds a special significance. They may not even be aware that they are grieving or mourning their loss. Adoption can create a situation where grieving is delayed or denied. Because adoption has been seen as such a positive solution, it may be difficult for a triad member to feel that it is okay to grieve when everything is "working out for the best."

There are no rituals or ceremonies for the loss of adoption. In the case of death, society provides the rituals of funerals and the gathering of people to support the person who is mourning. If the adoption process is secret, as was the case in many adoptions of the past, there is even less opportunity for mourning. In addition, with adoption, much attention is given to the next step of raising the child or getting on with one's life.

Some triad members resolve their grief by trying to find the person they are grieving for. Search and reunion offers the opportunity to address the basic and natural curiosity that all people have in their inheritance and roots. The missing pieces can be put in the puzzle, and lifelong questions can be answered. In addition, there is an empowering aspect to search and reunion and an internal sense of timing that brings with it a feeling of being in control and trusting one's own judgment. For most people who search, knowing—even if they find uncomfortable information—is better than not knowing.

Whether someone actively searches or not, there usually is some part of the person that is searching internally. A common experience among adoptees and birthparents is scanning crowds, looking for someone who could be their parent or their child. Even triad members who say they aren't interested in seeking will express curiosity and react to the idea of search and reunion.

What holds many triad members back from searching or admitting they are doing so is the fear of causing pain to one of the other triad members. Adoptees may worry about hurting their adoptive parents' feelings and appearing to be ungrateful, while birthparents may be concerned that their child wasn't told of the adoption or that he or she will reject them.

Reunion between triad members is the beginning of a previous relationship. It is where fantasy meets reality. Reunions impact all triad members and those close to them. As with other relationships, there has to be nurturing, attention, and a respect for people's boundaries and needs. Reunions and the interactions within them show that adoption was not just a simple solution, but a process that has lifelong impact.

Finding a Balance: Maintaining Relationships

- Marriage and Other Committed Relationships (Articles 20–25)
- Relationships between Parents and Children (Articles 26–29)
- Siblings: Another Lifelong Relationship (Articles 30 and 31)

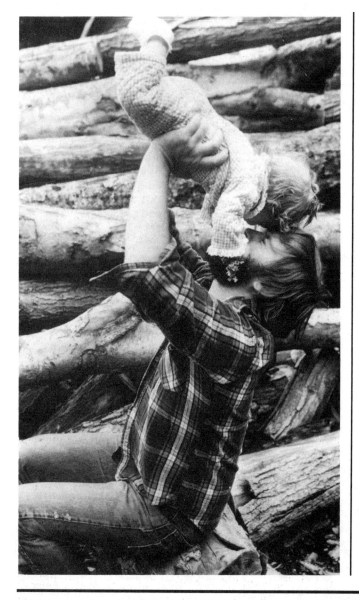

"And they lived happily ever after . . . " The romantic image conjured up by this well-known final line from fairy tales is not reflective of the reality of family life and relationship maintenance. The belief that somehow love alone should carry us through is pervasive. In reality, relationship maintenance takes dedication, hard work, and commitment.

We come into relationships, regardless of their nature, with fantasies about how things "ought" to be. Spouses, parents, children, siblings, and others—all family members have at least some unrealistic expectations about each other. It is through the negotiation of their lives together that they come to work through these expectations and replace them with other, hopefully more realistic, ones. By recognizing and acting on their own contribution to the family, members can set and attain realistic family goals. Tolerance and acceptance of differences can facilitate this process, as can competent communication skills. Along the way, family members need to learn new skills and develop new habits of relating to each other. This will not be easy and, try as they may, not everything will be controllable. Factors both inside and outside the family may impede their progress.

From the start, both partners' expectations have of their relationship have an impact, and the need to negotiate differences is a constant factor. Adding a child to the family affects the lives of parents in ways that they can previously only imagine. Feeling under siege, many parents struggle to know the right way to rear their children. These factors can all combine to make child rearing more difficult than it might otherwise have been. Other family relationships also evolve, and in our nuclear, family-focused culture, it is possible to forget that family relationships extend beyond those between spouses and parents and children.

The first subsection presents a variety of aspects of marriage and the marital relationship. The first article focuses on the multiple and often competing roles played by today's couples. Work and home are nearly impossible to separate for many of them. They expect to fulfill individual as well as couple needs, which can be a difficult balancing act. Figuring out how they can cope with the expectations and pressures of work, home, and child care and still have time for each other may be the most important way today's couples can prevent the problems and crises that lead to dissatisfaction. There are no easy solutions to these problems. Couples may believe that one possibility is a "Peer Marriage," in which couples create a truly egalitarian relationship. The reader will see that there are both positive and negative aspects to such a marriage.

In "Receipts from a Marriage," Margaret Ambry addresses the shifting pattern of spending habits that couples face throughout their marriage.

"Staying Power: Bridging the Gender Gap in the Confusing '90s" and "But What Do You Mean?" look at gender differences that may influence relationships between men and women. When we are able to step beyond stereotypes and appreciate differences, the likelihood of success is increased.

Finally, "Saving Relationships: The Power of the Unpredictable" presents a family systems view of the relationship process, suggesting ways in which small changes in one aspect of the family can have large impacts elsewhere.

In the next subsection, the parent/child relationship is examined. In "Vanishing Dreams of America's Young Families," Marian Wright Edelman, president of the Children's Defense Fund, depicts the struggle of young families in today's world. She argues that, as a society, we have an obligation to the children of these young families, an obligation we are not yet meeting. The next subsection article, "Effective Fathers: Why Are Some Dads More Successful than Others?" offers a look at fathers who have been successful in their role and may serve

as a resource for building family strengths. This subsection ends with two articles that are case studies of parents growing through their relationships with their children—in the first, a gay son, and in the second, HIV-positive foster children.

The final subsection expands our view beyond spousal and parent-child relationships to another family relationship. Both reports "Siblings and Development" and "The Secret World of Siblings" look at sibling relationships and their impact on children's development and their ability to relate to others. Although raised in the same family, children do not experience identical family influence. Each child goes through a different interactive process in the family and, as a result, each can have a radically different family experience.

Looking Ahead: Challenge Questions

When you think of a marriage, what do you picture? What are your expectations of your (future) spouse? What are your expectations of yourself? How much are you willing to give to your marriage? What would you be willing to give up?

How is your experience of committed relationships influenced by those you saw while growing up? How do those relationships affect your own willingness to enter a committed relationship?

How should each spouse behave in a marriage? How are men's and women's roles the same or different?

What do you expect parenthood to be like? What have you learned in talking with your parents or other parents about their expectations and experiences? Why should you share parenting tasks with your spouse or partner? Why would you want or not want to have a child by yourself?

What differences have you seen in the ways in which siblings are treated in families? Why do you think this is so? What is the best way to rear children? Why or why not should you focus on equal treatment of children?

What's Happening to

AMERICAN MARRIAGE?

Demands for intimacy, emotional support, companionship, and sexual gratification have increased, although there has been a decline in what individuals are willing to sacrifice for a relationship.

Norval D. Glenn

Dr. Glenn is Ashbel Smith Professor of Sociology and Stiles Professor in American Studies, University of Texas at Austin.

VER THE PAST three decades, there has been a period of substantial changes in the institution of marriage in the U.S. The divorce rate doubled from 1965 to 1975, increased more slowly through the late 1970s, and leveled off in the 1980s, but at such a high level that almost two-thirds of the marriages entered into in recent years are expected to end in divorce or separation. The increase in divorce, a decrease in remarriage after divorce, and a higher average age at first marriage have lowered the proportion of adults who are married. Out-of-wedlock births have increased substantially, so that one-fourth of all births now are to unmarried mothers. The proportion of married women who work outside the home has risen steadily, the increase being especially great among those with preschool-age children.

Everyone agrees that these changes are important, but different authorities and commentators disagree as to what they mean for the health and future of the institution of marriage. One point of view is that marriage is in serious trouble—that it

may disappear or lose its status as the preferred way of life for adult Americans. For example, a recent book is titled *The Retreat from Marriage,* and numerous books and articles refer to a decline or deinstitutionalization of marriage.

An opposing view, held until recently by most social scientific students of marriage, is that recent changes do not indicate decline or decay, but, rather, are adaptive and have kept the institution viable and healthy. These observers point out, for instance, that the increase in divorce has come about because people are rejecting particular marriages, rather than the institution of marriage—that most divorced persons want to remarry, and about three-fourths of them do so. Some of these commentators even view the increase in divorce positively, claiming that it reflects an increased importance people place on having good marriages and a decreased willingness to endure unsatisfactory ones. Divorce and remarriage, according to this view, are mechanisms for replacing poor relationships with better ones and keeping the overall quality of marriages high.

The evidence doesn't support consistently either the most negative or most positive views of what is happening to American marriage. For instance, the notion that it is a moribund or dying institution is inconsistent with the fact that a large percentage of Americans say that having a happy marriage is one of the most important, if not *the* most important, goal in their lives.

About two-fifths of the respondents to the 1989 Massachusetts Mutual American Family Values Study indicated this was one of their most important values, and more than 90% said it was one of the most important or very important. Approximately three-fourths of the high school seniors studied by the Monitoring the Future Project at the University of Michigan in recent years have stated they definitely will marry, and the proportion has not declined. When adults are asked what kind of lifestyle they prefer, a very large majority select one involving wedlock, and a substantial minority (more than one-third) choose a traditional marriage in which the husband is the breadwinner and the wife a homemaker.

Even when one takes into account that what people say in response to survey questions may not always reflect accurately what they think and feel, these survey data clearly demonstrate that Americans in general have not given up on matrimony. However, there is even more compelling evidence against the most extremely positive assessments of recent changes. Although having good marriages may be as important to people as ever, or may have become even more important in recent years, my research indicates that the probability of attaining them has declined to a large extent.

Those who argue that marriages in this country in general are doing quite well often cite data showing that a high and rather stable percentage of married persons give positive responses when they are asked

Percentage of Persons Saying They Were Personally "Very Happy," by Marital Situation

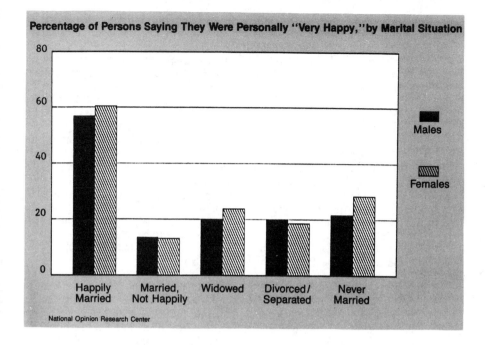

National Opinion Research Center

about the quality of their unions. In fact, since the early 1970s, the reported quality of marriages has gone down, though not very much. Most years since 1973, the General Social Survey conducted by the National Opinion Research Center at the University of Chicago has asked people to rate their marriages as very happy, pretty happy, or not too happy. The percentage of those who cited "very happy" fell by five percentage points from 1973-76 to 1988-91, dropping from 68 to 63%.

The indicated over-all happiness quality of American marriages still would be quite high if these ratings were to be taken at their face value, but they should not be interpreted that way. Many people are reluctant to admit to an interviewer—and perhaps even to themselves—that their marriages are less than satisfactory. Therefore, an unknown, but possibly substantial, proportion of the marriages reported to be "very happy" are not of very high quality, whereas virtually all those reported to be less than very happy are seriously deficient.

What is important about the indicated trend in marital quality is not that it has been slightly downward, but that it has not been steeply upward. If, as some commentators have claimed, the increase in divorce resulted only from people becoming less willing to stay in unsatisfactory marriages, the average quality of intact marriages should have climbed in tandem with the divorce rate. The fact that it didn't means that the probability of marriages remaining satisfactory must have declined substantially.

During 1973-76, about 60% of the persons who had first married three-five years earlier were still in their first marriages and

reported them to be "very happy." By 1988-91, it had declined to about 54%. For persons who first married 12-14 years earlier, the decline was greater, from 54 to 38%, while for those who married 20-24 years earlier, it dropped from 50 to 36%. There were declines of around 10 or more percentage points at most other lengths of time since the first marriage.

Those who view recent changes in American marriage positively may not find these data very alarming. To them, what is important is the kind of marriage a person eventually attains, not the success of his or her first union. From this perspective, the percentages of ever-married persons who were in marriages of any order (first, second, or subsequent) that they reported to be "very happy" are even more significant.

The changes from 1973-76 to 1988-91 show a distinct downward trend in the probability of being in a successful marriage. Among persons who have sought marital happiness by marrying at least once, a decreased proportion seem to be experiencing it. This indicates that the increase in divorce and the other changes in marriage during the past three decades have not been solely or primarily a matter of people becoming more willing and able to go from poor marriages to better ones.

Still, one might suspect that there has been one positive aspect of the changes of the past few years—namely, a decreased tendency for people to be in poor marriages. However, the proportion of ever-married persons who were in marriages they reported to be less than "very happy" increased from 1973-76 to 1988-91 at all lengths of time after the first marriage up to 20 years—the changes being in the range

of three to five percentage points. Only among persons who married 20-29 years earlier was there a slight decrease in the percentage of persons in the less satisfactory unions.

Most of the decrease in the probability of being in a very happy marriage resulted from an increase in the probability of being divorced or separated. For instance, at 12-14 years after the first marriage, the percentage divorced or separated at the time of the surveys went from eight to 18%, and at 20-24 years, it rose from eight to 19%.

The most important consequences of the increase in marital failure have been on the offspring. An enormous amount of evidence, from sources varying from in-depth clinical studies to large-scale surveys, indicates moderate to severe short-term negative effects on the well-being and development of most of the children of divorce. Although the causal link is less well-established, there also apparently are some important long-term effects on a substantial minority of those whose parents divorce, including difficulty in making commitments in relationships and an increased probability of various mental health problems. Equally important is evidence for harmful effects from failed parental marriages that do not end in divorce—especially from those unions characterized by high levels of tension and conflict.

The changes in matrimony also have tended to lower the well-being of adults. Although there are exceptions, in general, those who are the happiest and most fulfilled and who function the best are those in successful marriages. On average, the happily married are the happiest, by a large margin, and the less than happily married are the least happy. In other words, to be in a good marriage is the best situation, but a poor marriage is not better than no marriage at all.

The causal relationship between marital situation and well-being is not entirely clear. Happily married individuals may do best partly because those who are the happiest and best-adjusted, for whatever reasons, are more likely than others to marry and to succeed at marriage. However, most researchers who have studied the relationship between marital situation and well-being believe that it primarily is the former that affects the latter. If so, and if the strength of the effects has not diminished markedly in recent years, the decline in the percentage of persons at various stages of adulthood who are happily married has been distinctly detrimental to their welfare.

Why the decline in marital success?

One of the most likely reasons for the decline in marital success is the well-documented increase in what persons expect of marriage. The levels of intimacy, emotional support, companionship, and sexual gratification that people believe they should get from marriage have increased, while what they are willing to give very likely has declined. In other words, the motivation for marriage has become more purely hedonistic, or more selfish. This is just one aspect of a general increase in individualism in America and throughout most of the modern world.

Another likely reason is the breakdown in the consensus of what it means to be a husband or wife. Whereas, until recently, the rights and obligations of spouses were prescribed culturally and fairly well understood by just about everyone, they have become a matter for negotiation in individual marriages. This increased flexibility in marital roles, according to its advocates, should have increased the quality of matrimony or at least the quality of the lives of married persons, and for many persons it may have done so. For others, however, it has led to discord and disappointment. The optimistic view is that we eventually will learn to deal more effectively with the new freedom and flexibility in marriage, but that remains to be seen.

Another change that was supposed to have had unambiguously positive effects, but that may not have done so, is the easing of moral, religious, and legal barriers to divorce. The reasoning of those who advocated this was that making it easier for persons to correct marital mistakes—to escape from unsatisfying, stultifying, or dehumanizing marriages—would have

positive effects on human welfare. Indeed, if one concentrates only on individual cases, as therapists and marriage counselors do, one readily can see how diminishing the guilt, social disapproval, and legal penalties of divorce has improved the quality of many lives.

However, the changes that resulted in short-term benefits to many individuals may have lessened the probability of marital success and resulted in long-term losses in the well-being of the population as a whole. One spouse's freedom—to leave the marriage, to change the terms of the marital contract—is the other spouse's insecurity. That insecurity tends to inhibit the strong commitment and investment of time, energy, and lost opportunities that are conducive to marital success. The decline in the ideal of marital permanence—one of the most well-documented value changes among Americans in recent decades—also has tended to make persons less willing and able to make the needed commitments to and investments in marriage. To the extent that a person constantly compares the existing marriage with real or imagined alternatives to it, that marriage inevitably will compare unfavorably in some respects. People are hardly aware of needs currently being well-served, but tend to be keenly attuned to them not being well-satisfied. Since attention tends to center on needs not being especially well-met in one's marriage (and there always are some), the grass will tend to look greener on the other side of the marital fence. Therefore, merely contemplating alternatives to one's marriage may engender discontent.

Those authorities who have come to recognize the negative aspects of recent changes in American marriage are dividing into two camps—those who believe that the negative changes are inevitable and irreversible and that the best we can do is to try to lessen their impact, and those who believe that at least some of the changes can be reversed. The pessimists give strong arguments for their position, pointing out, for instance, that the trend to individualism that underlies many of the changes has occurred in most parts of the modern world and may characterize an advanced stage of economic development. Furthermore, the insecurity that inhibits commitment in marriage is likely to be self-perpetuating, as it leads to marital instability, which in turn leads to further insecurity.

There are signs, however, that a reversal in some of the changes already may be occurring. In recent years, there has been a strong reaction against radical individualism among many intellectuals in this country, and attitudinal survey data indicate that a similar reaction may be beginning in the general public. Marriage is just as crucial an institution as ever, and most Americans seem to know that. What has been missing is sufficient awareness of the costs of maintaining the health of the institution. It is to be hoped that Americans will recognize that the loss of personal freedom, renunciation of pleasure seeking, and acceptance of greater responsibility necessary for good marriages will benefit themselves, their children, and the entire society.

PEER MARRIAGE

What does it take to create a truly egalitarian relationship?

PEPPER SCHWARTZ

Pepper Schwartz, Ph.D., is a professor of sociology and an author. Address: University of Washington, Seattle, Washington, 98195. Her latest book is Peer Marriage: How Love Between Equals Really Works *(Free Press, 1994).*

WHEN I TOLD PEOPLE THAT I WAS beginning a research study of couples who evenly divided parenting and housework responsibilities, the usual reaction was mock curiosity—how was I going to find the three existing egalitarian couples in the universe? Despite several decades of dissecting the sexism and inequities inherent in traditional marriage, as a society, we have yet to develop a clear picture of how more balanced marital partnerships actually work. Some critics even argue that the practice of true equality in marriage is not much more common today than it was 30 years ago. In fact, authors like Arlie Hochschild have suggested that women's liberation has made prospects for equity worse. The basic theme of her provocative book, *The Second Shift,* is that women now have two jobs—their old, traditional marital roles and their new responsibilities in the work force. A look at the spectacular divorce rates and lower marriage rate for successful women provides further fuel for the argument that equality has just brought wives more, not less, burdens.

All of this figured heavily in my own commitment to exploring the alternative possibilities for marital partnership. Ten years ago this began with *American Couples: Money, Work and Sex,* a study I did with Philip Blumstein that compared more than 6,000 couples—married, cohabitating, gay males and lesbians—looking for, among other things, what aspects of gendered behavior contributed to relationship satisfaction and durability. This study contained within it a small number of egalitarian couples, who fascinated and inspired me. We discussed them rather briefly in the book, but our editor encouraged us to make them the subject of a second study that would examine how couples manage to sustain an egalitarian partnership over time. Unfortunately, my co-author was not able to continue the project and it was not until three years ago that I began the research on what I came to call Peer Marriage. I began looking for couples who had worked out no worse than a 60-40 split on childrearing, housework and control of discretionary funds and who considered themselves to have "equal status or standing in the relationship."

I started out interviewing some of the couples originally studied for *American Couples* and then, using what sociologists call a "snowball sample," I asked those couples if they knew anyone else like

themselves that I could interview. After talking to a few couples in a given network, I then would look for a different kind of couple (different class, race, educational background, etc.) in order to extend the range of my sample. I interviewed 57 egalitarian couples, but even after the formal study was over, I kept running into couples that fit my specifications and did 10 more partial interviews.

While initially my design included only Peer Marriages, I also began to interview a lot of couples who others thought to be egalitarian, but who did not meet my criteria. Instead of throwing them out of the sample, I used them as a base of comparison, dividing them into two additional categories: "Traditionals" and "Near Peers." Traditionals were couples in which the man usually had veto power over decision-making (except with the children) and in which the wife felt that she did not have—nor did she want—equal status. The Near Peers were couples who, while they believed in equality, felt derailed from their initial goal of an egalitarian marriage because of the realities of raising children and/or the need or desire to maximize male income. As a result, the husband could not be anywhere near as participatory a father as the couple had initially envisioned. These two groups proved to be a fortuitous addition to the design. It is sometimes hard to understand what peer couples are doing that allows them to fulfill an egalitarian agenda without understanding what keeps other couples from doing the same.

Even though I consider myself to be in a Peer Marriage, I found many surprises among the Peer Couples I studied. Of course, as a researcher, one is never supposed to extrapolate from one's own experience, but it is almost impossible not to unconsciously put one's presuppositions into the hypothesis phase of the research. Clearly, people make their marital bargains for many different reasons, and face different challenges in sustaining them. Here are some of the discoveries I made that I thought might be of use to therapists.

I ASSUMED MOST COUPLES WOULD, like myself, come to egalitarianism out of the women's movement or feminist ideology. Nevertheless, while approximately 40 percent of the women and about 20 percent of the men cited feminism and a desire to be in a non-hierarchical relationship, the majority of couples mentioned other reasons. These included a desire to avoid parental models that they found oppressive in their own upbringing, the *other* partner's strong preference for an egalitarian marriage, some emotional turmoil that had led to their rethinking their relationship, or an intense desire for co-parenting. Women in particular often mentioned their own parents as a negative model. One woman said, "I want a husband who knows how to pack his own suitcase, who puts away his own clothes, who can't tell me to shut up at will ... My mother may have been happy with this kind of marriage, but I'm still angry at my father for treating my mother like that—and angry at her for letting him." A 25-year-old husband told me, on a different theme, "My main objective in having an equal relationship was not to be the kind of father I had. I want my kids to know me before they are adults. I want them to be able to talk to me. I want them to run to me if they hurt themselves. I want our conversations to be more than me telling them they could do better on a test or that I was disappointed they didn't make the team. I want to be all the things to my kids that my dad was not. I want us to have hugged many, many times and not just on birthdays or their wedding day."

Quite a few men in Peer Marriages said they really had no strong feelings about being in either traditional or egalitarian marriages, but had merely followed their wives' lead. Typical of this group was a high school basketball coach who said he had had a very traditional first marriage because that was the only arrangement that he and his wife could envision even when it wasn't working. But when he met his current wife, a policewoman who had been single quite a while, her demands for equality seemed perfectly reasonable to him. He just, more or less, fell into line with his future wife's ideas about the relationship. Many of these men told me they had always expected a woman to be the emotional architect of a relationship and were predisposed to let her set the rules.

Most of the couples, however, did have strong ideas about marriage and placed particular emphasis on equity and equality. Even if they didn't start out with a common agenda, most ended up sharing a high degree of conscious purpose. People's particular personal philosophies about marriage mattered less than the fact that their philosophies differentiated their family from a culture that reinforced the general belief that equality is neither possible nor even in the long-term interests of couples. Many people talked about how easy it is to slide into old and familiar roles or follow economic opportunities that started to whittle away at male participation in childrearing. It takes an intense desire to keep a couple on the nontraditional track and a clear sense of purpose to justify the economic sacrifices and daily complications it takes to co-parent. As one wife of 10 years said, "We always try to make sure that we don't start getting traditional. It's so easy to do. But we really want this extraordinary empathy and respect we have. I just know it wouldn't be there if we did this marriage any other way."

I MPORTANT AS RELATIONSHIP IDE-ology is, Peer Marriages depend at least as much on coordinating work with home and childraising responsibilities and not letting a high earner be exempt from daily participation. Previous research had shown me the connection between a husband's and wife's relative income and their likelihood of being egalitarian. So I assumed that most of the couples I interviewed would be working couples, and have relatively similar incomes. This was mostly true, although I was struck by the couples who were exceptions. Four husbands in the study had non-working wives. The men didn't want to dominate those relationships because they felt very strongly that money did not legitimately confer power. For example, one husband had inherited a great deal of money but didn't feel it was any more his than his wife's. She stayed at home with the children, but he took over in the late afternoon and on weekends. He also was the primary cook and cleaner. In another case, a husband who earned a good deal more than his wife put all the money in a joint account and put investments in her name as well as his. Over time, she had assets equal to his. While these triumphs over income differentials were exceptions, it did make me respect the fact that truly determined couples could overcome being seduced by the power of economic advantage.

However, many Peer Marriages had a significant income differential and husbands and wives had to negotiate a lot just to make sure they didn't fall into the trap of letting the higher earner be the senior decision-maker. Even more tricky, according to many, was not letting work set the emotional and task agenda of the household. The couples needed to keep their eyes on what was the tail and what was the dog so that their relationship was not sidetracked by career opportunities or job pressures. Many Peer Couples had gone through periods in which they realized that they were beginning to have no time for each other, or that one of them was more consistently taking care of the children while the other was consumed with job demands. But what distinguished those couples from more traditional marriages was that they had a competing ideology of economic or career success that guided them when their egalitarianism began to get out of kilter.

One husband, who had an architectural practice designing and building airports, had begun to travel for longer and longer periods of time until it was clear that he was no longer a true co-parent or a full partner in the marriage. After long and painful discussions, he quit his job and opened up a home office so he could spend more time with his wife and children. Both partners realized this would cause some economic privations and, in fact, it took the husband five years to get a modestly successful practice going while the wife struggled to support the family. Without minimizing how tough this period had been, the couple felt they had done the right thing. "After all," the husband said, "we saved our marriage."

This attitude helped explain another surprise in this study. I had presumed that most of the Peer Marriages I would find would be yuppie or post-yuppie couples, mostly young or baby boom professionals who were "having it all." In fact, most of them were solidly middle class: small-business owners, social workers, school-teachers, health professionals (but not

There was an unexpected down side for the couples who did manage to co-parent. I was unprepared for how often Peer Couples mentioned serious conflict over childrearing.

●

doctors). Apparently, people on career fast tracks were less willing to endanger their potential income and opportunities for promotion. There may be childrearing Peer Marriages out there comprised of litigators, investment bankers and brain surgeons—but I didn't find them. The closest I came to finding fast trackers in a Peer Marriage and family were high-earning women who had husbands who were extremely pleased with their partner's success and were willing to be the more primary parent in order to support her career.

When these women negotiated issues with their husbands in front of me, they seemed more sensitive about their husbands' feelings than men of comparable accomplishment with lower earning wives. For example, they did not interrupt as much as high-earning men in traditional marriages, and they seemed to quite consciously not pull rank when I asked them jointly to solve a financial problem. They told me, however, that they consciously had to work at being less controlling than they sometimes thought

they deserved to be. A very successful woman attorney, married to another, significantly-less-prominent attorney, told me that they had some problems because he wasn't used to picking up the slack when she was called away suddenly to represent a Fortune 500 company. She found herself battling her own ambitions in order to be sensitive to his desire for her to let up a bit. As she noted, "We [women] are not prepared to be the major providers and it's easy to want all the privileges and leeway that men have always gotten for the role. But our bargain to raise the kids together and be respectful of one another holds me back from being like every other lawyer who would have this powerful a job. Still, it's hard."

The other fast track exception was very successful men in their second marriages who had sacrificed their first in their climb to the top. Mostly these were men who talked about dependent ex-wives, their unhappiness at paying substantial support and their determination not to repeat the mistakes of their first marriages. One 50-year-old man, who had traveled constantly in his first marriage raising money for pension funds, told me he was through being the high earner for the company and wanted more family time in the second part of his life. As he put it, "I consciously went looking for someone who I could spend time with, who I had a lot in common with, who would want me to stop having to be the big earner all the time. I don't want to die before I've been a real partner to somebody who can stand on her own two feet . . . and I've been a real father."

When I first realized how often the desire to co-parent led couples into an egalitarian ideology, I thought this might also lead couples to prioritize their parenting responsibilities over their husband-and-wife relationship. But these were not marriages in which husbands and wives called each other "Mom" and "Dad." For the most part, these couples avoided the rigidly territorial approach I saw in Traditional and Near Peer marriages. In both of these types of couples, I observed mothers who were much more absorbed in their children, which both partners regarded as a primarily female responsibility. As a result, women had sole control over decisions about their children's daily life and used the children as a main source of intimacy, affection and unshared secrets. They related stories about things the children told them that "they would never dare tell their father." While quite a few of the mothers talked about how "close" their husbands were with their children, they would also,

usually in the same story, tell me how much closer their children were with them. What surprised me was that while these traditional moms complained about father absence, very few really wanted to change the situation. Most often, it was explained that, while it would be great to have their husband home, they "couldn't afford it." But of course "afford" is a relative term and I sensed that the women really did not want the men interfering with their control over parenting. Or they would have liked more fatherly engagement but definitely not at the cost of loss of income. One young, working Near Peer Couple with four kids was discussing the husband's lesser parenting responsibilities with me when he said, "You know, I could come home early and get the kids by 3:30. I'd like to do that." The wife's response was to straightforwardly insist that with four kids going to private school, his energies were best used paying for their tuitions. She preferred a double shift to a shared one because her financial priorities and her vision of what most profited her children were clear.

But there was an unexpected downside for the couples who did manage to co-parent. I was unprepared for how often Peer Couples mentioned serious conflict over childrearing. Because each partner felt very strongly about the children's upbringing, differences of opinion were not easily resolved. As one peer wife said, "We are both capable of stepping up to the line and staying there screaming at each other." Another husband said, "If you only talked to us about how we deal with disagreements about the kids, you might think we were a deeply conflicted marriage. We're not. But unfortunately, we have very different ideas about discipline and we can get pretty intense with one another and it might look bad. We went to counseling about the kids and this therapist wanted to look at our whole relationship and we had to say, 'You don't get it. This really is the only thing we argue about like this.'"

Peers may, in fact, have more conflict about children than more Traditional partners because unlike Traditional Marriage, there is no territory that is automatically ceded to the other person and conflict cannot be resolved by one person claiming the greater right to have the final word. Still, while a majority of Peer Couples mentioned fights over child-related decisions, there were only a few Peer Marriages where I wondered if these arguments threatened the relationship. In the majority of them, the couples talked about how they ultimately, if not in the heat of battle, followed their usual pattern of talking until agreement was reached. What usually forced them to continue to communicate and reach a joint answer was their pledge to give the other partner equal standing in the relationship. Occasionally, a few people told me, they just couldn't reach a mutually satisfying answer and let their partner "win one" out of trust in his or her good judgement, not because they agreed on a given issue.

The couples that I felt might be in more trouble had recurring disagreements that they were never able to resolve over punishments, educational or religious choices or how much freedom to give kids. Furthermore, in each instance at least one partner said that the other partner's approach was beginning to erode the respect that made their relationship possible. Moreover, this particular kind of conflict was deeply troubling since many of them had organized their marriage around the expectation of being great co-parents. It may be that co-parenting requires that parenting philosophies be similar or grow together. Co-parents may have a particular need for good negotiating and communication skills so that they can resolve their differences without threatening the basis of their relationship.

IN CONTRAST WITH TRADITIONAL or Near Peer Couples, the partners in Peer Marriages, never complained about lack of affection or intimacy in their relationships. What they did mention, that other couples did not, was the problem of becoming so familiar with each other that they felt more like siblings than lovers. Some researchers have theorized that sexual arousal is often caused or intensified by anxiety, fear and tension. Many others have written about how sexual desire depends on "Yin" and "Yang"—mystery and difference. And quite a few women and men I talked to rather guiltily confessed that while they wanted equal partners, all their sexual socialization had been to having sex in a hierarchical relationship: Women had fantasies of being "taken" or mildly dominated; men had learned very early on that they were expected to be the orchestrators of any given sexual encounter and that masculinity required sexual directiveness. For men, sexual arousal was often connected with a strong desire to protect or control.

Peer couples complained that they often forgot to include sex in their daily lives. Unlike Traditional or Near Peers, their sexual frequency did not slow down because of unresolved issues or continuing anger, at least not in any systematic

ways. These couples may start to lose interest in sex even more than the other kinds of marriages because sex is not their main way of getting close. Many Traditional and some Near Peer Couples mentioned that the only time they felt that they got through to each other was in bed. Perhaps the more emotional distance couples feel with one another, the larger the role sexuality plays in helping them feel they still have the capacity for intimacy. Being less dependent on this pathway to intimacy, partners in Peer Marriage may be more willing to tolerate a less satisfactory sexual relationship.

One husband, who worked with his wife in their own advertising firm, even talked about having developed "an incest taboo," which had led to the couple entering therapy. They were such buddies during the daytime, he had trouble treating her as anything else in the evening. The therapist this couple consulted encouraged them to assume new personas in the bedroom. For example, he told them to take turns being the dominant partner, to create scenarios where they created new characters and then behaved as they thought the person they were impersonating would behave. He gave them "homework," such as putting themselves in romantic or sexy environments and allowing themselves to imagine meeting there the first time. The wife was encouraged to dress outrageously for bed every now and then; the husband occasionally to be stereotypically directive. The therapist reminded both partners that their emotional bargain was safe: they loved and respected each other. That meant they could use sex as recreation, release and exploration. They were good pupils and felt they had really learned something for a lifetime.

In another couple, it was the wife who mentioned the problem. Her husband had been the dominant partner in his previous marriage and had enjoyed that role in bed. However, she liked more reciprocity and role-sharing in sex, so he tried to be accommodating. However, early on in the relationship he began treating her, as she put it, "too darn respectfully... it was almost as if we were having politically correct sex... I had to remember that he wasn't my brother and it was okay to be sexually far out with him."

On the other hand, Peer Couples with satisfying sexual relationships often mentioned their equality as a source of sexual strength. These couples felt their emotional security with one another allowed them to be more uninhibited and made sex more likely since both people were responsible for making it happen.

Women with unhappy sexual experiences with sexist men mentioned that for the first time in their lives they could use any sexual position without worrying about any larger meaning in the act. Being on the bottom just meant being on the bottom; it was not about surrendering in more cosmic ways. Being a sex kitten was a role for the evening—and not part of a larger submissive persona.

Many of the Peer Couples I interviewed had terrific sexual lives. The women, especially, felt they had finally met men with whom they could be vulnerable and uninhibited. As one woman said, "I used to be a real market for women's books. I wanted men who fit the stereotype of Clark Gable or Kevin Costner—few words, and when they are delivered, they are real ringers, and there is a lot of eye contact and passion, and that's about as much talking as you get. Maybe it was dating all these guys who were really like that, but even as fantasy objects, I got tired of men who didn't want to explore a feeling or who were only loving when they had a hard-on. I fell in love the first time sharing *Prince of Tides* with the guy I was dating, and fell in love with Eric [her husband] over a discussion of *Eyes on the Prize*. The sexy thing was the conversation and the quality of our mind... I can't imagine anything more boring or ultimately unsexy than a man—and I don't care if he looked like Robert Redford and earned like Donald Trump—who had nothing to say or if he did, didn't get turned on by what I was saying."

Equality brings with it the tools to have a great erotic relationship and also, at the same time, the pitfalls that can lead to sexual boredom. If couples learn that their sexual lives need not be constrained by any preconceived idea of what is "egalitarian sex" or appropriate sexual roles, there is no reason that their equality can't work for them. But couples who cannot separate their nights and days, who cannot transcend their identities in everyday life, may need guidance from a knowledgeable counselor.

WHAT ENABLES COUPLES TO SUStain a style of egalitarian relationship in a world that encourages families to link their economic destiny with the male's career and casts women in an auxiliary worker role so that they can take responsibility for everyday childcare and household chores? In Peer Couples, a sense of shared purpose helps guide the couple back to why they are putting up with all the problems that come from putting together a new model of relationship without societal or familial supports.

Peer Couples may start to lose interest in sex even more than couples in other kinds of marriages because sex is not their main way of getting close.

●

Otherwise it is all too easy for mothers to fall in love with their children and assume primary responsibility for their upbringing or for men to allow their careers to sweep them out of the home, away from their children and back into the more familiar territory they have been trained to inhabit. When this begins to happen, a couple's ideology, almost like an organization's mission statement, helps remind them what their central goal is: the marital intimacy that comes from being part of a well-matched, equally empowered, equally participatory team.

But avoiding traditional hierarchy involves a constant struggle to resist the power of money to define each partner's family roles. Peer Couples continually have to evaluate the role of work in their lives and how much it can infringe on parenting and household responsibilities. If one partner earns or starts to earn a lot more money, and the job starts to take up more time, the couple has to face what this means for their relationship—how much it might distort what they have set out to create.

Peer Couples check in with each other an extraordinary amount to keep their relationship on track. They each have to take responsibility for making sure that they are not drifting too far away from reciprocity. Peer Couples manage to maintain equity in small ways that make sure the balance in their marriage is more than an ideology. If one person has been picking up the kids, the other is planning their summer activities and getting their clothes. Or if one partner has been responsible lately for making sure extended family members are contacted, the other person takes it over for a while. If one partner really decides he or she likes to cook, then the other partner takes on some other equally functional and time-consuming job. There's no reason that each partner can't specialize, but both are careful that one of them doesn't take over all the high-prestige, undemanding jobs while the other ends up with the classically stigmatized assignments (like cleaning bathrooms, or whatever is personally loathed by that person).

Besides monitoring jobs and sharing, couples have to monitor their attitude. Is the wife being treated as a subordinate? Does one person carry around the anger so often seen in someone who feels discounted and unappreciated? Is one person's voice considered more important than the other person's? Is the relationship getting distant and is the couple starting to lead parallel lives? Do they put in the time required to be best friends and family collaborators? Are they treating each other in the ways that would support a non-romantic relationship of freely associating friends?

There is nothing "natural" or automatic about keeping Peer Marriages going. There will be role discomfort when newly inhabiting the other gender's world. That is why some research shows that men who start being involved with a child from prenatal classes on show more easy attachment and participation in childrearing activities later. While men become comfortable with mothering over time, some need a lot of help. Children will sense who is the primary parent and that will be the person to whom they run, make demands, and from whom they seek daily counsel. One direct way of helping fathers evaluate how they are doing is to help the partners measure how much the children treat them as equally viable sources of comfort and help.

Likewise, being a serious provider is a responsibility some women find absolutely crushing. Most middle-class women were raised to feel that working would be voluntary. After they have made a bargain to do their share of keeping the family economically afloat, they may regret the pressures it puts on them. The old deal of staying at home and being supported can look pretty good after a bad day at the office. But only the exceptional relationship seems to be able to make that traditional provider/mother deal for very long and still sustain a marriage where partners have equal standing in each other's eyes. Couples have to keep reminding themselves how much intimacy, respect and mutual interest they earn in exchange for learning new roles and sustaining the less enjoyable elements of new responsibilities.

Couples who live as peers often attract others like themselves and the building of a supportive community can modify the impact of the lack of support in the larger world. Like-minded others who have made similar decisions help a lot, especially when critical turning points are reached: such as re-evaluating a career track when it becomes painfully clear that it will not accommodate Peer Family life.

This study yielded no single blueprint for successful Peer Marriage. As in all couples, partners in Peer Marriages require a good measure of honesty, a dedication to fair play, flexibility, generosity and maturity. But most of all, they need to remember what they set out to do and why it was important, at least for them. If they can keep their eyes and hearts on the purpose of it all—if we help them do that—more Peer Marriages will endure and provide a model for others exploring the still-unchartered territory of egalitarian relationships.

Receipts from

A Marriage

SUMMARY   Married-couple families are America's largest and most powerful consumer segment. These traditional households experience life as a roller coaster of child-rearing and spending. As married couples advance through various lifestages— from childless couples to new parents, prime-time families, mature families, and empty nesters—their spending waxes, wanes, and shifts in important ways.

Margaret K. Ambry

Margaret K. Ambry is director of consulting services at New Strategist Publications & Consulting in Ithaca, New York.

While single parents and alternative lifestyles get a lot of media attention, business's best customers are still "traditional" families. Married-couple families account for 55 percent of all U.S. households, and seven in ten Americans live in them. Married-couple families also account for 70 percent of total consumer spending. The biggest spenders—married couples with children under 18—comprise just 27 percent of all households, but the number of such households is projected to grow 12 percent during the 1990s.

Blame it on the baby boomlet. There is nothing like a child to change a couple's spending priorities, and baby-boomer par-ents have been making a lot of changes since the mid-1980s. Having a child doesn't mean getting an automatic raise, however. When the average young married couple makes the transition from childless couple to new parents (oldest child under age 6), their total expenditures increase less than 1 percent. Yet their spending patterns shift considerably: they spend more than their childless counterparts on health care, clothing, housing, and food, and much less on alcohol, education, and transportation. They also spend more on cigarettes and less on personal care and entertainment.

As parents and children get older, income and spending increase in nearly every category of household products and services. Married couples who make the transition to prime-time families (oldest child aged 6 to 17) spend 11 percent more overall than new parents. They spend more on virtually all products and services, although they spend less on alcohol and housing.

Mature families are couples with children aged 18 or older at home. They spend 9 percent more than prime-time families, and they generally have the highest incomes. But when children finally leave home, household spending falls by almost 30 percent. Empty-nester couples spend less than mature families on everything except health care and cash contributions.

Our analysis of the 1989-90 Consumer Expenditure Survey (CEX) shows how the birth, growth, and departure of children affect a married couple's spending. It shows that a couple's lifestage is at least as important as their ages in determining consumer behavior.

CHILDLESS COUPLES

Childless couples with a householder aged 25 to 34 have an average annual before-tax income of nearly $46,000. Each year, they spend an average of $34,000, 22 percent more than the average for all American households. The biggest chunk of a childless young couple's budget (32 per-

Parents' Progress

As married couples move through life, their spending patterns change. New parents spend less on alcoholic beverages than young childless couples. As children age, couples spend more on education. When children leave, couples reduce their spending on almost everything.

(percent change in average annual expenditures of married couples by lifestage change and expenditure category)

	childless couples to new parents	new parents to prime-time families	prime-time families to mature families	mature families to empty nesters
TOTAL EXPENDITURES	0.3%	11.0%	8.8%	-29.0%
Food	2.4	29.8	8.6	-33.5
Alcoholic beverages	-33.8	-6.2	17.5	-21.8
Housing	9.5	-5.0	-6.2	-18.8
Apparel and services	10.8	20.4	-0.2	-32.7
Transportation	-10.1	12.6	24.7	-40.1
Health care	49.3	9.2	18.9	28.1
Entertainment	-5.6	25.2	1.8	-34.6
Personal-care products	-7.3	21.7	16.6	-28.6
Reading	-7.4	9.7	4.7	-3.8
Education	-28.9	178.7	101.1	-86.4
Tobacco products	12.4	26.0	25.3	-39.3
Cash contributions*	-32.1	62.8	54.6	5.7
Personal insurance, pensions, Social Security ...	-8.3	6.2	4.3	-41.7
Miscellaneous	-13.3	29.7	5.9	-32.9

Cash contributions include alimony, child support, cash gifts to nonhousehold members, and charitable contributions.

Note: A prime-time family may have both preschool and school-aged children, while a mature family may have both adult children and children aged 0 to 17.

Source: Author's calculations based on 1989-90 Consumer Expenditure Survey data

cent) is devoted to housing. One-fifth of their spending (20 percent) goes directly into dwellings, and another 5 percent is spent on furnishings; both are higher-than-average shares. Yet childless couples spend very little on household operations. With fewer people to care for, their average annual tab for housekeeping supplies—about $400—is less than their liquor bill.

Like other households, childless couples devote the second-largest share of their spending to transportation. Although they spend an average amount on used cars, they spend 72 percent more than the average household on new cars. Spending on new cars drops off once there are young children in the household, then bounces back. It peaks among mature families and young empty nesters.

> **When children finally leave home, household spending falls by almost 30 percent.**

Just 13 percent of a childless couple's spending goes to food, but more than half of those dollars are given to restaurants and carry-out places. In all other lifestages, couples spend the majority of their food dollars on groceries. Childless couples spend an average of $440 a year on alcohol, more than 1 percent of their average annual budget.

Payments to personal insurance, pensions, and Social Security account for nearly 12 percent of a young childless couple's budget, about $4,000 a year. Because most are two-earner households, childless couples spend 70 percent more than average on pensions and Social Security.

Childless couples devote 5 percent of their spending to clothing, a smaller share than other couples. Another 5 percent goes to entertainment, with equal shares devoted to tickets for movies, theater, sports, and other events; TV, radio, and sound equipment; and other entertainment products and services such as sports equipment and boats. Although they have no children, childless couples also spend more than average on pets and toys.

They're young and don't have children to take to the doctor, so childless couples spend 34 percent less than the average household on out-of-pocket health-care expenses. Health care accounts for only about 3 percent of their budgets. They also spend less than average on tobacco products, education, and cash contributions (perhaps because the latter category includes alimony and child support). They spend less than 1 percent of their money on reading materials, although the $190 spent is 22 percent more than average. Young childless couples' trips to the hairdresser, cosmetics, shampoo, and other personal-care products and services take up another 1 percent of their household spending. This share doesn't vary much from lifestage to lifestage.

NEW PARENTS

New parents are couples whose oldest child is under the age of 6. They break down into two groups—younger parents (householders aged 25 to 34) and older new parents (householders aged 35 to 54). Although both types of households average 3.5 people, the older group's average income is just over $15,000 higher. Consequently, older new parents spend more on all major categories of products and services. They also allocate their funds differently than younger new parents do.

Both younger and older new parents devote a larger-than-average share of spending to housing—35 percent and 37 percent, respectively. Younger parents' housing expenditures are boosted by the 4 percent share that goes to household operations, mostly child care. But older parents of preschoolers outspend all other households on child care, mortgage payments, home maintenance, and other household services such as housekeeping, lawn-and-garden work, and household furnishings.

> **The average childless couple spends more than 1 percent of their entire budget on alcoholic beverages.**

Older new parents also spend more than younger new parents on transportation, although getting around consumes a smaller share of their total spending (15 percent versus 19 percent). Younger new parents outspend their older counterparts on cars, trucks, and other vehicles, while older new parents spend more on operating costs and public transportation.

Because of their higher incomes, older new parents are free to spend more on food and alcohol, although they allocate a smaller share of income to those categories. Food accounts for nearly 14 percent of young new parents' budgets, compared with 12 percent for older new parents. But older parents channel a larger share of funds to personal insurance, pensions, Social Security, entertainment, and cash contributions.

Older new parents outspend younger ones on all other major products and service categories, but the share they spend is similar. For example, both kinds of couples devote about 0.5 percent of their spending to reading materials. But younger couples spend an average amount, while older couples spend 81 percent more than the average household.

PRIME-TIME FAMILIES

Once the oldest child reaches school age, a family's lifestyles and spending patterns shift again. Like Ozzie and Harriet's family, the average household in the prime-time lifestage has two parents and two children, the oldest of whom is aged 6 to 17. Yet householders in this stage range

Doling Out

	ALL HOUSEHOLDS	CHILDLESS COUPLES	
		25 to 34	25 to
NUMBER OF HOUSEHOLDS (in thousands)	96,393	3,020	4,03
AVERAGE INCOME BEFORE TAXES	$31,600	$45,835	$37,84
AVERAGE HOUSEHOLD SIZE	2.6	2.0	3
AVERAGE TOTAL EXPENDITURES	$28,090	$34,323	$32,79
FOOD	4,224	4,533	4,49
At home	2,438	2,126	2,82
Away from home	1,787	2,407	1,66
ALCOHOLIC BEVERAGES	289	441	28
HOUSING	8,748	11,119	11,58
Shelter	4,934	7,024	6,27
Owned dwellings	2,902	4,132	4,05
Rented dwellings	1,517	2,390	1,93
Utilities, fuels, public services	1,863	1,746	1,96
Household operations	453	178	1,43
Housekeeping supplies	400	407	49
Household furnishings	1,099	1,763	1,42
APPAREL AND SERVICES	1,600	1,725	1,78
Men and boys	395	449	43
Women and girls	665	658	50
Children younger than age 2	71	38	38
Footwear	207	170	21
Other apparel products and services	262	409	24
TRANSPORTATION	5,154	6,989	6,25
Vehicle purchases	2,209	3,095	2,98
Cars and trucks, new	1,188	2,046	1,43
Cars and trucks, used	999	998	1,53
Gas and motor oil	1,016	1,216	1,14
Other vehicle expenses	1,636	2,286	1,93
Public transportation	293	392	18
HEALTH CARE	1,444	970	1,48
ENTERTAINMENT	1,423	1,867	1,59
Fees and admissions	374	485	29
TV, radios, sound equipment	441	525	48
Pets, toys, playground	263	312	39
Other products and services	345	545	42
PERSONAL-CARE PRODUCTS AND SERVICES	365	427	35
READING	155	189	15
EDUCATION	386	284	19
TOBACCO PRODUCTS	68	226	22
CASH CONTRIBUTIONS	858	791	47
PERSONAL INSURANCE, PENSIONS, SOCIAL SECURITY	2,532	4,026	3,34
MISCELLANEOUS	644	737	56

* Cash contributions include alimony, child support, cash gifts to nonhousehold members, and charitable contributions.

in age from 25 to 54, and their average before-tax household income ranges from $35,000 for households with a head aged 25 to 34 to just over $49,000 for households with a head aged 45 to 54. Their total spending ranges from 12 percent above average for prime-time families headed by 25-to-34-year-olds to 49 percent above average for those headed by 45-to-54-year-olds.

Housing accounts for a smaller share of spending for prime-time families than for

Dollars

Older families with children have the highest incomes among married couples, but new parents and mature families spend the most.

(average total income before taxes, average household size, and average annual expenditures by expenditure category and by married-couple lifestage and age of householder)

	PRIME-TIME FAMILIES			MATURE FAMILIES			EMPTY NESTERS		
35 to 54	25 to 34	35 to 44	45 to 54	35 to 44	45 to 54	55 to 64	45 to 54	55 to 64	65 and older
1,466	3,952	7,334	2,011	1,857	3,455	1,819	2,796	4,718	7,601
53,270	$35,251	$47,845	$49,374	$49,214	$51,948	$55,216	$52,736	$38,701	$24,477
3.5	4.3	4.2	3.9	4.5	3.9	3.5	2.0	2.0	2.0
44,839	$31,500	$41,144	$41,816	$43,149	$45,163	$40,730	$40,778	$31,534	$24,136
5,424	4,993	6,403	6,820	6,634	7,015	6,508	5,252	4,685	3,809
3,350	3,175	3,742	3,724	3,993	3,854	3,830	2,674	2,668	2,399
2,074	1,818	2,661	3,096	2,640	3,160	2,677	2,579	2,017	1,411
371	250	295	271	248	343	407	348	291	192
16,539	9,861	12,518	11,986	11,244	12,052	10,264	12,263	9,034	7,407
9,005	5,397	6,946	6,829	6,176	6,584	5,079	7,179	4,496	3,524
7,003	3,296	5,423	4,604	4,803	4,763	3,848	4,939	3,250	2,335
1,029	1,716	858	1,067	728	683	582	881	390	562
2,366	2,075	2,428	2,513	2,703	2,832	2,674	2,242	2,180	1,959
2,357	760	699	638	322	345	334	301	419	512
637	463	593	596	623	574	687	579	508	482
2,174	1,166	1,852	1,411	1,419	1,717	1,490	1,962	1,432	930
2,490	1,726	2,515	2,815	2,844	2,385	2,119	2,300	1,808	1,108
600	447	704	845	846	721	517	561	457	266
882	679	1,041	1,142	1,202	966	852	1,028	887	511
385	123	53	37	41	65	64	57	39	24
225	240	343	397	315	253	293	215	205	171
399	236	373	393	440	380	393	439	220	137
6,737	6,362	7,366	7,469	9,598	9,655	8,251	7,789	5,585	4,188
2,694	3,104	3,516	3,107	4,300	4,261	3,614	3,518	2,151	1,718
1,441	1,512	1,968	1,790	2,099	2,358	2,089	1,802	1,347	1,078
1,253	1,576	1,504	1,283	2,166	1,868	1,443	1,700	788	640
1,249	1,378	1,414	1,503	1,965	1,886	1,615	1,424	1,194	883
2,387	1,769	2,127	2,468	3,070	3,035	2,607	2,424	1,808	1,307
407	111	309	391	263	473	416	423	432	330
1,862	1,262	1,699	1,794	1,518	1,736	2,123	1,705	2,154	2,824
2,478	1,741	2,486	2,216	2,923	2,358	1,974	2,059	1,765	1,069
541	363	745	621	566	588	566	449	437	428
674	610	680	746	675	644	464	534	402	306
550	401	454	425	360	306	367	407	253	199
713	368	607	424	1,322	820	578	668	673	136
453	372	521	583	562	606	592	462	410	374
281	154	209	208	174	209	216	222	198	180
298	314	633	812	1,125	1,437	1,022	573	99	35
253	353	306	300	401	404	384	321	327	163
921	458	880	1,372	1,197	1,509	1,397	1,721	1,265	1,421
5,734	2,961	4,407	4,333	3,877	4,523	4,472	4,877	3,328	882
997	692	908	837	806	931	1,001	887	585	483

Source: 1989-90 Consumer Expenditure Survey

childless couples or new parents. Prime-time households headed by 45-to-54-year-olds spend just 29 percent of their budget on housing, compared with the 35 to 37 percent allocated by younger householders. With larger households and older children, however, prime-timers devote 16 percent of their budgets to food. They don't allocate more than half of their food budget to restaurants and carry-out food as childless couples do, but they tend to outspend new parents on food away from home.

Transportation claims 18 to 20 percent of a prime-time family's spending. This group outspends new parents on new vehicles, and they drive a lot more. Their tab for gas and oil is 36 percent more than the average household's.

Prime-time families have a lot to protect. That's why they spend 74 percent more than the average household on personal insurance and pensions, allocating 9 to 11 percent of their budgets to this

---

CINCINNATI, OHIO

DEMOGRAM

Tom Parker

Giving birth to twins in America isn't a big deal—it happens about 1,600 times a week. Quadruplet births, on the other hand, only happen four times a week. Quads make the evening news. But what about the 40 mothers a week who give birth to triplets? They get big guts, but what about the glory?

Janet Davis, 25, didn't even think she was pregnant. She went to the doctor for a routine exam. Later, when she gained weight faster than expected, her doctors thought her due date was wrong. So they scheduled a sonogram. "There's a very good reason you're getting so big," said the sonogram technician. "You have three babies in there." Janet, already the mother of two kids, ages 8 and 6, just sat in shock. Her mother said, "Oh, my God! I'm leaving town!" Her husband Pat got the news while at his job moving office furniture. He said he would have fainted if he hadn't been wedged into a phone booth.

That's where the fireworks ended. Janet didn't even discuss the triplets with her doctor until her next appointment a week later. Luckily, she stopped at a garage sale to look at a carseat. When she mentioned needing two more seats, the lady at the sale told her about a woman who lived just up the street with three newborn baby boys. Janet stopped and left a note on the woman's door. That's how she found The Triplet Connection.

The Triplet Connection is a nonprofit information clearinghouse and network for multiple-birth families based in Stockton, California. It was founded by Janet Bleyl, mother of ten, after a particularly difficult triplet pregnancy in 1982. According to Bleyl, the organization now has the largest database of multiple-birth information in the world. "We are in contact with more than 7,000 families of triplets and larger multiple births," she says. "And we currently work with over 1,250 expectant mothers per year."

Bleyl says that because triplets are not very common, most doctors have little experience in the special problems of large multiple pregnancies. And she adds that many doctors lack the nutritional training that is critical for these births. "We've found that the most important factor in large multiple pregnancies is keeping close track of nutrition and weight gain," says Bleyl. "As a rule, a mother hoping to walk out of the hospital with healthy triplets should plan on walking in with a weight gain of 50 to 70 pounds.

"We are also very concerned with the insidious nature of early contractions and preterm labor. In large multiple pregnancies, the uterus becomes so distended that it doesn't behave normally. Unless you take some extraordinary measures, it is often quite difficult to know if you are in premature labor. I had six kids before my triplets, but I didn't know!"

Bleyl's organization relies on two sources: a panel of medical advisors, and what she calls the "fabulous networking abilities of mothers" to help expectant parents and inexperienced physicians.

The Triplet Connection sent Janet Davis a packet of information, a medical questionnaire, an audiotape, and a quarterly newsletter. She says the material helped her check the quality of her doctor's advice. Janet's pregnancy was far from easy. Twice, she went to the hospital with premature contractions. Her doctors sent her home hooked to a Terbutaline pump to help prevent early labor. They kept track of Janet's progress with a fetal monitor hooked to a modem. The identical boys, Andrew, Adam, and Anthony, were delivered at 31 weeks—6 weeks early—by emergency C-section. Pat spent the last hour waiting at the hospital while Janet and her dad sat stuck in Cincinnati traffic.

I met the triplets at age 10 weeks. All three seemed healthy and as hard to tell apart as matching spoons. "Thanks to the good medical care, the boys were in the hospital for less than three weeks," Janet says. "The bill came to $90,000. Luckily, Pat's insurance paid most of it. Since then, Andrew and Anthony have had bouts with viral meningitis, we've moved to a different house, our car died, and our plumbing went out.

"Other than that, my biggest problem is simply getting the babies from one place to the next. Just to get into the doctor's office, I have to call ahead and ask the nurse to watch the parking lot for my arrival. Believe it or not, some mothers have figured out how to nurse triplets. Nursing is one thing, but lifting three babies is a different story. When your babies outnumber your arms, you've got problems."

If life's changes didn't throw us for a few loops, they wouldn't be changes at all. At first, most people respond with their own versions of, "Oh my God! I'm leaving town." But few of us ever really leave. We just gather our wits and do the best we can. And that's what Janet Davis is doing. She's got three bedrooms, one bath, two arms—and she's doing her best to hold seven people together. For more information: The Triplet Connection, P.O. Box 99571, Stockton, CA 95209; telephone (209) 474-0885.

> **Mature families have consistently above-average spending levels for food, transportation, entertainment, personal-care products and services, and education.**

spending category. Clothing and entertainment account for another 5 to 7 percent of their total spending. The amount spent on clothing is highest among prime-timers with householders aged 45 to 54. Households headed by 35-to-44-year-olds spend more on entertainment than others in this lifestage. Prime-time families are also among the biggest spenders on pets and toys.

MATURE FAMILIES

Mature families are couples whose oldest child at home is aged 18 or older. They have consistently above-average spending levels for food, transportation, entertainment, personal-care products and services, and education. Parents in mature families tend to be in their peak earning years, and many adult children also contribute to the family income. Average incomes in this lifestage range from a high of $55,000 for households headed by someone aged 55 to 64 to a low of $49,000 for those headed by someone aged 35 to 44. Mature families also shrink as householders age, from an average of 4.5 persons in families headed by 35-to-44-year-olds to 3.5 persons among those headed by 55-to-64-year-olds.

Compared with families in other lifestages, mature families allocate the smallest share of their budgets (25 to 27 percent) to housing, although they spend more than average on everything except rent, personal services, clothing for children younger than age 2, and household operations. What they save on housing probably goes to automobiles. Mature families spend 64 to 95 percent more than the average household on vehicles. They also spend above-average amounts on related items such as fuel and maintenance.

Because mature families support ravenous college-age youths, they spend more than other households on food and education. Their expenditures on food are at least 54 percent greater than average, and they allocate 15 to 16 percent of their budgets to food. Education eats up about 3 percent of the average mature family's spending dollar, triple the average amount.

EMPTY NESTERS

Couples' spending doesn't necessarily drop off as soon as the children leave the nest, especially if both spouses are still working. The average before-tax income of empty-nest households headed by people aged 45 to 54 is 67 percent greater than average, and their spending is 45 percent higher than average.

Income and spending do fall off among older couples. But the average income for empty nesters aged 55 to 64 is still 22 percent above the average for all households, and their spending is 12 percent above average. Among empty nesters aged 65 and older, both income and spending are below average (by 23 percent and 14 percent, respectively).

Not surprisingly, empty nesters spend more than younger couples on health care. Young empty nesters spend 18 percent more than average on health care, and their counterparts aged 65 or older spend almost twice as much as the average U.S. household. The share of spending devoted to health care by empty nesters climbs from 4 percent for pre-retirees to 12 percent among the elderly. As empty nesters age and their incomes decline, they also spend higher shares of income on food, personal-care products and services, reading, and cash contributions.

> **Children born to baby boomers will determine household spending for the rest of the decade.**

Young empty nesters spend nearly 60 percent more than the average household on vehicles, while the oldest empty nesters spend 22 percent less than average. Aging empty nesters also spend increasingly smaller budget shares on clothing, education, personal insurance, pensions, and Social Security.

Spending patterns change as children arrive and grow up. Children born to baby boomers during the 1980s and early 1990s will determine the lion's share of household spending for the rest of the decade. As they grow, their family's budget will almost certainly expand. For businesses that have struggled through the recession, this is something to look forward to.

Behind the Numbers This analysis is derived from the Bureau of Labor Statistics' annual Consumer Expenditure Survey (CEX). The unit of analysis in the CEX is a consumer unit, referred to in this article as a household. The analysis is based on a cross-tabulation of age of consumer unit head by composition of consumer unit. In order to obtain a large enough sample, data for the survey years 1989 and 1990 were combined. Because of low frequency counts, spending data could not be tabulated for all types of consumer units for all age groups. The lifestage called childless couples, for example, includes only those headed by someone aged 25 to 34 because there are so few couples headed by a person under age 25. Likewise, most couples aged 35 to 44 have children; the small number who do not are also excluded from the analysis. For more information about the CEX, contact the Bureau of Labor Statistics at (202) 272-5060. Margaret Ambry is co-author of *The Official Guide to American Incomes* and *The Official Guide to Household Spending*, to be published by New Strategist in spring 1993. Some of the data in this article come from these books.

Staying Power

Bridging the Gender Gap in the Confusing '90s

Melinda Blau

Melinda Blau is the author of Families Apart: Ten Keys to Successful Co-Parenting.

Karen Mason*, 40, considers herself lucky. "I have a husband who's a real parent—kissy-huggy with the kids. And three nights a week he cooks dinner so I can be on the swim team."

Yet even this seeming paragon of a modern husband continues to exhibit what she considers to be typically male characteristics. Peter, 40, isn't much of a talker, Karen notes wistfully, and yes, he likes sex whereas she likes romance. And sometimes Karen gets frustrated because her husband just doesn't seem to focus when it comes to the house and children.

When they got married, Karen and Peter were determined not to be bound by traditional gender-role assumptions—that he would bring home the bacon and she would cook it. Peter, a salesman, shared the housework and put in almost equal time with their first child. But then the demands of Peter's work increased, a second child arrived and the couple's time together began to slip away.

Even though Peter is a far cry from

Couples' names and some identifying details have been changed.

his own father, who wasn't home much or "always had his head in the newspaper," some evenings Peter understands how his dad must have felt. "I like to bury myself in the TV," he admits. "I'm exhausted at night." Karen agrees that Peter "is doing his best" but says she's sometimes saddened by what she perceives as their real gender differences.

Many '90s couples are grappling with new ways of being men and women. At the same time that expectations and demands have changed for both, the popular press suggests the battle of the sexes may never end because men and women are irreconcilably different. Books proclaim that *Men Are From Mars, Women Are From Venus,* and personal accounts highlight the issues on which couples differ: Communication (she wants more talk; he wants more action). Intimacy (she needs to relax to have sex; he needs sex to relax). Division of household labor and child care (she says she does more; he talks about how much he does). Money and careers (she says he doesn't value her job as much as his; he notes that he makes more money).

Yet despite these differences, the fact that men and women can transcend traditional gender roles indicates that many of these distinctions may be more a result of socialization than biology. "Men are not emotionally defective monsters, and women aren't depen-

dent, helpless creatures," says psychologist Susan Johnson at the University of Ottawa in Ontario.

While researchers debate the contributions of nature and nurture to gender differences, family therapists suggest we examine why couples become polarized in the first place. Boston psychologist Kathy McMahon notes that "gender rage," as she calls it, stands for the disappointment couples feel when reality doesn't live up to expectations.

Dr. McMahon offers a typical scenario: Both parents work, and their child gets sick. In a spirit of fairness, they decide to split caretaking, but by the end of the week, they're fighting about who does what around the house. The problem, says McMahon, is that neither has a model for this new behavior—Mom working when a child is sick, Dad staying home—and they can't buck their inner cultural imprinting. When it's time for Mom to go to work, she feels guilty for not living up to her role as mother. And Dad's upset because he's not living up to his role as provider.

Today's couples, say the experts, must acknowledge their unconscious expectations and speak up before gender rage erodes their relationship. "This is not so much about understanding differences," says family therapist Jo-Ann Krestan, "as it is about holding partners equally accountable for the quality of life in a family. Sharing responsibility doesn't mean the husband

From *American Health,* May 1994, pp. 87-89. © 1994 by Melinda Blau. Reprinted by permission.

saying, 'Honey, I'll cook tonight—where's the stove?'"

In essence, men and women usually want the same things from a relationship: closeness, support, respect, fairness, healthy children, a nice home and longevity. But, says California psychologist Lonnie Barbach, co-author of *Going the Distance,* they often differ about how to achieve these things and don't necessarily talk productively with each other about them.

Couples who talk about their needs and feelings fare far better than those who don't. But the longer people stay together, the less time they spend thinking and talking about their relationship, says University of Michigan psychologist Linda Acitelli. Complaining about a spouse's behavior doesn't count. Relationship work, Dr. Acitelli says, is like car maintenance—for safety's sake, you shouldn't wait until the vehicle breaks down.

The process of divvying up both practical *and* emotional responsibilities should be worked out thoughtfully. Some couples allocate chores arbitrarily, according to what has to be done; others earmark assignments based on preference. However it's done, structure—a chart or other means of clarifying who does what—can be helpful.

New York City designer Sara Roark, 41, and her husband, Carl, 42, an architect, drew up a "contract" and even included their four-year-old son, Orin. The major headings represent a bird's-eye view of what it takes to run a house and a family: meals and dishes, laundry, school, shopping, housecleaning, home maintenance, car, mail, finances, medical care, lifestyle decisions and leisure time.

At first the Roarks wanted to keep the assignments objective, but they wound up basing certain responsibilities on each person's skills and availability. "I took over more of the financial things, because it took me less time. My husband is more of a morning person, so he gets Orin ready for school, while I do more of the night things."

To a woman who complains that she's always in charge or that her husband does less than she does, Krestan would say it's her own fault for doing his share. "Sometimes you just have to leave his empty yogurt container on the kitchen counter. Throw it away and you cripple his ability to notice empty yogurt containers in the future."

Indeed, Sara Roark had to redefine "what needs to be done" and to accept the fact that things might not be done the way she'd do them, or when. "It's tough to let go. Sometimes when I come home late, I find that he's given our son crackers and cheese and put him to bed. A lot of women just take over at that point."

Dr. Ron Taffel, a New York City family therapist, concurs: "The biggest complaint I hear from men is, 'She wants me to do it, but when I do, she criticizes me.'" Our society, he explains, puts each member in a no-win situation. "The woman feels responsi-

Arguments over dirty dishes are signs of deeper issues.

ble for how the house looks and how the kids turn out. Society will hold her accountable, so she feels driven to be in charge. And even though the man may want to participate as an equal, he often feels like he has a boss."

Taffel's prescription goes beyond chores: Couples must also reserve time every night for reviewing the day. "One couple began to talk for 15 minutes each night after the kids went to bed about what happened with each other and with their sons. It made them feel more in synch."

While women typically will participate in such sessions, men are generally more resistant. Men tend to focus on what's in front of them, Taffel explains. "When they leave the office, they don't want to talk about work, and when the children finally are in bed, they don't want to talk about them. I try to get them to realize that the more they separate the different aspects of their lives, the more they end up zoning out in front of the TV or walking out on wives who want to talk."

Dave Goodrich, 34, an estate manager in Indianapolis, was happy to share the housework and child care for his two sons. But intimacy was another matter. "When Annie first complained that she was always the one to initiate conversations about our relationship, I was very defensive," he admits. "Guys don't talk about those kinds of things. We had a number of conversations, till

all hours of the night. Now I understand where she's coming from. It's hard sometimes, but I really make an attempt to share the emotional work of our marriage too."

Annie Goodrich, 37, a teacher, realizes that her attitude also made a difference. "In the beginning I would yell and scream, which just pushed him further away. I finally realized that when we had an argument, he needed a cooling-off period before he could talk."

Certainly, it takes perseverance—not

HOW TO CLOSE THE GAP

Get honest before you get angry: Something deeper than dry cleaning is probably bothering you.
Establish systems for sharing chores and child care.
Negotiate the division of labor *and* the division of love.
Don't get locked into your role: Try swapping responsibilities on occasion.
Express your emotional needs and expectations and really listen to your partner.
Review the cultural messages of your childhood to help understand the conflicts inherent in your new roles.
Give each other time to change; don't monitor or criticize.
Accept your differences and applaud each other's strengths.
Protect your intimate time together.

the same as nagging—to get some men to talk. More important, it requires the woman to speak honestly about what she needs, not rant about what her spouse is doing wrong. In most relationships, in fact, both partners are usually afraid of intimacy; the fear just looks different on men and women. As Dr. Johnson points out, "To love and to be intimately connected is to be incredibly at risk." A woman may believe she's doing "relationship work" because she starts conversations, but if she doesn't allow herself to be vulnerable and doesn't take responsibility for her own feelings, she may be dodging intimacy by focusing on him. Unexpressed feelings can contaminate a relationship—and obscure the real issues. Arguments over dirty dishes, vacuuming or food shopping or even a partner's infidelity are usually symptoms of deeper problems.

After two children and 14 years of marriage, Dana Berk, 37, finally had to confront why she felt so depressed, so sexually apathetic, so envious of other couples. It had nothing to do with chore wars. "Over the years, without realizing it, Hal and I had both shut down."

Realizing she was attracted to another man was Dana's wake-up call. Rather than act on impulse, she decided to talk to her husband. "It was brutal having to express our bottled-up feelings. I have tremendous gratitude because he was wonderful in terms of being able to face the issues, deal with the pain and support me. We had many talks late into the night. There was anger, but we also cried a lot. I even have a sex drive now, and there's a passion in our relationship that's deeper than we ever had. I think we've really learned how to be there for each other."

Dave and Annie Goodrich learned to be there for each other through a series of crises—beginning with Annie's miscarriage—that made their different styles pale in comparison with their ability to share life's hard knocks. "When we lost the baby, Dave really let go," Annie says. "He knew that we both had to talk about it. When I developed an eating disorder, he was really supportive. Then our youngest was born with a birth defect. Just knowing we can talk about it makes it bearable."

Successful couples constantly and consciously nurture their relationship. "The need to protect intimacy—their time with each other—is central to being together," stresses Taffel, "all the way from having conversations without being interrupted to having weekends together without the kids. When that starts to disappear, it's dangerous; the reservoir dips too low."

Taffel suggests creating rituals. One couple he knows takes a brief walk after dinner. The Roarks try to set aside a portion of every weekend for themselves. The Goodriches try to get away one weekend a month.

Of course, some gender differences will persist: She may not feel as comfortable being away from the kids; he may never be as observant. But such issues don't have to be divisive if you remember to reserve time to be alone together and if you appreciate your common victories instead of bemoaning each other's failings.

"Your partner is probably not going to get it the first time," Dr. Barbach emphasizes. "Acknowledge small changes, even if they're not perfect." Whether your differences are over housework, child care or emotions, she adds, "really value what each of you gives." In some areas, one person probably is more proficient. "If you're better at bringing romance into your relationship, do it."

Last year Karen Mason did just that. On Peter's 40th birthday, she "surprise kidnapped" him for a weekend alone, planning the whole thing meticulously, down to taking his clothes "bit by bit" so she could pack their suitcase. "He was so appreciative," she recalls, "but he admitted that he could never have done it for me. He wouldn't have thought of all the details."

Karen is satisfied, however, because Peter is a loving husband and father who can tolerate that her idea of a great birthday present is to go away *with* the kids. Thus the Masons have reached a workable détente. "As I get older, I realize there are some real differences between men and women," says Karen, "and I'm happier when I accept it."

But What Do You Mean?

Deborah Tannen, Ph.D.

Deborah Tannen is the best-selling author of You Just Don't Understand: Men and Women in Conversation.

Conversation is a ritual. We say things that seem obviously the thing to say, without thinking of the literal meaning of our words, any more than we expect the question "How are you?" to call forth a detailed account of aches and pains.

Unfortunately, women and men often have different ideas about what's appropriate, different ways of speaking. Many of the conversational rituals common among women are designed to take the other person's feelings into account, while many of the conversational rituals common among men are designed to maintain the one-up position, or at least avoid appearing one-down. As a result, when men and women interact—especially at work—it's often women who are at the disadvantage. Because women are not trying to avoid the one-down position, that is unfortunately where they may end up.

Here, the biggest areas of miscommunication.

1. Apologies

Women are often told they apologize too much. The reason they're told to stop doing it is that, to many men, apologizing seems synonymous with

> Men and women really do speak different languages, to praise, thank, apologize, even chat. How to avoid the 7 conversation traps that keep us apart— at work and at home

putting oneself down. But there are many times when "I'm sorry" isn't self-deprecating, or even an apology; it's an automatic way of keeping both speakers on an equal footing. For example, a well-known columnist once interviewed me and gave me her phone number in case I needed to call her back. I misplaced the number and had to go through the newspaper's main switchboard. When our conversation was winding down and we'd both made ending-type remarks, I added, "Oh, I almost forgot—I lost your direct number, can I get it again?" "Oh, I'm sorry," she came back instantly, even though she had done nothing wrong and *I* was the one who'd lost the number. But I understood she wasn't really apologizing; she was just automatically reassuring me she had no intention of denying me her number.

Even when "I'm sorry" *is* an apology, women often assume it will be the first step in a two-step ritual: I say "I'm sorry" and take half the blame, then you take the other half. At work, it might go something like this:

A: When you typed this letter, you missed this phrase I inserted.

This article was originally published in *Redbook*, October 1994, pp. 91-93, 145-147. Adapted from *Talking 9 to 5: How Women's and Men's Conversational Styles Affect Who Gets Heard, Who Gets Credit, and What Gets Done at Work* by Deborah Tannen, Ph.D. © 1994 by Deborah Tannen, Ph.D. Reprinted by permission of William Morrow & Company, Inc.

B: Oh, I'm sorry. I'll fix it.

A: Well, I wrote it so small it was easy to miss.

When both parties share blame, it's a mutual face-saving device. But if one person, usually the woman, utters frequent apologies and the other doesn't, she ends up looking as if she's taking the blame for mishaps that aren't her fault. When she's only partially to blame, she looks entirely in the wrong.

I recently sat in on a meeting at an insurance company where the sole woman, Helen, said "I'm sorry" or "I apologize" repeatedly. At one point she said, "I'm thinking out loud. I apologize." Yet the meeting was intended to be an informal brainstorming session, and *everyone* was thinking out loud.

The reason Helen's apologies stood out was that she was the only person in the room making so many. And the reason I was concerned was that Helen felt the annual bonus she had received was unfair. When I interviewed her colleagues, they said that Helen was one of the best and most productive workers—yet she got one of the smallest bonuses. Although the problem might have been outright sexism, I suspect her speech style, which differs from that of her male colleagues, masks her competence.

Unfortunately, not apologizing can have its price too. Since so many women use ritual apologies, those who don't may be seen as hard-edged. What's important is to be aware of how often you say you're sorry (and why), and to monitor your speech based on the reaction you get.

2. Criticism

A woman who cowrote a report with a male colleague was hurt when she read a rough draft to him and he leapt into a critical response—"Oh, that's too dry! You have to make it snappier!" She herself would have been more likely to say, "That's a really good start. Of course, you'll want to make it a little snappier when you revise."

Whether criticism is given straight or softened is often a matter of convention. In general, women use more softeners. I noticed this difference when talking to an editor about an essay I'd written. While going over changes she wanted to make, she said, "There's one more thing. I know you may not agree with me. The reason I noticed the problem is that your other points are so lucid and elegant." She

went on hedging for several more sentences until I put her out of her misery: "Do you want to cut that part?" I asked—and of course she did. But I appreciated her tentativeness. In contrast, another editor (a man) I once called summarily rejected my idea for an article by barking, "Call me when you have something new to say."

Those who are used to ways of talking that soften the impact of criticism may find it hard to deal with the right-between-the-eyes style. It has its own logic, however, and neither style is intrinsically better. People who prefer criticism given straight are operating on an assumption that feelings aren't involved: "Here's the dope. I know you're good; you can take it."

3. Thank-Yous

A woman manager I know starts meetings by thanking everyone for coming, even though it's clearly their job to do so. Her "thank-you" is simply a ritual.

A novelist received a fax from an assistant in her publisher's office; it contained suggested catalog copy for her book. She immediately faxed him her suggested changes and said, "Thanks for running this by me," even though her contract gave her the right to approve all copy. When she thanked the assistant, she fully expected him to reciprocate: "Thanks for giving me such a quick response." Instead, he said, "You're welcome." Suddenly, rather than an equal exchange of pleasantries, she found herself positioned as the recipient of a favor. This made her feel like responding, "Thanks for nothing!"

Many women use "thanks" as an automatic conversation starter and closer; there's nothing literally to say thank you for. Like many rituals typical of women's conversation, it depends on the goodwill of the other to restore the balance. When the other speaker doesn't reciprocate, a woman may feel like someone on a seesaw whose partner abandoned his end. Instead of balancing in the air, she has plopped to the ground, wondering how she got there.

4. Fighting

Many men expect the discussion of ideas to be a ritual fight—explored through verbal opposition. They state their ideas in the strongest possible terms, thinking that if there are weaknesses someone will point them out,

and by trying to argue against those objections, they will see how well their ideas hold up.

Those who expect their own ideas to be challenged will respond to another's ideas by trying to poke holes and find weak links—as a way of *helping*. The logic is that when you are challenged you will rise to the occasion: Adrenaline makes your mind sharper; you get ideas and insights you would not have thought of without the spur of battle.

But many women take this approach as a personal attack. Worse, they find it impossible to do their best work in such a contentious environment. If you're not used to ritual fighting, you begin to hear criticism of your ideas as soon as they are formed. Rather than making you think more clearly, it makes you doubt what you know. When you state your ideas, you hedge in order to fend off potential attacks. Ironically, this is more likely to *invite* attack because it makes you look weak.

Although you may never enjoy verbal sparring, some women find it helpful to learn how to do it. An engineer who was the only woman among four men in a small company found that as soon as she learned to argue she was accepted and taken seriously. A doctor attending a hospital staff meeting made a similar discovery. She was becoming more and more angry with a male colleague who'd loudly disagreed with a point she'd made. Her better judgment told her to hold her tongue, to avoid making an enemy of this powerful senior colleague. But finally she couldn't hold it in any longer, and she rose to her feet and delivered an impassioned attack on his position. She sat down in a panic, certain she had permanently damaged her relationship with him. To her amazement, he came up to her afterward and said, "That was a great rebuttal. I'm really impressed. Let's go out for a beer after work and hash out our approaches to this problem."

5. Praise

A manager I'll call Lester had been on his new job six months when he heard that the women reporting to him were deeply dissatisfied. When he talked to them about it, their feelings erupted; two said they were on the verge of quitting because he didn't appreciate their work, and they didn't want to wait to be fired. Lester was dumbfounded: He believed they were doing a fine job. Surely, he thought, he had said nothing to give them the impression he didn't like their work. And indeed he hadn't. That was the problem. He had said *nothing*—and the women assumed he was following the adage "If you can't say something nice, don't say anything." He thought he was showing confidence in them by leaving them alone.

Men and women have different habits in regard to giving praise. For

Men expect to fight about ideas, thinking it sharpens their minds. But many women take it as a personal attack.

example, Deirdre and her colleague William both gave presentations at a conference. Afterward, Deirdre told William, "That was a great talk!" He thanked her. Then she asked, "What did you think of mine?" and he gave her a lengthy and detailed critique. She found it uncomfortable to listen to his comments. But she assured herself that he meant well, and that his honesty was a signal that she, too, should be honest when he asked for a critique of his performance. As a matter of fact, she had noticed quite a few ways in which he could have improved his presentation. But she never got a chance to tell him because he never asked—and she felt put down. The worst part was that it seemed she had only herself to blame, since she *had* asked what he thought of her talk.

But had she really asked for his critique? The truth is, when she asked for his opinion, she was expecting a compliment, which she felt was more or less required following anyone's talk. When he responded with criticism, she figured, "Oh, he's playing 'Let's critique each other'—not a game she'd initiated, but one which she was willing to play. Had she realized he was going to criticize her and not ask her to reciprocate, she would never have asked in the first place.

It would be easy to assume that Deirdre was insecure, whether she was fishing for a compliment or soliciting a critique. But she was simply talking automatically, performing one of the many conversational rituals that allow us to get through the day. William may have sincerely misunderstood Deirdre's intention—or may have been unable to

pass up a chance to one-up her when given the opportunity.

6. Complaints

"Troubles talk" can be a way to establish rapport with a colleague. You complain about a problem (which shows that you are just folks) and the other person responds with a similar problem (which puts you on equal footing). But while such commiserating is common among women, men are likely to hear it as a request to *solve* the problem.

One woman told me she would frequently initiate what she thought would be pleasant complaint-airing sessions at work. She'd talk about situations that bothered her just to talk about them, maybe to understand them better. But her male office mate would quickly tell her how she could improve the situation. This left her feeling condescended to and frustrated. She was delighted to see this very impasse in a section in my book *You Just Don't Understand,* and showed it to him. "Oh," he said, "I see the problem. How can we solve it?" Then they both laughed, because it had happened again: He short-circuited the detailed discussion she'd hoped for and cut to the chase of finding a solution.

Sometimes the consequences of complaining are more serious: A man might take a woman's lighthearted griping literally, and she can get a reputation as a chronic malcontent. Furthermore, she may be seen as not up to solving the problems that arise on the job.

7. Jokes

I heard a man call in to a talk show and say, "I've worked for two women and neither one had a sense of humor. You know, when you work with men, there's a lot of joking and teasing." The show's host and the guest (both women) took his comment at face value and assumed the women this man worked for were humorless. The guest said, "Isn't it sad that women

don't feel comfortable enough with authority to see the humor?" The host said, "Maybe when more women are in authority roles, they'll be more comfortable with power." But although the women this man worked for *may* have taken themselves too seriously, it's just as likely that they each had a terrific sense of humor, but maybe the humor wasn't the type he was used to. They may have been like the woman who wrote to me: "When I'm with men, my wit or cleverness seems inappropriate (or lost!) so I don't bother. When I'm with my women friends, however, there's no hold on puns or cracks and my humor is fully appreciated."

The types of humor women and men tend to prefer differ. Research has shown that the most common form of humor among men is razzing, teasing, and mock-hostile attacks, while among women it's self-mocking. Women often mistake men's teasing as genuinely hostile. Men often mistake women's mock self-deprecation as truly putting themselves down.

Women have told me they were taken more seriously when they learned to joke the way the guys did. For example, a teacher who went to a national conference with seven other teachers (mostly women) and a group of administrators (mostly men) was annoyed that the administrators always found reasons to leave boring seminars, while the teachers felt they had to stay and take notes. One evening, when the group met at a bar in the hotel, the principal asked her how one such seminar had turned out. She retorted, "As soon as you left, it got much better." He laughed out loud at her response. The playful insult appealed to the men—but there was a trade-off. The women seemed to back off from her after this. (Perhaps they were put off by her using joking to align herself with the bosses.)

THERE IS NO "RIGHT" WAY TO TALK. When problems arise, the culprit may be style differences—and *all* styles will at times fail with others who don't share or understand them, just as English won't do you much good if you try to speak to someone who knows only French. If you want to get your message across, it's not a question of being "right"; it's a question of using language that's shared—or at least understood.

SAVING RELATIONSHIPS:
THE POWER OF THE UNPREDICTABLE

When one partner silently switches the "rules," both partners can benefit. Welcome to the surprising world systems thinking.

Barry L. Duncan, Psy.D.,
and Joseph W. Rock, Psy.D.

Sharon, 30, and Jeff, 35, have been married for nine years. Since the recent birth of their first child, Sharon has become increasingly aware of Jeff's propensity for giving instructions and pointing out imperfections in her methods of doing things. She knows that he is usually just trying to help.

The first thing Sharon does to address the problem is mention it to Jeff. She explains that when they were first married she needed and appreciated his knowledge and experience but now sometimes feels he is treating her like a child. She asks him to please hold his comments and advice until she asks for them. Jeff agrees to make every effort to treat her like the mature, independent woman she has become.

But before long, Jeff resumes sharing his observations of the way Sharon does things and making suggestions about better ways of doing them. When Sharon points this out to him, he becomes defensive and accuses her of overreacting and not being able to accept constructive criticism.

Sharon continues to make Jeff aware of his now "critical, paternalistic, and sexist nature." She takes every opportunity to point out his need to dominate and keep her in her place. Jeff responds by defensively backing off and withdrawing from conversation in general. When conversa-

tion does occur, he seems more apt to criticize Sharon about her "crazy, feminist" ideas as well as her way of doing almost everything. Their latest interactions seem to be best characterized by an unspoken tension.

Sharon decides to try a different approach. She goes "on strike," discontinuing to do anything Jeff criticizes. When he comments that the spaghetti sauce needs more garlic, she announces she's no longer cooking. When he criticizes how the grass is cut, she blows up in anger, and both Sharon and he say many things that they later regret. Jeff decides not only to stop commenting and suggesting but to stop talking altogether. Now an unspoken hostility hovers over their relationship.

Sharon and Jeff illustrate three ways in which people get stuck in their relationships and sabotage their own attempts to improve them. First Sharon believes she is trying different strategies to improve her relationship when in reality she is trying only slight variations on a single theme: "I will make my dissatisfaction apparent to him, and he will respond with less criticism." People get stuck by trying the same basic approach over and over, even though it might not be obvious to them that they are doing so.

Further, when her first method makes things worse, she tries more of the same. A well-intentioned attempt to resolve a

small difficulty ends up turning it into a serious conflict despite good intentions. Sharon wound up with increased criticism and an overly sensitive, defensive, withdrawn husband.

Third, Sharon recognized the problem but did not succeed in getting Jeff to help solve it. Almost always, one partner notices a joint problem first. That person mentions it to the other and then proceeds to try to solve the problem, while assuming the other person is motivated and cooperative. This can be a faulty assumption even if both people agree on how serious it is or how to solve it.

A widely shared belief is that in order for a relationship to change, both partners have to actively participate in changing it. As family therapists, we disagree. We subscribe to a "systems" approach with couples. In a relationship system, a noticeable change in one person can set in motion a change in the whole system, that is, the couple.

Early in relationships, rules begin to form that grow out of patterns of ways people to relate to each other. Rules can be simple and straightforward—one partner initiates sex, one partner does the dishes; or they can be more subtle—when both partners are angry they don't yell. Sometimes the rules are talked about openly, but typically they are assumed rather than discussed, and those involved

From *Psychology Today,* January/February 1993, pp. 46-51, 86, 95. Adapted from *Overcoming Relationship Impasses* by Barry L. Duncan and Joseph W. Rock, published by Plenum Publishing Corporation. © 1991 by Barry L. Duncan and Joseph W. Rock. Reprinted by permission.

may not even be consciously aware of the assumed rules. This non-awareness causes the most difficulty when problems arise.

Rules have their uses; in recurring situations, we don't have to figure out what to do from scratch. But because rules are based on previous experience, they also maintain the status quo. The very qualities that make rules useful day-to-day can render them harmful when a relationship problem needs to be resolved. Rules simplify life by limiting options to an acceptable few. But when we get stuck in solving a problem, we need *more* options, not fewer. The assumed rules we carry into a situation prevent us from exploring potentially helpful options and limit our flexibility. They discourage change—even helpful, necessary change.

Beyond Blame: Systems Thinking

Most theories of human behavior are couched in linear cause-effect terms and offer either historical (unhappy childhood) or physical (bad nerves) explanations for behavior. Both the medical and Freudian perspectives on problem behaviors or emotional stress consider only the individual, apart from his or her relationships.

Systems theory is evolving to explain the complexities of relationships and to help resolve the problems and distress in-

> In a relationship, you are not acting completely of your own free will. You are constantly influenced by your partner, and vice versa.

herent in relationships. It offers a refreshing, illness-free lens through which to observe human behavior—the focus of study shifts from what goes on inside a person to what takes place between people.

When two individuals come together in a relationship, something is created that is different from, larger, and more complex than those two individuals apart—a system. The most important feature of such a relationship is communication. Relationships are established, maintained, and changed by communicative interaction among members.

As relationships endure, communication sequences form patterns over time, and it is the patterning over time that is the essence of a couple system. Sometimes the enduring patterns begin to create difficulties for couples, and new patterns are need-

ed. With Jeff and Sharon, the pattern concerning the giving and receiving of advice was at the heart of their relationship problems.

In a system, all elements are mutually dependent. What one person does depends on what the other person does. In the context of a relationship, you are not acting completely of your own free will. You are constantly being influenced by your partner, and vice versa. When Sharon attempted to get less criticism, Jeff responded by criticizing more and pulling away. Each person's actions helped determine what the other did, and each person's actions affected the relationship as a whole.

A marriage, then, is not a static and fixed relationship. No matter how entrenched one's behavior or how strong one's personality, each individual is influenced by the other on an ongoing basis. *Once you recognize your partner's dependence upon your pattern of behavior, you can consciously plan and change your own behavior, thereby influencing your partner and the relationship in a constructive manner.*

Virtually every couple we see in therapy is interested in what, or who, caused their problems; they look for guilt, blame, or responsibility. But influence among people in relationships is reciprocal and mutually dependent, causality is circular. Choosing the point at which the causal chain begins is pointless and arbitrary.

One implication is that the circle can be broken or interrupted at any point, regardless of how the problem started or how long it has existed. If one person in a couple changes behavior noticeably and consistently, the other person's reactions will change, which will change the first person's reactions. In this way, one person can positively impact a troubled relationship; the partner's cooperation is not required.

Does Sharon have a problem with constructive criticism, or does Jeff have a problem with control and sexism? One partner, either partner, can interrupt the causal circle and move the relationship in another direction.

In much the same way that a stone thrown into a pond affects the surface well beyond the small point at which it enters, a small change in a specific area can lead to a positive ripple effect on the entire relationship. When there are many problems in a relationship, people assume that a major overhaul is required. Many times, however, a small adjustment, strategically employed, is all that is needed.

Communication: The Sound of Silence

Communication theory is crucial in systems thinking. Gestures, tone of voice, and facial expressions are important in understanding what someone is saying. Much has been written about body language, addressing what people "say" by their posture. What gets lost is that *all behavior is communicative.* Even silence conveys some message. There is no such thing as *not* communicating.

A spouse who routinely comes home late for dinner without calling may be saying, "Your inconvenience is unimportant compared to what happens at work" or "Your feelings are not a priority to me." The spouse who prepares dinner may not comment to the late spouse. Yet the silence may be a worse indictment than a verbal scolding.

Viewing behavior itself as a powerful means of communication significantly increases your options when verbal com-

> What gets lost is that all behavior is communicative. Even silence conveys some message. There is no such thing as *not* communicating.

munication is not working. If, like Sharon, you have tried to fix your relationship problems by talking ad nauseam, then behavioral options may provide a more powerful way.

Communication occurs at different levels, even though most of us focus our attention on only one—the content, or the literal meaning of the words. Most important, but less obvious, is the relationship level. It indicates how the sender of the message is attempting to influence the receiver. It conveys a command or directive concerning the sender's needs and is an implicit attempt to influence the receiver. "My back itches" may mean "Scratch my back." "I had a rough day" may mean "Leave me alone," "I need your support," or "Fix me a drink." Even "I love you" can be an implicit command, depending upon the circumstances. It may mean "Tell me that you love me."

Influence is unavoidable in communication; it is inherent in how we interact. Just as one cannot *not* communicate, one cannot *not* influence when communicating. Implicit directives also define the nature of the relationship. The statement, "The garbage can is overflowing," not only conveys the obvious, but may also contain

Relationship Myths

Myth #1: What people say is very important and has a big impact on what they do.

Words often fall short of accurately depicting someone's intentions and we can't really guess at times what someone else really means. In the long term, behavior is what gives evidence of our true intentions.

Myth #2: People can and should understand and explain their own and others' motives.

Behavior is the result of a tremendous number of interacting influences: biological, psychological, interpersonal, situational. We never get answers to "why," only plausible-sounding guesses. Knowing "why" seldom produces a solution. *Understanding* a behavior pattern and *changing* it are often completely different. Consider *what* is happening now between you and your partner and *how* that pattern can be changed.

Myth #3: In close relationships being completely open and honest is critical if the relationship is to work.

If the person with whom you are communicating is unable or unwilling to respond honestly and openly, honesty and openness may well be a bad idea at times. Being open with someone who will use the information to manipulate you or gain power over you is like playing poker and showing your cards before you bet. An open and honest expression must be interpreted as such by the receiver of the message for it to be truly open and honest. Openness is not the only way, and, in some situations, not the best way.

Myth #4: A good relationship is one in which both people give unselfishly.

Unselfish giving is not a prerequisite for a good relationship. In fact, attempts to do so usually create more problems than they solve. Giving is an important part of any relationship. However, all of us expect something back; it helps to let the other person know what that is. Balance is also important. Rather than expecting to meet all of each other's needs, stay in practice at meeting some of your own. It adds stability to a relationship and reduces the risk of resentment. Complete selfishness certainly does not lend itself to healthy relationships, but it turns out that neither does utter unselfishness.

Myth #5: In any situation there is only one reality or one truth.

Reality is entirely dependent upon who is observing and describing it, especially in complex situations such as interactions in relationships. When two people have very different stories to tell about the same situation, it does not mean that one is lying, although each partner usually believes that about the other. Rather, each is describing reality from his or her frame of reference. A lot of time usually is wasted trying to convince your partner that you are right. This time could be better spent trying to understand the others' point of view and using that understanding to change your own behavior in a way that will help the relationship.

---

the implicit directive, "Take the garbage out." The statement defines the relationship as one in which the sender has the right to comment on the state of garbage and expect the receiver to follow the (implicit) directive.

Implicit commands are largely automatic and occur outside of awareness. As a result, we often address the most important parts of our lives, our relationships, in an extremely haphazard fashion. By becoming aware of the implicit influence in communication we can deliberately use it in improving relationships.

When we think about communication, we usually think of a speaker actively conveying a message and a listener passively receiving it. This, however, is a very inaccurate perception. Listening is an active process. We have to make sense of the speaker's words; we compare their ideas to beliefs and attitudes we hold and to perceptions about the speakers we've already formed. We consider gestures, tone of voice, and facial expressions, and the circumstances. In addition, our needs influence what we hear.

The conclusion is inescapable—the listener helps create meaning. Much of this process tends to be automatic and outside awareness. We're seldom aware of how our beliefs and attitudes affect how we hear, or the ways we interpret nonverbal communication, much less how our own needs affect our perceptions. By paying attention to these factors, however, we can make them conscious, then control them.

The upshot is, we can choose how to interpret a given communication. Words

Words that hurt us before no longer have to have power. We can choose to interpret a message differently from the way the sender intended.

or behaviors that have hurt us before no longer have to have this power. Further, we can choose to interpret a message differently from the way the sender intended. Just because people intend to hurt or manipulate us doesn't mean we have to cooperate by giving their messages the meanings they want us to get.

Often, the listener's understanding of a message is *already* different from the sender's. If a woman believes her husband is stressed out and needs time away, she might suggest he go away for a week. If he interprets this as "She's trying to get rid of me," the whole point of her message is twisted, and caring is perceived as rejection. This may be the most common problem seen in couples: The message sent is not the message received. Finding ways to understand and express your partner's view of a situation can reduce defensiveness and change old, conflictual patterns in a relationship.

Guidelines for Change

The ideas that one person can produce meaningful change in a relationship, and that a small change can and will lead to a ripple of other changes, are not part of conventional wisdom. Nor are the implications that change can occur quickly and that it can happen without the knowledge or cooperation of one member of the couple. But strategies developed from systems concepts do work, even when both partners aren't equally motivated to change. Here, then, are some very practical guidelines for creating change in a troubled relationship where the partners are stuck at an impasse:

•Create confusion. Change the rules by which you've been playing. Be unpredictable. That encourages your partner to find new ways to react.

• Do not be completely honest and open at all times. If your partner tends to manipulate or use power plays, openness just tips your hand and makes you more vulnerable.

• "Give up" power, or "lose" by telling your partner that you agree that he or she is "right," but continue to do whatever you think is best. Allow yourself to give up power verbally, to gain control behaviorally.

• Recognize that words and behaviors are not consistent. People often say one thing but do another. Believe what your partner does, not what he or she says.

• Do things that are truly different, not just variations on a theme. Allow yourself to change 180 degrees in how you approach a problem. That alteration can loosen things up and produce real change in your partner's response.

• Stay off the defensive. If you spend all your time justifying what you are doing, you become reactive and lose track of what you are trying to accomplish. Most people are too busy trying to defend themselves to see other ways of approaching a problem. Relationships are very complex and much creativity is needed.

• If your partner openly resists change, don't push. Finding a different, less confrontational path the change can be much more effective—and less frustrating.

• Go with the flow whenever possible and recognize the disadvantages of change. Things are rarely black and white; consider the advantages of maintaining the problem. This form of creative interpretation directly addresses the ambivalence people have about changing their behavior and aligns with that part of the individual that may be reluctant to change. It helps clarify the feared consequences of change in the hope of motivating the person toward action regarding the problem.

• Start a small, positive ripple of change and let it grow by itself.

• Look at what is going well, instead of what is going wrong with your relationship. It's much easier to build on what is already there than to tear something down and start all over.

Power Disparities in Romantic Relationships

By far, the most common source of problems in a relationship involves the distribution of power. In a good relationship, ideally there is a balance of power. Unfortunately, this ideal is not always real-

ized, and neither party is happy with the unequal power. The powerless, disenfran-

The ideas that one person can produce meaningful change in a relationship, and that a small change will lead to a ripple of other changes, are not part of conventional wisdom.

chised partner feels cheated and resentful, and, whether aware of it or not, usually seeks ways to even the score. The powerful partner gets resentful because he or she has too much responsibility and carries a disproportionate share of the load.

In a relationship with a power disparity, no one wins. Yet the struggle for power underlies virtually every relationship quarrel. There are two common relationship patterns in which power is the key issue.

One involves the dependent partner who needs his partner to do things, but tries to regain the power lost to dependency by criticizing the way those things are done.

IN DEALING WITH A DEPENDENT PARTNER WHO IS RELENTLESSLY CRITICAL:

• Agree in words, but not in action, with criticism.

• Don't explain or defend yourself.

• Interpret your partner's critical message to mean you can stop doing whatever was criticized: "You're right, I am a terrible cook. I'll let you eat prepared frozen food more." Your partner will either stop in his tracks or—even better—refute the criticism himself.

The second power problem is the most common problem we see in troubled relationships. It involves one partner having control in multiple areas—money, decision-making, social life, conversation topics—such that the relationship begins to resemble that of a parent and child, with the powerful partner treating the other like a child. Even when the person in the powerful role, such as a parent, can be very kind and nurturing, the powerless partner can easily feel inferior, helpless, trapped—as well as resentful. Any attempts to speak out against the arrangement will usually sound like the helpless protestations of a child.

IN DEALING WITH A DOMINEERING PARTNER WHO PLAYS A PARENTAL ROLE:

• Do what you want to do—act independently of your partner's expectations.

If criticized, agree you were "wrong" or "misguided," but continue to do what you believe is best.

• Use "constructive payback," in which criticism from your partner is met with your "inadvertent" mistakes and "forgetfulness" (being late, stupid, inefficient) that bother your partner and make your partner's life more difficult. This indirectly expresses your anger and resentment and lets your partner know that he or she can't get away with being abusive.

Communication Problems

Three common communication patterns often make individuals unhappy. The first is lack of communication, in which one partner feels distress concerning the other's unwillingness or inability to talk about things. Unlike most other problems, the roles in this pattern consistently divide along gender lines; most often, the male partner is seen as relatively silent and the female partner distressed about it.

IN DEALING WITH AN UNCOMMUNICATIVE PARTNER:

• Do something that's a noticeable change from your previous strategies. Become less available for conversation and do not try hard to initiate or maintain discussion. Cut it short when it does start. This not only removes but reverses all pressure on the male partner. And it gives the female partner more control. The entire pattern is changing, and the power shifts.

• Interpret silence in a positive way: "We are so close we don't always have to be talking." "I feel good when you're quiet because I know that means everything is all right between us." This negates any power your partner may be expressing through silence.

• Focus less on the relationship and more on satisfying yourself. When you do things for yourself, you need less from others in the way of attention and assurance.

A second common communication problem involves a pattern in which one partner is consistently sad or negative—and verbalizes it—and the other is distressed by the complaints and frustrated in his or her attempts to help. Ordinarily, the complaint has at least some basis in fact—a life circumstance has given the person cause to feel depressed or pessimistic. Unfortunately, most people faced with a chronic complainer become cheerleaders; they assume that encouragement and information of a positive nature will help. But the complainer interprets the cheerleading as lack of understanding. Another losing strategy is ignoring the complaining so that the gates of negativism are never opened. Both strategies wind up intensifying the problem.

IN DEALING WITH A
CHRONIC COMPLAINER:

•Accept, agree, and encourage the complainer's position.

•Encourage complaining rather than trying to avoid it.

•Honestly express any negative opinions you have on the topic being complained about. (Do not express any positive opinions.) Initiate topics of complaint at every opportunity. This gives the complainer the freedom of choice to discuss other issues and positive feelings.

A third communication problem is an accuser-denyer pattern that frequently evolves when one partner accuses the other of lying. Lying may—or may not—actually be involved.

IN DEALING WITH AN ACCUSER:

•Don't explain or defend. This extremely simple solution is effective because the situation doesn't escalate—it's hard to argue with someone who doesn't argue back—and you do not appear guilty by reason of protesting too much. Accusations are often made to get an argument started; if one partner does not go for the bait, the accusation strategy stops working and is eventually dropped.

•Go one step further and reflect the insecurity of the accuser. "You're afraid that I'm having an affair." "You're concerned that you're not attractive to me anymore." "You're feeling insecure about my love for you."

Sex and Jealousy

Key aspects of couples' sex lives have little to do with what happens in bed. Jealousy and trust issues in a relationship are a prime example. Both involve one partner' suspecting that the other isn't be-

ing completely loyal or truthful. And in both, the partner who is the object of the jealous feelings or mistrust cannot remove the problem. Many different real or imagined actions can destroy trust, and jealousy certainly isn't the always the result of a real indiscretion. But sometimes it is.

An affair is a very difficult occurrence for a relationship to survive. It is much like surviving the death of a loved one; the relationship as it was before is forever lost. As in coming to grips with a death, the partner who must accept the "loss" needs to grieve, experience, and express the entire range of emotions associated with the affair.

Unfortunately, the partner who had the affair rarely facilitates this grieving process, Rather he or she tries to handle the situation with minimization, avoidance, and indignation, believing that the subject will die if ignored. "It was only sex, not love." "It's over, let's get on with our lives." "It meant nothing to me."

This strategy usually backfires because the other partner, already feeling hurt and angry at the betrayal, now feels dismissed and misunderstood—and brings up the affair even more. Already feeling defensive through guilt, the partner who had the affair gets more defensive ("How long do I have to go on like this?") The mistaken belief that the issue of the affair should be resolved quickly allows this partner to feel wronged, leading greater distance between partners.

IN DEALING WITH A JEALOUS PARTNER:

• Encourage the partner who feels betrayed to express jealous feelings, and listen nondefensively. This allows the affair to be treated as significant; the betrayed partner has no need to emphasize how important and painful an issue it is. And by encouraging discussion of the affair, the agenda of the person who feels betrayed is given priority. This restores some of the

lost power and control without necessitating a prolonged power struggle.

•Initiate at every opportunity discussion of actions or situation that provoke jealousy.

•Keep an exceptionally detailed diary of all your daily activities and recite it at length to your partner every day—in a matter-of-fact fashion. This breaks the questioning-defensiveness cycle. The information overload makes it less likely that accusations of giving partial or incomplete data will be made.

Of all the issues that are related to what happens in the bedroom, sexual frequency is the one about which we hear the most complaints. Usually, one partner decides that there is a problem—usually the partner who wants more sex. He or she begins by stating the problem and directly requesting more frequent sex. The verbal response from the partner is usually encouraging ("Okay, let's try to get together more often"), but the behavior frequently remains the same. At this point, the partner who feels deprived pulls out all the stops—adult movies, sexy clothing, candlelight dinners. The partner being pursued feels pressured and backs away further. The pursuer feels unloved and rejected, and may accuse his or her partner of being involved with someone else.

IN DEALING WITH A SEXUALLY
DISINTERESTED PARTNER:

•Remove all pressure to have sex, but increase nonsexual affection.

•Increase the time spent together in mutually enjoyable, nonsexual activities. This helps put sex back in a healthy perspective by focusing on the enjoyable parts of a relationship.

•Become less available for sex, rather than always being ready and eager. This reduces perceived pressure and frees your partner to accept the role of pursuer.

Vanishing Dreams of America's Young Families

The future of today's young parents and their small children is now in great jeopardy. Congress and the President must take immediate steps to ensure that every child has a fair start, a healthy start, and a head start.

MARIAN WRIGHT EDELMAN

Marian Wright Edelman is President of the Children's Defense Fund. This article draws upon her speech of April 14, 1992 delivered to the National Press Club in Washington D.C., and the report, issued jointly by the Children's Defense Fund and Northeastern University's Center for Labor Market Studies, entitled, Vanishing Dreams: The Economic Plight of America's Young Families. *This article and the report on which it is based is under copyright by the Children's Defense Fund, 25 E Street NW, Washington, DC.*

Americans from all walks of life are profoundly anxious—troubled by what they see around them today and even more by what they see ahead. This anxiety, not only about their own futures but also about the nation's future, is manifested in countless ways: in paralyzing economic insecurity; in an emerging politics of rejection, frustration, and rage; in a growing polarization of our society by race and by class; and in an erosion of the sense of responsibility to help the weakest and poorest among us.

But this anxiety about the future is *most* vivid when we watch our own children grow up and try to venture out on their own—struggling to get established as adults in a new job, a new marriage, a new home or a new family.

It's true that young families always have faced an uphill struggle starting out in life. But today's young families have been so battered by economic and social changes over the past two decades that the struggle has taken on a more desperate and often futile quality.

And as parents of my generation watch many of their adult children founder—failing to find steady, decent-paying jobs, unable to support families, shut out of the housing market and often forced to move back home—they know that something has gone terribly wrong. Often they don't know precisely what has happened or why. But they do understand that these young adults and their children may never enjoy the same opportunities or achieve the same standard of living or security that our generation found a couple of decades ago.

Two generations in trouble

Young families with children—those headed by persons under the age of thirty—have been devastated since 1973 by a cycle of falling incomes, increasing family disintegration, and rising poverty. In the process, the foundations for America's young families have been so thoroughly undermined that two complete generations of Americans—today's young parents and their small children—are now in great jeopardy. Figure 1 captures the poverty rates of those two jeopardized generations:

Young families are the crucible for America's future and America's dream. Most children spend at least part of their lives—their youngest and most developmentally vulnerable months and years—in young families. How we treat these families therefore goes a long way toward defining what our nation as a whole will be like twenty, fifty, or even seventy-five years from now.

What has happened to America's young families with children is unprecedented and almost unimaginable.

3. FINDING A BALANCE: Relationships between Parents and Children

Figure 1   Poverty Rates of Families With Children,
By Age of Family Head, 1973, 1979, 1982, 1990

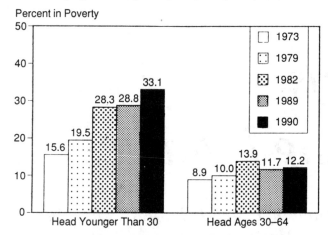

This also is not a story about teenagers. While America's teen pregnancy problem remains tragic and demands an urgent response, only 3 percent of the young families with children we are discussing are headed by teenagers. More than 70 percent are headed by someone aged twenty-five to twenty-nine. The plight of America's young families is overwhelmingly the plight of young adults who are both old enough and eager to assume the responsibilities of parenthood and adulthood, but for whom the road is blocked.

Finally and most importantly, this is *not* simply a story about someone else's children, about minority children or children in single-parent families or children whose parents dropped out of high school.

All young families affected

Huge income losses have affected virtually every group of young families with children: white, black and Latino; married-couple and single-parent; and those headed by high school graduates as well as dropouts. Only young families with children headed by college graduates experienced slight income gains between 1973 and 1990.

In other words, the tragedy facing young families with children has now reached virtually *all* of our young families. One in four *white* children in young families is now poor. One in five children in young *married-couple* families is now poor. And one in three children in families headed by a young *high school graduate* is now poor. Nearly three-fourths of the increase in poverty among young families since 1973 has occurred outside the nation's central cities. And poverty has grown most rapidly among young families with only one child (Figure 2).

There is no refuge from the economic and social shifts that have battered young families with children. We can pretend that they won't reach our children and our grandchildren. We can pretend that those who play by the rules will be O.K.

Adjusted for inflation, the median income of young families with children plunged by one-third between 1973 and 1990 (Table 1). This median income includes income from all sources, and the drop occurred despite the fact that many families sent a second earner into the workforce. As a result, poverty among these young families more than doubled, and by 1990 a shocking 40 percent or four in ten children in young families were poor .

The past two decades have been difficult for many other Americans as well. But older families with children have lost only a little economic ground since 1973, and families without children have enjoyed substantial income gains. By far the greatest share of the nation's economic pain has been focused on the weakest and most vulnerable among us—young families with children.

This is *not* a story about the current recession, although the recession surely is having a crushing impact on young families. Even comparing 1973 to 1989—two good economic years at the end of sustained periods of growth—the median income of young families with children dropped by one-fourth. Then just the first few months of the recession in 1990 sent young families' incomes plummeting to new depths.

Table 1	Median Incomes of Families With Children By Age of Family Head, 1973–1990 (in 1990 dollars)*					
	1973	1979	1982	1989	1990	Change 1973-1990
All families with children	36,882	36,180	31,819	35,425	34,400	- 6.7%
Family head younger than 30	27,765	25,204	20,378	20,665	18,844	-32.1%
Family head age 30–64	41,068	39,978	35,293	39,525	38,451	- 6.4%
Young families' median income as a share of older families' income	68%	63%	58%	52%	49%	

Note: The money incomes of families for all years prior to 1990 were converted into 1990 dollars via use of the Consumer Price Index for All Urban Consumers (CPI-U). The U.S. Bureau of Labor Statistics has generated an alternative price index for the years preceding 1983 that conforms to the current method of measuring changes in housing costs. This index is known as the CPI-UXI. Use of this price index would reduce the estimated 1973 real income by about 7 percent, thus lowering the estimated decline in the median income of young families between 1973 and 1990 from 32 percent to approximately 25 percent. None of the comparisons of median income between various groups of families are affected by these changes.

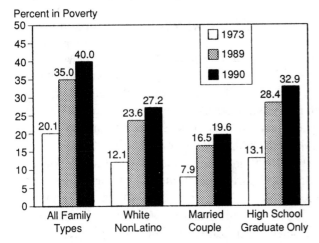

Figure 2 — Poverty Rates of Children in Young Families, By Characteristics of the Family Head, 1973, 1989, 1990

We can pretend, but that will not change the reality—the reality that young families have lost a third of their median income, that two in five American children in young families live in poverty, and that these facts have devastating consequences.

Those consequences include more hunger, more homelessness, more low birthweight births, more infant deaths and more child disability. They also mean more substance abuse, more crime, more violence, more school failure, more teen pregnancy, more racial tension, more envy, more despair and more cynicism—a long-term economic and social disaster for young families and for the country. In virtually every critical area of child development and healthy maturation, family poverty creates huge roadblocks to individual accomplishment, future economic self-sufficiency, and national progress.

Plummeting incomes and soaring poverty and growing gaps based on age and education and race mean more of all these problems, yet many of our leaders seem not to understand why they are occurring. But there is not really a puzzle, when we recognize that the nation has marginalized and pauperized much of two generations of Americans—young parents and young children.

Young families not only lost income in huge amounts, but as the permanence and quality of their jobs deteriorated, they lost fringe benefits like health insurance as well. In the decade of the 1980s the proportion of *employed* heads of young families with children whose employers made health insurance available by paying all or part of the cost dropped by one-fifth. And employers cut back on coverage for dependent spouses and children even more than for workers.

Fewer and fewer young pregnant women have been getting adequate prenatal care because they are poorer and less likely to have adequate insurance or any insur-

ance. And our falling vaccination rates and renewed epidemics of measles and other wholly preventable diseases among preschoolers are being driven by plunging incomes in young families, eroding health insurance coverage, and unraveling government programs.

Falling incomes also have devastated young families in an increasingly expensive housing market. One-third fewer young families with children were homeowners in 1991 than in 1980. Young renter families increasingly are paying astronomical shares of their meager incomes for rent. More and more are doubling up or becoming homeless—in some surveys three-fourths of the homeless parents in this country are under age thirty.

Young families are not only suffering from the hunger, housing, health and other problems that their plummeting incomes have caused. They are suffering as well because they are falling further and further behind the rest of the society—imperiling their attachment to the core work force and to mainstream values and threatening their potential to reacquire the American dream in the decades to come.

In 1973 the income of older families with children was not quite one-and-a-half times that of young families with children. By 1990 it was more than double that of the young families.

Combination of causes

There is no single cause of young families' plight. Instead, they have been pummelled by a combination of profound changes in the American economy; the government's inadequate response to families in trouble; and changes in the composition of young families themselves.

Much of the increase in their poverty is due to economic shifts and to changing government policies that have made it more difficult for young families to obtain adequate incomes. These changes have hurt all young families with children, regardless of their family structure, race or ethnicity, or educational attainment.

Unlike members of earlier generations, young workers today no longer can be confident of finding stable jobs with decent wages, even if they get a high school diploma or spend a couple of years in college. Since 1973, slower growth in U.S. productivity and declines in blue collar employment made some drop in inflation-adjusted median earnings for young workers inevitable. By last year the average wages of *all* nonsupervisory workers (of all ages) in the private sector fell to their lowest level since the Eisenhower Administration.

But the losses have been focused disproportionately on young workers. The median annual earnings of heads of young families with children fell a staggering 44 percent from 1973 to 1990. In other words, in the span of less than a generation this nation nearly *halved* the earnings of young household heads with children (Table 2):

These dramatic earnings losses occurred across-the-board. For example, young white families with children were hit as hard as young Latino families: the median earnings of both groups fell by two-fifths. College graduates as well as high school graduates and dropouts lost big chunks of income. But the drop in median earnings for high school dropouts and for young black family heads has been particularly devastating—in each case more than two-thirds.

Table 2	**Median Annual Earnings of Heads of Young Families With Children, 1973 and 1990** (in 1990 dollars)		
	1973	1990	% Change 1973-1990
All heads of young families with children	22,981	12,832	-44
Married couple	25,907	17,500	-33
Male-headed	18,547	14,000	-25
Female-headed	2,073	1,878	- 9
White, non-Latino	25,024	15,000	-40
Black, non-Latino	13,860	4,030	-71
Latino	15,924	9,000	-44
Other, non-Latino	17,664	12,000	-32
High school dropout	15,014	4,500	-70
High school graduate	23,817	14,000	-41
Some college	26,496	18,000	-32
College graduate	31,795	25,721	-19

The erosion in pay levels (due in part to the declining value of the minimum wage) combined with the growth of temporary or part-time and part-year jobs to put a triple whammy on young workers: far lower annual earnings; less secure employment; and less access to health insurance and other employer-provided benefits.

The huge drop in earnings among America's young workers has not received much attention. In part it has been obscured by the almost Herculean work effort of young parents. Many young married-couple families have tried to compensate for lower wages by sending a second worker into the work force. These second earners have softened (but not eliminated) the economic blow. But the growing number of young parents working longer hours or coping with two jobs has placed young families with children under tremendous stress and generated new offsetting costs, especially for child care. Many families, moreover, have two jobs that together provide less security and less support and less access to health care than one good job did a generation ago. This two-earner strategy is totally unavailable, moreover, to the growing number of single-parent families.

Economic shifts and family changes

Today's young families with children look considerably different from those in the early 1970s. They are more likely to be minority families or single parent families. Both groups are more likely to be paid low wages and to be poor than other families. So poverty among young families and children as a whole also rises.

The growth in young female-headed families with children is in part a reflection of changing values. But the economic hardships associated with falling earnings and persistent joblessness among young adults have contributed significantly to falling marriage rates and the increasing rates of out-of-wedlock childbearing. And the fastest growth in out-of-wedlock childbearing has occurred among women in their twenties, not among teenagers, a growth driven in significant part by the earnings free-fall for young adults.

The capacity to support a family has a powerful impact on the marriage decisions of young people. More than two centuries ago Benjamin Franklin wrote: "The number of marriages. . .is greater in proportion to the ease and convenience of supporting a family. When families can be easily supported, more persons marry, and earlier in life."

Increases in poverty among young families with children are *not* the result of young Americans having more children. Indeed, young adults have responded to a tightening economic vise by postponing childbearing and choosing to have fewer children. But these attempts to adapt their behavior have been overwhelmed by the far more rapid pace of economic decline and social disintegration they have encountered.

As a result of these economic and social changes, in 1990 a child in a family headed by a parent under age 30 was:

• twice as likely to be poor as a comparable child in 1973;

• if living with both parents, two and a half times as likely to be poor as in 1973;

• nearly three times more likely to have been born out-of-wedlock than his counterpart two decades ago;

• one-third less likely to be living in a home owned by her family than just a decade ago; and

• three times more likely to see his family pay more than one-half its income for rent.

But despite the devastating suffering these numbers

suggest, children in young families have been given less and less government help over the last two decades. They were getting less to begin with—government programs are particularly stingy when it comes to helping younger adults and young children. And in the 1970s and especially the 1980s young families saw programs that might help them cut rather than strengthened and reconfigured to adapt to new realities. As a result, government programs were less than half as effective in pulling young families out of poverty in 1990 as in 1979.

Hard hit minority families

The changes of the last two decades have had a very profound impact on minority young families, especially those that are black. As Table 2 shows, the median earnings of the heads of young black families with children fell *71 percent* from 1973 to 1990 (from $13,860 to $4,030 in 1990 dollars). Their total family incomes from all sources fell 48 percent. The *median* income of these young black families is now below the federal poverty line for a family of three. In 1973 it was nearly double that poverty line. *Two out of three* children in young black families now are poor.

This crisis for young black families is contributing mightily to the tearing apart of the black community. This society cannot year after year increase the poverty and isolation and hopelessness of black mothers and fathers and children—it can't keep turning the screws tighter and tighter—without appalling consequences. We see those consequences in the emergency rooms and unemployment lines and prisons and homeless shelters and neonatal intensive care wards and morgues of our cities and our suburbs and rural towns. We see it in the omnipresent violence that destroys so many black lives and leaves blacks and whites alike so fearful. More blacks die from firearms each year in this country than died in the century's worth of despicable lynchings that followed the Civil War. More black men die from firearms every six weeks in Detroit than died in the 1967 Detroit "riot." More black and Hispanic men die from firearms in Los Angeles every two weeks than died in the 1965 Watts "riot." [Editor's note: This speech was given two weeks before the most recent outbreak of violence in Los Angeles.]

Frankly, though, I would be skeptical that this nation would attack this cataclysm for young black families were it not for the fact that young *white* families are only a step or two behind in the scope of their economic depression and family disintegration. Perhaps the most important story told in this report is the impact of two decades of this Depression for the young on three types of families we often assume are insulated from hard times:

• From 1973 to 1990 the poverty rate for children living in young *white* families more than doubled to *27 percent*.

• From 1973 to 1990 the poverty rate for children in young *married-couple* families went up two-and-a-half times—to *20 percent*.

• And the child poverty rate in young families headed by *high school graduates* went up even faster, to *33 percent*.

In other words, a generation ago white or married-couple young families or those headed by high school graduates were fairly well insulated from poverty. The damage of the last two decades has cut so broadly and deeply that now one in four white children in young families, one in five children in married-couple young families, and one in three children in families headed by young high school graduates is poor.

Private and public response

What response do we see to these problems from private and public leadership? Precious little.

Too much of the business community is wholly untroubled by stripping away from millions of Americans the minimum family-supporting wages, fringe benefits, and job security that could help make our families strong again. The Administration has no higher domestic priority than cutting capital gains taxes for the rich. The Congress and the Administration together persist in keeping defense spending above the levels of the average year in the Cold War—impoverishing our society and the world by arming ourselves not only against real external threats but against weapons-justifying fantasies, while letting the internal enemies of poverty, disintegration, violence, and hopelessness rage unabated. The Congress can't mount the political will to get Head Start—a program universally conceded to be effective and cost-effective—to more than one in three eligible children or to pass the refundable children's tax credit that experts from all parts of the political spectrum think is a minimum first step to tax equity and family economic security.

Finally, far too many of the nation's Governors and state and national legislators have responded to budget crunches and political turmoil by scapegoating the poor—trying to bolster their political fortunes by pummeling the welfare recipients whose assistance gobbles up a grand total of 2 to 3 percent of state budgets.

3. FINDING A BALANCE: Relationships between Parents and Children

In hard times in the past our society usually has had escape valves—an inherent balance that gave to the powerless help from one institution when others turned their backs—from the federal government when the states were at their worst, from the courts when Congress and the executive were unresponsive. Now we seem to be in an awful time when every institution is competing to pander to the powerful and further penalize the poor.

A fair start

In response to the economic plight of America's young families, Congress and the President must take three immediate steps in 1992 to ensure that every child has a *fair* start, a *healthy* start, and a *head* start.

A *fair start* means renewed and sustained economic growth and enough jobs at decent wages to restore the pact our nation used to have with young families—that personal sacrifice and hard work will be rewarded with family suppporting jobs. A fair start also means enactment of a refundable children's tax credit to bolster the incomes of families with children, as proposed in recent months in various forms and amounts by the National Commission on Children and key members of Congress from both parties. Such a credit would reduce federal income taxes for middle- and low-income families and help the lowest income families that have no tax liability through a tax refund.

While creating no new bureaucracies, a refundable children's credit would target tax relief and economic support precisely to the group—families with children—that has been hardest hit by declining incomes and rising poverty rates since 1973. The Administration's alternative proposal—to expand the personal exemption for children—is extremely regressive. It gives $310 to a family with two children if their income exceeds about $100,000; $280 if it is over $50,000; $150 if income is between $15,000 and $50,000; and zero if it is under about $15,000.

Finally, a fair start means creation of a child support insurance system to give all single parents the chance to lift their families out of poverty through work, ensuring that all children who are not living with both parents receive a minimally adequate child support payment from the absent parent or the government when it fails to collect from the absent parent.

What we *don't* need in this time of great crisis for young families with children is a negative approach rooted in welfare-bashing and welfare cuts that ends up hurting children. Families on welfare are the victims of the recession, not the cause of it. They are victims of

budget deficits, not the cause of them. But nearly one-fourth of all young families with children are forced to rely upon Aid for Families with Dependent Children (AFDC) to meet their basic needs, and they are extremely vulnerable to misguided attacks on this essential safety net for children.

Our political leaders know these truths. Yet during an election year too many cannot resist the temptation to direct the public's frustration and anger toward the poorest of poor Americans—those families and children who rely upon welfare for basic income support.

There *are* ways we can and must improve welfare. For example, we agree with the Administration that welfare parents often don't have enough financial incentive to work because current welfare rules strip them of virtually all of their earnings when they do work. That is why we opposed the repeal of earnings incentives by President Reagan and the Congress in 1981, and why we think they should be restored now for all welfare families, not just those in a few demonstration counties.

But most of the welfare "reforms" now underway in states are little more than crass attempts to slash state budgets without regard to their impact on families with children. Reducing or stopping benefits to newborns when they are the second or third child in a family, as now proposed by several states, is punitive, pointless, and immoral. Only political leaders who are hopelessly out of touch with the realities of poor families' lives could think that an extra $2.50 per day in welfare benefits would cause teen parents to have a second child, or that reducing the added benefit to $1.25/day (as the Governor of Wisconsin and the President now propose for that state) constitutes any serious effort at welfare reform. All they will succeed in doing is taking desperately needed food, clothing and shelter from infants.

It's time for the President, Congress, and more of our Governors to be honest with the American people about the problems facing our economy, our poor families and our children.

The problem is *not* large numbers of welfare parents trying to "beat the system" by having more children or moving to another state to get higher benefits. The problem is a set of short-sighted, budget-driven welfare rules that make it virtually impossible for parents to work their way gradually off the welfare rolls and a dearth of stable, family-supporting jobs that would allow them to make it on their own.

In many ways, the welfare problem is the same problem facing all young families with children—the result of sharply falling wages, too few job opportunities for those with little education or training, and too little investment in the skills and supports poor parents need to make it in today's economy. And serious solutions begin with a fair start, a healthy start, and a head start for our young families.

A healthy start, a head start

A *healthy start* means a national health plan to assure insurance coverage for all Americans. Children and pregnant women need basic health care *now*, however. As an immediate step, the president and Congress must extend Medicaid coverage to every low-income child and pregnant woman. And to ensure that this insurance provides real access to essential health services, not merely theoretical coverage, children need universal access to vaccines and increased funding for community health centers, and other public health activities.

A *head start* means full funding of Head Start. A first step in bolstering the productivity of our next generation of workers lies in adequate investments in quality child care and early childhood development. Every dollar invested in good early childhood development programs saves $5.97 in later special education, welfare, crime, and other costs. Yet Head Start still reaches only one in three eligible preschool children.

As recommended by prominent business groups, educators, and a broad range of study commissions that have examined the educational problems of disadvantaged children and youths, the president and Congress should ensure every child a Head Start by 1995 by enacting immediately S. 911, the School Readiness Act, and accelerating the funding increases it provides.

A head start also means passing family preservation legislation that will strengthen and preserve families in crisis so that they can better protect, nurture and support their own children. So many of these young parents want to be better parents, and with intensive family preservation services they can get the help they need.

These are essential first steps. To reach them and go beyond them, we're going to have to make the President and Congress come to recognize that child and family poverty and insecurity are a national disaster that requires our addressing them with a pittance of the zeal and shared commitment we now apply to digging out after a devastating hurricane or earthquake or confronting a crisis abroad.

EFFECTIVE FATHERS

WHY ARE SOME DADS MORE SUCCESSFUL THAN OTHERS?

Ken R. Canfield

Ken R. Canfield is the author of The Seven Secrets of Effective Fathers *and* Beside Every Great Dad. *His articles have appeared in* Psychological Reports, Educational and Psychological Measurement, Parents, *and other publications. He is the founder of the National Center for Fathering in Shawnee Mission, Kansas, which seeks to inspire and train men to be responsible fathers.*

F athers win when they actively father. There is a deep sense of satisfaction that pervades a father's life when he becomes an involved dad. Vice President Al Gore spoke to this point recently when he said, "There is nothing more noble than to see a father succeed." Bravo! I couldn't agree more. As a researcher over the past seven years, I have tapped into the experiences of some seven thousand fathers across the nation. These dads come from a range of experiences: fathers in prison, fathers in the military, stepfathers, divorced dads, inner-city fathers, suburban fathers, and fathers from different ethnic backgrounds. Each group faces some unique challanges.

A N EFFECTIVE FATHER CAN REMAIN LEVELHEADED BOTH IN A CRISIS LIKE AN AUTO ACCIDENT AND IN THE MIDST OF MEDIA MESSAGES THAT ARE HOSTILE TO TRAINING RESPONSIBLE CHILDREN.

Still, in order to systematize and understand the role of fathers as such, a survey inventory was developed, and the differ-ent dads I have just mentioned were surveyed on their practices as fathers. A national Gallup poll was conducted. The sample used for this poll differed from the national average, however, in that only 7 percent of the men who were surveyed were noncustodial fathers—all the rest were living with their families. Thus, our sample was above the national average in terms of commitment to fatherhood.

Then, in the course of this research, my colleagues and I identified a group of effective fathers within the larger group. These "effective fathers" had raised at least one child to adulthood and were nominated by peers and/or professionals who knew them. Then, in combing through the survey responses, I found seven aspects of fathering that these fathers demonstrated to a significantly greater degree than did other fathers. Here is the essence of the study.

The seven aspects of effective fathering identified are:
- Commitment
- Awareness
- Consistency

- Protecting and providing
- Loving the children's mother
- Active listening
- Spiritual equipping

1. COMMITMENT

Commitment is being both eager to be with your children and willing to be with them when you are not so eager.

The strong fathers identified by their peers scored 77 percent on the commitment scale on the questionnaire, compared with 59 percent for other fathers. The difference—18 percentage points—was greatest in this area of the survey.

How does a father strengthen commitment? One way is by verbalizing to his children that he is committed to them and available for them. Giving his school-age children his work phone number is one way of emphasizing the point.

Telling others about your commitment to your children is another way of holding yourself accountable. Don't be embarrassed to tell an office mate that you are taking an afternoon off because of a son's ball game. What you're demonstrating is that you are committed to that child.

Symbols can help, too. When the president of the United States looks up from his desk, he can see the seal of his authority. When you look around you, what have you placed within your view that reminds you "I'm a dad!"?

2. AWARENESS

Effective fathers answered that it was "somewhat true" that they knew their children. Other fathers were "undecided" or "unsure" on questions measuring awareness.

Awareness has a couple of aspects. One is knowing your child's specific moods, temperament, abilities, situation at school, friends, dreams, and so on. The other is knowing the general developmental phases in a child's life.

Another secret within the secret of being aware of your children is being aware of the ways that their mom is in tune with them and paying attention to what she notices.

Knowing your children and their situation requires that you heavily invest yourself in digesting what your children tell you. Once I was trying to understand why my son was having trouble with his teacher. By listening hard and forcing myself to pay attention over a period of time, it suddenly clicked. This teacher didn't like my son because he reminded her of someone else. That problem didn't need a father's lecture or discipline—it called for a change in schools.

3. CONSISTENCY

Ahhh, consistency. Remember the often-misquoted phrase: "*Foolish* consistency is the hobgoblin of little minds." We need consistency that isn't stifling, or boring but that communicates love to our children.

When assessed on their stability in such things as their treatment of their children, their emotions, and even their schedule for coming home, effective fathers scored 80 percent, while the others got 68 percent.

Consistency is, first of all, being there. Far too many fathers live apart from their children. But don't let that definition of fatherlessness mislead you. Fathers can be emotionally absent as well. In the movie *Hook*, the successful Wall Street lawyer (played by Robin Williams), says to his son: "When we get back, I'll go to all the rest of your games. I promise. My word is my bond." His son, the victim of numerous broken promises, replies, "Oh, yeah. Junk bonds."

At the same time, let me offer hope to those dads who aren't living with their children: Consistency still makes a difference. Consistency in regular communication, being predictable down to the day and even the minute, speaks volumes. Consistency in financial support is crucial. And what you do during the time you spend with your children makes an enormous difference in your children's lives.

4. PROTECTING AND PROVIDING

One of the most accepted attributes of fatherhood is providing for and protecting children. That could be why the two groups of fathers we surveyed were closest in this area. Effective fathers rated 93 percent, while the others got 82 percent. These high scores are, of course, importantly a result of our sample being disproportionately made up of at-home dads.

An effective father can remain levelheaded both in a crisis like an auto accident and in the midst of media messages that are hostile to training responsible children.

I view the first formal talk I had with my son about sex as a form of protecting him. He was only seven years old, and this was not a full-blown "birds and bees" talk; it was simply a discussion about human anatomy that I undertook because my wife had noticed our son's curiosity about his older sisters. I wanted to protect my son from learning about anatomical differences in a locker-room-type situation. I wanted him to hear about these things firsthand from his dad, so that he would have a family-dom-

THE FATHERHOOD MOVEMENT

One definition of a movement includes the following three parts: A movement has (1) a group of people who identify themselves as members of the movement, (2) literature that advances their cause, and (3) opposition from other forces.

Defined this way, the "fatherhood movement" is embryonic. By and large, public advocates of responsible fatherhood do not see themselves as a coherent group but as lone prophets shouting in a wilderness of neglect. And opposition to responsible fatherhood is difficult to find.

Still, there are some developments that have the feel of a movement:

The National Fatherhood Initiative has been formed to raise public awareness of the need for responsible fatherhood. The National Fatherhood Initiative is led by Don Eberly (president), who once served as a key aide to Jack Kemp; Wade Horn (director), commissioner of Children, Youth, and Families under President Bush; and David Blankenhorn (chairman), who was a civil-rights activist and community organizer before becoming involved in research on the need for fathers to be present and involved with their families. The group hosted a National Fatherhood Summit in October 1994 to educate civic leaders. After a tour this spring and summer featuring talks by David Blankenhorn, it will be aiming to spearhead an Ad Council campaign on the need for responsible fathers.

Another effort is that of Vice President Al Gore under the name "Father-to-Father." Through meetings of researchers and social-work practitioners (which have been deliberately low-key to ensure that this cause is not seen as partisan), the group is working to develop a private-sector mentoring program matching experienced fathers with newer dads. Gore personally signs on to Father-Net, a computer bulletin board sponsored by the Children, Youth, and Family Consortium of the University of Minnesota. Gore has brought together pioneers in the area of fathering such as Jim Levine and Ed Pitt of the Fatherhood Project and Ralph Smith of the Philadelphia Children's Network.

Levine's Fatherhood Project is sponsored by the Family and Work Institute in New York City. He champions "father-friendly" policies in the workplace and has developed practical materials on how to get men involved in early childhood development programs such as Head Start.

During his years as founder and president of the Philadelphia Children's Network, Ralph Smith promoted "father reengagement," refusing to accept the assumption of many social-welfare bureaucrats that fathers are unwilling or unable to support their children. Smith, now of the Annie E. Casey Foundation, recently helped found the National Center on Fathers and Families at the Graduate School of Education at the University of Pennsylvania. This center aims at closing the research gap in the social sciences on knowledge about fathers.

Meanwhile, a grass-roots group that makes no effort at changing public opinion, Promise Keepers, has motivated a stratum of men from the churches to take up the cause of fatherhood. The Christian group, headquartered in Denver, Colorado, is impressive through raw numbers: It attracted a total of more than 280,000 men for seven day-long events in stadiums across the nation last year and aims to conduct thirteen similar events this year.

While their speakers are a cross-section of evangelical Christians, the message is consistent: Men need to be servant-leaders of their families, get together with a few other men to encourage and support one another, and cross ethnic barriers to reach toward racial harmony. This group attracted some incidental opposition, as homosexual and feminist activists rallied outside one site last year, attacking and misinterpreting the group's motives.

Other developments, spontaneous and unconnected but portending bigger changes, include the following:

• Community colleges offering parent-education classes are starting to aim not just at mother-oriented preschool classes but at classes for fathers as well. Susanne Spandau, an instructor at Pasadena City College in California, went so far as to offer a fathers-only class,

"Being A Father and Loving It." Her class was well attended.

• Corporations are beginning to see resolving work-family tensions in a new light. IDS in Minneapolis recently hosted a fathering seminar taught by professional trainers that drew an overflow crowd, exceeding management's expectations. *Personnel Journal* reported in October 1994 that currently 60 percent of *Fortune* 500 companies offer parenting education programs. Those programs do not consistently take the fathers' needs and desires into account, but they may start to.

• A quasi-corporate municipal agency has gone one better than simply offering parenting education. The Los Angeles Department of Water and Power has an actual "Fathering Program" as part of its Work and Family Life Services office. The program coordinator arranges "Daddy-n-Me" recreation outings once a quarter for employees, lends beepers to dads with expectant wives, and sponsors noontime "information groups" for dads who get together monthly to talk and share ideas.

There may be a place for this kind of "affirmative action" for dads. Work and Family Life coordinator Ray Castro puts it this way, "Every time we hung out a sign 'Family Life Workshop' moms came, so the idea was to target men." No doubt part of the appeal of their offerings is that other men identify with Castro, who told me, "As a 22-year-old with all my degrees nobody had prepared me for the toughest job I would ever have: fatherhood."

• Programs to encourage unwed urban dads to form families are springing up as well. Charles Ballard's work in Cleveland, Ohio, has been so successful that he has been funded to replicate his program in five other cities. His program, the National Institute for Responsible Fatherhood, helps unwed young men acknowledge paternity, get regular jobs so they can support their kids, and develop stable relationships with their child's mother. Many formerly unwed couples have married as a result of participating in the program. Uncovering a man's paternal instinct is actually the first step in Ballard's program—and a much-neglected one.

• Fathers' Education Network in downtown Detroit, with Don Burwell, is taking fifty-two men through weekly gatherings aimed at instilling purpose in their lives and commitment to their children.

• MAD DADS in Omaha, Nebraska, was an "emergency response" when Eddie Staton and two other fathers founded it some five years ago. Dads were needed to take responsibility not just for their own children but for those wandering the streets at night. The group, which has thirty-two chapters nationally, has as its main focus patrolling the streets and talking with young people, especially those who are out after ten at night. The group confronts drug pushers with the consequences of their actions and brings together warring gangs simply to talk. MAD DADS is now taking the step of equipping both young and old fathers so that they may be more effective in rearing their children.

—K.R.C.

MORE INFORMATION

NATIONAL FATHERHOOD INITIATIVE:
800-790-DADS.

FATHERNET:
612-625-7251
email address:
cyfcec@maroon.tc.umn.edu

THE FATHERHOOD PROJECT:
212-465-2044

NATIONAL CENTER ON FATHERS AND FAMILIES:
215-686-3910

PROMISE KEEPERS:
800-888-PK95.

LOS ANGELES DEPARTMENT OF Water and Power,
WORK AND FAMILY LIFE SERVICES:
213-367-3546.

NATIONAL INSTITUTE FOR RESPONSIBLE FATHERHOOD:
216-791-8336

FATHERS' EDUCATION NETWORK:
313-831-5838

MAD DADS:
402-451-3500.

—K.R.C.

inated environment within which to assimilate them.

5. LOVING YOUR WIFE

The National Center for Fathering has sponsored essay contests for children about their dads. One fourth-grader, Tasha, wrote: "He treats my mom very nicely, which makes me feel wanted." That is saying that her father's love for her mother indirectly supplies that love to her, too.

Effective fathers on the average reported their marriages were "good," while the average for typical fathers was "fair."

Fathers who are aware of the interplay between their lives and their children's lives know they need to consciously work on loving their wives. It's easy in the aftermath of birth and young children to let your own relationship slide. In fact, our research found that satisfaction with marriage typically drops off as the children grow up and then climbs back up when they leave the nest.

6. ACTIVE LISTENING

Fathering satisfaction goes down when children hit adolescence. But one trait that distinguishes the fathers who are more satisfied during those years from those who aren't is active listening.

Fathers who engage their children verbally are the most satisfied. Effective fathers scored 82 percent on items such as allowing children to disagree, creating an atmosphere of caring and acceptance that encourages children to share their ideas, and listening closely to their concerns. Other fathers averaged 68 percent.

Active listening is part skill and part motivation. Listening skills include:

• Eye contact. Getting on the same level with your child helps the two of you have a heart-to-heart talk.

• Asking questions or paraphrasing back your child's words. This provides you with a check to make sure that you understand what he or she is saying.

• Nodding or signaling that you are listening helps, too.

Staying relaxed and stopping any "mental overtime" from your job or other interests is largely a question of motivation. So is turning off the television or other distractions.

But, ohhh, the rewards of active listening! Ron Levant and John Kelly give a wonderful example in their book *Between Father and Child*:

Twice in the course of a ten-minute soliloquy on Batman, five-year-old Harry McCann interrupted himself to ask his father, "Dad, how far away is the movie you and Mom are going to tonight?" Harry's question didn't have much to do with Batman; it had a great deal to do with his hidden message, which was "Dad, I'm anxious about the new baby-sitter who's coming tonight."

His dad was able to draw him out on the subject of his worries about the new baby-sitter and reassure him. That's active listening.

7. SPIRITUAL EQUIPPING

Here I am talking about both serving as a moral guide for your family and introducing your children to the transcendent. Children have questions—will we as dads serve as their guides and help them discover answers?

Although this is one area that has been frozen out of much public discussion (and is sometimes ignored when our research is reported in the press), it is significant that this area revealed the second-largest difference between effective dads and the others: Effective fathers averaged 72 percent here, while others averaged 56 percent.

Responding to the Gallup poll we commissioned, only 48.5 percent of Americans agreed that "fathers feel comfortable discussing spiritual matters with their children." Spiritual equipping comes as much by an exemplary life lived as by the conscious education of our families in scriptures or habits of prayer.

David Blankenhorn of the Institute for American Values addresses the issue of living exemplary lives when summing up discussions he has had with groups of dads in his book *Fatherless America*:

All the pieces of the puzzle fit together, adding up to one man: the good father. Their ideals are public as well as private. For this reason a good father is not simply a man who performs certain tasks for his children. He is a man who lives a certain kind of life.

THE FAMILY HEART

Robb Forman Dew

For years I envisioned the passage of time as a sort of steady trudge—not necessarily dreary—just relentless. The minutes accrue imperceptibly into a stretch of history, and you turn around to recognize, with amazement, your own past.

But also, some days have long legs. Now and then an ordinary bit of time takes a yawning scissors step, leaving you to scuttle along behind, scrabbling to cling to ongoing events. I learned this late, when my children were nearly full-grown, because it was exactly such an ordinary moment that enlarged and enlarged upon itself almost three years ago, when my son told me he was gay.

It was spring in New England, a soft day in May, and Stephen was home from his sophomore year at Yale until the first week of June, when he, my husband, Charles, and I would drive to Virginia to see his brother, Jack, graduate from Woodberry Forest School. When the phone rang, Stephen came around the corner from the TV room to answer it, and he stood at the far end of the kitchen, lounging against the long, glass door to chat with Chloe. When I had come downstairs from my study to start dinner, I settled at the table to work the *Jumble* from the morning paper while occasionally tending the chicken I was roasting for dinner.

What happens when a child who is loved more than life itself grows up to be gay? In this moving account, a mother who is also a prizewinning novelist tells how she and her own close-knit family handled the grief, the fear, and—finally—the understanding

I'm not sure why I was suddenly alert to Stephen's end of the phone conversation. My attention was caught, I think, by some tone in his voice, or simply by the realization that his phone calls to or from Chloe were never particularly private; he never took the trouble to take the calls out of earshot of anyone else in the house. Chloe is a beautiful girl, sensuous and angelic-looking at the same time, and she is funny and bright and endearing as well.

It might be that my ear was caught by what I didn't hear: There was no sense of the kind of tension that is inevitably there between two people as attractive and sexual as Chloe and Stephen. And by "sexual," I only mean the kind of magnetism that emanates from some people, especially older adolescents. Chloe and Stephen both possessed it, and, although I couldn't hear Chloe, Stephen's voice was nothing more than friendly. He was completely at ease; there was a certain edginess missing.

Chloe had been at school with Stephen since they were 14, and, in fact, two years earlier Chloe's parents and various of her siblings had settled next to us on the temporary bleachers set up at St. Paul's School in Concord, N.H., to watch Stephen and Chloe's class graduate.

Chloe's mother leaned over to me and said, "Oh, don't you wish this were just their *wedding?*" And I knew exactly what she meant: Their lives seemed perfect and uncomplicated and filled with amazing possibilities in that gorgeous afternoon; perhaps they could go on that way forever. I believe I simply began at that moment to think of Chloe as the probable romantic interest in Stephen's life. There were always friends of Stephen's around, male and female, but, at a certain point, both our sons made it clear that they wouldn't answer questions about their social lives. So, in lieu of any information about Stephen's personal life, I jumped to a conclusion. I made one of many assumptions that parents should learn not to make about their children.

Two years later, though, in the kitchen on that afternoon in May, I only remember suddenly being aware—and being surprised by—the odd lack of interest in Stephen's voice. He was amiable—he is almost always amiable—but he wasn't reluctant to get off the phone.

He hung up and turned away, but I stopped him. "Stephen?" And he paused in the doorway and turned toward me, and I continued, "Have you been involved with anyone at all? I mean romantically?"

For an instant he was surprised, and then he frowned, and I thought he was going to walk away in anger. There was a peculiar feeling of urgency and expectation in the room that I can only recall now; I can't re-create the sensation.

"There's something I've been meaning to tell you," he said finally.

We both fell silent, and then he moved forward a few paces toward me and was backlit by the gauzy light filtering from the screened porch through the glass-paned door. I couldn't read his face because of the shadow, but I know my children in all their moods; I am fairly good at deciphering the nuances of their postures—vulnerable or defensive or joyous. I may well know their very scent. Probably I could find them if I were blindfolded in a room full of people. I remember when they were little boys, and I would suddenly catch sight of one of my sons precariously balanced on a chair, or racing up or down the stairs, and I would experience the sensation of a fall he didn't take. It was a similar sensation I felt watching Stephen standing in the kitchen with his thumbs looped in the waistband of his jeans, his shoulders canted toward me, his head dipped slightly forward in determination. At once I wanted to raise my hands and gesture for him to stop what he was going to say, and I also wanted to urge him on and hear whatever it was. In fact, I sat as still as a stone. I didn't move at all.

"Of course I've been involved with someone since St. Paul's," he said. He wasn't frowning any longer; in fact, he had a slight smile that I knew from years of being connected to him. It was a smile that sought to protect me and Charles from any worry or irritation on his behalf. It's easy for me to classify it now, but looking at him then, in the shadowy room, I only perceived danger.

"I think I might be gay," Stephen said. In the instant before he spoke I'm convinced I knew what he was going to say, but at the same time I was uncertain that I understood. "Ah…well…you *think* you're gay?"

He looked perplexed, and anxious, too. "No, that's not what I mean. I mean I *am* gay."

This is such a difficult moment to remember, because the two of us had suddenly moved straight ahead into uncharted territory. I got up from the table and hugged him, and he held on to me, too, in a fierce embrace, lowering his chin to the top of my head. I felt lightheaded, and my stomach clenched with dread. I had no idea what to do. "It doesn't make any difference to us," I said. "We love you no matter what."

We moved away from each other, both of us strangely embarrassed and without any rules of etiquette to cover this situation. Stephen seemed lost in his own house; he stood in the kitchen with a tentative air that more than anything in that elongated moment filled me with sorrow. His expression was precisely the curious gaze of assessment he had cast my way 30 minutes after he was born. He looked as though he wasn't at all sure that he could trust me.

I rarely say anything entirely off the cuff. It's almost as if I *see* the words before they come out of my mouth, but I was baffled by what came out of my mouth next in my desperation to alleviate the uneasiness between me and this person I had loved for all his life.

"Well, damn it, Stephen! I wish you'd told me years ago so I wouldn't have been stuck decorating the Christmas tree all by myself every year!" Since my children became teenagers, this has been my recurrent after-Christmas lament—tedious, now, to everyone who knows me, because I'm the only one who cares much if, or how, the Christmas tree is decorated at all.

He was as surprised as I by this peculiar outburst, and he merely looked at me blankly, and then he laughed.

"Yeah. But I didn't think you'd want it decorated all in mauve." And then we both laughed; we were back on sure footing. We had humor between us again, but only fleetingly, because I had brushed off our discomfort with a sophistication and an attempted jauntiness I didn't yet possess, and I have no idea where such glibness came from.

This was one of those events in my life that, as I conjure it up in retrospect, appears to me like a pointillist painting, coming into focus hazily, at first, and slowly gathering the form of a whole experience. "Do you want to tell Dad and Jack?"

"I think it would be better if you told Dad. Do you mind doing that?"

"You know he won't care, Stephen. He loves you."

"I know. But I just think it would be easier."

I don't know if he meant easier on him or easier on his father, and I suspect that it was a little bit of both, but mostly I think he yearned to avoid open embarrassment between the two of them.

"I don't think I should tell Jack yet," he said.

"Well, Stephen…." But he moved back into the other room and sat down in front of the television, although I thought he was as astounded as I was by the revelation of so much truth in the space of, perhaps, five or 10 minutes. An atmosphere of unrelenting honesty is not hospitable, really, to domestic life. It is exhausting, since it bars the possibility of tactfulness or diplomacy.

Charles had dashed home from a history-department meeting and gone upstairs to shower and change clothes before heading back. It seemed imperative that I tell him before he came face-to-face with Stephen, who would assume his father knew, but Charles was obviously in a hurry. He had scarcely noticed that I was standing next to him while he put on his tie in front of the vanity mirror. I put my hand on his arm to draw his attention, and then without taking the time to consider what I was doing, I simply said what I was determined to tell him.

"Listen, Stephen just told me he's gay, and he wanted me to tell you. I know it won't—"

"What? What did you say?" His words fell on top of my own, although he spoke slowly and softly, and he stopped still in the middle of adjusting his tie.

"Stephen is gay. He wants you to know, but…."

He was moving away from me and out of the room as I spoke, and I followed him downstairs. Charles reacted exactly as I had to Stephen's news. In fact, he used almost the same words. "We love you, Stephen. Nothing could ever change that." And he hugged Stephen and held onto him for a long moment. Both of us had the feeling that somehow Stephen was slipping away from us, as though he were being swept off by a strong current, and we wanted desperately to catch hold of him and pull him back to shore.

During several weeks that May, the rooms of my house seemed to me, each one, a foreign country. The three of us ranged around that newly strange place in a paralysis of politeness, afraid that we would blunder into some area of hurtfulness of the other two.

I know now that Charles and I—even in our manner of acceptance—were unwittingly cruel, but either Stephen was so shocked by his act of revelation that he didn't notice, or he took us at our intention. We were doing the best we could with information that filled us with fear and sorrow and confusion.

My husband and I were well brought up; we are excellent products of middle-class Anglo-American behavior. We kept our sorrow to ourselves. I found myself, at one point, standing under the hot water from the shower, cradling my head against the tiled wall and weeping and weeping, struggling with a thought that wouldn't come clear. "It would be easier if he were…." I had no idea how I meant to finish that sentence, nor did I know in what direction it was leading, until finally it occurred to me that I thought it would be easier for Stephen to have discovered he was black than to have realized that he was gay. When I had to admit to myself that I had had that thought—an idea so fraught with my own conveniently repressed knowledge of the hatred and inequity still extant in this country—I stood all alone under the running water and covered my face with my hands in embarrassment.

Stephen must not have known what to do next. Charles and I were relentlessly chipper and incurious over the few days following the day he told us he was gay. We didn't ask any questions at all, apparently less interested than if he had told us he had read a good book, and I don't remember that Charles and I even discussed these new circumstances with each other.

In the evenings we sat with books before us, but we didn't read; it requires reflection. We watched any sports we could find on television. There was no refuge in anything else on TV, because we discovered right away that, in 1991, the most innocent of sitcoms almost invariably had a passive but definite anti-gay agenda. Trotting out a stereotypical gay man—although rarely ever a lesbian—was apparently always good for a laugh. How had we not noticed and been offended by it before? We watched a lot of baseball.

One morning, I awoke to a solid wall of speculation. Had I done this to my son? Most of what I had read about homosexuality dealt with it as a tragic consequence of having a suffocating mother and a weak, indifferent, or absent father. Had I been a suffocating mother? I had meant to be a good mother, the best parent in the world. Was Charles weak, indifferent, or absent? Charles is probably the kindest man I have ever known, and he is

certainly not indifferent to his sons, whom he loves deeply, nor has he been absent—literally or figuratively.

From the upstairs front-hall window, I gazed out at the street, at my neighbors' houses. Standing alone, trying to decipher the future, I don't think that I have ever felt more desolate. I looked out the window and knew that all the people Stephen had counted on for approval—all, of course, but his parents—might now regard him as a threat, an aberration, a stranger, rather than as a much-liked friend, a trusted neighbor, even something of a star in our small sphere. I found that the thought of any disapprobation, any lessening of regard for my own son, filled me with despair and some small, early flicker of ill-defined rage.

If our son were not damaged by the nature of his own sexual orientation, if we were not flawed by virtue of having a son who was gay, then why hadn't I ever heard mention of any other gay child or family of a gay child? If there was no context for homosexuality then it must, indeed, be a terrible and shameful thing. And yet, I knew that there was nothing—nothing—terrible or shameful about Stephen.

Charles and I pretended to an ease with the new status quo that we didn't feel. We had each quickly and independently fashioned a sort of ludicrous etiquette of feigned heartiness, because we couldn't have stood to have Stephen know he had thrown us into a state of grief. His revelation had shattered our expectations of who he was. We pretended that his sudden emergence as a gay man in what we had considered our conventional family was a matter of no consequence, something that had slipped from our minds completely.

The three of us spent several days occupying the rooms in a state of careful good cheer. Charles and I were busy all the time; we never settled very long in one place, and I don't know what Stephen must have thought, but eventually he approached us in the late afternoon when we were sitting on the screened porch in the balmy air.

"Stephen!" Charles said. "Would you like some iced tea? Or a beer?" His

voice was warm, perhaps overly exuberant.

"Yeah. Thanks. I'll get some iced tea. Do you want anything?"

"I'd love some tea, Stephen, if it's not too much trouble," I said, beaming at him. I was so nervous that my mouth went dry. Stephen has my father's family's brown eyes—an orange brown, the iris rimmed with black—and arched brows, and his expression caught my attention that afternoon because it was filled with compassion. I think now that it struck me so forcefully because he was only 19 years old, but his expression held far more empathy than anyone that age usually possesses.

He brought out glasses of tea from the kitchen and sat down, too, not saying anything for a few moments, and then he looked directly at us, still with an expression of gentle tactfulness. He gazed at Charles and me steadily while he spoke, probably afraid we would find some chore to take us off if he didn't say what he wanted us to hear. "Listen, I know this must be really hard for you. I just want you to know how much it means to me to know that it doesn't change the way you feel about me."

"Nothing could ever change the way we feel about you, Stephen," Charles said. "We love you more than you know."

"We do, sweetie," I said.

"I *do* know. But it must be hard for you," he said, "because I know you didn't expect this. I just wanted to tell you that you can ask me anything you want to know. I mean, you must wonder about a lot of things. I don't want to have any secrets…I don't want you to feel uncomfortable around me." This was a terrible admission—a plea—from my own son, and I tried not to let myself start crying. "I'll be glad to answer any questions you want to ask," he said.

All around the porch the lilac bushes were in bud, with just a few blooms among the branches, so that their delicate scent reached us only when a breeze picked up, but I remember the smell of lilacs in conjunction with Stephen's words, and the combination was such a generous offering in the mild weather that it was very nearly heartbreaking.

"I don't sweat the small stuff anymore"

Born HIV-positive, they were three babies nobody wanted. Until one very special family opened up their home and their hearts—and learned a lesson in love in return.

Jan Goodwin

Jan Goodwin, formerly Executive Editor of Ladies' Home Journal, *is the author of* Price of Honor: Muslim Women Lift the Veil of Silence on the Islamic World *(Little, Brown and Company, 1994), which she researched in ten countries.*

The nightly scene at the Godbout home is common to many families across the country: Dad returning home from work, Mom greeting him, the kids pouncing on him and wrestling him to the floor, and then squeals and giggles as the toddlers are tickled, tosed and tumbled. In this suburban New Jersey household even the family bloodhound joins in, and the pet parakeet squawks excitedly on the sidelines. Only the four family cats are too dignified to participate.

An all-American moment? Not quite. Slumped listlessly on the sofa, two-year-old Tom* remains motionless; his large chocolate-brown eyes stare dully at the wall. When a visitor tries to greet him or pick him up, he begins to yowl, his cries quickly turning to piercing screams that seem beyond comfort.

Tom's behavior contrasts sharply with that of his two young sisters. In their pink corduroy pants and matching T-shirts, three-year-old Janice* and twenty-one-month-old Andrea* chase one of the long-suffering cats or the dog, Festus; imitate the sounds of the parakeet; and rush back and forth for hugs and kisses.

Yet, according to the Godbouts, all three of these children started out with the same tragic strikes against them: Janice and Tom's birth mother is a drug addict living on the streets. (Janice's father is unknown; Tom's is in and out

The children's names have been changed to protect their privacy.

Maureen Godbout cuddles two-year-old Tom,* the sickest of her three foster children

Eric Rasmussen

of jail.) As a result of their mother's drug use, both children were born addicted to crack, making the first few months of their lives a nightmare. Andrea's mother was also high when she gave birth, one month early. She abandoned Andrea (her ninth child) almost immediately after her birth.

All this would be a tough enough beginning for any infant. But, say the Godbouts, Janice's, Tom's and Andrea's parents also left them another grim legacy: All three youngsters were born HIV-positive; their parents have AIDS.

For Janice and probably Andrea, though, the future looks bright. They are part of a little-known good-news story about AIDS: Like 70 to 80 percent of children born HIV-positive, Janice has "seroreverted," meaning she no longer tests positive for the virus; doctors believe Andrea will also serorevert.

How is this possible? All babies whose mothers have AIDS will test HIV-positive at birth. That's because infants, who are born with underdeveloped immune systems, receive antibodies (blood cells that fight infections) from their mother. So, if the mother is infected with the AIDS virus, the baby will inherit her HIV antibodies as well, and the HIV test will thus show their presence in the baby's body. Over time, as the infant's own immune system takes over, the inherited antibodies disappear—including, in most cases, the HIV antibodies; this is seroreversion. A child probably has the AIDS virus, experts say, if he does not serorevert by the time he's eighteen months to two years old.

Babies who show antibodies to HIV are tested regularly. Andrea's first two tests were negative, says Maureen Godbout, the children's foster mother. "Janice was in the clear by the age of two years. They are both lucky little girls."

Although Tom has not yet been diagnosed as having the AIDS virus, his health strongly suggests that he has the disease. In his two years of life, Tom has seen more doctors and hospitals, and undergone more tests, than most of us do in our entire lives. Because of chronic upper-respiratory infections, he now takes antibiotics daily. And if any of the last battery of tests he recently underwent proves positive, the Godbouts say, his physicians plan to start him on AZT, the first drug approved as an AIDS treatment.

THE FORGOTTEN CHILDREN

Unfortunately, there are far too many children who start their lives as Tom, Andrea and Janice did. And since the biological parents sometimes die from AIDS before their offspring do, more and more youngsters are becoming orphans. These are children other relatives refuse to take into their homes, children few people consider adopting.

Many HIV babies live full-time in their cribs in a hospital ward. "No one picks them up, plays with them or takes them out," says Maureen, thirty-three, a part-time medical assistant. "That image haunted me after I visited a pediatric HIV hospital ward. It's why we took Janice, Tom and Andrea."

For Bob Godbout, thirty-six, a teacher at a high school for emotionally disturbed adolescents, the reason his family has taken these three African-American children into their home is much more personal. Like most Americans in the early eighties, Bob had barely heard the term AIDS. One evening in 1984, however, the phone rang. "It was a hospital in Georgia telling us my father was terminally ill with AIDS," recalls Bob. By the time he got to the hospital, his fifty-seven-year-old father was already in a coma. He died three weeks later without gaining consciousness.

"I never got to talk to my father," says Bob. "It was the nurses who told me that he was bisexual." Like his mother and sister, Bob was stunned.

In his father's memory, Bob and Maureen made a quilt square, which they took to Washington, D.C. The square is now one of tens of thousands making up the giant AIDS memorial quilt. "But I knew that wasn't enough," says Bob. "I wanted to give my father's death meaning."

The Godbouts first learned about HIV-infected babies who needed homes from the former principal at Bob's school. Terry Zealand, Ph.D., had just founded the AIDS Resource Foundation for Children, which runs three homes for kids with AIDS in New Jersey. "We had no idea such kids existed," said Maureen. "We saw these babies and fell in love."

By becoming foster parents, the Godbouts learned, they could take HIV-infected babies into their home and care for them. The state would still have the ultimate responsibility for the children and would pay the Godbouts for their care; the children's medical bills would be paid by Medicaid.

But before the couple took any action, they gave their two children, Daniel, a sharp twelve-year-old, and shy, ten-year-old Erin, equal votes on the matter. "We've always been very open with our kids," says Maureen, "and this was a major, major decision that was also going to affect their lives, all our lives, in a big way. We wanted our children to still be able to grow up normally and not be ostracized by other people or the kids at school.

"We explained that this child might come into our home and die," says Maureen. "We were honest about every-

"We saw these babies and fell in love," says Maureen.

thing. They told us they didn't care if the babies were sick; they said we should take them so they could see what it was like to have a real family."

But, while Daniel and Erin were enthusiastic about the idea, the Godbouts' friends and other relatives were very upset. "They asked us, 'How can [you] do this? Aren't you afraid of exposing your own kids, or our kids, to this?' " says Bob, who admits that he and his wife also shared doubts at the beginning, until they educated themselves thoroughly about AIDS.

"Every single person we discussed it with at the beginning tried to talk us out of it," says Maureen. "Some of Bob's family and mine have cut us out of their lives. People who used to visit regularly and invite us to their homes regularly no longer do. It was a testing point in our relationships with people."

OPENING THEIR HOME

The Godbouts applied to be a foster family in the fall of 1988. But before an HIV-positive child could live in their home, "we had to be trained in CPR and infectious-disease control," says Maureen, stroking Tom's head as he nestles in her lap. "I spent time in a hospital observing nurses looking after AIDS babies. These kids have to be watched constantly [to monitor whether] they get temperatures during the day, or thrush infections [a yeast infection of the mouth], or if they start to lose their appetite or lose weight. Their heads have to be measured regularly to make sure they are growing properly."

What the couple were not warned about, however, was how to deal with HIV babies who were also born crack-addicted. In July 1990, "the Division of Youth and Family Services [DYFS] just dropped off the first child, Jennifer* [who lived with the family only briefly]," remembers Maureen. "The baby screamed the entire time."

After a week of this, the Godbouts called the DYFS for help. The agency sent out a nurse, who taught Maureen and Bob that crack-addicted infants cannot make eye contact, have difficulty bonding and must not be stimulated. "They told us to tightly swaddle these babies—they feel more secure that way—and to hold them on our chests faced away from us so they didn't make eye contact," says Maureen. "We were also told to buy a battery-operated swing. We put Jennifer in it, and for three hours she didn't make a sound. It was the first time she slept properly."

Crack babies frequently have low birth weights and are premature; they may also suffer from mental or physical disabilities. In Tom's case, for example, he doesn't talk yet and prefers to crawl. On the few occasions he does try to walk, he drags one leg behind him. "He's only now learning to eat and gaining weight," says Maureen. "He's still very touch-sensitive; he won't pick things up, for example. And he cannot cope with any irregularities in his life. The moment I take him outside the house, he screams until we return."

Tom currently functions far below his age level. Andrea, on the other hand, is now functioning above her age level. "Once she got through her crack withdrawal, she was fine," says Maureen. And Janice, who is undergoing speech therapy, is now in preschool. "Janice's problems have been emotional," says Bob. "She might have been abused previously;

she was very hostile when she arrived. She threw a lot of temper tantrums, had no socialization skills and had to be taught how to play."

Despite the difference in the toddlers' health, the Godbouts treat all their children the same. Andrea, Janice and Tom receive a great deal of physical affection, and no one thinks twice about picking them up or hugging and kissing them. "Except when changing Tom's diapers, or if dealing with blood, I don't use gloves with these kids," says Maureen. "Everyone who touches HIV-positive children in the outside world wears surgical gloves. It's just so impersonal for them. It also isn't necessary. We know the AIDS virus isn't spread by touch, and we also know it is very fragile and dies quickly outside the human body."

SORROW AND JOY

The Godbouts face many difficulties most families never have to think about. One major problem is finding qualified baby-sitters they can afford. (The DYFS requires that the sitters undergo the same HIV training as foster parents.) Since they can't find a sitter, Maureen and Bob are never able to leave the house together. A night out for a movie or dinner, even sleeping late, is a distant memory. "Because of Tom's problems, we can't just pick him up and take him out with us," says Maureen. "One of us always has to stay home with him." The couple do, however, try to take thirty minutes a day together, "when we just go into the bedroom, close the door and touch base with each other and ask 'How was your day?'" says Maureen. "There have been times when I've thought,

Wow, if I don't get a few minutes to myself, I'll go crazy.

"But, you know, it's a funny thing: Since we've had these kids, I'm able to deal with more," she adds. "I no longer sweat the small stuff. When you are dealing with life and death, it no longer bothers you if the entrance floor was washed today."

How will the Godbouts cope if Tom or another foster child succumbs to AIDS in a few years' time? "We may not have experienced the death of one of these youngsters yet," says Maureen, "but we have experienced loss that was as severe as a death for us." She's referring to Jennifer and Shari,* the first two HIV foster babies who lived with the family. "We fell in love with these little girls; the whole family was head-over-heels," recalls Maureen. "DYFS asked us if we wanted to adopt them. We said yes, and we were so excited when they both seroreverted.

"But once both girls became HIV-negative, we were informed that other relatives would be taking them, and family has more legal rights than foster parents," Maureen says.

Adds Bob, "Maureen, I and the children were emotional wrecks when we lost Jennifer and Shari."

After that experience, the Godbouts seriously considered giving up fostering. "It was Daniel and Erin who changed our minds," says Bob. "'When's the next baby coming?' they asked us. Erin couldn't stand the idea of babies living in a hospital when we could take them."

The family say they have also had to deal with racism—not only from the public, but from some social workers who don't believe black children should be fostered with white families. "And when I take the babies out shopping with me," says Maureen, "I've had

some strange looks, but only from white people. I've been called white trash. But you learn to ignore the hostility."

Fortunately, the Godbouts have never faced the bigotry experienced by AIDS victims such as Ryan White—the young boy from Kokomo, Indiana, who was barred from school in his own town—during the early days of the AIDS epidemic. Neighbors have not threatened the family or treated the children as lepers. "In fact, ours is the house on the block where the neighborhood kids all congregate, and their parents know about our foster children," says Bob.

The Godbouts themselves have found fostering HIV babies a learning experience. "I've realized that people are *very* easy to love," says Maureen. "And it doesn't matter how sick they are."

Adds Bob, "I've become more open-minded about all sorts of things—biracial couples, gays and other people who are different from what society calls 'normal.'"

Janice, Andrea and Tom have "given more to us than we have ever given to them," says Maureen. "What we're doing may sound like a lot of work, but they're special kids. They've added so much to our lives."

For more information

To find out more about children who are HIV-positive, contact: Pediatric AIDS Foundation, 1311 Colorado Avenue, Santa Monica, CA 90404; 310-395-9051.

For information, or to find out about adopting a child with HIV, contact: The Children with AIDS Project of America, P.O. Box 83131, Phoenix, AZ 85071-3131; 800-866-2437.

Siblings and Development

Judy Dunn

Judy Dunn is Professor of Human Development at the Pennsylvania State University. Address correspondence to Judy Dunn, Center for the Study of Child and Adolescent Development, College of Health and Human Development, Pennsylvania State University, University Park, PA 16802.

The great majority of children—around 80% in the United States and Europe—grow up with siblings. Yet the developmental impact of the experience of growing up in close—often uncomfortably close—contact with another child within the family has until recently been little studied. The attention of investigators concerned with early developmental influences has been focused instead chiefly on parents (usually mothers) or family, often characterized in terms of structure (e.g., single-parent versus two-parent) or background variables (e.g., socioeconomic status), or in broad descriptive terms, such as "enmeshed" or "disorganized."

In the last few years, however, studies of siblings within their families have greatly increased in number,[1] and have challenged our assumptions concerning two quite different issues in developmental science. First, such studies have raised serious questions about how families influence individual development—and suggested some intriguing answers. Second, they have also shed light on the development of social understanding in young children. Here, research on siblings observed at home shows that formal assessments of very young children's abilities in experimental settings may have seriously underestimated the nature of young children's social understanding.

As an introduction to the new perspectives on these two developmental issues, consider the following incident, drawn from an observation of a 30-month-old child with his mother and his 14-month-old sister. Andy was a rather timid and sensitive child, cautious, unconfident, and compliant. His younger sister, Susie, was a striking contrast—assertive, determined, and a handful for her mother, who was nevertheless delighted by her boisterous daughter. In the course of an observation of Andy and his sister, Susie persistently attempted to grab a forbidden object on a high kitchen counter, despite her mother's repeated prohibitions. Finally, she succeeded, and Andy overheard his mother make a warm, affection-

ate comment on Susie's action: "Susie, you *are* a determined little devil!"

Andy, sadly, commented to his mother, "*I'm* not a determined little devil!" His mother replied, laughing, "No! What are you? A poor old boy!"

A NEW PERSPECTIVE ON THE DEVELOPMENT OF INDIVIDUAL DIFFERENCES

This brief incident serves to illustrate some of the key issues emerging from a series of systematic studies of siblings and parents in the United States and Britain,[2] which highlight why we need to study within-family processes to explain the development of individual differences. Three features of these processes, evident in the exchange between Andy and his mother, are important here: the difference between siblings in personality, the difference in their relationships with their parents, and their responses to exchanges between their siblings and parents.

Differences Between Siblings

The striking differences between siblings growing up within the same family—differences in personality, adjustment, and psychopathology—have now been documented in a very wide range of studies,[3,4] and these differences present a major challenge to investigators studying family influence. Why should two children who share 50% of their segregating genes and the same family background turn out to be so different? After all, the family factors assumed to be key in development (e.g., parental mental health, marital quality, social class background) are apparently shared by siblings.

This question of why siblings are so different is not just a matter of interest to fond parents puzzled by their children's differences. It turns out to be key to understanding the development of individual differences more generally. Extensive studies by behavior geneticists have now shown that the sources of environmental influence that make individuals different from one another work *within* rather than *between* families.[3] To understand the salient environmental influences on individual development, we have to be able to explain what makes two children within the same family different from one another. The message from this research is not that family influence is unimportant, but that we need to document those experiences that are specific to each child within a family, and therefore we need to study more than one child per family, with a new perspective on what are the salient influences within the family.

What could the significant processes within the family be—differences in parent-child relationships, differences within the sibling relationship itself, differences in peer relationships outside the family, or chance experiences that affect one sibling and not another? In a series of studies, the relation of each of these to children's developmental outcomes is being explored. A number of different samples have been studied in the United States and in England, including nationally representative samples, and major longitudinal studies have included adoptive and biological samples (enabling us to explore where genetic similarities and differences enter the picture). A wide variety of methods has been employed, including naturalistic observations of the families and interviews with all family members. The results of this body of research are discussed in a recent book;[2] here some illustrative points will be summarized briefly.

Differences Between Siblings' Relationships With Their Parents

It is clear that there are major differences in the affection, attention, and discipline that many siblings experience with their parents—whether the information on these differences comes from parents, children, or observers. The differences in warmth and pride that were evident in the behavior of Andy's mother toward her two children are very common. The extent of such differences and the domains in which they are most marked have now been documented in a range of differing samples of families, as have the variables related to the degree of parental differentiation (e.g., the developmental stages of the children and the mother's personality, educational background, and IQ). An important lesson from both the observational work and the experimental studies is that children are extremely sensitive to such differences.

Sensitivity of Children to Their Siblings' Interaction With Their Parents

From a remarkably early age, children monitor and react to their parents' interaction with their siblings. The example of Andy and Susie is typical: Andy monitors and responds to his mother's exchange with his sister, promptly, and with a self-comparison. A recent study showed that 20% of the conversational turns by secondborn children in one sample were attempts to join the conversation between other people.[5] The salient verbal environment for children is not solely the speech addressed to them, but includes conversations between parents and sibling.

Two lines of evidence from recent developmental work confirm the salience for young children of emotional exchanges between other people: laboratory studies of children witnessing exchanges between others and naturalistic studies of children in their families. A wealth of studies have now documented that children from the end of their first year are interested in the behavior of other family members, and especially in their emotional exchanges. In a series of studies, Zahn-Waxler and her colleagues have documented the development of children's responses to emotional displays between others, and the effects of witnessing such exchanges on play and aggressive behavior.[6,7] Naturalistic observations of siblings at home have shown that children rarely ignore disputes between others, but act promptly to support or punish one of the antagonists, and that the behavior of both firstborn and secondborn children is profoundly affected by their mothers' interactions with the other sibling.[8]

How important are these experiences of differential treatment, developmentally? The first investigations show differential experiences are linked to a range of outcome measures: In terms of adjustment, for example, children who receive less maternal affection and attention than their siblings are likely to be more worried, anxious, or depressed than other children in general. And there is now an accumulation of evidence that differential parental behavior is linked to the quality of the relationship between siblings, with more hostility and conflict found in families with greater differential parental treatment, an association found for preschool children, for siblings in middle childhood, for children with disabled siblings, and for children following divorce.[1]

Other Sources of Differential Experience

Among the other possible sources of differential experience, there is growing evidence that differences in children's experiences within the sibling relationship itself can also be related to adjustment. If instead of focusing on siblings as a dyad, we ask how similarly or differently the two siblings behave toward each other, we find there can be marked differences between the two in the affection or control they show. Whether the information comes from maternal interview, children's own accounts, or observations, the emerging picture is that in only one third of sibling pairs do the two children show very similar degrees of affection toward one another. For hostile behavior there is more reciprocity, but within a pair, the relative differences in negative behavior are correlated with later perceived self-competence, and with conduct problems and anxious or depressed behavior. For example, one study found that the more negative a younger sibling is toward the older, relative to the older's negative behavior, the higher the self-esteem of the younger 3 years later.[2] Of course, these initial findings must be treated with caution until they are replicated, and no causal inferences can be made from such correlational data.

In summary, the focus on siblings and their differential experiences within the family has changed and clarified our picture of what are the salient family influences on individual development. In an important sense children are, it appears, *family members* from early in their second year; they are interested in, responsive to, and influenced by the relationships between their siblings and parents—and this insight brings us to the second developmental arena in which sibling studies have provided illumination, the development of social understanding.

A NEW PERSPECTIVE ON THE DEVELOPMENT OF SOCIAL UNDERSTANDING

Recall the comments made by Andy in the incident with his sister and mother. Andy, in the emotional circumstances of the family exchange, made a self-evaluative comment following his mother's warm remark praising his sister. Yet he was *only* two *and a half*. This is startlingly early for a child to be evaluating himself. At this age, according to the received view of the development of self-reflective powers, based on experimental studies, he should not be able to evaluate himself in this way, or be sensitive to social comparison. Could we be misrepresenting children's sociocognitive abilities by studying them only outside the family? Here, observational studies of siblings at home have proved most illuminating.[8]

A focus on children's disputes, jokes, and cooperative play with their siblings has shown that from 18 months on children understand how to hurt, comfort, and exacerbate their siblings' pain; they understand what is allowed or disapproved in their family world; they differentiate between transgressions of different sorts, and anticipate the response of adults to their own and to other people's misdeeds; they comment on and ask about the causes of others' actions and feelings. Analyses of this growing understanding of emotions, of others' goals, and of social rules have shown that the foundations for the moral virtues of caring, consideration, and kindness are well laid by 3 years, but so too children have by this age a sophisticated grasp of how to use social rules for their own ends. The drive to understand others and the social world is, I have argued,[8] closely linked to the nature of a child's relationships within the family over this period: the emotional power of attachment to parents, of rivalry between siblings, and of the conflict between growing independence and socialization pressure. For a young child whose own goals and interests are often at odds with—and frustrated by—others in the family, it is clearly adaptive to begin to understand those other family members and the social rules of the shared family world. The study of siblings has highlighted why it is important that

social understanding should be high on the developmental agenda.

The subtlety of social understanding that children show in the family context—in contrast to their limited capabilities when faced with more abstract or formal tasks—has considerably changed our view of children's abilities, and why they change. And in addition to delineating the pattern of normative growth of social understanding, sibling studies are beginning to clarify in detail the causes of individual differences in social understanding. These differences are striking: Children vary greatly in their ability to understand the causes and consequences of emotions and to understand what other people are thinking and how this influences their behavior. In the recent burst of productive experimental research on children's understanding of "other minds," there has been little consideration of individual differences: How far such differences are related to verbal intelligence, to the quality of children's relationships, or to other family experiences has not been examined empirically. The study of children with their siblings has enabled us to test predictions concerning the significance of family relationships, parental expressiveness, and children's cognitive ability in accounting for differences in social understanding.[9]

The results highlight the importance—and the independent contribution to the variance—of a number of factors. For example, diffences in family discourse about the social world are important: Children who grew up in families in which feelings and causality were discussed performed better than other children on assessments of social understanding 14 months later. But the quality of children's relationships with their siblings is also key: Children who had experienced frequent cooperative exchanges with their siblings, for example, were more successful than other children on tasks assessing their grasp of the connections between another person's belief and subsequent behavior. Also—most notably—differences in children's social understanding are related to the quality of the relationships between their siblings and their mothers. Children who grew up in families in which they witnessed their mothers being highly attentive, responsive, or controlling to their siblings scored particularly high on social cognition assessments 1 year later.

Thus, the work on social understanding links with the first theme—the processes involved in family influence on individual differences. Examining within-family differential experiences of siblings will enlarge our understanding of the salient processes of family influences on personality and adjustment. Similarly, it is clear that studying children in the complex network of sibling and parental relationships within the family can greatly enhance our knowledge about their understanding of the social world. It is within the daily drama of family life that children's social intelligence is revealed and fostered, and siblings play a central role in that drama.

NOTES

1. F. Boer and J. Dunn, *Sibling Relationships: Developmental and Clinical Issues* (Erlbaum, Hillsdale, NJ, 1992).

2. J. Dunn and R. Plomin, *Separate Lives: Why Siblings Are So Different* (Basic Books, New York, 1990).

3. R. Plomin and D. Daniels, Why are children in the same family so different from each other? *The Behavioral and Brain Sciences, 10,* 1–16 (1987).

4. S. Scarr and S. Grajek, Similarities and differences among siblings, in *Sibling Relationships: Their Nature and Significance Across the Lifespan,* M. E. Lamb and B. Sutton-Smith, Eds. (Erlbaum, Hillsdale, NJ, 1982), pp. 357–386.

5. J. Dunn and M. Shatz, Becoming a conversationalist despite (or because of) having an older sibling, *Child Development, 60,* 399–410 (1989).

6. C. Zahn-Waxler and M. Radke-Yarrow, The development of altruism: Alternative research strategies, in *The Development of Prosocial Behavior,* N. Eisenberg-Berg, Ed. (Academic Press, New York, 1982), pp. 109–137.

7. E. M. Cummings, Coping with background anger, *Child Development, 58,* 976–984 (1987).

8. J. Dunn, *The Beginnings of Social Understanding* (Harvard University Press, Cambridge, MA, 1988).

9. J. Dunn, J. Brown, C. Slomkowski, C. Tesla, and L. Youngblade, Young children's understanding of other people's feelings and beliefs: Individual differences and their antecedents, *Child Development, 62,* 1352–1366 (1991).

The
Secret World
of Siblings

Emotional ambivalence often marks the most enduring relationship in life

They have not been together like this for years, the three of them standing on the close-cropped grass, New England lawns and steeples spread out below the golf course. He is glad to see his older brothers, has always been glad to have "someone to look up to, to do things with." Yet he also knows the silences between them, the places he dares not step, even though they are all grown men now. They move across the greens, trading small talk, joking. But at the 13th hole, he swings at the ball, duffs it and his brothers begin to needle him. "I should be better than this," he thinks. Impatiently, he swings again, misses, then angrily grabs the club and breaks it in half across his knee. Recalling this outburst later, he explains, simply: "They were beating me again."

As an old man, Leo Tolstoy once opined that the simplest relationships in life are those between brother and sister. He must have been delirious at the time. Even lesser mortals, lacking Tolstoy's acute eye and literary skill, recognize the power of the word *sibling* to reduce normally competent, rational human beings to raw bundles of anger, love, hurt, longing and disappointment—often in a matter of minutes. Perhaps they have heard two elderly sisters dig at each other's sore spots with astounding accuracy, much as they did in junior high. Or have seen a woman corner her older brother at a family reunion, finally venting 30 years of pent-up resentment. Or watched remorse and yearning play across a man's face as he speaks of the older brother whose friendship was chased away long ago, amid dinner table taunts of "Porky Pig, Porky Pig, oink, oink, oink!"

Sibling relationships—and 80 percent of Americans have at least one—outlast marriages, survive the death of parents, resurface after quarrels that would sink any friendship. They flourish in a thousand incarnations of closeness and distance, warmth, loyalty and distrust. Asked to describe them, more than a few people stammer and hesitate, tripped up by memory and sudden bursts of unexpected emotion.

Traditionally, experts have viewed siblings as "very minor actors on the stage of human development," says Stephen Bank, Wesleyan University psychologist and co-author of *The Sibling Bond.* But a rapidly expanding body of research is showing that what goes on in the playroom or in the kitchen while dinner is being cooked exerts a profound influence on how children grow, a contribution that approaches, if it may not quite equal, that of parenting. Sibling relationships shape how people feel about themselves, how they understand and feel about others, even how much they achieve. And more often than not, such ties represent the lingering thumbprint of childhood upon adult life, affecting the way people interact with those closest to them, with friends and coworkers, neighbors and spouses—a topic explored by an increasing number of popular books, including *Mom Loved You Best,* the most recent offering by Dr. William and Mada Hapworth and Joan Heilman.

Shifting landscape. In a 1990s world of shifting social realities, of working couples, disintegrating marriages, "blended" households, disappearing grandparents and families spread across a continent, this belated validation of the importance of sibling influences probably comes none too soon. More and more children are stepping in to change diapers, cook meals and help with younger siblings' homework in the hours when parents are still at the office. Baby boomers, edging into middle age, find themselves squaring off once again with brothers and sisters over the care of dying parents or the division of inheritance. And in a generation where late marriages and fewer children are the norm, old age may become for many a time when siblings—not devoted sons and daughters—sit by the bedside.

It is something that happened so long ago, so silly and unimportant now that she is 26 and a researcher at a large, downtown office and her younger brother is her best friend, really, so close that she talks to him at least once a week. Yet as she begins to speak she is suddenly a 5-year-old again on

Christmas morning, running into the living room in her red flannel pajamas, her straight blond hair in a ponytail. He hasn't even wrapped it, the little, yellow-flowered plastic purse. Racing to the tree, he brings it to her, thrusts it at her—"Here's your present, Jenny!"—smiling that stupid, adoring, little brother smile. She takes the purse and hurls it across the room. "I don't want your stupid present," she yells. A small crime, long ago forgiven. Yet she says: "I still feel tremendously guilty about it."

Sigmund Freud, perhaps guided by his own childhood feelings of rivalry, conceived of siblingship as a story of unremitting jealousy and competition. Yet, observational studies of young children, many of them the ground-breaking work of Pennsylvania State University psychologist Judy Dunn and her colleagues, suggest that while rivalry between brothers and sisters is common, to see only hostility in sibling relations is to miss the main show. The arrival of a younger sibling may cause distress to an older child accustomed to parents' exclusive attention, but it also stirs enormous interest, presenting both children with the opportunity to learn crucial social and cognitive skills: how to comfort and empathize with another person, how to make jokes, resolve arguments, even how to irritate.

The lessons in this life tutorial take as many forms as there are children and parents. In some families, a natural attachment seems to form early between older and younger children. Toddlers as young as 14 months miss older siblings when they are absent, and babies separated briefly from their mothers will often accept comfort from an older sibling and go back to playing happily. As the younger child grows, becoming a potential playmate, confidant and sparring partner, older children begin to pay more attention. But even young children monitor their siblings' behavior closely, showing a surprisingly sophisticated grasp of their actions and emotional states.

Parental signals. To some extent, parents set the emotional tone of early sibling interactions. Dunn's work indicates, for example, that children whose mothers encourage them to view a newborn brother or sister as a human being, with needs, wants and feelings, are friendlier to the new arrival over the next year, an affection that is later reciprocated by the younger child. The quality of parents' established relationships with older siblings can also influence how a new younger brother or sister is received. In another of Dunn's studies, first-born daughters who enjoyed a playful, intense relationship with their mothers treated newborn siblings with more hostility, and a year later the younger children were more hostile in return. In contrast, older daughters with more contentious relationships with their mothers greeted the newcomer enthusiastically—perhaps relieved to have an ally. Fourteen months later, these older sisters were more likely to imitate and play with their younger siblings and less apt to hit them or steal their toys.

In troubled homes, where a parent is seriously ill, depressed or emotionally unavailable, siblings often grow closer than they might in a happier environment, offering each other solace and protection. This is not always the case, however. When parents are on the brink of separation or have already divorced and remarried, says University of Virginia psychologist E. Mavis Hetherington, rivalry between brothers and sisters frequently increases, as they struggle to hold on to their parents' affection in the face of the breakup. If anything, it is sisters who are likely to draw together in a divorcing family, while brothers resist forming tighter bonds. Says Hetherington: "Males tend to go it alone and not to use support very well."

Pretend play is never wasted. Toddlers who engage regularly in make-believe activity with older siblings later show a precocious grasp of others' behavior.

Much of what transpires between brothers and sisters, of course, takes place when parents are not around. "Very often the parent doesn't see the subtlety or the full cycle of siblings' interactions," says University of Hartford psychologist Michael Kahn. Left to their own devices, children tease, wrestle and play make-believe. They are the ones eager to help pilot the pirate ship or play storekeeper to their sibling's impatient customer. And none of this pretend play, researchers find, is wasted. Toddlers who engage regularly in make-believe with older siblings later show a precocious grasp of others' behavior. Says Dunn: "They turn out to be the real stars at understanding people."

Obviously, some degree of rivalry and squabbling between siblings is natural. Yet in extreme cases, verbal or physical abuse at the hands of an older brother or sister can leave scars that last well into adulthood. Experts like Wesleyan University's Bank distinguish between hostility that takes the form of humiliation or betrayal and more benign forms of conflict. From the child's perspective, the impact of even normal sibling antagonism may depend in part on who's coming out ahead. In one study, for example, children showed higher self-esteem when they "delivered" more teasing, insults and other negative behaviors to their siblings than they received. Nor is even intense rivalry necessarily destructive. Says University of Texas psychologist Duane Buhrmester: "You may not be happy about a brother or sister who is kind of pushing you along, but you may also get somewhere in life."

They are two sides of an equation written 30 years ago: Michèle, with her raven-black hair, precisely made-up lips, restrained smile; Arin, two years older, her easy laugh filling the restaurant, the sleeves of her gray turtleneck pulled over her hands.

This is what Arin thinks about Michèle: "I have always resented her, and she has always looked up to me. When we were younger, she used to copy me, which would drive me crazy. We have nothing in common except our family history— isn't that terrible? I like her spirit of generosity, her direction and ambition. I dislike her vapid conversation and her idiotic friends. But the reality is that we are very close, and we always will be."

This is what Michèle sees: "Arin was my ideal. I wanted to be like her, to look like her. I think I drove her crazy. Once, I gave her a necklace I thought was very beautiful. I never saw her wear it. I think it wasn't good enough, precious enough. We are so different—I wish that we could be more like friends. But as we get older, we accept each other more."

It is something every brother or sister eventually marvels at, a conundrum that novelists have played upon in a thousand different ways: There are two children. They grow up in the same house, share the same parents, experience many of the same events. Yet they are stubbornly, astonishingly different.

A growing number of studies in the relatively new field of behavioral genetics are finding confirmation for this popular observation. Children raised in the same family, such studies find, are only very slightly more similar to each other on a variety of personality dimensions than they are, say, to Bill Clinton or to the neighbor's son. In cognitive abilities, too, siblings appear more different than alike. And the extent to which siblings *do* resemble one another in these traits is largely the result of the genes they share—a conclusion drawn from twin studies, comparisons of biological siblings raised apart and biological children and adopted siblings raised together.

Contrasts. Heredity also contributes to the *differences* between siblings. About 30 percent of the dissimilarity between brothers and sisters on many personality dimensions can be accounted for by differing genetic endowments from parents. But that still leaves 70 percent that *cannot* be attributed to genetic causes, and it is this unexplained portion of contrasting traits that scientists find so intriguing. If two children who grow up in the same family are vastly different, and genetics accounts for only a minor part of these differences, what else is going on?

The answer may be that brothers and sisters don't really share the same family at all. Rather, each child grows up in a unique family, one shaped by the way he perceives other people and events, by the chance happenings he alone experiences, and by how other people— parents, siblings and teachers—perceive and act toward him. And while for decades experts in child development have focused on the things that children in the same family share—social class, child-rearing attitudes and parents' marital satisfaction, for example—what really seem to matter are those things that are not shared. As Judy Dunn and Pennsylvania State behavioral geneticist Robert Plomin write in *Separate Lives: Why Siblings Are So Different*, "Environmental factors important to develop-

ment are those that two children in the same family experience differently."

Asked to account for children's disparate experiences, most people invoke the age-old logic of birth order. "I'm the middle child, so I'm cooler headed," they will say, or "Firstborns are high achievers." Scientists, too, beginning with Sir Francis Galton in the 19th century, have sought in birth order a way to characterize how children diverge in personality, IQ or life success. But in recent years, many researchers have backed away from this notion, asserting that when family size, number of siblings and social class are taken into account, the explanatory power of birth ranking becomes negligible. Says one psychologist: "You wouldn't want to make a decision about your child based on it."

At least one researcher, however, argues that birth order does exert a strong influence on development, particularly on attitudes toward authority. Massachusetts Institute of Technology historian Frank Sulloway, who has just completed a 20-year analysis of 4,000 scientists from Copernicus through the 20th century, finds that those with older siblings were significantly more likely to have contributed to or supported radical scientific revolutions, such as Darwin's theory of evolution. Firstborn scientists, in contrast, were more apt to champion conservative scientific ideas. "Later-borns are consistently more open-minded, more intellectually flexible and therefore more radical," says Sulloway, adding that later-borns also tend to be more agreeable and less competitive.

Hearthside inequities. Perhaps most compelling for scientists who study sibling relationships are the ways in which parents treat their children differently and the inequalities children perceive in their parents' behavior. Research suggests that disparate treatment by parents can have a lasting effect, even into adulthood. Children who receive more affection from fathers than their siblings do, for example, appear to aim their sights higher in terms of education and professional goals, according to a study by University of Southern California psychologist Laura Baker. Seven year-olds treated by their mothers in a less affectionate, more controlling way than their brothers or sisters are apt to be more anxious and depressed. And adolescents who say their parents favor a sibling over themselves are more likely to report angry and depressed feelings.

Parental favoritism spills into sibling relationships, too, sometimes breeding the hostility made famous by the Smothers Brothers in their classic 1960s routine, "Mom always loved you best." In families where parents are more punitive and restrictive toward one child, for instance that child is more likely to act in an aggressive, rivalrous and unfriendly manner toward a brother or sister, according to work by Hetherington. Surprisingly, it may not matter who is favored. Children in one study were more antagonistic toward siblings even when *they* were the ones receiving preferential treatment.

Many parents, of course, go to great lengths to distribute their love and attention equally. Yet even the most consciously egalitarian parenting may be seen as unequal by children of different ages. A mother may treat her 4-year-old boy with the same care and attention she lavished on her older son when he was 4. But from the 7-year-old's perspective, it may look like his younger brother is getting a better deal. Nor is there much agreement among family members on how evenhandedly love is apportioned: Adolescents report favoritism when their mothers and fathers insist that none exists. Some parents express surprise that their children feel unequally treated, while at the same time they describe how one child is more demanding, another needs more discipline. And siblings almost never agree in their assessments of who, exactly, Mom loves best.

Nature vs. nurture. Further complicating the equation is the contribution of heredity to temperament, each child presenting a different challenge from the moment of birth. Plomin, part of a research team led by George Washington University psychiatrist David Reiss that is studying sibling pairs in 700 families nationwide, views the differences between siblings as emerging from a complex interaction of nature and nurture. In this scheme, a more aggressive and active child, for example, might engage in more conflict with parents and later become a problem child at school. A quieter, more timid child might receive gentler parenting and later be deemed an easy student.

In China, long ago, it was just the two of them, making dolls out of straw together in the internment camp, putting on their Sunday clothes to go to church with their mother. She mostly ignored her younger sister, or goaded her relentlessly for being so quiet. By the time they were separated—her sister sailing alone at 13 for the United States—there was already a wall between them, a prelude to the stiff Christmas cards they exchange, the rebuffed phone calls, the impersonal gifts that arrive in the mail.

Now, when the phone rings, she is wishing hard for a guardian angel, for someone to take away the pain that throbs beneath the surgical bandage on her chest, keeping her curled under the blue and white cotton coverlet. She picks up the receiver, recognizes her sister's voice instantly, is surprised, grateful, cautious all at once. How could it be otherwise after so many years? It is the longest they have spoken in 50 years. And across the telephone wire, something is shifting, melting in the small talk about children, the wishes for speedy recovery. "I think we both realized that life can be very short," she says. Her pain, too, is dulling now, moving away as she listens to her sister's voice. She begins to say a small prayer of thanks.

For a period that seems to stretch forever in the timelessness of childhood, there is only the family, only the others who are unchosen partners, their affection, confidences, attacks and betrayals defining the circumference of a limited world. But eventually, the boundaries expand, friends and schoolmates taking the place of brothers and sisters, highways and airports leading to other lives, to office parties and neighborhood meetings, to other, newer families.

Adult bonds. Rivalry between siblings wanes after adolescence, or at least adults are less apt to admit competitive feelings. Strong friendships also become less intense, diluted by geography, by marriage, by the concerns of raising children and pursuing independent careers. In national polls, 65 percent of Americans say they would like to see their siblings more often than the typical "two or three times a year." And University of Indianapolis psychologist Victoria Bedford finds, in her work, that men and women of child-rearing age often show longing toward siblings, especially those close in age and of the same sex. Yet for some people, the detachment of adulthood brings relief, an escape from bonds that are largely unwanted but never entirely go away. Says one woman about her brothers and sisters: "Our values are different, our politics diametrically opposed. I don't feel very connected, but there's still a pressure to keep up the tie, a kind of guilt that I don't have a deeper sense of kinship."

How closely sibling ties are maintained and nurtured varies with cultural and ethnic expectations. In one survey, for example, 54 percent of low-income blacks reported receiving help from a brother or sister, in comparison with 44 percent of low-income Hispanics and 36 percent of low-income whites. Siblings in large families are also more likely to give and receive support, as are those who live in close geographical proximity to one another. Sex differences are also substantial. In middle and later life, sisters are much more likely than brothers to keep up close relationships.

So important, in fact, is the role that sisters play in cementing family ties that some families all but fall apart without them. They are the ones who often play the major role in caring for aging parents and who make sure family members stay in touch after parents die. And in later life, says Purdue University psychologist Victor Cicirelli, sisters can provide a crucial source of reassurance and emotional security for their male counterparts. In one study, elderly men with sisters reported greater feelings of happiness and less worry about their life circumstances.

Warmth or tolerance? Given the mixed emotions many adults express about sibling ties, it is striking that in national surveys the vast majority—more than 80 percent—deem their relationships with siblings to be "warm and affectionate." Yet this statistic may simply reflect the fact that ambivalence is tolerated more easily at a distance, warmth and affection less difficult to muster for a few days a year than on a daily basis. Nor are drastic breaches between siblings—months or years of silence, with no attempt at rapprochement—unheard of. One man, asked by a researcher about his brother, shouted, "Don't mention that son of a bitch to me!" and slammed the door in the psychologist's face.

Sibling feuds often echo much earlier squabbles and are sparked by similar collisions over shared responsibility or resources—who is doing more for an ailing

ONLY CHILDREN
Cracking the myth of the pampered, lonely misfit

Child-rearing experts may have neglected the psychology of sibling ties, but they have never been hesitant to warn parents about the perils of siring a single child. Children unlucky enough to grow up without brothers or sisters, the professional wisdom held, were bound to be self-centered, unhappy, anxious, demanding, pampered and generally maladjusted to the larger social world. "Being an only child is a disease in itself," psychologist G. Stanley Hall concluded at the turn of the century.

Recent research paints a kinder picture of the only child—a welcome revision at a time when single-child families are increasing. The absence of siblings, psychologists find, does not doom children to a life of neurosis or social handicap. Day care, preschool and other modern child-care solutions go far in combatting an only child's isolation and in mitigating the willfulness and self-absorption that might come from being the sole focus of parental attention. And while only children may miss out on some positive aspects of growing up around brothers and sisters, they also escape potentially negative experiences, such as unequal parenting or severe aggression by an older sibling. Says University of Texas at Austin social psychologist Toni Falbo: "The view of only children as selfish and lonely is a gross exaggeration of reality."

Indeed, Falbo goes so far as to argue that only children are often better off—at least in some respects—than those with brothers and sisters. Reviewing over 200 studies conducted since 1925, she and her colleague Denise Polit conclude that only children equal firstborns in intelligence and achievement, and score higher than both firstborns and later-borns with siblings on measures of maturity and leadership. Other researchers dispute these findings, however. Comparing only children with firstborns over their life span, for example, University of California at Berkeley psychologist B. G. Rosenberg found that only children—particularly females—scored lower on intelligence tests than did firstborns with a sibling.

Rosenberg distinguishes between three types of only children. "Normal, well-adjusted" onlies, he says, are assertive, poised and gregarious. "Impulsive, acting out" only children adhere more to the old stereotype, their scores on personality tests indicating they are thin-skinned, self-indulgent and self-dramatizing. The third group resembles the firstborn children of larger families, scoring as dependable, productive and fastidious.

Perhaps the only real disadvantage to being an only child comes not in childhood but much later in life. Faced with the emotional and financial burdens of caring for aging parents, those without siblings have no one to help out. But as Falbo points out, even in large families such burdens are rarely distributed equally.

parent, how inheritance should be divided. Few are long lasting, and those that are probably reflect more severe emotional disturbance. Yet harmonious or antagonistic patterns established in childhood make themselves felt in many adults' lives. Says psychologist Kahn: "This is not just kid stuff that people outgrow." One woman, for example, competes bitterly with a slightly older co-worker, just as she did with an older brother growing up. Another suspects that her sister married a particular man in part to impress her. A scientist realizes that he argues with his wife in exactly the same way he used to spar with an older brother.

For most people, a time comes when it makes sense to rework and reshape such "frozen images" of childhood—to borrow psychologist Bank's term—into designs more accommodating to adult reality, letting go of ancient injuries, repairing damaged fences. In a world of increasingly tenuous family connections, such renegotiation may be well worth the effort. Says author Judith Viorst, who has written of sibling ties: "There is no one else on Earth with whom you share so much personal history."

ERICA E. GOODE

Crises—Challenges and Opportunities

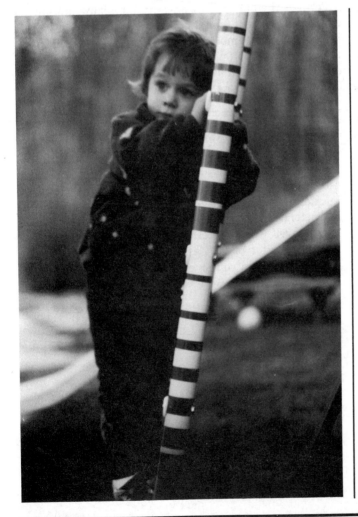

"Stress is life and life is stress." Sometimes stress in families gives new meaning to this statement. When a crisis occurs in families, many processes occur simultaneously as families and their members cope with the stressor and its effects. The experience of a crisis often leads to conflict and reduces the family members' ability to act as resources for each other. Indeed, a stressor can overwhelm the family system, and family members may be some of the least effective people in coping with each other's response to a crisis.

Family crisis comes in many forms; it can be drawn out or the crisis event can be clearly defined. The source of stress can be outside or inside the family, or it can be a combination of both. It can directly involve all family members or as few as one, but the effects will ripple through the family, affecting all of its members to one degree or another.

In this section, we consider a wide variety of crises. Family violence is the focus of the first subsection. Children can be intentional or unintentional victims of violence in families. "Helping Children Cope with Violence" shows how children growing up in violent surroundings can come away scarred for life. "After He Hits Her" addresses the spousal crisis of domestic violence. It explores the relationship dynamics involved that can be at the core of a continuing cycle of trauma and pain or help to begin the slow process of change. The next article is an honest "in the trenches" view of what is needed to be done to reduce the incidence of domestic battery of women. Rather than asking why battered women stay in abusive relationships, better questions would be "Why do men who batter do it, and what can be done to stop them?" The final article in this subsection, "Passion Kills" is a troubling, very personal look at the tragic impact of obsessive love.

The next subsection deals with problems in sexuality and sexual relationships, with infidelity as the focus. In "Beyond Betrayal: Life after Infidelity," Frank Pittman recounts the emotional and practical wreckage that results from extramarital sex. Tamar Lewin, in the next essay, takes a somewhat contrary view in suggesting that infidelity and other sexual stressors are less common in American marriages than has been assumed.

The next subsection looks at the work/family connection, with interesting results. "The Myth of the Miserable Working Woman" confronts many of the myths regarding women balancing work and home. Surprisingly, many of the assumptions we have about the overwhelming nature of this balancing act are not found to be true. Problems that *do* occur in the United States may, in fact, result from the government's lack of willingness to create a supportive family policy, according to "Family, Work, and Gender Equality: A Policy Comparison of Scandinavia, the United States, and the Former Soviet Union."

What is the nature of stress that results from caring for others in the family? In the following subsection, the stress (and the rewards) of caregiving are addressed. The two subsection articles address issues of providing care for a family member with a chronic, debilitating condition, first from a scholarly perspective and second from a personal perspective. Read together, they present a picture of challenging, sometimes frustrating, work that also contains some positive elements.

Divorce and remarriage are the focus of the next section. In the final subsection report, programs that have been developed to reduce the negative impacts of di-

vorce or to reduce the likelihood of divorce are reviewed. The other articles in the section take an optimistic look at stepfamilies. In both, the reader has an opportunity to examine the way our culture has set stepmothers and stepfamilies in an impossible evil/angelic dichotomy. These articles show that stepfamilies, although more complex than traditional families, are not doomed to failure and unresolved conflict.

Looking Ahead: Challenge Questions

How does an abusive relationship develop? What can be done to prevent it? How can we help someone caught in such a relationship? If you found that someone you know was obsessively in love with another person, what would you do? What would you do if someone you know was in danger?

How would you react if you learned that your spouse had been unfaithful? Under what circumstances would you consider extrarelational sex?

What is the best way to work out the competing demands of work and family? Discuss whether or not both partners should work if there are small children in the home.

What is your responsibility to your family? What is their responsibility to you? What would you give up to care for your parents? What would you expect your children to give up for you?

Discuss how any divorced person you know has been affected by the divorce. If the person has children, how have the children been affected?

Is your family, or that of a friend, a remarried or blended family? If so, how have you, or your friend, been affected?

Helping Children Cope With Violence

Lorraine B. Wallach

Lorraine B. Wallach, M.A., is one of the founders of the Erikson Institute in Chicago and is presently a faculty member there. Her recent work includes staff training around issues of children and violence.

Children who grow up in violent communities are at risk for pathological development because growing up in a constant state of apprehension makes it difficult to establish trust, autonomy, and social competence.

Violence is epidemic in the United States today. The murder rate in this country is the fifth highest in the world. It is 10 times higher than England's and 25 times that of Spain. For many inner-city children, violence has become a way of life. In a study of more than 1,000 children in Chicago, 74% of them had witnessed a murder, shooting, stabbing, or robbery (Kotulak, 1990; Bell, 1991). Almost half (47%) of these incidents involved friends, family members, classmates, or neighbors. Forty-six percent of the children interviewed reported that they had personally experienced at least one violent crime. These figures are similar to those found in other U.S. urban areas, such as Baltimore (Zinsmeister, 1990), Los Angeles County (Pynoos & Eth, 1985), and New Orleans (Osofsky, Wewers, Hann, Fick, & Richters, 1991).

Children are exposed to several kinds of violence, including child abuse and domestic violence. And there are communities where violence is endemic, where gang bangers, drug dealers, petty crimi-

nals, and not-so-petty criminals rule the streets. For children living in these conditions, feelings of being safe and secure do not exist.

Children who are not designated victims of assault can be unintended victims. Shoot-outs between gangs and drive-by shootings result in the wounding, and often killing, of innocent bystanders. In addition, the psychological toll of living under these conditions is immeasurable. The children in these neighborhoods see violence and hear it discussed. They are surrounded by danger and brutality.

Child abuse, other domestic violence, and neighborhood violence can harm development

The effects of this kind of violence on children are widespread and can permeate all areas of development, beginning in infancy and continuing through childhood. The first task a baby faces is the development of trust—trust

in the caregiving environment and eventually in himself. Achieving a sense of trust is compromised by growing up in a violent community. Many families find it difficult to provide infants with support, love, and affection in a consistent and predictable manner when they live in a constant state of apprehension—not knowing when they are going to be victims of violence. Toddlers have difficulty developing a sense of autonomy when their families cannot help them explore their environments because their surroundings are filled with danger. Preschoolers, too, are inhibited from going out into the world. Just at the age when they should be expanding their social contacts and finding out about people beyond the family, they are restricted by the dangers lurking outside. Many children living in high-rise housing projects and other dangerous neighborhoods are cooped up inside all day because it is unsafe to go out-of-doors. The situation is even more tragic when children experience violence within the family. Where can a child find protection when she is victimized within her own home? Although domestic violence occurs in *every* kind of neighborhood, the effects may be even more damaging when compounded by the harmful effects of growing up in *violent* neighborhoods.

Children who grow up under conditions that do not allow them to develop trust in people and in themselves or learn to handle day-to-day problems in socially acceptable ways are at risk for pathological development; they are at risk for resorting to violent behaviors themselves. The anger that is instilled in children when they are mistreated or when they see their mothers or siblings mistreated is likely to be incorporated into their personality structures. Children learn by identifying with the people they love. They also identify with the people who have power and control. When children see and experience abuse and violence as a way of life, when the people who are responsible for them behave without restraint, the children often learn to behave in the same manner.

Another serious problem for children living in chaotic communities is that the protectors and the dangerous people may be one and the same. The police, who are supposed to be protectors, are often seen as dangerous by community members. In his book *There Are No Children Here,* Alex Kotlowitz (1991) describes how a young man who is idolized by his housing project community be-

It is particularly important for children who come from chaotic environments to have firm but appropriate limits, even though children who feel powerless may try to provoke adults into a battle of wills in an effort to make themselves feel important.

The young child's protectors and the dangerous people in her life may be one and the same.

cause he is successful, has graduated from high school, is not caught up in gangs, and is still his own person is mistakenly killed by the police. What do children think when their idol is gunned down by the people who are supposed to protect them?

Children are confused when they cannot tell the good guys from the bad guys. Their teachers and the media tell them that drug dealers are bad and are the cause of the problems in the community, but the children may know

that cousins or friends or even older brothers are dealing. Some people have likened the inner city, especially housing projects, to war zones; but in a war the enemy is more often than not on the outside, and usually everyone knows who he is.

Children growing up with violence face risks other than becoming violent themselves. Children who live with danger develop defenses against their fears, and these defenses can interfere with their development. When children have to defend themselves constantly from outside or inside dangers, their energies are not available for other, less immediately urgent tasks, such as learning to read and write and do arithmetic and learning about geography and history and science. In addition to not having enough energy to devote to schoolwork, there is evidence that specific cognitive functions such as memory and a sense of time can be affected by experiencing trauma (Terr, 1981).

Boys and girls who are victims of abuse and who see abusive behavior in their families can grow up feeling as if they are responsible for what is happening. Young children cannot always differentiate between what is real and what is part of their inner lives. The literature on divorce has made clear that many children believe that they have caused the breakup of the family, even though it had nothing to do with them (Wallerstein & Kelly, 1980; Hetherton, Cox, & Cox, 1982). Children who feel guilty about the violence in their families often perceive themselves as being bad and worthless. Feelings of worthlessness can lead children to the idea that they

When children have to defend themselves constantly from inside and outside dangers, there is little energy for schoolwork. There is also evidence that specific cognitive functions such as memory and a sense of time can be affected.

are not capable of learning, which leads, in turn, to a lack of motivation to achieve in school.

Children who experience trauma may have difficulty seeing themselves in future roles that are meaningful. Lenore Terr (1983), in her study of the schoolchildren of Chowchilla who were kidnapped in their school bus, found that the views of their future lives were limited and often filled with anticipation of disaster. Children who cannot see a decent future for themselves cannot give their all to the present task of learning and becoming socialized.

Living in unpredictably frightening situations makes children feel as if they have no control over their lives. We know that young children need to feel as if they can direct some parts of their lives,

but children who are victims of violence learn that they have no say in what happens to them. This sense of helplessness interferes with the development of autonomy.

It is difficult for children to keep on growing and maturing when they have been traumatized because an almost universal reaction of children to traumatic occurrences is regression. Children slip back to stages at which they felt more secure. This is particularly true when they have only a tenuous hold on their current status.

What makes some children more resilient than others, and what can we do?

As depressing as all this sounds, however, it does not mean that all children who experience violence are doomed. It is known that some children are more resilient and withstand trauma and stress better than others. If a child has an easy temperament and makes a good fit with his primary caregiver, he or she is more likely to be off to a good start. Some lucky children are born to strong parents who can withstand the ravages of poverty and community violence and still provide some security and hope for their children. Children are shaped not only by their parents' behavior but also by their parents' hopes, expectations, motivations, and view of the future—including their children's future.

It is important to remember that children are malleable, that what happens in the early years is im-

A kindergarten teacher in a Chicago public school was discussing her dilemma concerning two boys in her classroom. All of the children were at their tables, engaged in drawing, when the teacher noticed these boys crawling under the tables, pretending to have guns. When one of the boys saw the teacher watching them, he reassured her, "Don't worry, we're just playing breaking into an apartment." The teacher questioned whether she should let the play continue or offer a more socially acceptable view of behavior. How should she react? A Head Start teacher in the group said that the boy who was taking the lead in this game had been in her class the year before, and that his family's apartment had been burglarized. The boy had been very frightened and, after that experience, had changed from a confident, outgoing youngster to a quiet and withdrawn child. Here it was a year later, and he was just beginning to play out his experience. He was becoming the aggressor in the play instead of the helpless victim. And he was regaining some of his old confidence.

portant, but that many children can overcome the hurts and fears of earlier times. Many can make use of positive experiences that occur both inside and outside their families. Child care centers, recreation programs, and schools can be resources for children and offer them alternative perceptions of themselves, as well as teaching them skills. One of the things that help determine the resiliency of children is the ability to make relationships and to make use of the people in their environments, people who provide to children what they do not get in their families or who supplement what their families cannot offer.

Child care professionals can help offset the negative effects of violence in the lives of young children by providing that supplement. Although teachers, social workers, and human service personnel cannot cure all of the hurts experienced by children today, they can make a difference.

1. **The first thing they need to do is to make sure that their programs provide opportunities for children to develop meaningful relationships with caring and knowledgeable adults.** Teachers and other staff members can offer each child a chance to form an important relationship with one of them, a relationship within which the child can learn that there are people in the world who can be of help. The best thing to offer children at risk is caring people, people who are available both physically and emotionally.

Some years ago the famous Chicago analyst Franz Alexander (1948) coined the term *corrective emotional experience* to explain the curative power of therapy, and that term best describes what child care professionals can do for children at risk. A corrective emotional experience means having a relationship with another person that touches one's deepest core—not a relationship that

is superficial or intellectual, but one that engages the emotions. It means having a relationship within which a person can redo old patterns and ties. It means feeling safe enough within a relationship to risk making basic changes in one's psychic structure. Children cannot be forced into these kinds of relationships; they can only be offered the opportunities with the hope that they take advantage of them.

Some children attach easily, and it does not take much effort on the part of the adults for these children to form attachments; these are usually the children who have had a good relationship in their past. Other children have not been lucky enough to have had the kind of relationship that makes them want to seek out others and repeat this satisfying experience; these children need more help in forming ties and trusting alliances.

What can adults do to stimulate relationships with children who do not come easily to this task? They can look into themselves and see if they are ready

for this kind of relationship—a relationship that makes demands on their emotions, their energies, and their time. Relationships with children who have inordinate needs and who do not have past experiences in give-and-take partnerships are not 50–50 propositions; adults must meet these children more than halfway.

2. **Child care professionals can organize their schedules and their time with the children so that they provide as much consistency as possible.** Attachment can be encouraged by reducing the number of people a child encounters during the day and by maximizing the amount of meaningful time and activity the child has with one adult. In this way each child is allowed to form an attachment to one person. There are several models—including therapeutic centers, child-life programs, and primary-care nursing—that use relationship as the principal tool in their interventions. Establishing significant relationships with the children who

A nine-year-old boy in a shelter for battered women told a story about his recurring dream. This is what he said: "I dreamed of someone taking me away. He was dressed like a lady, but he had a moustache. I went inside the house. It was dark. The lights were out, and there were people inside having a party. It was ugly. They were eating worms and they asked me to try one. I took one and threw it away. Then I opened the door, and the light came on in there, and I saw there were no more ghosts, and I saw I was sleeping. When I dream like that, I become afraid."

It was obvious that the boy was expressing his fears, but the exact meaning of the details was not evident—not until one of the child care workers who knew the mother reported that the abusive father was bisexual and brought his male sexual partners to the family's apartment. It then became clear that in addition to struggling with feelings about an abusive father, the boy was also frightened and confused about the meaning of his father's behavior and probably about his own sexual identification. In this case the child was able to tell about a disturbing dream through the telling of a story, and the adults were able to understand it with additional information about his family.

have suffered from trauma is the most important thing that can be done, and it is the basis for all of the work that follows. What is this other work?

3. **Child care professionals must provide structure and very clear expectations and limits.** All children, especially young children, need to know where they stand, but it is particularly important for children who come from chaotic environments to have firm but appropriate limits. It should be noted that they do not take to this kind of structure easily. It is not something they have experienced before, and the newness of it may cause anxiety and tension, just as any new situation does.

Some children see the structure of a new setting as an opportunity to assert themselves and force the adults into power struggles. Children who feel powerless may try to provoke adults into a battle of wills in an effort to make themselves feel important. But even though some of the neediest children may rebel against structure, no matter how benign, it is important to provide it so that the boundaries are clear.

4. **Early childhood professionals should offer children many opportunities to express themselves** within the confines of a comfortable and consistent schedule, with clear expectations about behavior. Children need to air their emotions; they need to tell their stories. They can do this in several activities that can be a part of any good program for children.

Except for life-sustaining activities, play is, of course, the most universal activity of children

Through play, children learn about the physical and social world. As they play, children develop a map of the world, a map that helps them make sense of the

Josephine, the child of an abused mother, told a story about a girl with red eyes who bit and scratched her mother because she was angry at her and the devil got into her body. The child care worker listened and accepted her story, thereby accepting the child's feelings. In subsequent sessions, after establishing a more trusting relationship with the child, the worker told her a story about the same little girl who told the devil not to bother her and who talked to her mother about how she was going to try harder to be nicer. By using the same characters and theme, she offered the little girl another way of relating to her mother. At the same time, the mother's worker helped her understand her own anger and supported her in trying to alter her behavior toward her daughter.

complexities that define the world today. Play, in the context of a corrective experience, offers children who live with chaos and violence a chance to redraw their world map.

Play provides an avenue for children to express their feelings. Children who are angry or hurt can take their anger out on toys, dolls, and stuffed animals. Children who feel isolated or lonely can find solace in pretending to live in a world with lots of friends. Children who are frightened can seek safety within a game by pretending to be big and strong. In other words, children can play out their own scenarios, changing their real life situations to their own design. They can invent happy endings. They can reverse roles and become the big—instead of the small—people. They can become the aggressors rather than the victims.

Play also allows children to repeat some of the bad things in their lives. Some people think that children want to forget the frightening or horrible things that they have experienced and try to put these events out of their minds. Some people think that children's play reflects only happy experiences; and many times it does. But some children gain strength from repeating situations that were overwhelming to them, as a way of trying to come to terms with the experiences.

Traumatic events have a way of staying with us. Sometimes they are repeated in dreams. Adults may review these events by talking about them with their friends and even with strangers. Adults, through discussion—and children, through play—gain control over trauma by repeating it again and again. Repetition allows the trauma victim to absorb the experience little by little, come to grips with what happened, and learn to accept it or live with it.

Expressive art is very therapeutic

In addition to being given many opportunities for dramatic play, children can benefit from a chance to paint and draw. Just as some children make sad or frightening events into happy occasions in their play, others may draw pictures of happy times, even when they are living in far-from-happy circumstances. They draw pictures of nice houses with flowers and trees and sunshine. Others draw pictures that are, or that represent, disturbing things in their lives. They draw angry or violent pictures and find solace in expressing their feelings through art and conquering their fears by putting them on paper.

Storytelling can bridge to valuable conversation

Storytelling is another way in which children can handle difficult situations and express their inner thoughts. Sharing the telling of stories can be an excellent way to open up communication between adults and children. It can establish rapport between the two and lay the basis for further discussions of a child's difficulties. It is easier for the adult to understand stories than to interpret drawings or play, and the adult is able to engage a child in a conversation about her or his story.

This does not mean that the stories children tell can be accepted verbatim. Just as play and drawing allow children to express themselves symbolically, so do stories offer them a chance to communicate an idea or feeling without acknowledging its closeness to reality. Adults often cannot understand a child's story without having some outside information about the child's life.

If we understand what children are telling us through their stories, we can help them by participating with them in storytelling. Gardner (1971) used this method in his therapy with children. After the child told a story, Gardner told the same story but with a different, healthier ending. Although teachers are not therapists, they can engage children in joint storytelling sessions and offer alternative endings to the stories told by the children.

Collaboration with families is critically important

Direct work with children is invaluable, but if it can be combined with help for parents, its effectiveness can be increased. Young children are best understood in the context of their families and communities. Professionals need to know the facts about a child's life situation, and that information can be gained from the adults who know the child well.

In addition to obtaining information from parents, the most effective help for a child is in collaboration with help for the family. Because the child is entwined with his family for many years, it is important to make changes in his familial relationships, if possible; even small changes can be important.

It is not possible for teachers and other child specialists to also be social workers and parent therapists. The person who makes contact with a child, however, is often in a good position to establish a working alliance with the child's parents. This alliance can then be used to refer parents to community agencies, clinics, churches, or self-help groups for the support, guidance, or therapy that they need. Making a good referral takes skill and patience. It cannot be done quickly, which means that teachers and child care workers must have the time to talk to parents and to make home visits if necessary. They must have time to establish contact with families as an essential part of their work with children who suffer the consequences of violence.

The problems spelled out here are formidable. They will not be easy to solve, but professionals who see children on a daily basis can be an important part of the solution. They cannot cure all of the ills and solve all of the problems that confront children today, but they can offer these children a chance to face and accept their feelings and to see alternative ways of relating to others. If child care professionals can help some—not all, but some—children find alternatives to destructive behavior, be it toward themselves or others, they have helped break the cycle of violence.

References

Alexander, F. (1948). *Fundamentals of psychoanalysis.* New York: W.W. Norton.

Bell, C. (1991). Traumatic stress and children in danger. *Journal of Health Care for the Poor and Underserved, 2*(1), 175–188.

Gardner, R. (1971). *Therapeutic communication with children: The mutual storytelling technique.* New York: Science House.

Hetherton, E.M., Cox, M., & Cox, R. (1982). Effects of divorce on parents and children. In M. Lamb (Ed.), *Non-traditional families.* Hillsdale, NJ: Lawrence Erlbaum.

Kotlowitz, A. (1991). *There are no children here.* New York: Doubleday.

Kotulak, R. (1990, September 28). Study finds inner-city kids live with violence. *Chicago Tribune,* pp. 1, 16.

Osofsky, J., Wewers, S., Hann, D., Fick, A., & Richters, J. (1991). *Chronic community violence: What is happening to our children?* Manuscript submitted for publication.

Pynoos, R., & Eth, S. (1985). Children traumatized by witnessing personal violence: Homicide, rape or suicide behavior. In S. Eth & R. Pynoos (Eds.), *Posttraumatic stress disorder in children* (pp. 19–43). Washington, DC: American Psychiatric Press.

Terr, L. (1981). Forbidden games: Posttraumatic child's play. *Journal of American Academy of Child Psychiatry, 20,* 741–760.

Terr, L. (1983). Chowchilla revisited: The effects of psychic trauma four years after a schoolbus kidnapping. *American Journal of Psychiatry, 140,* 1543–1550.

Wallerstein, J.S., & Kelley, J.B. (1980). *Surviving the breakup: How children and parents cope with divorce.* New York: Basic Books.

Zinsmeister, K. (1990, June). Growing up scared. *The Atlantic Monthly,* pp. 49–66.

After He Hits Her

This study examines the interactional dynamics following woman battering, and specifically addresses the question of whether, as time goes on, male batterers are less likely to offer accounts or aligning actions (i.e., apologies, excuses, justifications, and dismissals) for acts of violence, and whether female victims are less likely to honor the men's accounts. Based on in-depth interviews with 50 white women who had come to a battered women's shelter, the study finds that abusers generally are not likely to stop accounting for their violent behavior but that shelter victims are progressively less likely to honor the accounts. It also is found that, as time goes on, men are more likely to blame their victims for the battering. Similarities and differences between these findings and the research results used to support Walker's (1979, 1984) cycle theory of violence are discussed. Implications for practitioners working with batterers and victims are outlined.

Jane H. Wolf-Smith and Ralph LaRossa

Jane H. Wolf-Smith is an Associate Professor in the Department of Social Sciences, Gainesville College, Gainesville, GA 30503. Ralph LaRossa is a Professor in the Department of Sociology, Georgia State University, Atlanta, GA 30303.

For some time now, researchers and activists in the battered women's movement have realized that "acts of violence" are not discrete acts of physical aggression but are patterns of oppression, occurring over time and including events leading up to as well as following the use of force, itself. Thus, for example, in what may be the most widely cited theory of the pattern or cycle of violence, there is said to be at least three phases—the tension building phase, the acute battering phase, and the loving contrition phase—which ensnare women in a web of punishment and deceit (see Walker, 1979, 1984).

While much has been written about the structural and situational factors which precipitate violence toward women and, as more victims come forward, an all-too-vivid picture of both the range and severity of force in intimate relationships is being acquired, little still is known about

The authors wish to thank the women who participated in the study for their willingness to share their experiences; the staff of the battered women's shelter for their cooperation in arranging the interviews; and Phillip W. Davis and Paula L. Dressel for their comments on earlier versions of this article.

Key Words: cycle theory of violence, family violence, victimization of women.

what happens immediately after the incident—that is, "after he hits her."

Drawing on in-depth interviews with 50 white women who had been abused by their husbands or male companions, and who had come to a battered women's shelter for refuge, this study examines the interactional dynamics following acts of abuse, giving special attention to both the "acts of contrition" (and other verbal strategies) that men use and the kinds of responses that women give to these strategies. The research combines a theoretically informed approach to the concept of contrition with a methodological focus on the sequence of abuse. That is, from the beginning, the intent was to place "acts of contrition" within the class of theoretical concepts variously referred to as "techniques of neutralization" (Sykes & Matza, 1957), "remedial interchanges" (Goffman, 1971), "accounts" (Scott & Lyman, 1968), or "aligning actions" (Stokes & Hewitt, 1976); and, from the beginning, the goal was to examine whether the verbal strategies that batterers used the first time were different from the verbal strategies used later on.

The interest in whether men "repented" in different ways as time went on was sparked by the finding, reported in several previous studies, that men are likely to repent after the first incident of abuse but *increasingly less likely* to repent after subsequent incidents (see Dobash & Dobash, 1984; Ferraro & Johnson, 1983; Walker, 1984). What this means in terms of the cycle theory of violence is that,

after a while, men choose to "delete" the third phase.

If, indeed, abusive men are less contrite as time goes on, this would indicate a shift in their perception of their violent acts. The fact that they would repent for their behavior the first time would indicate some acknowledgment on their part that what they did would be met with disapproval. Their lesser tendency to repent after the 2nd, 10th, or 50th time would indicate that they had begun to "normalize" their violent behavior (i.e., see their violence within the bounds of social acceptability).

The logic here is that deviance and repentance go hand in hand. If individuals feel that they have done something wrong, they often will repent for their apparent misconduct. If, on the other hand, they feel that they are acting correctly, they will not repent. Students, for example, often will talk about why they were late for class, but rarely, if ever, talk about why they were on time (Goffman, 1971; Scott & Lyman, 1968; Stokes & Hewitt, 1976; Sykes & Matza, 1957).

Stopping violence requires an all-out effort to cancel the hitting license. If what happens in abusive relationships is that the license is not only not cancelled but actually renewed and possibly upgraded (i.e., defined as more "normal" than before), battered women and their advocates need to know this. Understanding the part that "acts of contrition" play in the cycle of abuse thus will go a long way toward helping victims of abuse.

From *Family Relations*, Vol. 41, No. 3, July 1992, pp. 324-329. © 1992 by the National Council of Family Relations, 3989 Central Avenue, NE, Suite 550, Minneapolis, MN 55421. Reprinted by permission.

Theoretical Rationale

A Typology of Aligning Actions

From a symbolic interactionist point of view, an act of contrition is *one* example of an *aligning action,* offered in the hope of mending, if only temporarily, a break between socially established norms and misconduct (Stokes & Hewitt, 1976). By offering aligning actions, social actors give neutral or positive meanings to behaviors that are "out of line." If, in turn, the aligning actions are "honored" by the offended party or parties (i.e., if others give the impression that they attach the same neutral or positive meanings to the apparent misconduct), then the aligning actions have the effect of "containing" or "minimizing" what otherwise might have been viewed as a relationship-threatening set of events.

When aligning actions are offered after deviant behavior, they are referred to as *accounts* (Scott & Lyman, 1968). When they are offered before a misdeed—or in the anticipation of a misdeed—they are referred to as *disclaimers* (Hewitt & Stokes, 1975). Given the interest here on what happens "afterward," the focus is on how men account rather than disclaim abusive behavior.

According to Hunter (1984), ex post facto aligning actions generally fall into four categories. Applied to woman battering, what differentiates the four categories is whether or not the batterer (a) makes the case that the violence in question deserves to be viewed as a negative act, and/or (b) says that he is responsible for the violence.

The first category is an apology. An *apology* signifies the batterer's acceptance of both the negative evaluation of the act and responsibility for the act, itself. Regret is also evident in this aligning action: "I know I shouldn't have slapped you. I'm sorry." Apologies are apparently what Walker (1979, 1984) was referring to when she talked about a "loving contrition phase" in her cycle theory of violence.

In [the loving contrition] phase, the batterer constantly behaves in a charming and loving manner. He is usually sorry for his actions in the previous phases, and he conveys contriteness to the battered woman. He begs her forgiveness and promises her that he will never do it again. (Walker, 1979, p. 65)

The batterer may apologize profusely, try to assist his victim, show kindness and remorse, and shower her with gifts and promises. (Walker, 1984, p. 96)

Being contrite or apologizing, however, is not the only account available to abusers. Other "third phase" strategies include the dismissal, the excuse, and the justification.

The *dismissal* is the opposite of an apology. Its intent is to invalidate both responsibility for the act and the negative evaluation of the act: "You pushed me to the limit—besides, you need to know who's boss around here."

Then there is the excuse. When using an *excuse,* the batterer accepts the negative evaluation of the act, but denies responsibility for the act: "That was a lousy thing to do—but I've been under a lot of pressure from my boss."

Finally, there is the justification. With the *justification,* the batterer accepts responsibility for the act but denies its negative evaluation: "I felt I had to do something to keep you from making a stupid decision."

A number of researchers have recognized that efforts on the part of both abusers and victims to account for abusive incidents can include more than apologies or acts of contrition. In one of the earliest studies of violence in the home, Gelles (1974) identified a variety of meanings that abusers gave to their violent acts to "explain" why they were violent—from "She asked for it" (an excuse) to "I tried to knock her to her senses" (a justification). Similarly, Ferraro and Johnson (1983), focusing not on the abusers but on the victims, described how women "rationalized" being abused, saying things like "I asked for it" (an excuse), "He's sick" (also an excuse), and "He didn't injure me" (a justification). Ferraro and Johnson (1983) also demonstrate how these accounts prevented the women from seeking help. Along the same lines, Mills (1985) described the "techniques of neutralization" that battered women use "to help them tolerate violent marriages." Mills (1985) found that one way that women "managed the violence" directed toward them was they used "justifications" (e.g., "compared to others, it seems my problems are small") to "minimiz[e] the significance of their victimization" (p. 109). Finally, Ptacek (1988), in a study of abusive men, discovered that he could classify the bulk of the men's accounts into either excuses or justifications. He also found that the men were more likely to excuse than to justify their behavior.

Drawing on Hunter's (1984) typology and following in the footsteps of Gelles (1974), Ferraro and Johnson (1983), Mills (1985), and Ptacek (1988), this study set out to determine not only whether abusers apologized for hitting their wives but also whether they dismissed, excused, and justified their violent behavior. Because of the interest, too, in whether men stopped using aligning actions as time went on (and with repeated incidents of abuse), the study also was designed to plot the chronological sequence of accounts.

A Typology of Honoring Stances

One might suppose that a victim has only two choices when her abuser offers to apologize for, or explain, his behavior: she can reject the aligning action or she can honor it. During the preinterview stage of the study, however, it was deduced that there are at least four honoring stances that a victim may take in response to an aligning action (or set of aligning actions). The four stances are: reject, pseudohonor, ambivalently honor, and wholeheartedly honor.

When the victim *rejects* the aligning action, she makes it clear by her verbal and nonverbal behavior that the aligning action is not acceptable, and consequently not effective in smoothing the disruption caused by the abuse.

With *pseudohonor,* the victim pretends to honor the account, with both verbal and nonverbal behavior indicating acceptance, but in self-interaction and in subsequent interaction with others she does not accept the aligning action as legitimate.

When the victim *ambivalently honors* the aligning action, there is some degree of hesitation before she acknowledges its legitimacy. Her honoring stance is characterized by uncertainty, in which she is tempted to honor the account but also doubts its legitimacy.

Finally, a *wholehearted honoring* of the aligning action occurs when the victim, without hesitation, gives it legitimacy. She readily accepts whatever account is issued and fully believes its validity.

The question of whether accounts are rejected has also been the subject of several inquiries. Ferraro and Johnson (1983), for example, talked about the shifts in events and perceptions that lead women to begin to reject their abusers' rationalizations; and Giles-Sims (1983) noted how the women in her study seemed to be willing to "forgive and forget" the first abusive incident but not the most recent. As far as it is known, however, no one has developed a typology of honoring stances like the one described above and applied it to abusive situations. In order to have a clear sense of the interactional dynamics in relationships, it is important to recognize the variety of accounts that men employ *and* the variety of honoring stances that women use in response.

To summarize, the object of this study was to examine the verbal strategies that abusive men use to neutralize or negate their violent actions and the honoring stances that women take to parry these accounts. A central concern of the project from the beginning was whether aligning actions and honoring stances change over time.

Methodology

Sample

The 50 women in the sample were all residents of a battered women's shelter located approximately 50 miles from a major urban area. Hypothesizing that communication patterns after abusive behavior might vary across racial lines, and feeling that an adequate analysis of racial variation would require a much larger sample, the decision was made (due to restrictions on time and other resources) to limit the interviewees to white victims.

The average age of the women in the study was 28 years. While the variation in educational levels was from less than 8 years of education to college graduate, the average number of years completed was 11.5. About one fourth of the women were employed outside the home. Seventy-eight percent were married to their abusers, 20% were cohabiting, and 2% were dating the abuser. The average length of the relationship was 6.5 years. Ninety-eight percent of the sample had children, the average number being 2.4. The average family income for this sample was $17,585.

As reported by the women, the average age of the abusers was 30 years. The average number of years of education completed was 10.7. The majority of the abusers were employed in blue-collar jobs involving manual labor.

Interviews

The interviews were conducted by the first author over a 2-year period, beginning in the fall of 1986 and ending in the fall of 1988. The interviews lasted from 1 to 2 hours, with the average interview lasting an hour and a half. In all but one case the women were interviewed during their stay in the shelter. With the women's consent, the interviews were tape-recorded, and eventually transcribed. The 50 interviews resulted in 1,500 pages of transcripts.

In order to gain an interpretive understanding of the women's point of view, the women were encouraged to talk at length and in-depth about what they thought and how they felt about the abuse in their relationships. All were asked to report on three separate incidents of abuse—the first, the most recent, and a middle incident. For the middle incident, the victims were asked to select an abusive incident that occurred about halfway between the first and the most recent—one that "stood out" to them for some reason. The women were especially encouraged to talk about what happened *after* an abusive incident, particularly what the batterers did or said. However, the women were not specifically asked whether the batterers apologized, excused, justified, or dismissed their behavior, nor were they specifically asked whether they honored any accounts offered. When the women happened to mention an aligning action, they were asked to repeat, to the best of their recollection, what the batterer said and what they had said and felt in response. Thus, every effort was made *not to solicit* aligning actions or honoring stances.

Analysis

To classify the women's comments into one category or another, the constant comparative method of qualitative analysis was used (Glaser & Strauss, 1967). As the transcripts were read and reviewed, notations were made in the margins about categories suggested by particular sections of the transcript. Often a single passage was coded in two or more categories. Once the entire transcript was reviewed, selected passages were cut from the transcript and placed in the appropriate files. As additional transcripts were reviewed, incidents that were similar to previously noted ones were filed with them. During this time the files themselves were reviewed. Incidents were compared with other incidents within the same category, and common properties were noted. Gradually, particular categories with their own properties began to emerge. It was then possible to compare newly discovered incidents with the properties of the category, rather than with just similar incidents (see also Lofland & Lofland, 1984; Strauss & Corbin, 1990).

Changes in the nature of aligning actions and in the nature honoring stances were examined both cross-sectionally and developmentally. The cross-sectional analysis involved an examination of distributions across the three time periods, looking at the sample as a whole ($N = 50$). The developmental analysis involved (a) an examination of the patterns of change in aligning actions as reported by 31 (of the 50) women who provided information on aligning actions on at least two of three incidents; and (b) an examination of patterns of change in honoring stances as reported by 23 (of the 50) women who provided information on honoring stances on at least two of three incidents. The developmental analysis, in other words, is an analysis of change within specific relationships. Sometimes, the women were not specific about when a particular aligning action or honoring stance was used. When this was the case, the women's descriptions of events were classified under a "general" category.

Limitations

There are several limitations to the study which should be considered when interpreting the results. First, the sample was limited to 50 white shelter residents. The experience of white women may be unlike that of other groups, and battered women who come to shelters may be different from other battered women in important ways. A second limitation is that female victims, rather than male batterers, were asked about the batterers' accounts. Essentially, then, the women provided "second-hand" information about the accounts employed. Third, the women were asked about interactions surrounding abusive incidents that had occurred, for most, years earlier. Ability to recall these early incidents of abuse varied from one respondent to the next, with some clearly recalling the first incident and others remembering little about it. Additionally, subsequent events may have altered the victims' perception and interpretation of these earlier incidents. Fourth, the interviewing strategy employed may have resulted in the women's failure to report both aligning actions and honoring stances surrounding abusive incidents. In an attempt to let the victims "tell their story," the women were not specifically asked whether abusers offered accounts for their behavior or, if offered, whether they were honored. Therefore, it is possible that accounts and honoring stances were employed but not reported by the women because the women were not asked about them.

Aligning Actions Following Woman Battering

Altogether, 139 aligning actions were discussed by the 50 victims. Table 1 presents the cross-sectional analysis of these accounts. As can be seen, 68% of all aligning actions issued after the first incident involved an apology only, while 67% after the middle incident and 42% after the last incident involved an apology only.

Here, for example, is how one victim, a 38-year-old mother of two, described how her husband apologized for his abuse:

Yeah, once I kind of calmed down

Table 1.
Aligning Actions Offered by Batterers After the First, Middle, and Last Incidents of Abuse: Cross-Sectional Analysis (N = 139)

	First		Middle		Last		General		Total	
	Percent	Number	Percent	Number	Percent	Number	Percent	Number	Percent	Number
Apology	68	21	67	14	42	13	30	17	47	65
With excuse	26	8	14	3	29	9	5	3	17	23
Excuse	6	2	14	3	16	5	50	28	27	38
Justification	0	0	5	1	3	1	13	7	6	9
With apology	0	0	0	0	6	2	0	0	1	2
With excuse	0	0	0	0	3	1	2	1	1	2
Dismissal	0	0	0	0	0	0	0	0	0	0
Total	100	31	100	21	100	31	100	56	100	139

Note. Percentages may not add up to 100% due to rounding.

and kind of regrouped. I went back in and when I did he was sitting on the chair, sort of mopey looking. And I walked in and I just stood there and he just jumps up and runs over and starts apologizing and hugging and crying and said he never meant to hit me and he'd never do it again.

Noteworthy is the fact that the percentages for the use of the apology (and only the apology) are very similar to the percentages that Walker (1984) reported. In Walker's (1984) study, apologies dropped from 69% after the first incident to 63% after the middle incident and to 42% after the last incident. At first glance, it thus seems that the results of this study are in accord with Walker's. However, when the categories that include the use of an apology (Apology Only, Apology with Excuse, Justification with Apology) are *combined,* a pattern different from the pattern Walker reported is uncovered. Used alone or in combination with other types of aligning actions, apologies were said to have been offered 94% of the time after the first incident, 81% of the time after the middle incident, and 77% of the time after the last incident.

A similar finding emerges in the developmental analysis. Only 32% of the women (i.e., 10 of the 31 women for whom there was enough information to carry out a developmental analysis) reported that their mates continued to use an apology (and only an apology) across the three incidents. However, when the categories that involve the continued use of the apology, (Apology Only, From Apology to Apology with Excuse, From Apology with Excuse to Apology, From Apology to Apology with Justification, From Apology with Excuse to Apology with Justification) are *combined,* it is found that 74% of individual abusers continued to use apologies with repeated incidents of abuse.

Quite often, in other words, men would offer a *mixture* of aligning actions, blending their apologies with other, more "self-preservative" accounts. One woman, for example, a 30-year-old mother of two

reported how her husband used an apology with an excuse:

There was never an "I'm sorry" for what happened. I mean he hugged and kissed me the next day and told me he was sorry but it wasn't like "I'm sorry, sorry," it was just, "Well you shouldn't have asked for that can opener. You shouldn't have been over there talking to those men." And I'm saying, "Well, all I did was ask for a can opener. I wasn't carrying on a conversation with them."

Another victim, a 21-year-old mother of one, echoed a similar theme of mixed accounts:

I had got [the baby] asleep while he was gone and he come in and laid in my lap and said, "Baby, I'm sorry." He said, "I don't believe I did that." He said, "I am sorry." And then in the next breath he said, "But you shouldn't have been up there [at your mother's house]." And then he turned and said, "I'm sorry, but they shouldn't have said that." He'd say he was sorry and then he'd say, "But ..."

Interestingly enough, none of the aligning actions described by the women could be classified as a dismissal. Possibly, batterers will resort to a dismissal rarely and only when they feel that an excuse or justification will not be honored.

Walker's (1984) findings led her to conclude that "over time in a battering relationship ... loving contrite behavior declines" (p. 97). Assuming that by "loving contrite behavior" Walker meant apologetic acts, this study failed to replicate Walker's results; according to the women interviewed for this project, while the singular use of the apology declined over time, the apology in conjunction with other aligning actions continued throughout the battering relationship.

Noteworthy, too, is what the interviews reveal about the use of the excuse. An excuse, again, is an account whereby the batterer admits that the abuse is bad

but denies responsibility. For example, a 21-year-old mother of three reported:

He'll say things like, "If you wouldn't run your smart mouth, I wouldn't do this." And he'll say stuff like, "I don't want to do it, you make me do it." Sometimes you could just say something wrong and not even think you had bothered anybody and he'd just fuss you out or cuss you out, but he just says, "You don't know when to shut your mouth, you just go on and on." He always blames it on me, it's never his fault.

And a 25-year-old mother of four stated:

Like I'd say, "Why do you hit me all the time?" [He'd say] "Shut up, you don't need to ask. If you'd done what I asked in the first place, you never would have gotten it." So it was always like my fault. I asked him to hit me. In a sense, that's what he was saying. She deliberately did this, you know, so that's why she got it.

In Table 1, it can be seen that 6% of all aligning actions used after the first abusive incident involved the excuse alone, while 14% and 16% after the middle and last incident respectively, involved the excuse alone. Not much of a difference. However, when the categories are *combined,* a clearer picture of change emerges. Collapsing all categories that involve the excuse, either used alone or in combination with other aligning actions (Excuses Only, Apology with Excuse, and Justification with Excuse), it is found that 32% of all aligning actions after the first incident involved the use of an excuse, while 28% and 48% involved the use of an excuse after the middle and last incident, respectively. In other words, excuses, although they may be used in combination with other aligning actions, are most likely to be used after the last incident of abuse.

A somewhat similar pattern regarding the use of the excuse emerged in the developmental analysis. Although apologies were the most common account to be used across the three incidents (see

Table 2.
Honoring Stances Taken by Victims After the First, Middle, and Last Incidents of Abuse: Cross-Sectional Analysis (N = 100)

	First		Middle		Last		General		Total	
	Percent	Number	Percent	Number	Percent	Number	Percent	Number	Percent	Number
Rejection	0	0	0	0	50	13	7	2	15	15
Pseudo	3	1	6	1	42	11	29	8	21	21
Ambivalent	27	8	29	5	4	1	25	7	21	21
Wholehearted	69	20	65	11	4	1	39	11	43	43
Total	100	29	100	17	100	26	100	28	100	100

Note. Percentages may not add up to 100% due to rounding.

Table 1), in 13% of the cases (i.e., 4 of 31), batterers were said to move from an apology to an excuse; and in 23% of the cases (i.e., 7 of 31), batterers were said to move from an apology to an apology with an excuse.

The Honoring of Aligning Actions

Changes in honoring stances were analyzed in the same two ways that changes in the use of aligning actions were analyzed (i.e., cross-sectionally and developmentally). The typology of honoring stances developed prior to the interviews and described earlier (i.e., reject, pseudohonor, ambivalently honor, and wholeheartedly honor) was the coding scheme employed.

Examining the first column in Table 2, it can be seen that 20 of the 29 women who provided information on honoring stances after the first incident wholeheartedly honored the aligning actions offered. A 21-year-old mother of one, for example, said that she genuinely thought her husband's accounts were valid:

I believe he was sorry he did it. He just can't control himself. I believe he does it before he realizes it and sometimes he doesn't even remember doing it the next morning. He'll look at me and say, "I did it again, didn't I?" And I'd say, "Yeah." And he didn't remember doing it. It's just out of his memory. I think in his heart he's really sorry for doing it. He just can't help it.

Eight of the 29 women, however, were unsure, or ambivalent, about what their response should be. A 25-year-old mother of one, for example, talked of the difficulty she had trying to decide whether to honor her husband's accounts:

It was very easy for him. Crying, bawling, and I can't stand to see a man cry and he knows it, too. "I swear I'll never do it again. Things are going to be different, I promise. I won't touch you." Just a bunch of lies. Just totally convincing me and knowing better. Me sitting there telling myself "I know this isn't right."

My second wind [*sic*] was I know this isn't right, but there was something else that won over what I thought was right. My heart would say, "Okay, I'll give him another chance. It might just be true this time." And then there was this other thing inside me saying, "You idiot." I always had like two things fighting inside of me. There was one that knew better and then there was the one that let itself be guided by strings.

These findings, which show that women are likely to wholeheartedly or ambivalently honor their mates' accounts after the first incident of abuse, are consistent with the results of prior research. Giles-Sims (1983), who interviewed 31 battered women who had sought help from a battered women's shelter, asked the women whether they had been willing to "forgive and forget" the first abusive incident. The vast majority—93%—said yes. Most of the women also said that they perceived the first abusive incident as an isolated one, and they did not expect it to happen again.

Looking at the second column in Table 2, it can be seen that 17 incidents of honoring were described after the middle incident of abuse. Of these, 65% were wholehearted honoring, 29% were ambivalent honoring, and 6% were pseudohonoring. There were no rejections. These percentages are similar to those found after the first abusive incident, and illustrate that as the battering progressed, the women were *still* likely to honor the aligning actions.

The real shift in honoring stances occurred after the last incident of abuse. Only a small fraction wholeheartedly or ambivalently honored the aligning actions then. However, 42% of the women who provided information pseudohonored their mate's accounts, and 50% flat out rejected them. Thus, if the categories of pseudohonoring and rejection are *combined*, it can be said that 92% of the women did not honor the account offered, whether or not they conveyed this to the batterer. Here is how one victim, for example, a 24-year-old mother of three, described her use of the pseudohonoring stance:

When he would first apologize to me, I would try to act like I was forgiving him, or he would get mad again. He would like come up and hug me, and I would try to act like I believed him, but I would be thinking, "I just hate you, and I'm leaving you, just wait 'til I can get out of here."

And here is how another, a 35-year-old mother of two, described how she moved to flat out reject her husband's accounts:

He came to the door and he was weeping. I don't mean crying just a little bit, I mean weeping, saying, "Please don't take my kids away, they're the only persons I've got, and I've missed you'all," and all that kind of stuff. And I felt so sorry for him, I just, you know. [He said] "Let me kiss you and hug you ... I am so sorry. It just got out of hand." But I just can't take that anymore. I've heard it too much, I guess.

The developmental analysis again supported the cross-sectional analysis. Eighty-seven percent of the women (i.e., 20 of the 23 for whom there was enough information to carry out a developmental analysis) shifted from honoring stances which more or less accepted the accounts issued by the abusers (wholehearted or ambivalent honoring) to honoring stances which questioned the accounts (pseudohonor or rejection).

These findings, which show that women who come to a shelter are likely to question their mates' accounts, are also consistent with other studies. Giles-Sims (1983) found that only 18% of her sample were willing to "forgive and forget" the last incident of abuse; and Ferraro and Johnson (1983) found that battered women who decide to go to a shelter generally do so only after they have rejected the rationalizations for abuse.

Implications

For counselors, therapists, and social workers who are working with abusive men and/or abused women, this study—like other recent studies on the "phenomenology" of abuse (e.g., Andrews &

Brewin, 1990; Herbert, Silver, & Ellard, 1991)—helps clarify how batterers and victims "give meaning to" and (from their point of view) "cope with" domestic violence.

If one focuses exclusively on the apology, as Walker (1984) did, the findings from this study are very similar to hers. However, if one looks at the full range of accounts that abusers use, the findings differ. According to the women interviewed in this study, the third phase in the cycle of violence is not bypassed with repeated abuse, as Walker (1984) suggested; rather the third phase is *modified* to include other types of accounts. In other words, the "content" of the stage may change, but its "form" (the offering of accounts) remains essentially the same.

This shift in the type of aligning actions is significant because of the message it conveys. In an apology, the abuser accepts responsibility and implies that what he did was wrong. When the abuser moves to the use of the excuse either alone or in combination with other accounts, he is attempting to deny responsibility for his behavior. Something else—stress, financial problems, alcohol or drug abuse, or the victim's behavior—is "causing" the abuse. Not only the batterer but also the victim may be distracted by these excuses, believing that the abuse will stop if the avowed "causes" could be eliminated (e.g., "If I/he would stop drinking, the violence would stop"). Ultimately, however, these accounts serve to perpetuate the abuse because they prevent the abuser from coming to grips with the fact that *he* is responsible for his violent behavior. Ultimately, they enable the abuser to continue *both* his violent behavior *and* his relationship with his victim.

Counselors, therapists, and social workers can help abusers and victims understand how accounts perpetuate domestic violence. Exposing the accounts for what they are—verbal strategies designed to minimize the violence—is the first step in eliminating their use and their power. It is important also for professional helpers to reject the accounts that abusers offer. Honoring apologies, excuses, and justifications leads the batterer to believe that his abusive behavior is acceptable "in some situations" and "under certain conditions." The hitting license must be *cancelled*, not qualified. The repudiation of the battering must be foremost in the practitioner's mind.

All the battered women in this study left their abusive relationships, at least temporarily. The process of getting out of an abusive relationship is a complex one, both emotionally and physically. Many women leave these relationships and return to them, often more than once (Pagelow, 1984). The honoring stance that a woman adopts can help counselors, therapists, and social workers determine whether a woman is emotionally ready to leave. The women in this study sought help from a shelter after the "last" abusive incident, an incident in which 92% (of those reporting a honoring stance) rejected or pseudohonored an account offered by the batterer. These women clearly did not believe that the abuser was sorry, that something or someone else was to blame, or that it would not happen again. Victims who honor accounts, much like the women in Ferraro and Johnson's (1983) study who offered rationalizations for the abuse which they suffered, may still believe that the abuser is sorry, that it will not happen again, and that he will change. Accounts offered by abusers and honored by victims thus serve the same purpose as victim rationalizations—that is, they prevent women from seeking aid.

Finally, it is important to emphasize that while counselors, therapists, and social workers have an obligation to help victims gain insight into their abuse, they also have an obligation to be nonjudgmental of whatever decision a woman makes about her abusive relationship. A number of women in this study talked about the loss of support they experienced from significant others when they made decisions to stay with or return to their abusers. Victims of male battering face difficult choices—choices about what to say to their abusers, choices about whether to stay. Respecting the choices that women make is an integral part of the counseling/therapeutic process. Victims must always know that there are people ready and willing to listen to them and assist them.

REFERENCES

Andrews, B., & Brewin, C. R. (1990). Attributions of blame for marital violence: A study of antecedents and consequences. *Journal of Marriage and the Family, 52,* 757-767.

Dobash, R. E., & Dobash, R. P. (1984). The nature and antecedent of violent events. *British Journal of Criminology, 24,* 269-288.

Ferraro, K. J., & Johnson, J. M. (1983). How women experience battering: The process of victimization. *Social Problems, 30,* 325-339.

Gelles, R. J. (1974). *The violent home: A study of physical aggression between husbands and wives.* Beverly Hills, CA: Sage.

Giles-Sims, J. (1983). *Wife battering: A systems theory approach.* New York: Guilford.

Glaser, B. G., & Strauss, A. (1967). *The discovery of grounded theory.* Chicago: Aldine.

Goffman, E. (1971). *Relations in public: Microstudies of the public order.* New York: Basic Books.

Herbert, T. B., Silver, R. C., & Ellard, J. H. (1991). Coping with an abusive relationship: I. How and why do women stay? *Journal of Marriage and the Family, 53,* 311-325.

Hewitt, J. P., & Stokes, R. (1975). Disclaimers. *American Sociological Review, 40,* 1-11.

Hunter, C. H. (1984). Aligning actions: Types and distributions. *Symbolic Interaction, 7,* 155-174.

Lofland, J., & Lofland, L. H. (1984). *Analyzing social settings: A guide to qualitative research and analysis.* Belmont, CA: Wadsworth.

Mills, T. (1985). The assault on the self: Stages in coping with battering husbands. *Qualitative Sociology, 8,* 103-123.

Pagelow, M. D. (1984). *Family violence.* New York: Praeger.

Ptacek, J. (1988). Why do men batter their wives? In K. Yllo & M. Bograd (Eds.), *Feminist perspectives on wife abuse* (pp. 133-157). Newbury Park, CA: Sage.

Scott, M. B., & Lyman, S. M. (1968). Accounts. *American Sociological Review, 41,* 46-62.

Stokes, R., & Hewitt, J. P. (1976). Aligning actions. *American Sociological Review, 41,* 838-849.

Strauss, A., & Corbin, J. (1990). *Basics of qualitative research: Grounded theory procedures and techniques.* Newbury Park, CA: Sage.

Sykes, G. M., & Matza, D. (1957). Techniques of neutralization: A theory of delinquency. *American Sociological Review, 22,* 667-670.

Walker, L. E. (1979). *The battered woman.* New York: Harper & Row.

Walker, L. E. (1984). *The battered woman syndrome.* New York: Springer.

Where Do We Go from Here?

An interview with Ann Jones

Ann Jones is the author of several landmark books on violence against women. "Women Who Kill," "When Love Goes Wrong" (with Susan Schechter), and "Next Time, She'll Be Dead." All contribute to moving the discussion about battery away from women and toward stopping the men who commit the violence. In July [1994], Jones sat down with "Ms." senior editor Gloria Jacobs to explore the current convulsion of soul-searching sweeping the U.S. in the wake of revelations about domestic violence in the O.J. Simpson case.

Gloria Jacobs: In your latest book, *Next Time, She'll Be Dead*, you say that we haven't put an end to violence in the home because society accepts that women are going to be battered, that they serve as an example of "what awaits all women who don't behave."

Ann Jones: We never confront the enormity of this problem. Battery is our greatest health problem, probably worse than breast cancer. It's one of the crimes most frequently committed against women. It's among the crimes most often committed in this country—period. Yet at the present time we have a national debate on health care, of which violence against women is not a part, and a national debate on crime, of which violence against women is not a part. So, if you can't get this issue discussed in the arenas where it is an absolutely central concern, then things aren't going to change. We need to shift the discussion. At the same time, individual women who are still up against this problem have to have a way to evaluate what's happening to

> **"The thing to remember is that women have a right to live free from bodily harm."**

them, and to figure out what to do.

G.J.: I know you don't like the term "domestic violence," but doesn't it acknowledge that the home is not necessarily a safe haven for women?

A.J.: It makes the violence sound domesticated, and it makes it sound like a special category of violence that is somehow different from other kinds—less serious. It's seen as a kind of violence that women volun-

teer for, or inspire, or provoke. I prefer to call it violence against women, because it does include so many other things, like rape and pimping and molestation of children.

G.J.: But do we need to identify the locus of this particular kind of violence? People tend to assume that danger and violence come from outside: the stranger on the street. Is it important to distinguish violence perpetrated, as you say, "by the person who says he loves you"?

A.J.: Yes. But this is the most common kind of violence against women. So when you simply call it violence against women, that in itself redirects our attention. It's not coming out of the bushes, it's coming out of the bedroom. I don't have the answer to how to shift this terminology, but I do think that it gets watered down by being called domestic violence.

The more difficult term is "battered woman," because it suggests a woman who is more or less permanently black and blue and helpless. And of course most women who are abused and controlled by men don't think of themselves as battered women. So, yes, we need some better terms to define what we're talking about. And, in my view, a lot of women are battered who are never hit, because you can, as we know, be subject to control without any physical violence.

I would like to see us start thinking about battered women as resisters, because it's clear to me that women are not battered or emotionally abused or controlled because they're passive and helpless. Often, women get emotionally abused and physically battered because they resist that kind of control. I don't think I've ever met a battered woman who didn't think of herself as a strong woman. Most are doing all the regular things of life—they're keeping their house, they're holding down a job, raising their kids—all while they're living in this terrible situa-

tion. They're doing all the things that put the rest of us under stress, plus they're trying to appease this man to keep him from being violent. So, yes, they're strong. They cope with an incredible amount, and that's the way they think of themselves, and they don't want to—can't—think of themselves as helpless battered women. But at the same time they are being victimized by these tyrannical, abusive men.

G.J.: Will the Violence Against Women Act affect police enforcement?

A.J.: The most important thing about the act is that it conceptualizes battering as a violation of civil rights. Whether it will ensure law enforcement depends upon what jurisdiction you're talking about and who is in charge—it depends on how rigorous a police chief is in monitoring officers and making them conform to public policy.

We still get reports from battered women who say they called the police and nothing happened. But you can also find police departments operating effectively, making arrests, and prosecutors following through.

We pin a lot on police, and say they should make arrests, but the police are quite right in saying that very often when they do, women don't press charges. The real culprit is the prosecutor. If the prosecutor's

> **"A man beats a woman because he *can* do it. He calls it love and so does everybody else."**

office is not going to follow through by prosecuting even without the woman's help—they can use 911 tapes, hospital records, proof of previous battery—why should the police arrest anybody? So we have to insist that the whole system work as a *system*. There are examples, like Duluth and San Diego, where the criminal justice system works as a system—it makes a difference not just in making women safe, but it probably saves the lives of batterers as well. It certainly saves the lives of innocent bystanders, and it certainly makes

---

WHAT ARE BATTERED WOMEN FOR?

The battered women's movement has organized for more than 15 years against "domestic violence," yet the violence continues. Could it be that individual women are to blame after all? Or could it be that battered women play some indispensable part, have some function, some role or social utility we haven't taken into account? Perhaps we should put a different question: What are battered women *for*?

This puts a new light on the problem: battered women are *for battering*. The battered woman is a woman who may be beaten. If you doubt that society views battered women as, by definition, "beatable," then how do you explain the fact that we almost always put responsibility for

woman-beating on the woman? Why else would we probe her psyche to reveal the secret self within, yearning for abuse, if not to set her apart as a *beatable* woman, unlike ourselves? There are millions of these beatable women. Many of them live within "the family," which entitles only the "head" of the family to beat them. Many others live outside "the family"—in which case anyone may beat them. Many live and work in industries that rent or sell beatable women and children—prostitution, for example, and pornography. A few beatable women, like Hedda Nussbaum, become public figures whom everyone can assail.

Battered women are to sexism what the poor are to capitalism—always with us.

They are a source of cheap labor and sexual service to those with the power to buy them, a "problem" for the righteous to lament, a topic to provide employment for academic researchers, a sponge to soak up the surplus violence of men, a conduit to carry off the political energy of other women who must care for them, an exemplum of what awaits all women who don't behave as prescribed, and a pariah group to amplify by contrast our good opinion of ourselves. And for all their social utility, they remain largely, and conveniently, invisible.

—From *Next Time, She'll Be Dead,*
by Ann Jones
(Beacon Press)

the job of the police easier. And it increases public respect for the police, because the police are suddenly doing an effective job.

G.J.: When we jail batterers, don't many come out and batter again?

A.J.: The evidence is that some men really learn a lesson, and they're deterred, while other men have thicker skulls, and these are the guys we should keep locking up.

G.J.: Is there hope for rehabilitation? In *Next Time, She'll Be Dead,* you talk about Duluth, Minnesota, where one activist estimates there is nearly a 60 percent recidivism rate among batterers.

A.J.: Researchers are beginning to examine the batterers. Now they have a theory that batterers suffer from frontal lobe damage. It's the same old crap. Nobody wants to admit that men do this because they like to. Other research claims there are two different kinds of batterers. One is impulsive and gets excited and loses his temper. They say you may be able to retrain some of those guys, using anger management. I don't believe that for a minute. And the other category is the cold, calculating batterer whose heart rate actually drops during an argument. The theory is that these heavy-duty guys are not responsive to therapy.

I think batterers should be given an opportunity to learn to think in a different way, but that's not like mental therapy. They need to be re-educated in terms of their values and their worldview. They need to learn that women are human beings and are not here simply to serve them. Perhaps you can persuade some of them to change their worldview, but until you do that, you can't make those guys stop. And if you can't make them stop, then these are the men who are candidates for three strikes and you're out [the policy of imprisoning people convicted of three felonies to terms from 20 years to life]. These are the people who cause serious damage to one person after another, or to large numbers of people at once.

FACT: Domestic violence causes almost 100,000 days of hospitalization, 30,000 emergency room visits, and 40,000 trips to the doctor every year.

G.J.: What if half of all men are batterers? Is this country ready to lock up many of its "upstanding citizens"?

A.J.: It's possible to look at the whole history of domestic violence in this country as one massive attempt to avoid that very thing. There's a new book out by some academic man who advocates "transcending the punitive response." But we have always transcended the punitive response. Let's face it, that's been our national policy.

In Duluth one in 20 male citizens of the metropolitan area have been through the batterers program at least once. That means that most of them were arrested to begin with. So if you could extrapolate from that nice midwestern community and see that as what might happen in other communities, it's a lot of guys. Some of those men will not re-offend. Others will. And then you have to arrest them and maybe lock them up this time and put them through the program again. You do that two or three times, and each time the punishment gets a little more severe, until either they get it or they get locked up indefinitely. If we were talking about any other crime, it would be clear to people that that's what we have to do. We must make people see this as a real crime and that what happens to women matters.

G.J.: Where do you start in educating boys that women are equal beings?

A.J.: Both boys and girls need to be taught about this. There should be a family violence curriculum in every grade school, starting the earlier the better, because so many children

come from homes where violence is going on, and so many are themselves victimized by violence. They should be told that this is not their fault. We should give those kids an opportunity to come forward and say what's happening to them in their homes. That kind of program should be carried on in the high schools, too—there are a lot of high schools now where peer education is going on. In Boston there is a program that's cosponsored by a men's counseling group and a women's group. Educating children and teenagers ought to help.

At the same time you have to look at the scary figures of violence against women in high schools and colleges, and the number of high school and college age boys who say that they get off on intimidating girls and who don't see anything wrong with doing that. [In 1993, for example, the American Association of University Women reported that 66 percent of high school boys admitted to being sexual harassers.]

You can educate young people, but guys also get an education from rock videos, and pornography, and our incredibly violent movies and television, and the constant depiction and identification of sex with violence, the depiction of women in demeaning and abusive situations. So lest they decide to emulate that kind of conduct, there also needs to be strong punishment from the start for kids who are violent.

G.J.: Let's talk about the shelters. What are the strengths and weaknesses of the shelter movement?

A.J.: Shelters were never meant to be permanent. They were always meant to be temporary. Unfortunately we need a lot more of them, because the problem is so great that they're turning away many women. They do save a great many lives. They give many women the breathing space to sort things out and get out, so they've been invaluable. But what they've really done is save the lives of *men*. The rate of women killing men has gone down, and its

FACT: If all women victimized by domestic violence in 1993 joined hands, the line would stretch from New York City to Los Angeles and beyond.

decline began with the advent of battered women's shelters. That's a very clear indication that if you give women a way to get out of these desperate life-and-death situations, they will get out.

But I'd like to see shelters put out of business. I think we ought to be working toward that. Maybe it's the men who should be put out of houses and locked up. The shelters are kind of reverse jails for women.

G.J.: How would we legislate getting the men out of the house so the women could stay there?

A.J.: That has been legislated in many places. Judges are empowered to evict men from the premises. But that means the men have to be arrested and brought to prosecution, and then the judge can evict them, issue stay-away orders, protective orders, and provide for child support.

G.J.: But then the men know where the women are, which would make many women feel like sitting ducks.

A.J.: That requires law enforcement to keep track of the situation and make sure that she's safe, and if she's not, then the guy needs to be locked up for a longer period of time.

G.J.: Often, we hear about women who were killed while they had a valid restraining order against their murderer. What do we need to do to make these orders effective?

A.J.: Again it requires changing the attitudes and procedures of police and prosecutors and judges so that they take the orders seriously. Very often what happens is that a woman gets a restraining order, a man violates it, and the police don't do anything about it. They say, "If he comes back again, let us know." It

should be police policy to seek out and arrest anyone who violates a restraining order, and that should be an unbailable offense, carrying an automatic jail sentence. If a batterer is sent to a reeducation program, it should be in addition to his jail term, not in lieu of it. He should serve real time, because any man who violates a restraining order poses a real danger.

But the attitude now is "Well, gee, we gave her a restraining order, it just made the guy mad. Maybe we shouldn't do that." If you were talking about any other crime you would see how ridiculous that is: "Stole your car? Well, we can't arrest him because he might get mad and steal somebody else's car."

G.J.: This brings up the response we got at *Ms.* to your article about women and guns. Women wrote in, saying: "I'm really frightened. There's someone out there aiming to get me. How can you say I shouldn't have a gun to protect myself? No one else will protect me." What do we tell women who feel the police won't help them?

A.J.: That's a good question. The alternative may be to go underground, and many women do that. Others don't, saying, "He'll find me anyway, and I can't live in that kind of fear." I wouldn't tell a woman in that situation that she shouldn't have a gun if that's what she feels she needs to defend herself. I would tell her to really learn how to use it. But I'm afraid that relying on the gun to save you may not work. I got letters, too, from women who said that they managed to save themselves with a gun, and I think it's a terrible commentary on how we live now. I would suggest that women go underground, but I understand why many women don't.

G.J.: What about this notion of the battered woman syndrome, which says that battered women have been so abused that they're incapable of resistance?

A.J.: I don't think there is a battered woman syndrome. I would call it

post-traumatic stress disorder. What happens is not peculiar to battered women. If you get beaten up enough and if your freedom of movement and autonomy are stripped from you bit by bit, you begin to suffer from post-traumatic stress disorder. The psychiatrist Judith Herman writes in her book *Trauma and Recovery* that there really ought to be a more intense category of post-traumatic stress disorder for battered women, hostages, and prisoners of war, because what happens to them is more prolonged and in many ways worse than a single traumatic event.

But this is not a preexisting condition in women's psychological makeup. People somehow see the battered woman syndrome as a cause of why women get battered—they say, "They have low self-esteem and that's why they get battered." That's nonsense, just nonsense. What happens is often the women resist and the men intensify the violence. If the women get stuck and can't get out of there for one reason or another—usually if they're scared—then they can begin to suffer from post-traumatic stress disorder. It's a consequence of severe and prolonged battery; it's not something women are naturally afflicted with.

G.J.: So what should we teach girls?

A.J.: I think we need to talk about love and romance, what I like to call "true luv," spelled l-u-v, the incredible romantic myth that all girls are subjected to from many sources. The problem is that so much of men's controlling behavior is absolutely synonymous with what is described as signs of love in the "true luv" kinds of literature. All that possessiveness and jealousy and wanting to monopolize your time: "I love you more than anybody ever did, and I want to take care of you," and all that la-di-da stuff—all the stuff that girls are taught to think of as signs of his devotion. We need to tell them: "Hey, those are danger signals. That's the stuff to watch out for."

Girls should be alert, and know that this guy is out to co-opt them.

G.J.: Let's go on to the media. I saw a clipping that said women were reporting that men are saying to them, "I will O.J. you, if you don't watch out." This has become a phrase for abuse and aggression, and the paper put this information in a column of various cute anecdotes rather than taking it seriously.

A.J.: After many highly publicized cases we get reports from local battered women's shelters that men are showing the newspaper headlines to their wives, saying, "Look what happened to her, she didn't do what she should have." That's standard, to use such cases to intimidate women.

And sometimes after a prominent homicide, you find women leaving shelters and going back to their abusers because they feel safer. If they're away from him, they think he'll come after them and kill them.

G.J.: The media often trivialize these stories, talking of "love gone awry."

A.J.: They tend to report the men's point of view. Some of the men who work with batterers have called attention to the fact that the news media and the academics just buy what the batterers tell them. Here's *Time* magazine from the week of July 4 reporting on the relationships that end in murder: it describes a "predictable progression that typically begins either with a steady diet of battery or isolated incidents of violence that can go on for years." You notice it doesn't specify who's doing this steady diet of battering. "Often, the drama is fueled by both parties," all right? "A man wages an assault. The woman retaliates by deliberately trying to provoke his jealousy or anger. He strikes again. And the cycle repeats." Here's a new kind of cycle of violence: he hits her, she provokes him deliberately, and he hits her again, and that's called a cycle. "The two are locked in a sick battle that binds—and reassures—even as it divides." This is hogwash! This is the worst kind of victim-blaming! Where do they get this

---

WORKING FOR CHANGE

In Little Rock, Arkansas, the Women's Watchcare Network (WWN) uses a group of more than 200 volunteers statewide to collect data on violence. Every year, WWN tracks murders of women—especially those related to domestic violence. (It also monitors racist and homophobic violence, incidents of police brutality, and the activities of the Ku Klux Klan and the religious right.) This information is compiled annually in the "Women's Watchcare Log," which is made available to the public. It lists victims' names and ages and the precise nature of the crime when available. Started in 1989, Watchcare is run by the Women's Project of Little Rock, which also publishes a newsletter and holds workshops, conferences, and outreach programs for women in prison.

---

shit? From talking to batterers who say, "I hit her and then she deliberately defied me until I had to hit her again." They would not get this story from a woman.

This is a deliberate misinterpretation of what some women might say; battered women will sometimes say that they knew a beating was coming so they tried to provoke him at a certain time when they thought they could control it. That does happen, but it's a desperate way of trying to cope with the situation. It's not "locked in a sick battle," it's a last-ditch effort to try to maintain some kind of control over a situation that you can't escape from. And some women are so conditioned to think they did something wrong to "cause" an attack that they report it that way. What everyone—like *Time*—forgets is that provocation is not a crime. Battering is.

And the other piece of this is the man who says he beats or murders a woman because he loves her so much. That's what these guys always say. That is not love. Yet reporters accept that language without criticism. They continue to call these cases crimes of passion.

That just has to stop, but again, it's part of the way we bend over backward *not* to look at what's going on. Men are trying to take over the lives of women, trying to control women. A man does that because he *can* do it, it's not that hard to do; it works, it gets him what he wants; nobody stops him. So why shouldn't he do it? And he calls that love, and everybody else calls that love, so there we are.

G.J.: The changes we need are huge. If you had to choose where to start, what would you say?

A.J.: It would be an immense change in the lives of women if we would just grasp the first principle—that women have a right to live free from harm. And keep in mind that bits and pieces of the picture have been changing for the last 20 years. Here and there, some community in this country is now doing a piece of it right. And other communities could copy them. Increasingly, people in one community or one state are starting to say, "Hey, look what's going on in Duluth. Or in San Diego. Or in Quincy, Massachusetts, in the prosecutor's office." So some of it is already happening. For every change we need to make, someone in the country not only already knows how to do it, but *is* doing it successfully.

The main thing is always to remember that women have a right to live free from harm. That's the thing that nobody talks about. We've talked all this time in terms of who the victims are, and how they behave, and how they ought to behave. We've psychologized the problem, as we always do in this country. We've seen it as a matter of personal psychology instead of the material conditions of people's lives.

G.J.: What about researchers who say male violence and aggression are innate, that this is what testosterone does and men just can't help it?

A.J.: Give me a break. There's always going to be some researcher saying biology is everything. Well, if that's what they think, that men can't help

FACT: Of the 35 women on death row in 1993, almost half were there for the murder of an abusive partner.

it, maybe the only answer left is to castrate them all.

G.J.: My last question is about the role of the bystander, the friend, or neighbor. What can we do to help? Should we be calling the police?

A.J.: First, about the police, I wish we could lay to rest this notion that domestic violence calls are so dangerous. The most dangerous calls for police are burglaries, robberies, and drug-related crimes. What probably causes the most trouble for police on these calls is that they don't know whether they're supposed to mediate or arrest or walk the guy around the block. A simple policy of mandatory arrest makes it much safer and easier for them.

The harder question is what the individual should do about it. The first thing to realize is that any woman in a situation of emotional or physical abuse has a much more complicated life than you can possibly understand. And it is very important that, as much as you are able, you let her know that you know or believe that she is being subjected to something that she doesn't have to put up with, that you value her, that you are afraid for her safety, that you stand ready to help her, in whatever way you are actually ready to help her. It's important not to intervene unless you're willing to put your body where your mouth is. You need to do some soul-searching before you take on intervention. And you can say, "I am afraid for my own safety in getting involved, but I

would like to give you this information about a place where you can talk to a counselor," or you can say, "I would like to help you do whatever it is you feel like you can do."

Probably the first thing you ought to do is research exactly what the situation is in your own community. Don't advise the woman to call the police unless you're pretty damn sure what the police are going to do. Don't get her into a situation that might make it worse for her. Do the homework, find out what goes on in your town, get what information you can and offer her that information. Call a shelter hotline or the prosecutor's office, or your state's domestic violence coalition, or NOW. Then realize that she might reject you, tell you it's not happening, get mad at you. The process of getting out of a situation like that sometimes takes a while. Any woman who's in a situation like that is bound to be confused, because it is very confusing to have a person beat you up, and then say he loves you. This is perhaps the single most confusing situation in the world. Offer support, but don't get mad at the woman if she doesn't take you up on it. Every one of us who has interviewed battered women over the years knows that every battered woman says, "Oh, I wish I could thank so-and-so. What they said made such a difference to me, even though I couldn't do anything about it at the time." So you can become part of the process of a woman liberating herself, although you may never know.

G.J.: And should we call the police?

A.J.: Yes, you should. But you should also go to the police yourself and ask what their policy is: Do they practice mandatory arrest? Or tell them you called because you could hear that your neighbor was being beaten up. Ask them exactly what they did about it: Was an arrest

made, and if not, why not? If they tell you she didn't want to press charges, then ask why she should have to press charges. Then you go to the prosecutor and ask what's going on, why they're not pressing charges against violent men, why they're discouraging the police from arresting violent men. And then when the prosecutor says the batterers are not going to get any kind of sentence anyway, then you go to the judge and you say, "What the fuck are you doing here? Why aren't you enforcing the law?" Then you enlist your friends, and you go to the newspapers with it.

And not to be too self-serving about this, but one thing that you can do for someone you suspect is being battered is give them *When Love Goes Wrong* by Susan Schechter and myself. The book shifts the attention from the usual self-help-book question of "Oh, what am I doing wrong, how can I change to make my husband change?" to ask the question "What is he getting out of doing that?" That helps a woman cut through so much confusion. It gives her a tool she can use to evaluate her situation and shift the questions that she's asking herself. Women tell us: "When I started looking at what he was getting out of this, it made it so clear that I changed my own mind about what to do."

The danger with the 12-step programs is they are the equivalent of external victim-blaming. They and the standard self-help books put the responsibility on the woman to change her behavior or character or to love her husband better, and none of that is what the issue is. The issue is always him. It's *his* problem, it's his crime. He's the one who's violating her fundamental rights. He's the one who has to stop and change.

Passion Kills

Louise Farr

Gayla Balfour has placed the photographs of her daughter Khristina carefully under thin plastic sheets in an album whose label promises a "lifetime guarantee." But there was no such guarantee for 17-year-old Khristy. After the photos of Khristy in a swimsuit and Khristy in a prom gown, there are pictures of flower-filled urns at her Houston memorial service, and of the sun setting on darkening waves when her ashes were scattered at sea.

On October 20, 1992, Khristy Balfour committed suicide, just a few days after a tearful breakup with her boyfriend of a year and a half, Patrick, 18. (His parents have asked that family members' real names not be used, to spare their son further anguish.) Patrick, handsome and dark-haired with a diamond stud in his ear, planned to become a police officer. Khristy was working hard to get As and Bs in the hope of becoming a teacher or a psychologist. Every morning before school, Khristy would pick Patrick up in the red Hyundai her mother, a real estate agent, had bought her. Patrick's house was just 20 minutes away, yet Khristy complained that she couldn't stand that he lived so far from her.

Often Khristy talked about the day they would marry. They'd live in a house with a picket fence, she said, and have two perfect children. Patrick's parents, who loved this smart, vibrant girl almost as much as their son did, had already contributed a set of black octagonal dishes to Khristy's hope chest.

Khristy's last weekend alive was homecoming. That night another girl criticized the new black dress Khristy was wearing—or so Khristy imagined. And she became convinced that Patrick was flirting with the same girl. In a burst of anger and jealousy, she told him she never wanted to see him again. She had done this before, and he'd been hurt. He had warned her the last time: Do it again, and I won't come back when you ask.

On Sunday Khristy drove to Patrick's house and dropped off possessions of his that she'd accumulated. Then she moped around her house, crying on and off. Trying to cheer her up, Gayla Balfour pointed out that there were other boys waiting in the wings.

But Khristy kept calling Patrick, saying she wanted him back. "I really wanted to go back with her, but I didn't want to play that game," Patrick says. And when Khristy threatened to kill herself, he didn't believe her. He says he spoke to Khristy's sister, Cyndie, then 20, and warned her: "Watch Khristy. She's talking crazy." Cyndie denies getting such a warning.

The Monday after the breakup, Khristy skipped school, embarrassed, her grandmother thinks, to face her friends. The Balfours say she seemed better. She was laughing and rough-housing with Cyndie, and she planned a shopping trip and an outing to a country club.

But Patrick's mother, Carol, says a hysterical Khristy called Patrick repeatedly that evening. He asked his mother's advice, but Carol was busy with people she had over for a work project. She still regrets that she didn't talk to Khristy directly to try to calm her down.

That night Khristy cleaned her room, took a bath, and arranged pictures of Patrick and her family on her dresser. At some point, she took the loaded .38 her mother kept on top of the refrigerator for protection and carried it to her room. She climbed into bed, drew the covers up to her chin, and at about five-thirty Tuesday morning held the revolver to her temple and pulled the trigger.

Gayla and her mother, Mary Ann, were in the kitchen making coffee when the shot startled them. Thinking it came from outside, Mary Ann pushed the panic button on the house alarm system. Cyndie, awakened by the noise, smelled gunpowder and ran across the hallway to her sister's room. Blood soaked the pale blue bedcovers and splattered the walls and floor. Cyndie started to scream, then raced to the bathroom to throw up. Their brother, 7-year-old Glen, slept on, peacefully unaware.

While Mary Ann frantically began to administer CPR, Gayla raced to a neighbor's to call an ambulance (activating the alarm had momentarily tied up the phone line). Then she called Patrick to urge him to go to the hospital. Maybe the sound of his voice would help keep Khristy alive, Gayla told him, hearing his anguished cry of "No!" as he tried to absorb the news.

The sky was still dark that cold, crisp morning when the police call went out for a medical helicopter. By the time technicians put Khristy's limp figure on board, her heart was barely beating. She was pronounced dead on arrival at the hospital. When Patrick was told, he punched a wall, breaking two fingers.

"They say it gets better as time goes on," Gayla says. "It doesn't. When you step in a puddle of warm blood and it's your daughter's . . . the grieving, the why did it happen? . . . It takes your skin off. People need to know that with kids, broken hearts can kill."

Ever since Romeo and Juliet, the notion of young lovers passionate enough to die for each other has been romanticized. And it's well known that adolescence is a time of extremes. During that confusing evolution from child to adult, teenagers die a dozen metaphorical deaths a day: over their hair, or grades, or allegiances to rock stars. They're often warring with their parents, worrying over their futures, navigating cliques, and—amid furtive phone calls, slammed doors, and declarations of "forever"—learning how and whom to love.

Some teenagers can't imagine that their pain will pass and life will go on. "They think, If I don't want to die, then I was never really in love. I was a fraud."

Most handle the joy and misery and emerge safely on the other side of maturity. But when love falters, some children refuse to let go, and passion turns to obsession. In a 1993 study of 67 adolescent suicides by the Western Psychiatric Institute and Clinic of the University of Pittsburgh, 40 percent had suffered a breakup, twice as high as reported in a control group of nonsuicidal teens. Girls attempt suicide at about triple the rate of boys—although boys' attempts are more often successful. Boys, on the other hand, may turn their rage outward and strike out at others.

Whatever the destructive urge, these young people can't imagine that their pain will pass and life will go on. "Part of their immaturity is that they feel if they don't follow through with the intensity of their feelings, they're being insincere," says Mark De Antonio, M.D., director of the inpatient adolescent psychiatric unit at the University of California at Los Angeles. "They think, If I don't want to die, then I was never really in love, I was a fraud."

When kids become sexually active, the stakes are raised. "Sometimes the feelings are too intense for teens to work through, so when something goes wrong, it really feels like the end of the world," says Dr. De Antonio.

But experts caution that although a broken romance may trigger violence, it's rarely the only cause. "Teens already standing on the edge are particularly sensitive to relationship losses," says Washington D.C. psychologist Alan L. Berman, Ph.D., past president of the American Association of Suicidology. An early trauma can render a teenager vulnerable: One parent leaves or dies and the other is too depressed to take up the emotional slack; a setback at school leads to a loss of self-esteem; an idolized older sibling leaves home. Such cumulative early wounds to a child's ability to trust can make him or her emotionally dependent, leading the child to pour too much into and expect too much out of—relationships. When a romance then crumbles, the child, hypersensitive to rejection, may find the grief too much to bear.

After Khristy's death, the local media left the distorted impression that Khristy's problems erupted fully formed over the weekend her relationship ended. In reality, her troubles had built up over a lifetime.

"Her relationship with Patrick was her redemption for the life we'd led," says Cyndie Balfour, referring to the turmoil of the sisters' early years. At 15, Gayla Balfour dropped out of high school to marry her step-brother, David. She left him—and the small Texas town in which they had been living—when Khristy was 5 and Cyndie 8. Khristy lost not just her father but a large extended family. In Khristy's lifetime her mother married four more times, and the children changed schools and homes depending on where their stepfather lived.

"I'd rather switch than fight," Gayla, 39, admits about her marriages (she's now on her sixth). But she quickly dismisses the suggestion that they caused Khristy's insecurity. The children knew, she says, that they were more important than their stepfathers.

Khristy's father, David, thinks his younger daughter was the black sheep in the shadow of perfect, blond Cyndie, who seemed to do everything well without trying. He and others also characterize Khristy as a Cinderella figure, always housecleaning and babysitting her younger brother. (Gayla counters that she paid Khristy to do these chores.) "This wasn't all based on Patrick," David Balfour charges. "It was based on a broken relationship with her mother."

Khristy clearly had an abysmal self-image. At nearly five feet eight and a perfect size six, she was convinced she was overweight. She also despised her long, elegant nose. Gayla, who'd had hers fixed, promised her daughter a new one for graduation. She took Khristy twice to a psychologist to discuss her unhappiness, and he judged her problems as normal teen insecurity.

There were secrets, too. Long before she succeeded in killing herself, Khristy, despondent over another boy, tried to overdose on aspirin, her cousin Stephanie says. Another time, Khristy later confided to Stephanie, she took a straight pin to her wrists, then lost her nerve. Gayla says she learned of these attempts from her daughter's friends only after Khristy's death.

Patrick's mother remembers many weepy phone calls from Khristy during the time the girl dated her son. She would have to reassure Khristy that Patrick wasn't flirting with other girls and that he really did love her. The calls didn't alarm Patrick's mother; they reminded her of her own adolescent dramas. "If everybody killed themselves over a broken heart, we'd all be dead," she says.

Sometimes when young passion turns to obsession, only a gossamer line separates killing oneself from killing a rival. When it came to their 16-year-old son, Brian, Arthur and Rita Tate knew enough to worry about suicide, but they never thought of homicide.

The Tates live on Maryland's Broadneck Peninsula in a columned house on a large wooded lot. Arthur Tate owns his own construction company and Rita is a technical writer. They have three children, the oldest of whom is Brian—handsome, six feet tall, and once a star of his high school football team.

In February 1992 Brian was dating a pretty, brownhaired girl who sent him a Valentine's Day card expressing what Rita Tate describes as "undying love." Less than a week later, the girl broke up with him over the phone and began dating Jerry Haines, 19. "Brian thought she had really cared for him," says his mother. He was devastated.

Jerry was the youngest of four boys his mother, Jacqueline, struggled to raise alone after a divorce. He had dropped out of high school to become a plumber's apprentice. At just five feet tall, he looked 14, but his charisma made him a pint-size ladies' man..

In the week after the breakup, Brian began stalking the new couple. He would cruise by them in his car and shout threats from the window. "Mom, this boy's crazy," Jerry told his mother. Jacqueline was worried, but Jerry insisted he could handle Brian himself. When Jerry bumped into a police officer he knew, he asked for advice. Maryland had no stalking laws, the cop told him, so authorities could do nothing unless Brian acted.

Later Jerry confided to his brother Michael that Brian had threatened to slice his throat. But since Brian was a minor, Jerry worried he'd get into trouble with the police if he hit Brian first.

That week Brian paced around the house. He had nothing to live for, he told his worried mother. The Tates claim they stayed home during the weekend that followed, hovering over Brian in what they characterize as a suicide watch. "We just sat on him, kept talking to him," says Rita Tate. They also put in two calls to a therapist, who never called them back.

By Monday, February 24, Brian's dark mood seemed to have lifted. He went to school, brought home an A on his geometry test, then went out with a friend to buy school supplies. But by ten o'clock, when he wasn't home, the Tates drove out to search. If they had driven to Jerry Haines's house an hour later, they would have found Brian pummeling Jerry with brass knuckles and stabbing him 24 times as Jerry begged for his life. Police, alerted by a neighbor who'd been awakened by the commotion, found Jerry's body under a pile of leaves. When they roused Jacqueline Haines, asleep for hours with a flu, she wandered barefoot out of her small duplex into the brilliance of crime-scene arc lights. Her son's body lay in the cold rain, his red baseball cap and asthma inhaler on the ground nearby. Jacqueline gave the police Brian Tate's name. "He's the only enemy my son ever had," she said. Brian was arrested the next day.

Rita Tate had noticed that her son had started to change six months earlier. He'd been his team's quarterback but was benched for poor team spirit. His grades had slipped and he began picking fights.

Then, late in 1991, Brian had trouble with a girlfriend who also began dating someone new. When that boy's house burned down, the fire was ruled an accident but—unbeknownst to his parents—Brian bragged to friends that he had set the blaze.

The Tates had taken their son to a therapist, who declared him "a typical teenager. They should clamp down and use a "tough-love" approach, was his only suggestion. "You trust people in these positions to know what they're doing," says Rita Tate. She and her husband took Brian out of his public school and enrolled him in a Catholic boys' school.

Rita Tate does not believe her son killed for love. The murder "was about his inability to deal with his life falling apart." she says. Defense psychiatrists claim that Brian suffered from a number of personality disorders. But according to the state's prosecutor, Brian's biggest defect was a narcissistic personality. Brian Tate pleaded guilty to first-degree murder and last year was sentenced to life in prison at Maryland's maximum security Patuxent Institution.

Most acts of violence remain partial mysteries, the full answers locked forever in the minds of those who commit them. But researchers are probing deeper by conducting "psychological autopsies," in-depth interviews with "survivors" such as relatives, friends, and teachers. Interviews reveal layer after layer of pain in what are often troubled families. And though it's easier for survivors to move on with their lives if they can settle on one reason for the violence, experts say there is never a single explanation.

Increasingly, researchers are looking to biology to unlock the mysteries of violence. Scientists at the National Institutes of Health have linked low levels of serotonin (a brain chemical that regulates emotion and impulses) to depression, aggression, and suicide. Scientists have also discovered that there is more depressive and manic-depressive illness in the families of those who try to take their own lives. And suicide is known to run in families: According to Gayla Balfour, both she and Khristy's maternal grandfather made unsuccessful attempts to kill themselves.

Even if a teenager is not suicidal or homicidal, obsession with a lover can still lead to violence. One classic scenario is the "good girl" attracted to the "bad boy." Raised on romantic images of surly, leather-jacketed movie idols who soften with the love of the right woman, girls can be lured by a boy's rebel status and their own fantasies of taming him.

That was the case with Jamie Michelle Faris. At 16, she was the cherished only child of hardworking, financially comfortable parents in the bucolic northern California town of Lakeport. Beautiful and smart, with long, dark hair, she earned straight As and worked part-time in a restaurant to pay for her new red Geo Storm. She wanted to be an artist and was in line to receive a summer internship through Oakland's College of Arts and Crafts.

"Khristy wanted so much just to be happy," her cousin laments. "If only she could have realized that things could change."

In the spring of 1991, Jamie showed her art teacher, Sue de Mille, some drawings of a young man she said she was in love with, Roy Corbett. He had a few problems, she told de Mille,

What Makes A Child Violent?

It isn't always easy to know. Like adults, teenagers newly in love spend a lot of time alone together and see less of their friends, And experts say it isn't unusual for adolescents to he drawn to themes of death, paradoxically because of their feelings of invulnerability, but also because they're emerging from the safety of childhood and sensing the dangers of the adult world, Writing morbid poetry or worshiping suicidal pop icons needn't worry parents, either, as long as teens seem otherwise healthy. But when sexually active teens isolate themselves from peers and lose interest in activities they previously enjoyed, they're more likely to fall to pieces when love goes wrong, says UCLA's Dr. De Antonio.

After a breakup, about one-third of all teens engage in mild stalking, such as driving past someone's house to see if the light's on or the car's there, says Michael L. Peck, Ph.D., executive director of the Institute for Suicide Prevention in Los Angeles. But they're over the line, he says, if they follow an ex around town or break into his or her locker or home.

Often, well-meaning parents try to offer reassurances. "A mother says to a girl, 'Don't worry. You'll get another boyfriend. You'll go to the prom next year,' " says Winifred Meyer, M.D., a Los Angeles forensic psychiatrist. But these comments belittle an adolescent's depth of feeling. Acknowledging the child's loss and pain is better than glossing over it.

Much has been written about suicide warning signs—insomnia, giving away possessions, talking only about death—but mental health experts say family members are often too close to see them, "Families possess a true blind spot," says David C. Clark, Ph.D., director of the Center for Suicide Prevention at Rush-Presbyterian-St Luke's Medical Center in Chicago. What's more, those oft-repeated signs may work when applied to adults, but adolescent behavior is different. Some teens may look like textbook cases and yet not be in trouble; others may give few classic indications. That's why parents need to be attentive to their own children's behavior and can't take their reassurances at face value, since teens are not reliable judges of their own state of mind.

Sometimes parents dismiss what their children are going through as puppy love or assume their kids are more worldly than they really are. But even when teens appear to he tuning you out or are openly hostile to your counsel, says Dr. De Antonio, your show of support is invaluable. If your child's unwilling or too uncomfortable to talk to you, make sure he or she gets guidance from another responsible relative, a pediatrician, or a mental health professional.

And don't wait until the eleventh hour to get help. Many at-risk kids exhibit antisocial behaviors (running away from home, picking fights, setting fires, abusing drugs or alcohol). A long history of these can mean that a child may resort to violence next, and substance abuse makes it easier for a child to pull a trigger or swallow pills. If the therapist you pick assures you that all is well when you know it's not, consult a different therapist.

Many teenagers who threaten suicide or murder at the end of a romance can get through that stage with the right help. And those with a reasonable sense of self-esteem and a network of support are more likely to survive unscathed.

—L.F.

---

but she was going to change him. De Mille warned her: "If you find yourself wanting to change someone, it's time to find somebody else." But she worried the girl wouldn't listen to her. "I think for Jamie," de Mille says, "there was something exciting about the danger."

Roy, 15, was the stepson of a successful contractor. His out-of-control behavior had worried authorities from the time he was in elementary school. When Jamie met him, he was taking LSD and amphetamines, and was hanging out with a troublemaking crowd of bikers. Jamie's parents made it clear that Roy wasn't welcome at their house. But that didn't stop Jamie from seeing him.

"I like how he lives on the edge," Jamie confided to a friend. She started wearing a leather jacket, smoking marijuana, and sported a temporary tattoo of a skull on her left breast.

After a year, Roy left Jamie for another girl. Still, he kept Jamie dangling. He continued to call her. And Jamie, hoping for a reconciliation, tried to keep seeing him.

In May 1992 Roy invited her to visit him the next week at his friend Paul Hennis's grandparents' walnut ranch. Jamie was so excited that she talked all week to friends about the meeting.

When Jamie got to the ranch, Roy was waiting, but so were Paul and another boy. And there was no tender reunion. Instead, Roy attacked Jamie, crushing her skull with a baseball bat and strangling her with Paul's help.

"He told me he was tired of her," Paul Hennis told police. He and Roy were tried as adults, and this year they were found guilty of first degree murder. Both are serving a sentence of 25 years to life.

God rescue me." Khristy Balfour wrote to her cousin Stephanie shortly before she died. "All I'm thinking about is my future lately. . . . I'm really afraid I'll be a failure." Says Stephanie: "Khristy wanted so much to just be happy. If only she could have realized that things could change."

That's a message parents wish any teenager in pain would heed.

Beyond Betrayal: Life After

INFIDELITY

Frank Pittman III, M.D.

Hour after hour, day after day in my office I see men and women who have been screwing around. They lead secret lives, as they hide themselves from their marriages. They go through wrenching divorces, inflicting pain on their children and their children's children. Or they make desperate, tearful, sweaty efforts at holding on to the shreds of a life they've betrayed. They tell me they have gone through all of this for a quick thrill or a furtive moment of romance. Sometimes they tell me they don't remember making the decision that tore apart their life: "It just happened." Sometimes they don't even know they are being unfaithful. (I tell them: "If you don't know whether what you are doing is an infidelity or not, ask your spouse.") From the outside looking in, it is insane. How could anyone risk everything in life on the turn of a screw? Infidelity was not something people did much in my family, so I always found it strange and noteworthy when people did it in my practice. After almost 30 years of cleaning up the mess after other people's affairs, I wrote a book describing everything about infidelity I'd seen in my practice. The book was *Private Lies: Infidelity and the Betrayal of Intimacy* (Norton). I thought it might help. Even if the tragedy of AIDS and the humiliation of prominent politicians hadn't stopped it, surely people could not continue screwing around after reading about the absurd destructiveness of it. As you know, people have *not* stopped having affairs. But many of them feel the need

to write or call or drop by and talk to me about it. When I wrote *Private Lies,* I thought I knew everything there was to know about infidelity. But I know now that there is even more.

 CCIDENTAL INFIDELITY

All affairs are not alike. The thousands of affairs I've seen seem to fall into four broad categories. Most first affairs are cases of *accidental infidelity,* unintended and uncharacteristic acts of carelessness that really did "just happen." Someone will get drunk, will get caught up in the moment, will just be having a bad day. It can happen to anyone, though some people are more accident prone than others, and some situations are accident zones.

Many a young man has started his career as a philanderer quite accidentally when he is traveling out of town on a new job with a philandering boss who chooses one of a pair of women and expects the young fellow to entertain the other. The most startling dynamic behind accidental infidelity is misplaced politeness, the feeling that it would be rude to turn down a needy friend's sexual advances. In the debonair gallantry of the moment, the brazen discourtesy to the marriage partner is overlooked altogether.

Both men and women can slip up and have accidental affairs, though the most accident-prone are those who drink, those who travel, those who don't get asked much, those who don't feel very tightly married, those whose running buddies

screw around, and those who are afraid to run from a challenge. Most are men.

After an accidental infidelity, there is clearly the sense that one's life and marriage have changed. The choices are:

1. To decide that infidelity was a stupid thing to do, to confess it or not to do so, but to resolve to take better precautions in the future;

2. To decide you wouldn't have done such a thing unless your husband or wife had let you down, put the blame on your mate, and go home and pick your marriage to death;

3. To notice that lightning did not strike you dead, decide this would be a safe and inexpensive hobby to take up, and do it some more;

4. To decide that you would not have done such a thing if you were married to the right person, determine that this was "meant to be," and declare yourself in love with the stranger in the bed.

 OMANTIC INFIDELITY

Surely the craziest and most destructive form of infidelity is the temporary insanity of *falling in love.* You do this, not when you meet somebody wonderful (wonderful people don't screw around with married people) but when you are going through a crisis in your own life, can't continuing living your life, and aren't quite ready for suicide yet. An affair with someone grossly inappropriate—someone decades younger or older, someone dependent or dominating, someone with problems even bigger

 Reprinted with permission from *Psychology Today,* May/June 1993, pp. 32-38, 78, 80, 82. © 1993 by Sussex Publishers, Inc.

than your own—is so crazily stimulating that it's like a drug that can lift you out of your depression and enable you to feel things again. Of course, between moments of ecstasy, you are more depressed, increasingly alone and alienated in your life, and increasingly hooked on the affair partner. Ideal romance partners are damsels or "dumsels" in distress, people without a life but with a lot of problems, people with bad reality testing and little concern with understanding reality better.

Romantic affairs lead to a great many divorces, suicides, homicides, heart attacks, and strokes, but not to very many successful remarriages. No matter how many sacrifices you make to keep the love alive, no matter how many sacrifices your family and children make for this crazy relationship, it will gradually burn itself out when there is nothing more to sacrifice to it. Then you must face not only the wreckage of several lives, but the original depression from which the affair was an insane flight into escape.

People are most likely to get into these romantic affairs at the turning points of life: when their parents die or their children grow up; when they suffer health crises or are under pressure to give up an addiction; when they achieve an unexpected level of job success or job failure; or when their first child is born—any situation in which they must face a lot of reality and grow up. The better the marriage, the saner and more sensible the spouse, the more alienated the romantic is likely to feel. Romantic affairs happen in good marriages even more often than in bad ones.

Both genders seem equally capable of falling into the temporary insanity of romantic affairs, though women are more likely to reframe anything they do as having been done for love. Women in love are far more aware of what they are doing and what the dangers might be. Men in love can be extraordinarily incautious and willing to give up everything. Men in love lose their heads—at least for a while.

MARITAL ARRANGEMENTS

All marriages are imperfect, and probably a disappointment in one way or another, which is a piece of reality, not a license to mess around with the neighbors. There are some marriages that fail to provide a modicum of warmth, sex, sanity, companionship, money. There are awful marriages people can't get all the way into and can't get all the way out of, divorces people won't call off and can't go through,

Every marriage is a thick stew of emotions ranging from lust to disgust.

marriages that won't die and won't recover. Often people in such marriages make a *marital arrangement* by calling in marital aides to keep them company while they avoid living their life. Such practical affairs help them keep the marriage steady but distant. They thus encapsulate the marital deficiency, so the infidel can neither establish a life without the problems nor solve them. Affairs can wreck a good marriage, but can help stabilize a bad one.

People who get into marital arrangements are not necessarily the innocent victims of defective relationships. Some set out to keep their marriages defective and distant. I have seen men who have kept the same mistress through several marriages, arranging their marriages to serve some practical purpose while keeping their romance safely encapsulated elsewhere. The men considered it a victory over marriage; the exploited wives were outraged.

I encountered one woman who had long been involved with a married man. She got tired of waiting for him to get a divorce and married someone else. She didn't tell her husband about her affair, and she didn't tell her affairee about her marriage. She somehow thought they would never find out about one another. After a few exhausting and confusing weeks, the men met and confronted her. She cheerfully told them she loved them both and the arrangement seemed the sensible way to have her cake and eat it too. She couldn't understand why both the men felt cheated and deprived by her efforts to sacrifice their lives to satisfy her skittishness about total commitment.

Some of these arrangements can get quite complicated. One woman supported her house-husband and their kids by living as the mistress of an older married man, who spent his afternoons and weekend days with her and his evenings at home with his own children and his sexually boring wife. People averse to conflict might prefer such arrangements to therapy, or any other effort to actually solve the problems of the marriage.

Unhappily married people of either gender can establish marital arrangements to help them through the night. But men are more likely to focus on the practicality of the arrangement and diminish awareness of any threat to the stability of the marriage, while women are more likely to romanticize the arrangement and convince themselves it is leading toward an eventual union with the romantic partner. Networks of couples may spend their lives halfway through someone's divorce, usually with a guilt-ridden man reluctant to completely leave a marriage he has betrayed and even deserted, and a woman, no matter how hard she protests to the contrary, eternally hopeful for a wedding in the future.

Philandering

Philandering is a predominantly male activity. Philanderers take up infidelity as a hobby. Philanderers are likely to have a rigid and concrete concept of gender; they worship masculinity, and while they may be greatly attracted to women, they are mostly interested in having the woman affirm their masculinity. They don't really like women, and they certainly don't want an equal, intimate relationship with a member of the gender they insist is inferior, but far too powerful. They see women as dangerous, since women have the ability to assess a man's worth, to measure him and find him wanting, to determine whether he is man enough.

These men may or may not like sex, but they use it compulsively to affirm their masculinity and overcome both their homophobia and their fear of women. They can be cruel, abusive, and even violent to women who try to get control of them and stop the philandering they consider crucial to their masculinity. Their life is centered around displays of masculinity, however they define it, trying to impress women with their physical strength, competitive victories, seductive skills, mastery of all situations, power, wealth, and, if necessary, violence. Some of them are quite charming and have no trouble finding women eager to be abused by them.

Gay men can philander too, and the dynamics are the same for gay philanderers as for straight ones: the obvious avoidance of female sexual control, but also the preoccupation with masculinity and the use of rampant sexuality for both reassurance and the measurement of manhood. When men have paid such an enormous social and interpersonal price for their preferred sexuality, they are likely to wrap an enormous amount of their identity around their sexuality and express that sexuality extensively.

Philanderers may be the sons of philanderers, or they may have learned their ideas about marriage and gender from their ethnic group or inadvertently from their religion. Somewhere they have gotten the idea that their masculinity is their most valuable attribute and it requires them to protect themselves from coming under female control. These

guys may consider themselves quite principled and honorable, and they may follow the rules to the letter in their dealings with other men. But in their world women have no rights.

To men they may seem normal, but women experience them as narcissistic or even sociopathic. They think they are normal, that they are doing what every other real man would do if he weren't such a wimp. The notions of marital fidelity, of gender equality, of honesty and intimacy between husbands and wives seem quite

foreign from what they learned growing up. The gender equality of monogamy may not feel compatible to men steeped in patriarchal beliefs in men being gods and women being ribs. Monogamous sexuality is difficult for men who worship Madonnas for their sexlessness and berate Eves for their seductiveness.

Philanderers' sexuality is fueled by anger and fear, and while they may be considered "sex addicts" they are really "gender compulsives," desperately doing whatever they think will make them look

MYTHS OF INFIDELITY

The people who are running from bed to bed creating disasters for themselves and everyone else don't seem to know what they are doing. They just don't get it. But why should they? There is a mythology about infidelity that shows up in the popular press and even in the mental health literature that is guaranteed to mislead people and make dangerous situations even worse. Some of these myths are:

1. Everybody is unfaithful; it is normal, expectable behavior. Mozart, in his comic opera *Cosi Fan Tutti,* insisted that women all do it, but a far more common belief is that men all do it: "Higgamous, hoggamous, woman's monogamous; hoggamous, higgamous, man is polygamous." In Nora Ephron's movie, *Heartburn,* Meryl Streep's husband has left her for another woman. She turns to her father for solace, but he dismisses her complaint as the way of all male flesh: "If you want monogamy, marry a swan."

We don't know how many people are unfaithful; if people will lie to their own husband or wife, they surely aren't going to be honest with poll takers. We can guess that one-half of married men and one-third of married women have dropped their drawers away from home at least once. That's a lot of infidelity.

Still, most people are faithful most of the time. Without the expectation of fidelity, intimacy becomes awkward and marriage adversarial. People who expect their partner to betray them are likely to beat them to the draw, and to make both of them miserable in the meantime.

Most species of birds and animals in which the male serves some useful function other than sperm donation are inherently monogamous. Humans, like other nest builders, are monogamous by nature, but imperfectly so. We can be trained out of it, though even in polygamous and promiscuous cultures people show their

true colors when they fall blindly and crazily in love. And we have an escape clause: nature mercifully permits us to survive our mates and mate again. But if we slip up and take a new mate while the old mate is still alive, it is likely to destroy the pair bonding with our previous mate and create great instinctual disorientation—which is part of the tragedy of infidelity.

2. Affairs are good for you; an affair may even revive a dull marriage. Back at the height of the sexual revolution, the *Playboy* philosophy and its *Cosmopolitan* counterpart urged infidelity as a way to keep men manly, women womanly, and marriage vital. Lately, in such books as Annette Lawson's *Adultery* and Dalma Heyn's *The Erotic Silence of the American Wife,* women have been encouraged to act out their sexual fantasies as a blow for equal rights.

It is true that if an affair is blatant enough and if all hell breaks loose, the crisis of infidelity can shake up the most petrified marriage. Of course, any crisis can serve the same detonation function, and burning the house down might be a safer, cheaper, and more readily forgivable attention-getter.

However utopian the theories, the reality is that infidelity, whether it is furtive or blatant, will blow hell out of a marriage. In 30 odd years of practice, I have encountered only a handful of established first marriages that ended in divorce without someone being unfaithful, often with the infidelity kept secret throughout the divorce process and even for years afterwards. Infidelity is the *sine qua non* of divorce.

3. People have affairs because they aren't in love with their marriage partner. People tell me this, and they even remember it this way. But on closer examination it routinely turns out that the marriage was fine before the affair happened, and the decision that they were not in love

with their marriage partner was an effort to explain and justify the affair.

Being in love does not protect people from lust. Screwing around on your loved one is not a very loving thing to do, and it may be downright hostile. Every marriage is a thick stew of emotions ranging from lust to disgust, desperate love to homicidal rage. It would be idiotic to reduce such a wonderfully rich emotional diet to a question ("love me?" or "love me not?") so simplistic that it is best asked of the petals of daisies. Nonetheless, people do ask themselves such questions, and they answer them.

Falling out of love is no reason to betray your mate. If people are experiencing a deficiency in their ability to love their partner, it is not clear how something so hateful as betraying him or her would restore it.

4. People have affairs because they are oversexed. Affairs are about secrets. The infidelity is not necessarily in the sex, but in the dishonesty.

Swingers have sex openly, without dishonesty and therefore without betrayal (though with a lot of scary bugs.) More cautious infidels might have chaste but furtive lunches and secret telephone calls with ex-spouses or former affair partners—nothing to sate the sexual tension, but just enough to prevent a marital reconciliation or intimacy in the marriage.

Affairs generally involve sex, at least enough to create a secret that seals the conspiratorial alliance of the affair, and makes the relationship tense, dangerous, and thus exciting. Most affairs consist of a little bad sex and hours on the telephone. I once saw a case in which the couple had attempted sex once 30 years before and had limited the intimacy in their respective marriages while they maintained their sad, secret love with quiet lunches, pondering the crucial question of whether or not he had gotten it all the way in on that immortal autumn evening in 1958.

and feel most masculine. They put notches on their belts in hopes it will make their penises grow bigger. If they can get a woman to die for them, like opera composer Giacomo Puccini did in real life and in most of his operas, they feel like a real man.

Female Philanderers

There are female philanderers too, and they too are usually the daughters or ex-wives of philanderers. They are angry at

men, because they believe all men screw around as their father or ex-husband did. A female philanderer is not likely to stay married for very long, since that would require her to make peace with a man, and as a woman to carry more than her share of the burden of marriage. Marriage grounds people in reality rather than transporting them into fantasy, so marriage is too loving, too demanding, too realistic, and not romantic enough for them.

I hear stories of female philanderers, such as Maria Riva's description of her

mother, Marlene Dietrich. They appear to have insatiable sexual appetites but, on closer examination, they don't like sex much, they do like power over men, and underneath the philandering anger, they are plaintively seeking love.

Straying wives are rarely philanderers, but single women who mess around with married men are quite likely to be. Female philanderers prefer to raid other people's marriages, breaking up relationships, doing as much damage as possible, and then dancing off reaffirmed. Like male philanderers, female philanderers put their vic-

In general, monogamous couples have a lot more sex than the people who are screwing around.

5. Affairs are ultimately the fault of the cuckold. Patriarchal custom assumes that when a man screws around it must be because of his wife's aesthetic, sexual, or emotional deficiencies. She failed him in some way. And feminist theory has assured us that if a wife screws around it must be because men are such assholes. Many people believe that screwing around is a normal response to an imperfect marriage and is, by definition, the marriage partner's fault. Friends and relatives, bartenders, therapists, and hairdressers, often reveal their own gender prejudices and distrust of marriage, monogamy, intimacy, and honesty, when they encourage the infidel to put the blame on the cuckold rather than on him- or herself.

One trick for avoiding personal blame and responsibility is to blame the marriage itself (too early, too late, too soon after some event) or some unchangeable characteristic of the partner (too old, too tall, too ethnic, too smart, too experienced, too inexperienced.) This is both a cop-out and a dead end.

One marriage partner can make the other miserable, but can't make the other unfaithful. (The cuckold is usually not even there when the affair is taking place). Civilization and marriage require that people behave appropriately however they feel, and that they take full responsibility for their actions. "My wife drove me to it with her nagging"; "I can't help what I do because of what my father did to me"; "She came on to me and her skirt was very short"; "I must be a sex addict"; et cetera. Baloney! If people really can't control their sexual behavior, they should not be permitted to run around loose.

There is no point in holding the cuckold responsible for the infidel's sexual

behavior unless the cuckold has total control over the sexual equipment that has run off the road. Only the driver is responsible.

6. It is best to pretend not to know. There are people who avoid unpleasantness and would rather watch the house burn down than bother anyone by yelling "Fire!" Silence fuels the affair, which can thrive only in secrecy. Adulterous marriages begin their repair only when the secret is out in the open, and the infidel does not need to hide any longer. Of course, it also helps to end the affair.

A corollary is the belief that infidels must deny their affairs interminably and do all that is possible to drive cuckolds to such disorientation that they will doubt their own sanity rather than doubt their partner's fidelity. In actuality, the continued lying and denial is usually the most unforgivable aspect of the infidelity.

One man was in the habit of jogging each evening, but his wife noticed that his running clothes had stopped stinking. Suspicious, she followed him—to his secretary's apartment. She burst in and confronted her husband who was standing naked in the secretary's closet. She demanded: "What are you doing here?" He responded: "You do not see me here. You have gone crazy and are imagining this." She almost believed him, and remains to this day angrier about *that* than about the affair itself. Once an affair is known or even suspected, there is no safety in denial, but there is hope in admission.

I recently treated a woman whose physician husband divorced her 20 years ago after a few years of marriage, telling her that she had an odor that was making him sick, and he had developed an allergy to her. She felt so bad about herself she never remarried.

I suspected there was more to the story, and sent her back to ask him whether he had been unfaithful to her. He confessed that he had been, but had tried to shield

her from hurt by convincing her that he had been faithful and true but that she was repulsive. She feels much worse about him now, but much better about herself. She now feels free to date.

7. After an affair, divorce is inevitable. Essentially all first-time divorces occur in the wake of an affair. With therapy though, most adulterous marriages can be saved, and may even be stronger and more intimate than they were before the crisis. I have rarely seen a cuckold go all the way through with a divorce after a first affair that is now over. Of course, each subsequent affair lowers the odds drastically.

It doesn't happen the way it does in the movies. The indignant cuckold does scream and yell and carry on and threaten all manner of awful things—which should not be surprising since his or her life has just been torn asunder. But he or she quickly calms down and begins the effort to salvage the marriage, to pull the errant infidel from the arms of the dreaded affairee.

When a divorce occurs, it is because the infidel can not escape the affair in time or cannot face going back into a marriage in which he or she is now known and understood and can no longer pose as the chaste virgin or white knight spotless and beyond criticism. A recent *New Yorker* cartoon showed a forlorn man at a bar complaining: "My wife understands me."

Appropriate guilt is always helpful, though it must come from inside rather than from a raging, nasty spouse; anger is a lousy seduction technique for anyone except terminal weirdos. Guilt is good for you. Shame, however, makes people run away and hide.

The prognosis after an affair is not grim, and those who have strayed have not lost all their value. The sadder but wiser infidel may be both more careful and more grateful in the future.

tims through all of this just to give themselves a sense of gender power.

Spider Woman

There are women who, by nature romantics, don't quite want to escape their own life and die for love. Instead they'd rather have some guy wreck his life for them. These women have been so recently betrayed by unfaithful men that the wound is still raw and they are out for revenge. A woman who angrily pursues married men is a "spider woman"—she requires human sacrifice to restore her sense of power.

When she is sucking the blood from other people's marriages, she feels some relief from the pain of having her own marriage betrayed. She simply requires that a man love her enough to sacrifice his life for her. She may be particularly attracted to happy marriages, clearly envious of the woman whose husband is faithful and loving to her. Sometimes it isn't clear whether she wants to replace the happy wife or just make her miserable.

The women who are least squeamish and most likely to wreak havoc on other people's marriages are victims of some sort of abuse, so angry that they don't feel bound by the usual rules or obligations, so desperate that they cling to any source of security, and so miserable that they don't bother to think a bit of the end of it.

Josephine Hart's novel *Damage,* and the recent Louis Malle film version of it, describe such a woman. She seduces her fiancee's depressed father, and after the fiancee discovers the affair and kills himself, she waltzes off from the wreckage of all the lives. She explains that her father disappeared long ago, her mother had been married four or five times, and her brother committed suicide when she left his bed and began to date other boys. She described herself as damaged, and says, "Damaged people are dangerous. They know they can survive."

Bette was a spider woman. She came to see me only once, with her married affair partner Alvin, a man I had been seeing with his wife Agnes. But I kept up with her through the many people whose lives she touched. Bette's father had run off and left her and her mother when she was just a child, and her stepfather had exposed himself to her. Most recently Bette's man-

All marriages are imperfect, a disappointment in one way or another.

ic husband Burt had run off with a stripper, Claudia, and had briefly married her before he crashed and went into a psychiatric hospital.

While Burt was with Claudia, the enraged Bette promptly latched on to Alvin, a laid-back philanderer who had been married to Agnes for decades and had been screwing around casually most of that time. Bette was determined that Alvin was going to divorce Agnes and marry her, desert his children, and raise her now-fatherless kids. The normally cheerful Alvin, who had done a good job for a lifetime of pleasing every woman he met and avoiding getting trapped by any of them, couldn't seem to escape Bette, but he certainly had no desire to leave Agnes. He grew increasingly depressed and suicidal. He felt better after he told the long-suffering Agnes, but he still couldn't move in any direction. Over the next couple of years, Bette and Alvin took turns threatening suicide, while Agnes tended her garden, raised her children, ran her business, and waited for the increasingly disoriented and pathetic Alvin to come to his senses.

Agnes finally became sufficiently alarmed about her husband's deterioration that she decided the only way she could save his life was to divorce him. She did, and Alvin promptly dumped Bette. He could not forgive her for what she had made him do to dear, sweet Agnes. He lost no time in taking up with Darlene, with whom he had been flirting for some time, but who wouldn't go out with a married man. Agnes felt relief, and the comfort of a good settlement, but Bette was once again abandoned and desperate.

She called Alvin hourly, alternately threatening suicide, reciting erotic poetry, and offering to fix him dinner. She phoned bomb threats to Darlene's office. Bette called me to tell me what a sociopathic jerk

Alvin was to betray her with another woman after all she had done in helping him through his divorce. She wrote sisterly notes to Agnes, offering the comfort of friendship to help one another through the awful experience of being betrayed by this terrible man. At no point did Bette consider that she had done anything wrong. She was now, as she had been all her life, a victim of men, who not only use and abuse women, but won't lay down their lives to rescue them on cue.

Emotionally Retarded Men in Love

About the only people more dangerous than philandering men going through life with an open fly and romantic damsels going through life in perennial distress, are emotionally retarded men in love. When such men go through a difficult transition in life, they hunker down and ignore all emotions. Their brain chemistry gets depressed, but they don't know how to feel it as depression. Their loved ones try to keep from bothering them, try to keep things calm and serene—and isolate them further.

An emotionally retarded man may go for a time without feeling pleasure, pain, or anything else, until a strange woman jerks him back into awareness of something intense enough for him to feel it— perhaps sexual fireworks, or the boyish heroics of rescuing her, or perhaps just fascination with her constantly changing moods and never-ending emotional crises.

With her, he can pull out of his depression briefly, but he sinks back even deeper into it when he is not with her. He is getting addicted to her, but he doesn't know that. He only feels the absence of joy and love and life with his serenely cautious wife

Once an affair is known or even suspected, there's no safety in denial but there is hope in admission.

and kids, and the awareness of life with this new woman. It doesn't work for him to leave home to be with her, as she too would grow stale and irritating if she were around full time.

What he needs is not a crazier woman to sacrifice his life for, but treatment for his depression. However, since the best home remedies for depression are sex, exercise, joy, and triumph, the dangerous damsel may be providing one or more of them in a big enough dose to make him feel a lot better. He may feel pretty good until he gets the bill, and sees how much of his life and the lives of his loved ones this treatment is costing. Marriages that start this way, stepping over the bodies of loved ones as the giddy couple walks down the aisle, are not likely to last long.

Howard had been faithful to Harriett for 16 years. He had been happy with her. She made him feel loved, which no one else had ever tried to do. Howard devoted himself to doing the right thing. He always did what he was supposed to do and he never complained. In fact he said very little at all.

Howard worked at Harriett's father's store, a stylish and expensive men's clothiers. He had worked there in high school and returned after college. He'd never had another job. He had felt like a son to his father-in-law. But when the old man retired, he bypassed the stalwart, loyal Howard and made his own wastrel son manager.

Howard also took care of his own elderly parents who lived next door. His father died, and left a nice little estate to his mother, who then gave much of it to his younger brother, who had gotten into trouble with gambling and extravagance.

Howard felt betrayed, and sank into a depression. He talked of quitting his job and moving away. Harriett pointed out the impracticality of that for the kids. She reminded him of all the good qualities of his mother and her father.

Howard didn't bring it up again. Instead, he began to talk to Maxine, one of the tailors at the store, a tired middle-aged woman who shared Howard's disillusionment with the world. One day, Maxine called frightened because she smelled gas in her trailer and her third ex-husband had threatened to hurt her. She needed for Howard to come out and see if he could smell anything dangerous. He did, and somehow ended up in bed with Maxine. He felt in love. He knew it was crazy but he couldn't get along without her. He bailed her out of the frequent disasters in her life. They began to plot their getaway, which consumed his attention for months.

Harriett noticed the change in Howard, but thought he was just mourning his father's death. They continued to get along well, sex was as good as ever, and they enjoyed the same things they had always enjoyed. It was a shock to her when he told her he was moving out, that he didn't love her anymore, and that it had nothing whatever to do with Maxine, who would be leaving with him.

Harriett went into a rage and hit him. The children went berserk. The younger daughter cried inconsolably, the older one

Most affairs consist of a little bad sex and a lot of telephoning.

became bulimic, the son quit school and refused to leave his room. I saw the family a few times, but Howard would not turn back. He left with Maxine, and would not return my phone calls. The kids were carrying on so on the telephone, Howard stopped calling them for a few months, not wanting to upset them. Meanwhile he and Maxine, who had left her kids behind as well, borrowed some money from his mother and moved to the coast where they bought into a marina—the only thing they had in common was the pleasure of fishing.

A year later, Harriett and the kids were still in therapy but they were getting along pretty well without him. Harriett was running the clothing store. Howard decided he missed his children and invited them to go fishing with him and Maxine. It surprised him when they still refused to speak to him. He called me and complained to me that his depression was a great deal worse. The marina was doing badly. He and Maxine weren't getting along very well. He missed his children and cried a lot, and she told him his preoccupation with his children was a betrayal of her. He blamed Harriett for fussing at him when she found out about Maxine. He believed she turned the children against him. He couldn't understand why anyone would be mad with him; he couldn't help who he loves and who he doesn't love.

MEN AND WOMEN WHO CHEAT

Howard's failure to understand the complex emotional consequences of his affair is typically male, just as Bette's insistence that her affair partner live up to her romantic fantasies is typically female. Any gender-based generalization is both irritating and inaccurate, but some behaviors are typical. Men tend to attach too little significance to affairs, ignoring their horrifying power to disorient and disrupt lives, while women tend to attach too much significance, assuming that the emotions are so powerful they must be "real" and therefore concrete, permanent, and stable enough to risk a life for.

A man, especially a philandering man, may feel comfortable having sex with a woman if it is clear that he is not in love with her. Even when a man understands that a rule has been broken and he expects consequences of some sort, he routinely underestimates the extent and range and duration of the reactions to his betrayal. Men may agree that the sex is wrong, but may believe that the lying is a noble effort to protect the family. A man may reason that outside sex is wrong because there is a rule against it, without understanding that his lying establishes an adversarial relationship with his mate and is the greater offense. Men are often surprised at the intensity of their betrayed mate's anger, and then even more surprised when she is willing to take him back. Men rarely appreciate the devastating long-range impact of their infidelities, or even their divorces, on their children.

Routinely, a man will tell me that he assured himself that he loved his wife before he hopped into a strange bed, that the women there with him means nothing, that it is just a meaningless roll in the hay. A woman is more likely to tell me that at the sound of the zipper she quickly ascertained that she was not as much in love with her husband as she should have been, and the man there in bed with her was the true love of her life.

A woman seems likely to be less concerned with the letter of the law than with the emotional coherence of her life. It may be okay to screw a man if she "loves" him, whatever the status of his or her marriage, and it is certainly appropriate to lie to a man who believes he has a claim on you, but whom you don't love.

Women may be more concerned with the impact of their affairs on their children than they are with the effect on their mate, whom they have already devalued and discounted in anticipation of the affair. Of course, a woman is likely to feel the children would be in support of her affair, and thus may involve them in relaying her messages, keeping her secrets, and telling her lies. This can be mind-blowingly seductive and confusing to the kids. Sharing the secret of one parent's affair, and hiding it from the other parent, has essentially the same emotional impact as incest.

Some conventional wisdom about gender differences in infidelity is true.

More men than women do have affairs, but it seemed to me that before the AIDS epidemic, the rate for men was dropping (philandering has not been considered cute since the Kennedy's went out of power) and the rate for women was rising (women who assumed that all men were screwing around saw their own screwing around as a blow for equal rights.) In recent years, promiscuity seems suicidal so only the suicidal—that is, the romantics—are on the streets after dark.

Men are able to approach sex more casually than women, a factor not only of the patriarchal double standard but also of the difference between having genitals on the outside and having them on the inside. Getting laid for all the wrong reasons is a lot less dangerous than falling in love with all the wrong people.

Men who get caught screwing around are more likely to be honest about the sex than women. Men will confess the full sexual details, even if they are vague about the emotions. Women on the other hand will confess to total consuming love and suicidal desire to die with some man, while insisting no sex ever took place. I would believe that if I'd ever

seen a man describe the affair as so consumingly intense from the waist up and so chaste from the waist down. I assume these women are lying to me about what they know they did or did not do, while I assume that the men really are honest about the genital ups and downs—and honestly confused about the emotional ones.

Women are more likely to discuss their love affairs with their women friends. Philandering men may turn their sex lives into a spectator sport but romantic men tend to keep their love life private from their men friends, and often just withdraw from their friends during the romance.

On the other hand, women are not more romantic than men. Men in love are every bit as foolish and a lot more naive than women in love. They go crazier and risk more. They are far more likely to sacrifice or abandon their children to prove their love to some recent affairee. They are more likely to isolate themselves from everyone except their affair partner, and turn their thinking and feeling over to her, applying her romantic ways of thinking (or not thinking) to the dilemmas of his increasingly chaotic life.

Men are just as forgiving as women of their mates' affairs. They might claim ahead of time that they would never tolerate it, but when push comes to shove, cuckolded men are every bit as likely as cuckolded women to fight like tigers to hold on to a marriage that has been betrayed. Cuckolded men may react violently at first, though cuckolded women do so as well, and I've seen more cases of women who shot and wounded or killed errant

husbands. (The shootings occur not when the affair is stopped and confessed, but when it is continued and denied.)

Betrayed men, like betrayed women, hunker down and do whatever they have to do to hold their marriage together. A few men and women go into a rage and refuse to turn back, and then spend a lifetime nursing the narcissistic injury, but that unusual occurrence is no more common for men than for women. Marriage can survive either a husband's infidelity or a wife's, if it is stopped, brought into the open, and dealt with.

I have cleaned up from more affairs than a squad of motel chambermaids. Infidelity is a very messy hobby. It is not an effective way to find a new mate or a new life.

It is not a safe treatment for depression, boredom, imperfect marriage, or inadequate gender splendor. And it certainly does not impress the rest of us. It does not work for women any better than it does for men. It does excite the senses and the imaginations of those who merely hear the tales of lives and deaths for love, who melt at the sound of liebestods or country songs of love gone wrong.

I think I've gotten more from infidelity as an observer than all the participants I've seen. Infidelity is a spectator sport like shark feeding or bull fighting—that is, great for those innocent bystanders who are careful not to get their feet, or whatever, wet. For the greatest enjoyment of infidelity, I recommend you observe from a safe physical and emotional distance and avoid any suicidal impulse to become a participant.

Sex in America: Faithfulness in Marriage Is Overwhelming

Tamar Lewin

While several previous studies of sex in America have created a popular image of extramarital affairs, casual sex and rampant experimentation, an authoritative new study of American sexual practices—widely described as the most definitive ever—paints a much more subdued picture of marital fidelity, few partners and less exotic sexual practices.

In the new study, based on surveys of 3,432 men and women 18 to 59 years of age, 85 percent of married women and more than 75 percent of married men said they are faithful to their spouses. And married people have more sex than their single counterparts: 41 percent of all married couples have sex twice a week or more, compared with 23 percent of the singles.

But cohabiting singles have the most sex of all, with 56 percent reporting that they had sex twice a week or more.

"We have had the myth that everybody was out there having lots of sex of all kinds," said John H. Gagnon, a co-author of the study. "That's had two consequences. It has enraged the conservatives. And it has created anxiety and unhappiness among those who weren't having it, who thought, 'If I'm not getting any, I must be a defective person.'

"Good sense should have told us that most people don't have the time and energy to manage an affair, a job, a family and the Long Island Rail Road," said Mr. Gagnon, a sociology professor at the State University of New York at Stony Brook.

The study is considered important because it is one of the first to rely on a randomly selected nationally representative sample. Most previous sex studies—from the Kinsey reports in the 1940's and the Masters and Johnson study in the 1960's to more recent popularized studies—by, for example, Playboy magazine, the researcher Shere Hite and Redbook magazine—relied on information from volunteers, a method that may seriously skew the results, experts say, because those who are interested in sex and are most sexually active tend to participate.

"A lot of the people we approached initially said, 'Oh, you don't want to talk to me, I haven't had a partner in three years,' and those people wouldn't have taken part in previous studies, where self-selection decided who would fill out the questionnaires," said Edward O. Laumann, a sociology professor at the University of Chicago who is one of the coauthors of the study.

For an American man, the median number of sexual partners over a lifetime is six; for a woman, the me-

dian is two. But the range in the number of lifetime sexual partners varied enormously, with 26 percent reporting only one lifetime partner, while one man in the study reported 1,016 partners and one woman reported 1,009.

To one of the most politicized questions in human sexuality—how common is homosexuality—the study offers a fuzzy answer: It depends.

A subdued picture of few partners and less exotic sexual practices.

For many years, the conventional wisdom was that 1 in 10 Americans was homosexual, a number that came from a 1948 Kinsey report that 10 percent of the men surveyed had had exclusively homosexual relations for at least three years between the ages of 16 and 55. Many recent studies have debunked that figure, including a study last year finding that only 1 percent of the male population was homosexual.

In the new study, 2.8 percent of the men and 1.4 percent of the women identified themselves as homosexual or bisexual. But when the question is asked differently the numbers change.

About 9 percent of the men and 5 percent of the women reported having had at least one homosexual experience since puberty. Forty percent of the men who had a homosexual experience sometime in their life did so before they were 18, and not since. Most women, though, were 18 or older when they had their first homosexual experience.

And when asked whether having sex with someone of the same sex seemed appealing, 5.5 percent of the women said the idea was somewhat or very appealing. About 6 percent of the men said they were attracted to other men.

The survey also found that homosexuals cluster in large cities. More than 9 percent of the men in the 12 largest cities identified themselves as homosexual, compared with less than 4 percent of the men in the suburbs of those cities and only about 1 percent of the men in rural areas. Lesbians also tend to cluster in cities, but not to the same extent as gay men.

The study asked about many different sexual practices, but found that only three were appealing to more than a small fraction of heterosexual Americans.

The vast majority of heterosexual Americans said they included vaginal intercourse in almost every sexual encounter. Many people said that oral sex and watching a partner undress were also appealing, but men were substantially more likely to enjoy both practices than women.

Most men and women said they did not find such practices as anal intercourse, group sex or sex with strangers very appealing, but again, the men were more interested than the women.

Among the other findings were these:

• More than half the men said they thought about sex every day, or several times a day, compared with only 19 percent of the women.

• More than four in five Americans had only one sexual partner, or no partner, in the past year. Generally, blacks reported the most sexual partners, Asians the least.

• Three-quarters of the married women said they usually or always had an orgasm during sexual intercourse, compared with 62 percent of the single women. Among men, 95 percent said they usually or always had an orgasm, married or single.

• Less than 8 percent of the participants reported having sex more than four times a week. About two-thirds said they have sex "a few times a month" or less, and about 3 in 10 have sex a few times a year or less.

• Both men and women who, as children, had been sexually touched by an adult were more likely, as adults, to have more than 10 sex partners, to engage in group sex, to report a homosexual or bisexual identification and to be unhappy.

• About one man in four and one woman in 10 masturbates at least once a week, and masturbation is less common among those 18 to 24 years of age than among those who are 24 to 34.

• Among marriage partners, 93 percent are of the same race, 82 percent are of similar educational level, 78 percent are within five years of each other's age and 72 percent are the same religion.

To gather data for the study, conducted by the National Opinion Research Center at the University of Chicago, 220 researchers spent several months in 1992 conducting face-to-face interviews. Those who agreed to participate—almost four out of five of those contacted—were also given written forms to place in a sealed envelope, so that the oral answers to some of the most intrusive, potentially embarrassing questions could be checked against what they wrote privately.

"There were some differences, but it never amounted to much, percentage-wise," Professor Laumann said. "Of course, you can't be sure that everyone told the truth all the time, but most of the time our interviewers had the sense that people were being extremely candid."

The sex survey grew out of a 1987 attempt by the Federal Government to develop data on sexual practices that would help in the fight against AIDS. The authors got money from the Government to develop a methodology for such a survey, but Senator Jesse Helms, a North Carolina Republican, persuaded the Senate in 1991 to block the financing to carry out the survey. The authors then got money to continue their work from several private foundations.

Among the survey's important implications was the finding that more than a third of the younger women said that peer pressure had made them have sex for the first time, compared with only 13 percent of those from previous generations. The authors suggest, therefore, that one important part of preventing teen-age pregnancy is helping young women learn to resist peer pressure.

The survey results are being published in two forms, one a paperback book, "The Social Organization of Sexuality" (University of Chicago Press), written by Mr. Gagnon, Mr. Laumann, Robert T. Michael, dean of the graduate school of public policy studies at the University of Chicago, and Stuart Michaels, a researcher at the University of Chicago.

The other version is a general-interest hard cover book, "Sex in America: A Definitive Survey" (Little, Brown and Company), by Mr. Gagnon, Mr. Laumann, Mr. Michael and Gina Kolata, a science reporter for The New York Times.

The Myth of the Miserable Working Woman

She's Tired, She's Stressed Out, She's Unhealthy, She Can't Go Full Speed at Work or Home. Right? Wrong.

Rosalind C. Barnett and Caryl Rivers

Rosalind C. Barnett is a psychologist and a senior research associate at the Wellesley College Center for Research on Women. Caryl Rivers is a professor of journalism at Boston University and the author of More Joy Than Rage: Crossing Generations With the New Feminism.

"You Can't Do Everything," announced a 1989 USA Today *headline on a story suggesting that a slower career track for women might be a good idea. "Mommy Career Track Sets Off a Furor," declaimed the* New York Times *on March 8, 1989, reporting that women cost companies more than men. "Pressed for Success, Women Careerists Are Cheating Themselves," sighed a 1989 headline in the* Washington Post, *going on to cite a book about the "unhappy personal lives" of women graduates of the Harvard Business School. "Women Discovering They're at Risk for Heart Attacks," Gannett News Service reported with alarm in 1991. "Can Your Career Hurt Your Kids? Yes, Say Many Experts," blared a* Fortune *cover just last May, adding in a chirpy yet soothing fashion, "But smart parents—and flexible companies—won't let it happen."*

If you believe what you read, working women are in big trouble—stressed out, depressed, sick, risking an early death from heart attacks, and so overcome with problems at home that they make inefficient employees at work.

In fact, just the opposite is true. As a research psychologist whose career has focused on women and a journalist-critic who has studied the behavior of the media, we have extensively surveyed the latest data and research and concluded that the public is being engulfed by a tidal wave of disinformation that has

serious consequences for the life and health of every American woman. Since large numbers of women began moving into the work force in the 1970s, scores of studies on their emotional and physical health have painted a very clear picture: Paid employment provides substantial health *benefits* for women. These benefits cut across income and class lines; even women who are working because they have to—not because they want to—share in them.

There is a curious gap, however, between what these studies say and what is generally reported on television, radio, and in newspapers and magazines. The more the research shows work is good for women, the bleaker the media reports seem to become. Whether this bizarre state of affairs is the result of a backlash against women, as *Wall Street Journal* reporter Susan Faludi contends in her new book, *Backlash: The Undeclared War Against American Women,* or of well-meaning ignorance, the effect is the same: Both the shape of national policy and the lives of women are at risk.

Too often, legislation is written and policies are drafted not on the basis of the facts but on the basis of what those in power believe to be the facts. Even the much discussed *Workforce 2000* report, issued by the Department of Labor under the Reagan administration—hardly a hotbed of feminism—admitted that "most current policies were designed for a society in which men worked and women stayed home." If policies are skewed toward solutions that are aimed at reducing women's commitment to work, they will do more than harm women—they will damage companies, managers and the productivity of the American economy.

THE CORONARY THAT WASN'T

One reason the "bad news" about working women jumps to page one is that we're all too willing to believe it. Many adults today grew up at a time when soldiers were returning home from World War II and a way had to be found to get the women who replaced them in industry back into the kitchen. The result was a barrage of propaganda that turned at-home moms into saints and backyard barbecues and station wagons into cultural icons. Many of us still have that outdated postwar map inside our heads, and it leaves us more willing to believe the horror stories than the good news that paid employment is an emotional and medical plus.·

In the 19th century it was accepted medical dogma that women should not be educated because the brain and the ovaries could not develop at the same time. Today it's PMS, the wrong math genes or rampaging hormones. Hardly anyone points out the dire predictions that didn't come true.

You may remember the prediction that career women would start having more heart attacks, just like men. But the Framingham Heart Study—a federally funded cardiac project that has been studying 10,000 men and women since 1948—reveals that working women are not having more heart attacks. They're not dying any earlier, either. Not only are women not losing their health advantages; the lifespan gap is actually widening. Only one group of working women suffers more heart attacks than other women: those in low-paying clerical jobs with many demands on them and little control over their work pace, who also have several children and little or no support at home.

As for the recent publicity about women having more problems with heart disease, much of it skims over the important underlying reasons for the increase: namely, that by the time they have a heart attack, women tend to be a good deal older (an average of 67, six years older than the average age for men), and thus frailer, than males who have one. Also, statistics from the National Institutes of Health show that coronary symptoms are treated less aggressively in women—fewer coronary bypasses, for example. In addition, most heart research is done on men, so doctors do not know as much about the causes—and treatment—of heart disease in women. None of these factors have anything to do with work.

But doesn't working put women at greater risk for stress-related illnesses? No. Paid work is actually associated with *reduced* anxiety and depression. In the early 1980s we reported in our book, *Lifeprints* (based on a National Science Foundation–funded study of 300 women), that working women were significantly higher in psychological well-being than those not employed. Working gave them a sense of mastery and control that homemaking didn't provide. More recent studies echo our findings. For example:

• A 1989 report by psychologist Ingrid Waldron and sociologist Jerry Jacobs of Temple University on nationwide surveys of 2,392 white and 892 black women,

conducted from 1977 to 1982, found that women who held both work and family roles reported better physical and mental health than homemakers.

• According to sociologists Elaine Wethington of Cornell University and Ronald Kessler of the University of Michigan, data from three years (1985 to 1988) of a continuing federally funded study of 745 married women in Detroit "clearly suggests that employment benefits women emotionally." Women who increase their participation in the labor force report lower levels of psychological distress; those who lessen their commitment to work suffer from higher distress.

• A University of California at Berkeley study published in 1990 followed 140 women for 22 years. At age 43, those who were homemakers had more chronic conditions than the working women and seemed more disillusioned and frustrated. The working mothers were in good health and seemed to be juggling their roles with success.

In sum, paid work offers women heightened self-esteem and enhanced mental and physical health. It's unemployment that's a major risk factor for depression in women.

DOING IT ALL—AND DOING FINE

This isn't true only for affluent women in good jobs; working-class women share the benefits of work, according to psychologists Sandra Scarr and Deborah Phillips of the University of Virginia and Kathleen McCartney of the University of New Hampshire. In reviewing 80 studies on this subject, they reported that working-class women with children say they would not leave work even if they didn't need the money. Work offers not only income but adult companionship, social contact and a connection with the wider world that they cannot get at home.

Doing it all may be tough, but it doesn't wipe out the health benefits of working.

Looking at survey data from around the world, Scarr and Phillips wrote that the lives of mothers who work are not more stressful than the lives of those who are at home. So what about the second shift we've heard so much about? It certainly exists: In industrialized countries, researchers found, fathers work an average of 50 hours a week on the job and doing household chores; mothers work an average of 80 hours. Wethington and Kessler found that in daily "stress diaries" kept by husbands and wives, the women report more stress than the men do. But they also handle it better. In short, doing it all may be tough, but it doesn't wipe out the health benefits of working.

THE ADVANTAGES FOR FAMILIES

What about the kids? Many working parents feel they want more time with their kids, and they say so. But does maternal employment harm children? In 1989 University of Michigan psychologist Lois Hoffman reviewed 50 years of research and found that the expected negative effects never materialized. Most often, children of employed and unemployed mothers didn't differ on measures of child development. But children of both sexes with working mothers have a less sex-stereotyped view of the world because fathers in two-income families tend to do more child care.

However, when mothers work, the quality of non-parental child care is a legitimate worry. Scarr, Phillips and McCartney say there is "near consensus among developmental psychologists and early-childhood experts that child care per se does not constitute a risk factor in children's lives." What causes problems, they report, is poor-quality care and a troubled family life. The need for good child care in this country has been obvious for some time.

What's more, children in two-job families generally don't lose out on one-to-one time with their parents. New studies, such as S. L. Nock and P. W. Kingston's *Time with Children: The Impact of Couples' Work-Time Commitments,* show that when both parents of pre-schoolers are working, they spend as much time in direct interaction with their children as families in which only the fathers work. The difference is that working parents spend more time with their kids on weekends. When only the husband works, parents spend more leisure time with each other. There is a cost to two-income families—the couples lose personal time—but the kids don't seem to pay it.

One question we never used to ask is whether having a working mother could be *good* for children. Hoffman, reflecting on the finding that employed women—both blue-collar and professional—register higher life-satisfaction scores than housewives, thinks it can be. She cites studies involving infants and older children, showing that a mother's satisfaction with her employment status relates positively both to "the quality of the mother-child interaction and to various indexes of the child's adjustment and abilities." For example, psychologists J. Guidubaldi and B. K. Nastasi of Kent State University reported in a 1987 paper that a mother's satisfaction with her job was a good predictor of her child's positive adjustment in school.

Again, this isn't true only for women in high-status jobs. In a 1982 study of sources of stress for children in low-income families, psychologists Cynthia Longfellow and Deborah Belle of the Harvard University School of Education found that employed women were generally less depressed than unemployed women. What's more, their children had fewer behavioral problems.

But the real point about working women and children is that work *isn't* the point at all. There are good mothers and not-so-good mothers, and some work and some don't. When a National Academy of Sciences panel reviewed the previous 50 years of research and dozens of studies in 1982, it found no consistent effects on children from a mother's working. Work is only one of many variables, the panel concluded in *Families That Work,* and not the definitive one.

What is the effect of women's working on their marriages? Having a working wife can increase psychological stress for men, especially older men, who grew up in a world where it was not normal for a wife to work. But men's expectations that they will—and must—be the only provider may be changing. Wethington and Kessler found that a wife's employment could be a significant buffer *against* depression for men born after 1945. Still, the picture of men's psychological well-being is very mixed, and class and expectations clearly play a role. Faludi cites polls showing that young blue-collar men are especially angry at women for invading what they see as their turf as breadwinners, even though a woman with such a job could help protect her husband from economic hardship. But in highly educated, dual-career couples, both partners say the wife's career has enhanced the marriage.

THE FIRST SHIFT: WOMEN AT WORK

While women's own health and the well-being of their families aren't harmed by their working, what effect does this dual role have on their job performance? It's assumed that men can compartmentalize work and home lives but women will bring their home worries with them to work, making them distracted and inefficient employees.

Perhaps the most dangerous myth is that the solution is for women to drop back—or drop out.

The only spillover went in the other direction: The women brought their good feelings about their work home with them and left a bad day at home behind when they came to work. In fact, Wethington and Kessler found that it was the *men* who brought the family stresses with them to work. "Women are able to avoid bringing the contagion of home stress into the workplace," the researchers write, "whereas the inability of men to prevent this kind of contagion is pervasive." The researchers speculate that perhaps women get the message early on that they can handle the home front, while men are taking on chores they aren't trained for and didn't expect.

THE PERILS OF PART-TIME

Perhaps the most dangerous myth is that the solution to most problems women suffer is for them to drop back—or drop out. What studies actually show is a significant connection between a reduced commitment to work and increased psychological stress. In their Detroit study, Wethington and Kessler noted that women who went from being full-time employees to full-time housewives reported increased symptoms of distress, such as depression and anxiety attacks; the longer a woman worked and the more committed she was to the job, the greater her risk for psychological distress when she stopped.

What about part-time work, that oft-touted solution for weary women? Women who work fewer than 20 hours per week, it turns out, do not get the mental-health work benefit, probably because they "operate under the fiction that they can retain full responsibility for child care and home maintenance," wrote Wethington and Kessler. The result: Some part-timers wind up more stressed-out than women working full-time. Part-time employment also provides less money, fewer or no benefits and, often, less interesting work and a more arduous road to promotion.

That doesn't mean that a woman shouldn't cut down on her work hours or arrange a more flexible schedule. But it does mean she should be careful about jumping on a poorly designed mommy track that may make her a second-class citizen at work.

Many women think that when they have a baby, the best thing for their mental health would be to stay home. Wrong once more. According to Wethington and Kessler, having a baby does not increase psychological distress for working women—*unless* the birth results in their dropping out of the labor force. This doesn't mean that any woman who stays home to care for a child is going to be a wreck. But leaving the work force means opting out of the benefits of being in it, and women should be aware of that.

As soon as a woman has any kind of difficulty—emotional, family, medical—the knee-jerk reaction is to get her off the job. No such solution is offered to men, despite the very real correlation for men between job stress and heart attacks.

What the myth of the miserable working woman obscures is the need to focus on how the *quality* of a woman's job affects her health. Media stories warn of the alleged dangers of fast-track jobs. But our *Lifeprints* study found that married women in high-prestige jobs were highest in mental well-being; another study of life stress in women reported that married career women with children suffered the least from stress. Meanwhile, few media tears are shed for the women most at risk: those in the word-processing room who have no control at work, low pay and little support at home.

Women don't need help getting out of the work force; they need help staying in it. As long as much of the media continues to capitalize on national ignorance, that help will have to come from somewhere else. (Not that an occasional letter to the editor isn't useful.) Men need to recognize that they are not just occasional helpers but vital to the success of the family unit. The corporate culture has to be reshaped so that it doesn't run totally according to patterns set by the white male workaholic. This will be good for men *and* women. The government can guarantee parental leave and affordable, available child care. (It did so in the '40s, when women were needed in the factories.) Given that Congress couldn't even get a bill guaranteeing *unpaid* family leave passed last year, this may take some doing. But hey, this is an election year.

FAMILY, WORK, AND GENDER EQUALITY
A Policy Comparison of Scandinavia, the United States, and the Former Soviet Union

Elina Haavio-Mannila, Ph.D.
Department of Sociology, University of Helsinki, Finland

The workplace is not separate from other human institutions. Workers bring into the workplace their values and expectations from home, from the community and from the larger society that bear on their relationships and aspirations at work. They also take home from the workplace feelings of frustration or worth that affect their roles as parents, community members, and citizens. To view work in isolation from other role relationships is to remove it from the normative context that sustains it and gives it meaning.[1]

The sociology of family and gender roles has long tended to link work, the family, and even the community and state. As early as 1956 social scientists presented strategies by which women could combine their traditional family obligations with paid work. Today we recognize that women have many more than two roles, and the contemporary interface of family and work produces many a dilemma. Most women now see the challenge they face not in terms of becoming exactly like men in their work lives or returning to the domestic hearth but in terms of restructuring the family and work roles both for themselves and for men as well.[2]

This article will first compare public work policy among Scandinavia, the U.S., and the former Soviet Union. Traditional work policies focus on norms and standards for safety, occupational health, and working conditions. Labor-market policy also includes workers' participation in management and ownership, as well as rules for collective bargaining. Family policies are a part of all developed nations, designed to give economic support to families. Some countries emphasize cash child allowances, others emphasize tax reductions. Family support -- with the exception of maternity insurance -- does not affect the labor market or the bargaining power of workers.

Background: Comparison of Work Policies
In the United States, large firms provide services that mirror those of government services. For instance, businesses have a social service component to deal with is-

sues of alcoholism, drug abuse, and family needs; a justice component to address issues of equal opportunity; and an educational component to provide training.[3] Nevertheless, only a minuscule proportion of even the large firms have made determined efforts to reform their internal structure to better accommodate workers' needs. Rosabeth Moss Kanter suggests that the "new workplace" is less hierarchical, more egalitarian, and more conducive to the freedom that the new work force seeks.[4] This means bureaucratic control: a system of labor control that weakens bonds of solidarity among workers. In the U.S. auto industry, for instance, men and women who run the factories and staff the offices are said to do surprisingly well in the global competitiveness race — but only when managers give them a chance.[5] At General Motors and Ford, the companies for which we conducted research in 1988, the organization is said to be more authoritarian and patriarchal than in some newer branches of U.S. industry, like computer manufacturing, for example.

Scandinavia has been a forerunner in industrial democracy, management-worker cooperation, and work-safety research and policy. Discussions of the democratization of work life entered the political arena in Scandinavian countries around 1960, and since then many changes have been made.[6] Many Scandinavian organizations assumed new experimental forms with researchers, trade unions, and cooperative employers' organizations working together to bring about change. The Scandinavian countries revised work-safety laws in the 1970s, allowing the state to establish norms, supervise and sanction employer compliance through, for example, occupational inspections. Those inspections rely heavily on medical, chemical, and technical expertise. Since the 1980s, laws dealing with worker/management cooperation and workers' influence on decision making have guaranteed a degree of industrial democracy in all Nordic countries. Dialogue among partners in the labor market is encouraged, even to the point that the state intervenes as a third party in wage and fringe-benefit negotiations. It is considered important for work policy to encourage innovative organi-

Reprinted with permission from the *SIECUS Report*, August/September 1993, pp. 1-5. © 1993 by the Sexuality Information and Education Council of the United States, Inc., 130 West 42nd Street, Suite 350, New York, NY 10036.

zational arrangements and to avoid polarization of work conditions and tasks.

Occupational health -- the prevention and treatment of occupational diseases and accidents -- is a major work-policy issue in Nordic countries. Recently, quality of work, the environment at work, and human relations in the work community have also become concerns of workers' health policy.[7] Work is an important part of the quality of life. A healthy, safe, and comfortable work environment which promotes motivating, meaningful work is believed to promote the health of workers, better productivity, and a higher quality product.

In the Nordic countries, there is at present a trend toward less governmental control of work life. This means that both public and private employers have an increasing "freedom of responsibility" in the development of working conditions. An additional goal of recent Finnish work policy is to increase self-initiation in work organizations.[8]

In the former Soviet Union, state control of individuals was strict. During the politically shaky, economically difficult, and inflationary last years of Communist rule, social policy could not guarantee reasonable welfare to pensioners, the ill, the handicapped, and many other groups in need of social services.

Family Policy in the United States
The United States is unique in its reluctance to address the issues of family roles and women's and men's work in the policy arena. European countries provide support to families, parents, and women in the form of children's allowances, paid parental leaves of absence, and maternity benefits. The United States, while paying lip service to the importance of families and children, has no comprehensive family policy and has been notably disinclined to pay the costs of government benefits and services for families, for working parents, and for women.[9]

Child allowances and tax reductions, which exist in the United States, are only a small part of family policy. Otherwise, the official infrastructure of the country does not encourage people to have and rear children.[10] Working hours are long;[11] paid parental leave is short, if paid at all. Only a portion of employers offer job guarantees for parents staying home without pay to care for a baby, the quality of municipal day-care centers varies (when such facilities are available), and high-quality private child care is expensive.

Some employers have privately developed measures to make the workplace more responsible to the needs of employees. Major companies are providing modest paid disability benefits at the time of pregnancy and childbirth, and some allow female employees brief additional unpaid but job-protected leaves. The 1970s saw a rapid expansion in the establishment of flex-time policies, but the trend has since slowed. Part-time work, in contrast, is growing, as is temporary work. The number of counseling services in the workplace has increased, and that expansion seems likely to continue. Childcare remains the family-related service most discussed in the workplace in the United States.

For years, a dramatic difference in vacation time between many European countries and the United States has existed. In Scandinavia, for instance, most employees have an annual paid vacation of five to six weeks. Further, daily work hours are considerably shorter than in the United States.

It is puzzling that, in the United States, women have high labor-force participation rates despite no benefit legislation, highly uneven coverage through collective bargaining, and modest benefits for sickness or maternity and parental leave. At the end of the 1980s, the proportion of women in the labor force was similar in the United States (45%) and Scandinavia (45%-48%). In the former Soviet Union, the proportion of women in the labor force at that time was over 50%. It is generally agreed that changes in the relationship between men and women and transformations in family life have had profound social repercussions. As the rate of divorces climbed and the ranks of women in the labor force has grown, a whole new set of issues relating to child support and the problems involved in mixing work and family have been raised in all income ranges in all countries.

Family Policy in Scandinavia
Gender equality is one of the main goals of Scandinavia's social democracies. Actual policy, however, has been developed according to conflicting views about the extent to which public policy should support family functions or substitute for the family through public-service arrangements.[12] According to detailed studies by Kamerman and Kahn, Sweden has the most comprehensive family policy of all capitalist countries. Finland and Denmark also have explicit policies, but they are focused more narrowly.

Policy in the Scandinavian countries supports employed parents in their attempts to cope with both work and family demands. Women, who have carried the main responsibility for care in the family circle and in the multigenerational chain, now receive help from public services in fulfilling the tasks of everyday life. Day care for children, elder care, home health services, and so on, have begun to liberate women from both family and intergenerational dependency.[13] The municipal day-care system covers a large proportion of children under school age (which is seven years).

Parental leave with 80% - 90% compensation for lost salary extends for 15 months in Sweden, 12 months in Finland, and about half a year in Denmark. Fathers as well as mothers are eligible for this leave. In the early 1990s, practically every eligible Swedish father used "daddy days" immediately after the birth of a child, and 34% of Finnish fathers took advantage of "daddy days" in 1989.[14] In addition, parents have their jobs guaranteed by law for several years if they choose to stay at home to care for their children. It is still predominantly mothers who take this longer period of parental leave.

The Nordic countries represent a special tradition of women's economic activity: early integration into the labor market, high labor-force participation rates, high rates of union organization, low unemployment, high segregation, frequent but "safe" atypical employment (part-time and temporary work), and relatively small wage differentials. Most of the stability of women's employment in Scandinavia was achieved by means of general economic policy, not so much by policies targeting gender equality in pay or employment opportunities.[15]

The Nordic countries have laws guaranteeing equality between men and women in society generally and at work. There are also state gender-equality councils and ombudsmen for coordinating public equality policy. Shortcomings and backlashes concerning gender equality still exist in the Nordic countries, however. The Nordic model has supported, perhaps even strengthened, segregation and gender division in the workplace. It has made women increasingly dependent on the state instead of on husbands: the private patriarchy has merely become public.[16]

From the point of view of gender equality in the labor market, Scandinavia and the United States show different developmental tendencies. The Swedish employment structure was, in the 1970s and 1980s, evolving toward two economies: one, a heavily male private sector; the other, a female-dominated public sector. Although there was a small increase in "female" job concentration, women were also moving into traditional male jobs. The share of women in privileged "male" occupations in the United States was twice that in Sweden.[17]

The present cuts in social services in Scandinavia due to economic recession will mean a reduction in employment opportunities for women.[18] Since 1970, women have composed almost two-thirds of the public employees in the Nordic Countries.[19] In 1985, the public sector employed almost every second working woman. In Denmark 45%, in Finland 39%, and in Sweden 55% of employed women were public employees.

Family Policy in the Former Soviet Union

A socialist vision of the future emphasized the importance of public life. Women's drudgery in the home would be replaced by public, collective arrangements in which men and women would participate freely and symmetrically. But the introduction of women into the labor force is not enough to produce change in the gender system. The traditional attitudes of male superiority in the former Soviet Union outweighed the pronouncements of official egalitarian ideology. No real change occurred in the roles of men; they merely looked on while women took more jobs. The main goal of recent Soviet social policy, according to Narusk,[20] was to reconcile the woman's duties in society and at home, to facilitate her ability to perform her dual role, and to lessen the differences in material welfare existing among families based on number of children.

As of the latter half of the 1980s, it was obligatory for both men (aged 16 - 59) and women (aged 18 - 54) to work or study outside the home. Free education (with grants to students in secondary and vocational schools and universities), free medical care (with payments for being on the sick list and also for time spent in the hospital), almost-free day-care centers, cash child allowances, and other social services helped families. There were practically no housewives who stayed at home, and women were supposed to take an active role in social life and politics.

A new stage in Estonian family policy began in the early 1980s, when the rights of state enterprises and collective farms were broadened to include the use of company social funds for the help of workers' families. Working mothers became entitled to paid maternity leave until their child was one year old and to additional unpaid leave until the child was 18 months old. A state grant was established for the birth of a first child, and a double sum for the birth of a second or third.[21] Mothers of small children were entitled to shorter working days or were given the opportunity to work at home, if their managers deemed this possible. The use of these measures depended on the good will of the managers and on the real amount of social funds at their disposal. There were great differences in benefits from enterprise to enterprise.

Lapidus identifies three features of the Soviet system that impede women's work freedom and choices.[22] First, sexual stereotyping of occupations was not eliminated. Second, female occupational choices were profoundly influenced by the continuing identification of both creativity and authority with men. Third, culturally and in legislation, household and family responsibilities were explicitly treated as the primary and proper domain of women. At the same time, shortages of consumer goods and everyday services made household responsibilities especially onerous.

The social policy system was supposed to satisfy the basic needs for food and housing, as well as for health, education, cultural and social services for all citizens without separate charge. However, the continuing lack of consumer goods and housing have made daily life difficult, and the quality of state services has been poor. For example, day-care facilities were often understaffed; children disliked them and got sick, adding to parental stress. In addition, the hours were too long for children, often nine hours a day, since most women worked, and full-time and flex-time did not exist.[23]

Nevertheless, the official Soviet ideology of gender equality was successful in some respects. For example, female-male gaps in the number of third-level science students, in the labor force, and in parliament, were smaller in the Soviet Union than in the capitalist countries studied. After the fall of the Soviet Union, however, women criticized the official gender-equality ideology for its lip-service. They questioned the value of gender equality in science, the labor force, and politics. For example, surveys of Estonian high school students in 1979 and 1990 showed that the value girls assigned to education, particularly technical studies, had diminished in the 1980s. The few girls who were interested in technology had low self-esteem.[24] According to a survey of 921 adult women in 1990, women valued family and children more than economic welfare. They also valued love, hobbies, friends, and relationships with their parents more than their jobs or studies.[25]

In 1990, Estonian women were relatively unconscious of inequality between men and women. More than half of the 921 respondents in the survey could not point out gender inequalities, a situation related to the fact that "'feminist' in Estonia is a word of abuse."[26] Opposition to forced equality during the Communist period resulted in a strengthening of traditional attitudes with regard to the position of women. In 1988-90, the Estonian women's movement proposed that women should concentrate on giving birth to many (Estonian) children and care for them at home.

The high number of women in the Supreme Soviets (parliaments) in the former Soviet Union was achieved by applying a 30% quota for women members in elected bodies at the national, regional, and local levels.[27] After the breakdown of the Soviet Union, the proportion of women sank in the representative political bodies of the Soviet republics. The legislature elected in independent Estonia in 1991, for example, included only seven women among 105 members. Women were simply not interested in running as candidates. Their attitude toward politics was negative and based on frustration and alienation. In the prior Communist period, women legislators were like toys in the hands of their male counterparts, even though some of the women were quite competent.[28] The Soviet Women's Committees were the only officially accepted women's organizations functioning on both the national and local levels during the period from 1940 to 1991, and they were not allowed to discuss women's social, economic, and political inequality, the existence of which was denied.

Summary

In the mid-1980s, the five countries we studied were ranked according to gender equality as measured by a combined index.[29] The comparison included 99 countries, representing 92% of the world's female population, and the index was based on 20 indicators, including health, marriage and children, education, employment, and social equality. The status of the women in the five countries in this study declined in the following order:

Sweden	(with a score of 87)
Finland	(85)
U.S.	(82.5)
Denmark	(80)
USSR	(70)

This comparison indicates that, in practice, there was more gender equality in Scandinavia and the U.S. than in the former Soviet Union.

Gender equality seems to be especially high in Scandinavia, according to another international comparison. The Human Development Index combined indices of longevity (life expectancy at birth); knowledge (adult literacy rate and years of schooling); and decent living standards (adjusted real gross domestic product). In 1990, the overall Human Development Index was on the same level for the U.S. (.976) and Scandinavia (Denmark .967, Finland .963, and Sweden .982), but lower in the USSR (.908). When the male-female disparities were taken into account, Scandinavian countries turned out to have higher scores (.878 for Denmark, .902 for Finland, and .886 for Sweden) than the United States (.809). Finland ranked highest among the countries of the world on this gender-sensitive index.[30]

The high level of social development in Scandinavia is reflected in people's satisfaction with life. At the beginning of 1980s, life satisfaction was higher in Scandinavia than in the U.S.[31] (Life satisfaction is part of a syndrome of positive attitudes toward the world in which one lives.)

Nowhere, however, has equality of economic opportunity for women followed automatically from their higher levels of educational attainment and labor force participation. The basic problem is still lower pay for women's work than for men's work. Men derive greater benefits from educational and occupational attainments, even when women's work ex-

perience and levels of current labor-force participation are comparable. The gender gap in wages is larger in the United States, where female wages are 69% of male wages, as compared to Scandinavia, where female wages vary between 76% and 84% of male wages.[32] In 1989, the average full-time earnings of women in the Soviet Union ranged from 65% to 75% of those of men.[33] Scandinavian countries have relatively high economic equality between men and women, but a gender gap in earnings remains.

We found by conducting social research and other comparative work among the three regions that type of society and type of workplace (with its specific gender composition) have strong connections with the organization of work, with the social relations at work and in the family, and with the well-being of women.[34]

Elina Haavio-Mannila is a professor of sociology at the University of Helsinki. She has published nearly 200 sociological books and articles in her main field of interest which is gender roles in the family, at work, and in politics. Haavio-Mannila has also conducted studies on medical sociology and sexual behavior. She has been a visiting scholar at the Center for the Education of Women at the University of Michigan and a visiting professor at the University of Minnesota, among others. Presently she is conducting a large study of sexual behavior in Finland with Osmo Kontula.

Author's References

[1] Epstein, C. The Cultural perspective and the study of work. In Kai Erikson & Steven Peter Vallas (eds.), The Nature of Work: Sociological Perspectives (New Haven and London: American Sociological Association Presidential Series and Yale University Press, 1990).

[2] Moen P. Women's Two Roles — A Contemporary Dilemma (New York: Auburn House, 1992).

[3] Vallas SP. The future of work. In Kai Erikson and Steven Peter Vallas (eds.), The Nature of Work: Sociological Perspectives. (New Haven and London: American Sociological Association Presidential Series and Yale University, 1990).

[4] Kanter, RM Men and Women of the Corporation. (New York: Basic Books, 1990.)

[5] Magnet M. The truth about the American worker. *Fortune Magazine*, May 4, 1992, pp. 48-65.

[6] Gustavsen B. Reforms on the place of work and democratic dialogue. In Jan Odhnoff and Casten von Otter (eds.), Rationalities of Work: On Working Life of the Future (Stockholm: Arbetslivscentrum, 1987).

[7] Komiteanmietinto. Report on the Committee on Working Conditions. (Helsinki: Valtion Painatuskeskus, 1991).

[8] Komiteanmietinto. Report on the Committee on Working Conditions. (Helsinki: Valtion Painatuskeskus, 1991).

[9] Moen P. Op. cit.

[10] Kamerman SB and Kahn AJ. Family Policy: Government and Families in Fourteen Countries (New York: Columbia University Press, 1978); Kamerman SB and Kahn AJ. Child Care, Family Benefits and Working Parents: A study in Comparative Policy (New York: Columbia University Press, 1981); and Kamerman SB and Kahn AJ. The Responsive Workplace (New York: Columbia University Press, 1987).

[11] Schor J. The Overworked American: The Unexpected Decline of Leisure (New York: Basic Books, 1991).

[12] Dahlstrom E. Theories and ideologies of family ideologies, gender relations and human reproduction. In Katja Boh et al

(eds.) Changing Patterns of European Family Life: A Comparative Analysis of 14 European Countries. (London and New York: Routledge, 1989).

[13] Simonen L. Change of Women's Caring Work at the Turning Point of the Welfare State — A Nordic Perspective. Paper Presented at the Fourth Annual International Conference of the Society for the Advancement of Socio-Economics, Graduate School of Management, University of California, Irvine, March 27-29, 1992.

[14] Haavio-Mannila E, Kauppinen, K. Women and the welfare state in Nordic countries. In Hilda Kahne and Janet Z. Giele (eds.) Women's Work and and Women's Lives: The Continuing Struggle Worldwide (Boulder: Westview Press, 1992).

[15] Allen T. The Nordic Model of Gender Equality and the Labour Market. Paper presented at the Fourth Annual International Conference of the Society for the Advancement of Socio-Economics, Graduate School of Management, University of California, Irvine, March 27-29, 1992.

[16] Ibid.

[17] Esping-Andersen, G. The Three Worlds of Welfare Capitalism (Cambridge: Polity Press, 1990).

[18] Julkunen R. The Welfare State at a Turning Point (Tampere: Vastapaino, 1992).

[19] Marklund S. Paradise Lost? The Nordic Welfare States and the Recession, 1975-1985. (Lund: Lund Studies in Social Welfare II, 1988 and Alestalo M. The Expansion of the Public Sector (Vammala: Sosiaalipolitiikka, 1991).

[20] Narusk A. Parenthood, partnership and family in Estonia. In Ulla Bjornberg (ed.) European Parents in the 1990s: Contradictions and Comparisons (London: Transaction Publishers, 1991).

[21] Ibid.

[22] Lapidus GW. Gender and restructuring: The impact of perestroika on soviet women. In Valentine M. Mogdaham (ed.) Gender and Restructuring (Oxford: Clarendon Press 1993).

[23] Laas A. The future for Estonian women: Real women are mothers. Family Research Institute of Tartu University, Estonia. (Stencil) 1992.

[24] Hansen H. Attitudes of Girls to Future Occupations. Paper presented at Finnish-Estonian Seminar on the position of women at work and in society, Tallinn, May 14-15, 1992.

[25] Narusk A. Satisfaction of women with work and family life. Paper presented at Finnish-Estonian Seminar on the position of women at work and in Society, Tallinn, May 14-15, 1992.

[26] Meri T. Feminist on Eestis soimusona (feminist is in Estonia a word of abuse) Naised Eestis 2(32), 28 February, 8, 1992

[27] Laas A. The future for Estonian women: Real women are mothers. Family Research Institute of Tartu University, Estonia. (Stencil) 1992.

[28] Kilvet K. Interview of Krista Kilvet, president of the Estonian Women's Union, Finnish Radio, July 1, 1992).

[29] Population Crisis Committee. Country rankings of the status of women: Poor, powerless and pregnant. Population Briefing Paper No. 20, June, 1988 (Washington: Population Crisis Committee).

[30] Human Development Report. Published for the United Nations Development Programme. (New York and Oxford: Oxford University Press, 1991).

[31] Inglehart R. Culture Shift in Advanced Industrial Society (Princeton: Princeton University Press, 1990).

[32] Human Development Report. Op. cit.

[33] Lapidus G. Op. cit.

[34] Haavio-Mannila E. Work, Family and Well-Being in Five North and East-European Capitals. (Helsinki: The Finish Academy of Science and Letters B:255, 1992); Haavio-Mannila E. Women's Work in Three Types of Societies (Ann Arbor, Michigan: University of Michigan, Center for the Education of Women, 1993).

CONTINUITIES AND DISCONTINUITIES IN FAMILY MEMBERS' RELATIONSHIPS WITH ALZHEIMER'S PATIENTS*

Thirty families who cared for a family member with Alzheimer's Disease were asked to provide narratives of daily care over one and one-half years. A key finding of the hermeneutic analysis of their narratives was that different family members experience their relationship with the AD patient to be continuous, continuous but transformed, or radically discontinuous with their relationship prior to the disease. Responsiveness to these qualities of family relations by professionals may ease family members' caregiving efforts.

Catherine Chesla, Ida Martinson,
and Marilou Muwaswes

Catherine Chesla is an Assistant Professor and Ida Martinson is a Professor in the Department of Family Health Care Nursing, University of California, San Francisco, California, 94143. Marilou Muwaswes is an Associate Clinical Professor, Physiological Nursing, University of California, San Francisco.

The central concern in research on families and Alzheimer's Disease (AD) in the past ten years has been to identify factors that place family members at risk for negative outcomes because of their involvement in AD care (Bowers, 1987; Colerick & George, 1986; Liptzin, Grob, & Eisen, 1988; Ory et al., 1985; Quayhagen & Quayhagen, 1988). This research has identified AD family caregivers to be at risk for poor physical health, mental health, and quality of life, when compared with family members who are not caregivers (Kuhlman, Wilson, Hutchinson, & Wallhagen, 1991). Family burden, resources (including social support), and AD patient characteristics and symptoms im-

*This research was conducted as part of a larger study "Impact of Alzheimer's Disease on the Family and Caregiver," by Ida Martinson, P.I., Catherine Gilliss, Glen Doyle and Marilou Muwaswes, Co-Investigators. The project was funded by Biomedical Research Support Grant, School of Nursing, University of California, San Francisco; Academic Senate Grant, UCSF; NRSA Post-Doctoral Fellowship Grant #1F31 NR06020, National Center for Nursing Research, NIH; Alzheimer's Disease and Related Disorders Association Paine-Knickerbocker Graduate Research Award.

Key Words: Alzheimer's disease, dementia, family caregiving, family relationships, intergenerational relationships.

(Family Relations, 1994, 43, 3-9.)

pact negative family outcomes, although factors that place family members most at risk remain to be specified (Baumgarten, 1989). In all of this research, however, AD patients are assumed to be a demand or a drain on family members.

Persons with AD are frequently described as experiencing a loss of self as the disease unfolds (Cohen & Eisdorfer, 1986). Progressive loss of memory, along with personality and behavior changes common to the disease, are thought to overwhelm those with the disease. AD patients are characterized as suffering from a biomedical disorder that severs them from their history and severely restricts their potential in life. The biomedicalization of dementia (Lyman, 1989) has restricted the scope of research to disease progression and biologic processes that give rise to the disease. Research about those who care for demented elders has similarly been restricted by the pervasiveness of the biomedical perspective to the questions about how the disease, in its various stages of progression, impacts family members. Largely unasked, and therefore unanswered, are questions about the lived experience of AD for the person with the disease, the family member's experience of living with and caring for the person with AD, and how qualities of the caregiving environment might influence disease progression (Lyman, 1989).

Research on caregivers of AD patients often progresses from the implicit assumption of particular relations between the ill family member and others in the family. One member in the relationship is assumed to be the passive recipient of care, holding less interpersonal power yet imposing demands and burdens. In a parallel way, the caregiving member is assumed to be an active provider, possessing relatively greater interpersonal power, but at risk of negative outcomes because of the burdens and risks experienced. Recent caregiver research suggests that the quality of relations between ill and other family members is complex, and that factors such as centrality of the relationship, personal qualities of both members, and the degree of reciprocity in the relationship may impact outcomes for both the ill and non-ill family members (Walker, Pratt, & Oppy, 1992; Wright, Clipp, & George, 1993).

One aim of this investigation was to question the assumption of a fixed relation between the family and the person with AD and additionally to specify the range of relations that were apparent in the day-to-day lives of family members living with a person with AD. As part of a larger study aimed at understanding the *experiences* of family members who cared for a person with AD over time, we critically examined family members' self-initiated discussion of relations with

From *Family Relations*, Vol. 43, No. 1, January 1994, pp. 3-9. © 1994 by the National Council of Family Relations, 3989 Central Avenue, NE, Suite 550, Minneapolis, MN 55421. Reprinted by permission.

the person with AD, as well as the content and nature of those relations. Working directly from family members' narratives, we attempted to understand these relations in ways that formal theories, such as exchange or friendship theory, may have missed. We were interested in the whole of the family's experience; what was salient and meaningful for the family members themselves, the difficulties or demands they encountered (Martinson, Chesla, & Muwaswes, 1993) and the skills and practices they developed in living with a person with AD. Through family members' narratives over an 18-month time span, it was evident that relationship issues were paramount to family members in their everyday lives and that qualitatively distinct forms of relations between ill members and other family members were evident.

Relationships Between Caregivers and Family Members with AD

Although little attention has been paid to the positive or sustaining aspects of caring for a family member with AD, detailed studies of the relationship between the AD patient and the family show that: (a) relationships change over time and intimacy declines with time for some but not for all family members (Blieszner & Shifflett, 1990); (b) care of a family member with AD brings both suffering and rewards; and (c) reciprocity in the relationship with a family member with dementia seems to be a key aspect reported by families, but can take many forms (Farran, Keane-Hagarty, Salloway, Kupferer, & Wilken, 1991; Hirschfeld, 1983; Orona, 1990).

Blieszner and Shifflett (1990) produced a sensitive analysis of caregivers' responses to the first 18 months of care after AD had been diagnosed. They found that intimacy between AD patients and family caregivers diminished over the first 18 months of care and that a host of emotional responses was elicited for family caregivers at each point in time. At diagnosis, there was relief at having an understanding of what was happening, but also anger, sadness, and grief. Six months into the disorder, family members focused on the loss of the previously established relationship with the AD patient. One year and six months after diagnosis, caregivers were found to be coping with a dramatically changed but continuing relationship. Coping strategies that predominated were redefining the relationship, working on closure in the relationship, and working on expanding caregiver role responsibilities. These investigators found that, although caregivers on average felt less intimate with the person with AD, some caregivers reported increased intimacy

as the disease progressed (Blieszner & Shifflett, 1989).

Hirschfeld (1983) developed in her grounded theory study a concept of "mutuality" in caregiver, care receiver relations. Mutuality was defined as the caregiver's capacity to find: (a) gratification in the relationship with the impaired person; (b) positive meaning from the caregiving situation; and (c) a sense of reciprocity, even in situations where the elder had severe dementia. The sample of 30 caregivers included both spouses and children of elders with senile brain disease. Most striking was Hirschfeld's finding that the higher the mutuality in the relationship, the less likely the caregiver was to consider institutionalization of the elder.

In a small grounded theory study of family members who cared for a member with AD, Orona (1990) focused on identity loss of the AD patient and its impact on the dyadic relationship over time. Using a social constructionist framework, Orona noted temporality as an important subjective aspect of the caregiving experience. Facets of temporal experience were: (a) the use of memories to maintain the identity of the AD person, (b) the re-enactment of meaningful social interactions with the AD person, and (c) the use of memories as a basis for constructing new images for the future. Caregivers were found to engage in "identity maintenance" via everyday activities with the AD family member, and when reciprocity was lost, these relatives "worked both sides of the relationship," or took on both the caregiver's and the AD patient's social roles, in order to continue some part of the past relating.

In summary, detailed studies that have examined a family member's experience with a relative with dementia over time undermine any standard depiction of the process. Rather, they demonstrate complex variability in issues of intimacy, reciprocity, and management of life tasks given the unbalanced capabilities of well and ill members. Questions remain about the basic nature of these relations and how they evolve over time.

METHOD

This study was designed within a tradition known as hermeneutic phenomenology (Benner & Wrubel, 1989; Packer & Addison, 1989; Van Manen, 1990). The aim of the method is to explain particular and distinct patterns of meaning and action in the lives of those studied, taking into account the context in which they live, their history, and their particular concerns. Rather than trying to characterize a modal or group response, research within this method

provides detailed explanations of varied patterns of human understanding and action. The method is: (a) systematic in its use of practiced modes of questioning the informant about experiences; (b) explicit in its attempt to articulate, through careful interpretation of a text, the meanings embedded in human experience; (c) self-critical and self-corrective in its continual examination of interpretations made on a text; and (d) a shared interpretation that is consensually agreed upon by multiple readers (Van Manen, 1990).

This phenomenological study was part of a multifaceted, longitudinal study of the impact of Alzheimer's Disease on the family and caregiver (Martinson, Gilliss, Doyle, & Muwaswes, 1983). Only the phenomenologic interview data are reported here. Fifteen spouses and fifteen adult-child family members were recruited from support groups and clinics serving AD patients. Semistructured, intensive interviews were conducted at intake and every six months for 18 months. In each interview, family members were asked to reflect on their experiences in the previous 6 months and on changes in the AD patient, family members' feelings, and care arrangements. They were asked to provide narratives of salient, difficult, or memorable episodes of care that had arisen in the past 6 months. Full narratives of the episodes, preceding events, caregivers' emotions, thoughts, and actions throughout the episodes and outcomes were elicited. The interviews, which lasted approximately one hour, were audiotaped and transcribed verbatim.

Hermeneutic interpretation (Packer & Addison, 1989; Van Manen, 1990) of texts from the interviews comprise this paper. The first author, educated in Heideggerian philosophy and hermeneutics, directed the interpretive process and interpreted all texts with the third author. The second author was familiar with all interview texts and provided consensus on summary interpretations.

Interpretation was comprised of two interwoven processes: thematic interpretation and interpretation of exemplars. Three levels of thematic interpretation were used to uncover and isolate themes in a text: (a) the holistic approach, (b) the selective approach, and (c) the detailed or line-by-line approach. In the holistic approach, the whole text was read through and described as a piece in an attempt to capture the fundamental meaning of the text as a whole. In the selective approach, aspects of the text that stood out as essential or revealing of the phenomenon under study were the focus. A line-by-line detailed reading was then completed in which the text was examined for what it revealed about the experience. After completing all three steps, the text was examined in its entirety, in its particular salience, and for fine-grained nuances.

Interpretation of exemplars occurred simultaneously with the search for general themes. Exemplars are narratives of whole incidents of family care elicited from participants in the interviews. All relevant aspects of each exemplar were coded together, including the family member's recollection of what preceded the episode, how the episode unfolded, emotions at the start and throughout the episode, actions considered and taken, direct and indirect clues to what was at stake for the family, and the family member's retrospective reworking of the situation. These episodes, in their complete form, served as examples of particular patterns of action that included a rich description of the situation and responses that evidenced family member's understandings, concerns, and practical involvements with the AD patient.

FINDINGS

Description of Informants

Eighteen of the family members interviewed were female (7 wives and 11 daughters), and twelve were male (8 husbands and 4 sons). The mean age of family members was 57 years. Family members were predominantly Caucasian and from middle socioeconomic strata.

Eight male and 22 female persons with AD entered the study. Their mean age was 74 years (range 59-86) and the mean duration of the illness was 4 years (range 1-11 years). Twenty persons with AD at the start of the study resided in the home of a family member, seven were institutionalized in a nursing or board and care home, and three lived alone. Residence status changed with each data collection period, and at six months 17 AD patients lived in their caregiver's home, 11 lived in institutions, 1 lived alone, and 1 person with AD died. By 18 months, 8 were living in the caregiver's home, 8 were institutionalized, 1 was still living alone, 8 persons with AD had died, and 5 family members had withdrawn from the study.

Severity of the AD patients' illness, as measured by the Mini-Mental Status Exam (Folstein, Folstein, & McHugh, 1975) indicated moderate to severe cognitive dysfunction. Mean scores for AD patients were 9.4 (SD = 6.7) at induction and 6.4 (SD = 8.06) six months later on a 30-point scale, where a score below 24 indicates some cognitive impairment. On a second measure of illness severity, the Older Adults Multifunctional Assessment Questionnaire (Fillenbaum & Smyer, 1981), the AD patients scored significantly lower (p < .001) on measures of physical health and activities of daily living than a comparison group of institutionalized elderly.

Interpretive Findings

Continuity and discontinuity in the relationship between the family member and the person with AD were salient issues in two paradigm cases in an early reading of the narratives. A paradigm case is an outstanding instance of a pattern of narratives that seem to go together, the coherence of which is visible only through the whole reading of a particular case. Continuity and discontinuity in these two cases seemed to set up the kind of care that the family member had with the AD patient. The finding challenged our assumption of what AD relations might be, which most closely resembled a third pattern we eventually observed and labeled *continuous but transformed*. After recognition and identification of three predominant forms of relating through paradigm cases, the texts from the remaining informants were identified as being strongly similar to the aspects of relating evident in these three predominant forms.

One aspect of the experience of living with and caring for a family member with AD is presented in this article: the existential relation that family members had with their spouse or parent with AD as evidenced by their narratives of providing day-to-day care. Three forms of relationship will be presented: (a) a relationship that is maintained as continuous with the relationship between caregiver and AD patient prior to the disease, (b) a relationship that is continuous but is transformed by the disease, and (c) a relationship in which there is radical discontinuity between the present and prior relationship.

Relationship as Continuous

Some family members found possibilities in their relationships to continue to be a wife, daughter, husband or son to the person with AD. Despite the changes in the person with AD, family members continued to define themselves "in relation to" the patient in ways that paralleled their relations prior to the disease. These family members interpreted small gestures or statements made by the AD patient as continuous with past behavior and found remnants of the AD patient's intentions, wishes, likes and dislikes in present behavior. Dramatic losses and changes in the relationship were not denied and there was particular sensitivity in this group to patients' functional and memory losses. Despite realistic assessment and grieving, these family members felt a sense of connection to and continuity with the patient. They watched for, held precious, and felt comforted by, familiar responses and behaviors by the patient.

One woman exemplifies continuous relating with an AD spouse. She is a 75-year-old woman who had been married to her husband for more than 54 years. The husband had shown signs of AD for the past 10 years and during the course of the study declined from almost complete dementia to death.

This woman's narratives provide evidence that her relationship to her husband is almost unaltered from the life they shared prior to the illness. Despite the AD, she finds access to his person, his intelligence, and his capacity to comfort her. She is distressed that her husband, who never used profanity, now curses her in anger and tries to hit her if he is confused. However, the man with whom she built a life and a family, the person that comprised her world prior to the illness, continues to define her world and focus her daily concerns. She finds comfort that they can share a bed together and feels his presence very strongly in her life. In the first two interviews, when they lived together in their retirement apartment, she noted repeated instances where her husband seemed present and interacted with her in familiar ways:

> Wife: The other morning, for instance, he woke up early and I was just barely awake, and he reached over and held my hand. So you know that is a lot really. He's here. He always has been a very gentle, caring sort of person.

She noted incidents where he commented on her clothes, "I always liked you in that," or tried to comfort her when she became tearful. From an outsider's perspective, his behavior could have been interpreted as random or meaningless, but the woman interprets it as meaningful, coherent, and indicative of his past and present personhood.

This woman's respect for her husband's continuity of person appears in the way she approaches his physical care. She values his lifelong habits and practices and continues them for him now that he cannot carry them out.

> Wife: My son said 'Well you don't have to shave Dad everyday.' I said, 'I know he doesn't have much of a beard but he likes being shaved.' He sometimes sings when I'm shaving him. I remember he always used to clean his finger nails every morning when he was getting ready to go. So why not do that?

In a similar way, this woman relied on past relationship patterns with her husband to comfort *her*. She told of two stressful incidents in which her husband wandered away from her. In both incidents, her husband was found within minutes, but she experienced extreme anxiety and distress, fearing he might be harmed or permanently lost. Both times, she calmed her husband and comforted herself by sitting and talking with him.

Wife: Well, I talk to him. I just say, 'you know, you really scared me, and you worry me when you wander away like that. I can't keep track of you all the time.' I just talk like you would in general.

Interviewer: And that helps you?

Wife: Yea.

Interviewer: Do you think that sinks in?

Wife: No. It's helpful for me to talk to him. We always talked a lot.

Conversing with her husband re-enacted a 54-year-old ritual in which they sat together and had a glass of wine each night when her husband returned from work. This ritual was time-honored and practiced no matter what was happening with their household of seven children.

One year into the study, the husband had a stroke and had to be placed in a nursing home. While this dramatically changed the nature of her care responsibilities, her relationship with her husband continued largely unchanged. She went to the nursing home for many hours each day to monitor his care and bring him foods he liked. In the final interview, after her husband died, she recounted her sense of continuity with her husband.

Interviewer: So the Alzheimer's disease didn't take that away from you, that happy feeling of being married to Ron and that relationship you felt with him?

Wife: No, it never did. Never. I would have been happy to bring him home again. . . . I mean, I would have gone on indefinitely. One of the books I read said they usually have Alzheimer's for about 15 years. So I figured that I had about another 7 years to go. He'd come home from the hospital before, so I thought he'd be coming home again, I really did.

Interviewer: So you really felt you had an ongoing relationship with him?

Wife: Yes.

This case demonstrates several aspects of a continuous relationship with an AD family member: (a) the interpretation that the AD patient is still present despite the disease, (b) the interpretation that the person with AD reciprocates in positive ways, and (c) the AD patient continues to define the spouse's or child's world in stable and relatively unchanging ways.

In a similar way, adult children maintained the parent in a place of respect and esteem despite the advance of the disease. Although the parent could not provide advice or support, he or she was still respected and honored by the child as his or her parent. Adult children in this group expressed concern that they "try to maintain her dignity" and "not strip everything away from her."

One daughter's capacity to see her mother in small aspects of the mother's behavior remained present, as in the prior case, throughout the 18-month study. During that time, the mother's physical and mental health declined, she suffered numerous strokes, and the AD progressed to the extent that the mother required placement in a board and care home and eventually a nursing home. Still, the daughter felt an attachment to what she saw in her mother's behavior and appearance that still represented "mother." The daughter continued practices that her mother had maintained throughout her lifetime: coloring her hair red and manicuring her nails. Until the end of the study, the daughter claimed that her relationship with her mother was alive and vibrant.

Interviewer: So you still very much have that bond with her?

Daughter: Oh yes. I will sit there with her in the evenings. I'll sit on the bed and she's in the wheelchair, and I'll put my arm around her and cuddle with her.

Interviewer: She still likes affection from you?

Daughter: Oh yes. She responds to that. Awhile back when I told her I loved her, I was very richly rewarded because she told me, 'I love you.' That just leveled me. I try to hang on to what's still left of her. She still knows me; she still knows chocolate; she still remembers hymns; she's not gone yet. There's still Mama there.

Relationship is Continuous but Transformed

Another group of family members described the AD patient as fairly lost to them because of AD. These spouses and children saw minimal, residual, and fleeting signs of the AD person's personality and either had doubts about their accessibility or saw them as totally inaccessible. What remained, however, was a strong commitment to the relationship, to maintaining contact with the person that the patient had *become* in the disease. Because of the changes in the AD patient, past relations were mourned, and current relations were on a new footing.

Interviewer: Is she still the same person to you?

Daughter: No. Oh no! She's a totally different person. She's not Helen anymore. She's not my mom. No. She's just there in body.

These family members found ways to relate to the patient as the symptoms progressed, and continued to adapt their ways of relating as the AD person's capacities became more constricted. For example, one man reported in the first three interviews that his greatest fear was that his wife would no longer recognize him. In the abstract, he feared that her lack of recognition would break the thin continuity that he felt with her. Additionally, he said he was most sustained by his wife's contentment and recognition. Then in the last interview, his wife increasingly did not recognize him. He then found a new way to stay connected to her in her current capacities. He no longer worried that she recognize him but found it essential that she appreciate him and accept his care. Her willingness to eat what he prepared and her cooperation with the caregivers he hired were taken as signs of her acceptance of his care.

Family members who experienced their relationships as transformed lived more in synchrony with the actual decline in the AD patient's functioning than did those family members who experienced continuity in relations with the AD member. Their relationship with the patient evolved and changed with the changes in the disease. They saw their possibilities for relating to the person with AD as being more firmly bounded by the actual symptomatic changes in the person than did those family members who experienced a continuous relationship with the family member with AD.

In the continuous but transformed relationship, reciprocity between the patient and family members was seen as minimally possible and always in doubt. The patient's fleeting smiles or signs of pleasure were noted by family members and brought them satisfaction. What distinguished these family members from those in the continuous relationship category is the fact that small gestures by the AD patient were not interpreted as indications that the patient was still "there" in the same way that those who had continuous relationships interpreted these signs.

Daughter: I just feel like I've already lost her. She's here but she isn't here. It's probably the most difficult thing.

Spouses found living in this ambiguous relationship difficult because they could no longer relate to their partner as an intimate friend or sexual partner and at the same time they remained married and deeply committed to the spouse. Children also experienced the ambiguity in relations as a dilemma, although the day-to-day impact on their lives was less than for spouses. The children never talked of finding a replacement relationship for that which they had lost, but many of the spouses wished this were possible.

In families where the relationship was transformed, the primary relationship concerns were to provide sensitive care that maintained the dignity of the person and to sustain the AD patient's functional abilities. One spouse, who exemplifies these concerns, demonstrated that to be a good husband to his wife meant providing good care. To this end, he gave up his job in international business and turned his energies entirely to the care of his wife. In his interviews he was exclusively focused on his wife's care requirements and how to sensitively meet them in a way that maintained her current functioning and dignity. He was deeply committed to taking good care of his wife, deeply grieved when there was any evidence that he was not doing a good job, and satisfied when he was successful.

Relationship is Radically Discontinuous

In the third form of relating to a family member with AD, the relationship with the spouse or parent was radically discontinuous with the relationship that existed prior to the illness. These family members found no continuity in the AD patient's personhood and instead found that the AD rendered the patient unrecognizable. They found the behaviors and symptoms of AD to be an affront to the person he or she had been prior to the disease. The relationship these family members experienced was less emotional, less personal and more clinical than that of the first two groups. In their interpretation, the spouse or parent was lost in the disease, and therefore the family member could not continue a truly personal relationship. The concern of these family members for the patient was more objective, abstract, and less tailored to the particular needs of their AD family member.

The coping narratives of these family members focused on caregiving arrangements and problems. When the AD patient gave signs of recognition or pleasure, these family members, like others, were pleased and touched. They did not, however, attempt to elicit such signs and did not interpret such signs as evidence of purposeful, personalized behavior. They diminished the importance of instances of recognition. Instead, there was more of a clinical distancing

and evaluation of the person's disease process.

Emotional distancing was evident in a daughter whose mother had contracted the disease eight years earlier. The daughter described a recent incident where her mother said something that actually seemed to make sense. The daughter was about to take her mother off the commode and the mother said "no" because she needed to stay longer. This moment of possible lucidity in a woman who had not been lucid for 2 years surprised the daughter. But when the interviewer probed about how the incident affected her, she replied:

Daughter: I don't think it made a difference. I found it interesting that she said 'no' definitely. I thought to myself, how does the correlation go there?

The mother's statement raised for the daughter a clinical question, rather than a relational response. The daughter wondered about how the disease worked, rather than how her mother experienced the disease. Witnessing her mother make sense, and thus have some possibility of making meaningful contact with current reality, made the daughter feel neither closer to nor more distant from her mother. In this daughter's understanding of the situation, the possibility of connecting with her mother simply was not present.

One husband provides some insight about how this emotional break in his relationship with his wife occurred. He recounted that prior to the AD they were "best friends," "did everything together" and in many ways she defined his life. When facing up to her illness, he recognized the only way that he could stay in a relationship with his wife was if he were to "die" himself.

Husband: I think somehow I'm hardened. If I can say it like that. I've become hardened to a lot of it. It may be by design. Because I had to decide, when I talked about that turning point, whether I was going to live, or whether I was going to sit here and curl up and die because she's got that disease. I don't know if the word's martyr or. . . . Anyway I'm not going to sit around here and let it kill me. I think that's what it was doing.

The dissolution of the relationship with his wife is also evident in this man's hopes and fears for the future. The best possible life he hoped for was: "I would feel good if she died, the sooner the better." He also felt that the worst life for him would be if his wife were to continue to live, and hold him in this "limbo" of being "married, but not married."

Family members who realized radical discontinuities in their relationships

with the AD patient may have had a wide variety of predisposing factors. Perhaps they as a group had more conflicted relations with the person with AD prior to the disease, and thus the disease introduced unsurmountable distance. Perhaps they had difficulty coping with the pervasive losses that one must face as a loved one progresses through AD and distancing was one way of warding off the pain of these losses. We lack the data to thoroughly understand *how* family members came to a discontinuous relationship with the AD patient. What was evident was that these family members found few, if any, possibilities for relating to the person with AD that paralleled their relationship prior to the disease.

Despite the emotional distance that typified the discontinuous relationship, providing good care was a central and focusing concern for family members who experienced this relationship. Proper diet, supervision, safety, and comfort of the AD patient were all raised as issues in the family members' narratives. Providing or arranging care demanded extensive daily effort and time and some of these family members were the primary or sole providers of care. What distinguished the care concerns of this group of families was their relative lack of concern that the care be tailored to the present or past personal needs of the AD patient.

DISCUSSION

In this intensive study of the relationships between family members and AD patients over time, we discovered qualitatively distinct ways that family members interpreted the AD patient's accessibility, capacity to reciprocate affection and concern, and capacity to *relate* as parent or spouse to the family member. For some family members of persons with AD, the loss of self and transformation of the person with AD by the disease were not complete. For these family members, the life and capacities of the person with AD were still a part of their ongoing relationship either fully or in a diminished and transformed way. For other family members, however, the disease covered over the person, overrode their relational possibilities, and care became much more strategic or objectified.

All three forms of relating (continuous, transformed, or discontinuous) presented here were evident in both the children's and spouses' relations with the person with AD. With the exception of continuous relating, both male and female caregivers experienced each form of relating. In our group of informants, there were no male caregivers who demonstrated the continuous form of relating, and wives of persons with AD were the most predominant in this group of caregivers. We acknowledge that the forms of relating that we present may not represent all of the possibilities for how relations between family and the person with AD might evolve. For example, we interviewed only persons who maintained some kind of relationship with the person with AD, whether that relationship was personal or merely organizational. Thus, we have no information on the ways in which family members may sever their relationship with the person with AD.

The severity of illness in the person with AD did not seem to determine the form of relationship that was described by the family member. Moderate to severe Alzheimer's disease was evident in all three forms of relationships when data from both family member ratings and interviewer ratings were considered. The disease itself, and the progression of the disease, was not a clear determinant of what the relationship might be.

Our findings support and further articulate detailed qualitative studies of AD family relationships reported to date. Like Blieszner and Shifflett (1990), we found that closeness between the person with AD and the family members diminished for some but remained strong for others over time, despite sometimes dramatic progression of the dementia and, thus, a decrease in the AD person's "objective" capacities to relate. Orona (1990) reported interactions similar to those we observed in the first two groups of our sample: the reenactment of familiar rituals and the searching for and success at finding familiar behaviors and expressions in the AD patient. She similarly reported the phenomena we observed in the continuous relationships of "working both sides" of the relationship, filling in additional meanings for vague or difficult to interpret behaviors by the person with AD.

Hirschfeld (1983) combined three dimensions of mutuality in a single concept. Considering Hirschfeld's concept of mutuality in light of our own findings, we believe that her three aspects of mutuality might offer greater explanatory power in terms of caregivers' involvements if they are examined independently. In this study, we found that: (a) the caregiver's capacity to find gratification in the *relationship* with the impaired person, (b) *positive* meaning of caregiving, and (c) a sense of *reciprocity* with the care recipient, all aspects of mutuality, did not combine in meaningful ways in our groups of family members who provided care. For example, family members in the continuous group seemed to experience all three dimensions of mutuality in a consistent, coherent fashion. Family members in the con-

tinuous but transformed group also experienced positive meanings from the care situation, questionable reciprocity, and some gratification from the relationship, but here it was a relation acknowledged to be changed by the disease. Finally, family members in the discontinuous group experienced substantial positive meanings from giving care, but found no sense of reciprocity in the caregiving relationship and made almost no mention of relationship gratifications with the AD patient. We believe that Hirschfeld identified important explanatory dimensions in the relationship of family and persons with AD and argue for further refinement of the "mutuality" concept so that each dimension be examined as qualitatively distinct.

Our findings are not in conflict with, but are distinct from, the prevailing themes in the literature on family factors and AD care. This literature has largely ignored the quality of the relationship between the person with AD and the family member who provides care, assuming instead that the former is a passive, uninvolved recipient of care and the latter is burdened by the responsibility for this passive object/person. We wish to argue that the qualitative aspects of the relationship between the AD person and the family members described in this research deserve a more prominent place in research on family processes in relation to AD care. Alongside continuing efforts to identify factors that place the family at risk for negative outcomes, conceptualizations and investigations of family care processes must begin to include an awareness of relationships that may be sustaining and meaningful. As Hirschfeld's research demonstrated a decade ago, the relational qualities may have powerful explanatory power in how families function over time.

CLINICAL IMPLICATIONS

Recognizing that family members who care for a person with AD have distinct relations with that person is vital to their sensitive care and support. Relying on standardized responses to the family situation, or relying on the pervasive literature that emphasizes the losses, burdens, and difficulties in AD care, may lead professionals to overlook the family members' possibilities for hope, satisfaction, and continuity in their relations with and care of the AD patient.

Care for family members who experience their relationship as continuous might explicitly legitimatize their experience of the person as present and encourage their efforts to continue the AD patient's habits and practices. The biomedicalization of dementia (Lyman,

1989) may be so complete that family members feel criticized or isolated because they continue to relate to the person with AD. In recognizing the two-way nature of the family relations, health professionals should give credence to the AD patient as a person with a history and recognize further the AD patient's capacity to carry on in a meaningful way in relationships despite the debilitations of the dementia. Rather than emphasizing the negative changes wrought by the disease, health professionals might learn from family members how the disease makes possible continued exercise of lifelong marital or parental relations. Family members additionally might inform practitioners about authentic commitments to the care of beloved family members that are neither self-sacrificing nor "loving too much." For some, care of the person with AD is the genuine working out and fulfillment of a lifelong relationship; therefore, it is not experienced as burdensome but sustaining and meaningful.

The group of family members who experience a continuous relationship with the person with AD might have the most difficulty, however, with recognizing the true limitations that occur over time in the AD person's abilities. Although all caregivers we observed provided safe and protective environments, some had their choices for care restricted because they believed that the person with AD was capable of doing things that seemed unlikely. Respectful solicitation of what family members perceive as the capabilities of the AD person, and feedback by the professional regarding these perceptions are warranted.

Family members who experienced their relationship with the AD patient as continuous but transformed might similarly benefit from interventions that respect their efforts at continued close relations with the person with AD. These family members, who are more in synchrony with the changes of the disease, are particularly apt to observe firsthand a decline in the AD patient's abilities. Care of these family members may involve helping them find ways to maintain their commitment to closeness, while at the same time being respectful of the AD patient's new restrictions. Providing examples of how other family members have coped with this dilemma, like the spouse who no longer needed his wife's recognition, but merely needed her acceptance of his care, might make these transitions easier.

Work with family members who experience their relationship with the person with AD as discontinuous could focus on helping them find some continuities in the person despite the AD, assisting them with appropriate care arrangements, and showing appreciation for their existential experience of distance from their prior relations with the person with AD. These family members may need help in recognizing that AD dementia does not immediately and totally transform a person, and that she or he may actively contribute to and participate in the life of the family. These family members may also benefit from a frank discussion about how we live in a culture where caring for others is seldom valued, and how the person providing care may be misunderstood as "addicted" to or dependent upon his or her need to care for others (Dreyfus & Rubin, in press). Offering a positive connotation for care of a family member who has AD may make closer relations possible for these families. Both of these interventions, however, must be tempered by attention to the family member's current possibilities in relation to the AD patient. Some family members, because of their background with the AD patient or because of their current social context, cannot tolerate closer emotional proximity to the AD patient, and thus their distance must be honored.

REFERENCES

Baumgarten, M. (1989). The health of persons giving care to the demented elderly: A critical review of the literature. *Journal of Clinical Epidemiology*, **42**, 1137-1148.

Benner, P., & Wrubel, J. (1989). *The primacy of caring, stress and coping in health and illness*. Menlo Park, CA: Sage.

Blieszner, R., & Shifflett, P. A. (1989). Affection, communication and commitment in adult-child caregiving for parents with Alzheimer's disease. In J. A. Mancini (Ed.), *Aging parents and adult children* (pp. 231-242). Lexington, MA: Lexington Books.

Blieszner, R., & Shifflett, P. A. (1990). The effects of Alzheimer's disease on close relationships between patients and caregivers. *Family Relations*, **39**, 57-62.

Bowers, B. J. (1987). Intergenerational caregiving: Adult caregivers and their aging parents. *Advances in Nursing Science*, **9**(2), 20-31.

Cohen, D., & Eisdorfer, C. (1986). *The loss of self*. New York: Norton.

Colerick, E. J., & George, L. K. (1986). Predictors of institutionalization among caregivers of patients with Alzheimer's Disease. *Journal of the American Geriatrics Society*, **34**, 493-498.

Dreyfus, H., & Rubin, J. (in press). Kierkegaard on the nihilism of the present age: The case of commitment as addiction. *Synthese*.

Farran, C. J., Keane-Hagerty, E., Salloway, S., Kupferer, S., & Wilken, C.S. (1991). Finding meaning: An alternative paradigm for Alzheimer's Disease family caregivers. *The Gerontologist*, **31**, 483-489.

Fillenbaum, G. G., & Smyer, M. A. (1981). The development, validity and reliability of the OARS Multidimensional Functional Assessment Questionnaire. *Journal of Gerontology*, **36**, 428-434.

Folstein, M., Folstein, S., & McHugh, P. (1975). Mini-mental state: A practical method for grading the cognitive state of patients for the clinician. *Journal of Psychiatric Research*, **12**, 189-198.

Hirschfeld, M. (1983). Homecare versus institutionalization: Family caregiving and senile brain disease. *International Journal of Nursing Studies*, **20**, 23-32.

Kuhlman, G. J., Wilson, H. S., Hutchinson, S. A., & Wallhagen, M. (1991). Alzheimer's disease and family caregiving: Critical synthesis of the literature and research agenda. *Nursing Research*, **40**, 331-337.

Liptzin, R., Grob, M., & Eisen, S. (1988). Family burden of demented and depressed elderly psychiatric inpatients. *The Gerontologist*, **28**, 397-401.

Lyman, K. A. (1989). Bring the social back in: A critique of the biomedicalization of dementia. *The Gerontologist*, **29**, 597-605.

Martinson, I. M., Chesla, C., & Muwaswes, M. (1993). Caregiving demands of patients with Alzheimer's Disease. *Journal of Community Health Nursing*, **10**, 225-232.

Martinson, I., Gilliss, C. L., Doyle, G., & Muwaswes, M. (1983). *The impact of Alzheimer's Disease on the family and caregiver*. San Francisco: University of California.

Orona, C. J. (1990). Temporality and identity loss due to Alzheimer's Disease. *Social Science in Medicine*, **30**, 1247-1256.

Ory, M. G., Williams, T. F., Emr, M., Lebowitz, B., Rabins, P., Salloway, J., Sluss-Radbaugh, T., Wolff, E., & Zarit, S. (1985). Families, informal supports and Alzheimer's Disease. *Research on Aging*, **7**, 623-644.

Packer, M. J., & Addison, R. B. (1989). *Entering the circle: Hermeneutic investigation in psychology*. Albany: SUNY Press.

Quayhagen, M. P., & Quayhagen, M. (1988). Alzheimer's stress: Coping with the caregiving role. *The Gerontologist*, **28**, 391-396.

Van Manen, M. (1990). *Researching lived experience*. London, Ontario: Althouse.

Walker, A. J., Pratt, C. C., & Oppy, N. C. (1992). Perceived reciprocity in family caregiving. *Family Relations*, **41**, 82-85.

Wright, L. K., Clipp, E. C., & George, L. K. (1993). State of the art review: Health consequences of caregiver stress. *Medicine, Exercise, Nutrition & Health*, **2**, 181-195.

The Long Road Back
A Daughter Deals With Her
Mother's Stroke

Patricia K. Lynch

Patricia Lynch is a CBS News producer currently working on "Eye to Eye" with Connie Chung and on other projects.

"Good night, darling, I love you," was the last complete sentence I heard my mother say. That was July 17, 1988. Sometime during the next morning, after she dressed and made her bed, a lightning bolt burned into her brain, destroying delicate tissue. That rogue blood clot took away my mother's ability to reason and to understand.

Her best friend found her later standing at the door, incoherent . . . disconnected. "Dementia" is what the doctors called it at the hospital, a psychotic episode. I somehow knew that Violet Lynch, 79, schoolteacher, mother, widow, was gone forever.

There were so many questions I never asked . . . so many things left unsaid. A stranger looked at me now with frightened eyes—pleading eyes, like those of an animal struck by a car. In the seconds that it took for the stroke to obliterate my mother's cognitive skills, our relationship changed irrevocably, from mother-daughter to daughter-child. In this awful role reversal, I became the caregiver to a woman whose first words to me at the hospital were, "Who are you?" My mother. A stranger.

The world *caregiver* is frequently a euphemism for unpaid female relative. A Travelers Insurance Company survey reports that nearly 7 of 10 primary caregivers are women, who spend an average of 16 hours a week providing care. According to the American Association of Retired Persons, 53 percent are daughters who are also employed.

And the elderly population is increasing: According to the census bureau, the number of people over 85 will triple by the year 2030. They are living longer but not better because of debilitating chronic illness and a health-care system that serves them poorly. Those first days she was in the hospital were unforgettable. "What is your mother's Medicare number?" "I don't know." Does she have private insurance?" "I don't know."

The day after my mother's stroke, she seemed to recognize me as someone familiar. Strangely, she also reacted to a photo of my dogs. "My babies," she mumbled, her eyes filling with tears. That night I showed her an old photo of her mother. "Momma . . . Momma," she said, crying.

I had no time to mourn the death of my mother. There was too much to do. I had to learn about Medicare and Medicaid and nursing homes and home care. And bills were coming in . . . from doctors whom I never met . . . "referrals" who were called in by the attending physicians . . . doctors who didn't return phone calls for days and had little to say when they did. One, a psychiatrist my mother had consulted in 1975 after my father and her only sister died, billed me $1,200 for hospital visits—visits to a woman who knew no one but two golden retrievers and a faded picture of her mother.

The hospital stay was a nightmare . . . of "roommates" who left because they could not deal with my mother's agitated behavior . . . of nurses who seldom stopped by . . . and of doctors who dropped by with eager students, and spoke about my mother as if she were a specimen. "See how her eyes do not follow my finger. See how she does not comprehend simple commands." The third day I ordered the medical group to leave the room.

Many of mother's friends stopped visiting. They saw their future in her eyes and were frightened. By the fourth day, my worst fears were realized. "Violet Lynch might improve somewhat, but . . ." My mother, who loved to read and do crossword puzzles and play bridge, would need 24-hour supervision the rest of her life. "I recommend a nursing home," a neurologist advised. A "discharge planner" reminded me of how "lucky" I was that the hospital was keeping her as long as they were—10 days. She also informed me that " 'Mom' is not a good candidate for a nursing home" because she needs "too much care."

I wheeled my mother out of the hospital. She had been given a heavy dose of Haldol, an anti-psychotic drug sometimes given to stroke and Alzheimer's victims. It was July 27, the first day of my vacation. I was very apprehensive because my employer at the time was not known for compassion. To ask for a leave of absence would have been professional suicide.

My mother showed no recognition of her surroundings. She said nothing when we got home and I put her to bed. Then I sat quietly nursing a strong Scotch, wondering what the hell I was going to do.

The next three weeks were a blur: Bathing. Feeding. Cooking. Medicating. Cleaning up mistakes. My mother could never be left alone. I found out the discharge planner was right. Violet was not a "good candidate" for a nursing home. Because of her dementia, no facility I found would accept her in a nonskilled home-care section—where people must be able to take care of their own basic needs.

According to Federal rules at the time, my mother wasn't sick enough for the skilled nursing-care section. After visiting several, I grew to hate the smell of urine and the sight of once-dignified people tied to their chairs, staring at nothing. Medicare didn't cover intermediate facilities. My mother had enough money for a good nursing home...but she didn't fit the requirements. She was put on a waiting list—a year or two for the best places. So I started pursuing home care.

Back then, private agencies wanted $150 just to sit down and talk about my mother's needs. I was told to expect to pay $100 a day excluding carfare and food for a nurse's aide who would feed and bathe my mother and "watch her so she doesn't get into any trouble." Technically, an aide is not supposed to administer medication, but I was told—"off the record"—that most would if I left "specific instructions." Friends began to tell me horror stories—of aides who robbed them blind, of people who never showed up, of abuse. A quick review of our finances revealed that my mother's Social Security and pension couldn't completely pay for home care. My salary and the money she meant for me to inherit would have to make up the difference. Then my luck changed. A friend of mine had a housekeeper whose sister needed a job. Olivia's salary was affordable, and she hit it off with Mother. We began to reduce the dosage of Haldol gradually, and mother became less zombielike. I began to feel I could return to work.

Then, in the middle of one night, I awoke to find my mother standing over my bed...screaming. She was hospitalized for what was described as another psychotic episode. Earlier I had discovered her turning the dial of her TV and looking frantic. She seemed to know that she used to understand what the people on the screen were saying. And now she didn't. The doctors said the "event" was caused by reduced blood supply to the brain. Her prognosis was poor. The glass over her mother's picture was removed, as were all sharp objects—in case she tried to kill herself. Once again she was put on Haldol, which turned her into a robot.

While the doctors tried to find a chemical solution, I spent hours on the phone getting rejections from nursing homes because of my mother's dementia: "too much work."

I called a friend, a Catholic priest, for advice. He gave me names, then asked quietly, "May I pray for your mother?" It was September 6. That night, when I got to the hospital, my mother was coherent for the first time since the "event." "The medicine finally kicked in," a doctor explained. Probably...but I asked Father Ralph to keep praying.

Almost six years have passed. My mother has had two minor "events" since the massive stroke, and she needs a cane to walk. But Violet Lynch, now 85, still lives at home with Olivia. Without her, we could not have made it. I fenced in my mother's yard, and two stray dogs have joined the family. She loves them and her home, which I gradually renovated to meet her needs. (A bathroom downstairs, railings, a heated porch that will be her bedroom when she needs to be downstairs full time.)

My mother lives completely in the present now...without Haldol... and takes only heart and blood-pressure medication. Her doctor is amazed that she made it...and actually has improved. Violet is still aphasic and has trouble remembering words, and she can't read or write, but she understands TV, friendship and love.

Her savings—"my inheritance"—was spent long ago, but we manage. I am happy that my mother is someone I know again. The frightened stranger is gone—I hope forever.

Should This Marriage Be Saved?

Many Americans are trying to make marriages more permanent—and divorce more difficult

ELIZABETH GLEICK

ON A CHILLY MONDAY NIGHT, Laura Richards and Mark Geyman are sitting in a living room in Jeffersonville, Indiana, their hands clasped tightly together in Laura's lap. This attractive, clean-cut couple met last May through a mutual friend and got engaged in November, and they are happy to tell John and Patti Thompson, their mentors in the St. Augustine Catholic Church's marriage-preparation program, all about their wedding plans. It will be a big June affair, Laura says, with eight bridesmaids and eight groomsmen, two flower girls, a ring bearer and two priests. Patti Thompson cuts through the chatter. "How much time have you put into your marriage?" she asks, adding pointedly, "Your wedding is just one day. Your marriage is the rest of your life."

The conversation grinds to a brief, awkward halt, then takes a turn into the wilderness—into the thicket of this young couple's most intimate concerns and darkest fears. Patti tells Laura, a 29-year-old department store salesclerk, that in her opinion it is O.K. to take birth-control pills on the advice of her doctor to help with PMS. Then John, coordinator of family ministry at St. Augustine, says, "Is either one of you jealous?"

"Yeah," admits Mark, who works in international customer service for United Parcel Service. He laughs and adds, "She gets jealous of some of the girls in the office," then explains how Laura once visited him at his previous job and became uncomfortable after she overheard him repeatedly compliment a female co-worker on her job performance. Laura smiles nervously, fidgets with a pen and says nothing.

Patti urges Laura and Mark to continue discussing Laura's jealousy when they are alone together. Soon the Thompsons hit upon other prickly topics: Mark's compulsive neatness and Laura's worry that her future mother-in-law has reservations about the pending nuptials.

After Mark and Laura leave, the first of four 90-minute sessions completed, the Thompsons—who have been married 31 years and have raised four children—offer an assessment of this couple's chances at marital harmony. It is based not just on gut impressions but also on a computer printout of the pair's "premarital inventory"—more than 100 questions about everything from the number of children they want to whether they are comfortable being naked in front of each other. Mark and Laura, who scored 72 out of 100 on this compatibility test, should do just fine, says Patti, but "there are just some things that smack you in the face that say they've got some work to do."

Working on a relationship, of course, is an activity that everyone—save for perhaps the most wildly romantic and misguided among us—has come to regard as a sometimes thrilling, sometimes infuriating, but always necessary exercise. But Mark and Laura, well meaning, full of love and hope, with their lives ahead of them and their family values just taking shape, are actually on the cutting edge—even if it is an old blade. Although the Catholic Church has always required engaged couples to undergo pre-Cana counseling—usually just one day of talks from a priest and a married couple about finances, communication and family planning—a more intensive form of preparation is coming into practice not only among Catholics but also among churchgoers of all denominations across America. Last November clergy in the Louisville, Kentucky, area became the 26th religious coalition in the U.S. to adopt standard premarital procedures that, in the words of the Kentuckiana

Marriage Task Force, express "the seriousness with which we view marriage and the preparation we are convinced is vital." Says Michael McManus, author of the 1993 *Marriage Savers* and a national leader of this particular bandwagon: "We're preventing bad marriages. If it is the job of a church to bond couples for life, it has to provide more help before and after."

If this new marital *gravitas* were simply a church-based phenomenon, it would not be a phenomenon at all; the clergy has traditionally attempted to shore up the moral foundations of people's private lives. But a growing recognition that marriages are not to be entered into—or dissolved—lightly because of the enormous social and economic costs is dawning in some unlikely places and crossing political lines. Conservatives who espouse "family values" have long lamented the trend toward throwaway marriage and quickie divorce. But in President Clinton's recent State of the Union speech he too took time out to introduce the Revs. John and Diana Cherry, whose ministry convinces couples "to come back together to save their marriages and to raise their kids." Meanwhile, there is a new sensitivity among divorce lawyers that breakups can have a devastating effect on everyone involved—and so comes a nudge toward reconciliation or mediation, lost revenues be damned! An increasing number of marital therapists believe it is their job to save the relationship rather than simply help each party pursue his or her chosen path.

Several people have gone so far as to suggest imposing a waiting period for marriage licenses, modeled after gun laws. "Both kinds of licenses," explains historian Glenda Riley, author of *Divorce: An American Tradition*, "create a volatile situation." And just last week, a group of mostly

From *Time*, February 27, 1995, pp. 48-53, 56. © 1995 by Time Inc. Magazine Company. Reprinted by permission.

female state lawmakers in Washington introduced a bill that would require marriage licenses to come with warnings about spousal abuse. "I would say, simply, 'Beware. Stop, look, listen and be cautious,' " said state senator Margarita Prentice, a co-sponsor of the bill, which is expected to pass the Democratic Senate but run into trouble in the Republican House. "Marriage is serious business."

In 1993, 2.3 million couples—in living rooms and city halls, in churches and synagogues and backyards, on mountaintops and while scuba diving—performed that most optimistic of human rituals and got married. That same year, 1.2 million couples agreed, officially, that their marriages could not be saved. Again in 1993, the Bureau of the Census projected that four out of 10 first marriages would end in divorce. Indeed, the number of divorces began soaring in the mid-60s and has declined only slightly since peaking at a little over 1.2 million in 1981. Thus, despite sporadic cheers about falling divorce rates, couples have not gotten much better at staying together—not yet anyway. Divorce, Glenda Riley claims, reflects the true American spirit; after the country achieved independence, she says, people wrote divorce petitions that read something like: "My husband is tyrannical. If the U.S. can get rid of King George, I can get rid of him."

THE INSTITUTION OF MARRIAGE underwent a particularly rebellious and dramatic shift when women entered the work force. "People don't have to stay married because of economic forces now," explains Frank Furstenberg Jr., co-author of the 1991 Divided Families and a sociology professor at the University of Pennsylvania who has been studying divorce for 20 years. "We're in the midst of trying to renegotiate what the marriage contract is—what men and women are supposed to do as partners." But the chips in these negotiations are often young children, emotionally fragile, economically vulnerable—for despite their work outside the home, most women still suffer a severe income drop after divorce. The by-product of what remains the world's highest divorce rate is millions of children thrown into poverty, millions more scarred by bifurcated lives and loyalties.

Almost no one disputes there are many valid reasons for divorce—among them, domestic violence, child abuse and substance abuse. Mere incompatibility seems reason enough, when no children are involved. But the breakup of families is increasingly seen not only as a personal tragedy but also as a social crisis. Which may be why, suddenly, there seems to be so much attention being paid to preventing divorce. "We're seeing a trend in the past couple of years toward cou-

ples doing more work to preserve and strengthen relationships," says Froma Walsh, co-director of the Center for Family Health at the University of Chicago.

Certainly marital therapy has become big business in the past decade or so, though few hard figures are available. Some 4.6 million couples a year visit 50,000 licensed family therapists, up from 1.2 million in 1980. Thousands of couples swear by such programs as PAIRS (Practical Application of Intimate Relationship Skills), the semester-long relationship class offered by the PAIRS Foundation in 50 U.S. cities (as well as 16 other countries), or Retrouvaille, a church-sponsored program in which couples who have weathered their own marital difficulties run weekend seminars for other couples in trouble.

"People are poorly trained for marriage today," says Joyce Clark, a coordinator for Retrouvaille in Youngstown, Ohio. From her 34-year marriage she recognizes all the stages of matrimony: romance, casual irritation, (he doesn't put the toilet seat down; she stays on the phone too long), then total disillusionment. "This is when many couples decide to bail out. They don't realize that they can still work back to romance," says Clark, who suffered through five years of misery after discovering her husband Pat had had an affair. Then she and Pat attended a Retrouvaille weekend and learned how to forgive, how to get over it—and how to fight. "Everyone I knew who had the same problem was divorced," says Joyce of the crisis in her marriage. "I wanted to find one person who survived and was in good shape. Now we work in the movement because somebody out there is waiting to see us."

Perhaps the newest, and most unlikely, recruits in the battle against divorce are lawyers. Last fall Lynne Gold-Bikin, a divorce attorney in Norristown, Pennsylvania, who chairs the family law division of the American Bar Association, founded the Preserving Marriages Project. "Divorce lawyers as individuals have no vested interest in saving marriages," Gold-Bikin says. "It's not our business. But we know the problems more than anyone else. Every day we see kids being yanked back and forth. Enough. I'm sick of people not recognizing what they're doing."

Last October, Gold-Bikin took her project—to which some 3200 lawyers have contributed time and money—to more than 50 high-school classrooms nationwide. During five sessions, juniors and seniors do role-playing exercises and homework designed to give an overview of family law and show how difficult it can be to maintain a serious relationship. "We're trying to teach these things to kids because many are not learning them at home," Gold-Bikin says. In March, Gold-Bikin will conduct a weekend seminar for couples who have been married one year; after that, she hopes to create a marriage-

Taking Stock

PREPARE (Premarital Personal and Relationship Evaluation), a set of 125 questions developed by University of Minnesota family social science professor David Olson to assess a couple's compatibility, has been administered to some 500,000 couples worldwide. The results are computer scored, and, claims Olson, can determine with 80% to 85% accuracy which couples will divorce. "Ten percent [of those who take the inventory] are so shocked by their poor scores, they break their engagement," contends Michael McManus, author of Marriage Savers. "That can be painful, but much less painful than a divorce with two kids." Individuals are asked if they ·"Agree Strongly," "Agree," are "Undecided," "Disagree," or "Disagree Strongly" with statements such as the following:

▶ I believe most disagreements we currently have will decrease after marriage.

▶ I expect that some romantic love will fade after marriage.

▶ I am concerned about my partner's drinking/smoking.

▶ I wish my partner was more careful in spending money.

▶ I am satisfied with the amount of affection I receive from my partner.

▶ My partner and I sometimes disagree regarding our interest in sex.

▶ I have some concerns about how my partner will be as a parent.

▶ We disagree on whether the husband's occupation should be a top priority in deciding where we live.

▶ I can easily share my positive and negative feelings with my partner.

▶ My partner is less interested in talking about our relationship than I am.

▶ We have some important disagreements that never seem to get resolved.

▶ I enjoy spending some time alone without my partner.

▶ At times I feel pressure to participate in activities my partner enjoys.

▶ My partner and I agree on how much we will share the household chores.

▶ We sometimes disagree on how to practice our religious beliefs.

preservation program for corporations, which she claims suffer tremendous productivity losses because of divorce.

All such efforts are applauded by Judith Wallerstein, the California clinical psychologist who first raised public consciousness about the lasting damage of divorce. After studying 131 children of divorce over a span of 15 years, she found them to be at higher risk for depression, poor grades, substance abuse and intimacy problems. "We started to report this," she says, "and people got angry. They said, 'Impossible! If it's good for the parents, it's good for the children.' They wanted to believe that divorce and women's lib would take care of everything."

Though Wallerstein's results are debatable, they have definitely seeped into the zeitgeist and affected not only efforts to stay married but also how people approach divorce. More and more often, couples are seeking to avoid ugly fights over custody, property and money. A St. Louis, Missouri, couple who do not want their names used are dissolving their marriage after 17 years, two daughters, couples therapy and individual counseling. They have chosen to use a mediator and work out the details at the kitchen table. "It's a much healthier environment for [the children]," says the wife, a Presbyterian minister. "They see that we still treat each other with respect." The six- to eight-month process will cost $2,500 and produce a divorce decree, a property agreement and a parenting plan to be submitted for court approval.

On the state level too, there is a growing belief that if divorcing couples cannot reconcile, they should at least be taught how to split in a reasonable fashion. Bucking the trend to make divorce ever easier and quicker, Utah and Connecticut have mandatory education programs for all parents of minor children entering the family court. Six states are considering such regulations in a current session of their legislature. "This is the latest trend in family courts," says Michael Pitts, who until recently was executive director of the Children's Rights Council in Washington, "and it is a lasting one."

In many other states, including Maryland, Virginia, New Jersey and Florida, divorce-education classes are required in some counties, or at the discretion of some family court judges. Some family judges have even taken it upon themselves to involve the children directly. As of last November, divorcing parents in Dade County, Florida, attend one mandatory course, while children attend another, called Kids in Divorce Succeeding (KIDS). Sherri Thrower, a 30-year-old mother of five, says the parenting classes have really helped her. "There were a lot of cobwebs in my mind," she says. "A lot of confusion." She and her husband tried several times to reconcile for the sake of the children, but the attempts ultimately failed. Now her main concern is for her kids. "I don't want to teach them anything bad about their father," she says. "My son has been missing him more and more. He doesn't know how to deal with it." Thrower's children have attended the KIDS program, which uses a curriculum called Sandcastles.

IN SANDCASTLES THE CHILDREN ARE divided into small groups by age, and each group is run by a therapist and a teacher. Older children may write poems, do role-playing or create their own talk shows, while the younger kids draw pictures of their families and talk about them, or write letters to their parents and read them aloud. "When you come home from court, I want you to have a happy face, not a sad one," reads Edward, 10, during the Saturday morning session. "Mom, I love you. Dad, I miss you," says Dave. Another child reads, "If you were divorced, you wouldn't fight. I wish you were divorced." Explains psychotherapist Gary Neuman, who developed Sandcastles: "When kids see there are all these other kids experiencing the same type of things, it immediately alleviates the intense feelings of isolation children of divorce experience."

Though the Federal Government has no jurisdiction over marriage and divorce, indirectly the impact of federal programs is enormous. Current welfare policy, for example, pays AFDC benefits only when there is no man in the house, thus fueling divorce and abandonment. And in a broader sense says University of California, Berkeley, sociology professor Arlie Hochschild, author of the landmark study about two-career marriages, *The Second Shift,* "we do not have a family-friendly society." Better day care, plentiful jobs at decent wages, flex- time and job sharing would all help to reduce the stresses on American households, which are overtaxed, overburdened and overwhelmed. And while entering into marriage with the utmost care and deepest consideration can only be to the good, it may be marriage itself—along with the most basic institutions like the workplace—that continues to need refining. "I would say we're in a stalled revolution," says Hochschild, "Women have gone into the labor force, but not much else has changed to adapt to that new situation. We have not rewired the notion of manhood so that it makes sense to men to participate at home. Marriage then becomes the shock absorber of those strains."

Mark Geyman and Laura Richards are convinced that they are increasingly prepared to handle those strains. Since they began meeting with Patti and John Thompson, says Mark, "we have done a lot of talking, more than we were." They have had conversations about whose family they will see during holidays and how they will handle their finances. And they have tried to grapple with the problem of Laura's jealousy. "It's been helpful," says Mark. "I think she's beginning to open up a little more. She's being more trusting." The fact that one of Laura's sisters is going through a divorce makes the idea of building a secure marriage from the outset feel all the more urgent to this young couple. And in spite of the problems that have begun to crop up during a time when they wish only to focus on the excitement of planning a wedding, Laura insists she is looking into her future with, well, a somewhat tempered confidence. As she puts it, "I'm still sure we want to get married, and everything."

—*Reported by Ann Blackman/Washington, Gideon Gil/Jeffersonville, Jenifer Mattos/New York, Elizabeth B. Mullen/San Francisco, Sophfronia Scott Gregory/Miami, and Leslie Whitaker/Chicago*

lessons from stepfamilies

Yes, they are more complicated. But they're also richer. Stepfamilies turn out to be living laboratories for what it takes to create successful relationships. They have surprising things to tell us all about marriage, gender relations, parenting, and the intricacies of family life.

Virginia Rutter

Virginia Rutter is a freelance writer living in Seattle who reports on family, marital, and sex research, among other things. She has worked as public affairs director at the Johns Hopkins School of Public Health and the American Association for Marriage and Family Therapy. She is currently coordinating a project on collaborative, psychosocial health care.

Here we are, three decades into the divorce revolution, and we still don't quite know what to make of stepfamilies. We loved the Brady Bunch, but that was before we discovered how unreal they were. Now that stepfamilies embrace one of three children and, one way or another, impact the vast majority of Americans, we can't seem to get past seeing them as the spawn of failure, the shadow side of our over-idealized traditional family. When we think of them at all, we see only what they are not—hence their designation as "nontraditional" families, heaped with unwed moms, gay parents, and other permutations that make up the majority of families today. By the year 2000, stepfamilies will outnumber all other family types.

Despite their ambiguous standing, stepfamilies are getting first-class attention from social scientists. Much of what they are discovering is eye-opening. Although, for example, it is widely known that second marriages are less stable than first ones—with a break-up rate of 60 percent, versus 50 percent for first marriages—that statistic paints stepfamilies with too broad a brush; it conceals their very real success. A far more useful, more important fact is that stepfamilies do indeed face instability, but that shakiness occurs early in the re-

marriage—and may ultimately be traced to lack of support from the culture. In denying them the status of "real family," we may be doing much to undermine their chances of success. Nevertheless, once remarriage families make it over the early hurdle, they are even stronger than traditional families.

Let this turnabout truth serve as a metaphor for what is now coming to light about stepfamilies. They are certainly more complex than first-marriage families—but they are also richer. New information about what really goes on, and what goes wrong, in stepfamilies will definitely change the way you think about them. It also promises to change the way you think about *all* families. Among the new findings:

• Contrary to myth, stepfamilies have a high rate of success in raising healthy children. Eighty percent of the kids come out fine.

• These stepkids are resilient, and a movement to study their resilience—not just their problems—promises to help more kids succeed in any kind of family, traditional or otherwise.

• What trips stepkids up has little to do with stepfamilies per se. The biggest source of problems for kids in stepfamilies is parental conflict leftover from the first marriage.

•A detailed understanding of the specific problems stepfamilies encounter now exists, courtesy of longitudinal research—not studies that tap just the first six months of stepfamily adjustment.

•Stepfamilies turn out to be a gender trap—expectations about women's roles and responsibilities are at the root of many problems that develop in stepfamilies.

•After five years, stepfamilies are more stable than first-marriage families, because second marriages are happier than first marriages. Stepfamilies experience most of their troubles in the first two years.

•Stepfamilies are not just make-do households limping along after loss. All members experience real gains, notably the opportunity to thrive under a happier relationship.

•The needs of people in stepfamilies are the needs of people in all families—to be accepted, loved, and cared about; to maintain attachments; to belong to a group and not be a stranger; and to feel some control by maintaining order in their lives. It's just that these needs are made acutely visible—and unavoidable—in stepfamilies.

THE MYTHS AND THE RESEARCH

Despite the prevalence of stepfamilies, myths about them abound. You probably know some of them: There's an Evil Stepmother, mean, manipulative, and jealous. The stepfather is a molester, a sexual suspect—Woody Allen. The ex-wife is victimized, vindictive, interfering—a She-Devil. The ex-husband is withdrawn, inept, the contemporary Absentee Father. And the kids are nuisances intent on ruining their parents' lives; like Maisie in Henry James' story of 19th century post-divorce life, they play the parents and stepparents like billiard balls.

The familiarity of these myths can't be blamed solely on Dan Quayle, nor on nostalgia for the 1950s. Stepfamilies are a challenge. There are attachments that must be maintained through a web of conflicting emotions. There are ambiguities of identi-

Reprinted with permission from *Psychology Today*, May/June 1994, pp. 30-33, 60, 62, 64, 66, 68-69. © 1994 by Sussex Publishers, Inc.

ty, especially in the first years. Adults entering stepfamilies rightly feel anxious about their performance in multiple roles (spouse, instant parent) and about their acceptance by the kids and by the ex-spouse, who must remain a caring parent to the children. When an ex-spouse's children become someone else's stepchildren and spend time in a "stranger's" home, he or she worries about the children's comfort, their role models—and their loyalty.

Out of this worry are born the mythic stereotypes—and the fear of reliving a bad fairy tale. A stepmother, for example, forced to take on the role of disciplinarian because the children's biological father may lack a clear understanding of his own responsibilities—is set up to be cast as evil.

'Stepfamilies turn out to be a gender trap—expectations about women's roles are at the root of many problems that develop in stepfamilies.'

Still, there is a growing recognition among researchers that for every real pitfall a myth is built on, stepfamilies offer a positive opportunity in return. Researchers and stepfamilies are asking questions about resilience and health, not just pathology. In "The Family In Transition," a special issue of the *Journal of Family Psychology* in June 1993, editors and stepfamily researchers Mavis Hetherington, Ph.D., and James Bray, Ph.D., explained it this way: "Although divorce and remarriage may confront families with stresses and adaptive challenges, they also offer opportunities for personal growth and more harmonious, fulfilling family and personal relationships. Contemporary research is focusing on the diversity of responses to divorce, life in a single-parent household, and remarriage."

It is now clear from detailed research that the adaptation to stepfamily relation-

ships depends on the timing of the transition in the children's lives, the individuals involved, and the unique changes and stresses presented to the group.

THE 80 PERCENT WHO SUCCEED
Take Hetherington's research, considered the definitive, longitudinal study of post-divorce families, conducted at the University of Virginia. She found that children in post-divorce and remarriage families may experience depression, conduct disorders, lower academic performance, and delinquency. Such problems are the result of reductions in parental attention that may immediately follow divorce or remarriage. There are the distractions of starting a new marriage. Such lapses may also be the outgrowth of parental conflict. They may reflect a noncustodial parent's withdrawal from the scene altogether. There's the stress of reductions in resources—typically, the lowered income of divorced mothers—and the disruption of routines, so highly valued by children, when two residences are established.

Hetherington, however, is quick to point to her finding that 80 percent of children of divorce and remarriage do *not* have behavior problems, despite the expectations and challenges, compared to 90 percent of children of first marriage families. Kids whose parents divorce and remarry are not doomed.

This high success rate, Hetherington and others recognize, is a testament to the resilience of children. Further study, she believes, can teach us more about the strengths summoned up in stepfamilies—and how to support them. But that would also contradict the gloom-and-doom scenarios that, though they do not actually describe most stepfamilies, often get trotted out on state occasions.

Needless to say, scientifically researching strength and resilience in stepfamilies, complete with a control group, poses great challenges. Building a scientific model of stepfamilies isn't simply trying to pin down a moving target, it's like trying to pin down many moving targets—up to four sets of kids from previous marriages in as many residences at different times—with none of them on the same radar screen at once.

From the standpoint of the kids, yes, they feel loss going into a stepfamily—it certifies that their original family exists no more. And it takes time to adjust to a new set of people in family roles. But the new arrangement is not just a problem appearing in their lives by default. Elizabeth Carter, M.S.W., director of the Westches-

ter Family Institute, points to specific opportunities a stepfamily affords. Children acquire multiple role models, they get a chance to see their parents happier with other people than they were with each other. They learn how to be flexible.

Because they come into the world with no relationship ties but must forge their own, stepfamilies provide a living laboratory for studying what makes all families successful, insists psychologist Emily Visher, Ph.D., who cofounded the Stepfamily Association of America in 1979 with her husband, psychiatrist John Visher, M.D., after finding herself in a stepfamily and no rules to go by. For their pioneering efforts, the Vishers jointly received a Lifetime Contribution Award from the American Association for Marriage and Family Therapy at its annual meeting last fall.

Addressing an audience packed to the rafters in a mammoth sports arena, Visher

'Stepfamilies provide lessons for all families, because their emotions and problems are common—but they are exposed by an open structure.'

emphasized that "stepfamilies provide lessons for all families, because their emotions and problems are common to all people—but they are exposed by the open structure of stepfamilies." The process of bonding and belonging is made entirely, sometimes painfully, visible.

THE COPARENTING FACTOR
It turns out that it's the parents, not the stepfamily, that make the most difference in the success of stepfamilies.

"Remember, divorce isn't ending the family. It is restructuring it," explains Carter. "Parents and children don't get divorced. Parents and children aren't an optional relationship. One of the biggest issues for stepfamilies is: How can we stay in touch?" The steady, regular involvement of both biological parents in their children's lives come what may is known in the family biz as coparenting.

Today's most familiar stepfamily setup is a mother and her biological children living with a man who is not their birth father, and a noncustodial father in another residence—although the dilemmas of maintaining parenting responsibilities are much more complicated than who lives with whom. The U.S. Bureau of the Census reports that 14 percent of children in stepfamilies live with their biological father, 86 percent live with their biological mother and their stepfather. Whatever the situation, the parents' job is to find a way to stay in touch with each other so that both can remain completely in touch with their children.

Study after study shows that divorce and remarriage do not harm children—parental conflict does. That was the conclusion of research psychologists Robert Emery, Ph.D., of the University of Virginia, and Rex Forehand, Ph.D., of the University of Georgia, in a 1993 review of the divorce research. Sociologist Andrew Cherlin, Ph.D., author of the classic *Divided Families*, reported in *Science* magazine that children with difficulty after divorce started having problems long before divorce took place, as a result of parental conflict.

While divorce forces temporary disruption and a period of adjustment to loss and to new routines, marital conflict produces long-term disturbances. Depression and anger, often acted out in behavior problems, substance abuse, and delinquency, are all especially common among children in families where conflict rages. Following divorce, adversarial coparenting or the withdrawal of one of the parents from his or her (but usually his) role undermines children's healthy development.

The solution, of course, is cooperation of the parents in coparenting following divorce and remarriage. Desirable as it is, cooperative parenting between divorced spouses is rare, attained only in a minority of cases, Hetherington and Bray note.

WHY IS COPARENTING SO DIFFICULT?

Most marriages don't end mutually with friendship—so jealousy and animosity are easily aroused—and ex-spouses aren't two folks practiced at getting along anyway. Yet the ability of exes to get along is a key to the success of a new stepfamily.

Remarriage of one or both ex-spouses only enlarges the challenge of getting along —while possibly increasing tension between the ex-spouses responsible for co-parenting. A stepparent who becomes a part of the kids' lives usually has no relationship to the child's other biological parent; if anything there is hostility.

The ideal, says John Visher, is creation of a "parenting coalition" among the parents and stepparents in both households. "From the beginning, the new couple needs to work together in making family decisions." One of the most important is how, and by whom, the children will be disciplined, and on that score the evidence is clear: only a birth parent has the authority to discipline his or her children.

Betty Carter is quick to warn, however, that stepparents cannot interfere with their spouse in parenting. Involved but not interfering? A parenting coalition requires the parents include their new spouses in family decisions. The new spouses, for their part, must support the parenting duties and the coparenting bond between the ex-spouses.

IT TAKES RESPECT

The glue that makes it all happen is respect, the Vishers report. Both parents must require kids and stepparents to treat one another with respect. Only then can bonds between them develop. Despite feelings of jealousy and animosity, first and second spouses must also accord one another respect to accomplish the coparenting tasks the children need to do well.

For their part, the kids also need each of the coparents to refer to the other parent with respect. Children are quick to pick up hints of hostility on either side. For them, hostility becomes an invitation to play the grown-ups off each other, and to imitate unkind behavior.

> 'Children are quick to pick up hints of hostility on either side. For them, it becomes an open invitation to play the grown-ups off each other.'

When the parents are adversarial, their hostility inhibits children from freely spending time with both parents, and the kids suffer. They lack the one-on-one attention that breeds a sense of self-value. And they are torn in half. All in all, it's a recipe for disappointment and anger.

ANY HELP?

"If you can help parents and stepparents early on to deal with issues of child-rearing appropriately, they have a lot of potential for giving stability to children and exposing them to appropriately happy relationships," says Australian research psychologist Jan Lawton. Lawton is spokesperson for The Stepfamily Project at the University of Queensland, a major government study of behavioral interventions for stepfamilies with troubled children.

What kind of help do stepfamilies need? Information and support. Stepfamily support groups exist across the United States, many of them organized by the Stepfamily Association. The organization responds to about 400 information requests each week from stepfamilies—while 7,000 new stepfamilies are forming weekly.

Stepfamily functioning improves dramatically when participants know which problems are normal, which are temporary, and that it takes time for people to integrate themselves and feel comfortable in a stepfamily. Lawton's study has demonstrated the benefits of practical guidance, and she has found that even a little help goes a long way. "The positive part of this study is that we can help stepfamilies with a very minimal amount of therapy and self-help, aimed at the right areas." The components of the Queensland program are a map of stepfamily problem areas.

•Child-Management Training, for parents and stepparents, to help them focus their attention on the children at a time when there's a tendency to slip a little on monitoring and disciplining the kids. The adults often get overly absorbed in their new romance.

•Partner-Support Training for newly remarried couples, since they don't automatically work together as a team during the first two years, when they are also at high risk for divorce. Such support helps them while their relationship is undergoing trial by fire in the new stepfamily.

•Communication and Problem-Solving Training for the entire new stepfamily helps everyone learn to talk together, understand each other, and learn how to solve problems and reach consensus.

Lawton reports as much as a 60 percent reduction in behavior problems and about 50 percent improvement in child adjustment, self-esteem, and parent/stepparent conflict. While therapy had a slight margin over self-help, persons in both groups outperformed by far the control group that received no help during the study. Those with the most troubled children do best with formal therapy; the rest do fine with self-help. Indeed, programs families could apply at home are especially useful, since stepfamilies involve people already weighed down by multiple demands, and coordinating a formal appointment can be formidable.

The key, Lawton says, is to reach stepfamilies at the beginning when they need basic information about what to expect. Lawton's next project is a prevention study, seeking the most effective ways to help all stepfamilies—not just ones where the children have behavior problems.

MORE HELP: A HAPPY MARRIAGE

If coparenting can be accomplished, children benefit in at least two ways. They feel loved by both biological parents; no child can thrive without affectionate connections. And they gain from being exposed to remarried adults in a successful intimate relationship. Especially when remarriage occurs before the children are teenagers, there is great potential for easy adaptation and smooth development.

A remarriage at adolescence, however, poses added challenges to adjustment and success of the stepfamily, Bray and Hetherington report. It's a critical time of identity formation. Daughters are particularly apt to get into fights with stepmothers. Sexual tension may develop between stepfather and a budding adolescent stepdaughter, manifest in aloofness and what every parent knows as snottiness. Even if the divorce occurred many years before, a parent's remarriage during a child's teen years can revive adjustment difficulties that may have cropped up during the divorce.

Generally, though, a successful second marriage helps to reduce—if not eliminate—kids' problems. Divorced people are generally more compatible with their second partner than their first—even though there is a higher divorce rate among second marriages.

Clinical psychology lore has it that the high divorce rate is because the spouses are making the same mistake again. Divorcing spouses have problems with intimate relationships, not with a particular partner, the thinking goes, and they are more apt to bail out a second time.

But this view is totally contradicted by those who have closely scrutinized many stepfamilies. The Vishers are among them. So is University of Southern California sociologist Constance Ahrons, Ph.D. They point out that a lot of second divorces are the result not of conventional marital deterioration but of problems in integrating into a household children and adults who are not related to each other.

"The divorce rate among remarried families is high in the first two years—then it slows down," says Lawton. "By about the five-year period, second relationships are more stable than first relationships. I see these couples at very high risk during the first few years, but thereafter offering great benefits to the children."

LOOKING AT THE PROBLEMS

While stepfamilies are doing a lot better than they're generally given credit for, a not insubstantial 20 percent of them—or twice the number of first-marriage families—do have problems with the kids. The research illuminating the specific problems in stepfamilies points to the basic requirements of stepfamilies as the major stumbling blocks. Cooperative coparenting. Equal involvement of both parents after the divorce. Noninterference by stepparents.

> **'Sexual tension may develop between stepfather and adolescent stepdaughter, and manifest in aloofness and snottiness.'**

Support for the coparenting relationship.

Bray's longitudinal study of stepfamilies has tracked mothers, stepfathers, and children, who were around six years old at the time of remarriage, over the next seven years. During the early months of remarriage, behavior problems rise steeply among the children. This is a time when stepfamilies are not yet cohesive—they are not likely to think of themselves as a unit.

Gradually, behavior problems subside over the next two years. By then stepfamilies are just as likely as first-marriage families to have developed useful ways of communicating, rules of behavior, and discipline. They may not consider themselves as cohesive, but objective evaluation finds few practical differences.

In Bray's study, trouble with the children developed when there was a reduction in time and attention from one or both parents, and reduced resources. These parental lapses, Bray notes, arise most often from problems of coparenting, and difficulties of stepparents in supporting the coparenting role.

But even the reduced parental attention does not doom the children. Hetherington observes that the reduced parental attention can also be seen as an opportunity for the children to take on responsibility. The end result is that some children—almost always daughters—wind up more capable and competent.

Others, however, particularly at adolescence, respond to the lapse of parental attention by going off and experimenting with sex or drugs. Younger children may display more conduct problems and depression. Both younger and older kids are at risk for lower academic achievement.

While few distinctions turn up between the ways daughters and sons react to being in a stepfamily, Bray did find increased conflict between stepfathers and stepdaughters at puberty. Hetherington also found difficulties with teenage daughters, and warns that remarriage when a daughter is entering adolescence promises to produce tremendous tension and resentment on the part of the daughter.

Daughters, who have grown close to their mothers and increasingly identify with them at the onset of puberty, will have difficulty with the addition of either a mother's new spouse, who is competition for her, or a father's new spouse—who is competition for her mother. What the girls are feeling is divided loyalty.

DIVIDED LOYALTIES

Stepfamilies are littered with possibilities for loyalty conflicts, say the Vishers. A particularly common one revolves around entry of new stepparent. A mom feels hostile toward her ex-husband's new partner; kids understand that their mom wants them to feel the same way. The same kids are also being asked by their dad to love the new wife, whom he loves. The kids feel torn because their parents are pulling them in opposite ways.

It is an axiom of psychology that when kids feel torn, they erupt in symptoms—like bad behavior or depression. It may be a desperate attempt to draw attention away from the unresolvable conflict between the parents. Whatever the source of divided loyalties, once kids feel them, they develop problems—if not behavior problems or depression, then the symptoms of anxiety. The solution? Back to coparenting. It is up to the adults to rise above jealousy or romanticism and work together for the good of the kids.

The respect they use to make the system operate must include appreciation for the inevitability of ambivalent feelings in the kids. And that, says Emily Visher, is one of the most important lessons from stepfamilies for all families. "The ability of adults to share with children ambivalence over loss and change determines how well they will do in the future. It paves the way for sharing other thoughts. It leads to a sense of mastery of whatever life presents."

> **'Lesson #1: The ability of adults to share with kids ambivalence over loss and change determines how well they will do in the future.'**

One of the sizable traps in remarriage is the temptation a new spouse may feel to interfere with the coparenting process, observes William Doherty, Ph.D., family social scientist at the University of Minnesota. The new spouse may feel insecure or jealous of the coparent's continuing attachment to the former spouse. Still, that only succeeds in dividing the loyalty of the biological parent. A weekly conversation with an ex-spouse about the kids might trouble an anxious new spouse—but the communication is essential and the stepparent has the obligation to adjust, just as the parents do, for the good of the kids.

On the other hand, no stepparent should be expected to love, or even like, a partner's kids, nor must demands be placed on kids to love the stepparent. Loyalty just can't be forced. A strong couple relationship is necessary to the success of the stepfamily, but it cannot hinge on whether the stepparent likes the kids, marital therapists agree. After all, a stepfamily essentially brings together strangers.

THE BASIC NEED: ACCEPTANCE

Stepfamilies can't push members into close relationships; still, they may feel the pain of absence of intimacy. Stepfamily life throws into bold relief very fundamental human needs—above all, says John Visher, the need to be a part of something. Entry into a stepfamily puts members in a position of assessing whether they are an insider or an outsider. A new wife belongs to her new husband, and he to her, but she is not a natural part of the husband's children's life. Feeling like an outsider to their relationship may be upsetting to her.

There's no fast solution for the inside/outside dilemma; stepfamilies come with a big catch in their very structure. The relationship between the parents and children predates the new marital relationship. It may even seem to outweigh it. A parent's love for a child must always be unconditional; couple love is not.

Joan Giacomini, a remarried parent and university administrator in Seattle, warns that it is hard for stepmothers to adjust to the fact that they are not number one to their new spouse. "There may be a handful of number ones, but you aren't the only number one," she says.

That gives rise to an all-too-common scenario: a remarried stepparent—often the stepmother—asks, "who is it going to be, me or your kids?" It's a false question—it leads to what Carter calls a "fake fight"—because it erroneously equates parent–child relationships and marital relationships, apples and oranges. Children are dependents; parental obligations to them are always unconditional.

Because the loyalty challenge rests on a mistaken assumption, Carter says, the proper solution is acceptance that relationships between parent and child are qualitatively different from those between spouses. Still, such conflicts can recur from time to time, as life continually presents new situations that assault the loyalties, resources, and time of kids and spouses.

THE ULTIMATE TRAP

Name a stepfamily dilemma and women—biomothers, stepmothers, even stepdaughters—are at the center of the problem. Psychologists know that women are always more likely to express distress wherever troubles exist. But stepfamilies are the ultimate gender trap. Ever-sensitive to interpersonal problems, women sense problems all over the place in stepfamilies.

Traditional male and female roles are troublesome enough, for the marriage and the children, in first-marriage families. But they wreak havoc on stepfamilies, Carter explains; they don't work at all. Indeed, researchers report that there's more equality in the marriage and in the distribution of domestic tasks in stepfamilies. But they still have a lot to learn—or unlearn—about gender roles and domestic life.

"No matter what we say or how feminist you are, everybody knows that women take care of children and men bring in most of the money. This sucks the stepmother into a quagmire of traditional domestic roles; it's not only that somebody makes her do it, she also does it to herself," explains Carter, coauthor of *The Invisible Web: Gender Patterns in Family Relationships*.

"We are raised to believe that we are responsible for everybody. A stepmother sees the children as unhappy and the husband as ineffectual, and she moves in to be helpful. Mavis Hetherington's research shows the consequence of this: a lot of fighting between teenage stepdaughters and stepmothers." Nevertheless, women move toward a problem to work on it—whether it's theirs to work on or not.

Trouble is, explains Carter, "in stepfamilies, everybody has to be in charge of their own children. A biological father has to understand that it is his responsibility to take charge. The stepmother has to back off, let the father do the monitoring and caretaking of the kids—even let him do it wrong. This is very hard to do; it flies in the face of all our gender training."

What's more, a large body of research on depression and marriage demonstrates that women's self-esteem becomes contingent upon relationships going smoothly; it holds in stepfamilies, as well. Women get depressed when stepfamily life goes badly, and they blame themselves.

For all its difficulty, the way parents in stepfamilies devise to take care of their own children contains another lesson for all families. "Stepfamilies demonstrate the importance of one-on-one relationships," says Emily Visher. "Parent–child alone time maintains the security of relationships. It requires conscious planning in all families. The health of all families resides in the quality of the relationships between members."

THE MYTH OF THE HAPPY FAMILY

If stepfamilies make it out of the gender trap, there's one more to avoid—the myth of the nuclear family. Successful stepfamilies let go of their fantasy of a traditional family life, reports James Bray. They become more realistic, less romantic, and more flexible about family. They can cope with what life deals.

But remarriage often sets up conditions pulling the other way. "There's often a sense of defensiveness," explains Betty Carter. "There's a feeling of 'let's not rock the boat this time. Let's be a happy family immediately so we can prove that this complicated thing—the divorce, the new marriage—was the right move.' People try to achieve an instant family, they don't allow for disgruntlement, fear, anxiety. Now we know it takes about five years for a stepfamily to become fully integrated."

Carter advises stepfamilies to "kiss the nuclear family good-bye. Stepfamilies simply cannot draw a tight circle around the household in the same way that nuclear families do. That always excludes somebody." The stepfamily's task is to keep permeable boundaries around the household, to facilitate coparenting, and to allow children access to the noncustodial parent.

It's a lot like tightrope-walking. "At the very time a stepfamily is trying to achieve its own integration, it has to keep the doors wide open and stay in touch with another household. You are not the lord of all you survey, as in the traditional family myth. You are on the phone regularly with someone about whom you feel, at best, ambivalent."

WHAT TO CALL IT?

Perhaps the most concrete evidence that old-fashioned family ideas don't work for stepfamilies is in the labels stepfamilies prefer for themselves.

Some people reject the label "stepfamily" altogether. Joan Giacomini is one. She is divorced from her grown children's father; he is remarried and has a toddler boy. Joan's husband has grown children from his first marriage, too, but she doesn't want to be referred to as a stepmother, nor does she like the idea of someone being referred to as the "stepmother" of her children.

"In our cases, we don't do any mothering. No one else is mother to my children, and my husband's children have their own mother," she explains. "One of my main goals is to respect their first family, so that they can have their relationships without worry about me." Despite dropping the "step" terminology, Giacomini's various families comprise a successful stepfamily that has respect, shared responsibility, even shared holidays.

Many stepfamilies who start off using step terminology eventually drop it all, reports James Bray. It may be the surest sign of integration. The terms "stepmother" and "stepfather" help clarify roles and remind everybody who belongs to whom, and under what terms, in the transition. Later, though, they don't bother with such names. "Labels connote a struggle for identity that doesn't exist anymore for these groups," says Bray.

For other stepfamilies, such as Ned and Joanna Fox—my mother and her husband—in Charlotte, North Carolina, there is little thought of stepfamily integration.

Nobody considers it a stepfamily, nor is anyone a stepsibling or stepparent. The kids were grown when the divorces and remarriages occurred, and none of the kids seem particularly interested in getting involved with the others. While Joanna's children treat Ned like an uncle, and value his love for Joanna, Ned's children don't warm up to the situation.

The moral of the story: Every stepfamily is different.

Some reject not merely the "stepfamily" label but stepfamily roles as well. In fact, the best way for a new spouse to move into stepparent life, suggests Barry Dym, Ph.D., a family psychologist (and remarried father) in Cambridge, Massachusetts, may be to find a different role than that of stepparent. The term itself may force the relationships into an unrealistic, and even intrusive, parental mold.

Dym suggests that stepmothers might do better modeling themselves after a favorite aunt—involved, but not the mother. My favorite aunt provides acceptance, guidance, honesty, but the obligation on either side is voluntary. If I become a stepmother, I think I'll be an aunt.

The naming issue underscores what stepfamilies have that original families don't always get: there is no monolithic view of what a stepfamily is supposed to be, or even be called. To catalog stepfamily experiences would be to catalog all relationships—there is endless variety, and unlimited routes to success or failure. Unlike traditional families, stepfamilies allow much more room for diversity. And equality. Count that as the ultimate lesson from stepfamilies.

THE MYTHS AND MISCONCEPTIONS OF THE STEPMOTHER IDENTITY

DESCRIPTIONS AND PRESCRIPTIONS FOR IDENTITY MANAGEMENT*

There are two cross-cultural and trans-historical myths associated with stepmotherhood: the evil stepmother myth and the myth of instant love. The tenacity of these myths has served to stigmatize stepmothers. This paper describes the myths associated with stepmothers, details how these myths affect stepmother life, reveals dilemmas in identity management for stepmothers, and indicates identity management strategies stepmothers might utilize.

Marianne Dainton

Marianne Dainton is a doctoral student at Ohio State University, Department of Communication, 319 Neil Hall, Columbus, OH 43210.

In America there are a multitude of family forms, one of which is the stepfamily. Statistics indicate that currently 16% of all married couples in this country have at least one stepchild (Moorman & Hernandez, 1989). Moreover, current predictions are that 35% to 40% of children born in the 1980s will spend time in a stepparent family before they are young adults (Coleman & Ganong, 1990a).

Although researchers are increasingly turning their attention to the stepfamily form, there are many areas of stepfamily life that have not received adequate attention (Coleman & Ganong, 1990a). One such area is the effect of myths about stepfamily relations on stepfamily members. A focus upon myths is salient to the study of stepfamilies in general, and stepmothers in particular, because of the prevalence of myths concerning step-relations. For example, at least three of the Brothers Grimm's fairy tales—"Hansel and Gretel," "Cinderella," and "Snow White"—revolve

*The author would like to thank Patrick McKenry and Dirk Scheerhorn for editorial comments, and three anonymous reviewers for their valuable suggestions.

Key Words: identity management, myths, stepmothers, stigma.

around the actions of an evil stepmother. These stories may appear innocuous enough, unless of course you happen to be a stepmother or a stepchild. "Fairies do not exist, and witches do not exist, but stepmothers do exist, and therefore certain fairy tales are harmful rather than helpful to large segments of the population" (Visher & Visher, 1979, p. 6).

The myths associated with stepmotherhood may constrain stepmothers' identity management. Identity management refers to efforts on the part of stepmothers to foster preferred perceptions about themselves. Accordingly, this article examines some of the impediments to the identity management strategies enacted by stepmothers. Specifically, throughout the course of this article the myths and misconceptions of stepmotherhood will be identified, the implications of these myths for stepmothers will be discussed, issues of identity will be elaborated, and, finally, some initial steps toward identity management strategies for stepmothers will be detailed.

STEPMOTHER MYTHS

The term *myth* is popularly conceived to be analogous to "falsehood." Indeed, myths often contain false and/or negative information. Scholars, however, define myth as a recurring theme or character type that incorporates infor-

mation about cultural standards (Birenbaum, 1988). Thus, myths represent a way of viewing the world that embodies a culture's beliefs, regardless of whether these beliefs are accurate.

According to Bruner (1960), myths can be characterized by two components. The first component is an externalization, which Bruner describes as a "corpus of images and identities" (p. 280). This externalization provides a cultural explanation of the way the world works. The second component is an internalization. Bruner argues that a myth can only exist to the extent that cultural members internalize personal identities based upon the externalized corpus of ideas propagated by the myth.

Regarding stepmotherhood, there are two generic myths that are simultaneously cross-cultural and transhistorical (Schulman, 1972). The first of the myths is that of the *evil stepmother,* a myth propagated through fiction of all forms. The second myth is that of *instant love,* wherein a stepmother is expected to immediately assimilate into a family and to love the children as if they were her own. Each will be discussed in turn.

Myth #1: The Evil Stepmother

The myth of the evil stepmother has a strong and inveterate legacy; the negative connotations of the term *step* were firmly in place as early as 1400 (Wald,

From *Family Relations*, Vol. 42, No. 1, January 1993, pp. 93-98. © 1993 by the National Council of Family Relations, 3989 Central Avenue, NE, Suite 550, Minneapolis, MN 55421. Reprinted by permission.

1981). Moreover, scholars have identified the existence of evil stepmother folktales in virtually every part of the world. In fact, Smith (1953) identifies 345 versions of the "Cinderella" story alone, revealing the evil stepmother myth as a global phenomenon.

Although evil stepmothers appear in all genres of fiction, the evil stepmother is particularly prevalent in fairy tales (Wald, 1981). In an analysis of fairy tales, one researcher found that the most frequent representations of evil included bears, wolves, giants and ogres, witches, and stepmothers (Sutton-Smith, 1971, cited in Wald, 1981). Thus, fairy tales suggest that stepmothers are the equivalent of wild animals and supernatural beings—entities that children have very little chance of facing in real life—in their wicked treatment of children.

Myth #2: Instant Love

The second myth is instant love (Schulman, 1972; Visher & Visher, 1988; Wald, 1981). This myth is based upon cultural standards about mothering (Visher & Visher, 1988), and the resulting societal expectations about stepmothers' assimilation into the family. Specifically, the myth maintains that remarriage in and of itself creates an instant family, that stepmothers should (and will) automatically love their stepchildren, and that stepchildren will automatically love their stepmother. Further, because of this love, mothering is assumed to come naturally and easily.

In reality, none of the above necessarily happens. Counselors working with stepmothers suggest that many women are surprised and dismayed when they don't feel immediate love for their stepchildren (Lofas & Sova, 1985). Moreover, stepchildren are often afraid, unsure, and uncomfortable with the changes in the family, and may express these feelings by being surly and resentful. As a result, many stepmothers experience a great deal of ambivalence regarding their stepchildren (Ambert, 1986).

The Prevalence of These Myths Today

Despite the increasing number of stepfamilies in America today, the myths identified above show no signs of losing strength. In a series of research efforts, one group of researchers found that the role of stepmother elicited more negative connotations than any other family position (Bryan, Coleman, Ganong, & Bryan, 1986; Ganong & Coleman, 1983). Specifically, stepmothers were perceived as less affectionate, good, fair, kind, loving, happy, and likable, and

more cruel, hateful, unfair, and unloving. More recently, researchers have determined that these negative perceptions still stand, although there is little difference in the perceptions of stepmothers and stepfathers (Fluitt & Paradise, 1991; Ganong, Coleman, & Kennedy, 1990). Similarly, clinicians assert that the myth of instant love has yet to be replaced by more realistic expectations (Visher & Visher, 1988).

Individually, these myths negatively affect the experiences of stepmothers. For example, both clinical and empirical evidence reveals that stepmothers identify the wicked stepmother myth as directly contributing to the stress they experience in adapting to the stepmother role (Duberman, 1973; Hughes, 1991; Visher & Visher, 1979). Further, counselors have identified the unrealistic expectations associated with the myth of instant love as a possible cause of stress for stepmothers in general, and have suggested that such expectations may actively interfere with the family integration that the myth promises (Visher & Visher, 1988).

Ironically, these myths provide external images of the stepmother that are at polar extremes; one myth depicts stepmothers as unrealistically evil, the other as unrealistically loving and competent. Together, these contradictory images may contribute to identity management difficulties, as stepmothers must struggle with internalizing two conflicting sets of ultimately unrealistic expectations. Clearly, taking on the mantle of stepmother includes not only taking on the responsibility of a family, but taking on a host of potential identity management challenges (Hughes, 1991; Visher & Visher, 1979, 1988).

THE CONCEPT OF IDENTITY

Before discussing the identity issues associated with stepmotherhood, some fundamental issues surrounding the concept of identity itself must be addressed. In so doing, some critical distinctions between key terms need to be made. Finally, a framework for understanding identity management must be constructed.

First, *identity* can be defined as an individual's self-concept (McCall & Simmons, 1978). Thus, an individual's identity involves beliefs about whom he or she is, and how he or she should be perceived and treated in social life (Schlenker, 1980). Although our identities are frequently manifested in the roles that we enact, the notion of identity is broader than that of roles. Definitionally, *roles* are expectations held

about the occupant of a social status or a position in a social system, while *identity* is a constellation of all of the roles an individual performs (McCall & Simmons, 1978).

The same distinction can be made between role performance and identity management. A *role performance* (also known as *role enactment*) is the individual's day-to-day behavior associated with a given role (McCall & Simmons, 1978). *Identity management,* on the other hand, is a broader concept; it is an individual's efforts to foster perceptions (usually positive) relevant to his or her self-concept. Similar terms include *self-presentation* (Goffman, 1959) and *impression management* (Schlenker, 1980).

The definitions above imply that an identity is chosen. This is not always the case. McCall and Simmons (1978) assert that individuals do not entirely have discretion in the roles they will enact, and hence in the perceptions others will have of them. For example, most stepmothers do not choose the stepmother persona; it is thrust upon them when they choose to marry a man with children. Identity management for stepmothers, then, is not simply the process of maintaining preferred perceptions, but of preventing unwanted perceptions associated with preconceived evaluations of a given social role.

To clarify, McCall and Simmons argue that each role identity has two elements: the *conventional* and the *idiosyncratic*. The conventional aspect of a role identity consists of social stereotypes. These stereotypes might be captured in myths such as the myths associated with stepmotherhood. The idiosyncratic elements of a role identity, on the other hand, are those characteristics an individual modifies and elaborates within the given role.

IDENTITY DILEMMAS

Generally, identities are inferred by appearance and actions (McCall & Simmons, 1978). In the case of stepmothers, however, the perceptions associated with stepmotherhood are not conveyed by appearance or actions, but are label-bound. Accordingly, stepmothers fulfill the requirements of being a stigmatized group. *Stigmas* are products of definitional processes in which a defining attribute (such as being a stepmother) eclipses other aspects of the stigmatized person, including individual personalities and abilities (Ainlay, Coleman, & Becker, 1986; Stafford & Scott, 1986). Thus stigmas are categorizations that often involve negative affect (Jones et al., 1984).

Goffman (1963) posits that stigmatization is the result of the relationship between a particular attribute and a stereotype about that attribute. "Society establishes the means of categorizing persons and the complement of attributes felt to be ordinary and natural for members of each of these categories" (Goffman, 1963, p. 2). Ironically, the "ordinary and natural" attributes that society has established for stepmothers (through myths) are that they are inherently wicked, yet capable of providing instant love. It is the very fact that stepmothers are characterized in such an extraordinary manner that causes their stigmatization.

Further, Goffman (1963) argues that there are two primary types of stigmas: the *discredited* and the *discreditable*. Discredited individuals are those in which the stigma is immediately apparent (e.g., those with physical deformities). Discreditable individuals are those whose stigma is not known or immediately perceivable. The fact that stepmothers' stigma is not visually apparent would lead one to believe that they have a discreditable stigma. That is, despite fairy tales' depiction of stepmothers as evil hags, real stepmothers look just like real mothers. Their stigma is not immediately apparent.

However, with different audiences stepmothers are sometimes discredited and sometimes discreditable. For example, members of the stepfamily are aware of a woman's stepmother status, so in their eyes she is discredited. In the general public, however, a stepmother remains merely discreditable. This contradiction brings up one of the major problems stepmothers have with identity management; part of the dilemma of managing a stepmother identity is the public/private dichotomy. Stepmothers believe that they are judged based on stepmother myths in both the public and private arenas of social life (Hughes, 1991). Because of this, stepmothers may find themselves with the paradox of having inconsistent identity management strategies become necessary to manage the same identity.

Goffman (1963) has identified two broad classes of identity management strategies. *Corrective practices* are what people do after their preferred identity is threatened. According to Goffman, it is likely that discredited individuals will be forced to engage in corrective strategies. *Preventative strategies*, on the other hand, are behaviors an individual uses to avoid negative perceptions. In general, the discreditable will rely on preventative strategies.

In order to determine which class of strategies to enact, a stepmother must consider a contextual matrix. That is, stepmothers must consider where they

are and who their audience is in order to select the appropriate identity management techniques (McCall & Simmons, 1978). This matrix might look like the one in Figure 1.

As the matrix shows, stepmothers face competing concerns when selecting identity strategies: *who* and *where*. Within each of these superordinate categories is a dichotomy. For example, when considering who, a stepmother might be in the company of her family or she may be in the company of some generalized others. When considering *where*, she might be in private (e.g., at home) or in public (e.g., a restaurant).

Taking each quadrant of the grid in turn, the following issues are stressed. First, the upper left quadrant is one in which there is little inconsistency. Here, stepmothers are with their family in private. Given that they are already discredited in this forum (i.e., their stigma is known), it is likely that they will utilize corrective identity management strategies in this case. Such strategies might include assertive techniques described by Jones and Pittman (1980) like *exemplification* (projecting integrity), *self-promotion* (showing competence in mothering), or *ingratiation* (being helpful and positive).

Similarly, there is probably little quandary about strategy selection when in the others/public quadrant; here, the stepmother is discreditable (her stigma is not known). Accordingly, it is likely a stepmother would select what Goffman (1963) describes as preventative strategies, such as *passing* (behaving in a way consistent with a nonstigmatized identity without specifically claiming to be nonstigmatized) or using *disidentifiers* (behaviors deliberately used to indicate a nonstigmatized identity, e.g., saying "my son" instead of "my stepson").

The two remaining quadrants might cause psychological tension between

competing identity management options, however. For example, in the family/public quadrant, an initial reaction might be to use preventative strategies. After all, other patrons of a restaurant have little need to know that the normal family seated next to them might in fact be a stepfamily. However, if a stepmother selects such strategies she is neither accomplishing her goal of overcoming negative perceptions within the family, nor is she safe from intentional or unintentional unmasking. The last quadrant, others/private, is liable to involve a very different sort of tension. An example of such a situation is holding a professional gathering at home. Given that the interaction is at home, her stigma is already known among family members who may be present. Therefore, corrective strategies might seem appropriate. However, because she is also with nonintimate others, preventative strategies might be preferred. Here, the tension reflects a pull towards actively managing existing negative stereotypes within the family, and at the same time preventing others from learning of the stigma.

Confounding contextual constraints are the ways in which expectations based upon stepmother myths affect our identity management. That is, people might interpret a stepmother's behavior as negative (even if by objective measures it is not) simply because stepmothers' behaviors are expected to be negative (Coleman & Ganong, 1987a; for a discussion about how this process might work, see Darley & Gross, 1983). A dilemma that stepmothers face, then, is whether they should use corrective strategies at all, since any efforts to actively repair others' perceptions might be interpreted unfavorably. She is stuck in a "damned if you do, damned if you don't" situation.

A final identity management dilemma stepmothers face is related to the

Figure 1. *Matrix for Stepmothers' Identity Management Strategies* extent to which they play an active parenting role. That is, in attempting to fulfill the stepparent role, stepmothers are in a double bind. On one hand, they are expected to love the child as if he or she were their own, but on the other hand, they are often sanctioned against adopting a bona fide parental role (Visher & Visher, 1979). Thus, becoming a stepmother requires a careful balancing act, wherein a woman must regulate perceptions of involvement without being perceived as overinvolved or uncaring.

The dilemma described above is complicated by the ambiguity associated with the stepmother role. According to Cherlin (1978), remarriage represents an "incomplete institution" because there are few norms or rules to define expected behavior in stepfamily life. Cherlin posits that this ambiguity causes stress on family members. There is recent evidence for this hypothesis; in a review of the literature, Fine and Schwebel (1991) identified role ambiguity as the core difficulty in stepfamilies.

Role ambiguity involves four types of uncertainty: (a) uncertainty about the scope of one's responsibilities; (b) uncertainty about the particular behaviors needed to fulfill one's responsibilities; (c) uncertainty about whose expectations for role behavior must be met; and (d) uncertainty about the effects of one's actions on the well-being of oneself and others (King & King, 1990). This uncertainty is a function of the difference between stepfamily roles and biological family roles, and the difference between effective stepfamily functioning and effective biological family functioning (Coleman & Ganong, 1987b). There are two primary differences: (a) the degree of clarity about which behavior is appropriate for a given role, and (b) the degree to which the role is either ascribed or achieved (Walker & Messinger, 1979).

IDENTITY MANAGEMENT STRATEGIES

Given the dilemmas of identity management outlined above, the selection of specific strategies may be complex, if not overwhelming, to a stepmother. However, research has provided some preliminary answers as to which strategies stepmothers are likely to use, whether such strategies are likely to work, and which strategies are not often used but might be beneficial given the specific identity problems stepmothers face.

First, because the nature of the stigma of being a stepmother is not immediately apparent to those who don't know a woman's stepmother status, an identity strategy frequently selected for the general public is one of concealment (e.g., Duberman, 1975; Jones et al., 1984).

> For many women who have chosen to become stepmothers, the realization that they are part of a minority group comes as a bit of a shock. But by masquerading as a natural mother, altering her true identity in order to fit into a society and to be accepted as part of a "normal" family, a stepmother acts like any member of a minority group who is striving to conform. (Morrison, Thompson-Guppy, & Bell, 1986, p. 17)

Concealment is an example of a preventative strategy (Goffman, 1963). Despite the frequency of use of this strategy, however, some counselors have suggested that concealment is ineffective as a long-term solution (Morrison et al., 1986).

A more proactive strategy for public identity management is what Jones et al. (1984) call *confrontation and breaking through*. This strategy involves acknowledging one's stepmother status and working to frame the identity in a constructive and commendable context. Recall McCall and Simmon's (1978) distinction between the conventional and idiosyncratic elements of identity. Based on this distinction, one way to accomplish confrontation and breaking through might be to foster the idiosyncratic elements of the stepmother identity, while simultaneously diminishing the conventional elements. However, due to the strength of the myths of stepmotherhood, such efforts might be construed negatively. As Coleman and Ganong (1987a) noted, people's expectations of negative behavior might lead them to perceive even idiosyncratic elements negatively.

Moving from individual identity management efforts to societal efforts to change the stigma of stepmotherhood, one controversial public strategy that has been suggested is to change the label. If the term *stepfamily* engenders negative reactions, some authors contend we should just change the name to one without such negative connotations (see Coleman & Ganong, 1987a, for a summary of the debate). This can be classified as a corrective strategy. Alternatives to stepfamily include *blended* or *reconstituted family*. What the associated changes in the name of *stepmother* would be is unclear. Other scholars believe that changing the terminology would be confusing (Wald, 1981) or insulting (Lofas & Sova, 1985), or would only add to the mystification (Hughes, 1991).

There have also been some specific strategies identified to overcome the myths within the stepfamily itself. Based on empirical evidence, Cissna, Cox, and Bochner (1990) assert that an effective way to overcome myths about stepmotherhood involves two steps. First, they claim, the remarried partners must establish the solidarity of the marriage in children's minds. Then, they say, the partners should use this solidarity to establish the credibility of the stepparent as a valid parental authority. Such efforts are clearly corrective in nature, and take into account overly negative expectations due to the evil stepmother myth as well as overly positive expectations due to the myth of instant love.

Taking quite a different approach, Salwen (1990) proposes that stepmothers might remove themselves from the parenting role altogether by insisting that the biological father take on all parenting responsibilities. This does not mean that stepmothers cannot be supportive or nurturing to their stepchildren. However, Salwen argues that by avoiding the parental role, stepmothers simultaneously avoid the negative expectations associated with the role. They are therefore free to work on positive, nonparental relationships with their stepchildren that are not weighted down by preconceived, unfavorable perceptions. Again, such a strategy is an effort to achieve a middle ground between the two myths.

A similar, but perhaps less radical, approach to identity dilemmas within the stepfamily is to focus on alternative role enactment. Furstenberg and Spanier (1984) posit that the stepparent role is ambiguous, as there is no single prescribed role for stepparents (see the section on role ambiguity above). Thus, they should feel free to try on various roles until they find one that fits (see also Walker & Messinger, 1979). Alternative roles a stepmother can don to ease her interactions with stepchildren include *primary mother* (which works only if the biological mother is physically and/or psychologically dead to the child), *other mother,* and *friend* (Draughon, 1975).

Related to alternative roles in managing identity, simply finding a name that a child is comfortable calling the stepmother might assist in the individualization of a stepmother's identity (Visher & Visher, 1988). Very often, a child avoids finding a name for his or her stepmother, referring to her simply as "you" or "she." By insisting on a name, the stepmother moves out of the realm of the group of all stepmothers (a stigmatized group) to personhood (Maglin & Schniedewind, 1989). Possible names include the stepmother's own first name, a mutually agreed upon nickname, or a variation of mother not used for the biological mother (Wald, 1981).

Finally, while not directly related to the problems of stepmothers, Crocker and Lutsky (1986) have identified three strategies for changing cognitions about stigmas. First is the *sociocultural* approach, which emphasizes a change in socialization practices. In the case of stepmothers in particular, this might involve replacing evil stepmother fairy tales with stories with more positive messages. Second is the *motivational* approach. This involves redefining group boundaries to allow the stigmatized persons to become part of the normal population. For example, the category of *mothers* might be expanded to include stepmothers. Lastly, Crocker and Lutsky identify *cognitive* approaches to changing stigmas. This involves proving the stereotype wrong. In global terms this might mean a public relations campaign of sorts for stepmothers. More specifically, however, it might involve allowing a stepmother's positive actions within the stepfamily to prove the myth wrong (i.e., replacing conventional elements of identity with idiosyncratic elements).

IMPLICATIONS FOR RESEARCH

There are several directions for future research. First, Goffman's theoretical differentiation between corrective and preventative identity management strategies needs to be operationalized. Specific research questions might be "What communicative behaviors serve corrective functions?" and "What communicative behaviors serve preventative functions?"

Second, because our knowledge of the identity management strategies stepmothers actually use is quite limited, it would be of interest to identify the specific identity management strategies stepmothers select, when they select them, and why. In addition, future research should strive to fill in the empty squares of the identity matrix detailed by Figure 1. That is, research should focus upon what identity management strategies women select when in a private setting with nonfamily members, and, perhaps more interestingly, what they do when they are with family members in a public situation. Moreover, researchers should ascertain whether the theoretical predictions of strategies that have been identified are correct.

More important than merely identifying what women do, however, is to identify what actually works. A repertoire of strategies is useless unless they actually assist a stepmother in overcoming the negative perceptions associated with stepmotherhood. Thus, critical research questions include: "What spe-

cific identity management strategies work to overcome negative public perceptions?" and "What strategies work to overcome negative perceptions within the family?"

IMPLICATIONS FOR PRACTICE

The issues raised here also have several implications for educators and counselors working with stepfamilies. Most importantly, practitioners can enact two global strategies to ameliorate the identity management difficulties stepmothers face. The first strategy is to assist individual stepmothers in overcoming some of the myths and misconceptions associated with this family role. Ideally, this assistance would take place before the formation of the stepfamily. By presenting future stepmothers—and all stepfamily members—with the reality of stepmother life before the remarriage, the frustrations associated with the myths of the evil stepmother and of instant love might be avoided. A first step in such counseling might be the completion of the Personal Reflections Program (Kaplan & Hennon, 1992).

More realistically, however, this assistance will likely be sought after the identity management difficulties have been encountered. In this case, practitioners might offer some of the strategies described in the previous section on identity management. In addition, referral to organizations proffering support to stepmothers and stepfamilies might be warranted. Finally, preliminary evidence suggests that the use of fiction can assist stepfamilies and stepfamily members in counseling (Coleman & Ganong, 1990b).

The second strategy is to actively work to diffuse these myths and misconceptions on a societal level. This paper points to the need for greater attention to the messages we are sending children about stepmothers. Family life educators and primary school educators might be especially important in normalizing the stepfamily experience (Crosbie-Burnett & Skyles, 1989). Family life educators can assist in debunking the myths by informing the public about the realities of stepmothers and stepfamily life. Similarly, primary school educators might be recruited to assist in this information campaign. Through programs such as the Classroom Guidance Program discussed by Crosbie-Burnett and Pulvino (1990), by selecting texts and children's literature that include normal stepfamilies, and by incorporating stepfamily roles in everyday classroom discussions, grade school teachers might make great

strides in overcoming the evil stepmother myth.

CONCLUSION

The stepmother role is a stressful one that is particularly challenging in terms of identity management. Stepmothers must combat the firmly entrenched myths of the wicked stepmother and of instant love. Despite the fact that the stepfamily form is becoming increasingly more common, empirical and clinical evidence suggests that stepmother myths show little sign of changing (Bryan et al., 1986; Ganong & Coleman, 1983; Fluitt & Paradise, 1991). Thus, identity issues will remain salient for stepmothers for some time to come. Accordingly, researchers and practitioners must incorporate the concept of identity when considering the experiences of stepmothers.

REFERENCES

Ainlay, S. C., Coleman, L. M., & Becker, G. (1986). Stigma reconsidered. In S. C. Ainlay, G. Becker, & L. M. Coleman (Eds.), *The dilemma of difference: A multidisciplinary view of stigma* (pp. 1-13). New York: Plenum Press.

Ambert, A. (1986). Being a stepparent: Live-in and visiting stepchildren. *Journal of Marriage and the Family, 48,* 795-804.

Birenbaum, H. (1988). *Myth and mind.* Lanham, MD: University Press.

Bruner, J. S. (1960). Myth and identity. In H. A. Murray (Ed.), *Myth and mythmaking* (pp. 276-287). Boston: Beacon Press.

Bryan, H., Coleman, M., Ganong, L., & Bryan, L. (1986). Person perception: Family structure as a cue for stereotyping. *Journal of Marriage and the Family, 48,* 169-174.

Cherlin, A. (1978). Remarriage as an incomplete institution. *American Journal of Sociology, 86,* 634-650.

Cissna, K. N., Cox, D. E., & Bochner, A. P. (1990). The dialectic of marital and parental relationships within the stepfamily. *Communication Monographs, 57,* 44-61.

Coleman, M., & Ganong, L. (1987a). The cultural stereotyping of stepfamilies. In K. Pasley & M. Ihinger-Tallman (Eds.), *Remarriage and stepparenting: Current research and theory* (pp. 19-41). New York: Guilford.

Coleman, M., & Ganong, L. (1987b). Marital conflict in stepfamilies: Effects on children. *Youth and Society, 19,* 151-172.

Coleman, M., & Ganong, L. H. (1990a). Remarriage and stepfamily research in the 1980s: Increased interest in an old family form. *Journal of Marriage and the Family, 52,* 925-940.

Coleman, M., & Ganong, L. H. (1990b). The uses of juvenile fiction and self-help books with stepfamilies. *Journal of Counseling and Development, 68,* 327-331.

Crocker, J., & Lutsky, N. (1986). Stigma and the dynamics of social cognition. In S. C. Ainlay, G. Becker, & L. M. Coleman (Eds.), *The dilemma of difference: A multidisciplinary view of stigma* (pp. 95-122). New York: Plenum Press.

Crosbie-Burnett, M., & Pulvino, C. J. (1990). Children in non-traditional families: A classroom guidance program. *School Counselor, 37,* 286-293.

Crosbie-Burnett, M., & Skyles, A. (1989). Stepchildren in schools and colleges: Recommendations for educational policy changes. *Family Relations, 38,* 59-64.

Darley, J., & Gross, P. H. (1983). A hypothesis confirming bias in labeling effects. *Journal of Personality and Social Psychology, 44,* 20-33.

Draughon, M. (1975). Stepmother's model of identification in relation to mourning in the child. *Psychological Reports, 36,* 183-189.

Duberman, L. (1973). Step-kin relationships. *Journal of Marriage and the Family, 35,* 283-292.

Duberman, L. (1975). *The reconstituted family: A study of remarried couples and their children.* Chicago, IL: Nelson-Hall.

Fine, M. A., & Schwebel, A. I. (1991). Stepparent stress: A cognitive perspective. *Journal of Divorce and Remarriage, 17,* 1-15.

Fluitt, M. S., & Paradise, L. V. (1991). The relationship of current family structures to young adults' perceptions of stepparents. *Journal of Divorce and Remarriage, 15,* 159-174.

Furstenberg, F. F., Jr., & Spanier, G. (1984). *Recycling the family: Remarriage after divorce.* Beverly Hills, CA: Sage.

Ganong, L., & Coleman, M. (1983). Stepparent: A pejorative term? *Psychological Reports, 52,* 919-922.

Ganong, L., Coleman, M., & Kennedy, G. (1990). The effects of using alternate labels in denoting stepparent or stepfamily status. *Journal of Social Behavior and Personality, 5,* 453-463.

Goffman, E. (1959). *The presentation of self in everyday life.* New York: Doubleday Anchor.

Goffman, E. (1963). *Stigma: Notes on the management of spoiled identity.* New York: Simon & Schuster.

Hughes, C. (1991). *Stepparents: Wicked or wonderful?* Brookfield, VT: Gower Publishing Co.

Jones, E. E., Farina, A., Hastorf, A. H., Markus, H., Miller, D. T., & Scott, R. A. (1984). *Social stigma: The psychology of of marked relationships.* New York: W. H. Freeman.

Jones, E. E., & Pittman, T. S. (1980). Toward a general theory of strategic self-presentation. In H. Suls (Ed.), *Psychological perspectives on the self.* Hillsdale, NJ: Lawrence Erlbaum Associates.

Kaplan, L., & Hennon, C. B. (1992). Remarriage education: The Personal Reflections Program. *Family Relations, 41,* 127-134.

King, L. A., & King, D. W. (1990). Role conflict and role ambiguity: A critical assessment of construct validity. *Psychological Bulletin, 107,* 48-64.

Lofas, J., & Sova, D. B. (1985). *Stepparenting.* New York: Zebra Books.

Maglin, N. B., & Schniedewind, N. (1989). Women and stepfamilies. Philadelphia: Temple University Press.

McCall, G. J., & Simmons, J. L. (1978). *Identities and interactions* (rev. ed.). New York: The Free Press.

Moorman, J. E., & Hernandez, D. J. (1989). Married-couple families with step, adopted, and biological children. *Demography, 26,* 267-277.

Morrison, K., Thompson-Guppy, A., & Bell, P. (1986). *Stepmothers: Exploring the myth.* Ottawa, Canada: Canadian Council on Social Development.

Salwen, L. V. (1990). The myth of the wicked stepmother. *Women and Therapy, 10,* 117-125.

Schlenker, B. R. (1980). *Impression management: The self-concept, social identity, and interpersonal relations.* Monterey, CA: Brooks/Cole.

Schulman, G. L. (1972). Myths that intrude on the adaptation of the stepfamily. *Social Casework, 53,* 131-139.

Smith, W. C. (1953). *The stepchild.* Chicago, IL: University of Chicago Press.

Stafford, M. C., & Scott, R. R. (1986). Stigma, deviance, and social control: Some conceptual issues. In S. C. Ainlay, G. Becker, & L. M. Coleman (Eds.), *The dilemma of difference: A multidisciplinary view of stigma* (pp. 77-91). New York: Plenum Press.

Visher, E. B., & Visher, J. S. (1979). *Stepfamilies: Myths and realities.* Secaucus, NJ: Citadel.

Visher, E. B., & Visher, J. S. (1988). *Old loyalties, new ties: Therapeutic strategies with stepfamilies.* New York: Brunner/Mazel.

Wald, E. (1981). *The remarried family: Challenge and promise.* New York: Family Services Association of America.

Walker, K. N., & Messinger, L. (1979). Remarriage after divorce: Dissolution and reconstruction of family boundaries. *Family Process, 18,* 185-192.

Families, Now and Into the Future

What is the future of the family? Does the family even have a future? These questions and others like them are being asked, and many people fear for the future of the family. As articles in previous sections of this volume have shown, the family is a continually evolving institution that will continue to change throughout time. Still, certain elements of family appear to be constant. The family is and will remain a powerful influence in the lives of its members. This is because we all begin life in some type of family, and this early exposure carries a great deal of weight in forming our social selves, who we are and how we relate to others. From our families, we take our basic genetic makeup, while we also learn and are reinforced in health behaviors. In families, we are given our first exposure to values, and it is through families that we most actively influence others. Our sense of commitment and obligation begins within the family as well as our sense of what we can expect of others.

Much of what has been written about families has been less than hopeful and has focused on ways of avoiding or correcting errors. The four articles in this section take a positive view of family and its influences on its members. The emphasis is on health rather than dysfunction.

Increasing evidence of genetic factors in physical as well as mental health serves to promote the need for awareness of our family's health history. The first article, "Trace Your Family Tree," considers how charting your relatives' medical history can save your life. Ruth Papazian provides a useful technique for mapping out your family health history so that you can anticipate, plan, and possibly change your health behaviors.

The next article focuses on healthy families and suggests that the idea that "all families are at least a little dysfunctional" might better be stated as "all families are at least a little bit healthy." "Happy Families: Who Says They All Have to Be Alike?" describes the strengths of today's families and provides glimpses of an assortment of happy, healthy families. Next, Geoffrey Cowley and Karen Springen's article, "Rewriting Life Stories," describes narrative therapy, a new and promising approach in family therapy that sees life as a series of stories that can be rewritten to find one's own strengths rather than weaknesses. The final article of this volume, "Rituals for Our Times," by family therapists Evan Imber-Black and Janine Roberts, describes the ways in which families use rites and ceremonies to strengthen families. Through examples, the authors show how readers might use ritual in their own families.

Looking Ahead: Challenge Questions

What type of future do you see for yourself after having charted your family's health history? What changes do you see yourself making in your life?

Discuss whether or not, if it were possible, you would return to families of an earlier age.

What decision have you made about long-term commitments—marriage or some other relationship? How about children?

When you look around at families, what do you think about them? In what ways do you feel hopeful about your future? In what ways do you not?

How would rewriting your life story, or aspects of it, benefit you?

What is the state of rituals in your family? What rituals might you build in your family?

TRACE YOUR FAMILY TREE

Charting your relatives' medical history can save your life

RUTH PAPAZIAN

Ruth Papazian, a New York City-based writer specializing in health and medicine, is constructing a family tree for herself and her niece and nephew.

When it comes to health, the apple doesn't fall far fom the family tree: Research suggests that an astonishing number of diseases—from rare to common—have some sort of hereditary link.

That is why constructing a family health tree can offer life-saving glimpses into your future. If you're at risk of inheriting a serious disease, you can get regular checkups to spot early symptoms and increase the chances for a cure. You may also want genetic counseling, to learn the risk of passing a disease on to your children.

Aside from health problems caused by accident or infectious disease, you can assume that most every disease in your family's background has some sort of genetic basis. These can be divided into two classes: *susceptibility diseases,* in which genes don't cause the problem but influence your risk of becoming ill; and *purely genetic diseases,* which people almost invariably develop if they inherit the requisite genes.

Susceptibility diseases typically occur later in life and include major ailments such as heart disease, diabetes (especially the non-insulin-dependent type) and several types of cancer, including breast, lung, colorectal (colon and rectal), prostate, ovarian and skin. The inherited tendency to develop a disease probably results from complex interactions among several genes. Also on the list of disorders with a genetic component: rheumatoid arthritis, allergies, asthma, glaucoma, Alzheimer's disease, osteoporosis, glaucoma and behavioral and emotional problems including schizophrenia, alcoholism and depression. ("Hereditary Risk" lists for several diseases the increased risk faced by someone with an afflicted parent.)

Although genes set the stage for these disorders, the actual illness is usually caused in part by some environmental factor—cigarette smoke in the case of lung cancer, for example, or high-fat diets in heart disease and non-insulin-dependent diabetes, as well as prostate, colorectal and perhaps ovarian cancer. Luckily, people who know that a susceptibility disease lurks in their family tree may be able to control those nongenetic risk factors, or at least be on the alert for early symptoms.

For example, if your mother or sister developed breast cancer before menopause, your lifetime risk would be as

From *American Health*, May 1994, pp. 80-84. © 1994 by Ruth Papazian. Reprinted by permission.

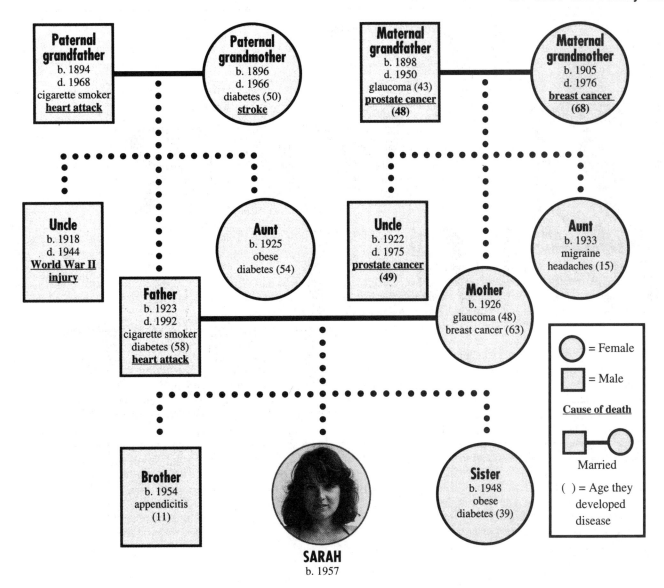

Paternal grandfather
b. 1894
d. 1968
cigarette smoker
<u>heart attack</u>

Paternal grandmother
b. 1896
d. 1966
diabetes (50)
<u>stroke</u>

Maternal grandfather
b. 1898
d. 1950
glaucoma (43)
<u>prostate cancer</u>
(48)

Maternal grandmother
b. 1905
d. 1976
<u>breast cancer</u>
(68)

Uncle
b. 1918
d. 1944
<u>World War II injury</u>

Aunt
b. 1925
obese
diabetes (54)

Uncle
b. 1922
d. 1975
<u>prostate cancer</u>
(49)

Aunt
b. 1933
migraine
headaches (15)

Father
b. 1923
d. 1992
cigarette smoker
diabetes (58)
<u>heart attack</u>

Mother
b. 1926
glaucoma (48)
breast cancer (63)

○ = Female
□ = Male
<u>Cause of death</u>
□—○ Married
( ) = Age they developed disease

Brother
b. 1954
appendicitis
(11)

SARAH
b. 1957

Sister
b. 1948
obese
diabetes (39)

SARAH'S FAMILY MEDICAL HISTORY

Sarah risks inheriting non-insulin-dependent diabetes from her father's side of the family and breast cancer and glaucoma from her mother's side. But the two fatal heart attacks on her father's side shouldn't cause concern; both occurred relatively late in life and probably stemmed from major risk factors—smoking (her grandfather) and both smoking and diabetes (her father).

Diabetes: Sarah's sister already has it. Sarah and her brother should have their blood sugar monitored regularly; they can help ward off the disease by exercising and adopting a prudent diet.

Glaucoma: Sarah and her two siblings should have yearly eye exams to detect glaucoma at its early stages.

Breast cancer: Sarah and her sister face a higher than normal risk, since their mother and maternal grandmother developed it. Both sisters should have a baseline mammogram between the ages of 30 and 35, and yearly mammograms after 35; her sister should lose weight, since obesity adds to her risk.

Finally, Sarah should alert her brother to the fact that he's at increased risk for *prostate cancer*. His maternal grandfather and uncle both developed it early in life. He needs regular screening: each year, a digital rectal exam, plus a PSA (prostate-specific antigen) test.

great as one in three, vs. one in nine for other women. (Early onset of any disease increases the probability that heredity played a role.) A family history of breast cancer means you should get annual mammograms beginning at age 35, plus frequent professional exams.

s for purely genetic diseases, there are more than 4,000—most of them rare—that result from defects in single genes. If you have such a disorder in your family tree, your chance of inheriting it depends on the nature of the gene responsible.

For instance, if one of your parents died of a heart attack before age 60, there's a one-in-five chance that he or she had familial hypercholesterolemia (an inherited extremely high cholesterol level); if so, there's a 50-50 chance you have it too. The gene responsible for familial hypercholesterolemia is "dominant": Inherit a defective version from one parent and you'll get the disease, even if your other parent gave you a normal copy.

Familial hypercholesterolemia, which affects one in every 500 people, can clog arteries and lead to a heart attack at an early age. If you have a family history of heart disease, be sure to get your cholesterol level measured. Once detected, an abnormally high cholesterol level can often be controlled with a lowfat diet and cholesterol-lowering drugs.

Familial adenomatous polyposis, another inherited disorder, afflicts one in 8,000 people and almost always results in intestinal cancer. ("Surviving a Family Curse," below, describes a family coping with this dominant-gene problem.) Other dominant diseases include Huntington's disease (the degenerative nervous-system disorder that killed singer Woody Guthrie), adult polycystic renal disease (a kidney disorder) and Marfan's syndrome (characterized by abnormally long limbs and heart problems). Diseases controlled by a dominant gene rarely skip a generation, so you've probably been spared if neither of your parents had the disease, even if a grandparent did.

Fortunately, most purely hereditary diseases are "recessive": that is, they afflict only those unlucky enough to inherit two copies of a defective gene—one from each parent. The most common of these recessive diseases seem to target certain ethnic groups.

For example, about one in 25 white Americans carries the gene for cystic fibrosis (CF), one of the most common lethal hereditary diseases (for those of northern European descent the risk is somewhat higher). The gene defect in CF results in a thick, sticky mucus in the lungs; the mucus encourages severe respiratory infections that usually prove fatal by age 30.

A CF carrier—with one abnormal and one normal gene—will be healthy. But if someone with the gene marries another carrier, their offspring will have a one-in-four chance of inheriting two defective copies of the gene and being born with CF. Following the discovery in 1989 of the gene that causes CF, a blood test became available that can tell whether a person is a carrier and whether a couple's fetus will develop the disease. ("Family Roots" lists several ethnic groups, the diseases to which they're susceptible, and how common those diseases are.)

Purely hereditary diseases (or disorders) that usually affect only men are called X-linked recessive diseases. The best known are hemophilia, color blindness and Duchenne muscular dystrophy. An X-linked disorder is transmitted from mother to son by a gene on one of her two X chromosomes. Each son has a 50-50 chance of getting the disease, from inheriting just a single copy of the recessive gene.

Mom may be a healthy carrier, since her other X chromosome carries a normal copy of the gene, which masks the defective one. But her son, with his X chromosome paired with a Y from his father, isn't as lucky. A woman should suspect she may be a carrier of an X-linked disorder if the disease has shown up in a male relative.

Virtually every month, researchers identify a gene linked to yet another hereditary disease; these findings are leading to increasing numbers of blood tests to identify people who carry these genes or who are destined to develop the diseases. ("Testing for Risk" lists some of these diseases.) To take advantage of these advances, you must first learn whether you or other family members are at risk.

Surviving a Family Curse

Larry Howard* had considered his family's medical history a curse, but knowing about it probably saved his life.

Larry's mother, three brothers and a sister all had been diagnosed with familial adenomatous polyposis, a disease in which thousands of polyps—tiny wartlike growths—sprout from the lining of the large intestine (colon). People with this condition (about one in 8,000) almost always develop colon cancer from polyps that turn malignant.

Larry's mother and his four affected siblings had to have their colons removed to prevent cancer from taking hold—the treatment reserved for severe cases. But Larry and his other sister, Mary, thought they had been spared.

Since early adolescence, when the polyps generally arise, Larry and Mary had taken part in the Johns Hopkins

*Not his real name.

University familial polyposis study, undergoing annual sigmoidoscopies (visual examination of the lower third of the colon) and receiving clean bills of health. Ten years ago, when Larry was 32, he was told he didn't need any more checkups, since his risk of having inherited the disease seemed minimal.

Then last year he and Mary were given a new blood test, developed at Johns Hopkins, that identifies the gene that causes familial polyposis. The test determined that Mary did not carry the defective gene, but Larry did. Sure enough, a subsequent exam revealed sprouting polyps.

Larry plans to have his colon removed later this year. His three children have taken the blood test too: One of the three has tested positive.

Gathering information about illnesses that run in your family is not as daunting as it may seem—especially if you ask relatives for help. Here is a guide for constructing your medical family tree:

1. Make a list of your first-degree relatives (parents, siblings and children) and second-degree relatives (grandparents, aunts and uncles). Adding more peripheral branches to your tree usually isn't worthwhile: The more distant the relative, the less relevant his medical fate is to you (you and your second cousin, for example, inherit only about 3% of the same genes). A possible exception: when you need more evidence to confirm a pattern involving a serious health problem such as cancer or heart disease.

2. Construct your family tree, using the sample on p. 225 as a guide. Your name and the names of your siblings go on the bottom row. On the row above, put the names of your parents, along with the names of their brothers and sisters. The names of all four grandparents go on the top line. It's customary to put male relatives in squares and female ones in circles and to indicate marriages by connecting relatives with horizontal lines.

3. Record the following information for each relative:
● *Date of birth, date of death and cause of death.* If necessary, you can usually obtain this information from the death certificate. To get a copy, contact the department of vital records in the state where the relative lived. (Be sure to check the family Bible first—birth and death certificates are often tucked inside the covers.)
● *All known illnesses and major surgeries, including the age when they occurred.* This information could be more relevant than the cause of death—if an uncle had a heart attack at age 40 but died 20 years later from an automobile accident, for example. Medical records are the most reliable sources for this information.

Ask relatives who are still living either to give you copies of their medical records or to sign a consent form allowing their doctors to give you this information. To obtain a deceased relative's records, contact the doctor or hospital that treated him; those names should be on the death certificate. You may have to provide a letter of consent from your relative's next of kin, as well as a copy of the death certificate.
● *Lifestyle factors that may have contributed to illness.* For instance, heart disease would be less of a genetic threat if you found that the uncle who suffered the heart attack at age 40 was a chain smoker. Most every family has a self-appointed "historian" who is the repository of family lore. You may be able to learn about relatives' lifestyles by talking to that person.
● *Occupation (optional).* This information may be important if there were job-related factors (such as exposure to toxic chemicals) that may have contributed to illness, miscarriage or birth defects.
● *Unusual physical characteristics.* Prominent features or chronic skin rashes could hint at certain medical conditions or birth defects (but you'll want to corroborate your hunches with medical records or other documents). Again, the family historian may be a good source. Family photo albums can also be revealing: A grandmother's "dowager's hump," for example, probably indicates that she had osteoporosis.

As you research your family medical tree, be prepared for difficulties. Information may be unavailable (some family

TESTING FOR RISK

The genes responsible for more than 300 diseases, most of them rare, can now be identified through blood tests. In some cases, these tests detect the gene itself; in others, they identify DNA "markers" that suggest the gene is present.
● **Cystic fibrosis**
● **Familial hypercholesterolemia**
● **Duchenne muscular dystrophy**
● **Fragile-X syndrome** (the most common inherited form of mental retardation)
● **Huntington's disease**
● **Neurofibromatosis** (a nerve disease characterized by dozens of skin tumors all over the body)
● **Retinoblastoma** (an eye tumor that usually occurs in childhood)
● **Sickle-cell anemia**
● **Tay-Sachs disease**
● **Thalassemia** (a blood disorder that occurs most often in people of Mediterranean descent)
● **Wilms' tumor** (a malignant kidney tumor that usually occurs in childhood)
Source: *Heredity and Your Family's Health,* by Aubrey Milunsky, M.D. (Johns Hopkins University Press, 1992)

FOR MORE HELP
Free pamphlets
● **"Genetic Counseling,"** GC Pamphlet, March of Dimes, 1275 Mamaroneck Ave., White Plains, NY 10605.
● **"Genetic Counseling: Valuable Information for You and Your Family,"** the National Society of Genetic Counselors, 233 Canterbury Dr., Wallingford, PA 19086-6617.
● **"Where to Write for Vital Records,"** Superintendent of Documents, U.S. Government Printing Office, Washington, DC 20402.

Books
● **Heredity and Your Family's Health** by Aubrey Milunsky, M.D. (Johns Hopkins University Press, 1992).
● **How Healthy Is Your Family Tree? A Complete Guide to Creating a Medical and Behavioral Family Tree** by Carol Krause (Collier Books).

Organizations
● **The Hereditary Cancer Institute,** Creighton University School of Medicine, 2500 California Plaza, Omaha, NE 68178.
● **Gilda Radner Familial Ovarian Cancer Registry,** Roswell Park Cancer Institute, Elm and Carlton streets, Buffalo, NY 14263.
● **University of Utah Cardiovascular Genetics Research Clinic,** 410 Chipeta Way, Room 161, Research Park, Salt Lake City, UT 84108.
● **The Hereditary Disease Foundation,** 1427 Seventh St., Suite 2, Santa Monica, CA 90401.

Family Roots

Risk of certain genetic diseases in specific races or ethnic groups.

Racial or ethnic background	Diseases	Carriers	Afflicted
Italian or Greek	Thalassemia	1 in 10	1 in 400
African	Sickle-cell anemia	1 in 12	1 in 650
Caucasian	Cystic fibrosis	1 in 25	1 in 2,500
Eastern or Central European Jewish (Ashkenazic), Cajun American or French Canadian	Tay-Sachs disease*	1 in 30	1 in 3,600
Mediterranean Jewish (Sephardic) or Armenian	Familial Mediterranean fever**	1 in 45	1 in 8,000

*Neurological disorder invariably fatal within the first five years of life.   **Repeated bouts of fever and abdominal pain.
Adapted from *Choices, Not Chances: An Essential Guide to Heredity and Health,* ©1977 by Aubrey Milunsky, M.D.
By permission of Little, Brown and Company.

Hereditary Risk

Estimated risk for some common disorders that are influenced by inherited genes but not directly caused by them. Risks are for people with one parent who had the disease. The risk would be greater if a second parent or a sibling also had the disease.

Disease	General population	One parent with condition
	Lifetime risk	
Alcoholism	5%	10% to 20%
Alzheimer's disease	2% to 5%	19%
Asthma	4%	26%
Cancer, breast	11%	22%*
Cancer, colon	4%	10%
Cancer, ovarian	1%	5%
Cancer, uterine	3%	9%
Diabetes (non-insulin-dependent)	2%	5% to 10%
Duodenal ulcer	10%	30%
Glaucoma	2%	4% to 16%
Manic depression	1%	25%
Migraine	5% to 10%	45%
Schizophrenia	1%	8% to 18%

*The risk may be three times as great as in the general population if the mother was premenopausal when her cancer was diagnosed.
©1992 by Consumers Union. Reprinted by permission from *Consumer Reports on Health.*

members may not cooperate, for example), or it may not exist (as when a child died and no diagnosis was ever made) or it may not be accurate (family legend, for example, may attribute an aunt's pregnancy loss to a miscarriage when in fact she had an abortion).

A little tact goes a long way. Family members may not want to talk about sad events or what they consider to be the family's dirty laundry. A good approach: "My doctor is in-terested in Cousin Bobby's condition because it could affect the children I may have. Can you tell me about his problem so that we can calculate the risks?" Offer to share your completed tree with relatives, along with the opinions of medical or genetic experts you consult.

Now that you've constructed your family tree, here are some tips on interpreting it:
● Your tree's two most important "branches" are your mother and father: Each gave you half your genetic inheritance, so their diseases will be most relevant to you and your siblings.
● The earlier a disease develops, the more likely that heredity played a role in it (except for ailments with obvious non-genetic causes such as infections).
● A disease that strikes two or more relatives at the same age is likely to be strongly influenced by heredity.
● A clustering of cases of the same disease on one side of the tree is more likely to suggest that genes play a strong role in causing it than a similar number of cases scattered on both sides. On the other hand, your risk of inheriting a purely hereditary disease like cystic fibrosis would actually be greater when it's present on both your mother's and father's side.

If you have questions about your family tree, you should show it to your doctor. If the doctor suspects a genetic problem, you will probably be referred to a genetic counselor, who can assess your risk of developing the diseases you're worried about, and of passing them on to a child. A counselor can also tell prospective parents if a fetus can be tested for conditions of concern.

Genetic counselors typically have a master of science degree in genetics and are certified by the American Board of Medical Genetics. Your family doctor, obstetrician or pediatrician can probably refer you to one, or you can contact a major hospital or medical school in your area or your local chapter of the March of Dimes for referrals (for further information, see "For More Help").

Your medical family tree should be a living, growing document. As you and your brothers and sisters get married and have children, keep adding to it: It can contribute to your health today and to the health of future generations.

Happy Families

WHO SAYS THEY ALL HAVE TO BE ALIKE?

Susan Chollar

Susan Chollar writes about science and health for a number of national magazines.

It's Thursday evening in Watsonville, a small agricultural town on California's central coast. Cathy Chavez-Miller is fixing dinner for her "blended" family: her husband, Mike, her stepson, Cliff, and her son from her first marriage, Patrick, who spends half his time with his father. "At times it's been a real challenge," she says, "but we really enjoy each other and wouldn't change the way things are." On the opposite coast, it's nighttime in suburban Washington, and mental health therapist Shelly Costello tucks her five-year-old twins Chelsea and Carly into bed. Worn out after 10 hours in day care followed by a rowdy evening at home with Mom, the kids are soon fast asleep. But Shelly, a single parent, must tackle a sinkful of dirty dishes and a couple of loads of laundry before she can call it a day. Her philosophy concerning our oldest social institution: "I don't believe in the rule that a family has to have two parents living together, but I do believe that people have to be happy. As long as a family is happy, it will be a good place for children to grow up."

American families are not what they were 40 years ago when Father Knew Best and every household was presumed to live *The Life of Riley*. Ozzie and Harriet and the Cleavers have long since given way to Murphy Brown and the *Full House* gang, and the traditional two-parent family sometimes seems like an endangered species.

We all know the statistics: Half of all marriages in the U.S. end in divorce, and nearly a third of our children are born out of wedlock. As a result, four out of 10 kids don't live with both of their biological parents; one in four lives in a single-parent home; and almost one in six families includes at least one stepchild.

Critics such as former Vice President Dan Quayle have blamed these demographic changes for everything from the Los Angeles riots and the growing wave of violence among teenage boys to declining scholastic performance. But while social scientists don't deny that American children and parents face greater challenges than ever before, they increasingly question the assumption that broken homes and single-parent families per se are threatening children. Several recent sophisticated studies suggest that growing up under the same roof with both biological parents is less crucial to a child's psychological health than growing up in a stable home.

"The quality of the individuals and relationships in the household matters more than who the particular actors are," says Dr. Frank Mott, a senior research scientist at the Center for Human Resource Research at Ohio State University in Columbus. "If you have a happy home, you'll probably have well-adjusted children." In other words, the atmosphere of the home counts for more than the type of family who inhabits it—even when it comes to "broken" homes.

In 1980 Dr. Paul Amato, an associate professor of sociology at the University of Nebraska in Lincoln, began charting the progress of 2,000 marriages; over the course of his study, 15% ended in divorce. In 1992 he contacted 500 adult children from those failed marriages and measured their psychological and social adjustment. The offspring of the failed unions tended to fall into two distinct groups: Those from marriages in which there had been little external conflict before the divorce were likelier to have personal problems as young adults than those from overtly troubled marriages.

Amato believes that children from seemingly harmonious homes that break up bear the greater scars because, to them, "the divorce means the loss of a stable home. Although the parents were unhappy with the

THE STRONGEST PREDICTOR OF SUCCESS IS THE LEVEL OF CONFLICT BETWEEN A MOTHER AND HER CHILD: LESS IS BEST.

From *American Health*, July/August 1993, pp. 52-57. © 1993 by Susan Chollar. Reprinted by permission.

marriage, from the child's perspective it wasn't really that bad."

For children who had lived in homes where there were arguments and perhaps physical violence, however, divorce often meant an end to discord. Therefore, the adult children from such homes tended to have better psychological health—and even stronger social relationships and marriages—than those from homes in which there had been little external conflict before divorce. "To the children," Amato concludes, "the consequences of divorce depend on the quality of the marriage prior to it." He adds: "It might be better for children to be in a well-functioning divorced single-parent family than a nuclear family marked by high levels of conflict."

Research on families headed by single women also suggests that the quality of a home is more important than its cast of characters. Sociologist David Demo, an associate professor of human development and family studies at the University of Missouri in Columbia, examined the emotional health and academic performance of 742 teens from the four most prevalent types of households: intact two-parent, never married single-parent, divorced single-parent and stepfamily.

When Dr. Demo analyzed all his data, he found that the type of family a child belonged to was a surprisingly weak predictor of the child's well-being and achievement. Although teens who resided with both biological parents tended to do better academically and behaviorally, they did only slightly better than those from never-married single-parent families. The most powerful predictor of the young people's adjustment and academic performance was the level of conflict between mother and child: Less is best.

"Dan Quayle argues that families headed by never-married mothers are inherently harmful to children," says Demo, "but the data don't show that. In fact, the never-married [single-parent] family offers a type of continuity that can parallel that of intact two-parent families." He summarizes his research this way: "Families are diverse by race, class, structure and well-being. Some are in trouble, some are doing very well. And some are somewhere in-between."

If some divorces—but not all—cause problems, so do some stepfami-

lies. Dr. Louise Silverstein, a family therapist and an assistant professor of psychology at Yeshiva University in New York City, observes that research shows relationships are often more difficult in stepfamilies, particularly for girls who find themselves living under the same roof with their mother's new husband. Boys who accompany their mother to a new household seem to fare better, presumably because there is less sexual tension in their relationship with a same-sex stepparent.

Children who deal with strife that continues between parents *after* divorce also often suffer. Silverstein illustrates with a case history: The parents of three-year-old Sean separated in a tangle of bitterness and anger when his mother, Mary Ann, was six months into a second pregnancy her husband, Tom, opposed. When Tom reacted by embarking on an affair with Mary Ann's closest friend, their conflict escalated into screaming matches and even physical violence that showed no sign of abating months after their marriage dissolved. "They were completely out of control," says Silverstein. Unfortunately Sean was his parents' real victim: Over eight months, his once normal behavior deteriorated into frequent tantrums and a severe case of separation anxiety.

Researchers who found that children from broken homes generally don't do as well as those whose parents stayed together may have misinterpreted the causes. Nearly half of single-parent families live in poverty, for example, compared with only 8% of married families. Almost 12 million households are headed by women, whose economic status is slashed by at least a third following divorce; never-married mothers are among the poorest members of our society. In many single-parent homes, low income—not divorce—causes children to live in high-crime neighborhoods and to have more health and academic problems.

Sociologist Nicholas Zill is vice president of the Westat research corporation in Rockville, Md., which explores social issues for the federal government, among other clients. "If you are the classic Murphy Brown type with all the advantages, and you decide to have a child out of marriage," he says, "your child is not nec-

essarily at risk. But if you're a teenager with little education or money, that can be a recipe for disaster."

Assessing the effects of growing up in a household headed by a single woman is clearly not a simple matter. Ohio State's Mott analyzed data about 1,714 youngsters aged five to eight from various socioeconomic backgrounds, to see if a father's absence from the home caused academic and/or behavioral problems. He discovered that those from fatherless homes indeed scored lower on math and reading achievement tests. But additional probing revealed that the children's mothers scored lower on aptitude tests than the married mothers; they also tended to be poorer and were more likely to have dropped out of school. When he compared children in the sample from similar socioeconomic backgrounds, he found that they performed equally well, regardless of a father's presence.

When it came to behavior, the absence of a father didn't correlate with any particular problems among black children. But fatherless white children had significantly more behavioral difficulties than peers who had fathers, even when income and education levels were similar. White girls and white boys from fatherless homes were less sociable and less independent than white children from homes with fathers. In addition, white boys from fatherless homes were also more prone to hyperactivity, peer conflict, anxiety and depression.

Mott offers several suggestions for these race- and gender-based differences. Girls may be less vulnerable than boys in the absence of a father, he says, because they're closer to their mothers. And black children are part of a culture in which single parenting is not only more prevalent but also more accepted. While nearly half of the fatherless black households in Mott's study had never had a paternal presence, 94% of similar white homes had; many more white children had "lost" their fathers due to divorce or other family disruption. "From a child's perspective," says Mott, "never having had a father in the home may be better, at least in a psychological sense, than having had one who left." Along with more accepting attitudes toward families without fathers, many

The '50s: Not So Happy Days

The 1950s are often portrayed as a simple time when fresh-faced children flourished in nuclear families, men ruled their castles with wisdom and benevolence, and women relished their roles as ever-nurturing wives and mothers. Not so, says Stephanie Coontz, a family historian at The Evergreen State College in Olympia, Wash. "The reality of these families was far more painful and complex than the situation-comedy reruns or the expurgated memories of the nostalgic would suggest," she writes in *The Way We Never Were: American Families and the Nostalgia Trap* (Basic Books, 1992, $27). "Contrary to popular opinion, *Leave It to Beaver* was not a documentary." A quarter of Americans, a third of U.S. children and nearly two-thirds of the elderly were desperately poor, making do without food stamps or housing programs. Half of two-parent black families lived in poverty, and 40% of black women with small children had to work outside the home.

Even for families who came closer to the Cleaver mold, life was often not as simple or happy as it appeared. A quarter to a third of '50s marriages eventually ended in divorce. Many who described their unions as "happy" in national polls nonetheless admitted many dissatisfactions with their mates and day-to-day lives. Child and spouse abuse was common, though largely unacknowledged.

For women in particular, the '50s were not what they seemed to be on *Ozzie and Harriet*. (In his new book, *The Fifties,* author David Halberstam argues that the real-life Nelsons—dominated by autocratic, workaholic Ozzie, who stole "the childhood of both his sons and used it for commercial purposes"—were in fact a dysfunctional family.) "It was a period where women felt tremendously trapped,"

says Coontz. "There were not many permissible alternatives to baking brownies, experimenting with new canned soups and getting rid of stains around the collar." In some states, husbands had legal control over family finances. In 1954, an article in *Esquire* magazine labeled working wives a "menace." Feminist values and lack of interest in childbearing were considered abnormal, if not pathological. Some women unwilling or unable to fulfill their expected domestic roles were subjected to electroshock or confinement to psychiatric institutions. Throughout the '50s, the press reported a growing wave of frustration and resentment among full-time homemakers, whose use of tranquilizers and alcohol skyrocketed.

To those who point to the '50s as an era of conservative sexual values, look again, says Coontz. Birth rates among teenagers reached numbers since unequaled. The percentage of pregnant white brides more than doubled, and the number of babies born out of wedlock and put up for adoption rose 80% between 1944 and 1955. "What we now think of as 1950s sexual morality," writes Coontz, "depended not so much on stricter sexual control as on intensification of the sexual double standard."

Although Coontz's research shines light on the weaknesses of American families from earlier historical periods as well, she denies that family bashing is her goal. "To say that no easy answers are to be found in the past is not to close off further discussion of family problems, but to open it up," she says. "Only when we have a realistic idea of how families have and have not worked in the past can we make informed decisions about how to support families in the present or improve their future prospects."

with boys and girls raised by gay parents also tends to refute the conventional wisdom. After reviewing studies of the children of lesbian mothers, Dr. Charlotte Patterson, an associate professor of psychology at the University of Virginia in Charlottesville, concluded in the October 1992 issue of *Child Development* that there was no evidence that these children's development had been compromised in any significant respect. "Children don't need a father to develop normally," says Silverstein, "and future research on children raised by gay fathers will probably show that they don't need a mother either. What children need are affectionate, nurturing adults—regardless of their gender or biological relationship—who love them."

Considering the very real challenges of growing up in a nontraditional home, family researchers are quick to acknowledge the advantages that the *right kind* of traditional family can confer. If the worst scenario is a family marked by hostility and conflict, "the best situation," says Nebraska's Amato, "is to grow up in a family where there are two adults who get along well and love the child. Two parents can supervise a child better, provide more practical help, discipline and guidance, and serve as effective role models."

What is most promising about the new research, says Missouri's Demo, "is the suggestion that a lot of these changes in traditional family structure are not harmful to children. But what is disturbing is that the studies point out that negative and disruptive events in children's lives do have important effects on their well-being. Those are the real problems—and those are the patterns that are increasing in our society."

One point on which family experts agree is that we should spend our energy on securing a happy future for our children rather than waxing nostalgic about the past. "It is important to look at the realities of how families are actually functioning," says Westat's Zill, "rather than labeling some as inevitably bad and others as inevitably good." Adds Amato: "All of these types of families are here to stay. And by and large, all of them can work quite well. We need to concern ourselves with making sure that each of them works as well as it can."

black communities offer single parents more extended-family support.

This extra help can make the difference between success and failure in families of any color, says Yeshiva's Silverstein, offering another case history as an example: Alice, now a well-adjusted, young white adult, was raised in a household consisting of her mother, grandmother and aunt; the mother was the breadwinner, while

the grandmother created a warm, nurturing atmosphere. "The additional adults also acted as an emotional safety net for Alice," Silverstein says. "If she had a fight with her mother, there was always her grandmother or aunt to comfort her. And their presence meant she didn't have to experience her mother's anger or disappointment so intensely."

The newest research conducted

Rewriting Life Stories

*Mind: Instead of looking for flaws in people's psyches, 'narrative therapy'
works at nurturing their forgotten strengths*

Geoffrey Cowley and Karen Springen

Last August, Lorraine Grieves fell into a familiar pattern: "The rule in my head was, I couldn't have any food, and if I did, I had to purge." Fearing for her life, the 21-year-old Vancouver woman's doctor sent her to a psychiatric ward where, for three weeks, she sat surrounded by fellow sufferers with feeding tubes dangling from her nose. Under the house rules, anyone who left a meal unfinished was fed liquid calories or plugged into a feeding machine. And if a patient resisted that drill, she was eligible for a straitjacket. Hospital staffers monitored the ward closely, but the women found ways to evade them. Though Grieves weighed just 103 pounds, she did sit-ups in bed and ran in the shower. When hooked up to a feeding machine, she would wait until no one was looking and then disconnect the tubes. "we'd all sit there sometimes with our tube dripping into the garbage," she recalls. "After all, they were giving you the thing you're most afraid of."

Narrative therapy recognizes that one's psyche is not a fixed, objective entity but a fluid social construct that can be "re-authored" to correct mental problems.

Today, Grieves carries a healthy 125 pounds on her 5-foot, 5-inch frame, and she's no longer dominated by the craving to be thinner. What finally kept her from starving herself was not the prison-style discipline of the hospital, she says, but the perspective she gained through her conversations with a local psychotherapist named Stephen Madigan. Unlike the professionals she'd consulted in the past, Madigan didn't reinforce her sense that there was something wrong with her. Instead, he worked at driving a wedge between her and her problem. He got her to think about the rare moments when anorexia and bulimia *didn't* control her life. He coaxed her to focus on what that experience felt like. And as she began to think of anorexia as a hostile oppressor, not the whole of her own being, he inspired her to fight back. If a person told you to deprive yourself of food and water, he asked, wouldn't you revolt? Yes, she realized, she would revolt. And with the support of other sufferers, she did.

Like Madigan, a small but growing number of psychotherapists are shedding ideas that have dominated their field for a century. Loosely united by what they call a "narrative" approach, they're forging a new conception of mental suffering and devising new strategies for easing it. The psyche, from their perspective, is not a fixed, objective entity but a fluid social construct—a story that is subject to revision. And the therapist's job is to help people "re-author" stories that aren't doing them justice. The new approach is still far from orthodox, but its adherents—mainly family therapists in Australia, New Zealand and North America—are applying it to everything from marital conflict to psychosis. And as Lorraine Grieves's experience suggests, their efforts are changing people lives. Narrative therapy is "more than a new set of techniques," Omaha therapist Bill O'Hanlon wrote recently in The Family Therapy Networker. "It represents a fundamentally new direction in the therapeutic world."

At the heart of the new approach is the postmodernist idea that we don't so much perceive the world as interpret it. The buzz of sensory experience would overwhelm us without some frame of reference, says Michael White, an Australian therapist who helped launch the narrative movement in the late 1980s. So we collapse our experience into narrative structures, or stories, to make it intelligible. As we forge identities, we inevitably give some patterns of experience more weight than others, and cultural pressures help determine which patterns define us. If our "dominant stories" happen to center on problems, they can become spiritual prisons, As the Berkeley, Calif.-based therapists Jennifer Freeman and Dean Lobovits have written, a "problem-saturated" dominant story tends to "filter problem-free experiences from a person's memories and perceptions," so that "threads of hope, resourcefulness and capability are excluded from a person's description of self."

That's where therapy comes in. Conventional Freudian psychotherapy tends to assume that people's problems stem from internal pathologies that need to be identified, scrutinized and corrected. Narrative therapy, as conceived by White and his colleague David Epston of Auckland, New Zealand, takes a different tack. Instead of looking for flaws in people's psyches, the therapist helps people spot omissions in their stories. "No problem or diagnosis ever captures the whole of a person's experience," says Epston. "The person has other ways of acting and thinking, but they get neglected because they lie in the shadows of the dominant story." Practitioners have different tricks for helping people recover forgotten strengths, but the process follows a predictable arc.

Small discoveries can have big effects. One small discovery can be when a person seeking help feels, even for an instant, that they are not dominated by their problem.

Danny's story: The first step is to initiate what's known in the trade as an externalizing conversation. "People come in thinking, 'I'm depressed. This diagnosis defines me. I'm a failure'," says Freeman, the Berkeley therapist. "There's usually very little distance between the person and the problem. That feeling of being defective can immobilize people." To counter that feeling, the therapist

typically invites the client to personify the problem—to give it a name and talk about how it's affecting his life. As you see from a videotaped conversation between White and a 5-year-old named Danny, the effect can be transformative. Danny has already seen many counselors when his mom brings him to White's office at the Dulwich Centre in Adelaide, Australia. No one has been able to toilet-train the bubbly, sweet-natured kindergartner; he won't bother with a trip to the bathroom, no matter how awful the consequences. But White engages Danny in a conversation about two characters named Sneaky Poo and Sneaky Wee, and within minutes the child is talking about how they take advantage of him.

How does Sneaky Poo make you feel?
I start to have tears. It just sneaks out.
So it makes you feel sad. How else does it make you feel?
It makes me feel angry.
Anything else?
Yes, it stinks and it sticks to me. It hurts and its hard to get off.
Does Sneaky Poo cause trouble in your friendships with other kids?
Sometimes they just want to go away.
I can see that Sneaky Poo is causing a lot of trouble in your life. What would you like instead?
I'd be happy if it didn't come out any time except in the toilet!

Danny is soon scheming to put Sneaky Poo in his place, and doing timed laps around the office to show that he's a faster runner than his newfound adversary. Throughout the exchange, White proposes nothing directly. He simply asks questions that create an opening for the boy to act on the problem without acting against himself. "[The other] therapists had succeeded in making him think of himself as the problem," White says. "No one had invited him to recount the problem's effects on his own life." Danny returned for several visits, but within six weeks Messrs. Poo and Wee had been vanquished.

Sparkling moments: To "externalize" a problem is not necessarily to solve it. The next step in the therapeutic process is to identify "unique outcomes"—those sparkling moments when the person seeking help has *not* been dominated by the problem. Those small discoveries can have big effects. Consider what happened last year when Epston had an hourlong conversation with Jermaine, a black 17-year-old from Ann Arbor, Mich. Jermaine has always suffered from life-threatening asthma, and as a teenager he'd grown so indifferent about treating and monitoring it that he was rarely out of the hospital for more than three days at a stretch. Despairing over his irresponsibility (he had also started committing petty juvenile offenses), his mother had recently placed him in a state institution.

In chatting with Epston, Jermaine quickly establishes that asthma has been messing up his life, and that he'd like to assert some control over it. Then Epston asks a pivotal question: "Tell me, has there ever been a time when asthma tried to pull the wool over your eyes and somehow you didn't keel over?" It turns out that he had staved off a trip to the hospital just that morning, by testing himself and taking his medication. Epston bears down enthusiastically on the meaning of the event, and Jermaine is soon proclaiming himself "asthma smart" and predicting a winning streak. A year later, the streak is all but unbroken.

New identities: There's more to changing a life than noticing a "unique outcome." The value of those moments is that they illuminate the resources a person can use to succeed on a larger scale. "we're not just telling people, 'You can do it!'" says therapist Jill Freedman of the Evanston Family Therapy Center, outside Chicago. "we're asking questions, in the hope that they'll help people see things about themselves that they weren't seeing before."

Liz Gray, a 52-year-old, self-employed accountant, used to think of herself as a servant. That was the assigned role of girls in her Irish Catholic household. and she continued to play the role as an adult. She laughs when she remembers teaching a course for tax preparers at an H&R Block office—and voluntarily cleaning the bathroom while she was there. When she started suffering panic attacks a few years ago, the therapists she consulted declared her "codependent" and told her she'd been psychologically damaged as a toddler. But the conversation changed when she started seeing Gene Combs at the Evanston Family Therapy Center.

Combs wanted to know how Gray, 20 years divorced, had managed to run a household, raise two children, look after her aging mother and run her own business. What did it say about her that she was able to do all that? Was she a victim, or was she a survivor? What resources had she drawn on? "As the patient identifies the exceptions to the dominant story of pathology," says New York psychiatrist Christian Beels, "the plot becomes thick and many-stranded." After two years of monthly sessions with Combs, Gray still suffers occasional panic attacks, which she treats with a tranquilizer. But she says she doesn't feel "broken" anymore. "I'm rewriting a story that someone told me a long time ago about what happens to women in this world," she says. "The idea of a queen keeping track of a house is a very different story from a victim saying, 'Oh my god, I'm overwhelmed'."

Going public: Unlike most other approaches, narrative therapy isn't a secretive transaction between the therapist and the client. Since the stories that define us are "negoti-ated and distributed within communities," White observes it's only reasonable to "engage communities in the renegotiation of identity." In Vancouver, Lorraine Grieves and others have organized an "anti-anorexia/anti-bulimia league" to fight the social pressures that encourage women to starve themselves. In Berkeley, Jennifer Freeman encourages the children she sees to chronicle their struggles for anthologies like "The Temper Tamer's Handbook" and "The Fear Facer's Handbook." And narrative therapists everywhere are incorporating audiences into the therapeutic process.

It's not an entirely new idea.

With the client's consent, a family therapist will often have other therapists observe a session from behind a screen. Normally, the observers share their impressions only with the therapist who recruited them. But narrative practitioners often invite their clients to watch the "reflecting team" deliberate. The Moore family had that experience last fall, when they spent an hourlong session with Michael White at the Evanston Family Therapy Center. Jane Moore and her second husband, Clint, an Episcopal priest, had been married for several years when Jane's 16-year-old daughter, Jennifer, left her father to live with them. They felt they needed help in becoming a family, but as they listened to the reflecting team, they realized they had already started to function as one. "It was a wonderful surprise to find out that other people perceived you as having the qualities you thought you were looking for," says Jane.

Narrative therapy doesn't have all the answers people need, but it incites them to ask different questions that may well lead to positive life choices.

There are of course limits to what any of these exercises can accomplish. No form of talk therapy is likely to eliminate a biologically based depression or psychosis. And traumatic experiences, such as childhood abuse, don't just go away when people focus on their strengths. "There is such a thing as true mental illness," says San Diego psychiatrist Harold Bloomfield, "Some people just need drugs." Many proponents of narrative therapy would agree, but they would add that there's more than one way of living with an illness. "The question is how you want to face the experiences you're stuck with," says

Beels. """What kind of relationship are you going to have with depression? What have you found effective? It's not an either-or situation, where you're cured or defeated. It's a lifetime battle."

Some experts worry that narrative enthusiasts, in their reluctance to "pathologize" people, will give their problems short shrift. They fear that by focusing solely on the problem at hand—anorexia, pants-soiling or panic attacks—a therapist may ignore larger issues that need to be confronted. But to narrative purists, such questions simply reflect a particular view of the world. "In traditional therapy, the audience is the therapist," say Beels. "What does the therapist expect? He expects that we have not gotten to the bottom of this problem yet. He expects that things are not better than we thought, but worse." In fact, he says, the sources of people's suffering—traumatic memories, low self-esteem, whatever—are not that mysterious. Any line of inquiry will draw them out, and they need to be acknowledged. But they don't need monuments built to them. As Epston puts it, "Every time we ask a question, we're generating a possible version of a life." Narrative therapy doesn't have all the answers people need. Its beauty is that it incites them to ask different questions.

Rituals

FOR OUR TIMES

**Evan Imber-Black
and Janine Roberts**

*Evan Imber-Black is the director of the
Family and Group Studies program of the
Department of Psychiatry at Albert Einstein
College of Medicine. Janine Roberts is the
director of the Family Therapy program of
the School of Education at the University of
Massachusetts.*

• • • • • • • • •

**How today's
families are
developing
innovative rites
and ceremonies
to ease difficult
transitions, heal
relationships, and
celebrate life.**

• • • • • • • • •

EVERY FOURTH OF JULY, PAUL
and Linda Hoffman pack their
three children and their dog
into the station wagon and
drive 250 miles to Paul's sister's
home, where all of the Hoffmans gather.
The event is fairly unpleasant. The
women spend the day cooking, which
Linda resents, while the men watch sports,
an activity Paul doesn't care for. The
young cousins spend most of the day
fighting with one another. In the evening,
Grandpa Hoffman sets off fireworks, but
no one really pays attention. On the fifth
of July, Paul and Linda drive home, weari-
ly vowing that this is the last year they will
spend their holiday this way.

The following June, however, when
Paul and Linda dare mention that they are
thinking about doing something different
for Independence Day, Paul's sister calls
and tells them how upset their parents will
be if the couple and their children don't
come this year. Alternate plans fall by the
wayside, and on the Fourth of July into
the car they go.

Does this story sound at all familiar to
you? Because of experiences like the Hoffmans', in which celebrations are static and
meaningless, many of us have minimized
the practice of rituals in our lives. One

woman we know who grew up in a family
whose rituals were particularly confining
put it this way: "I don't want any rituals in
my life. Rituals are like being in prison!"

Yet in these times of rapid and dramatic
change in the family—with more children
being raised by single parents, more mothers working outside the home, fewer
extended families living in close proximity
—rituals can provide us with a crucial
sense of personal identity as well as family
connection. Despite the changing status

of the family, membership within a family
group is still the primary way that most
people identify themselves. Rituals that
both borrow from the past and are
reshaped by relationship needs of the present highlight for us continuity as well as
change. A family in which ritual is minimized may have little sense of itself
through time. Everything simply blends
into everything else.

As family therapists who have been
working with and teaching the use of rituals since the late '70s, we have encountered
an increasing number of people who are
longing to revitalize the rituals in their lives.
They just don't know how. Rituals surround
us and offer opportunities to make meaning from the familiar and the mysterious
at the same time. Built around common
symbols and symbolic actions such as
birthday cakes and blowing out candles,
or exchanging rings and wedding vows,
many parts of rituals are well known to us.

A ritual can be as simple as the one that
sixty-two-year-old Eveline Miller practices
when she needs to sort things through.
She goes to her grandmother's rocking
chair, sits, and rocks. When she was a
child and needed comfort, this was where
she used to go to lay her head upon her
grandmother's lap. Her grandmother
would stroke her hair and say, "This too
will pass." Now, as Eveline rocks and
thinks, she repeats those words to help
calm herself and provide perspective.

Rituals also can be more elaborate and
creative, such as one that Jed and his wife,
Isabel, a couple in their early twenties,
designed for Jed's brother. Several months
after Jed married Isabel, his mother died
suddenly, leaving Jed's nineteen-year-old

From *New Age Journal*, September/October 1992, pp. 70-73, 140. Excerpt from *Rituals for Our Times: Celebrating, Healing,
and Changing Our Lives and Relationships* by Evan Imber-Black and Janine Roberts. © 1993 by Evan Imber-Black and
Janine Roberts. Reprinted by permission of HarperCollins Publishers, Inc.

brother, Brian, orphaned. Brian came to live with Jed and Isabel. The young couple thus found themselves not only newlyweds but also new "parents." One day Brian told them, "You know, I feel like I don't have a security blanket. My friends at school, other people in my classes—most of them have at least one parent still alive. Their parents can help them if they're having trouble in school, or if they need a place to stay, or can't find a job. And I don't have that security blanket because both of my parents are dead."

What Brian had said seemed so important to him that Jed and Isabel talked about it between themselves and eventually came up with an idea: They would make Brian a quilt—a security blanket. Jed's sister had an old nurse's uniform of their mother's that they could use for material. An older brother had a Marine camouflage shirt of their father's. They found some other old fabric among their mother's things. Then, as they began to cut the material into squares, they realized that they would need help sewing them together into a quilt. Jed thought of his maternal grandmother, who had sewn a number of quilts for other family members.

The siblings and the grandmother began gathering in secret to sew the quilt and share memories of Brian's parents and their earlier life. And when the family gathered to celebrate the grandmother's eightieth birthday, Brian was given the quilt—a blanket that symbolized both the ability of Jed and Isabel to "parent" in creative ways and the new network of contact that had been built between the siblings and their grandmother. Together, these family members had proved to be Brian's "security blanket."

The symbols and symbolic actions of rituals embrace meaning that cannot always be easily expressed in words. Eveline Miller's rocking chair, for example, was much more than a place to sit; it evoked safety, reassurance, and the memory of her grandmother. Brian's quilt was not just a cover; it represented the interconnected people in his life—from the past and the present—whom he could carry with him into the future. The textures, smells, and sounds of ritual symbols—an heirloom rocking chair, a family-made quilt—can be powerful activators of sensory memory. Family members may recall scenes and stories of previous times when similar rituals were enacted or some of the same people were together. Rituals connect us with our past, define our present life, and show us a path to our future.

FAMILY RITUALS TAKE A VARIETY OF FORMS. There are daily practices, such as the reading of a child's bedtime story or the sharing of a mealtime. There are holiday traditions, some celebrated with the community at large (seasonal events such as the solstice, religious events such as Passover, national events such as the Fourth of July) and others exclusive to a particular family (birthdays, anniversaries, reunions). Then there are life-cycle rituals, which mark the major transitions of life.

All human beings throughout the world and throughout time are born, and all die. All of us experience emerging sexuality. And most create sustained adult relationships to form new family units and new generations. Such changes are enormously complicated, involving both beginnings and endings; holding and expressing both pain and joy. They may shape and give voice to profoundly conflicting beliefs about our personal existence and our relationships. It's little wonder that every culture in the world has created rituals to celebrate and guide our way through these life-cycle passages.

The truly magical quality of rituals is embedded in their capacity not only to announce a change but to actually create the change. Given that volumes have been written advising people how to change, and that people spend countless hours in therapy, often agonizing over their inability to make needed changes, it is easy to see why rituals exist in all cultures, to ease our passage from one stage of life to another. Using familiar symbols, actions, and words, rituals make change manageable and safe. Simply knowing which rituals lie ahead during a day, a year, or a lifetime stills our anxiety. Change is *enacted* through rituals and not simply talked about—couples don't change from being single to being married by talking about marriage, but rather by participating in a wedding ceremony. Teens don't graduate from high school when a teacher says "you're finished now"; they attend proms, picnics, and the graduation ceremony itself.

As families have changed, life-cycle events have changed too, and there are many crucial transitions for which there are no familiar and accepted rituals in our culture. Changes that often go unmarked include divorce, the end of a nonmarried relationship, adoption, forming a committed homosexual relationship, leaving home, pregnancy loss, and menopause. Since life-cycle rituals enable us to begin to rework our sense of self and our relationships as required by life's changes, the lack of such rituals can make change more difficult.

Rituals tend to put us in touch with the profound circle of life and death, so it is not surprising that healing moments emerge spontaneously during these cele-

• • • • • • • • •

A family in which ritual is minimized may have little sense of itself through time.

• • • • • • • • •

brations. If you keep that in mind when changes are occurring in your life or in the lives of those close to you, you can plan a ritual to specifically generate healing.

Healing a Broken Relationship
The crisis of shattered trust and broken promises can lead to genuine atonement, forgiveness, reconciliation, and relationship renewal or, alternatively, to chronic resentment, bitterness, parting, and isolation. Since rituals are able to hold and express powerful contradictory feelings, such as love and hate, anger and connectedness, they enhance the possibility of relationship healing.

For Sondra and Alex Cutter, ritual provided a way to bury that past. The Cutters had spent seven of their twelve years of marriage in bitter arguments about a brief affair Alex had had just before their fifth anniversary. Sondra didn't want to leave her marriage, but she felt unable to let go of the past. Alex, in turn, had become extremely defensive about his behavior and was unable to genuinely show Sondra that he was sorry. In couple's therapy, Sondra and Alex were asked to bring two sets of symbols of the affair. The first set of symbols was to represent what the affair meant to each of them at the time it occurred. The second set was to symbolize what the affair had come to mean in their current life together. As a symbol of her feelings at the time of the affair, Sondra brought a torn wedding photograph to show that the affair meant a break in their vows. Sondra was surprised by Alex's symbol: an old picture of his father, who had had many affairs. "I thought this was just what husbands did," said Alex. "I thought this was what made you a man, but I found out quickly that this didn't work for me and for what I wanted my marriage to be. Then we couldn't get past it." Sondra had never heard Alex speak about the affair in this way. Her belief that the affair meant he didn't love her and that he loved another woman began to shift for the first time in seven years.

As a symbol of what the affair meant currently, Alex brought the wheel of a hamster cage, remarking, "We just go round and round and round and get nowhere." Sondra brought a bottle of bitters, and said, "This is what I've turned into!" After a long conversation engendered by their symbols, Sondra said quietly, "This is the first time in seven years that we've talked about this without yelling and screaming." When the therapist asked if they were ready to let go of the past, both agreed that they were. They decided to revisit a favorite spot from early in their relationship and to bury these symbols there. During the ceremony, Alex cried and for the first time asked Sondra to forgive him, which she readily did. They followed this with a celebration of their anniversary, which they had stopped celebrating seven years earlier.

This healing ritual was created as part of couple's therapy, but you don't need the help of a therapist to create rituals to effect healing. Common to all healing rituals is a dimension of time—time for holding on and time for letting go. Selecting symbols to express painful issues generally allows for a new kind of conversation to emerge. Taking some joint action together, such as symbolically burying the past, can impart a new possibility of collaboration. Creating a ritual together can help you to rediscover the playful parts of your relationship, such as the couple who "put an affair on ice," placing symbols in their deep freezer and agreeing that they could only fight about the affair after they had thawed these symbols out!

A Ceremony for Grieving

There is no life that is lived without loss. We all experience the death of people we love and care for deeply. When healing rituals have not occurred, or have been insufficient to complete the grief process, a person can remain stuck in the past or unable to move forward in meaningful ways. Even the unhealed losses of previous generations may emerge as debilitating symptoms in the present. When this happens, new rituals can be created to address the need for healing.

Joanie and Jeralynn Thompson were identical twins who had a close and loving

Rituals shape our relationships and give us a basis for a healthy society. Simply having a family meal together helps establish a stronger sense of self.

(UN photo/John Isaac)

relationship. They went away to the same college and planned to graduate together. During their junior year, however, Jeralynn developed leukemia. She died within the year. Before her death, Jeralynn talked with Joanie about how important it was that Joanie continue college and graduate. Joanie did go back to school after her sister's funeral, but she found it impossible to study. At the urging of friends, she took a year off in order to be with her family and begin to deal with the terrible loss of her sister. But a year turned into two years, two years into three. Finally, her family insisted that she go back to college. Joanie returned to school and finished all of her courses, but remained unable to do her senior thesis. She didn't graduate that June. "I don't know how I can graduate without Jeralynn," she told her mother. "It'll mean that she's really gone." Once her mother began to understand what was stopping Joanie from finishing, she talked with her daughter about how they might honor Jeralynn's life while still celebrating Joanie's entering adulthood with her college graduation. After developing a plan with her mother, Joanie finished her thesis in time to graduate the following December.

Joanie and her mother planned a special ceremony to be held two nights before graduation. They invited extended family and close friends, asking them to bring symbols of Jeralynn and to speak about her openly. During a very moving ceremony, many people spoke about what they thought Jeralynn would have wished for Joanie. One aunt made a video that showed places the two sisters had both loved, and after showing it told Joanie, "These places still belong to you." Joanie's father brought photographs of several pets the twins had raised, carefully pointing out the individual contributions each twin had made to these animals. Then, in a five-minute talk, he highlighted the strengths and gifts of each young woman and gave Joanie permission to be her own person. People grieved the loss of Jeralynn openly and then embraced Joanie for finishing school and going on in life.

Several months later, settled in a new job as a teacher, Joanie talked about this ceremony and her graduation: "They all helped me to graduate. If we hadn't had our memorial first, I know all I would have been wondering about on graduation day was what my family was feeling about Jeralynn's death. Instead, all of it was out in the open. We could be sad together and then we could be happy together on my graduation day. They call graduation a

> **Rituals** connect us with our past, define our present life, and show us a path to our future.

commencement, an ending that's really a beginning, and that's what mine was. I miss my sister terribly—I'll always miss her—but my family and friends helped me take the next step in my life, and Jeralynn's spirit was right there with me."

Celebrating Recovery from Illness

Sometimes very important changes take place but remain unacknowledged. This may be because the changes are difficult to talk about, because they bring up the pain of how things used to be, or because no one had thought about how to mark the change. In our experience, recovery from medical or psychiatric illness is an aspect of change that is seldom marked by a ritual. Families, relationships, and the individual's own identity remain stuck with the illness label, and behavior among family members and friends remains as it was when the person was ill.

Adolescents who have recovered from cancer or adults who are now healthy after heart surgery often maintain an "illness identity," and others treat them accordingly. A ritual can declare in action that a person has moved from illness to health. Such a ritual might include a ceremony of throwing away no-longer-needed medicines or medical equipment, burning or burying symbols of a long hospital stay, or writing a document declaring new life and health.

After recovering from breast cancer,

Gerry Sims had a T-shirt made that read HEALTHY WOMAN! She wore this T-shirt to a family dinner and announced to everyone that they were to stop treating her as a patient, and that, in particular, she wanted people to argue with her as they had before she became ill. Then she handed out T-shirts to her husband and children that read HUSBAND OF A HEALTHY WOMAN, CHILD OF A HEALTHY WOMAN, and TEENAGER OF A HEALTHY WOMAN. Everyone put on his or her T-shirt and for the first time spontaneously began to talk about what they had been through together during Gerry's year-long illness. They cried out loud to each other. Following this, Gerry's teen-age daughter picked a fight with her, just as Gerry had hoped!

A Rite of Passage

Like many life-cycle passages, a child leaving home is an event that carries deeply mixed feelings, including a sense of joy and accomplishment, fear regarding what lies ahead, sadness over the loss of relationships in their present form, and curious anticipation about what life will look like next. This life-cycle passage of leaving home may be even more difficult when the leaving is unanticipated or when the child has grown up with a handicap. Creating a leaving-home ritual whose symbols and symbolic actions speak to the many contradictory issues can ease this passage for everyone in the family.

Jennifer Cooper-Smith was born with some severe disabilities that affected her capacity to read, write, and speak. During her childhood she took the handicap in stride despite the cruel teasing of other children and despite coming from a family where high academic achievement was the norm. Through it all she taught her family a lot about perseverance in the face of enormous struggles and about building on strengths rather than focusing on weaknesses.

When Jennifer reached nineteen, since her disabilities would preclude her going to college, it was clear that high school graduation was to be her rite of passage. The family wanted to create a ritual that would both honor all that she had accomplished and send her forth into the adult world with confidence.

Jennifer wanted a party at a Chinese restaurant with her favorite festive food. Her mother and stepfather invited people who were important to Jennifer—extended family who lived far away, friends who had supported her, special teachers and co-workers from her part-time job. The invitation included a secret request for special items—poems, letters, photos, stories, drawings, and so on—to help make a "becoming an adult woman" album for Jenni. During the weeks before the party, her mom worked secretly to construct the album, which began at the time Jennifer joined the family as an adopted infant and included sections that marked significant stages of her development. Although the handicaps had sometimes made it difficult for both Jennifer and those around her to notice her growth and changes, this album recorded them for all to see.

When Jennifer arrived at the party, the album was waiting for her as a special symbol of her development. What she still didn't know, though, was that the album was open-ended, and a new section, "Becoming an Adult Woman," was about to be added during the party. After dinner, when people were invited to give their presentations to Jennifer, a moving and unexpected ceremony unfolded. Person after person spoke about how they experienced Jenni and what she meant to them,

and they gave her their own special brand of advice about living.

Her grandma Dena gave Jenni a photograph of Dena's late husband—Jenni's grandfather—down on his knees proposing marriage. She spoke about enduring love and her wish that Jenni would have this in her life. Her aunt Meryle Sue read an original poem, "Portrait of Jenni," and then spoke through tears about what this day would have meant to Jenni's grandfather and how proud he would have been of her. Her cousin Stacey wrote a poem that captured who Jenni was to her and offered words about Jenni's future. Advice about men and what to beware of was given by Jenni's step-grandfather and received with much laughter. Photographs of strong women in history were presented.

Person after person spoke with grace and love and special stories about Jennifer's strengths. Her mother watched as Jennifer took in all that she was to people and the sometimes unknown impact that her own courage had had on family and friends. And then all who gathered wit-

nessed the emergence of Jennifer, the adult woman, as she rose from her seat and spoke unhaltingly and with no trace of her usual shyness, thanking each person in turn for what they had given her in life, and talking about the loss of her grandfather and her wish that he could be with her today. She ended with all that she anticipated next in her life.

The weeks and months following this ritual were perhaps even more remarkable than the ceremony itself. Her family experienced a changed Jennifer, a Jennifer who moved from adolescence to young womanhood—starting a full-time job, auditing a community college course, traveling by herself, making new friends, and relating on a previously unseen level.

AS ALL OF THESE EXAMPLES ILLUSTRATE, rituals ease our passage through life. They shape our relationships, help to heal our losses, express our deepest beliefs, and celebrate our existence. They announce change and create change. The power of rituals belongs to all of us.

Credits/ Acknowledgments

Cover design by Charles Vitelli

1. Varied Perspectives on the Family
Facing overview—Dushkin Publishing Group/Brown & Benchmark Publishers photo.

2. Exploring and Establishing Relationships
Facing overview—Photo by Pamela Carley. 92—Photo by Kathy Sloane.

3. Finding a Balance
Facing overview—United Nations photo by L. Barnes.

4. Crises—Challenges and Opportunities
Facing overview—Photo by Cheryl Greenleaf. 159—Subjects & Predicates photo.

5. Families, Now and Into the Future
Facing overview—Photo by Louis P. Raucci.

PHOTOCOPY THIS PAGE!!!*

ANNUAL EDITIONS ARTICLE REVIEW FORM

■ NAME: _____ DATE: _____

■ TITLE AND NUMBER OF ARTICLE: _____

■ BRIEFLY STATE THE MAIN IDEA OF THIS ARTICLE: _____

_____

■ LIST THREE IMPORTANT FACTS THAT THE AUTHOR USES TO SUPPORT THE MAIN IDEA:

_____

_____

_____

_____

_____

_____

■ WHAT INFORMATION OR IDEAS DISCUSSED IN THIS ARTICLE ARE ALSO DISCUSSED IN YOUR TEXTBOOK OR OTHER READING YOU HAVE DONE? LIST THE TEXTBOOK CHAPTERS AND PAGE NUMBERS:

_____

_____

_____

_____

_____

_____

■ LIST ANY EXAMPLES OF BIAS OR FAULTY REASONING THAT YOU FOUND IN THE ARTICLE:

_____

_____

_____

_____

■ LIST ANY NEW TERMS/CONCEPTS THAT WERE DISCUSSED IN THE ARTICLE AND WRITE A SHORT DEFINITION:

_____

_____

_____

_____

_____

*Your instructor may require you to use this Annual Editions Article Review Form in any number of ways: for articles that are assigned, for extra credit, as a tool to assist in developing assigned papers, or simply for your own reference. Even if it is not required, we encourage you to photocopy and use this page; you'll find that reflecting on the articles will greatly enhance the information from your text.

ANNUAL EDITIONS: MARRIAGE AND FAMILY 96/97
Article Rating Form

Here is an opportunity for you to have direct input into the next revision of this volume. We would like you to rate each of the 48 articles listed below, using the following scale:

1. **Excellent: should definitely be retained**
2. **Above average: should probably be retained**
3. **Below average: should probably be deleted**
4. **Poor: should definitely be deleted**

Your ratings will play a vital part in the next revision. So please mail this prepaid form to us just as soon as you complete it.
Thanks for your help!

Annual Editions revisions depend on two major opinion sources: one is our Advisory Board, listed in the front of this volume, which works with us in scanning the thousands of articles published in the public press each year; the other is you—the person actually using the book. Please help us and the users of the next edition by completing the prepaid article rating form on this page and returning it to us. Thank you.

Rating	Article
	1. Is the Family Obsolete?
	2. The New Crusade for the Old Family
	3. The New Family: Investing in Human Capital
	4. Bringing Democracy Home: Shere Hite Reports on the Family
	5. The Ache for Home
	6. Growing Up in Black and White
	7. Love: The Immutable Longing for Contact
	8. What Makes Love Last?
	9. Why Don't We Act Like the Opposite Sex?
	10. Back Off!
	11. Choosing Mates—The American Way
	12. The Mating Game
	13. Psychotrends: Taking Stock of Tomorrow's Family and Sexuality
	14. Choosing a Contraceptive
	15. Men, Sex, and Parenthood in an Overpopulating World
	16. Baby Love
	17. What a Baby *Really* Costs
	18. Adolescent Childbearing: Whose Problem? What Can We Do?
	19. The Lifelong Impact of Adoption
	20. What's Happening to American Marriage?
	21. Peer Marriage
	22. Receipts from a Marriage
	23. Staying Power: Bridging the Gender Gap in the Confusing '90s
	24. But What Do You Mean?
	25. Saving Relationships: The Power of the Unpredictable

Rating	Article
	26. Vanishing Dreams of America's Young Families
	27. Effective Fathers: Why Are Some Dads More Successful than Others?
	28. The Family Heart
	29. "I Don't Sweat the Small Stuff Anymore"
	30. Siblings and Development
	31. The Secret World of Siblings
	32. Helping Children Cope with Violence
	33. After He Hits Her
	34. Where Do We Go from Here? An Interview with Ann Jones
	35. Passion Kills
	36. Beyond Betrayal: Life after Infidelity
	37. Sex in America: Faithfulness in Marriage Is Overwhelming
	38. The Myth of the Miserable Working Woman
	39. Family, Work, and Gender Equality: A Policy Comparison of Scandinavia, the United States, and the Former Soviet Union
	40. Caregiving: Continuities and Discontinuities in Family Members' Relationships with Alzheimer's Patients
	41. The Long Road Back: A Daughter Deals with Her Mother's Stroke
	42. Should This Marriage Be Saved?
	43. Lessons from Stepfamilies
	44. The Myths and Misconceptions of the Stepmother Identity
	45. Trace Your Family Tree
	46. Happy Families: Who Says They All Have to Be Alike?
	47. Rewriting Life Stories
	48. Rituals for Our Times

(Continued on next page)

ABOUT YOU

Name _____ Date _____

Are you a teacher? ❑   Or student? ❑

Your School Name _____

Department _____

Address _____

City _____ State _____ Zip _____

School Telephone # _____

YOUR COMMENTS ARE IMPORTANT TO US!

Please fill in the following information:

For which course did you use this book? _____

Did you use a text with this Annual Edition? ❑ yes ❑ no

The title of the text? _____

What are your general reactions to the Annual Editions concept?

Have you read any particular articles recently that you think should be included in the next edition?

Are there any articles you feel should be replaced in the next edition? Why?

Are there other areas that you feel would utilize an Annual Edition?

May we contact you for editorial input?

May we quote you from above?

ANNUAL EDITIONS: MARRIAGE AND FAMILY 96/97

BUSINESS REPLY MAIL

First Class   Permit No. 84   Guilford, CT

Postage will be paid by addressee

**Dushkin Publishing Group/
Brown & Benchmark Publishers**
Sluice Dock
Guilford, Connecticut 06437